The Social Stratification of English in New York City

One of the first accounts of social variation in language, this ground-breaking study founded the discipline of sociolinguistics, providing the model on which thousands of studies have been based. In this second edition, Labov looks back on forty years of sociolinguistic research, bringing the reader up to date on its methods, findings, and achievements. In over forty pages of new material, he explores the unforeseen implications of his earlier work, addresses the political issues involved, and evaluates the success of newer approaches to sociolinguistic investigation. In doing so, he reveals the outstanding accomplishments of sociolinguistics since his original study, which laid the foundations for studying language variation, introduced the crucial concept of the linguistic variable, and showed how variation across age groups is an indicator of language change. Bringing Labov's pioneering study into the twenty-first century, this classic volume will remain the benchmark in the field for years to come.

WILLIAM LABOV is Professor of Linguistics and Psychology at the University of Pennsylvania. Since *The Social Stratification of English in New York City* was first published in 1966, he has also published *Sociolinguistic Patterns* (1972), *Language in the Inner City* (1972), *A Quantitative Study of Sound Change in Progress* (with M. Yaeger and R. Steiner, 1972), *Principles of Language Change* (Volume 1, 1994; Volume 2, 2001; Volume 3, forthcoming), and (with S. Ash and C. Boberg), the *Atlas of North American English* (2006). He is co-editor of the journal *Language Variation and Change* (Cambridge University Press).

The Social Stratification of English in New York City

Second Edition

William Labov

CAMBRIDGE
UNIVERSITY PRESS

CAMBRIDGE UNIVERSITY PRESS
Cambridge, New York, Melbourne, Madrid, Cape Town, Singapore, São Paulo

Cambridge University Press
The Edinburgh Building, Cambridge CB2 2RU, UK

Published in the United States of America by Cambridge University Press, New York

www.cambridge.org
Information on this title: www.cambridge.org/9780521528054

First published 1966
Second edition 2006

Printed in the United Kingdom at the University Press, Cambridge

A catalogue record for this publication is available from the British Library

ISBN-13   978-0-521-82122-3 hardback
ISBN-10   0-521-82122-3 hardback

ISBN-13   978-0-521-52805-4 paperback
ISBN-10   0-521-52805-4 paperback

Contents

Introductory note to the first edition

The Clearinghouse for Social Dialect Studies, a joint instrumentality of the Center for Applied Linguistics and the National Council of Teachers of English, collects and distributes social dialect research information. It operates under the guidance of an Advisory Committee whose members are, at the present writing: Harold B. Allen, University of Minnesota; Alva L. Davis, Illinois Institute of Technology; W. Nelson Francis, Brown University; Alfred S. Hayes, Center for Applied Linguistics; Robert F. Hogan, National Council of Teachers of English; Albert W. Marckwardt, Princeton University; Raven I. McDavid, University of Chicago; David W. Reed, University of California at Berkeley; William A. Stewart, Center for Applied Linguistics. This Committee, known as the Clearinghouse Committee for Social Dialect Studies, also encourages the publication of selected documents. The present publication, essentially the author's 1964 Columbia University dissertation, was unanimously approved by the Clearinghouse Committee, and by the Commission on the English Language of the National Council of Teachers of English, acting on behalf of the Executive Committee of that organization. It is a ground-breaking study, a milestone in the emerging field of sociolinguistics, and we are pleased to make it available to the scholarly community.

Alfred S. Hayes
Director
Education and Research Program
Center for Applied Linguistics

Preface to the first edition

The work presented in the following pages is a linguistic analysis of one speech community. Like any linguistic analysis, it is concerned with a system of contrastive relations, the code by which speakers communicate with one another. In this particular community, New York City, the system of the individual speaker appears to be less coherent than that of the speech community as a whole. The isolated idiolect of the individual New Yorker shows so much unaccountable variation that it has been described as a case of massive "free variation." But when this individual speech pattern is studied in the larger context of the speech community, it is seen as an element in a highly systematic structure of social and stylistic stratification. It has therefore been necessary to extend the study of linguistic structure to include continuous social and stylistic variation, and unconscious subjective reactions to the variables concerned – areas that have previously been considered inaccessible to formal linguistic analysis.

In the past few years, there has been considerable programmatic discussion of *sociolinguistics* at various meetings and symposia. If this term refers to the use of data from the speech community to solve problems of linguistic theory, then I would agree that it applies to the research described here. But *sociolinguistics* is more frequently used to suggest a new interdisciplinary field – the comprehensive description of the relations of language and society. This seems to me an unfortunate notion, foreshadowing a long series of purely descriptive studies with little bearing on the central theoretical problems of linguistics or of sociology. My own intention was to solve linguistic problems, bearing in mind that these are ultimately problems in the analysis of social behavior: the description of continuous variation, of overlapping and multi-layered phonemic systems; the subjective correlates of linguistic variation; the causes of linguistic differentiation and the mechanism of linguistic change. The final Chapter 14 is devoted to the integration of the individual findings, in an analysis of structural consequences for the vowel system as a whole, and outlines the evolution of the New York City vowel system over the past sixty years.

The data also face in another direction: they bear on many problems of sociological theory – the discreteness of socio-economic stratification, the integration of ethnic groups into the social system, the role of exterior reference groups, the relation of normative values to social behavior, the transmission of prestige patterns, and the nature of social control. In order to make this material accessible to sociologists and anthropologists, special phonetic symbols and technical linguistic terms have been kept to a minimum, and defined in the text. A glossary at the beginning of the Appendixes defines symbols and linguistic terms.

Many of the techniques for gathering data, as developed in this study, may apply generally to the study of any complex speech community. Fairly complete descriptions are provided on the methods of sampling through secondary surveys (Chapter 6, Appendix C), the quantitative analysis of linguistic variables (Chapters 7, 8), interview construction (Chapter 6), eliciting a range of contextual styles (Chapter 4), subjective evaluation tests (Chapters 11, 12), methods of sampling non-respondents (Appendix D), and rapid and anonymous surveys (Chapter 3, Appendix B).

The material as presented here is essentially my 1964 Columbia University dissertation, with minor changes. Chapters 12 and 13 formed part of the original plan of Part III, dealing with social evaluation; though they did not appear in the dissertation, they have been restored here. The work as presented here was carried out under the direction of Uriel Weinreich. It is impossible for me to acknowledge properly my indebtedness to him by footnotes and citations alone; his influence may be seen most strongly in the focus of the work upon the general problems of linguistic structure and linguistic change. Many suggestions of Herbert Hyman of the Department of Sociology, Columbia University, have been incorporated in this study, not only in the approach to survey methods, but in conceptual analysis as well. William Diver's help has been important in sharpening the initial approach to phonemic analysis.

The financial support of the American Council of Learned Societies, throughout the major portion of this study, is gratefully acknowledged. With this help, it was possible to enlarge the field work to a point where the results stand upon adequate empirical data, and are not merely suggestive or programmatic. The assistance of Michael Kac, of Haverford College, was of great value in standardizing the field techniques; Mr. Kac not only served as a reliable and efficient field worker, but also as a valuable associate in the attack on problems of transcription and codification.

The linguistic survey of the Lower East Side gained considerably in accuracy and reliability through the use of the primary survey carried out by Mobilization for Youth in 1961. For permission to use the survey materials, I am deeply indebted to Mobilization for Youth and the Columbia School of Social Work. I would like to acknowledge particularly the help of Lloyd

Ohlin, Director of Research of the Columbia School of Social Work, and Wyatt Jones, Director of Research of Mobilization for Youth, who provided material support and advice at many critical points. Many suggestions have been derived from discussions with members of the Mobilization for Youth staff; I am particularly indebted to Donald Pappenfort, John Michael, Paul Lerman, and Warren Mintz.

Kenneth Lennihan of the Bureau of Applied Social Research, Columbia University, provided many important suggestions on the empirical procedures used in this study. I have profited greatly from discussions with Marvin Herzog of the Language and Culture Atlas of Ashkenazic Jewry, Columbia University, whose searching questions precipitated a number of re-analyses of the relations of linguistic and social behavior.

It would be difficult to assess the full importance of the support given by my wife Teresa, whose thoughtful criticism contributed to the solution of many analytical problems.

W. L.
New York City

Preface to the second edition: forty years later

The original edition of this book was printed by the Center for Applied Linguistics, photographed from the pages of the dissertation that was finished in the spring of 1966. In spite of the rough form of the diagrams, the prevalence of typos, and pages that terminated in mid-sentence, the book reached its audience and had considerable effect in stimulating further research. As the first quantitative study of a metropolitan speech community, it launched a mode of work that is well developed today in the annual NWAVE conference on *New Ways of Analyzing Variation*, now in its 34th year, and the journal *Language Change and Variation*, in its 17th year.

SSENYC introduced a number of concepts that have proved useful in the study of change and variation: the linguistic variable; social and stylistic stratification; the cross-over pattern; apparent time; covert prestige. It also introduced a number of procedures that were new to linguistic studies: the creation of a representative sample; the sociolinguistic interview and the control of style shifting within it; subjective reaction tests to measure the effect of particular linguistic variables; self-report and linguistic insecurity tests. Many of these methods and results were encapsulated in chapters of *Sociolinguistic Patterns* (1972a) and developed further in later publications, especially those connected with the study of Linguistic Change and Variation in Philadelphia which followed (see Chapter 15).

There were also aspects of this work that were not so widely generalized, and when the book went out of print, were not so often reproduced in the work of others. SSENYC was a bit formal in its prose style, but it dealt with people. It reached out into the community and brought to life a number of individuals whose special characteristics did much to clarify and illuminate the linguistic processes at work. I think of Nathan B., an academic who could not control the (dh) variable; of Steve K., the Jungian who wanted to go back to Brooklyn; of Dolly R., who showed me what style switching was really about; and of Mollie S., who developed a linguistic sensitivity to compensate for her loss in vision. The Appendices to SSENYC contained analytic procedures that have not been replicated in later work: in particular, the study of out-of-town respondents and the analysis of those who refused the ALS interview through the television interview. I would especially direct the new reader to the pages of Appendix B, the punch-ball game, where the sounds of New York City street life are captured in IPA.

SSENYC is not up-to-date in several respects. Its analyses are based on cross-tabulations and graphic display; there is no multivariate analysis and very little statistical evaluation. The high degree of regularity of the results made this problem seem less urgent at the time, or so it seemed to the statisticians I briefly consulted. I considered updating this treatment, but decided against it: it would have created a different book. On the positive side, the absence of multivariate analysis favored the discovery of many important interactions between gender, age, ethnicity, and social class.

The main contribution of this second edition is a series of interventions, in each chapter, where Labov 2006 breaks in with the viewpoint of forty years after. These are marked by square brackets. I point out to the reader what political issues were involved, which new efforts seem to have succeeded and why, what were the unforeseen further implications, what has worked and what hasn't, and what has been left out and why. I have made an effort to give fuller credit to those who I had learned the most from, like William Moulton and Allen Walker Read, and to those who have carried my work further on the basis of what they read in this book, like Walt Wolfram, Peter Trudgill, Henrietta Cedergren, and Gillian Sankoff. On the whole, I hope that these thirty pages of new interventions will make the book more useful to the current reader, and I hope that my junior colleague of 1966 will forgive me for looking over his shoulder with the hindsights gained over the past four decades.

Chapter 15 is entirely new. It reviews 37 studies that followed SSENYC, and then tries to answer some general questions about where the field is heading.

There is another figure in the background, who I would have step forward if I could. In my regular meetings with Uriel Weinreich, I rarely got direct suggestions about what to do next. He inserted only occasional questions as I talked at length about what I had been doing. Afterwards, I would ask myself where it was that I had talked altogether too much. There was the problem that would have to be fixed. Uriel died a year after the book was published, not much older than I was at the time. Reading over his unpublished papers, I found an outline for the study of the New York City speech community that anticipated my earliest notes for the project. I find it very hard to say where his influence is to be found, since it has merged so deeply with my own approach to language, so I must assume that it is everywhere.

This second edition of SSENYC was the idea of Andrew Winnard, and I am duly grateful for his persistence in pushing this project to maturity.

W. L.
Philadelphia

Part I

Problems and methods of analysis

1   The study of language in its social context

The work which is reported in this study is an investigation of language within the social context of the community in which it is spoken. It is a study of a linguistic structure which is unusually complex, but no more so than the social structure of the city in which it functions. Within the linguistic structure, change has occurred on a large scale, and at a rapid pace which is even more characteristic of the changing structure of the city itself. Variability is an integral part of the linguistic system, and no less a part of the behavior of the city.

To assess the relative complexity of the linguistic problem presented by New York City, it may be useful to compare this investigation to an earlier study of a sound change in progress that I carried out on the island of Martha's Vineyard (Labov 1963). This earlier work traced the distribution of a particular sound feature as it varied through several occupational, ethnic, and geographic sub-groups of the population, and through three generations of native islanders. The objective pattern of language behavior was seen to be correlated with the overall social pattern of differential reaction to specific economic strains and social pressures; it was then possible to assign a single social meaning to the linguistic feature in question. It was thus demonstrated that social pressures are continually acting upon the structure of a language, as it develops through the mechanism of imitation and hypercorrection.

In turning to the speech community of New York City, we are faced with a much more complex society, and linguistic variation of a corresponding complexity. On the Vineyard, the six thousand native residents are close to single-style speakers: they show relatively little change in their linguistic behavior as the formality of the social context changes. In New York City, the population to be sampled is more than a thousand times as large, with many more divisions of social class and caste. Neither the exterior nor the interior boundaries of the New York City community are fixed, as Martha's Vineyard's are: for within the limits of the island, the sharp distinction between the native residents and the newcomer permits little equivocation. In New York, mobility is a part of the pattern, and the descendents of the

3

earliest long-term native settlers are not necessarily the most powerful influence in the speech community today. Large numbers of people live within the city yet remain outside the boundaries of the speech community, and the line which divides the native speaker from the foreigner is broken by many doubtful cases. The area of New York City that was chosen for intensive study – the Lower East Side – does not represent a simplification of these problems. On the contrary, it is an area which exemplifies the complexity of New York City as a whole with all its variability and apparent inconsistencies.

The study of linguistic structure

The investigation of New York City is more complex than the Martha's Vineyard study in another sense: instead of limiting the investigation to a single sound feature, I will be dealing eventually with the New York vowel system as a whole. One view that would probably meet with general approval from all linguists today is that the prime object of linguistics is the structure of language, not its elements. In this study, we will be dealing with the structure of the sound system of New York City English – because it is the most amenable to quantitative techniques. Within this system, the question of structure can be approached on a number of levels of organization of increasing complexity.

The individual sound which we hear is in no way a structural unit. Many different sounds may have the same function in distinguishing words; the linguist considers them *non-distinctive variants* of a single structural unit, the *phoneme*. Phonemes in turn are organized into larger systems of vowels or consonants.

It is generally considered that the most consistent and coherent system is that of an *idiolect* – the speech of one person in the same context, over a short period of time. According to this view, as we consider the speech of that individual over longer periods, or the combined dialects of a neighborhood, a town, or a region, the system becomes progressively more inconsistent. We find an increasing number of alternations which are due to stylistic or cultural factors, or changes in time – and these are external to language, not a part of linguistic structure.[1]

---

[1] A precise statement of this position and the disposition of the problems involved may be found in Harris (1951) page 9: "These investigations are carried out for the speech of one particular person, or one community of dialectically identical persons, at a time . . . In most cases, this presents no problem . . . In other cases, however, we find the single person or the community using various forms which are not dialectally consistent with each other . . . We can then doggedly maintain the first definition and set up a system corresponding to all the linguistic elements in the speech of the person or the community. Or we may select those stretches of speech which can be described by a relatively simple and consistent system, and say that they are cases of one dialect, while the remaining stretches of speech are cases of another dialect." The evidence first presented in Chapter 2, and then in the rest of this study,

The present study adopts an entirely opposite view of the relative consistency of idiolect and dialect in the structure of New York City English. We find that in New York City, most idiolects do not form a simple, coherent system: on the contrary, they are studded with oscillations and contradictions both in the organization of sounds into phonemes, and the organization of phonemes into larger systems. These inconsistencies are inexplicable in terms of any data within the system. To explain them in terms of borrowing from some other, unknown, system is a desperate expedient, which eventually reduces the concept of system to an inconvenient fiction.

[This vigorous attack on the idiolect anticipated the more thorough treatment of the issues in Weinreich, Labov, and Herzog (1968). The result of this program led to what I see as the central dogma of sociolinguistics: that the community is prior to the individual. Or to put it another way, the language of individuals cannot be understood without knowledge of the community of which they are members. In 1989, I attacked the problem of "the exact description of the community" by a treatment of the complex Philadelphia short-*a* system, and several hundred speech communities have been described in a reasonably precise and replicable way. Still, a very large number of linguists – including some sociolinguists – believe that the community is a fiction, and that language resides in individual brains. As far as I can see, nothing has come of the many efforts to develop a linguistics of individuals (see Fillmore, Kempler & Wang (1979)), except in those fortunate situations where the speech community has been well studied in advance. Language as conceived in this book is an abstract pattern, exterior to the individual. In fact, it can be argued that the individual does not exist as a linguistic entity. That is not to say that we do not study individuals – see the case of Nathan B. (Chapter 7) or the Chapter 12 of Labov (2001) that deals with the leaders of linguistic change. But the individuals we study are conceived of as the product of their social histories and social memberships.

Still, it would not do to be too dogmatic about the central dogma. Santa Ana and Parodi have described a Mexican community of Zamora where a number of older people seem to have limited recognition of community norms (1998), and Zwicky has made strong demonstration of the existence of individual grammars for less frequent syntactic phenomena (2002).]

The treatment of this inconsistency is the overall program of the present investigation. We will begin by turning our full attention to the sources of inconsistency, and treat them as continuous phonological variables rather

Footnote 1 *(cont.)*
  shows that the inconsistency found in most New York City idiolects is so great that the first alternative of Harris is impossible, and the second implausible.
    The attempt to find linguistic uniformity by retreating to the idiolect is more thoroughly criticized in Weinreich, Labov, and Herzog (1968).

than fluctuating constants. These will be codified and measured on a quantitative, linear scale. The data must then be enlarged to include the distribution of these linguistic variables over a wide range of stylistic and social dimensions – that is, distribution within the larger structural unit, the speech community.

That New York City is a single speech community, and not a collection of speakers living side by side, borrowing occasionally from each other's dialects, may be demonstrated by many kinds of evidence. Native New Yorkers differ in their usage in terms of absolute values of the variables, but the shifts between contrasting styles follow the same pattern in almost every case. Subjective evaluations of native New Yorkers show a remarkable uniformity, in sharp contrast to the wide range of responses, from speakers who were raised in other regions.

Traditional dialect studies have shown that isolation leads to linguistic diversity, while the mixing of populations leads to linguistic uniformity. Yet in the present study of a single speech community, we will see a new and different situation: groups living in close contact are participating in rapid linguistic changes which lead to increased diversity, rather than uniformity.

Our understanding of this apparent paradox stems from the recognition that the most coherent linguistic system is that which includes the New York speech community as a whole. It is a long-standing axiom of structural linguistics that a system is essentially a set of differences. De Saussure's conception of the phoneme has been applied to all kinds of linguistic units:[2]

They are characterized, not by the particular and positive quality of each, but simply by the fact that they are not confused with each other. Phonemes are above all, contrasting, relative, and negative entities.

For a working class New Yorker, the social significance of the speech forms that he or she uses, in so far as they contain the variables in question, is that they are not the forms used by middle class speakers, and not the forms used by upper middle class speakers. The existence of these contrasting units within the system presupposes the acquaintance of speakers with the habits of other speakers. Without necessarily making any conscious choice, they identify themselves in every utterance by distinguishing themselves from other speakers who use contrasting forms.

Some earlier restrictions on linguistic study

The procedure which is outlined above may be termed historical and contextual, and, above all, empirical. Its aim is the understanding of the

---

[2] Ferdinand de Saussure (1916), page 164 (my translation).

mechanism of linguistic change, and of linguistic evolution in general. The hypotheses that will be constructed here will be designed to lead to empirical confirmation or disconfirmation, and the intention is to make no statement for which there is no empirical evidence within the study itself. No limits are set as to the type of data which are relevant, so long as they are reliable and valid, and clearly correlated with linguistic behavior. The claim is made here that only a socially realistic description can show a consistent and coherent structure for the speech of this community.[3]

In order to carry out this program, it will be necessary to disregard certain restrictions on the scope of investigation that have been imposed upon twentieth-century linguistics. They can be quoted in the forms that have been given them at various times by leading figures in the field. Although it might be difficult to find many who would explicitly endorse all of these restrictions, the combined result will give us a fairly accurate picture of the constraints placed on linguistic writings in the past five decades.

1) *Synchronic structural systems and diachronic [historical] developments must be studied in isolation*   This principle was enunciated most clearly by Saussure (1916) at the beginning of the century:

The difference in kind between successive and co-existent terms . . . excludes the use of both as the material of a single science. [p. 124] . . . Thus the synchronic 'phenomenon' has nothing in common with the diachronic one. [p. 128]

It has often been pointed out that Saussure's caveat laid the foundation for the structural study of language, but as an absolute principle, it has not been highly regarded. The application of structural arguments to historical changes has never been abandoned, and it has been followed with great vigor in the second half of the twentieth century (Martinet 1952, 1955; Moulton 1960, 1961, 1962).[4] However, the introduction of time depth into synchronic studies of present-day languages is another matter, and here the restriction seems to hold. For our present purposes, it will be necessary to regard a synchronic structure as an instantaneous description of a present state with each unit marked as to its direction and rate of change.

---

[3] By *socially realistic*, I mean a description which takes into account the distribution of language differences throughout the community, and necessarily preserves the data on the age, sex, education, occupation, and ethnic membership of the speakers studied.

[4] Martinet is cited as the exponent of a different restriction in 3). Martinet's theoretical approach to the explanation of linguistic change is presented concisely in "Function, Structure and Sound Change" (1952). A fuller treatment is given in *Économie des changements phonétiques* (1955).

2) *Sound change cannot be directly observed*   The well-known statement of Bloomfield on this point may be quoted:[5]

> The process of linguistic change has never been directly observed; we shall see that such observation, with our present facilities, is inconceivable.

Logically, Bloomfield's statement is unassailable if it is taken to mean that we cannot observe sound change in the same way that we watch crystals grow or cells divide. Like other forms of social change, linguistic change is a change in a pattern of behavior, and it must be observed by inference from the sampling of discrete stages. But Bloomfield's statement is extended to exclude the possibility of such inferential observations as well:

> We must suppose that, no matter how minute and accurate our observation, we should always find deviant forms, because . . . the forms of the language are subject to the incessant working of other factors of change, such as, especially, borrowing and analogic combination . . . [p. 364]

Bloomfield's argument was avowedly designed to support the neogrammarian assumption of the absolute regularity of sound change, despite the observed irregularity of empirical data. In actual observations, we find that change proceeds by fits and starts; that the newer form is heard in some words, and the older form in others; that some groups of speakers lead in the change, while others lag. This irregularly advancing front does not answer Bloomfield's requirements for a perfectly regular, gradual shift in a sound pattern which is never ragged, never retrograde. The net effect of this argument was to remove the empirical study of linguistic change from the program of twentieth-century linguistics. Since borrowing and analogy were considered relatively unsystematic processes, and sound change was unapproachable, there remained nothing to do but construct abstract models of an unobservable process.[6]

[Bloomfield and the neogrammarians appear here in an unfavorable light, since their rigid adherence to their doctrine inhibited them from studying ongoing variation in the present. Later on, my efforts to resolve

---

[5] *Language* (1933), page 347.

[6] Bloomfield's original prohibition has been repeated by C. F. Hockett, *A Course in Modern Linguistics* (1958), Chapter 52. Hockett's statement of Bloomfield's position is given at the outset: "No one has yet observed sound change: we have only been able to detect it via its consequences. We shall see later that a more nearly direct observation would be theoretically possible, if impractical, but any ostensible report of such an observation so far must be discredited." Hockett's hypothetical suggestion for the study of sound change involves a thousand accurate acoustic records made each month from the members of a tight-knit community for a period of fifty years. Of this point of view, Weinreich (1959) wrote in his review: "It is hard to feel comfortable with a theory which holds that the great changes of the past were of one kind, theoretically mysterious and interesting, whereas everything that is observable today is of another kind, transparent and (by implication) of scant theoretical interest."

the neogrammarian controversy (Labov 1981) led me to believe that they were essentially correct – that in most sound changes, it is the phoneme that changes, not words. This issue is still being disputed, but in *Principles of Linguistic Change* (Labov 1994), the neogrammarians emerge as the heroes of the story.]

3) *Feelings about language are inaccessible*   This restriction has not been discussed as freely as the others, except where linguists have used it to combat the excesses of a normative approach to language. However, the following statement by Bloch and Trager in their *Outline of Linguistic Analysis* is pointed enough:[7]

The native speaker's feeling about sounds or about anything else is inaccessible to investigation by the techniques of linguistic science, and any appeal to it is a plain evasion of the linguist's proper function. The linguist is concerned solely with the facts of speech. The psychological correlates of these facts are undoubtedly important; but the linguist has no means – as a linguist – of analyzing them.

As an antidote to crude psychologizing in the place of phonemic analysis, this statement may have served admirably well. But it seems to be cast in an unnecessarily absolute form reflecting a certain purism that seems to have crept into twentieth-century linguistics. It is possible that too much concern with the image of the linguist – with what the linguist is permitted to do *as a linguist* – may interfere with one's view of language as it is spoken.[8]

4) *The linguist should not use non-linguistic data to explain linguistic change* This point of view may be considered more a statement of policy, or a focus of attention, than a prohibition. It was originally directed against theories which attempted to correlate linguistic change with such factors as climate, inherited differences in physiology, invasions, and revolutions.[9] Martinet (1955) turned linguists' attention away from such remote and occasional factors, and showed that the internal relations of linguistic systems produced constant pressures towards changes that were present in every act of communication. His point of view is supported by evidence in the present study, and many references will be made to Martinet's analysis of structural pressures towards linguistic change. However, in emphasizing the importance of the structural relations of functional units, Martinet has

[7] Bernard Bloch and George L. Trager (1942), page 40.
[8] The evidence to be presented in Chapter 11 indicates that subjective reactions to individual sound features are by no means as inaccessible as Bloch and Trager thought. However the method employed here serves an entirely different purpose than the psychological one which Bloch and Trager rejected.
[9] A review of a number of such theories is given by A. Sommerfelt (1930).

laid unnecessary restrictions on the linguist. In a report to the Ninth International Congress of Linguists in 1962, he declared:[10]

It is clear, of course, that any language . . . is exposed to changes determined by impacts from outside; no one will doubt that man's changing needs in general will affect his communicative needs which in turn, will condition linguistic structure. The impacts from outside may consist in the pressure exerted on each other by two languages 'in contact.'

The linguist will feel competent to deal with the latter, but he may be excused if, in his capacity as a linguist, he declines the invitation to investigate sociological conditioning.

Martinet himself has shown a broad range of interest in the study of language in its social context, yet the statement given above reflects a policy which is followed by many who would apply Martinet's ideas. Attempts have been made to explain linguistic change by juxtaposing abstract models of linguistic systems which were in fact separated by many centuries and extensive geographic dislocation. The painstaking inquiries of historical linguists into dialectal variations and intermediate stages have been overlooked or disregarded.[11] Such bold abstractions draw support from Martinet's confidence that structural explanations based on the internal economy of the system are sufficient to account for linguistic change in the present, though they may be consequences of social dislocations in earlier times. Evidence in this study, and in the earlier work on Martha's Vineyard, runs counter to Martinet's notion that social forces operated on language only in the remote past. Martinet's reliance on communicative function in the narrowest sense also seems to have played a part in his general argument. The indications of the present studies are that the role of language in self-identification, an aspect of the expressive function of language, is more important in the mechanism of phonological change.

[Martinet was the teacher of my teacher, Uriel Weinreich, and I had the unofficial status of *petit fils* among the Martinetians. Though I argue here against Martinet's insistence on the autonomous character of linguistics, later work has confirmed his contention that the structural consequences of external disruption of the linguistic system may work themselves out for

[10]   Martinet's (1962) report on "Structural Variation in Language" embodied this prohibition in even stronger terms as delivered on the floor. Objections were raised by several European linguists on behalf of geographic and other "external" data, but no comment was made on the exclusion of socially determined conditions.

[11]   An example of such an a-historical treatment of linguistic history may be found in Herbert Pilch (1955). Pilch used Martinet's ideas "to trace in outline the history of the American English vowel pattern from the time of its geographical separation from British English." The "outline" consisted of three points: Kökeritz' reconstruction of sixteenth-century pronunciation, Pilch's own observations of modern American dialects, and one "connecting link": the vowel pattern described by Noah Webster in 1800.

many centuries, leading progressively from one adjustment to another, so that much of linguistic development is autonomous. Evidence for this view appears most strongly in the *Atlas of North American English* (Labov, Ash & Boberg 2006).]

Some earlier studies of language in its social context

Despite the fact that some of the restrictions on the scope of linguistic study are stated in a rigid form, they may best be regarded as temporary expedients adopted by linguists to serve particular ends. In setting them aside, we are returning in one sense to the sound empirical base which formed the methodology of linguistics before a split had developed into dialectology on the one hand and structuralism on the other.

It may be appropriate to quote at some length from a lecture delivered by Meillet in 1905 before a class in general linguistics. Meillet had worked intensively in many areas of Indo-European historical linguistics; his remarks show that he had already formed a clear conception of a socially realistic linguistics which would continue the empirical tradition which he had absorbed. He began with the observation that all historical laws which had been discovered in the nineteenth century were still to be considered as mere possibilities.[12]

. . . we must discover the variables which permit or induce the realization of the possibilities thus recognized.

Meillet added that this variable cannot be the structure of the physical organs, or a mental function.

But there is an element in which circumstances induce continual variation, sometimes rapid, sometimes slow, but never completely suspended: it is the structure of society.

He continued with an analysis which is remarkable for its brevity and clarity.

. . . it is probable, *a priori*, that every modification of social structure is expressed by a change in the conditions from which language develops. Language is an institution with its proper autonomy: we must therefore discover the general conditions for development from a purely linguistic point of view, and this is the object of general linguistics, with its anatomical, physiological, and psychic conditions . . . but from the fact that language is a social institution, it follows that linguistics is a social science, and the only variable to which we can turn to account for linguistic change is social change, of which linguistic variations are only consequences.

---

[12] Antoine Meillet (1921), pages 16–17.

We must determine which social structure corresponds to a given linguistic structure, and how, in a general manner, changes in social structure are translated into changes in linguistic structure.

It is evident, from the record of the ensuing years, that neither Meillet nor his students took this prospectus with full seriousness. That nothing further was accomplished along these lines may have been due to the fact that the views of Saussure were just beginning to take hold at that time, and linguistics turned in a completely different direction. We can now return to this area of work with more adequate equipment than Meillet could have brought to bear upon such difficult problems. Not only do we have a more explicit theory of phonological structure, but we also possess such useful tools as tape recording, spectrograms and methods of sampling and handling large quantities of data.

Before proceeding to the discussion of the methods used in the present study, it would be best to review some of the more concrete achievements of the intervening years in the empirical study of language in its community context. The references will be discussed under the heading of the particular restriction on linguistic investigation which was necessarily disregarded by those undertaking the work.

1) *Empirical studies of linguistic change in progress*   This is a category which is unfortunately almost empty. There are, of course, innumerable studies of linguistic change over long periods of time, utilizing texts and the comments of contemporary observers. But there are very few systematic studies of communities in which the observer analyzed the speech of successive generations to study the development of change. (See Chapter 9 for an elaboration of such methods.) In 1899, Gauchat began the study of the speech of Charmey, a village in French-speaking Switzerland, and found systematic differences in the treatment of six phonological variables by three successive generations. His study, *L'unité phonétique dans le patois d'une commune* (1905), attracted a great deal of comment, particularly from neogrammarian theoreticians who tried to explain away his findings as nothing but a complicated series of borrowings.[13] M. E. Hermann (1929) re-studied Charmey, and his results confirmed Gauchat's inference of phonological change in four of the six items.

[Even though Gauchat's study of Charmey is a purely qualitative description, it stands out among earlier studies of the speech community as the nonpareil investigation of change in progress, and almost every such study since has begun by citing this work. It is full of astonishing insights

---

[13] P. G. Goidanich (1926) (cited by Sommerfelt 1930).

and observations, including the first solid finding that women are the leaders of language change.]

Kurath's plan for the *Linguistic Atlas of New England* (1941) called for the selection of at least one old and one middle-aged informant in each community; this arrangement has permitted analysis of linguistic changes in progress, such as that by W. S. Avis (1961) of the receding pattern of New England short /o/. In the *Atlas of the Middle and Atlantic States*, three social levels were interviewed in many cities. The *Linguistic Atlas* records were also utilized by the present writer in the earlier study of Martha's Vineyard (1963), although the distribution of speech sounds in successive generations of the contemporary community formed the primary data.

In addition to these few studies, there have been many observations on differences in the speech of older and younger subjects, in the course of dialect studies. However, the number of investigations that have been systematically planned to study linguistic change in progress are very few indeed.

2) *The structural analysis of historical changes*   In the opening pages of his *Économie des changements phonétiques*, Martinet (1955) cites some of the earlier observations of Sweet, Passy, and other nineteenth-century phoneticians. Pfalz (1918) applied some earlier ideas of van Wijk to the structure of contemporary German dialects, with particular attention to front-back symmetry in the vowel system;[14] he explained the symmetric movements of front and back vowels as a product of changes in the "base of articulation" characteristic of the language in question.

Martinet's theories of the internal economy of phonological structures (1952, 1955) were more comprehensive and systematic than any published previously. The most important empirical verification of these concepts has been provided by Moulton (1960, 1961, 1962) who studied the geographic distribution of structural variations in the dialects of Swiss German, and demonstrated the existence of regular historical tendencies to fill empty spaces in phonological structures, and to equalize distances between functional units in phonological space. Following Moulton, Kufner (1957, 1960) has carried out further investigations of this type.

---

[14] The rules given by Pfalz for front-back symmetry may be useful for comparison with the empirically determined developments of (æ) and (oh), (ay), and (aw), in this study. "In an indogermanic language, co-existing front and back vowels pass through the same types of sound change, in so far as they possess the same height and tension, and so long as the one vowel remains a front vowel and the other a back vowel. If in an indogermanic language co-existing vowels of equal height and tension are diphthongized, this diphthongization will follow parallel routes, in that the second members of the diphthong will remain in the same relation to the first" (my translation).

In his programmatic article "Is a Structural Dialectology Possible?," Weinreich (1954) demonstrated the difficulties of applying the concept of a closed structure to the almost continuous range of partial similarities and differences which constitute "dialects" in the traditional sense. He showed that the primary problem of a structural dialectology is that of breaking down the continuum into discrete units, a problem which is faced in the present study.

A very different type of structural analysis from that considered above has been applied to historical developments by Halle (1962), and others. Halle has described historical changes as adjustments in a series of rules for the realization of words (or morphemes) as sets of acoustic features.

[Halle's remarkable paper of 1962, which created generative phonology, developed this very reasonable view that the mechanism of change lies in children's reorganization of adult grammars. Lightfoot (1997, 1999) has strongly argued for this mechanism in his examination of completed changes, though I do not know of any application to changes in progress. In any case, I was intrigued to find a new version of Halle's argument emerging from my own effort to explain the development of changes in progress by children's re-analysis of their parents' dialects – in this case not a structural re-analysis but a re-interpretation of the social correlates of linguistic variation.]

A statistical approach to phonological variation in recently settled areas was provided by D. W. Reed and J. L. Spicer in their study of a transition area in California phonology (1952).

3) *Studies of subjective evaluation of language*   There are even fewer citations which can be made under this heading than under the first. G. N. Putnam and E. M. O'Hern (1955) published a dissertation on "The Status Significance of an Isolated Urban Dialect." The speech of African–American residents of a particular neighborhood in Washington was studied, and recordings of some were played to a selected group of judges from outside the area who evaluated the status of the speakers. This work suffered from a number of limitations: the selection of informants was unsystematic, and from the occasional background information which was collected, it appears that only a minority of the informants had any connection with the neighborhood or Washington during their formative years.[15] The speech of the informants was judged as a whole, and it is not

---

[15] Of 39 informants whose place of birth was known, only 3 were born in the neighborhood; 15 in Washington, and the rest in southern states. Of 62 informants whose length of residence was known, only 20 had lived in the neighborhood more than 15 years, and 16 had lived there less than 5 years.

clear what the judges were reacting to, or how representative their judgments were.

W. A. Grootaers (1959) reported on efforts to determine the "Origin and Nature of the Subjective Boundaries of Dialects." The inhabitants of a number of Japanese villages were asked if the language of their own village differed from that of a number of neighboring villages, and to what extent. Grootaers reported a negative result and concluded that subjective consciousness seems of little value in linguistic research. Yet his results seemed very rich, and his disappointment stemmed from the fact that he expected to use subjective reactions as a base for the study of dialect units and dialect boundaries, rather than as a separate plane of linguistic behavior.

A series of carefully controlled experiments to test evaluational reactions to speech have been carried out by Wallace Lambert and associates. These investigators began with the concept that "spoken language is an identifying feature of members of a national or cultural group and any listener's attitude towards members of a particular group should generalize to the language they use." They tested the reactions of English Canadians to the recorded voices of English and French speakers (Lambert et al. 1960), and asked the judges to evaluate the personality of the speakers. In the "matched guise" format, judges did not know that the same bilingual speakers were using French in one recording, and English in another. The judgments of personalities proved to be influenced favorably by the use of English, negatively by the use of French. Similar tests were carried out for English and English spoken with a Jewish accent (Anisfeld et al. 1962), and in Israel for Arabic, Ashkenazic, and Sephardic Hebrew (Lambert et al. 1963). Though these experiments establish the importance of general linguistic signals in expressive communication, they do not isolate subjective reactions to any particular features of a language.

4) *Studies of linguistic behavior in its social context*   There are a great many studies which might be cited in this area; anthropologists, linguists, psychologists, and sociologists have all contributed to the study of language in its social context, in approximately that order of magnitude. The works that will be mentioned here are primarily the empirical studies which have isolated socially significant variables of a language.

The programmatic article of Hymes (1962), "The Ethnography of Speaking," sets up a general framework for the study of the speech community. Some of the most important contributions have come from anthropologists working in south-east Asia (Ferguson & Gumperz 1960). Gumperz (1958) studied 10 phonological variables in an Indian village with 31 social castes, and found 6 caste groups differentiated by these linguistic indicators. Bright and Ramanujan (1962) studied the evolution of upper and lower class dialects in Kanarese, Tamil, and Tulu, finding evidence for independent developments on both conscious and unconscious planes.

Fischer (1958) studied social influences on the use of *-ing* by a class of New England schoolchildren, and suggested a much broader program for linguists and anthropologists in this area.

[Fischer's small study anticipated both the quantitative methods of this book and the dimensions of social variation in it. Working with very small numbers, Fischer showed the differential behavior of males and females for the sociolinguistic variable (ING), patterns of style shifting, and the distinction between "model" boys and normal boys.]

The linguists who have contributed most to the study of language in its social context are primarily those who have worked in dialect geography. Almost all studies in this field show some concern with the social context in which speech occurs, although the community is primarily regarded as a point in a geographic matrix (Roedder 1926, Bottiglioni 1954). The most important step forward towards a socially realistic dialectology was taken by Kurath et al. (1941) who designed the *Linguistic Atlas of New England*, and its later extensions, to include informants of several social types in each community studied. McDavid (1948) drew upon this information to analyze the social significance of post-vocalic /r/ in South Carolina.

Herzog (1963), drawing upon the materials of the *Language and Culture Atlas of Ashkenazic Jewry*, showed that both structural linguistic factors and social factors were required to account for the distribution of dialects in a transition area of northern Poland.

A number of studies by A. W. Read (1936, 1938) have illuminated the social context in which the development of American English has taken place. In a recent study of the genesis of *O.K.*, Read (1963) showed how a particular linguistic attitude in one American community produced a proliferation of abbreviations, of which *O.K.* was the most successful surviving member.

[Allen Walker Read taught my first linguistics course, and is responsible for my presence in the field. Though he was never engaged in theoretical linguistics, he had a keen eye for significant detail and provocative questions, such as "The grammar of double talk"(1977). His papers on the origin of *O.K.* provided a definitive answer to a much disputed question by anchoring the facts in the speech community of young Boston social clubs in the 1830s, and stand as a progenitor of socio-historical work.]

One of the few quantitative studies of phonological features within a community is that of Reichstein (1960). She tested 570 Paris schoolgirls for phonemic contrast in minimal pairs involving /a–ɑ/, /ɛ – ɛ:/, /ɪn – æn/; it was found that these phonemic contrasts are disappearing rapidly, and that certain working class districts in the interior of the city are leading in this respect.

In general, it may be said that psychologists and sociologists have lacked the linguistic training required to isolate particular elements of language structure, and have worked primarily with vocabulary or content analysis. Bernstein (1959, 1960) has dealt with the relations of social class to British English in a series of articles. Schatzman & Strauss (1955) analyzed the reports of a disaster given by rural Arkansas speakers of several class levels, and found differences in perspective and style of narration; evaluations of speech are freely given by the authors, but without any formal method.

Lerman (1962) incorporated in a social survey of youth, ten questions on slang words associated with delinquent activities; knowledge of the meaning of these words was correlated with delinquent behavior, and with the age at which children enter groups which participate in this behavior.

A great many other works might be cited which make general observations on the relations of language and society, but for the study of the complex communities of the United States and western Europe, it appears that quantitative methods are required. Of all the studies cited here, only Reichstein's can fairly be placed in that category.

Quantitative techniques are required for dealing with speech communities as complex as New York City. In Chapter 2, the problems of studying the language of New York City will be discussed, and the methods used by previous studies of the city's speech in dealing with these problems. The principal devices used in the present study for the analysis of this complex situation – the five main phonological indexes – will then be selected and defined.

2 First approach to the structure of New York City English

[The first half of this chapter demonstrates the practical difficulties for the linguist in dealing with inherent variation – where it is not possible at any one time to predict which of several alternatives a speaker will adopt in the stream of speech. New York City was a classic case, and the review of the literature shows how linguists were in fact baffled by the problem. The second half presents a solution: the definition of five linguistic variables. The concept of the linguistic variable is probably the most influential and widely adopted aspect of the approach to linguistics introduced here. The central idea, which is argued in many different ways throughout the book, is that the linguistic variable is an aspect of linguistic structure rather than the absence of it.]

It is safe to say that the language of New York City is better known to the people of the United States as a whole than the language of any other single city. The great majority of our informants report that whenever they travel outside of the city, they are quickly identified as New Yorkers.[1] On radio and television, stereotypes of middle class and working class New York speech have traditionally been used for comic effects. For many years, several other features of working class and lower class New York City speech have been stigmatized under the label of *Brooklynese*. In Minnesota or Pittsburgh, the speech of lower class New Yorkers may be imitated by boys who think of this style as a symbol of the tough, hard life and defiance of authority. Indeed, some of these sound features have entered into a folk mythology.

Previous studies of the language of New York City

In 1896, E. H. Babbitt published a brief description of "The English of the Lower Classes in New York City and Vicinity," in the first volume of

---

[1] One of the questions in the survey of the Lower East Side dealt with these experiences. The data is summarized in Chapter 13.

Dialect Notes.[2] It is one of the earliest descriptions of an urban dialect by an American linguist, and the information is exceptionally valuable for the interpretation of linguistic changes now in progress in New York City. Babbitt's notes were made during six years spent in New York City, teaching at Columbia University.

> The guards on the elevated roads, the tradespeople, some of my students, the servants in my kitchen and those of my friends, the newsboys, hawkers and "barkers," the school-children in school and out, have all contributed material.

By the "lower classes," Babbitt means about 90 percent of the population – all New Yorkers except the upper class, who "live a life of their own, travel a great deal, and educate their children in private schools, in which most of the teachers are not New Yorkers." Babbitt's observations of the linguistic situation in New York City show a remarkable resemblance to the one we observe today. On the one hand "a New Yorker who has four American-born grandparents is a rarity, and . . . a great majority have not one"; yet on the other hand:

> there is a distinct New York variety of English pronunciation, used by a large majority of the inhabitants, and extending over a considerable district. It is most marked in the lower classes, who do not travel nor come under outside influences; but it is rare to find any person who learned to speak in New York who cannot be recognized before he has spoken two sentences.

The view maintained in the present study is that New York City is a single speech community; Babbitt comments:

> In spite of diverse origins, the population of New York is singularly homogeneous socially and intellectually, as soon as you get below the distinct upper classes.

Babbitt saw clearly that the vast numbers of European immigrants had little influence on the New York City dialect of English: "after a generation, or even sooner, [they] are fully amalgamated, without exerting any sensible influence to change in their direction the general current."

Although Babbitt's description of the phonology of the City is brief, it is based upon evidence he was surrounded with, and he seems to have made good use of his opportunities. It is unfortunate that the more elaborate surveys made in more recent decades do not show the same sense of social realism. For one reason or another, all of the studies since Babbitt's have

---

[2] The citations of previous studies of New York City will be identified in the text by author's name and date of publication, to avoid the multiplication of footnotes. Complete data is given in the Bibliography.

been devoted to a small minority of the New York City population, and none have reported the speech of the great bulk of the working class and lower middle class population that Babbitt described.

There are three principal sources of information on the speech of New York City for the period 1930 to 1960: the writings of C. K. Thomas, the records of the Linguistic Atlas, and the studies of A. F. Hubbell.

C. K. Thomas (1932, 1942, 1951) published several articles about New York City speech, based upon his observations of college students who attended Cornell University. His observations are primarily of two types: lists of specific words which occur with particular sounds, especially in the area of the low back vowels, and discussions of errors from the point of view of the speech teacher. In Thomas' extensive records of the usage of college students, we have valuable information on the more formal styles of younger middle class speakers.

The interviews for the Linguistic Atlas of the Eastern United States, directed by Kurath (1939), were carried out in 1941 by Guy S. Lowman. The results of the Atlas interviews in New York City are reported in three Atlas publications which have described the dialect regions of the Eastern United States, as a whole, dealing with lexical items, verb forms, and pronunciation, (Kurath 1949; Atwood 1953; Kurath and McDavid 1961). A full treatment of the New York City material is given in the dissertation of Frank (1948) and a separate section is devoted to New York City in Wetmore's study (1959) of the low back and low central vowels as reported in the Atlas records.

The population sampled by the Atlas was primarily the "old stock" of New York City: those whose parents and grandparents had been born and raised within the city. The field worker selected certain types of informants, according to the instructions quoted at length in Chapter 9. In this typology, Kurath used considerations of age, education, and connection with the local community. In New York City, twenty-five informants were selected – a comparatively large number, since in most cities only three to five informants were used. The sampling methods were informal, and a great deal was necessarily left to the judgment of the field worker.[3]

The policy of selecting informants from families with the longest history of residence in the area was in accordance with the principal focus of the Atlas: to determine the basic outlines of the regional dialects of the Eastern United States, as determined by the original settlement patterns. In New York City, this policy had the consequence of limiting the population

---

[3] At the time that New York was surveyed, Lowman was the only field worker. The interview took several days, and the availability of the informants was necessarily an important consideration.

sampled to a very small minority of the native English speakers.[4] However, it would not have been feasible to modify the overall procedure of the Atlas because of the special conditions in New York City.

In 1950, Allan F. Hubbell published his independent study of *The Pronunciation of English in New York City*. He investigated the speech of thirty informants, and reviewed phonograph records of nine Atlas informants as well. Hubbell was a meticulous and systematic observer, who reported many details which are not found in the Atlas records. Furthermore, he was conscious of the need to examine phonemic contrasts, and was thus able to add new insights in this area.

The population sampled by Hubbell has the same general limitations as that of the Linguistic Atlas. Most of his informants were fourth or fifth generation New Yorkers, and there is no representation from any of the very large groups that have entered the speech community within the past eighty years – Jews, Italians, and African–Americans – and which now make up the bulk of the speech community. Fourteen of the thirty informants were Columbia College students, and the rest of the informants were over fifty years old.

An article by Arthur Bronstein, "Let's Take Another Look at New York City Speech" (1962), reviews some of the materials cited above, with a judicious overall discussion of the social and dialectal complexity of the region, and adds some new observations based on the speech of Queens College students.

Thus it appears that previous studies of New York City speech, with the exception of Babbitt's brief report, have concentrated upon college students and members of old-stock families, with a small number of speakers from the very lowest ranking groups. Despite such limitations, these reports show fairly good agreement on most of the sounds that are heard in New York City. Some of the studies, especially Hubbell's, give a large body of information on the special status of particular words, which might otherwise have been overlooked by an investigator coming fresh to the scene. In Hubbell's work there is a good description of most of the phonemic contrasts that are found in New York City, and a new study which began without consulting these records might miss many subtle points.

The limitations of these studies as a whole lie in two distinct areas. The first is in the treatment of variation.

All of these studies of New York City recognized the existence of social and stylistic variation, although the exploration of such variation was not

---

[4] Glazer and Moynihan (1963) estimate that "not more than one-twentieth of the present population of New York City is 'old stock'"; in 1855, the Irish-born and German-born and their children made up a majority of the city's population.

their principal aim. In the Linguistic Atlas records, the usage of the informants for any particular phoneme is given in a large number of words.
Frank's monograph provides charts with ten to twelve forms in which each
phoneme occurred; the usage of each informant is listed for all of these
forms, usually as a choice between two or three principal variants. Wetmore
gives detailed information for the low back vowels by listing the number of
occurrences of each variant symbol in the Atlas notation for a number of
words, and a similar distribution for single words with a breakdown by
social types. This data will be utilized at many points in the present study, to
give additional time depth to the interpretation of linguistic change.

The value of these materials for our purposes is greatly enhanced by the
fact that Kurath foresaw the need for studying social variation, and provided
a social classification for the informants. However, there are limitations in the
Atlas method which imply the need for caution in making direct comparisons
between Atlas records and the results of the present study. The stylistic
context of the Atlas interview was essentially that which will be termed
"careful conversation," in the discussion of Chapter 4. Although casual conversation undoubtedly must have occurred in the course of the long Atlas
interviews, the forms noted down were primarily isolated words or phrases,
spoken in stressed position, as answers to direct questions about lexical
usage. As far as social variation is concerned, the method of classifying informants was informal, and depended on a mixture of objective criteria (age,
education) and subjective impressions of the field worker ("old-fashioned"
vs. "modern," "wide social contacts" vs. "restricted social contacts"). In some
cases, the language of the informant was used as an additional criterion in the
Atlas social typology, in preference to the objective data (Kurath 1939, p. 41).

[Beginning with the Martha's Vineyard project, I've profited a great deal
from the output of the Linguistic Atlas tradition of Kurath and McDavid.
That earlier work has provided the main real-time basis for my efforts to
trace linguistic change in progress. Moreover, the sociolinguistic interview
grew from its original base in the approach of dialect geography. This chapter
unites an appreciation of the strengths of the Atlas work with an assessment
of its limitations. Instead of an opposition between "dialectology" and
"sociolinguistics," the end result was a mutual recognition. Kurath's *Studies
in Area Linguistics* (1972) devoted space to a summary of the New York City
study, and one of the major findings of the *Atlas of North American English*
(Labov et al. 2006) was that Kurath and McDavid were right in their fundamental division of American English into North, Midland, and South.]

Hubbell's report on the variability of his informants is quite detailed in a
qualitative sense, but he gives less quantitative information than the Atlas
records. In a final section of his study, each of the informants' usage is
described for a long list of phonological variables, including all of those

discussed in the present investigation. The fluctuations of the informants are reported in such general terms as "occasionally," "rarely," or "irregularly." Hubbell also reviewed the pronunciation of nine Atlas informants, as preserved on phonograph records, and so provided a valuable basis for comparing his survey with the Atlas.[5]

Hubbell's social classification of informants is based upon their speech: he arranges the thirty subjects in order of decreasing cultivation, based on his own general impressions. On the other hand, he gives sufficient objective data to allow these informants to be re-classified in accordance with the methods used in the present study. The majority of his informants would be classified in the highest ranking social group of the present study; like the Atlas, Hubbell's record provides comparatively few informants from the bulk of the working class and lower middle class population.

In order to investigate the pronunciation of a great many lexical items by his informants, Hubbell found it necessary to rely primarily upon the reading of isolated sentences. He defends this policy on the grounds that stylistic variation is really not very important:

. . . objections have sometimes been raised to the use of written material. These objections, I feel, are not particularly convincing, for the distortions that appear in reading are pretty obvious and can be taken into account. The most important variation from ordinary conversational speech is in the frequently altered pattern of intonation and stress . . . (p. 14)

On the other hand, Hubbell states that the extemporaneous material recorded can serve as a check on the written material, and notes a tendency for many New Yorkers to pronounce post-vocalic /r/ in reading more than in conversation. His descriptions of the variations of his informants are primarily based on the extemporaneous material, and in only a few cases does he actually provide information on stylistic shift.

The net result of Hubbell's treatment of variability appears in his final assessment of New Yorkers' use of /r/:

The pronunciation of a very large number of New Yorkers exhibits a pattern in these words that might most accurately be described as the complete absence of any pattern. Such speakers sometimes pronounce /r/ before a consonant or a pause and sometimes omit it, in a thoroughly haphazard fashion. (p. 48)

Hubbell sees a tendency towards the adoption of /r/ as a norm of correctness, but only for those informants who consciously acknowledge that they think /r/ is correct.

---

[5] The phonemic identity of the raised vowel in *bad, ask, dance* with that of *where, bear* was not recorded in the Atlas transcript, but was noted by Hubbell in reviewing the phonograph records of nine informants. Hubbell also noted some marginal contrasts such as *chalk-chocolate-chock* and *curd-cud-occurred*.

In many cases, this irregularity is a result of the conscious attempt, only partly successful, of originally r-less speakers to pronounce the consonant because they feel
that it is more "correct" to do so. But often no conscious effort is involved. The
speaker hears both types of pronunciation about him all the time, both seem almost
equally natural to him, and it is a matter of pure chance which one comes to his lips.
(p. 48)

Thus we find that a very careful observer, who recognizes the existence of
extensive variability among his informants, regards New York City use of
/r/ (with its many phonological consequences) as a massive case of "free
variation." Similar reports are given for many other variables.

The investigations of Bronstein were confined to college students, but
they represent a sample of a very large number of students, selected randomly. He makes the following statement on the use of /r/:

Final and preconsonantal /r/, as in *her* and *charm*, is used more widely in the New
York City area than seems to be reported in the literature. As noted in the previously
cited works by Hubbell and Thomas, complete consistency in the use of this sound
is not present. But the impression is growing that perhaps as many educated speakers use it, with reasonable consistency, as do not. Perhaps Thomas' statement that
New York City speech is 'characterized by a frequent, but by no means universal,
loss of /r/ in the final and preconsonantal positions . . .' does not seem to hold now,
unless one understands this to mean that both the loss and the presence of final and
preconsonantal /r/ are almost equally frequent.

The number of qualifiers in Bronstein's statements is a tribute to the
difficulty of the problem. It is disappointing to learn that these impressions
are the only result of three controlled and quantitative procedures, in
which the author sampled the speech of thousands of Queens College
students.[6]

Bronstein's treatment of other variables shows a similar difficulty in analyzing large-scale variation. On the raised vowel of *ask*, *hand*, *crab*, he says:
". . . there is little doubt that three forms, (ɛ³, æ ̣, æ) exist in free variation
. . ." (p. 25)

At the outset, Bronstein does recognize the existence of differences in
pronunciation among different social groups. Yet most of his particular
comments present a picture of increasing "free variation," a fluctuation of
numerous variants that are to be found in the speech of "the cultivated" as
well as "the uncultivated."

---

[6] Bronstein examined the records of approximately 200 entering freshmen at Queens College,
randomly selected from each entering class of between 800 and 1,000 students for the five
years between 1947 and 1952. He then studied the records of sophomore and junior students who had been interviewed for the teacher-training program, for 1952 through 1955.
Finally, he himself has kept notes on over 500 students from 1947 to 1961 in the
Department of Speech freshman course.

This general retreat before the complexity of variation in New York City is matched by the failure of previous studies to show any clear structural pattern for the speech of the city.

The vowel structure of New York City English, as it appears in the Atlas records, was analyzed by Wetmore (1959), Frank (1948), and by Kurath and McDavid (1961). All of these writers agree in showing a list of sixteen phonemes, classified by distributional criteria as *checked* and *free*. Kurath and McDavid (1961, p. 6) show a structural chart for the vowels of New York City, which is identical with that for the Upper and Lower South. A system of ingliding and long phonemes for words such as *fear, four, far*, does not appear in this analysis. Instead, /r/ is said to appear as an unsyllabic phoneme /ə/. (pp. 15, 115)

In their introduction, Kurath and McDavid discuss the advantages and disadvantages of analyzing American English vowels as binary (vowel plus semivowel, /ey, ow/) or as unary (/e, o/). For the purposes of dialect geography, they find the latter preferable. This decision does not entirely resolve the question of the ingliding and long phonemes. Instead of interpreting the unconstricted glide which follows the nucleus of *fear, four*, as a semivowel, Kurath and McDavid show New York City *ear* as /iə/, *care* as /ɛə/, *door* as /oə/, but *law* as /lɔ/ (pp. 117, 55–57). These distinctions support their interpretation that the glide /ə/ is not a semivowel used generally with all nuclei, but only a representative of the diaphone /r/. The phonetic basis for this interpretation is a series of transcriptions in which a schwa [ə] is written after the vowel of *ear, care, Mary, four, door*, but only a superscript schwa [ᵊ] or no glide at all after the vowel of *dog, frost, law, forty*, and *morning*.

The usage of the informants for the present study, and for Hubbell's study, does not support such a distinction. The words *lore* and *law* are homonyms, and the same vowel (with or without a glide) appears in *door, four, for, frost, off, office, gnaw, nor*, etc. Furthermore, the occurrence of a central glide [ə] in *Mary* as opposed to a shorter glide [ᵊ] in *forty* does not describe the speech of informants for the present survey or for Hubbell's study.

[I was wrong about this. I assumed, and everyone else did too, that when /r/ was vocalized in *nor* it became identical to *gnaw*, and r-less *source* was identical to *sauce*. In 1972, Labov, Yaeger & Steiner published the surprising finding that the nuclei of these two word classes were statistically distinct even when the /r/ was vocalized to an inglide. The native speaker heard *source* and *sauce* as "the same," but produced a reliable statistical difference between the nuclei of these vowels: *source* was higher and/or backer than *sauce*. This was the first discovered case of "near-merger," where speakers produce a consistent difference between two classes of words that they label "the same" in minimal pair tests and commutation tests. Dozens of such cases have been discovered since (see Milroy and Harris 1980, Labov 1994, Janson and Shulman 1983, Kontra 1993, Di Paolo and Faber 1990, etc.). But this hidden persistence of the effect of a following /r/ on the vowel nucleus does not justify the use of different notation for the glides.]

The Linguistic Atlas analysis of the vowel structure of New York City English differs from that used by Hubbell in another important point. The vowel of *ask*, *bag*, *bad*, *dance*, etc. is shown in the Atlas records as a raised variant of the /æ/ heard in *cap*, *bat*, etc., and distinct from the vowel of *where*, *care*, *bear*, etc. This gives additional support to the Atlas view that the glide that terminates *care* occurs only where the diaphone /r/ appears in other dialects. However, Hubbell's records show that the ingliding mid-front vowel heard in *care*, *where*, is the same for many informants as the vowel in *ask*, *bag*, *bad*, *dance*, etc., words which do not contain historical /r/. Hubbell heard this identity in the recorded speech of a number of Atlas informants as well.

Hubbell's list of phonemic contrasts for New York City is quite a long one. It is, in fact, over-representative, since no one actually uses all the contrasts shown. In the following list, Hubbell's phonemes are given in the notation used in this study.[7]

/i/	bit
/e/	bet
/æ/	bat
/a/	pot
/ʌ/	but
/u/	put
/ih/	beer, beard
/eh/	bare, bared, bad, ask, dance
/æh/	Cary, parents, jazz
/aˑh/	half, ask, bath (imitation of Eastern New England)
/ah/	bar, barred
/oh/	bore, bored, bought
/uh/	boor, moored
/ɜh/	stir, birth, etc. (mostly women)
/ʌh/	stir, her, occurred
/iy/	beat
/ey/	bait
/ay/	bite
/oy/	Hoyt

[7] Hubbell uses /ii/ where the present study uses /iy/; Hubbell's /iə/ corresponds to the present /ih/, etc. These substitutions are purely for typographic convenience, and the notation /ih/ implies no theory about the identification of the consonant /h/ with the latter part of an ingliding or long phoneme.

/ʌy/	Bert, work, shirt
/aw/	about
/ow/	boat
/uw/	boot, loot, moo
/iw/	newt, lute, new

This list of phonemes does tell us a great deal about New York City speech. The binary symbols used for different kinds of phonemes imply a type of structure, but nowhere does Hubbell attempt to work out the larger structures which show how these phonemes are organized in the speech of any one person or any group.

The most characteristic feature of New York City English, as seen in this list, is the set of ingliding or long vowels symbolized by the series /Vh/. In most other regions of the United States, the vowels symbolized in this set do not exist as separate structural elements, but rather as a set of similar sounds which are automatic variants before /r/. One may be tempted to think of this series as merely another way of representing the short vowels followed by a substitute for /r/; Kurath and McDavid did in fact pursue this line of reasoning. However, many of the words which are found in New York City speech with these ingliding phonemes do not contain the historical /r/ of the spelling form. In the case of the front mid vowel /eh/, there are large numbers of such words: *yeah, bad, bath, badge, ban, bag*, etc. – a larger number of words than the group which is found with the short vowel /æ/ as in *bat, back*, etc. Again, the long vowel /ah/ is used with many words that are not associated with /r/ in any way: *god, father, log, pa, ma, calm, bomb, balm*, etc.

Does this system indeed describe the idiolects of most New York City residents? The exploratory interviews for the present study, which were conducted in 1962 on the Lower East Side and elsewhere in New York City, provided an opportunity to answer this question.

Results of the exploratory interviews

[In returning to these 70-odd exploratory interviews, I am struck by the volume of activity required to identify the linguistic variables that are the main focus of the work. In listening to everyday speech, we tend to hear only those linguistic features that have already been described, and it takes a major effort to hear the new variables that are being generated in the speech community. The pages of detailed phonetic transcription in the exploratory notebooks identified the new and vigorous changes and generated the definitions of (æh, oh, ay, aw) that emerge in the chapters to follow.]

The first exploratory interviews for the present study were conducted on the Lower East Side of New York City, in a tenement area between 14th

Street and Houston Street. Tape recordings were made of conversations with young people on the streets, and with older men and women in their homes. In other cases, the interviewer was merely an observer, and collected samples of casual and anonymous speech.

A preliminary interview had been constructed in which a number of regional words characteristic of the city were investigated, and the contextual situation was not very different from that of the Atlas interviews.

The speech of many working class subjects in these exploratory interviews showed a range of variation which was greater than any that had been reported in previous studies. The record of one of the first interviews will serve to illustrate this variability: the subject, Walter M., was a young man born on the Lower East Side, of Ukrainian parents. He was then working as a radio repairman.

The example of one of the ingliding or long vowels will show the difficulty of fitting the system to the data. According to both Hubbell and the Linguistic Atlas, the phoneme /a/ should appear in words such as *dock*, *pot*, etc., while the phoneme /ah/ should appear in *dark*, *car*, etc. The record of Walter M.'s speech showed that he did use the expected phoneme /ah/ in *car*, in the phonetic form [kɒ]. But he also pronounced this word as [kɑ˖ɚ], with a short vowel [ɑ] followed by an *r*-like constriction. The word *farmer* occurred with the same combination, as [fɑɚmɚ]. A friend of Walter M.'s, of similar age and background, pronounced *guard* as [gɒ:ᵊd], which would be the expected phoneme /ah/. However, *farmer* again occurred as a short low center vowel plus a constriction, [fɑɚmɚ].

While the writings of Hubbell and Bronstein indicated that /r/ appears frequently in the speech of college-educated New Yorkers, nothing in their statements would lead one to expect such alternations in the speech of working class subjects. Yet the situation as it appeared in these preliminary interviews turned out to be a very common one. The next interview, for example, was with a fourteen-year-old boy, of Jewish parents. He used the expected low back vowel without /r/ in *car*, *heart*, *hard*, *army*. But he also pronounced *car* with a short vowel and an *r*-like glide, [kɑɚ].

The evidence of the speech pattern heard so far might permit a system in which speakers have two different ways of distinguishing *dark* from *dock*: either by the use of the low back phoneme /ah/, or by adding /r/ to the short phoneme /a/ as in [dɑɚk]. However, the subject last mentioned also pronounced the word *smart* with the low back vowel [ɒ:] followed by /r/, as [smɒ:ɚt].

Equally mixed results were obtained in interviewing a 34-year-old African–American woman, a high school graduate raised in the Bronx; a 41-year-old Italian man, native to the Lower East Side, with only a grammar school education; a 50-year-old accountant raised in Brooklyn, his wife, and 15-year-old son. Altogether, seventy individuals of various ages and backgrounds showed a speech pattern which was not easily described by the list of phonemes given above.

When the speakers were confronted directly with minimal pairs such as *guard* vs. *god*, their responses were no less inconsistent. They were first asked to read the sentence, "In prison, every guard thinks he is a little tin god," and then asked if *guard* sounded the same as *god*, or different. In some cases, both words were pronounced [gɒːd], or [gɑʳːd], and we can recognize the phoneme /ah/. But in other cases, these words were distinguished: sometimes as *god* [gɑʳd], vs. *guard* [gɒːd], and sometimes as *god* [gɑʳ·d] vs. *guard* [gɑɚd]. Thus the vowel of *god* is sometimes further forward than *guard*, and sometimes further back. In a few cases, both words were pronounced [gɒːɚd]. There was no necessary connection between what the speaker heard as the same, and the record, on tape, of what was pronounced the same.

All of the examples of variability given above involve the use of /r/. It might be said, following the line of explanation begun by Bronstein, that there is a free use of /r/ in New York City, with alternate ways of distinguishing words, and that this freedom occasionally causes some mixture of forms – in Hubbell's usage, "contaminations." However, there are many forms of variation in New York speech which have nothing to do with /r/.

In the phonemic pattern given above, both *bared* and *bad* occur with the vowel /eh/, and are indistinguishable. There are some speakers who follow this pattern in never using /r/, and always pronounce the word *bared* as [bɛːᵊd]. Let us consider the results with this type of speaker alone, where the treatment of /r/ is not a factor in the variation.

In many cases, the expected homonymity of *bared* and *bad* does occur, with both as [bɛːᵊd]. However, in a majority of the cases, the range of variation of the vowel used in *bad* is astonishingly large, from [aᐧ] to [iᵊ], overlapping the probable range of four of Hubbell's phonemic units, and producing complications which go beyond the simpler question of whether *bared* is pronounced with /er/ or /eh/. Even when the informants read a sentence such as "When he bared his arm, I saw he had a bad cut," we find that *bad* is not always homonymous with an /r/-less *bared*. Some speakers contrast *bared* [bɛːᵊd] with *bad* [bæːd], others with *bad* [bɪːᵊd]. Similar problems affect the phonemic resolution of the back mid ingliding phoneme /oh/. As Hubbell points out, the phoneme /ɜh/ is used by only a few informants, and those who do usually do not use /ʌh/. In the exploratory interviews, no /ɜh/ was found, and very little /ʌh/. The main form for words such as *her*, *were*, *occur*, was the constricted form, similar to that used in *r*-pronouncing dialects: [hɜ], [wɜ], [əkɜ], etc. A sound that would correspond to a phoneme /æh/ was heard quite often: a long [æː], but it was impossible to pin down a contrast with /æ/. If /æ/ and /æh/ are distinct phonemes, as opposed to /eh/, the functional load of /æh/ must be very small.

However, one might say that at least the two upper members of the in-gliding system, /ih/ and /uh/, follow a fairly simple pattern. Either the following glide is /r/-like, which gives us /ir/ and /ur/, or else it is not, and we would have /ih/ and /uh/. However, such simplicity could only stem from imprecise phonetics, because if we transcribe some pronunciations of the word *beer* very closely, we would write something like [be: ꜛꜛ] or [bɪ: ꜛꜛ]. This would indicate a long, monophthongal sound somewhat lower than the /i/ of *bit*, and centralized. Is this really different from the vowel used in *bad?* Or the pronunciation of *bare?* Nothing in the traditional literature about New York City would prepare us for a collision between these two sets of words. Furthermore, consider the pronunciation used by many informants for *shore*, as /šoh/ – phonetically, [šoꜛꜛ]. Is this really distinct from the high back vowel /uh/ as in *sure?* At this point, we may justly feel that the entire structure of the ingliding vowels is in doubt:

a) If the word class of *bad* is not homonymous with that of *bared*, then the vowel of *bared* can be re-interpreted as /er/ even in an /r/-less dialect.
b) By the same argument, is there a vowel /ah/ distinct from /a/ plus /r/?
c) Is there a vowel /oh/ distinct from /o/ plus /r/?
d) Is there a vowel /ih/ distinct from /eh/ if /eh/ exists?
e) Is there a vowel /uh/ distinct from /oh/ if /oh/ exists?
f) Is there a vowel /æh/ distinct from /æ/ and /eh/? /ah/ distinct from all of these? /ʌh/ distinct from /ʌ/? /ɜh/ distinct from /ʌh/?

As a result of the exploratory interviews, we can revise Hubbell's list of in-gliding phonemes as a column of nine question marks.

Resolution of the problem

The complexities found in the exploratory interviews may appear to justify the view that New York City speech is chaotic, and that "free variation" is indeed an adequate description. But free variation on a scale such as this is hardly consonant with the concept of a coherent, interrelated system. We cannot accept the notion that New York speech is "a pattern which is the absence of a pattern." All of our previous studies of language indicate that phonological behavior is not amorphous: on the contrary, it is the most highly structured aspect of language. Nor can we accept the view of New York City as a disparate collection of individuals with various backgrounds, borrowing randomly from one another's dialect. There is too great a similarity in the manner in which these variations occur in the speech of most of the informants. It is evident in these interviews that more /r/ occurs in more formal contexts.

The comments of Hubbell, Thomas, and Bronstein, all indicate that /r/-pronunciation has the distribution characteristic of a prestige pronunciation. But aside from the fact that college students and radio announcers favor /r/, we know little about the effect of this pattern on the speech of other middle class groups, and nothing about its status among working people. We have no data on the percentage of people who use /r/, nor the consistency with which they use it, nor in what contexts they employ this feature. We also would like to know what effect /r/-pronunciation has on the rest of the phonological system; what other variables have similar distribution; whether there are variables with radically different distribution. These are questions which cannot be answered by the use of qualitative impressions. They require quantitative treatment, and the next step is to identify the chief variables of New York City speech, and codify them into units which can be measured on a linear scale.

To accomplish this task, it will be necessary to view the various inconsistencies and disagreements in the data in a new light. In the past, considerable progress was made by deliberately ignoring such differences, large or small; the structural analysis of language has advanced by adopting a basic unit which is an abstract language, dialect, or idiolect, exemplified by constant and consistent behavior.[8] Because language does operate by means of consistent and compelling rules, it is possible to obtain this abstract pattern by studying only a few informants. However, to understand the structure of the entire language, and to grasp the dynamics of linguistic change, it is now necessary to turn our full attention to the variable elements in the system. These are the elements that have traditionally been relegated to a kind of linguistic scrap heap, under the name of "free variants," "social variants," "expressive variants," and similar terms.[9]

In the approach we shall now follow, no such liberties with the data will be permitted. Whenever we hear an inconsistency in someone's speech, we must ask: Is this variation consistent? Is it part of a larger pattern? This attitude is grounded in the conviction that language is no less determinate than other forms of social behavior. The amount of randomness in this system is relatively small: behavior that seems at first to be "free" or "random" is

[8] "Although differences of style can be described with the tools of descriptive linguistics, their exact analysis involves so much detailed study that they are generally disregarded. The procedures presented in the following chapters will not take note of style differences, but will assume that all styles within a dialect may be roughly described by a single structural system." Harris (1951), page 11. Though many similar quotations might be assembled, few have stated the matter as precisely as Harris.
[9] As employed by Harris to establish the minimal functioning units of a language, this labelling is a legitimate procedure. See Harris (1951) page 29. As employed by Bronstein to summarize the distribution of variants, this cover terminology begs the question.

discovered on closer examination to be determined by factors accessible to the linguist.[10]

There are of course many kinds of variation that fall outside the scope of linguistic analysis. Lisp, stammer, hiss, and whistle seem to be correlated with biological or psychological idiosyncrasies. Variations in tempo, volume, or pitch, or such voice qualifiers as rasp or nasality are very often idiosyncratic. In general, only variation that is distributed along social dimensions can be considered relevant to linguistic structure.

From the many examples of socially significant variation to be found in the language of New York City, it will be desirable to select a small number for intensive study. The most useful items are those that are high in *frequency*, have a certain *immunity from conscious suppression*,[11] are integral *units of larger structures*, and may be easily *quantified on a linear scale*. By all these criteria, phonological variables appear to be the most useful. In the exploratory interviews, there were five such variables which appeared to satisfy these requirements, and showed considerable social significance in the differentiation of speech styles and speakers.

[This characterization of the ideal linguistic variables for sociolinguistic study has frequently been cited in the sociolinguistic literature that followed. It's true enough that these are useful features. But it has led to the peculiar practice, on the part of students looking for a dissertation topic, of searching for a variable to study. It seems more reasonable to start the other way around: begin by trying to describe the practice of the speech community. The variables that emerge in this chapter are the results of efforts to describe the phonological system of New York City as a whole.]

The following conventions of notation will be used in the discussion of the variables, and throughout this study. Variables are indicated by parentheses, as the variable (r), or the variable (æh). Particular values of the variables are indicated by a number within the parentheses, as (r-1), or (æh-4). Index scores derived from average values of the variables are indicated by numbers outside the parentheses: (r)-00, or (æh)-25. Brackets [ ] will continue to indicate phonetic notation, indicating the speech sounds

---

[10] The need to study linguistic diversity was stated by Martinet, in his preface to Weinreich's *Languages in Contact* (1953), page vii: ". . . but it remains to be emphasized that linguistic diversity begins next door, nay, at home and within one and the same man. It is not enough to point out that each individual is a battlefield for conflicting linguistic types and habits, and at the same time, a permanent source of linguistic interference. What we heedlessly and somewhat rashly call 'a language' is the aggregate of millions of such microcosms . . ."

[11] Immunity from conscious distortion is not required, since both conscious and unconscious distortion of a native speech pattern appear to have about the same results in response to a shift of context (see Chapter 4). But if an item can be completely suppressed by most informants (such as the use of *ain't*, or taboo words) it will give us a much more limited body of data for analysis.

produced or heard; slashes/ /will continue to indicate phonemic notation, indicating a functional unit of the sound system; *italics* indicate a word or morpheme, without regard to its pronunciation. Thus (æh)-20 is an index score for a speaker who consistently uses the (æh-2) value of the variable (æh), as in the form [bɛːᵊd] which will be ultimately analyzed as the phonemic sequence /bæhd/, a pronunciation of both *bad* and *bared*.

The five phonological variables

1) (r). The first of these is the presence or absence of final and pre-consonantal /r/ in words such as *car* or *card, bare* or *bared, beer* or *beard, bore* or *bored, Saturday, November, fire* or *fired, flower* or *flowered*, (but not the /r/ in *red*, in *Cary* or *merry*, or *four o'clock*).

One class of words which would fall under the definition is excluded and studied under a separate heading: words with the mid-central vowel of *her, bird, work*, or *shirt*.[12]

The variant forms associated with /r/ were classified by a simple procedure: whenever a definitely constricted [r]-like sound was heard, *1* was recorded; if an unconstricted glide, or no glide was heard, *0* was recorded. Indeterminate cases were recorded in parentheses, but not used in the final index. This index is then the percentage of *1*s in the total number of instances.

2) (æh). The height of the vowel in *bad, bag, ask, pass, cash, dance*, forms the next variable. The class of words that was utilized for the index is a sub-group of the general class of words that occur with the low front vowel /æ/ in most other dialects of American English. Of this larger class, we will consider only words in which the /æh/ or /æ/ vowel occurs in the last syllable, plus any words derived from these by the addition of a suffix.[13] If we now classify this group by the following consonants, we obtain the sub-groups listed in Table 2.1.

In New York City English, sub-group a) always occurs with a short, checked vowel [æ]. Sub-group b) is inconsistent, sometimes occurring with the pattern of sub-group a), sometimes with that of c).

[12] Data on the vowel which occurs in *her, were, occur*, etc., were tabulated separately, and are presented in Chapter 10. Data on the vowel of *bird, work, shirt*, etc., may be found in Chapter 9.

In the original transcriptions of data for (r), separate tabulations were maintained for five separate environments, according to the preceding vowel, and weak constriction was distinguished from more prominent or strong constriction. However, these sub-classifications showed parallel distribution and the simplified form of the index as presented here preserves all of the patterns of structural variation seen in the more detailed data.

[13] Thus *dragging, wagging, clammer* would fall into this class, but *dragon, wagon*, and *clamor* would not.

Table 2.1   *Subcategories of* (æh) *by following segment*

Following consonant		Examples
a) voiceless stop:	/p, t, k, tš/	*cap, bat, back, batch*
liquid:	/l/	*pal*
b) voiced fricative:	/v, z/	*salve, jazz*
velar nasal:	/ŋ/	*bang*
c) voiced stops:	/b, d, g, dž/	*cab, bad, bag, badge*
voiceless fricatives:	/f, s, š, θ/	*half, pass, cash, bath*
other nasals:	/m, n/	*ham, dance*

Table 2.2   *Scale for* (æh) *index*

No.	Approximate phonetic quality	Level with the vowel of
(æh-1)	[ɪ³]	NYC *beer, beard*
(æh-2)	[ɛ³]	NYC *bear, bared*
(æh-3)	[æ⁺]	
(æh-4)	[æ:]	NYC *bat, batch*
(æh-5)	[a:]	Eastern New England *pass, aunt*
(æh-6)	[ɑ:]	NYC *dock, doll*

Sub-group c) is a fairly uniform class of words in which some speakers regularly use [ɛ:³] or higher vowels.

The index for (æh) is based only upon words of sub-group c). There is one exclusion from this group: the function words *can, am, an,* and *had.*

[The New York City short-a system outlined here was first described by Babbitt (1896) but treated in more detail as a phonological split by Trager (1942) and Labov, Ash and Boberg (2006, Ch. 13).]

The height of the vowel which occurs in words of sub-group c) forms a continuous scale. This may be codified into several discrete units with the help of other word classes that are relatively fixed (see Table 2.2).

Although this is a six-point scale, only four of the points are actually along a scale of height in traditional terms. The only point on the scale which is not identified by the phonetic quality of some other word group is (æh-3): this is an intermediate sound which is usually classed as a raised allophone of (æh-4), and it is the sound which is most commonly heard in the speech of educated speakers from northern regions outside of New York City.

The index score for (æh) is derived by multiplying by ten the average of the values assigned to all of the individual occurrences of the vowel

Table 2.3   *Scale for* (oh) *index*

No.	Approximate phonetic quality	Level with the vowel of
(oh-1)	[ʊ°] [ɔ̝⁺°]	NYC *sure*
(oh-2)	[ɔ̝⁺°]	
(oh-3)	[ɔ⁺°]	General American *for, nor*
(oh-4)	[ɔ:]	IPA cardinal /ɔ/
(oh-5)	[ɒ,] (rounded)	Eastern New England *hot, dog*
(oh-6)	[ɑ:]	NYC *dock, doll*[14]

in words of sub-group c).[15] It is irrelevant for the purposes of this index whether the vowel in question would structurally be assigned to /æ/ or /eh/ or even /ih/: the index measures the phonetic position of the initial portion of the vowel in this word group. Thus (æh)-25 would be the index rating for a person who pronounced half of the words in this group with (æh-3) and half with (æh-2). A person who always used a vowel level with the vowel of *bat* would be assigned (æh)-40.

3) (oh). The third variable is the mid-back rounded vowel heard in *caught, talk, awed, dog, off, lost, all*, sometimes known as "long open o" and symbolized phonetically as [ɔ:]. The word class which is measured by the index may be defined as those words which are reported with the phoneme /oh/ in the Linguistic Atlas data for New York City.[16]

A six-point linear scale parallel to that for (æh) is used to measure the height of this vowel. The great number of diacritics needed to capture the phonetic quality is matched by the extended collection of reference points (see Table 2.3). The difficulty of the phonetic description of this vowel is so great that none of these methods are satisfactory, and the following discussion may be of some help.

(oh-4) is the vowel of height level with Daniel Jones' fixed position for cardinal [ɔ]. It is heard frequently in the speech of upstate New York residents, and in many other parts of the country, but never with

---

[14] The same restriction which was imposed on the inclusion of *aunt* as an (æh-6) word is adopted here for *chocolate*.

[15] In the construction of the interview and the transcription of the data, information on all of the categories of /æ/ and (æh) words was preserved, and information on the occurrence of polysyllabic words ending in weak syllables as well. In the case of (æh-6), this vowel was included in the count for all relevant words except *aunt*. Since many New Yorkers place *aunt* in the /a/ phoneme as a part of their native pattern, such a pronunciation has no relation to the pattern of raising and lowering which is characteristic of the scale.

[16] In terms of American dialects spoken in western Pennsylvania, northeastern New England, or the western states outside of San Francisco and Los Angeles, it is difficult to distinguish this class of words from the class of *hot, hock, hod, doll*. In the most common convention adopted by dictionaries, this class of *caught, talk, awed* words is identified by the symbol ô as the vowel.

Table 2.4

		(th)	(dh)
1)	an interdental fricative[17]	[θ]	[ð]
2)	an affricate	[tθ]	[dð]
3)	a lenis stop	[t]	[d]

enough consistency for the speech of a particular region to serve as a firm reference point. (oh-3) is somewhat higher, and may be identified fairly accurately as the sound preceding [r] in *for, or, nor* in almost any region of the United States where [r] is pronounced in those words.

(oh-2) is a sound which is not heard in many other parts of the United States. This vowel is higher than (oh-3), more forward, and more rounded. The centering glide which follows is often more marked than with (oh-3), but a glide does not necessarily follow. (oh-1) is even more unusual; it is a sound nearly unique in American dialects. It is raised and centered beyond (oh-2) level with most pronunciations of *sure* and is rounded with what appears to be considerable tension. The rounding is quite different from that observed in British tense [ɔ:]: it is actually a pursing of the lips, in women; in men, a similar but distinct phonetic quality is imparted by what seems to be a hollowing of the tongue.

[Labov, Ash and Boberg (2006) show that (oh) values of 1 or 2, vowels raised above the mid-line with F1 < 700 Hz, are confined to a belt of eastern seaboard cities from Fall River to Baltimore.]

4,5) (th) and (dh). These two variables are the initial consonants of *thing* and *then*; they are well known as variables throughout most of the United States. These consonants do not of course show any close relation to the vowel system; they are incorporated in this study as a pair of correlated variables which are not involved in any of the processes of structural change which affect the first three variables (see Table 2.4).

The prestige form in this scale is the fricative. The stop with its [t]-like or [d]-like effect is everywhere considered to have less prestige. This stop consonant may be formed in a number of different ways, but its essential quality is that no turbulent, fricative, or scraping sound is heard as it is articulated. The affricate is a rapid succession of the two forms – or more precisely, it is heard as the fricative with a sudden onset, instead of a gradual beginning.

---

[17] For many speakers, the position of the tongue might more accurately be described as *pre-dental*, that is, pressing lightly against the aperture of the teeth from behind. For others, the tongue protrudes between the teeth. The important point is the fricative quality: the absence of sudden transitions.

The use of these two variables will give us a base of comparison with other scales of measurement without reference to linguistic change or the structural consequences of the other variables. Moreover, the high frequency of these variables, especially (dh), will enable us to obtain accurate measurements for short stretches of speech. The fact that these variables are not peculiar to New York City will enable us to use them in the study of the informants who were raised outside the city. The difference in the behavior of New Yorkers and out-of-towners in respect to (r), (æ), and (oh) can be calibrated against the differences in the handling of (th) and (dh).

The index for (th) and (dh) is derived by obtaining the average value of all occurrences of (th) and (dh), subtracting 1, and multiplying by 100. This yields a value of (th)-00 and (dh)-00 for those who use only the fricatives, and a value of (th)-200 and (dh)-200 for someone who might use only stops.

[This combined index was used many times in the sociolinguistic literature that followed, and gives a good view of the sociolinguistic continuum. But another approach is to ignore the difference between fricatives and affricates, and count only the marked forms, the stops. The Philadelphia study showed a sharp division between speakers with (dh) scores over 100 and those below. A score above 100 requires the use of some stops, but scores of 70 to 80 can be achieved with affricates alone].

The problem of stylistic variation

In the exploratory interviews, it was found that the five items just described vary to a significant degree in the speech of most New Yorkers. Further explorations of New York City speech revealed more of the pattern behind this variation. A professor of sociology, born and raised in New York City, began a lecture with an (r) index of 50 to 60; as he proceeded, and warmed to his subject, the index dropped precipitately, as low as (r)-05; then as he began to make his final points, the (r) index began to rise again, though it never quite reached its initial value. An African–American woman, living on welfare in a bare tenement apartment, used a carefully articulated style of speech with (r)-19; now and then she interrupted herself to scold her children, using a radically different style of speech with (r)-00. An electrician used (r)-00 in all of his conversation, but faced with the isolated word *guard*, pronounced it as [gɑɚd], and was surprised to hear that he usually said [gɑːd].

Behind cases like these, and many others, one can see the outlines of a pattern: that more (r-1) is used in more formal situations, and less (r-1) is used in less formal contexts. The problem is to reduce this vague impression to an exact description. We would like to delineate the structure of this variation by quantitative means, so that the amount of shift could be measured in the speech of any given individual – not merely at two opposing extremes, but at a whole series of points to see if the direction of shift is constant. With such a measure at hand, the performances of any two individuals or groups can be compared and the development of this dynamic process can be traced through several generations of New York speakers. When similar techniques have been developed for the other variables as well, the problem of stylistic variation will be considered solved.

The problem of social variation

The comments found in previous studies have already indicated that the pronunciation of (r-1) is a common characteristic of young college students. The predominance of (r-1) in mass media is a pattern that can be quickly grasped from a few hours of listening to radio or television. Further progress in analyzing the situation is difficult in the presence of the large-scale variation produced by changing contexts. Until we have a means of holding an individual's speech at a constant and comparable point along the axis of stylistic variation, we cannot compare his or her use of (r) with anyone else's. Yet a number of examples from exploratory interviews suggested that the pattern of social variation may be just as highly determined as the stylistic pattern.

The problem of social variation is to reduce our general impression of the social significance of (r) to an exact statement of social distribution (and eventually, social evaluation). We will want to compare groups and individuals through the exact use of the index for (r), and the other indexes as well.

Some of the most convincing illustrations of the social significance of a variable occur when the linguist is simply an anonymous observer. In such situations we can observe linguistic behavior without the biasing effect of conscious attention to speech, which is characteristic of the linguistic interview. The formal procedures of the interview are always open to the suspicion that the linguist is creating the language that he is studying. Yet the anonymous and casual speech exchange is usually the most uncontrolled type of observation: we cannot hope to learn very much from such random jottings unless the variation along the social axis, and the stylistic axis, is tightly controlled.

A method of using casual and anonymous observations in a systematic manner, with such controls, was developed in the course of this exploration of New York City speech. It was decided to use this method to test a general hypothesis about the social variation of (r): that given any groups of New York speakers who are ranked on a scale of social stratification, these groups will be ranked in the same order by their differential use of (r). To carry out such a program before continuing the development of the formal interview on the Lower East Side, would increase our confidence in the general application of the methods and indexes described in this chapter. Chapter 3 reports the confirmation of the hypothesis in a study of New York City department stores.

3   The social stratification of (r) in
New York City department stores

[The department store study has received a great deal of attention, and many people have written to me for information about it who have no other knowledge of the New York City study. Of the year and a half spent studying New York City, a day and a half was spent in the three department stores. I have been concerned that people would not see past the method to the importance of the results. Yet the department store study has withstood the test of time. It has been replicated many times – twice in NYC department stores – with extraordinary fidelity, and it articulates with the larger study in remarkable detail, showing that the inquiry limited to the Lower East Side is valid for the city as a whole. It contributes to one of the most unexpected findings of this study: that the great metropolis is a geographic unity. Furthermore, rapid and anonymous studies have been established as an efficient and reliable tool of sociolinguistic research.]

So far in the investigation of the speech of New York City, we have been taking a very close view of the linguistic behavior of individuals. As a preliminary to extending this method to large numbers of speakers, it will be useful to consider a survey of the speech of New York City department store employees, conducted in the November of 1962. This survey was designed to test two ideas that arose from the exploratory interviews: first, that the variable (r) is a social differentiator in all levels of New York City speech; and second, that casual and anonymous speech events could be used as the basis for a systematic study of language. The study as carried out was a self-contained unit, and will be reported as a whole in this chapter.

We can hardly consider the social distribution of language in New York City without encountering the pattern of social stratification which pervades the life of the city. We will have ample opportunity to deal with this concept in Chapter 7; at the moment, we may refer to the definition given by Bernard Barber:[1] social stratification is the product of social differentiation and social evaluation. The use of this term does not imply any specific type of class or caste, but simply that the normal workings of society have

[1] *Social Stratification* (1957), pages 1–3.

produced systematic differences between certain institutions or people, and that these differentiated forms have been ranked in status or prestige by general agreement.

We begin with the general hypothesis suggested at the end of the last chapter: *if any two sub-groups of New York City speakers are ranked on a scale of social stratification, then they will be ranked in the same order by their differential use of (r).*

It would be easy to test this hypothesis by comparing occupational groups, which are among the most important indexes of social stratification. We could, for example, take a group of lawyers, a group of file clerks, and a group of janitors. But this would hardly go beyond the indications of the exploratory interviews, and such an extreme example of differentiation would not provide a very exacting test of the hypothesis. We would like to show that the hypothesis is so general, and the differential use of (r) pervades New York City so thoroughly, that fine social differences will be reflected in the index as well as gross ones.

It therefore seemed best to construct a very severe test by finding a subtle case of stratification within a single occupational group: in this case, the sales people of large department stores in Manhattan. If we select three large department stores, from the top, middle, and bottom of the price and fashion scale, we can expect that the customers will be socially stratified. Would we expect the sales people to show a comparable stratification? Such a position would depend upon two correlations: between the status ranking of the stores and the ranking of parallel jobs in the three stores; and between the jobs and the behavior of the persons who hold those jobs. These are not unreasonable assumptions. C. Wright Mills points out, in *White Collar*, that salesgirls in large department stores tend to borrow prestige from their customers, or at least make an effort in that direction.[2] In later chapters, we will show that a person's own occupation is more closely correlated with his or her linguistic behavior – for those working actively – than any other single social characteristic. In this chapter, we will give some evidence that the stores are objectively differentiated in a fixed order, and that jobs in these stores are evaluated by employees in that order. Since the product of social differentiation and evaluation, no matter how minor, is social stratification of the employees in the three stores, the hypothesis will predict the following result:

[2] C. Wright Mills, *White Collar* (1956), page 173. See also page 243: "The tendency of white collar people to borrow status from higher elements is so strong that it has carried over to all social contacts and features of the work-place. Sales people in department stores . . . frequently attempt, although often unsuccessfully, to borrow prestige from their contact with customers, and to cash it in among work colleagues as well as friends off the job. In the big city the girl who works on 34th Street cannot successfully claim as much prestige as the one who works on Fifth Avenue or 57th Street."

sales people in the highest ranked store will have the highest values of (r); those in the middle ranked store will have intermediate values of (r); and those in the lowest ranked store will show the lowest values.

If this result holds true, the hypothesis will have received confirmation in proportion to the severity of the test.

The three stores which were selected are Saks Fifth Avenue, Macy's, and S. Klein. The differential ranking of these stores may be illustrated in many ways. Their locations are one important point:

Highest ranking: Saks Fifth Avenue
                    at 50th St. and Fifth Ave., near the center of the high fashion shopping district, along with other high prestige stores such as Bonwit Teller, Henri Bendel, Lord and Taylor.
Middle ranking: Macy's
                    Herald Square, 34th St. and Sixth Ave., near the garment district, along with Gimbels and Saks-34th St., other middle range stores in price and prestige.
Lowest ranking: S. Klein
                    Union Square, 14th St. and Broadway, not far from the Lower East Side; the other large store in the area, Ohrbachs, recently raised its price and advertising level and moved uptown.

The advertising and price policies of the stores are very clearly stratified. Perhaps no other element of class behavior is so sharply differentiated in New York City as that of the newspaper which people read; many surveys have shown that the *Daily News* is the paper read first and foremost by working class people, while the *New York Times* draws its readership from the middle class.[3] These two newspapers were examined for the advertising copy in October 24th through 27th, 1962 (see Table 3.1). Saks and Macy's advertised in the *New York Times*, where Klein was represented only by a very small item; in the *News*, however, Saks does not appear at all, while both Macy's and Klein are heavy advertisers.

We may also consider the prices of the goods advertised during those four days. Since Saks usually does not list prices, we can only compare prices for all three stores on one item: women's coats. Saks: $90.00, Macy's: $79.95, Klein: $23.00. On four items, we can compare Klein and Macy's (see Table 3.2).

---

[3] This statement is fully confirmed by answers to a question on newspaper readership in the Mobilization for Youth Survey of the Lower East Side, as described in Chapter 6. The readership of the *Daily News* and *Daily Mirror* (now defunct) on the one hand, and the *New York Times* and *Herald Tribune* on the other hand, is almost complementary in distribution by social class.

Table 3.1   *No. of pages of advertising October 24–27, 1962*

	NY Times	Daily News
Saks	2	0
Macy's	6	15
S. Klein	1/4	10

Table 3.2

	Macy's	S. Klein
dresses	$ 14.95	$ 5.00
girls' coats	16.99	12.00
stockings	.89	.45
men's suits	49.95–64.95	26.00–66.00

The emphasis on prices is also different. Saks either does not mention prices, or buries the figure in small type at the foot of the page. Macy's features the prices in large type, but often adds the slogan, "You get more than low prices." Klein, on the other hand, is often content to let the prices speak for themselves. The form of the prices is also different: Saks gives prices in round figures, such as $120; Macy's always shows a few cents off the dollar: $49.95; Klein usually prices its goods in round numbers, and adds the retail price which is always much higher, and shown in Macy's style: $23.00, marked down from $49.95."

The physical plant of the stores also serves to differentiate them. Saks is the most spacious, especially on the upper floors, with the least amount of goods displayed. Many of the floors are carpeted, and on some of them, a receptionist is stationed to greet the customers. Klein, at the other extreme, is a maze of annexes, sloping concrete floors, low ceilings; it has the maximum amount of goods displayed at the least possible expense.

The principal stratifying effect upon the employees is the prestige of the store, and the working conditions. Wages do not stratify the employees in the same order. On the contrary, there is every indication that high prestige stores such as Saks pay lower wages than Macy's.

Saks is a non-union store, and the general wage structure is not a matter of public record. However, conversations with a number of men and women who have worked in New York department stores, including Saks and Macy's, show general agreement on the direction of the wage differential.[4] Some of the incidents reflect a willingness of sales people to accept much lower wages from the store with greater prestige. The executives of the prestige stores pay a great deal of attention to employee relations, and take many unusual measures to ensure that the sales people feel that they share in the general prestige of the store.[5] One of the Lower East Side informants who worked at Saks was chiefly impressed with the fact that she could buy Saks clothes at a 25 percent discount. A similar concession from a lower prestige store would have been of little interest to her.

From the point of view of Macy's employees, a job in Klein is well below the horizon. Working conditions and wages are generally considered to be less, and the prestige of Klein is very low indeed. As we will see, the racial and ethnic composition of the store employees reflect these differences quite accurately (see Table 3.5).

A socio-economic index which ranked New Yorkers on occupation would show the employees of the three stores at the same level; an income scale would probably find Macy's employees somewhat higher than the others; education is the only objective scale which might differentiate the groups in the same order as the prestige of the stores, though there is no evidence on this point. However, the working conditions of sales jobs in the three stores stratify them in the order: Saks, Macy's, Klein; the prestige of the stores leads to a social evaluation of these jobs in the same order. Thus the two aspects of social stratification – differentiation and evaluation – are to be seen in the relations of the three stores and their employees.

The normal approach to a survey of department store employees requires that one enumerate the sales people of each store, draw random samples in each store, make appointments to speak with each employee at home, interview the respondents, then segregate the native New Yorkers, analyze and re-sample the non-respondents, and so on. This is an expensive

[4] Macy's sales employees are represented by a strong labor union, while Saks is not unionized. One former Macy's employee considered it a matter of common knowledge that Saks wages were lower than Macy's, and that the prestige of the store helped to maintain its non-union position. Bonuses and other increments are said to enter into the picture. It appears that it is more difficult for a young girl to get a job at Saks than at Macy's. Thus Saks has more leeway in hiring policies, and the tendency of the store officials to select girls who speak in a certain way will play a part in the stratification of language, as well as the adjustment made by the employees to their situation. Both influences converge to produce stratification.

[5] A former Macy's employee told me of an incident that occurred shortly before Christmas several years ago. As she was shopping in Lord and Taylor's, she saw the president of the company making the rounds of every aisle and shaking hands with every employee. When she told her fellow employees at Macy's about this scene, the most common remark was, "How else do you get someone to work for that kind of money?" One can say that not only do the employees of higher status stores borrow prestige from their employer – it is also deliberately loaned to them.

and time-consuming procedure, but for most purposes there is no short cut which will give accurate and reliable results. In this case, a simpler method, which relies upon the extreme generality of the linguistic behavior of the subjects, was used to gather a very limited type of data. This method is dependent upon the systematic sampling of casual and anonymous speech events. Applied in a poorly defined environment, such a method is open to many biases and it would be difficult to say what population had been studied. In this case, our population is well defined as the sales people (or more generally, any employee whose speech might be heard by a customer) in three specific stores at a specific time. The end result will be a view of the role that speech would play in the overall social imprint of the employees upon the customer. What is surprising about the method, is not only the simplicity and economy of the approach, but the high degree of consistency and regularity in the results, which will allow us to test the original hypothesis in a number of subtle ways.

The method

The application of the study of casual and anonymous speech events to the department store situation was relatively simple. The interviewer approached the informant in the role of a customer asking for directions to a particular department. The department was one which was located on the fourth floor. When the interviewer asked, "Excuse me, where are the women's shoes?" the answer would normally be, "Fourth floor."

The interviewer then leaned forward and said, "Excuse me?" He would usually then obtain another utterance, "*Fourth floor*," spoken in careful style under emphatic stress.[6]

The interviewer would then move along the aisle of the store to a point immediately beyond the informant's view, and make a written note of the data. The following independent variables were included:

the store
occupation [floorwalker, sales, cashier, stockboy]
floor within the store[7]
sex
race
age [estimated in units of five years]
foreign or regional accent, if any

---

[6] The interviewer in all cases was myself. I was dressed in middle class style, with jacket, white shirt, and tie, and used my normal pronunciation as a college-educated native of New Jersey (*r*-pronouncing).

[7] Notes were also made on the department in which the employee was located, but the numbers for individual departments are not large enough to allow comparison.

The dependent variable is the use of (r) in four occurrences:

(casual)   (emphatic)
  fou*r*th floo*r*   *fourth floo*r

Thus we have pre-consonantal and final position, in both casual and emphatic styles of speech. In addition, all other uses of (r) by the informant were noted, from remarks overheard or contained in the interview. Following the notation of Chapter 2, *1* was entered for each plainly constricted value of the variable; for unconstricted schwa, lengthened vowel, or no representation, *0* was entered. Doubtful cases or partial constriction were symbolized "d" and were not used in the final tabulation.

Also noted were instances of affricates or stops used in the word *fourth* for the final consonant, and any other examples of (th-2), (th-3), (dh-2), or (dh-3), used by the speaker.

This method of interviewing was applied in each aisle on the floor as many times as possible before the spacing of the informants became so close that it was noticed that the same question was asked before. Each floor of the store was investigated in the same way. On the fourth floor, the form of the question was necessarily different: "Excuse me, what floor is this?"

Following this method, 68 interviews were obtained in Saks, 125 in Macy's, and 71 in Klein. Total interviewing time for the 264 subjects was about six and one-half hours.

At this point, we might consider the nature of these 264 interviews in more general terms. They were speech events which had entirely different social significance from the point of view of the two participants. As far as the informant was concerned, the exchange was a normal salesman-customer interaction, almost below the level of conscious attention, in which relations of the speakers were so casual and anonymous that they may hardly have been said to have met. This tenuous relationship was the minimum intrusion upon the behavior of the subject; language and the use of language never appeared at all.

From the point of view of the interviewer, the exchange was a systematic elicitation of the exact forms required, in the desired context, the desired order, and with the desired contrast of style.

Overall stratification of (r)

The results of the study showed clear and consistent stratification of (r) in the three stores. In Figure 3.1, the use of (r) by employees of Saks, Macy's, and Klein's is compared by means of a bar graph. Since the data for most informants consist of only four items, we will not use a continuous

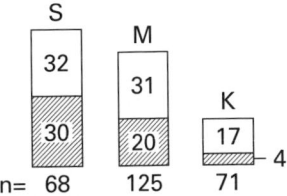

Figure 3.1   Overall stratification of (r) by store (S=Saks, M=Macy's, K=S. Klein. Shaded area= % *all (r-1)*; unshaded area= % *some (r-1)*)

numerical index for (r), but rather divide all informants into three categories:[8]

all (r-1):   those whose records show only (r-1) and no (r-0)
some (r-1):   those whose records show at least one (r-1) and one (r-0)
no (r-1):   those whose records show only (r-0)

The shaded area of Figure 3.1 shows the percentage of *all (r-1)*; the unshaded area of the bar shows the percentage of *some (r-1)*. The remainder, not shown on the graph, is the percentage of *no (r-1)*. The figure underneath each bar shows the total number of cases.

Thus we see that a total of 62 percent of Saks employees used all or some (r-1), 51 percent of Macy's, and 21 percent of Klein's. The stratification is even sharper for the percentages of all (r-1). As the hypothesis predicted, the groups are ranked by their differential use of (r-1) in the same order as their stratification by extra-linguistic factors.

Next, we may wish to examine the distribution of (r) in each of the four standard positions. Figure 3. 2 shows this type of display, where once again the stores are differentiated in the same order, and for each position. There is a considerable difference between Macy's and Klein's at each position, but the difference between Macy's and Saks varies.

In emphatic pronunciation of the final (r), Macy's employees come very close to the mark set by Saks. It would seem that *r*-pronunciation is the norm at which a majority of Macy employees aim, yet not the one they use most often. In Saks, we see a shift between casual and emphatic pronunciation,

---

[8] The notation outlined in Chapter 2 will be adapted here to distinguish between a variable and a particular value of the variable. The symbol (r) is the variable, symbolizing the entire range of variation within the community which occurs in the specified positions in the linguistic sequence – in this case, the points where historical *r* is found in pre-consonantal and final position. The symbol (r-1) or (r-0) means a particular value of the variable – in this case, a constricted central glide-consonant or the absence of such a consonant respectively. An underlined *r* refers to the spelling, which coincides with the position of the historical consonant.

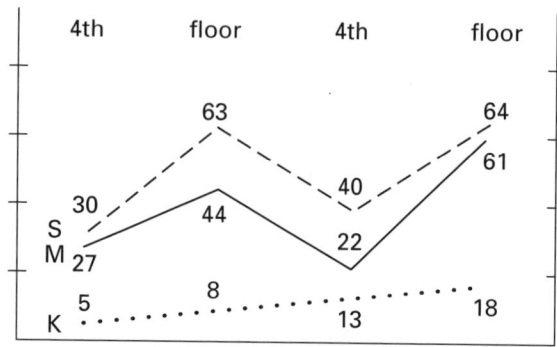

Figure 3.2   Percentage of *all (r-1)* by store for four positions (S=Saks, M=Macy's, K=S. Klein)

but it is much less marked. In other words, Saks employees have more *security* in a linguistic sense.

The fact that the figures for (r-1) at Klein are low, should not obscure the fact that Klein employees also participate in the same pattern of stylistic variation of *r* as the other stores. The percentage of *r*-pronunciation rises at Klein from 5 to 18 percent as the context becomes more emphatic: a much greater rise in percentage than in the other stores, and a more regular increase as well. It will be important to bear in mind that this attitude – that (r-1) is the most appropriate pronunciation for emphatic speech – is shared by at least some speakers in all three stores.

Table 3.3 shows the data in detail, with the number of instances obtained for each of the four positions of (r), for each store. The symbol "d" indicates indeterminate, partially constricted forms not used in the percentages of *all (r-1)*, *some (r-1)*, or *no (r-1)*. It may be noted that the number of occurrences in the second pronunciation of *four* is considerably reduced, primarily as a result of some speaker's tendency to answer a second time, "Fourth."

Since the *No data* entries in the fourth position are larger than the second, it might be suspected that those who use [r] in Saks and Macy's tend to give fuller responses, thus giving rise to a spurious impression of increase in (r) values in those positions. We can check this point by comparing only those who gave a complete response. Their responses can be symbolized by a four digit number, representing the pronunciation in each of the four positions respectively (see Table 3.4).

Thus we see that the pattern of differential ranking in the use of (r) is preserved in this sub-group of complete responses, and omission of the final "*floor*" by some respondents was not a factor in this pattern.

Table 3.3   *Detailed distribution of* (r) *by store and word position*

| | Saks | | | | Macy's | | | | S. Klein | | | |
| | Casual | | Emphatic | | Casual | | Emphatic | | Casual | | Emphatic | |
	4th	floor	4th	floor	4th	floor	4th	floor	4th	floor	4th	floor
(r-1)	17	31	16	21	33	48	13	31	3	5	6	7
(r-0)	39	18	24	12	81	62	48	20	63	59	40	33
"d"	4	5	4	4	0	3	1	0	1	1	3	3
No data[9]	8	14	24	31	11	12	63	74	4	6	22	28
Total	68	68	68	68	125	125	125	125	71	71	71	71

Table 3.4   *Distribution of* (r) *for complete responses*

| | | Percentage of total responses in | | |
		Saks	Macy's	S. Klein
all (r-1)	1 1 1 1	24	22	6
some (r-1)	0 1 1 1, 0 0 1 1, 0 1 0 1, etc.	46	37	12
no (r-1)	0 0 0 0	30	41	82
		100	100	100
		[N: 33	48	34]

The effect of other independent variables

It is possible that other factors, besides the stratification of the stores, may explain the regular pattern of *r*-pronunciation seen above, or that this effect may be the contribution of a particular group in the population, rather than the behavior of the sales people as a whole. The other independent variables recorded in the procedure will enable us to check such possibilities.

Race   There are many more African–American (AA) employees in the Klein sample than in Macy's, and more in Macy's than in Saks. Table 3.5 shows the percentages of AA informants and their responses.

When we compare these figures with those of Figure 3.1, for the entire population, it is evident that the presence of many AA informants will contribute to a lower use of (r-1). The AA subjects at Macy's used less (r-1)

---

[9] The "no data" category for Macy's shows relatively high values under the emphatic category. This discrepancy is due to the fact that the procedure for requesting repetition was not standardized in the investigation of the ground floor at Macy's, and values for emphatic response were not regularly obtained. The effects of this loss are checked in Table 3.4, where only complete responses are compared.

than the white informants, to a certain extent; the AA subjects at Klein were considerably more biased in the *r*-less direction.

The higher percentage of AA sales people in the lower ranking stores is consistent with the general pattern of social stratification, since in general, AA workers have been assigned less desirable jobs. Therefore the contribution of AA speakers to the overall pattern is consistent with the hypothesis.

There are other differences in the populations of the stores. The types of occupations among the employees who are accessible to customers are quite different. In Macy's, the employees who were interviewed could be identified as floorwalkers (by red and white carnations), sales people, cashiers, stockboys, and elevator operators. In Saks, the cashiers are not accessible to the customer, working behind the sales counters, and stockboys are not seen. The working operation of the store goes on behind the scenes, and does not intrude upon the customer's notice. On the other hand, at Klein's, all of the employees seem to be operating on the same level: it is difficult to tell the difference between sales people, managers, and stockboys.

Here again, the extra-linguistic stratification of the stores is reinforced by objective observations in the course of the interview. We can question if these differences are not responsible for at least a part of the stratification of (r). For the strongest possible result, it would be desirable to show that the stratification of (r) is a property of the most homogeneous sub-group in the three stores: native New York, white, saleswomen. Setting aside the male employees, all occupations besides selling itself, the AA and Puerto Rican employees, and all those with a foreign accent,[10] there is still a total of 141 informants to study.

Figure 3.3 shows the percentages of (r-1) used by the native white saleswomen of the three stores, with the same type of graph as in Figure 3.1.

---

[10] In the sample as a whole, 17 informants with distinct foreign accents were found, and one with regional characteristics which were clearly not of New York City origin. The foreign language speakers in Saks had French, or other western European accents, while those in Klein had Jewish and other eastern European accents. There were three Puerto Rican employees in the Klein sample, one in Macy's, none in Saks. As far as sex is concerned, there were 70 men and 194 women. Men showed the following small differences from women in percentages of (r-1) usage:

	men	women
all (r-1)	22	30
some (r-1)	22	17
no (r-1)	57	54

Table 3.5   *Distribution of (r) for African–American employees*

	Percentage of responses in		
	Saks	Macy's	S. Klein
all (r-1)	50	12	0
some (r-1)	0	35	6
no (r-1)	50	53	94
	100	100	100
	[N: 2	17	18]
[% of AA informants:]	03	14	25

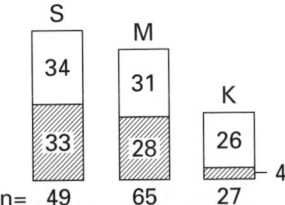

Figure 3.3   Stratification of (r) by store for native New York white saleswomen (S=Saks, M=Macy's, K=S. Klein. Shaded area= % *all (r-1)*; unshaded area= % *some (r-1)*)

The stratification is essentially the same, though somewhat smaller in magnitude. The greatly reduced Klein sample still shows by far the lowest use of (r-1), and Saks is still ahead of Macy's in this respect.

We can therefore conclude that the stratification of (r) is a process which affects every section of the sample.

We can now turn the heterogeneous nature of the Macy's sample to advantage. Figure 3.4 shows the stratification of (r) according to occupational groups in Macy's: as the discussion of the initial hypothesis indicated, this is much sharper than the stratification of the employees in general.

The floorwalkers and the sales people are almost the same in the total percentage of those who use all or some (r-1), but the floorwalkers have a much higher percentage of those who consistently use (r-1).

Another interesting comparison may be made at Saks. This store shows a great discrepancy between the ground floor and the upper floors. The ground floor of Saks looks very much like Macy's: a great many crowded counters, salesgirls leaning over the counters, almost elbow to elbow, and a great deal of merchandise displayed. But the upper floors of

Table 3.6   *Distribution of* (r) *by floor in Saks*

	Ground floor	Upper floors
% all (r-1)	23	34
% some (r-1)	23	40
% no (r-1)	54	26
	100	100
	[N: 30	38]

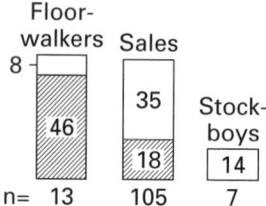

Figure 3.4   Stratification of (r) by occupational groups in Macy's

Saks are far more spacious; there are long vistas of empty carpeting, and on the floors devoted to high fashion, there are models who display the individual garments to the customers. Receptionists are stationed at strategic points to screen out the casual spectators from the serious buyers.

It would seem logical then, to compare the ground floor of Saks with the upper floors. By the hypothesis, we should find a differential use of (r-1). Table 3.6 shows that this is the case.

In the course of the interview, information on another variable was also collected: the (th) variable, particularly as it occurred in the word *fourth*. We have already seen this variable as a social differentiator in the individual cases of Chapter 2. The percentage of speakers who used stops in this position was fully in accord with the other measures of social stratification which we have seen:

Saks   00%
Macy's   04%
S. Klein 15%

Thus the hypothesis has received a number of semi-independent confirmations. Considering the economy with which the information was obtained, the survey appears to yield rich results. It is true that we do not

Table 3.7   *Distribution of* (r) *by estimated age*

	Age groups		
	15–30	35–50	55–70
% all (r-1)	24	20	20
% some (r-1)	21	28	22
% no (r-1)	55	52	58

know a great deal about the informants which we would like to know: their birthplace, language history, education, participation in New York culture, and so on. Nevertheless, the regularities of the underlying pattern are strong enough to overcome this lack of precision in the selection and identification of informants.

Differentiation by age of the informants

The age of the informants was estimated within five-year intervals, and these figures cannot be considered reliable for any but the simplest kind of comparison. However, it should be possible to break down the age groups into three units, and detect any overall direction of change.

At various points in this discussion, it has been indicated that (r-1) is one of the chief characteristics of a new prestige pattern which is being superimposed upon the native New York City pattern. We would therefore expect to see a rise in *r*-pronunciation among the younger sales people. However, the overall distribution by age shows no evidence of change (see Table 3.7).

This lack of direction is surprising. For further discussion and clarification, the material to be presented in Chapter 9 will be required. It may be illuminating, however, to examine the breakdown for each store, as shown in Figure 3.5. Here the expected increase in (r-1) pronunciation is seen in Saks. However, Macy's shows a contrary direction of change, and no particular direction can be seen for Klein.

This is a puzzling result, especially in the light of the clear-cut evidence for the absence of (r-1) pronunciation in New York City in the 1930s, and the subsequent increase in the records of Hubbell and Bronstein. Although the numbers of the sub-groups may appear small, they are larger than many of the sub-groups used in the discussion of the previous pages, and it is not possible to discount these results.

The conundrum represented by Figure 3.5 is one of the most significant results of the procedures that have been followed to this point. Where all of

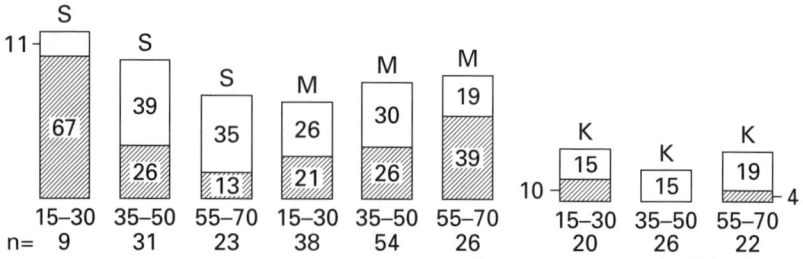

Figure 3.5   Stratification of (r) by store and age level (S=Saks, M=Macy's, K=S. Klein. Shaded area= % *all (r-1)*; unshaded area= % *some (r-1)*)

the other findings confirm the original hypothesis, a single result which does not fit the expected pattern may turn our attention in new and profitable directions. From the data in the department store survey alone, it was not possible to account for Figure 3.5 except in speculative terms. The following quotation is from the evaluation of the original report on the department store survey, written shortly after the work was completed:

How can we account for the differences between Saks and Macy's? I think we can say this: the shift from the influence of the New England prestige pattern [r-less] to the mid-Western prestige pattern [r-ful] is felt most completely at Saks. The younger people at Saks are under the influence of the r-pronouncing pattern, and the older ones are not. At Macy's, there is less sensitivity to the effect among a large number of younger speakers who are completely immersed in the New York City linguistic tradition. The stockboys, the young salesgirls, are not as yet fully aware of the prestige attached to r-pronunciation. On the other hand, the older people at Macy's tend to adopt this pronunciation: very few of them rely upon the older pattern of prestige pronunciation which supports the r-less tendency of older Saks sales people. This is a rather complicated argument, which would certainly have to be tested very thoroughly by longer interviews in both stores before it could be accepted.

The analysis of the pattern of Figure 3.5 will be resumed in Chapter 9, as we study the distribution of the data from the Lower East Side survey through various age levels of that population.

Some possible sources of error

The method followed in this study is not without many sources of error. Some can be reduced, while others are inherent in the nature of the procedure.

Table 3.8   *Percentage of all (r-1) for each position*

Casual		Emphatic	
fourth	*floor*	*fourth*	*floor*
23	39	24	48

The approach to sampling might well have been more systematic. In future studies, it would be preferable to select every fifth sales person, or to use some other method which would avoid the bias inherent in selecting the first available person. As long as such a method does not interfere with the basic unobtrusiveness of the speech event, it should improve the accuracy of the procedure without seriously decreasing its efficiency. However, there is no apparent bias in the present procedure which would seriously affect the comparison, since the same procedure was followed in all stores.

Another limitation is that the data was not tape recorded, as was done in most of the procedures described in this study as a whole. The transcriber, myself, knew what the object of the test was, and it is always possible that an unconscious bias in transcription would lead to the doubtful cases being recorded as (r-1) in Saks, and as (r-0) in S. Klein. On the other hand, the phonetic detail was not complex, and the precaution was taken of discounting entirely all doubtful cases, as noted above. Further, there is the unusually favorable factor that the sample is always available for rechecking, and this can be done by anyone in the course of a few hours. Thus the data is actually less subject to suspicion than many studies of speakers long since disappeared.

Another limitation is in the method used to elicit emphatic speech. Figure 3.2 indicates that the effect of stylistic variation may be slight compared to such a phonological alternation as pre-consonantal vs. final position. The total percentages for all three stores bear this out (see Table 3.8).

The problem may lie in the fact that a simple request for repetition is not an effective means of contrasting casual speech with a more formal style. In Chapter 4 more attention will be given to this problem.

Conclusion

The hypothesis with which this chapter opened has been confirmed by a severe test within a single occupational group, and we may conclude that (r) stratification is an integral part of the linguistic structure of the New York City speech community. An equally important aspect of this study is that it

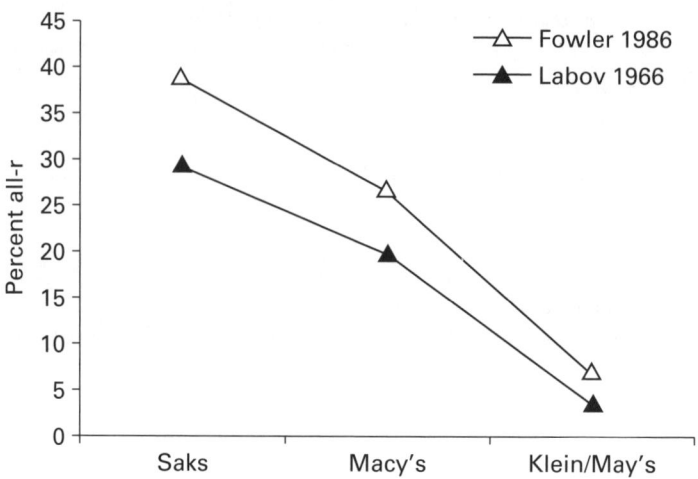

Figure 3.6

has accomplished the aim suggested at the conclusion of Chapter 2: to study language apart from the bias of the formal linguistic interview. The results of this study should terminate any suspicion that the pronunciation of (r-1) in New York City is limited to a narrow group of speakers, or that it is a phenomenon which occurs only in the presence of linguists and speech teachers.

[A precise replication of the department store study was done by Joy Fowler of NYU in 1986. Fowler retraced my steps as carefully as she could, substituting May's for S. Klein, which had gone out of business. Each of the dimensions of stratification outlined in this chapter were preserved, at a slightly higher rate of *r*-pronunciation. Details are reproduced in Labov 1994. Figure 3.6 compares the two studies for the overall rate of all-r. The stratification of the stores is well preserved, and the rate of importation of r-pronunciation is small. Over 23 years, the rate of r-pronunciation had increased an average of 7 percent, but this was not distributed evenly. Saks and Macy's showed a proportional increase of 1.3, while Klein/May's almost doubled, at 1.75. The actual percentage of increase was of course greatest for the highest status store.

The Fowler study was remarkable in preserving the patterns of age distribution reported above. Saks showed a negative correlation with age, and Macy's a positive correlation, indicating that it is the younger upper middle class speakers who are acquiring the new norm, but among the lower middle class, this increase is not found until middle age.

The general term for this kind of sociolinguistic research is a "rapid and anonymous" survey, or "R&A." A great many other studies have been carried out since 1963. MacDonald restudied the NYC department stores in 1984. Gardner Chloros studied language selection and switching in a study of department stores in Strasbourg (1991).

The general design involves a request for "free goods," a term of Goffman. The chief free goods one may ask for are directions and time (and a cigarette light in former times.) A typical R&A study is carried out, not within a store, but on the street. The investigator locates a street name that involves a critical phonological form, and asks for directions with a wrong street designation. Over the past five years, a number of R&A studies have been carried out in Philadelphia where /r/ is normally constricted. A target word *Market* is found in *Market Street*. The field workers will typically ask, "How do I get to Market Avenue?" This strategy increases the number of stressed repetitions of the target word by the subject. If the form of interest is in a number between 1 and 12, requests for time of day are used. Labov and Baranowski both investigated the monophthongization of /ay/ by asking for the time around five o'clock in Columbia and Charleston, SC (Baranowski 2006). Clopton (2005) studied the alternation of /θ/ and /s/ in the Spanish of Barcelona by asking for the time around 5 and 10 o'clock, yielding *cinco* and *diez*.]

Chapter 4 will turn to the problem of stylistic variation, which was only a marginal consideration in the department store survey. The next step towards the systematic study of all the variables will be the isolation of a range of contexts and styles, to represent the speech of the informant in many social contexts. But directly before us lies a contradiction. The study of stylistic variation under controlled conditions requires that the axis of social variation be defined as well, and held constant while stylistic variation is charted. This can only be done in a series of formal linguistic interviews of individuals whose social characteristics are well determined. Yet the formal interview itself is a context which normally requires formal speech; more generally, any style of speech used in a formal interview is biased towards the formal end of the spectrum of behavior. Chapter 4 will be devoted to the problem of obtaining the full range of stylistic variation within the bounds of the formal interview, and the definition of distinct styles as they emerge.

4 The isolation of contextual styles

Linguists have never been unconscious of the problems of stylistic variation. The normal practice is to set such variants aside – not because they are considered unimportant, but because the techniques of linguistics are not thought to be suitable or adequate to handle them.[1] Structural analysis is normally the abstraction of those unvarying, functional units of language whose occurrence can be predicted by rule. Since the influence of stylistic conditioning on linguistic behavior is said to be merely statistical, it can only lead to statements of probability rather than rule.[2]

For the present purposes, I would rather say that stylistic variation has not been treated by techniques accurate enough to measure the extent of regularity which does prevail. The combination of many stylistic factors imposed upon other influences may lead to seemingly erratic behavior; but this apparent irregularity is comparable to the inconsistencies which seemed to govern the historical development of vowels and consonants until some of the more subtle conditioning factors were perceived.

At the end of Chapter 3, it was suggested that the five phonological variables show regular variation through different styles and contexts in the speech of New Yorkers. The problem now is to control the context, and define the styles of speech which occur within them, so that this hypothesis can be tested.

[This chapter has been perhaps the most influential in determining what people actually do in a sociolinguistic study, and perhaps the most misunderstood in terms of what it is all about. The adjective "Labovian" is often used to describe a set of interviews that uses several different styles to trace the shift of styles with increasing formality, most typically spontaneous speech, reading, and word lists. Style shifting within the interview is an effective tool to register the direction of overt (and perhaps covert) linguistic

---

[1] See the quotation from Harris in Chapter 2, footnote 8.
[2] The evidence presented in this work does not contradict this point of view; the regularities with which we shall deal are characteristic of a group of utterances, rather than a single utterance, and no matter how certain the findings may be, they are based upon a distribution of events rather than a rule for each event.

norms for a particular variable, and to differentiate individuals and groups by the steepness of their stylistic slope. The fact that these four or five styles can be ordered by increasing attention paid to speech has been mistaken for a claim that this is the way that styles and registers are to be ordered and understood in everyday life. The style shifting devices used in this chapter were introduced as heuristic devices to obtain a range of behaviors within the individual interview, not as a general theory of style shifting. In the Harlem work that followed (Labov et al. 1968), a different approach to style shifting was introduced: group sessions vs. individual interviews.]

For accurate information on speech behavior, we will eventually need to compare the performance of large numbers of speakers. Furthermore, we will want to study a sample which is representative of a much larger group, and possibly of the New York speech community as a whole. This cannot be done without random sampling. Yet to complete random sampling, and to make the data for many speakers comparable, we need structured, formal interviews. Here is the paradox which we sensed: the formal interview itself defines a speech context in which only one speaking style normally occurs, what we may call *careful speech*. The bulk of the informants' speech production at other times may be quite different. They may use careful speech in many other contexts, but on most occasions they will be paying much less attention to their own speech, and employ a more relaxed style which we may call *casual speech*. We can hear this casual speech on the streets of New York, in bars, on the subway, at the beach, or whenever we visit friends in the city. Yet anonymous observations in these contexts will also be biased. Our friends are a very special group, and so too are those New Yorkers who frequent bars, play stickball in the streets, visit public beaches, or talk loud enough in restaurants to be overheard. Only through a painstaking method of sampling the entire population, and interviewing speakers chosen at random, can we avoid serious bias in our presentation. The problem is now to see what can be accomplished within the bounds of the interview.

Context B. The interview situation   The simplest style to define is what we have called careful speech. In our investigation, this is the type of speech which normally occurs when the subject is answering questions which are formally recognized as "part of the interview." Generally speaking, an interview which has as its professed object the language of the speaker,[3] will

---

[3] The extended formal interview of the Lower East Side population was presented as an interview about language. The study of standard reading behavior, of the pronunciation of isolated words, of linguistic attitudes, and above all, the inquiry into subjective reactions, could not have been conducted under any other pretext. The television interview (as discussed in Chapter 6) and the department store survey described in Chapter 3 are examples of the limited objectives that can be achieved under other flags.

rate higher on the scale of formality than most conversation. It is certainly not as formal a situation as a public address, and less formal than the speech which would be used in a first interview for a job, but it is certainly more formal than casual conversation among friends or family members. The degree of spontaneity or warmth in the replies of individuals may vary greatly, but the relation of their careful speech to the speech of less formal contexts is generally constant.[4] *Careful speech* will then be defined as that speech which occurs in Context B, and will be designated *Style B*. For *Context A* and *Style A*, see page 65.

It is a relatively simple matter to shift the context from Context B in a more formal direction, though there are a number of ways of refining this procedure. In the following discussion, we will pursue the definition and control of more formal styles to its ultimate conclusion, before attempting to move in the opposite direction.

Context C. Reading style   [The discussion of reading texts to follow might be of some interest to those planning new community studies. The usual reading constructed by dialectologists ("Grip the Rat," "Arthur the Rat," "The North Wind and the Sun") are rather painful assemblages of words of interest and evoke the most formal of reading styles. The reading texts constructed for the American Language Survey interview were designed to close the stylistic gap between speech and reading by writing texts that are more animated and colloquial.]

After a half to three-quarters of an hour of questions and answers, the informant is asked to read two standard texts. Both of these are given in the Questionnaire, in Appendix A. The first of them, "When I was nine or ten . . ." is presented in five paragraphs in which the chief variables are successively concentrated. The first paragraph is a zero section, in which none of the variables are found; the second contains a great many (oh) words, the third concentrates on (æh), the fourth on (r), and the fifth contains a high concentration of both (th) and (dh). This text has a double purpose: first, to measure in Context C the speaker's use of all five variables by an efficient means; second, to acquaint the subject with the text which is used as a base for the measurement of subjective reactions, as discussed in Chapter 11.

The second reading, "Last Saturday night I took Mary Parker to the Paramount Theatre . . ." follows the design of a text constructed to resolve phonemic variation on Martha's Vineyard. In the present text, there are a number of words which form minimal pairs in respect to the chief variables: these are underlined in the text as it appears in Appendix A, but

---

[4] Concrete illustrations of this statement will be provided later in this chapter; more systematic proof is given in Chapter 7.

not, of course, as the informant reads them. Speakers' pronunciation of these words will tell us whether they use the particular variable to distinguish words in reading style, and how they do so. The examples which concern (r) will illustrate the technique:

. . . You're certainly in the <u>dark</u>! They tore down that <u>dock</u> ten years ago, when you were in diapers!

The speaker may differentiate *dock* and *dark* in any of the ways discussed in Chapter 2.

. . . She told him to ask a subway <u>guard</u>. My <u>god</u>! I thought, that's one sure way to get lost in New York City.

Here the speaker may pronounce *god* and *guard* the same, as /gahd/ (again using a phonemic notation appropriate to the traditional pattern described by Hubbell). But he may also differentiate them as /gad/ vs. /gard/, or /gad/ vs. /gahd/.

. . . And what's the <u>source</u> of *your* information, Joseph? She used her sweet and sour tone of voice, like ketchup mixed with tomato <u>sauce</u>.

The speaker may use (r-1) to differentiate *source* and *sauce*, which would then appear phonemically as /sors/ vs. /sohs/, or he may pronounce them both the same, or possibly differentiate them by the value of (oh), using (oh-3) for *source* and (oh-1) for *sauce*. Primarily, we will be interested in whether or not (r-1) functions in this style as an element to differentiate words, although the other details will be useful in the final view.

A complete list of the phonemic pairs used in the reading is given on the page following the text in Appendix A.

The phonemic reading is so designed that the words which form minimal pairs occur in close proximity. The transcriber can then hear the contrast by listening to the tape without cutting or editing. However, it is important that the pair be not so obvious that the reader will notice the contrast, and adjust the pronunciation of one word to fit or contrast with the other.[5]

The instructions given to the reader can govern certain variations in reading style. In both texts, the design was to standardize the context towards the informal end of the possible range. Thus the instructions were,

---

[5] In this aim, the reading was successful. Few of the speakers were aware of the minimal pairs, as noted by their volunteered remarks and by direct questioning. Another important requirement is that the words occur in approximately the same prosodic position, with the same stress and contour. This is not always carried out perfectly in the reading, but gross violations are avoided.

We'd like you to read this as naturally as possible. In other words, we don't want you to read this as if you were in a school room, but to give us an idea of how you might actually say this if you were telling the story yourself.

The effect of such instructions is of course very slight. More influential is the nature of the text. It has been found, through the construction of a number of such readings, that a text which is ostensibly a narrative of a teenage boy seems to lend itself to the least artificial performance for most people. In such a framework, it was possible to incorporate such phrases as, "He was a funny kid, all right." Elderly women might balk at such a phrase if it were placed in the mouth of an adult, but as the utterance of a teenage boy, it made natural reading for them.

  The content of the readings carries this point further, by focusing on two main themes: the teenager's traditional protest against the restrictions of the adult world, and his exasperation at the foibles and inconsistencies of the girls he dates. Thus a number of phrases which are difficult to insert into other contexts proceed quite naturally in this sentence:

I wanted to go and see The Jazz Singer, but Mary got her finger in the pie. She hates jazz, because she can't carry a tune, and besides, she never misses a new film with Cary Grant.

It might have been possible to standardize in a different direction, by urging the subject to read carefully and slowly. The chief disadvantage of such an approach would be that very slow reading is accompanied by special phonetic characteristics which would make it difficult to compare conversation and reading style. For example, the question of final (r) followed by another word beginning with a vowel, as in *four o'clock*, may become quite confused if the tempo is very slow. In normal speech, a pronunciation in which no consonant occurs between *four* and *o'clock* would be entered as a violation of the rule followed by most New Yorkers which preserves (r-1) in this position. But such a rule begins to break down if speech is slow enough. Then too, in a very slow tempo of reading, the minimal pairs are more likely to be noticed by the reader. Therefore the overall design of the two texts is to encourage a reasonably fast reading style.

  There is no danger that the instructions given will bring reading style to a point where it becomes confused with careful conversation. The gap between Context B and C, by every measure of performance, is so great that the effect of the bias introduced by the instructions is barely noticeable in reducing this difference.[6]

---

[6] A few upper middle class speakers seemed to have the degree of control and self-awareness needed to modify their reading style in the direction of conversational style, but this is a rare effect and not a very large one.

The style used in reading under Context C will be designated *Style C*.

Context D. Word lists   A further step in the direction of a more formal context is to consider the subject's pronunciation of words in isolation. There are two types of word lists which are used for the investigation of the variables (r), (æh), and (oh). One is a list which the subject knows by heart, such as the days of the week or the months of the year. A second type is a printed list of words with the same or similar sound feature. One of these contains the (æh) variable, with a few associated occurrences of (r); the other contains (oh) words. These words appear in Section V.2–3 of the Questionnaire.

The first half of the (æh) list sets up an alternation between words of sub-group a) (see Chapter 2, page 33) and sub-group c) as: *bat, bad, back, bag, batch, badge* . . .. This allows the transcriber to hear the pattern of differentiation very clearly, and if the speaker uses a corrected pattern with (æh-4) in all words, any deviation from this leveling is immediately obvious.[7]

Context D'. Minimal pairs   For the variable (r), it is useful to extend the spectrum of formality one stage further. In the word lists of Context D, (r) occurs in two situations. In one, the pronunciation of (r) is seemingly incidental, as in the reading of *hammer* and *hamster* in the (æh) list, or the names of the months ending in *-er*, or with such minimal pairs as *finger* and *singer*, *mirror* and *nearer*. Here (r) is pronounced in the formal context of a word list, but it does not receive the full attention of the reader. But in minimal pairs such as *dock* and *dark, guard* and *god, source* and *sauce, bared* and *bad*, (r) is the sole differentiating element, and it therefore receives maximum attention. We will therefore single out this sub-group of Style D, under the designation of *Style D'*.

[Minimal pairs look easy, but they're not so simple to do right. The investigator has to keep a poker face after the subject pronounces the two words, and then ask in an absolutely neutral manner, "Are they the same or different?" Some field workers will register their own impressions and say something like, "They're different, aren't they?" Good minimal pair administrators keep their own reactions under control.]

---

[7] The rhythmic effect produced by this alternation may have made it more difficult for speakers to preserve an acquired pronunciation than in an unstructured list. Thus we find that the number of irregularities in the overall pattern of stylistic variation is greater with (æh) than with (r) in Style D. See below, pages 162–63. On the other hand, there are even more irregularities (reversals of the informal-formal progression) with (oh) D, which is not as rhythmically structured. The accumulation of a great many examples of a variable in close proximity may be the factor which disturbs the pattern, as many speakers find it more difficult to preserve a learned pronunciation in this case than where words are widely spaced.

The problem of casual speech

Up to this point, we have been discussing techniques for extending the formal range of the interview by methods which fall naturally into the framework of a discussion about language. Now, within the interview, we must go beyond the interview situation, if we can. We must somehow become witnesses to the everyday speech which informants will use as soon as the door is closed behind us: the style in which they argue with their nearest and dearest, scold their children, or pass the time of day with their friends. The difficulty of the problem is considerable; yet the rewards for its solution are great, both to further our immediate goal and to build the general theory of stylistic variation.

First, it is important to determine whether we have any means of knowing when we have succeeded in eliciting casual speech. Against what standard can we measure success? In the course of the present study of New York City speech, there are several other approaches to casual speech which have been used. In the exploratory interviews, I recorded a great deal of language which is literally the language of the streets. This material included the unrestrained and jubilant activity of a great many small children, and also some recordings of street games among young men, 18 to 25 years old, where I was an anonymous bystander. It may be that none of the conversation within the interview will be as spontaneous and free as this material. But if the informants show a sudden and marked shift of style in this direction, we will be justified in calling this behavior casual speech.

Another check will be the department store survey, as described in Chapter 3, in which the bias of the linguist's presence disappeared completely. Here we can judge whether the type of alternation which is found within the interview gives us a range of behavior comparable to that which is found under casual conditions in everyday life.

The immediate problem, then, is to construct interview situations in which casual speech will find a place, or which will permit spontaneous speech to emerge, and then set up a formal method for defining the occurrence of these styles. By *casual speech*, in a narrow sense, we mean the everyday speech used in informal situations, where no attention is directed to language. *Spontaneous speech* refers to a pattern used in excited, emotionally charged speech when the constraints of a formal situation are overridden. Schematically:

Context:	Informal	Formal
Style:	Casual	Careful/Spontaneous

We do not normally think of "spontaneous" speech as occurring in formal contexts: yet, as we will show, this frequently happens in the course of the interview. *Spontaneous* speech is defined here as that counterpart of casual speech which does occur in formal contexts, not in response to the formal situation, but in spite of it.

While there is no *a priori* reason to assume that the values of the variables will be the same in spontaneous as in casual speech, the results of this investigation show that they can be studied together. At a later point, as we examine more deeply the mechanism of stylistic variation, it will be possible to suggest an underlying basis for this identification. For the moment, either term will be used according to the nature of the context, but they will both be measured under the heading of *Style A*, or casual speech in general.

[This distinction between spontaneous vs. casual speech was quite insightful at the time, but I lost sight of it for quite a while. Whether or not the speech was relaxed and casual outside of the interview format, or tense and excited in answer to a question, seemed to have little influence on the shift of the variable. In both cases, attention to speech was reduced, but for opposite reasons. In 1980, Hindle analyzed the all-day recordings made of Carol Meyers by Arvilla Payne. He distinguished three stylistic contexts: the travel agency, where Carol Meyers worked [O]; dinner conversation at home [H]; and the bridge game with close friends in the evening [G]. These would correspond to careful, casual and spontaneous speech in the terminology of this section. But tracing the mean values of the Philadelphia vowels in the three contexts, Hindle found that [G] was very different from [H]: two new and vigorous changes were shifted in the direction of younger speakers for [G], towards the norms of older speakers for [H] and even more so for [O].]

The formal definition of casual speech within the interview requires that at least one of five contextual situations prevails, and also at least one of five non-phonological cues. We will first discuss the contextual situations, which will be identified as Contexts A_1 through A_5.

Context A_1. Speech outside the formal interview   There are three occasions within the larger context of the interview situation which do not fall within the bounds of the formal interview proper, and in these contexts, casual speech is apt to occur.

Before the interview proper begins, the subject may often address casual remarks to someone else in the household, wife, husband or children, or may make a few good-natured remarks to the interviewer. Although this is not the most common context for a good view of casual speech, the interviewer will not hurry to begin formal proceedings if there seems to be any opportunity for such an exchange. In several cases, where a housewife took time to wash the dishes, or a family to finish dinner, the interviewer overheard casual speech in some quantity.

After the interview begins, there may be interruptions, when someone else enters the room, or when the informant offers a glass of beer or a cup of coffee. In the following example, the three paragraphs represent: 1) speech in the formal interview directly before the break; 2) speech used while opening a can of beer for the interviewer; and 3) the first sentences spoken on the resumption of the formal interview.

1) If you're not careful, you will call a lot of them the same. There are a couple of them which are very similar: for instance, *width* and *with*. (What about *guard* and *god*?) That's another one you could very well pronounce the same, unless you give thought to it.

2) . . . these things here – y'gotta do it the right way – otherwise [laughter] you'll need a pair of pliers with it. . . . You see, what actually happened was, I pulled it over to there, and well . . . I don't really know *what* happened. . . . Did it break off or get stuck or sump'm?
    . . . just the same as when you put one of these keys into a can of sardines or sump'm – and you're turning it, and you turn it lopsided, and in the end you break it off and you use the old fashioned opener . . . but I always have a spoon or a fork or a screw driver handy to wedge into the key to help you turn it . . . [laughter] I always have these things handy to make sure.

3) [How do you make up your mind about how to rate these people?] Some people – I suppose perhaps it's the result of their training and the kind of job that they have – they just talk in any slip-shod manner. Others talk in a manner which has real finesse to it, but that would be the executive type. He cannot [sic] talk in a slipshod manner to a board of directors meeting.

In these examples, the shift in speech style can be perceived even as the conversation is reproduced in conventional orthography. The effects of channel cues, the phonological variables, the forms of words, syntax, and content all conform to the overall shift of style.

The interviewer may make every use of this opportunity by moving away from his chair and tape recorder, and supporting the emergence of casual conversation. One great advantage of such a break is that it occurs in close juxtaposition with very careful speech, and the contrast is very sharp, as in the example given above. The sudden occurrence of radically different values of the variables is particularly marked in this example. The word *otherwise* in section 2) had (dh) in medial position which is rarely (dh-3) in this speaker's careful speech; (dh-3) does occur here in this word and makes a sharp impression on the listener.

The most frequent place for casual speech to emerge in Context A_1 is at the end of the interview. It is perhaps most common when the interviewer has packed away his equipment, and is standing with one hand on the door knob.[8]

Context A₂. Speech with a third person   At any point in the interview, the subject may address remarks to a third person, and casual speech may emerge here. One of the most striking examples occurred in an interview with an African–American (AA) woman, 35, raised in the Bronx, and then living on the Lower East Side in the poorest possible circumstances as a widow with six children. The following three sections illustrate the sharp alternations which occurred throughout the interview between her careful, quiet, controlled style used in talking to the interviewer, and the louder, higher-pitched style used with her children. Again, the grammatical and stylistic differences shown in conventional orthography illustrate the shift of style.

1)   . . . Their father went back to Santo Domingo when they had the upris-
     ing about two years ago that June or July . . . he got killed in the upris-
     ing . . . I believe that those that want to go and give up their life for their
     country, let them go. For my part, his place was here with the children
     to help raise them and give them a good education . . . that's from my
     point of view.

2)   Get out of the refrigerator, Darlene! Tiny, or Teena, or whatever your
     name is! . . . Close the refrigerator, Darlene! . . . What pocketbook? I
     don't have no pocketbook – if he lookin' for money from me, dear
     heart, I have no money.

3)   I thought the time I was in the hospital for three weeks, I had peace and
     quiet, and I was crying to get back home to the children, and I didn't
     know what I was coming back home to.

Interruptions of the interview by telephone calls sometimes provide unusually good opportunities to study casual speech. In one interview, the telephone interrupted the proceedings at the very middle. Dolly R. had just returned from the summer spent in North Carolina, and one of her cousins was anxious for news of the family. I left the room with her nephew, and continued to talk to him quietly in another room; for twenty minutes, the informant discussed the latest events in a very informal style, and I obtained a recording of the most spontaneous kind of speech.

[Here are some excerpts from Dolly R. talking with her cousin on the phone:

---

[8] The interviewer is not a passive agent in any of these circumstances. By his participation in
the developing informality, he can help casual speech to emerge. At the termination of the
interview, he can also terminate his role as interviewer, and behave like any other tired, hot,
or sleepy employee who has now finished his job and is free to be himself.

So you know what Carol Anne say? Listen at what Carol Anne say. Carol Anne say, "And then when Papa die, we can come back. [laughs at length]. Ain't these chill'un sump'm? Dat what she say! and when Papa die can we come back? . . .

Tha's Nick boy. Tha's Nick boy. Sure it is. An' the one Miz Bell had from Ni' had three . . . Hah? They were whole brothers, 'cause I mean they all got the same mother. 'At's what dey say, you know. Yeah, yeah, yeah . . .

She said she sho' had herself a good res'. Yeah . . . well if she didn' i's too bad. 'Cause they sho' worked the hell out of me! Listen, honey, they'll change clothes so fast down there, I said, "Now wait a minute. Shit, now y'all ain't in New York any more. Y'all can go down them –" "Shucks, we get too dirty!" I said, "Well don't get dirty!" . . . Gah! . . . Mmhmm.

When Dolly R. hung up the phone, we continued our discussion of what makes "a successful man."

Well I would say that on the average . . . a successful man . . . is one that has had something in his mind to reach out . . . *for*. And he have reached it, and made a living for himself, and family.

and then we continued to talk about "common sense."

[Could you say that someone is very *smart* and has no common sense?] Smart? Well I mean when you use the word intelligent and smart, you use it in the same sense? [I don't know, I want to know how you use it] [Laughs] 'Cause some people are pretty witty, I mean, yet they're not so intelligent!

Compare this discussion of intelligence with Dolly R. talking to her cousins about how smart the kids were:

'Cause that boy is a Skreet and this here one is a Davis. Um hm. Umhm. No, she ain't had no kind of nobody to bring her up. I was kinda glad she was comin'. And I said, I know this other little boy, 'cause he useta go to school with Lilly Belle. The one she's stayin' with. And all those kids was smart, y'know. So, if she behaves herself, I think she be all right.

It seems that these are not just two different styles, but two different people talking. From this and other experience we came to the conclusion that the techniques for approaching the vernacular of most native New Yorkers didn't work in a conversation between black and white, and when we did our work in Harlem three years later, we used entirely different methods.]

Context A_3. Speech not in direct response to questions   In some types of interview schedules, it is necessary to cut off long, rambling replies, or sudden outbursts of rhetoric, in order to get through with the work. In this interview program, the opposite policy prevailed. Whenever subjects showed signs of wanting to talk, no obstacle was interposed: the longer they digressed, the better chance we had of studying their natural speech pattern. Some older speakers, in particular, pay little attention to the questions as they are asked. They may have certain favorite points of view which they want to express, and they have a great deal of experience in making a rapid transition from the topic to the subject that is closest to their hearts.

Context A_3 forms a transition from those contexts in which casual speech is formally appropriate, to those contexts in which the emotional state or attitude of the speaker overrides any formal restrictions, and spontaneous speech emerges.

Context A_4. Childhood rhymes and customs   This is one of the two topics within the interview itself which is designed to provide the context in which spontaneous speech is likely to emerge. The atmosphere or tone required for such a shift is provided by a series of questions which lead gradually to the topic of jump-rope rhymes, counting-out rhymes, the rules of fighting, and similar aspects of language drawn from the pre-adolescent period when the youngster participates in a culture distinct from that of adult society. Rhymes, for example, cannot be recited correctly in Style B of careful conversation. Both the rhyme itself, and the tempo, would be wrong if Style B were used in:

Cinderella,
Dressed in yellow
Went downtown to buy some mustard,
On the way her girdle busted,
How many people were disgusted? 10, 20, 30 . . .

The following song, which is popular in New York City schools, does not permit the *r*-pronunciation which creeps into Style B:

Glory, glory, Hallelujah,
The teacher hit me with the ruler,
The ruler turned red,
And the teacher dropped dead,
No more school for me.

Equally *r*-less pronunciation is implied in the traditional:

Strawberry short cake, cream on top
Tell me the name of your sweetheart . . .[9]

If the reciting of these rhymes demanded a return to a childhood pronunciation which was no longer normal, their use as evidence would be wrong. However, the pattern which is used in Context A_4 is quite

---

[9] The acceptable half-rhyme here implies a pronunciation of -*heart* as /hat/, with a fairly short vowel. Such pronunciations are not rare in the city, as indicated in Chapter 2.

comparable to that which is used in the four other contexts which are utilized. There is no necessity for the following rhyme to assume any particular value of (oh), yet (oh-1) is very common:

I won't go to Macy's any more, more, more,
There's a big fat policeman at the door, door, door,
He pulls you by the collar
And makes you pay a dollar,
I won't go to Macy's any more, more, more.

The nine examples of (oh) in this rhyme provide a very efficient means of studying that variable.

Even in counting-out rhymes, where meter and rhyme are less compelling for the informant, we find that Style B is inadequate for:

My mother and your mother were hanging out the clothes,
My mother punched your mother right in the nose.
What color blood came out?
    [Green.] G-R-E-E-N spells green and you are not IT.

or for the much simpler:

Doggie, doggie, step right out.

Men as well as women will be able to repeat counting-out rhymes such as "Eeny meeny miny moe," or "Engine, engine, number nine." Lacking this, spontaneous speech is often obtained from men in the rules for playing marbles, or skelley, or punch ball.

Context A₅. The danger of death   Another series of questions, in a later section of the interview, leads to the following question:

Have you ever been in a situation where you thought there was a serious danger of your being killed? That you thought to yourself, "This is it"?

If the informant answers "yes," the interviewer pauses for one or two seconds, and then asks, "What happened?" As the informant begins to reply, he is under some compulsion to show that there was a very real danger of his being killed; he stands in a very poor light if it appears that there was no actual danger. Often he becomes involved in the narrative to the extent that he seems to be re-living the critical moment, and signs of emotional tension appear. One such example occurred in an interview with six brothers, from 10 to 19 years old, from a lower class Irish-Italian household. While most of the boys spoke freely and spontaneously in many contexts, the oldest brother, Eddee D., was quite reserved and careful in his replies. He had given no examples of casual or spontaneous speech until this topic was reached. In a few sentences, a sudden shift in style occurred. The beginning of his narrative followed his usual careful style:

[What happened to you?] The school I go to is Food and Maritime – that's maritime training – and I was up in the masthead, and the wind started blowing. I had a rope secured around me to keep me from falling – but the rope parted, and I was just hanging there by my fingernails.

At this point, the speaker's breathing became very heavy and irregular; his voice began to shake, and sweat appeared on his forehead. Small traces of nervous laughter appeared in his speech.

I never prayed to God so fast and so hard in my life . . . [What happened?] Well, I came out all right . . . Well, the guys came up and they got me. [How long were you up there?] About ten minutes. [I can see you're still sweating, thinking about it.] Yeh, I came down, I couldn't hold a pencil in my hand, I couldn't touch nothin'. I was shakin' like a leaf. Sometimes I get scared thinkin' about it . . . but . . uh . . well, it's training.

The effect of probing for the subject's feelings at the moment of crisis can be effective even with speakers who are much more articulate than this informant. One of the most gifted story tellers and naturally expressive speakers in the sample was Mrs. Rose B. She was raised on the Lower East Side, of Italian parents; now in her late thirties, she recently returned to work as a sewing machine operator. The many examples of spontaneous narratives which she provided show a remarkable command of pitch, volume, and tempo for expressive purposes.

. . . And another time – that was three times, and I hope it never happens to me again – I was a little girl, we all went to my aunt's farm right near by, where Five Points is . . . and we were thirteen to a car. And at that time, if you remember, about 20 or 25 years ago, there wasn't roads like this to go to Jersey – there was all dirt roads. Well, anyway, I don't know how far we are – I don't remember what part we were – one of the wheels of the car came off – and the whole car turned, and they took us all out. They hadda break the door off. And they took us out one by one. And I got a scar on my leg here . . . 'ats the on'y thing . . . [When the car turned over, what did you think?]
    . . . it was upside dow – you know what happened, do you know how I felt? I don't remember anything. This is really the truth – till today, I could tell that to anybody, 'n' they don't believe me, they think I'm kiddin 'em. All I remember is – I thought I fell asleep, and I was in a dream . . . I actually saw stars . . . you know, stars in the sky – y'know, when you look up there . . . and I was seein' stars. And then after a while, I felt somebody pushing and piling – you know, they were all on top of each other – and they were pulling us out from the bottom of the car, and I was goin' "Ooooh."
    And when I came – you know – to, I says to myself, "Ooooh, we're in a car accident," – and that's all I remember – as clear as day – I don't remember the car turning or anything. All I know is I thought I went to sleep. I actually felt I went to sleep.

Channel cues for casual speech

The five contexts just described are only the first part of the formal criteria for the identification of Style A in the interview.[10] It is of course not enough to set a particular context in order to observe casual speech. We also look for some evidence in the type of linguistic production that the speaker is using a speech style that contrasts with Style B. To use phonological variables would involve a circular argument, because the values of these variables in Styles A and B are exactly what we are trying to determine by the isolation of styles. The best cues are channel cues: modulations of the voice production which affect speech as a whole.[11] Our use of this evidence must follow the general procedure of linguistic analysis: the absolute values of tempo, pitch, volume, and breathing may be irrelevant, but contrasting values of these characteristics are cues to a differentiation of Style A and Style B. A *change* in tempo, a *change* in pitch range, a *change* in volume or rate of breathing, form socially significant signs of a shift towards a more spontaneous or more casual style of speech.[12]

Whenever one of these four channel cues is present in an appropriate context, the utterance which contains them is marked and measured under Style A. The fifth channel cue is also a modulation of voice production: laughter. This may accompany the most casual kind of speech, like the nervous laughter in the example on page 71, and is frequently heard in the description of the most dramatic and critical moments in the danger-of-death narrative. Since laughter involves a more rapid expulsion of breath than in normal speech, it is always accompanied by a sudden intake of breath in the following pause. Though this intake is not always obvious to the listener in the interview situation, the recording techniques being used in this study detect such effects quite readily; it is therefore possible to regard laughter as a variant type of changes in breathing, the fourth channel cue.

The question now arises, what if a very marked constellation of channel cues occurs in some Context B? Intuition may tell us that this is

[10] There is a subordinate context which is usually found in association with those listed above. This is the use of direct quotations in a reply. Should this occur in the interview outside of the five contexts given, with the appropriate channel cues, it is allowed as Style A.

[11] These would be considered modifications of the *Message Form* rather than the *Channel* in the terminology used by Dell Hymes, "The Ethnography of Speaking" (1962). In the framework suggested by Hymes, the more formal styles of reading would represent a shift in the channel; the elicitation of casual speech would be encouraged by shifts in the *Setting* and *Topic*, and the phonological variables appear as variations in the *Code*.

[12] The use of these criteria is not based upon an exact, objective procedure, but upon our general knowledge of these socially significant signs. A precise study of these cues as a preliminary would have involved too great an effort for too small a gain, since it was considered that the confirmation of this selection of cues would come from the consistency of the final correlations.

spontaneous speech, but the formal rules of this procedure instruct us to consider it Style B. This is a necessary consequence of a formal definition. The situation may be schematized in this way:

intuitive observations	Careful speech	Casual speech
formal definition and measurement	Style B	Style A

As this diagram indicates, Style B as formally defined overlaps casual speech as intuitively observed. Some examples of casual speech will occur outside of the five contexts given, conditioned by some less prominent context we have not considered, and these will be lost by the formal definition. However, since the body of careful speech bulks much larger than casual speech, this small amount of comparatively casual speech now included under Context B and Style B will not seriously distort the values for careful speech. If, on the other hand, there should be overlap in the other direction, with a definition which specified the contexts of careful speech, the resulting admixture in the smaller bulk of casual speech would be a source of serious distortion. By leaving careful speech as the unmarked category, we are protected from such distortion.

What are the actual proportions in our material of casual and careful speech as defined? This was determined in a random sample of ten percent of the adult interviews of the Lower East Side survey, using a combined index for each interview of the total incidence of (dh) and (r) in each style. These variables occur very frequently in all styles of speech; the total number of all variants is proportional to the total volume of speech. Instead of counting words, we then take the sum of all (dh) and (r) variants in a given style – totals we already have on hand – as a measure of the volume of speech in that style.[13] The mean proportion for the group is:

Style A, Casual speech   29%
Style B, Careful speech   71%

An alternate course would have been to rely only upon channel cues, without reference to the context. This would have been far less reliable, for in many contexts the channel cues vary continuously, and to determine where contrast occurred, and where it did not, would have often been very

---

[13] The use of (dh) or (r) alone would have produced serious bias. For some speakers, primarily lower class white and AA speakers, (r) is not a variable, and is not recorded as such on the transcription forms. For others, primarily middle class speakers, (dh) is always a fricative, and is not tabulated. There are no speakers in the sample for whom neither of these features is a variable. It is interesting to note that the (dh) variable gives a somewhat higher percentage for casual speech: 33 percent as against 26 percent for (r). This is probably a reflection of the greater spontaneity and more casual approach of many working class speakers.

difficult. The interview as now constructed provides for sudden shifts of contexts which have sharp boundaries. These shifts thus enable us to observe sudden contrasts in the channel cues. It is not contended that Style A and Style B are natural units of stylistic variation: rather they are formal divisions of the continuum set up for the purposes of this study, which has the purpose of measuring phonological variation along the stylistic axis. The discovery of natural breaks in the range of stylistic phenomena would have to follow a very different procedure. It is not unlikely that the results of the present work, yielding sensitive indexes to linguistic variation, may eventually be applied to this end.

[The five contextual styles have survived well into the twenty-first century, but channel cues did not. I know of only one sociolinguist who followed my lead in using changes of pitch, tempo, and laughter as a way of corroborating the shift to casual speech. Claude Paradis did a meticulous study of laughter and other channel cues in his dissertation on the French of Chicoutimi-Jonquieres (1985). But it appears that channel cues did not provide a high enough level of interpersonal reliability for most researchers.]

The array of stylistic variation

The validity of our method may be tested by comparison with other means of recording casual speech.[14] It can also be measured against psychological experiments which attain similar results by completely different methods.[15]

---

[14] For one such record of casual speech outside the procedures of the linguistic interview, see "The punch-ball game" in Appendix B. The values of the variables shown there may be compared to the arrays of this chapter, and the stratification diagrams of Chapter 7.

[15] A completely different approach to stylistic variation may be derived from psychological experiments conducted by Dr. George Mahl of the Yale School of Medicine. He used colorless, random noise as a means of eliminating subjects' ability to hear their own speech, and studied the resulting effect upon their speech performance. The speech of his subjects was studied during three interviews, under four conditions: with white noise, facing the interviewer and not facing the interviewer; without white noise, facing the interviewer and not facing the interviewer. In many cases, there were sharp changes in pitch, volume, intonation, and the length of responses to questions when audio-monitoring was eliminated. In several cases, there were changes in the speech pattern which seemed to have social class significance. In cooperation with Dr. Mahl, I applied the techniques described in this study to several of these cases. A study of the New Haven speech pattern developed a list of socially significant variables; the most important of these for the speech behavior of Mahl's subjects was (dh). The (dh) index was applied to the recorded interview for one particular subject, who showed the same type of variation which we have seen for New York subjects in the linguistic interview. Under the effect of white noise, his (dh) index rose consistently, and when audio-monitoring was restored, the index fell to its usual level. The index was also higher when the subject was facing away from the interviewer. These relationships were maintained throughout three interviews, though in the course of the interviews, increasing familiarization with the interviewer and the situation was accompanied by a steady increase in the

Table 4.1   *Style*

Variable	A	B	C	D	D'
(r)	x	x	x	x	x
(æh)	x	x	x	x	
(oh)	x	x	x	x	
(th)	x	x	x		
(dh)	x	x	x		

But even before such steps are taken, it becomes evident from the regularity of the distinctions which appear in the dependent variables, that the stylistic divisions we have set up correspond to some regular alternation in the linguistic behavior of New York City speakers.

In the course of the interview, there is a steady process of familiarization which diminishes the formality of the context. It would be desirable to rotate the succession of Styles B, C, D, and D' in order to detect and cancel out such a familiarization effect. However, the structure of this interview does not permit such a rotation: once the readings and word lists have been brought forward, a certain amount of conscious attention has been focused on the variables. Style B which follows C or D is considered contaminated for this reason and is not used.

The full range of contexts and styles elicited by the methods described above, provides us with Table 4.1, showing the array of values to be determined.

The first native New Yorker to whom this method was applied was Miss Josephine P., 35, who lived with her Italian-born mother in the same Lower East Side tenement apartment where she was born. Josephine P. attended high school on the Lower East Side, and had completed almost four years of college. At the time of the interview, she worked as a receptionist at Saks 5th Avenue. Josephine P.'s style of speech is lively and rapid; she seems to be an outgoing person who has no difficulty in making friendly contact with strangers. Her careful conversation, in Context B, seems at first to be equivalent to the casual conversation of most speakers. Yet two short samples of casual speech were recorded, which contrasted with her speech in Context B. We thus have the complete array of average values of the variables for this speaker (see Table 4.2).

Footnote 15 (*cont.*)
   absolute value of the index. The results of this study (Mahl 1972) suggest that spontaneous speech as well as casual speech as defined in our interview is accompanied by a reduction in audio-monitoring by the subject. An increase in audio-monitoring would correspondingly accompany a shift to more formal styles.

Table 4.2   *Stylistic array for Josephine P.*

Variable	A	B	C	D	D'
(r)	00	03	23	53	50
(æh)	25	28	27	37	
(oh)	21	23	26	37	
(th)	40	14	05		
(dh)	34	09	09		

Table 4.2 shows us a regular progression for each of the variables, through each of the styles (with the slight deviations noted below). On the top line, we see that Josephine P. used no (r-1) in casual speech, only a trace in careful speech, 23 percent (r-1) in reading, and finally pronounced fully half of the isolated words with (r-1). On the second line, we see that her casual use of the (æh) variable in the word class of *ask, bad, dance*, reached values close to the vowel (æh-2), the sound in *where*. (As defined in Chapter 2, the (æh) and (oh) indexes are the average values of the variable on the scale of 1 to 6, multiplied by 10.)

Josephine P.'s use of (oh), on the third line, shows a close approximation to (oh-2) in casual speech, but in the most formal contexts, the vowel used is a very open one, more open than any sound naturally used in conversation in New York City. The bottom two lines show that she uses a very notice-able amount of stops and affricates for (th) and (dh) in her casual speech; although these drop to slight traces when she is being careful, she never reaches the index of (th)-00 or (dh)-00 – that is, she always shows traces of affricates, even in reading style.

The two sections of casual speech which were recorded in contrast to Style B occurred in Context A_1, extra-interview. In one section, Josephine P. talked with some emotion about her dead father, as she remembered him from her childhood, and the dolls he brought her from the factory where he worked. The associated channel cues were laughter, increase in tempo, and a change in the rate of breathing. The second section was a burst of irrita-tion at the behavior of other tenants in the building, with increased pitch and volume. Both of these were recorded after the interview, as I sat having coffee with Josephine P. and her mother.

In the normal course of an interview, the speech of Josephine P. would have been accepted as free and spontaneous; but since the present proce-dure assumes that the speech of Context B cannot be truly casual, all of the contexts relevant to Style A were examined. The emergence of a very different speech pattern in the measurements of the five variables under Style A as defined confirms our expectation. Many other examples confirm

Table 4.3   *Frequency array for Josephine P.*

Variable	A	B	C	D	D'
(r)	18	66	44	15	4
(æh)	4	4	28	13	
(oh)	10	11	19	11	
(th)	10	29	20		
(dh)	26	65	35		

the idea that this method can successfully isolate contrasting speech styles where a less carefully constructed interview would report the presence of only one.

In the overall pattern, there are two slight reversals, both less than 5 percent in magnitude. This is remarkable when we consider the irregular fluctuations of the variables that seem to mark the individual sections of speech. For example, here are the occurrences of (th) in casual speech, in the order that they occurred: 1221221111; and here are the occurrences in careful speech: 221111111111112121. There seems to be no pattern or system within this sequence – yet it fits into the larger pattern shown in the array of styles.

The total number of items upon which the array of Table 4.1 was based is not large; a relatively small number of occurrences establish the progressions, despite the variations within each style.

If we were to return to the notion of *idiolect*, each of the styles would have to be considered a distinct idiolect, and each is fully as irregular as the examples given in Chapter 2. It again becomes apparent that such a notion is not a useful one for describing the structure of New York City English.

Table 4.3 shows the number of instances for each value.

This array of frequencies shows three weak points, at (r) D', and at (æh) A and B, where there were only four occurrences of the variable in each cell. This limitation of the data allows errors in perception and transcription, as well as variation in the usage of the individual, to affect the final result significantly. If Table 4.3 is now compared with the average values of the variables given in Table 4.2, it appears that the low points of frequency coincide exactly with the points where small deviations from the overall pattern were found. The implication of this finding is that if more occurrences of (æh) A and B and (r) D' were introduced, the behavior of the subject might be seen as perfectly regular.

The next New Yorker who was interviewed by this procedure was Abraham G., 47, a high school graduate, native of the Lower East Side, of

Table 4.4   *Stylistic array for Abraham G.*

Variable	A	B	C	D	D'		Frequencies			
(r)	12	15	46	100	100	8	60	39	7	5
(æh)	35	36	39	40		6	22	18	13	
(oh)	10	18	29	20		3	11	16	11	
(th)		17	00			1	20	20		
(dh)	72	33	05			18	78	35		

Polish Jewish parents. He lives in a public housing project, and drives a taxi for his regular income. In contrast to Josephine P., this informant was immediately and obviously a multiple-style speaker. In Context B, he used a fluent but self-conscious style, which reflected his experience in many committee meetings as head of his American Legion chapter. His Style B, which employed such phrases as *the armed forces* for "army," and *fair and equitable* for "fair," was obviously not his casual style. He even managed to tell several long and exciting stories of near hold-ups, in the danger-of-death section, without losing the elevated manner of Style B. However, midway through the interview, he stopped to offer me a can of beer, and delivered the humorous monologue quoted on page 66, which is the main basis for the Style A column in Table 4.4.

The blank spot in Table 4.4, at (th) A, is the point where the single occurrence of (th) (as a stop) could not be used for a rating. The only apparent irregularity is the change of direction at (oh) D: as we shall see later, this is not uncommon. Comparison with larger numbers of speakers will be necessary to resolve this point.

In most cases, the interview procedure isolates Style A in more than one context. The case of Mrs. Doris H., 39, is typical. She is AA, raised on Staten Island, a high school graduate; her husband is a New York City policeman. Doris H. showed a wide range of stylistic behavior, from the careful, well reasoned, highly organized replies of Context B, to sudden outbursts of spontaneous humor that marked her as a person of considerable wit and charm. Table 4.5 shows spontaneous speech in Context A_2 (speech to a third person) as she rallied her thirteen-year-old son on his tendency to show off; in Context A_3 (not in direct response) as a long account of the tactless behavior of some of her friends, with direct quotations; in four cases within Context A_4 (childhood rhymes) and in Context A_5 (danger of death). In these seven sections of Style A, the most prominent channel cues are sudden increase in volume, and laughter; occasionally there was an increase in tempo and in rate of breathing. The resulting array of the variables is quite regular in its left to right progression except for (æh) (see Table 4.5).

Table 4.5   *Stylistic array for Doris H.*

Variable	A	B	C	D	D'	Frequencies				
(r)	00	31	44	69	100	29	64	55	19	4
(æh)	30	26	32	29		3	10	25	13	
(oh)	18	21	23	25		16	21	18	11	
(th)	80	24	12			5	29	24		
(dh)	50	22	16			28	85	42		

Part of the reason for the irregularity is (æh) A, represented only by three vowels (all of them before nasals). We do find that values of (r) in Style D' are usually quite regular, even though there are only four instances. The overriding effect of the formality of the context seems to provide quite uniform results. But in all other contexts, three or four items seem to be insufficient to provide values that fit into a regular array. This problem disappears as we begin to sum the arrays of individuals to obtain values for social groups. The other deviation at (æh) D, is based on sufficient evidence, and indicates again that a reversal at (æh) D and (oh) D is more common than a reversal in the pattern anywhere else. The great range in (r-1) pronunciation which is seen here, from 00 to 100, is a frequent characteristic of the linguistic class of speakers to which Doris H. belongs, as will be seen in Chapter 7.

A very different type of character may be considered in the case of Steve K. He is a very intense young man, 25 years old, now a copyreader's assistant, living in a fifth-floor walk-up tenement on the Lower East Side. He came to the Lower East Side only three years ago from Brooklyn, where he was raised, a third-generation New Yorker. His grandparents were Jewish immigrants from Eastern Europe.

Steve K. might be considered a deviant case in many ways. He studied philosophy for four years at Brooklyn College, but left without graduating; he has turned away from the academic point of view, and as an intense student of the psychologist Wilhelm Reich, seeks self-fulfillment in awareness of himself as a sexual person.[16] His attitude towards language is much more explicit than that of most people. He was unique among the informants in being aware of all five of the chief variables, and believed that he was able to control or at least influence his own usage. He has consciously tried to reverse his college-trained tendency towards formal speech, and to reinstate the natural speech pattern of his earlier years. In

---

[16] Steve K.'s definition of a *successful man* puts his point of view very concisely: "a man who is fully aware of himself . . . of his own sexuality and of his emotions . . . who always knows what he feels towards each person he meets."

Table 4.6   *Stylistic array for Steve K.*

Variables	A	B	C	D	D'	Frequencies			
(r)	00	06	08	38	100	32	70	49	16 3
(æh)	28	33	34	30		6	16	25	13
(oh)	22	23	25	30		5	27	18	11
(th)	09	00	00			11	12	24	
(dh)	15	06	05			34	55	42	

other words, he deliberately rejected the pattern of values reflected in the array of numbers shown in the preceding examples.

Steve K.'s self-awareness, and his set of values, might prepare us to find a radically different pattern in the array of the variables, if we believed that the linguistic and social forces operating here are subject to conscious manipulation. But as a matter of record they are not. Except for the fact that the (th) and (dh) patterns operate at a low level, Table 4.6 is quite similar to that of Abraham G. The only deviation from a regular progression is that at (æh) D.

For New Yorkers of Steve K.'s age, all of these variables will remain variables in normal speech, no matter what conscious adjustments are attempted. Not one speaker in the sample who was raised in New York City was able to use 100 percent (r-1) in conversation, and this includes a great many speakers who were consciously aiming in that direction after (r) had been discussed. For example, Steve K. claimed that his present performance was a deliberate step backward from his college days, when he had pronounced all or most (r) as (r-1). I then asked him to re-read the *r* paragraph from "When I was nine or ten," and pronounce all (r) as consonants.

His first attempt was a complete failure, and his second start no better. I asked him to read a little more slowly. He continued and produced an (r) index of 33. A third try produced a step upward to 45. A fourth attempt gave 61, and in a fifth trial, he seemed to level off at 69. He then confessed that he probably could not have pronounced that much (r-1) when he was in college.

Steve K.'s inability to deal with a few sentences containing only thirteen (r)'s suggests that the original reading score of 38 is probably very close to the pattern which was solidified in his college days. Despite his profound shift in ideology, the speech pattern dictated by equally profound forces remains constant. It is not likely that he could, by his own efforts, return to zero or reach much higher than 38 in extended reading style.

Many similar tests could be cited. The most consistent and highly controlled speaker in the survey was Warren M., 27, a social worker and

Table 4.7   *Effect of conscious effort by Martha S. for three linguistic variables*

	Original reading	Conscious effort
(r)	45	47
(æh)	40	40
(oh)	28	29

graduate student. At college he had been intensively trained in speaking technique, had done a great deal of acting, and was justly proud of the control he could exert over his voice. His original reading of the *r* paragraph was at an index of 68. After a thorough discussion of (r), he read again to produce a perfectly consistent version. A very slow reading gave 90; fast, 56; more careful, 80; a repeat, 80; again, concentrating on voice quality 63; he then recited Jabberwocky at 88.[17]

Merwin M., a less sophisticated speaker of the same age, was able to improve his performance from (r)-28 to (r)-50. There is reason to think that older speakers would have less ability to shift, and that only very young ones, just emerging from their pre-adolescent years, would be able to make radical changes in their pattern by conscious attention.

Martha S., a very careful, Jewish middle class speaker of 45, was asked to read several paragraphs after discussion (see Table 4.7).

The (æh) index was already at the point preferred by the speaker, but the (oh) items still fluctuated considerably, and the small increases in both (r) and (oh) show her inability to attain the desired result. On the other hand, her daughter, Susan S., 13, was able to read with an (r) index of 50, and after discussion, reach as high as 75. Her normal (oh) index of 15 was shifted to 28 as she imitated her mother. An even more dramatic case was that of Bonnie R., 10. Whereas her parents used no more than 5 or 10 percent (r-1) in reading, she was able to go from an (r) index of 14 to (r)-64 after this variable was discussed in the family interview.

The compelling nature of the pattern of stylistic alternation appears to operate at the extremes of the social scale, as well as in the center. In Table 4.8, we may compare the record of two New Yorkers of radically different education and social status. On the left is the performance of Bennie N., 40, a truck driver who finished only the first term of high school.

---

[17] It appears here, as indicated in footnote 7, that a high concentration of (r) words makes more difficulties than a long text with the (r)'s dispersed. A similar effect was noted in the (th) paragraph; some speakers saw the phrase *this thing, that thing, and the other thing*, some even took a breath before attempting it, but by the time they reached the fifth or sixth item, fatigue set in, and with it, (dh-3).

Table 4.8   *Contrast of lower working class and upper middle class stylistic arrays*

Stylistic array for Bennie N.					Stylistic array for Miriam L.				
00	00	13	33	33	32	47	39	56	100
19	21	26	22		28	38	40	39	
15	20	24	20		20	26	30	30	
168	81	58			00	00	00		
153	96	38			25	04	02		

On the right is the record of Miriam L., 35, who graduated from Hunter College and St. John's Law School, and is now practicing law on the Lower East Side. (The headings of the array of variables will hereafter be omitted; the pattern in every case will be that shown in Table 4.1).

The absolute values of these variables are as totally opposed as any pair of speakers we might choose. But the structure of stylistic variation is essentially the same. In this comparison, one can find a statement of the theme which will dominate this study of social stratification of language: that New York City is a speech community, united by a common evaluation of the same variables which differentiate the speakers. The structure seen in Table 4.8 is the concrete manifestation of that evaluation.

The differences between the speakers are, of course, very real. Bennie N. uses no (r-1) in conversation; at her most casual, Miriam L. uses large numbers of (r-1) variants. The (æh) sound for Bennie N. is normally that of *where*; Miriam L. aims for the sound of *that* and *bat* and usually reaches it. For Bennie N., stops are practically normal forms of (th) and (dh); Miriam L. never uses anything but the prestige form for (th), and only a few affricates for (dh) except in the most casual style.

At this point, one might ask whether the difference may be in large part that Miriam L. recognizes the formal situation of the interview, and never uses her casual style in this interview, while Bennie N. doesn't care that much about making a good impression. Perhaps Miriam L.'s true casual style, outside of the interview, is not so different, after all.

The record of the survey in general shows that this is not the case. Here in particular, I can resolve a part of the doubt since I spent fifteen minutes waiting in Miriam L.'s office while she discussed business affairs with a client. The client seemed to be an old friend, and in any case, Miriam L. did not know who I was, and language had not entered the picture. We may compare the record of this conversation with the Style A and Style B of the interview in Table 4.9.

As we compare the style used with the client with the results of the inter-

Table 4.9   *Three stylistic levels for Miriam L.*

	With client	Style A	Style B
(r)	40	32	47
(æh)	30	28	38
(oh)	27	20	26
(th)	00	00	00
(dh)	00	25	04

Table 4.10   *Similar stylistic arrays for two older speakers*

Stylistic array for Jacob S.					Stylistic array for Carl L.				
07	09	04	30	75	16	12	18	23	00
20	29	31	31		–	25	32	23	
19	22	29	26		20	24	29	25	
50	47	10			–	22	05		
85	51	15			37	21	20		

view, it appears to lie somewhere in between Style A and Style B, perhaps closer to B. In any case, the casual style elicited by the interview is considerably less formal than that which Miriam L. uses in the daily execution of her business affairs.

Finally, it should be noted that not all of the speakers who were interviewed show patterns as regular as those just displayed. There are many deviations which cannot be explained within the data provided by a single interview, although the great bulk of material does appear as a coherent system. It may be profitable to make a comparison of two older speakers whose backgrounds are as radically opposed as the two just considered. On the left, in Table 4.10, is the record of Jacob S., 61, a retired mailman who lived all his life on the Lower East Side; on the right is Carl L., 56, a pharmacist who is extremely active in civic affairs of the Lower East Side.

These older speakers share certain common features of stylistic variation: neither shows a regular pattern for (r), although the last two figures of Jacob S. do show a sudden increase. They show similar patterns for (æh) and (oh), with a steady rise in the values (indicating more open vowels), until D, when the trend is reversed. Both show a regular decrease in the value of (th) and (dh) with more formal contexts. In comparison to the case of Bennie N. and Miriam L., there is far less difference shown here in the absolute values of the variables.

The structure of stylistic variation

At the beginning of this investigation, I proposed to reduce the irregularity in the linguistic behavior of New York speakers by going beyond the idiolect – the speech of one person in a single context. I first isolated the most important variables which interfered with the establishment of a coherent structure for these idiolects. After defining and isolating a wide range of styles in highly comparable interview situations, we were able to discover a regular pattern of behavior governing the occurrence of these variables in the speech of many individuals.

The term *structure* has been used so often in linguistic discussion that it sometimes slips away from us, or becomes fixed in denoting a particular kind of unit which was originally analyzed by structural considerations. Thus a list of phonemes may be taken as a structural statement, though no structure uniting the list is given, other than the fact that each unit is different. The excellent definition of *Webster's New International Dictionary* (2nd Edition):

structure, the interrelationship of parts as dominated by the general character of the whole

describes the pattern of stylistic variation which has been shown in the foregoing pages. But in addition to this description, twentieth-century linguistics has added the requirement that linguistic structures be composed of discrete units, which alternate in an all-or-none relationship.[18]

The dimensions of stylistic variation that have been illustrated cannot satisfy this requirement – at least, not by the evidence that has been presented. The sharp contrasts between Styles A through D′ are in part artifacts of the procedure. If this dimension is thought of as a continuum, then the method of dividing that continuum used here is perfectly adequate; if one suspects that natural breaks in the continuum exist so that in natural situations one does not pass evenly and continuously from careful to increasingly casual speech, this must be demonstrated by other methods.

If contrast exists between casual and careful styles, and the variables which we are using play a significant role in that contrast, they do not seem to operate as all-or-none signals. The use of a single variant – even a highly stigmatized one such as a palatalized diphthong in *bird* and *shirt* – does not usually produce a strong social reaction; it may only set up an expectation that such forms might recur, so that the listener does begin to perceive a socially significant pattern. Every speaker occasionally begins a (dh) word

---

[18] Thus the phonological structure is built with discrete units, phonemes that are themselves the products of the natural economy of the language. The structural units of the vowel systems are not artifacts of the analytical procedure: the categorizing procedure which breaks the continuum into highly discrete units, can be tested and observed.

with a sharp onset, which can be interpreted as an affricate, (dh-2). However, in the prestige form of speech, these forms recur so seldom that they are negligible. Any pattern of expectation set up by them dies out before the next is heard. It is the frequency with which Bennie N. uses such forms that has social significance, and it is essentially one level of frequency which contrasts with another level in the structures outlined above.

Are there breaks in the continuum of possible frequencies? This will become apparent as we discuss the results of the Lower East Side survey as a whole. However, the very clear-cut type of all-or-none reaction which is characteristic of phonemic units will be found not in performance so much as in evaluation, as will appear in Chapter 11. In the meantime, whether or not we consider stylistic variation to be a continuum of expressive behavior, or a subtle type of discrete alternation, it is clear that it must be approached through quantitative methods. We are in no position to predict exactly when a given speaker will produce a fricative, or when he or she will produce a stop. A complex of many factors operate to obscure stylistic regularities at the level of the individual instance. The remarkable fact is that the basic unit of stylistic contrast is a frequency set up by as few as ten occurrences of a particular variable.

[I think this discussion of the probabilistic character of stylistic levels was right on target. There are linguistic variables that provide clear social information on each occurrence – the paradigmatic example is the pronouns of power and solidarity (Brown and Gilman 1960). But most stylistic markers show the stochastic character discussed here, and efforts to interpret the significance of each token in the stream of conversational speech have foundered. Current research on the sensitivity of listeners to the (ING) variable shows that differences as small as 10% can be reliably detected and evaluated (Labov, Ash, Baranowski, Nagy, Rabindranath and Weldon 2006). As frequency of the nonstandard /in/ form increases linearly, negative evaluation in a formal context increases on a logarithmic scale, where the impact of each deviation from the norm is determined by the proportional increase in total deviations.]

We have seen that such frequencies contrast regularly in the different styles of one speaker, and have shown examples of how frequencies in the same style can contrast one speaker with another. The next step is to take up the cue offered by the last four examples in this chapter, and chart the distribution of both stylistic and social contrast of the five variables throughout the population as a whole.

To accomplish this purpose, the method of isolating contextual styles must be applied systematically to a cross-section of New York speakers. This was done by means of the survey of the Lower East Side carried out with the formal linguistic interview, constructed around the methods described in this chapter. Chapter 5 will describe the questionnaire in which these methods are embedded. I will then proceed to an account of the area to be surveyed, and of the method of sampling. We will then be ready for the exact statement of the distribution of the five variables.

[Before proceeding to the American Language Survey interview, it might be helpful to relate this chapter to more recent discussions of style. The general approach developed here was articulated more clearly as a set of axioms (Labov 1972a): (1) that there is no such thing as a single-style speaker; (2) that one style – the vernacular – is of primary interest to linguists; (3) that the vernacular is not used when an outside observer is present; (4) that the goal of the sociolinguistic interview is therefore to observe how people speak when they are not being observed. Efforts to solve this "Observer's Paradox" have been a central focus of sociolinguistic methodology.

At the heart of this discussion is the concept of the *vernacular*. This word is commonly used to mean low, uneducated or low prestige speech, but I have tried to stabilize it as a technical term to signify the language first acquired by the language learner, controlled perfectly, and used primarily among intimate friends and family members. Thus every speaker has a vernacular, some quite close to the network standard, some quite remote from it.

In a series of insightful studies, Bell has put forward a concept of style as audience design, based on his original studies of differences in the style of the same newscaster on different radio stations (1977, 1984). Style shifting within a fixed context is then seen as the result of the speaker imagining a different audience (Gumperz' 1964 "metaphorical shifting"). Preston (1991) pointed out that in studies that combine stylistic and social stratification, the range of style is always less than the range for class, since style shifting is derived from social stratification. However, this generalization does not seem to hold for a large set of stylistic variables, like English contraction or the many variables studied by Finegan and Biber (2001).

Many of these issues are brought to a focus in the recent collection of Eckert and Rickford, *Style and Sociolinguistic Variation* (2001). My own article in that volume contains the surprising (to me at least) finding that all of the contexts for defining casual speech contributed equally to the identification of casual vs. careful speech: the use of narrative, tangents, children's topics, and speech outside the interview were about equally effective in separating stylistic levels of linguistic variables.]

5   The linguistic interview

The methods for isolating contextual styles, as discussed in Chapter 4, were designed to be applied in a series of linguistic interviews. These interviews were conducted on the Lower East Side, as a secondary survey of a sample population that had already been carefully studied for its social characteristics. Chapter 6 will discuss the methods and the design of this social survey, and the sampling methods which were followed for the linguistic study. The present chapter will be concerned only with the linguistic interview itself, as it would be applied to any speaker of English.

The interview is constructed around the problem of isolating contextual styles, and almost every detail of the questionnaire can be understood from that point of view. In the evolution of the questionnaire, however, the situation was not so clear-cut. The method for isolating contextual styles gradually emerged from the interview as it evolved in exploratory studies; as the importance of the exact definition of style became apparent, and the ways of eliciting casual speech were developed, the interview was re-shaped to its present form. As it now stands, every part of the interview serves a double purpose:

1) to measure the values of the five phonological variables in the context and style of that section;
2) to gather the information which is the ostensible subject of the questions being asked.

In general, the first purpose is dominant, and the content of the questionnaire may be sacrificed to obtain better information on the variables. There are a few exceptions: certain details about the informant's language background are essential in order to utilize the information gathered under (1).

These considerations do not apply to the final sections of the questionnaire, dealing with subjective evaluation and linguistic attitudes. Once the variables have been brought forward for conscious discussion, the linguistic evidence on speech performance is considered contaminated, and in these sections, there is only the second purpose to consider.[1]

The interview situation

The details of the questionnaire can best be understood in the context of the larger interview situation. The first contact which the informant had with the interview was an American Language Survey letter. The American Language Survey was an ad hoc label which was used in all dealings with informants. (The linguistic interview will therefore be referred to as the ALS interview, and the survey which used this instrument, the ALS survey.)

The need for such a letter was found early in the pre-testing of the interview, when the attempt was made to select households on a random basis, and it raises the question of the effect of the city dweller's attitude towards strangers upon the interview as a whole.

[There are two ways in which the New York study differed from a number of projects that followed. At the time, I felt that the initial approach had to involve language, since otherwise the readings and minimal pairs and experimental techniques that followed might seem unmotivated. Hence the "American Language Survey." This focus on language and the ALS letter did help to lower refusal rates in the big city, and language is again in the forefront of the *Atlas of North American English*. But the years following the Lower East Side study have developed initial approaches that are broader than language: how the neighborhood is changing, how people get along with each other, common sense learning, and so on. These all include language without focusing directly on it, and so help to lower the tendency to shift towards prestige norms under the effects of observation.]

Without a preliminary letter, the number of refusals was relatively high, particularly for middle class subjects. Once the credentials of the interviewer were established, and his connection with Columbia University was set down in black and white, a great deal of resistance to the interview disappeared.[2] Yet the factors which gave rise to this resistance must also be considered to affect the degree of stylistic variation which occurred within the interview. In a small number of cases, suspicion of the interviewer remained

[1] There are a few exceptions to this rule, where a part of the original record was accidentally destroyed. In other cases, this material has been utilized for a special study of that type of speech which occurs when the informant is talking about speech.

[2] In one particular case, I knocked on the door of a tenement apartment to which no preliminary letter had been sent, and obtained only a brusque refusal from within. Several weeks later, I sent a letter to this subject, and when I called in person met with a cordial and cooperative reception. The respondent showed no signs of recalling the previous contact.

to the very end, usually as a conviction that the entire procedure was an elaborate prelude to a sales effort. In the case of most respondents, residual suspicions evaporated after the first minutes of the interview proper, and a definite change in the informants' style of speech could then be noted.

In general, it can be said that suspicion of strangers is an important element in the psychology of the residents of the Lower East Side. There are three main elements in this attitude: 1) the fear of attack or robbery; 2) resistance to salesmen; and 3) general hostility to any action not in the immediate interest of the subject himself.[3] Despite these recurrent themes in the attitudes of New Yorkers, it must not be assumed that they are a part of the make-up of all of the informants. In about one-half of the households visited, such resistance was not evident; on the contrary, the interviewer was welcomed from the beginning, and the subjects showed none of the fears and suspicions which were listed. These New Yorkers had the same open attitude towards strangers that we find in many small towns or rural areas. For example, in the study of Martha's Vineyard cited in Chapter 1, none of the resistance to strangers which we find in New York City was present to any noticeable degree.[4] In New York, we face the problem of potential refusals in at least half the cases.

The ALS letter was effective in reducing refusals to about 20 percent. The figure would probably have been much lower if this had been a primary survey.[5] However, one must see the latent resistance to the interviewer as conditioning the nature of stylistic variation in many cases, and every effort must be made throughout the interview to overcome this attitude. Part of the effort is made by the interviewer himself; part of it is built into the design of the questionnaire.

In all but a few of the cases, the net effect of the interview was to reverse the attitudes of fear and suspicion, where they had existed. It appears that people like to talk about language; even towards the end of the interview, when they were asked to complete some difficult tests, their enthusiasm for the subject carried them forward. If suspicion may be said to dominate the first

[3] The classic working class expression of this third attitude may be heard in the phrase, "Buddy, I don't know you from Adam!" A more abstract statement characteristic of some middle class attitudes is the question directed at one interviewer through the Judas hole of a cooperative [sic] apartment: "Will you please explain to me exactly what benefit this will be to me?"

[4] The only refusal, in interviewing a hundred individuals on the island of Martha's Vineyard, was from a man who mistook my first inquiry as a request to speak to his wife.

[5] In about half of the cases where subjects refused to participate in the ALS survey, their experience with the previous social survey was given as a reason, although no connection between the surveys was indicated by the interviewer. Even informants who did cooperate would refer to the previous survey as if it had been completed only a few months before, when in reality it had been conducted two years previously. In some cases, they had found this first interview exhausting.

approach, then it is equally true that kindliness and goodwill held the upper hand at the conclusion. A number of informants who were willing to give only a few minutes at the outset, talked for hours in the final event. One may often judge the success of the interviewer in the long run by whether or not he was offered anything to eat or drink, and such hospitality is common even in the heart of inhospitable New York. (One of the minor laws of linguistic field work appears to be that the best informants bake the best apple pies.)

All of the interviews were tape recorded.[6] The initial effect of the tape recorder is usually to increase self-consciousness and the atmosphere of formality. Though this effect is sharply reduced as the interview progresses, it never disappears entirely. Even informants who seem to be speaking quite freely and spontaneously will sometimes interrupt themselves and say: "Is it all right if I–" pointing at the machine, or else say, "If you'll turn off the machine a minute, I'll really go into that . . .." But such extreme cases are rare. The effect of the machine is usually to be interpreted as a constant but slight interference with the spontaneity of the proceeding. It is, of course, essential for a quantitative measure of the five phonological variables.[7]

[The experience of four decades has confirmed what is said here. People being interviewed do not forget the presence of the tape recorder, though its effect may be greatly reduced, or defined as irrelevant as in the case of Dolly R. in Chapter 4. Efforts to hide or minimize the presence of the recorder are generally counter-productive. Reducing the effects of observation calls for the more sophisticated techniques described in Labov (1984).]

Before the interview began, and many times throughout the interview, the informant was told that the survey was concerned with natural speech, in everyday language, as opposed to the language of the school room. I also stressed that there were no right or wrong answers to the questions asked, and that the only object of the questions was to find out how the informant

---

[6] Three tape recorders were used in various interviews. The Butoba MT-5, with the MD-21 microphone, was employed by one of the interviewers, Michael Kac. The author used the Sony 262L, with the RCA BK6B lavaliere microphone, for two-thirds of his interviews. The remaining third of the interviews were recorded with the Nagra III, using the RCA BK6B microphone. The problem of noise is severe in New York City, especially in the summer. The lavaliere microphone proved by far the best approach to this problem, better than a highly directional microphone tested, and was also useful in reducing self-consciousness of the informant. Results with the BK6B microphone gave more accurate perception of consonants when transcribing from tape than when listening in person; this was of course true in an even greater degree when the Nagra was used.

[7] It is possible to note down the values of the five phonological variables, using specially prepared forms, as the informant speaks – but only if he or she speaks at a moderate speed or in short utterances. However, it is not possible to record any other information on content or associated variables at the same time. Our experience has also shown that such on-the-spot transcriptions are not as accurate for this data as transcription from a tape, taking approximately one and a half hours for each hour of conversation.

talked in everyday life. This point of view was absorbed in varying degrees by the informants, and it was often necessary to correct the tendency of some informants to look to the interviewer for corroboration of their own replies.

The questionnaire

The complete form of the questionnaire is given as Appendix A. This chapter will discuss the general structure of the interview in order to explain the function of the various sections. As noted above, each part of the interview had at least two purposes: first, to provide the context for a given style of speech, and second, to obtain the specific information proper to the questions themselves. Not all of this material will be used in the present study, though I will have occasion to refer to many specific items of content besides the phonological variables.

I. *Language background*   The questions of Part I were designed to obtain the chief details of the informant's past life which would have the most bearing on his language. This information is essential to classify the informant by age and education, and to place him in relation to the United States, New York City, and the Lower East Side. From the details on residence and schooling, and parents' background, it was possible to rate informants in all three of these relationships on the same scale:

4th generation	at least two previous generations born and raised in the area
3rd generation	at least one of the informant's parents born and raised in the area
2nd generation	both parents born elsewhere, but informant born and raised in the area
1st generation	informant born elsewhere, and moved to the area

a)	informant moved to the area when	0–4 years old
b)	informant moved to the area when	5–8 years old
c)	informant moved to the area when	9–13 years old
d)	informant moved to the area when	after 13 years old

We now subdivide d) into the following three categories:

1) informant has lived in the area more than 20 years
2) informant has lived in the area 10–20 years
3) informant has lived in the area less than 10 years

These categories will be essential in the decision as to which subjects will be accepted as native speakers, and in measuring the extent of exposure to the New York linguistic tradition. This section also obtained the necessary information on the primary and secondary language of each informant, based on his or her current usage.[8]

II. *Lexicon*   The first set of questions in the lexical inquiry concerns six regional markers of New York City English. These items determine the extent of the informant's contact with the linguistic tradition of New York City, and introduce the topic of children's words, rhymes, and customs. The entire series is designed to form a graduated transition from the careful style of Section I to the spontaneous style that emerges in dealing with children's rhymes and games.

[From the standpoint of today's field methods, it seems that too much time was spent on individual words. Questions such as "What's the difference between *cottage cheese* and *pot cheese?*" did not produce very much casual speech. They did provide an index to the speaker's relation to the NYC speech community, but they also show that the American Language Survey interview had not departed very far from its starting point in dialect geography.]

III. *Children's lore*   (Context A_4) This section is divided into a portion designed exclusively for men, and a section primarily for women, but with some questions appropriate for men as well. The men's section covers rules for fighting, accounts of fights in childhood, and terminology for insulting individuals or groups. The women's section deals with childhood customs, rhymes, and special rhyming games.

Section III must be regarded as an instrument rather than a blueprint; the interviewer's purpose is to keep the informant talking within this context. Any speech with appropriate channel cues occurring in this section will be considered Style A, casual speech.

The most successful questions for eliciting casual speech were III B. 4 and 5, for counting-out rhymes and jump-rope rhymes. However, questions 1, 2, and 3 in that section were very effective in setting the emotional tone for natural delivery of these rhymes.

IV. *Semantics and syntax.* A. *Common sense*   This section marks a sudden return to the context of careful speech. These questions introduce more serious topics which eventually lead to greater emotional involvement.

In contrast to Section III, the questions of Section IV are asked in the exact order and wording of the questionnaire. The rule from this point on was to keep one's eyes on the informant's face, avoid consulting any

---

[8] Marginal cases are of special significance in charting the distribution of the variables, as discussed in Chapter 8.

papers or checking the tape recorder, and convince the speaker by such total attention that what he is saying is profoundly interesting to the listener.

IV B. *The danger of death*   (Context A_5) This question is introduced as if it were connected to the previous question, although there is little basis in the logic of the situation. The timing and delivery of this question is discussed in Chapter 4, under Context A_4, with examples of the type of replies which can be obtained.

[The "danger of death" question has become its own stereotype of the interview method developed in the New York City study. I once received a whole batch of interviews recorded in a Buffalo high school, which used the following fixed protocol: "What's your name?" "What grade are you in?" "How many brothers and sisters do you have?" "Have you ever been in a situation where you were in danger of being killed?" The investigator had no idea of how questions are to be embedded in conversational sequences, and how one topic leads to the other. Yet crude and embarrassing as it might seem, there were many stories of compelling interest on those tapes. It seems that a good tool can survive a bad carpenter.

To follow where this type of interviewing has led us, I recommend *Field Methods of the Project on Linguistic Change and Variation* (Labov 1984). This shows how the interview format can be shifted towards genuine conversational exchange, and how interviewers can equip themselves to obtain long and highly engaged conversations through the use of an array of versatile conversational modules.]

IV C. *The tying of a shoelace*   In this sub-section, the informant's attention is turned to a formal task which allows us to test certain properties of his syntactic usage. The request, as phrased in the questionnaire, is for him or her to describe the tying of a bow, using only words. In previous investigations, this question sometimes met with resistance, but in its present location, and with the immediate background of IV A and B, all but one or two of the informants cooperated with a smile. For the great majority of respondents, the style utilized in this section is a very regular form of Style B – careful speech.

IV D. *Definition of "a successful man"*   This question is introduced with a backward reference to the common sense discussion, as another term which people disagree about. Like the common sense question, it provides us with a great deal of highly stratified information on the semantics and value system of the informants. In many cases, replies to this question are quite long, but Context B always prevails and speech in this section is Style B.

At this point, the portion of the interview which yields information on casual or careful speech is ended, with the exception of outbreaks of casual speech under Contexts A_1 or A_2 (speech outside the interview situation or to a third person). Since a certain degree of conscious attention is now directed towards the five phonological variables, the careful speech to follow will not as a rule be used as evidence for the values of those variables.

V. *Pronunciation*   This section requires little comment, since the purpose and structure of most of the items have been discussed in Chapter 4. There are a great many lexical, phonemic, and phonetic items in the two standard readings in addition to the five variables, but the present study will not take up most of these points. The chief purpose of this section is to obtain data on Styles C and D through the standard readings and the word lists – Contexts C and D respectively.

VI. *Subjective reaction test*   In this section, the subjective reactions of the informant to the five phonological variables are tested by the methods to be described in detail in Chapter 11. This test forms a distinct break in the procedure of the interview, for the interviewer stops tape recording in order to play the test tape of twenty-two sentences spoken by Lower East Side residents.

It was originally believed that it would be difficult to obtain complete results on Section VI from many informants, especially those who had less interest in the discussion of language for its own sake. However, response to Section VI was generally very keen, and the great majority of the informants – 111 out of the 122 adults responding to the ALS interview – completed the test with strong interest.

Self-evaluation test   Immediately after the completion of this test, the interviewer adds that he would like to find out how the informant sounds to himself. The informant listens to variant pronunciations of seven words, illustrating the variables (r), (oh), (æh), (th), (dh), in that order, and in addition, variant pronunciations of *her* and *hurt*. The respondent is asked to circle the number of the pronunciation which he usually uses on the form shown as VI C in Appendix A. This series forms the *Self-Evaluation Test*.

VII. *Linguistic attitudes*   At this point in the interview, the questions are less highly structured, and it is not required that they be asked in the exact order or wording given in the questionnaire. The fatigue of the informant may be relieved by a more casual approach. Any incident or opinion which bears upon the five phonological variables, or upon New York speech in general, is to be followed up by the interviewer to the limit that the time or the patience of the informant permits.

VIII. *Index of linguistic insecurity*   The final section of the interview is introduced as if an afterthought. Eighteen words are listed on the form shown in Appendix A, with each word followed by two numbers. The words are pronounced by the interviewer with two variant pronunciations, as noted in the questionnaire. The informant is asked to circle the number of the pronunciation which he believes is correct, and then check the pronunciation that he usually uses. All but one of the words appear in the text of the readings or the word lists, so that it is possible to compare the informant's earlier pronunciation with his present performance and preference. However, the principal purpose of this section is to give a rapid and independent check of the degree of linguistic insecurity of the respondent. The number of items in which the informant has checked one pronunciation and circled the other is counted, and this count forms the index of linguistic insecurity.

Interviewing several members of the household

Because we were interested in the children of the informants as well as themselves, there were many interviews in which a number of subjects were being interviewed together. The figures on the number of youth interviewed are given in Chapter 6.

   The interview form and questionnaire, as here discussed, was employed by two interviewers: myself, and Michael Kac, of Haverford College, who worked on the project from July to September, 1963.

   There were some significant differences in the speech and personal presentation of the two interviewers. The normal speech form used by Kac in the interviews is an *r*-pronouncing dialect with vowels typical of upstate New York. Values of (æh) and (oh) are quite constant at (æh-4) and (oh-4) as opposed to my own (æh-3) and (oh-3). Kac's conversational style may be described as slightly more careful than my own. He impresses respondents as a young college student. Despite such differences, his treatment of the questionnaire was quite close to my own, in both intonation and timing of the questions. It is sometimes difficult for a third person to tell from a tape which of us is interviewing.

   The type of stylistic variation which emerges from tabulations of the interviews appears to be the same for both interviewers. The high degree of organization of the interview in terms of contextual styles is thus effective in standardizing the relative shifts of language behavior which occur.

   Chapter 6 will discuss the area and the survey in which this instrument was employed.

6   The survey of the Lower East Side

[This chapter concerns the random survey of the Lower East Side of New York City. The particular methods discussed in this chapter were the results of my contact with the Bureau of Applied Social Research at Columbia, which made it possible for me to profit from the highly professional sampling method used by Cloward and Ohlin in the Mobilization for Youth project (1960). None of the many studies of speech communities that followed used exactly the method developed here, but a good number have been constructed on the same general principles. Chapter 15 provides a summary of the approach taken by 37 sociolinguistic studies of large cities in the years 1966–2006. Some improved on the method for sampling the community outlined here, particularly in the construction of a stratified random sample in which the groups of interest are equally represented, rather than proportional to their numbers in the population. For various reasons, others did not follow the general principle that each member of the community (or sub-group) should have an equal opportunity of entering the sample. In the most different method, the investigator begins with introductions from friends and acquaintances. Such a convenience sample, which follows the researcher's personal networks (sometimes called "friend of a friend" approach), is well justified under some circumstances. Political disturbances may make it impractical to do otherwise, as in Milroy's study of Belfast during the troubles (Milroy and Milroy 1978). The target group may be isolated from contacts by strangers (as in Kroch's (1996) study of the Philadelphia upper class). However, the speakers we contact through personal networks are certain to be more similar to us than the speakers we do not. Though we may reduce the observer effect by interviewing our friends, we will be increasing it by choosing people more similar to ourselves.]

The material of the preceding chapters may be considered preliminary to the main attack on the question of the social stratification of language in New York City. In a first trial it was found that one variable, at least, showed regular stratification in the speech of department store employees. To study this question more systematically, a method of isolating contextual styles has been presented, as embodied in the questionnaire of Chapter 5. We are now ready to discuss the application of this method to a representative sample of the speech community.

This chapter is concerned with the principal device for detailed study of the social stratification of New York City English: the survey of the Lower East Side. Although three other quantitative investigations of the language of New York City form a part of the present work, the survey of the Lower East Side is by far the most important. Information on the speech of 340 individuals was obtained in recorded interviews and written tests. The data now available, in the form of 150 hours of recorded conversation, 200 subjective reaction tests, and 200 self-evaluation forms, provides a large store of information which cannot be presented here in full. Furthermore, the main part of the linguistic interviews rests upon a previous survey of the social position and attitudes of the informants, so that the amount of information available for analysis is almost double that collected by the linguists alone.

Bulk alone is no measure of adequacy: in this chapter, the planning of the survey will be discussed so that the reader can judge to what extent it gives good representation of the various sections of the population of the Lower East Side. I will consider the selection of the area; its social and geographic characteristics; the construction of the questionnaire and the methods of interviewing; the methods of sampling and the results of the interview program; the methods of sampling the non-respondents; and finally, the various sources of error within the entire procedure.

The selection of the area

Some of the reasons for choosing the Lower East Side of New York City for the study of the social stratification of language were stated in Chapter 1. As indicated there, most of the previous studies of New York City speech had used a small number of speakers, and relied heavily on college students. The Lower East Side is weak in the representation of the upper portions of the city's social structure, but it has a good section of the larger groups: middle class, working class, and lower class New Yorkers. Furthermore, all of the city's main ethnic groups are represented well: Italians, Jews, Irish, Germans, Ukrainians and Poles, African–Americans, and Puerto Ricans.[1] None of the ghetto areas such as Harlem or Bedford-Stuyvesant would have allowed us to

---

[1] The groups that are listed here under the general heading of *ethnic groups* are obviously identified by a very mixed set of characteristics: race, religion, language, and country of origin. The use of the term *ethnic group* for these sections of the population is quite natural for those who are familiar with the political and social structure of New York City, although it may seem unusual for those who are accustomed to the use of the word in more traditional contexts. For a detailed discussion of the role of ethnic groups in New York City, see Nathan Glazer and Daniel P. Moynihan, *Beyond the Melting Pot* (1963). We will return to the discussion of ethnic groups in discussing the sampling procedure below.

find representation of all these groups in a single neighborhood, any more than we would have obtained a cross-section by studying Washington Heights or Jamaica. The original pattern of the Lower East Side as a port of entry, with movement in one direction in and out of the area, has now been broken by the construction of many large city housing projects. We therefore have a good representation of New Yorkers from other parts of Manhattan, including Harlem, and other boroughs as well.

The interaction of the various ethnic and social groups will be an important part of the pattern on the Lower East Side; whether or not this interaction tends to weaken and dilute the pattern of speech that governs more homogeneous areas is a point which must ultimately be examined. From the point of view of housing, the Lower East Side represents current trends in the city quite well: it has large tenement areas, large blocks of lower income projects, and also large blocks of middle income cooperative apartments. Finally, there remains the fact that the Lower East Side has been one of the most important points of entry for new immigrant groups. This pattern has held true for the successive arrival of the Irish, the Italians, the Jews, the Ukrainians, Poles, and Russians. Only recently has this section become a second neighborhood for many New Yorkers, as AA, Puerto Rican, and other newcomers move in from other parts of Manhattan.[2]

Thus in the Lower East Side, we are conscious of rapid social movement, with second and third generation citizens moving out and upward in a continuous stream, while new groups take their place from outside. Those who do remain are often marked by either a strong sense of local tradition, or total inertia. This process enables us to test the proposition, often stated, that the native New York City pattern of speech can absorb a tremendous bulk of foreign influence without being seriously transformed itself. At the same time, the dilution of native speakers with immigrants proves to be a serious problem in the economy of sampling native speech, and must be considered a drawback of this particular area.

Shortly after I began exploratory interviews in the Lower East Side, in the summer of 1962, I learned that a comprehensive survey of the area had been conducted the year before as a preliminary to the Mobilization for Youth Program.[3] Mobilization for Youth (MFY) is a large-scale assault on

[2] The Mobilization for Youth Survey of the Lower East Side, to be discussed in detail below, shows that 68 percent of those living in the area less than five years moved from other parts of New York City (41 percent from Manhattan), while only 20 percent came from outside the continental United States.

[3] A complete description of the Mobilization for Youth program, its research activities, and its plan of action is to be found in *A Proposal for the Prevention and Control of Delinquency by Expanding Opportunities* (MFY 1962). References here are to the second edition, published August, 1962. It will be referred to as the MFY *Proposal*. The full form of the MFY questionnaires, and description of sampling procedures, are given in this volume.

the problem of juvenile delinquency, supported by federal funds as well as local incentives. It aims to change the opportunity structure in which the young people of the area are placed, taking as its unifying principle the hypothesis developed by Cloward and Ohlin:[4]

the kind of opportunity structure in which young people find themselves is the central condition determining their behavior, either conforming or deviant.

The research design for this project was constructed by faculty members of the New York School of Social Work of Columbia University. Among the first steps, as described in the MFY *Proposal*, was the establishment of a base line for all future studies through three community surveys: of adults, adolescents, and leaders of local organizations. I first turned to MFY for information about the community. The members of the research staff of the New York School of Social Work showed a great deal of interest in the proposal for a survey of the distribution of language features in the area, more so than the naive linguist might have expected.

[The first edition followed with a footnote stating that "the theoretical importance of studying language behavior appears to be axiomatically obvious to many sociologists." But forty years after the Social Science Research Council set up a Committee on Sociolinguistics, the amount of interaction between linguists and sociologists remains minimal. Despite important work on discourse and conversational analysis, very few sociologists have acquired the basic tools of linguistic analysis, and very few linguists have contributed to the thinking of sociologists. The situation is quite different on the boundary between linguistics and anthropology, or linguistics and psychology, though these frontiers are guarded by the same disciplinary demons.

I hope that the balance of this chapter will persuade some readers that sociologists take a deep and thoughtful approach to the problem of representing the speech community, and that we will take more advantage of their skills in the future.]

As the complexity of conducting a social survey of the area unfolded, it was apparent that I could not hope to approach the precision of the MFY sampling technique by my own efforts. For example, the preliminary mapping of the neighborhood, in which each dwelling unit was given a serial number, occupied four months of the MFY schedule.[5] It was suggested that I not only

---

[4] Richard A. Cloward and Lloyd E. Ohlin, *Delinquency and Opportunity: A theory of Delinquent Gangs* (1960).

[5] A trial random sampling of my own involved counting every tenth building in a block, and calling on every seventh apartment. This method seemed to be free from bias, but did not enable me to choose my informants randomly within the family, nor could I predict how large an area I would be able to cover by this method before available resources were expended. Most importantly, any sampling on this basis would be unable to discriminate

use the demographic data of the MFY survey, but also re-interview the same informants. This would not only solve the sampling problem, but also enable me to emphasize certain sub-groups that were of particular interest, without distorting the overall view of the composition of the population. The wasted effort that would be involved in pursuing hundreds of informants who later turned out to be recent immigrants would also be avoided. Most importantly, I would then have a rich store of information on the informants' social position, their social attitudes and aspirations, and their relations to the community. All of my own interview time could then be devoted to linguistic behavior.

Exploratory interviews on the Lower East Side were carried out in 1962; altogether, some seventy individuals and many groups were interviewed while the questionnaire was being developed and pre-tested. In November, 1962, a rapid survey of the social stratification of (r) among department store employees was carried out, as described in Chapter 3. The actual field work for the linguistic survey of the Lower East Side began in July, 1963. Before discussing the procedures of this field work, it will be necessary to describe the methods and operations of the social survey on which it is based. (In the discussion to follow, the Mobilization for Youth Survey will be designated the MFY survey; the linguistic survey will be referred to as the ALS survey, since the ad hoc name of the American Language Survey was used in all dealings with informants.)

Procedures of the MFY survey

The social survey of the Lower East Side had been carried out with every precaution against bias and inaccuracy which is available to survey method-ology. Such precautions were particularly necessary in this case because many of the people that MFY was most anxious to reach are not the easiest subjects to interview. Many are seldom found at home, or live with families other than their own. A certain number of urban dwellers are also suspicious and hostile to strangers in general. It would therefore have been easy to con-clude a survey which failed the general task of describing all sections of the population, unless rigorous methods were followed at all stages of the work.

Footnote 5 (*cont.*)
    between native speakers and foreign-language speakers, and a great deal of effort would be spent on fruitless calls on the latter type of resident.
    I am particularly indebted to Mr. Donald Pappenfort of Mobilization for Youth, who was in charge of the original enumeration, for his initial suggestion on the use of the Mobilization survey; Dr. Lloyd Ohlin, Director of Research of the New York School of Social Work, who made it possible for me to utilize the facilities of the school and MFY, and furthered the project considerably by his interest and encouragement; and to Dr. Wyatt Jones, Director of Research for Mobilization for Youth, who provided not only the help of his office and staff, but also an enthusiastic support which never flagged.

Considerable attention was given to the initial enumeration of all dwelling units in the area.[6] Many months were spent in the exact determination of the number of dwelling units, vacant and occupied, in each building, yielding a serial listing of 33,932 units in which informants might be found. It was considered that a simple random sampling might not give adequate representation to some of the smaller ethnic groups concentrated in a particular neighborhood. Therefore a stratified random sampling procedure was employed: the list was divided into 250 equal intervals of 133 units, and 5 households were randomly selected from each interval, yielding a sample of 1,250 households.

A corps of forty interviewers was trained in the procedures of the MFY survey. The first task of the interviewer was to locate the occupants of the household, and enumerate each member by age, sex, and relation to the head of the family. Then, by a second random process, one of the adults over twenty was selected to be interviewed. Strenuous efforts were made to reach even the most inaccessible informants; in many cases, the field worker had to call six or seven times before finding the person in. If the subject refused, an interviewer of the same sex and ethnic characteristics as the subject sent a second introductory letter, and called in person. Persuasion by letters from prominent ministers and community leaders was sometimes effective.[7] Special attention was paid to Italian and AA groups, where the greatest number of refusals was found. A total of 988 interviews or 79 percent of the target sample, was obtained. The final refusal rate was approximately the same for all ethnic groups except Puerto Ricans, who were noticeably more cooperative.

The MFY interview combined pre-coded questions with free-answer, open-ended questions. Many of the questions on social attitudes were drawn from well-tested batteries developed by the National Opinion Research Center, and others were specifically designed for Lower East Side problems. The field worker wrote down everything that the informant said,

---

[6] "The listing of housing units was facilitated by the Department of Buildings and the City Planning Department . . . A list of all buildings was compiled by street address, block number, and number of floors. . . . The Buildings Department supplied information on the number of dwelling units in each building, which was added to the list. The number of units per building in the public housing projects and middle-income cooperatives was obtained from the managers of the projects. A physical spot check of mail boxes and doorbells was made to confirm the accuracy of the count of dwelling units, and all buildings not listed by the Buildings Department were inspected to determine whether any part of them was used as living quarters. . . . A check of storefronts was made to locate any stores that were used as living quarters as well as places of business." – MFY *Proposal*, page 564. This list was then verified by four other sources for a count of dwelling units per block.

[7] A small number of informants were offered payment, towards the end of the interview program. Fifteen accepted, twelve refused.

verbatim. The entire interview lasted from an hour to two hours; in some cases, the effects of the resulting fatigue remained to become an obstacle to the completion of our own survey of the same informants.

The content of the MFY interview falls into a number of large divisions: attitudes towards the neighborhood, social aspirations, relations with settlement houses, participation in community organizations, and attitudes towards juvenile delinquency. Much of this material will eventually be related to the informant's linguistic behavior, but the chief items of demographic information and background data that are of immediate use for the linguistic survey are listed below:

> Language in which the interview was conducted[8]
> Sex and marital status
> Age
> Race
> Religion
> Family income
> Education of respondent
> Education of spouse
> Occupation of respondent
> First occupation after leaving school
> Occupation of spouse
> Father's occupation
> Country of birth
> Father's country of birth
> Number of years on the Lower East Side
> Region or New York borough of previous residence
>   (for those who have lived on the LES 5 years or less)
> Newspapers read

A view of the Lower East Side

From the results of the MFY survey, we can construct an accurate view of the neighborhood in which the linguistic survey was to take place.[9]

Figure 6.1 is a detailed map of the section which has been surveyed. On the north, it is bounded by 14th Street, on the east by the East River, on the south by the Brooklyn Bridge. The western boundary begins with Avenue B, in the northwest corner, and follows the line indicated down Clinton Street, Rivington Street, Grand Street, East Broadway, and so down to the

---

[8] Only 646 of the 988 interviews were conducted entirely in English; 176 were entirely in Spanish, 24 entirely in Yiddish, 18 in Italian, 13 in Chinese, 7 in Polish, 3 in Ukrainian, 2 in Russian. Thirty-eight other interviews were conducted partly in a wide variety of languages, 23 partly in Spanish, 37 partly in Yiddish.

[9] Much of the material in this section utilizes the discussion of the area in the MFY *Proposal*, pages 20–28.

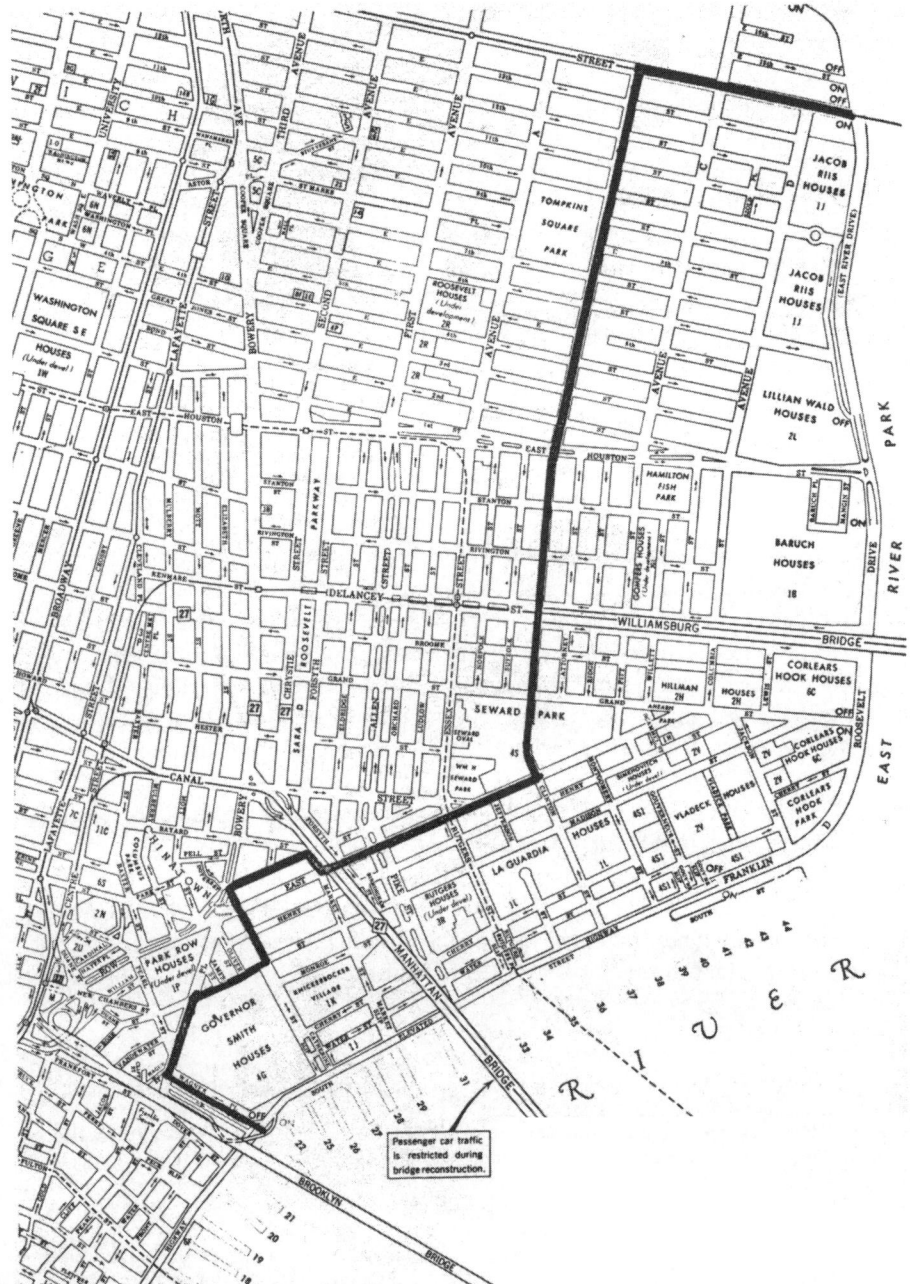

Figure 6.1   Detailed map of the Lower East Side (Survey area outlined in black)

Brooklyn Bridge.[10] This is only a part of the area traditionally known as the Lower East Side, which itself has no strict boundaries, like most of the New York City neighborhood terms.

The most obvious characteristic of the Lower East Side, as we walk through it, is that it consists of two radically different kinds of buildings – tenements and housing projects. The projects in turn may be divided into low income public housing projects, and middle income cooperatives. Most of our middle class subjects live in the latter, which are concentrated in a relatively small area where Grand Street meets the East River.

There are four middle income cooperatives, and one private project in the area. Some are becoming a little dark and dingy as they age, but most of them are comfortable, and a few are as well designed and as handsomely located as any apartments in New York City. The Corlears Hook project, on the East River, is attractive enough to hold a good many people with moderately high incomes who might otherwise have left the East Side entirely.

Another type of project is the low income apartment house, under public administration, such as the Jacob Riis Houses or Lilian Wald Houses along the East River. Most of these are thirteen-story elevator apartments. The hallways are tile and concrete, and regularly scrubbed with detergent and disinfectant. The apartments are usually quite spacious, with plenty of light and air, and some of them have a spectacular view of the Brooklyn Bridge and the East River. The public housing projects were integrated at the outset.[11]

The tenement apartments usually consist of one to three small rooms in a straight line, barely furnished and neglected by the landlord.[12] The smell of garbage and urine which pervades the halls can creep into the homes of the cleanest housekeepers. The contrast between living in a tenement house of this type, and in the best of the middle income apartment houses, illustrates the full range of stratification in the society of the Lower East Side.

---

[10] The lines are drawn to coincide with thirteen Census Tracts utilized in the 1960 Census, coordinate with five Health Areas.

[11] The discussion of the housing conditions in the projects, as opposed to the tenements, should not be allowed to obscure the fact that the same social strains and tensions exist in both areas. There are delinquent gangs, such as the Centaurians, which were centered in the low-income project area, as well as gangs in the tenement areas. Problems of unemployment and lack of opportunity exist in projects as well as tenements.

[12] The only extensive repairs being made by a landlord which I saw in the Lower East Side were in a building which was slated for demolition; these repairs were being conducted so that the landlord would receive a higher price in compensation for the building's destruction.

Table 6.1   *Housing units on the Lower East Side*

Type of housing	Number of units	Percentage
Tenements	18,903	55.7
Public housing projects	10,729	31.6
Middle-income cooperatives	2,715	8.0
Private middle-income project	1,585	4.7
	33,932	100.0

Table 6.1 shows the number of each type of housing units, and the percentage distribution in the area.[13]

We may follow the Bureau of the Census in defining substandard housing as housing that does not have hot water, cold running water, private bath, or private toilet, or that which is deteriorating or dilapidated. We then find that 62.4 percent of the tenements are substandard.

Population   The 1960 population of the Lower East Side area we are studying was 107,000. One may be surprised to learn that this figure shows a steady decline from the peak population of 1910, when 300,000 people lived in the same area. Of the present-day total, 27% are Jewish and 11% are Italian. Ukrainian, Russian, Polish, Irish, and other ethnic groups make up the rest of the population of European stock, which accounts for 63% of the total population. The Puerto Rican group is 26% and growing. The AA population is 8%, and other nonwhite, largely Chinese, are 3% of the total.

As far as the distribution of these groups in the area is concerned, an informal picture might be sketched as follows. In the tenement area north of Houston Street, the blocks are sharply stratified: some streets have a high concentration of Slavic groups, while others have more Jewish residents; in a few areas there are still quite a few of the older Irish people left; some blocks now have a great concentration of AAs, and an increasing number of blocks are predominantly occupied by Puerto Ricans.

The public housing projects are mixed, and the middle income projects have a high percentage of Jewish residents. A large percentage of Italians are concentrated in the lower end of the district, on Henry Street and Madison Street, although an increasing number of Puerto Ricans are now living in that area. The Chinese population is in the southwest corner, where Chinatown is expanding across East Broadway and up into former Italian neighborhoods.

---

[13] Table 6.1, and the data on the two following pages, are based on information in the MFY *Proposal*, pages 21–23.

Table 6.2   *Length of residence in the Lower East Side*

	Percent
Less than 5 years	22
5–12 years	30
13–29 years	17
30 years or more	30
	99
	[N: 988]

The Lower East Side seems to have a disproportionately large number who have lived in the area either a very short time or a very long time, with a smaller percentage in between (see Table 6.2).

The newcomers seem to be of several distinct types. The main body is the Puerto Rican group, coming directly from Puerto Rico. There are also AAs from Harlem, and a young white bohemian group moving across the island from Greenwich Village. This latter group provides the largest part of the very small white Protestant element in the population. The bohemians, students or intellectuals, are mostly from outside the city. They move quite rapidly from one residence to another, and have little connection with the community around them, except in so far as some are beginning to build a community of their own.

The results of the MFY survey show that this area is depressed as far as the education, incomes, and occupations of its residents are concerned. Compared to the United States as a whole, the Lower East Side is shifted very considerably towards the lower end of each of these scales. When the figures for the 1950 Census, which were used in this part of the MFY report, are replaced by national figures from the 1960 Census, the low position of the Lower East Side is even more marked.[14] The comparison is even more extreme when we compare the Lower East Side with other urban areas, or with the New York metropolitan areas, for in most respects the New York region ranks higher than the nation as a whole. The final view of the incomes of the Lower East Side shows that only 28.3 of Lower East Side households rank above the nation's median in family income, while 71.7 are below the median.

The information that has been presented on the Lower East Side is a view of the community as a whole in which the informants for the linguistic

---

[14] Comparisons of the Lower East Side with the national levels of occupation, income, and education are made in "The Construction of the Social Class Index," (mimeographed) by John A. Michael, Mobilization for Youth, 214 East Second Street, New York, N. Y. This discussion, to which we will refer frequently in the following pages, is included as Appendix A to the *Codebook for the Mobilization for Youth*, Vol. 1, Adult Survey.

survey live. More detailed figures on occupation, education, income, and other social parameters are not relevant, because these figures from the MFY survey do not describe the target population for the present study. We wish to consider only the native English speakers of the area in order to investigate the structure of New York City English. The original sample of 988 Lower East Side Residents will then be reduced to a much smaller number. Since many of the non-native speakers are lowest in the various socio-economic indexes, we can say that the population we will study is not characterized by such low values as the original sample. The method for selecting the group to be interviewed for the ALS survey will now be outlined, and the description of this group by social and economic characteristics will then follow.

The ALS survey population

Of the 988 MFY informants, 280 were identified in the data as Puerto Rican. Although this group is extremely important for the social study of the area, and eventually for its linguistic character, it contains very few adult speakers, over 20 years old, who grew up in this country with English as their native language. The Puerto Rican group was therefore not included in the target population of the ALS survey.

Thirty other informants were identified as neither white, nor AA, nor Puerto Rican. This small group is primarily Chinese, and was also excluded from immediate consideration. Subtracting other miscellaneous categories, we have 617 respondents. For sampling purposes we divided this group into four categories: AA, Jewish, Catholic, and white Protestant (hereafter referred to as "Protestant"). The large Jewish group may be divided in turn into two halves: the Orthodox, and the Conservative or Reform sub-groups. As for the distribution of native English speakers and of social classes, these two sub-groups are quite different. The Catholic group may be further subdivided into its main components: Italian, Slavic, and others. However, it is perhaps not large enough to demand sub-division at this first stage.[15]

---

[15] In the sample which was finally interviewed for the ALS survey, Italians form the only component of the Catholic sampling group which was large enough to be studied separately. In the present chapter, we will discuss the characteristics of the Catholic group as a whole along with the other categories which we will refer to informally as ethnic groups. Of course neither the Catholic nor the Protestant categories form single ethnic groups, and this usage is solely for its utility in discussing sampling problems. The concept of ethnic group will be used for the analysis of the data in Chapter 8, where the linguistic behavior of Jews, Italians, and AAs will be compared, and in ensuing chapters. At that point, we will resume the discussion of the concept of ethnic group, first raised in footnote 1 to the present chapter.

Table 6.3   *Ethnic and racial representation*

African–American	85
Jewish: Orthodox	174
Jewish: Conservative or Reform	100
Catholic	211
Protestant	<u>47</u>
	617

For the first approach to the sample, then, it may be useful to consider five main groups, as in Table 6.3.

For further analysis, it will be useful to look at the socio-economic characteristics of this group. For this purpose, we will use a ten-point socio-economic index developed by MFY, combining three objective characteristics – occupation, education, and family income – into a single linear scale. The general considerations behind this procedure, and the detailed steps involved, will be discussed in Chapter 7, which deals with the class stratification of the five variables. For the moment, we may consider the scale as a useful device for dividing the population along the socio-economic scale into three units of approximately equal size. The purpose of such divisions is to ensure that we will have sufficient representation for all of the major groups listed above in an upper, middle, and lower socio-economic category. If one sub-group is particularly weak, it will be possible to adjust the percentage of sampling so that we will have enough informants in that sub-group to give us an accurate report on its speech as a whole. Since the limited resources of the ALS survey did not permit study of the entire group of 617 speakers, or even all of the native speakers in this group, some such adjustment in percentages studied would yield the most efficient procedure.

This adjustment would have been impossible in a primary survey, where the population and its major breakdowns was unknown. Any concentration on one type of informant in place of another would yield a biased analysis of the population, and it would be impossible to see the finished result as representative of the population as a whole. But with a secondary study, the effect of stratified sampling (using such adjusted percentages) does not interfere with the reconstruction of a representative statement about the whole population. The final statement is corrected by a weighting of the values for each sub-group, which is the inverse of the original bias.

I therefore divided the socio-economic scale into three sections: 0–2, 3–5, and 6–9. The totals for the resulting fifteen divisions are shown as the first column of Table 6.4.

Table 6.4 *Derivation of the sample population*

Ethnic group	Class group	Total MFY population	Part of MFY pop'n studied	Native speakers	Moved or died	ALS target sample	Total ALS interviews	ALS linguistic interviews	ALS television interviews
	Column	1	2	3	4	5	6	7	8
African–American	0–2	32	32	29	6	23	16	14	2
	3–5	36	36	31	10	21	19	16	3
	6–9	17	17	16	11	5	5	5	–
		85	85	76	27	49	40	35	5
Jewish, Orthodox	0–2	71	71	14	4	10	8	8	–
	3–5	55	38	13	3	10	10	9	1
	6–9	48	48	22	8	14	11	6	5
		174	157	49	15	34	29	23	6
Jewish, Conservative & Reform	0–2	25	25	9	3	6	4	3	1
	3–5	35	21	14	4	10	8	7	1
	6–9	40	40	35	13	22	18	12	4
		100	86	58	20	38	30	22	6
Catholic	0–2	72	72	36	11	25	18	11	7
	3–5	102	69	41	17	24	19	15	4
	6–9	37	37	27	11	16	13	8	4
		211	178	104	39	65	50	34	15
Protestant	0–2	7	7	4	0	4	4	3	1
	3–5	13	13	6	6	0	–	–	–
	6–9	27	27	15	10	5	5	5	–
		47	47	25	16	9	9	8	1
		617	553	312	117	195	158	122	33

The decisions as to the final percentages of each sub-group to be studied were not made immediately. Since the Protestant group as a whole is very small, 100% of these informants were studied. A similar consideration applied to the AA group.[16] For the remaining groups, 50% were randomly selected. The native speakers were first determined by consulting the MFY questionnaire on place of birth, and we began to interview these. It soon appeared that the majority of the lowest socio-economic group for Jews and Catholics were foreign-born. It also appeared that a great many of the upper socio-economic group for Jews had moved in the interval between the MFY survey and the ALS survey. (The upper Catholic group was relatively small.) To compensate for this loss, 100% of the upper and lower groups were selected for all five ethnic divisions. The percentage of the intermediate group, actually the main body of the working class, was gradually increased by random selection until the maximum which could be handled in the available time for field work had been reached. This figure was 67% of the 3–5 group.

Column 2 of Table 6.4 therefore shows 100% of groups 0–2 and 6–9 selected, 100% of the AA and Protestant 3–5 group, and 67% of the Jewish and Catholic 3–5 group. From this total population of 553 informants studied, the non-native speakers are to be subtracted.

Selection of native speakers

All those MFY informants who had been born in a foreign country (including Ireland, England, and the West Indies) were excluded as not being native speakers, unless they had come to the Lower East Side before they were eight years old.[17] The reason for including those who had come to the United States early in life is that the inclusion of a certain number of marginal native speakers in the survey will ultimately show a great deal about

---

[16] This step produced complications; the success in obtaining interviews with AA subjects was greater than expected, and the rate of moving among the lower and working class AAs was less than expected. As a result, the excess of AA working class speakers, as compared to the other working class groups, would have biased the overall figures. As noted below, one-third of the AA working class group was rejected on a random selection for all comparisons of class behavior. Among these rejections were two AA men who were native New Yorkers; their evidence will be required to redress the general weakness of representation among male residents. The small Protestant working class group had moved out completely, so that there was no issue here.

[17] This leaves a certain number of speakers who were born outside of the United States, moved to other parts of the United States before they were eight years old, and subsequently moved to the Lower East Side. The information in the MFY survey did not allow us to identify these subjects. However, the rule given here was later modified to include as native speakers only those who had come to the United States before they were five years old, or were born in this country, and so the issue diminishes in importance.

Table 6.5   *Percentage of native speakers for several ethnic and*
socio-economic class groups

Ethnic group	
African–American	91
Jewish	41
Orthodox	30
Conservative	68
Catholic	59
Protestant[18]	77
Socio-economic class group	
Lower class 0–2	44
Working class 3–5	58
Middle class 6–9	74

the directions in which native speech is moving. It was expected that such
marginal speakers would show up in the final analysis as deviant types in
some ways. The age of eight was selected as a cutting-off point because it
represents the half-way mark in the establishment of native dialect characteristics (posited here as the years 4–13). If the speaker had marked foreign
characteristics in his English, and fell into this marginal category, he or she
was rejected from the sample.

Column 3 of Table 6.4 shows the number of native speakers who
remained as eligible informants for the ALS study. The total is 312, a bare
56 percent of the 553 cases in Column 2. The distribution of native speakers
by ethnic group and by socio-economic group is shown in Table 6.5.

The steady rise in percentage of native speakers with class is a reflection
of the general upward movement of the population of immigrants and
their children. The low point on the scale of native speakers would be represented by lower class orthodox Jews. Of the 71 such informants in the MFY
survey, only 14 were native speakers. Since four of these had moved or had
died, this left only 10 for the ALS survey. Fortunately, we succeeded in
interviewing eight of these speakers, and so obtained a fairly good view of
the speech pattern which they represented.

---

[18] In the Protestant group, there were a number of young people who had moved to the
Lower East Side within a year or so. Though shown here as native speakers, they were not
included in the sample if they had been in New York City less than two years before the
MFY survey. (The great majority of these had moved in any case.) Therefore Table 6.4
shows only twenty-five of the Protestant group as native speakers, which is only 55 percent
of the total.

The shift in the composition of the survey population as a result of eliminating non-native speakers, also eliminates much of the difference between the Lower East Side and other areas as far as occupation, education, and income are concerned. Before we consider the detailed characteristics of the native population, it must be noted that it was not possible to study the entire group of native speakers. In the two-year interval between June of 1961 and June of 1963, eight informants had died or become incapacitated,[19] and 109 had moved, leaving only 195 informants on the scene. The 35 percent who had moved in two years represent a comparatively high rate of mobility, characteristic of an area which is undergoing rapid social change.

In the initial statement of the reasons for choosing the Lower East Side, it was indicated that this choice did not represent a retreat from the problem of variability among New York speakers. On the contrary, the mixture of ethnic groups and social classes, of native and non-native speakers, of mobile and stationary groups, should show us all of the factors which have led to the theoretical problems of linguistic structure outlined in Chapter 2. To a lesser or greater extent, these mixtures have been characteristic of the city as a whole for all of its recent history.[20] Therefore, if we can demonstrate a coherent and systematic structure for the speech pattern of this neighborhood, we can expect that even less difficulty would be found in more homogeneous sections of the city. The question as to whether the information to be presented in the following chapters represents the speech of the city as a whole, or merely this neighborhood, will be considered in detail at a later point.

It is important to characterize the groups which had moved, in order to see in what way the sample of 195 does or does not represent the original population of native speakers which was present on the Lower East Side in 1961. The social characteristics of the moved population are presented in detail in Appendix C, on "Analysis of losses through moving of the MFY sample population." We find in this analysis that the ethnic composition of the population, and the proportion of men and women, are not distorted by the loss of the 109 subjects who moved in the two-year period. There is a serious class bias, since the highest-ranking groups showed the most tendency to move, and the lowest-ranking groups the least tendency. The analysis of the possible effects of this loss, as given in Appendix D, indicates that the social stratification of our present sample is probably a *minimal* stratification, since those middle class subjects who left showed a greater

---

[19] One was deaf, another had lost the use of her voice.

[20] In 1900, only 21 percent of New Yorkers were native white of native parents; in 1960, this category included 31 percent. See Glazer and Moynihan (1963) Table 2.

tendency to differentiate themselves from the Lower East Side working class than those who remained.

The ALS sample population

The target population of the ALS study was all those native speakers of the Lower East Side who had lived in the area for at least two years prior to the ALS survey. The sample which was to represent this population was a group of 195 individuals, who may be termed the ALS sample population.

These 195 individuals represent 100 percent of the lower class and middle class section of the original population, 100 percent of the AA working class, but only 67 percent of the Jewish and Catholic working class. They have therefore been selected from a larger group of 221 native speakers who had not moved (if the percentage of moving in the one-third of working class speakers not studied was the same as that two-thirds which was studied). Since the MFY survey described a population of 33,000 households and 100,000 individuals we can say that our present target population consists of approximately 8,000 households and about 23,000 individuals.

The interviewing of this population began in July, 1963, and was largely completed by the middle of September. The final portion of the interviews, about one-fifth, was obtained in October and November of 1963. A total of 158 of the 195 subjects were interviewed, representing 81 percent, although full information was obtained from only 122, or 63 percent. The fifth column of Table 6.4 shows the numbers of ALS informants in the sample, and the sixth column, the total number who were interviewed.

These interviews were of two types. The main designs of the program were embodied in the linguistic interview described in Chapter 5, the ALS interview. The 122 ALS interviews were supplemented by 33 short interviews with informants who refused the linguistic interview, or who could not be reached for the longer interview. This short interview, which obtained data on the five phonological variables for Style B only, is described in the following section of this chapter as the *ALS television interview*. With this device, it was possible to reduce the margin of unknown subjects by half, and obtain information on informants who could not otherwise be reached; the group of 33 television interviews contains a large proportion of the refusals, and a number of those who would otherwise be labelled as "can't reach."

It would have been possible to obtain a higher percentage of ALS interviews if the sample population chosen had been a smaller part of the eligible MFY subjects. However, the two field workers for the ALS had to work at maximum efficiency if they were to obtain one-eighth of the total number of interviews which were gathered by the forty MFY field workers.

It was necessary to keep a list of thirty or forty active prospects in hand to obtain three or four interviews a day, and avoid the long and inefficient period of following up the last few names on a list. Since a total of at least one hundred and twenty linguistic interviews were felt necessary to study social variation across several class strata and ethnic groups, it was decided to expand the number of individuals in the sample population to cover the percentages noted above. This approach yielded 122 ALS interviews, at 63 percent of the sample population; the program was brought to 81 percent of the sample through the use of the shorter television interview.

It is not claimed that two field workers can within a short time equal the results of a large staff of the social survey, neither in the reduction of error nor in the quantity of reliable material gathered. However, it is likely that most linguistic studies will be carried out with such limited forces, and techniques for making the most efficient use of them are important to consider. If the type of behavior which was being studied was similar to most forms of behavior that are investigated by social survey, the value of the study could be measured by how far it fell short of the MFY standards. However, linguistic behavior is far more general and compelling than many social attitudes or survey responses. The primary data being gathered in the ALS interview are not subject to the informant's control in the way that answers on voting choices would be. The discussion at the end of Chapter 4 demonstrated this point. In studying both linguistic differentiation and linguistic evaluation, we are going beyond the self-conscious answers of the informant, to a type of behavior that is well below the level of awareness.

In Chapter 4, we found that from ten to twenty instances of a given variable were sufficient to assign a value that fits consistently into a complex matrix of stylistic variation, while at the level of three or four instances, fluctuation unrelated to the matrix was noted. Similarly, we will find that from ten to twenty individuals will give us a value for a social class which fits consistently into an overall pattern of stratification, while groups of four or five show unrelated fluctuation. In the case of (r), it will be possible to divide a group of eighty-one informants into six strata which are clearly separated in the same order for five stylistic levels. Thus we see that numbers which might be totally inadequate for the study of attitudes, say, towards racial segregation, with the associated reluctance to give a straightforward personal response, are quite adequate for the study of the phonological variables.

Many of the ALS informants would refer to the earlier MFY survey, although we stated no connection with that survey. One woman commented, "They asked me a lot of questions about segregation. Gee! I hope I said the right thing!" While the social scientists are aware of such biasing factors, they must overcome them by subtle comparisons of large numbers of speakers under varying conditions. The bias of an attitude towards correctness is equally strong in the linguistic interview, but the means for analyzing it are contained within the interview itself. Chapter 4 discussed the methods by which this very bias is utilized for the study of linguistic structure. Thus the linguistic interview, as shown in the examples of Chapter 4, contains four to five hundred pieces of information on the main phonological variables alone, more than the total number of items in the entire social survey. This large quantity of information is so organized that the resulting values of the variables are more regular than the individual's answers to a single question of the social survey. They are more comparable to a very large battery of questions on a single topic, yet it would be impractical to construct a battery of a hundred questions to achieve the same regularity.

Of the 122 ALS interviews, 20 were carried out by Michael Kac, and 102 by myself. Of the television interviews, two were conducted by Kac, and 31 by myself.

The ALS television interview

The ALS television interview was designed to obtain information on the use of the five variables by non-respondents. It was originally designed for those who refused the regular ALS interview, and was afterward applied to give information on the speech of those who could not be reached within the time allotted for field work.

In the case of those subjects who did not have telephones, or whose telephones were not listed, the ALS television interview was conducted in person. If the subject had refused previously a request for an interview by one interviewer, the ALS television interview was conducted by the other interviewer. For those subjects whose telephones were listed, the television interview was conducted by telephone.

The full form of the ALS television interview is given in Appendix D. In the first half of the interview, we asked the subject questions about the quality of the television picture he was receiving for various channels. This subject was chosen as the one likely to obtain the maximum percentage of response from those who had refused the regular ALS interview. Each of the questions was designed to elicit at least one example of a particular variable.

What channels give you the best reception? the worst? which channels do you watch most often? least often?

From these questions, we obtained examples of (r) in *four*, (th) in *thirteen*, and two auxiliary variables to be discussed in Chapter 10: the vowel of *nine*, and the first vowel of *thirteen*.

For the variable (æh), which frequently does not occur in short conversations, we elicited the word *bad*.

Would you say that the trouble . . . was *very* bad, or *not so* bad?

It was necessary to use the word *bad* in our question in order to obtain a uniform response. The effects of influencing the respondent were minimizing by laying heavy stress on *very* and *not so*, and slurring over the word *bad* so that it was not clear which value of the variable the interviewer was using. The actual value used was (æh-3).

For the variable (oh), the following question was used:

At two o'clock in the afternoon, would you say your television set is usually *on*, or off? at four o'clock? at ten in the morning? ten at night?

Again, the bias produced by using the word *off* was reduced by giving it only tertiary stress. The value of (oh) used by the interviewer was (oh-3). The questions were continued until several clear instances of (oh) were obtained.

The value of (dh) was obtained from the many examples which occurred naturally throughout the interview.

In all but a few cases, the technique shown was successful in obtaining the desired forms. In addition to these deliberately elicited values of the variable, a great many others were obtained throughout the television interview. This technique assured that each variable would be represented by at least some examples.

The second half of the television interview was designed to obtain as much conversation from the subject as possible. The questions concerned opinions about programs, commercials, and the effects of television upon children. In a few cases, it was possible to obtain information on the subject's background by the line of questions indicated at the end of the questionnaire.

The technique of the second half of the interview was successful in obtaining large samples of the speech of most subjects. Even those who had rejected the ALS linguistic interview most abruptly would talk freely in response to the television interview, for as long as fifteen minutes. For example, one subject refused the ALS interview, referring to the earlier MFY interview, and categorized the ALS letter as "ridiculous nonsense." He responded quite vigorously to the television interview, which lasted almost fifteen minutes. We obtained 23 instances of (r), 11 of (æh), 8 of (oh), 11 of (th), and 45 of (dh), more than enough to give us an accurate view of his treatment of the variables.

Only one subject refused the television interview, and in so doing, gave us reasonable information on her treatment of several of the variables.

Of the 27 subjects who refused the regular ALS interview, we succeeded in interviewing 16 by the television interview. Of 46 subjects who could not be reached in the time allotted for the field work, 17 were interviewed by this method. Thus, of the 73 persons who were not reached for the linguistic interview, we succeeded in obtaining good evidence on the language behavior of 33.

The validity of the television interview is affected by the fact that most of the interviews were conducted over the telephone. The losses in sound quality must be assessed as a factor in these results. It is also necessary to determine which stylistic context the television interview represents. For this purpose, ten subjects randomly selected from those who had already been interviewed by the regular ALS interview, were re-interviewed with the television questionnaire. None of these respondents suspected any connection with the original linguistic interview. We are thus able to calibrate the television interview against the main body of the linguistic interviews, and determine its relative reliability and validity. The results of this comparison are given in Appendix D "calibration of the television interviews."

The results of the television interview will be used in Chapters 9 and 10, where they will be merged with the results of the regular linguistic interviews for certain specific variables. In Appendix D, the television interviews are analyzed separately for the information they give us on the non-respondents. On the whole, they indicate that the non-respondents show the same pattern of social stratification of the variables which is observed in the main body of 122 ALS respondents and 68 of their children who participated in the interviews.

Characteristics of the ALS respondents

In the remainder of this chapter, the social characteristics of the 122 ALS respondents will be discussed. We will also consider briefly the other members of the family interviewed in the course of the survey, primarily the children of the 122 informants.

Columns 5 and 6 of Table 6.4 compare the total number of interviews obtained with the ALS target sample. Column 7 shows the number of regular ALS interviews for each division. However, the overall distribution of the informants is not so significant for our purpose as the distribution after one major division has been made in the sample: that between the natives of New York City, and those raised outside the city. We may therefore divide the 122 respondents as follows:

New Yorkers   84
Non-New Yorkers   38

Redefinition of "native speaker" and "New Yorker"

The original definition of "native speaker" had allowed only those who were born in the United States, or had come to this country before they were eight years old, excluding those in the second category who had a pronounced foreign accent. The definition of a New Yorker was at first made a little broader. Two speakers who had come to the city between the ages of eight and twelve were studied along with the main body of New Yorkers in the first investigation of the data. It was found that these two speakers showed linguistic patterns quite different from most AA speakers born and raised in New York City. Both were AA subjects who had come to New York from Virginia at the age of ten: a man forty-four years old, and a woman forty-two years old. Because their speech showed a mixture of characteristics that were not found together in native New York speech, nor in the speech of other AA respondents from the South, their evidence was not used for either category.[21]

Two other marginal cases appeared as the result of analysis. Both were speakers whose status as native speakers of English had been considered marginal when first admitted to the sample. One was a Jewish woman of forty-nine who had been born in Hungary, and came to the United States when she was five years old. The other was an older Jewish woman of sixty-nine, born in Czechoslovakia, who also came to the United States at five. The details of their linguistic behavior ultimately showed that they did not act like native speakers of English, although no pronounced foreign accent was evident. In one distributional chart after another, these respondents appeared at isolated points with values of the variables quite different from those of other New Yorkers of the same age and social characteristics.[22]

---

[21] The chief peculiarities of these speakers may be described as follows. Both showed a high allophone for the vowel in *bat* and *that*, at the level of (æh-3), which is not character-istic of New York speakers. The man showed a zero index for (th), typical of southern AA speakers, but not New York natives. The woman had a very high (th) level, but a very low (dh) index; her (æh) variable jumped suddenly from 13, to 28, to 17, to 25; her value of (oh) started at 21, typical of New York speech, and fell to a value of 35 in Style D. This latter value is typical of southern AA speech, but only middle class New Yorkers show this pattern of fluctuation; this speaker, who was class 1, was the only member of the New York group below class 6 to show such a pattern. Finally, she used an (r) pattern typical of lower class speakers, without showing any middle class influence.

[22] The chief peculiarities of these speakers may be summarized as follows. The older woman used a zero index for (th) and (dh) in Styles B and C, which is not characteristic of native New York class 3 speakers; she used a very pronounced and regular form of upgliding center diphthong in *work* and *bird*; her intonation showed strong Yiddish influence, and when I first spoke to her, I debated for some time whether or not to interview her as a native speaker. The younger woman, from class 2, showed a very high level of (r) at all points; she

As a result of these studies, we re-defined the concept of "native speaker" to include only those who had come to the United States before they were five, and the concept of "New Yorker" to include only those who had come to New York before the age of eight.

Class distribution of the ALS respondents

In order to use the ALS sample to study class distribution, it was necessary to adjust the percentage of all class groups to an equivalent value. Originally, 100 percent of the AA working class and the Protestant working class was studied, since these were the smallest sections of the population. No Protestant informants in this group remained in the sample, but there are sixteen working class AA informants. One-third of the original MFY sample must be rejected at random in this category, in order to allow comparison across ethnic groups. This process removes three AAs from the group of completed interviews: two New Yorkers and one non-New Yorker. These individuals may be used for any study of AA speech, but not for any general studies of the sample as a whole.

Finally, it was noted that there were only eight native New York interviews in category 9 of socio-economic class. This was the group that had lost the most heavily in the moving of subjects during the two-year interval. Since this class was observed to form a separate sub-group in many ways, it was supplemented by the following procedure. The husband of one of the subjects was a leading figure in local politics. He was asked to suggest the names of local community leaders who were native to the area. With his cooperation, two informants were added to the list: an assemblyman and a pharmacist, one Jewish and one Italian. A third supplementary informant was selected from the group of research assistants at MFY, to add representation in the younger age levels: a Jewish man raised in the Bronx, twenty-seven years old. This addition brought the upper middle class group to a total of eleven New Yorkers in addition to the three non-New Yorkers.

With one exception, this category is a fairly uniform group of speakers. Calculations based on the group without the three supplementary speakers are quite similar to the presentation in Chapter 7 with these added informants.

Footnote 22 (*cont.*)
    used a very low level of (oh) and (æh), and lacked most identifying characteristics of New York City speech. When she was first brought to the United States, she forgot her native Slavic language, and learned Yiddish only. When she went to school, she knew no English. Often she is told by friends and casual acquaintances that she does not speak like a New Yorker. Both of these informants show up at isolated points on distributional charts for values of the variables, such as those used in Chapter 8.

Table 6.6   *Number of respondents in the ALS sample*

New Yorkers	81
Non-New Yorkers	37
AAs not part of the basic sample	3
	121

Table 6.7   *Percent age groups in ALS and MFY samples*

	ALS New Yorkers	ALS non-New Yorkers	MFY total native speakers
0–2	28	32	30
3–5	35	32	33
6–9	37	34	37

These subtractions and additions yield the breakdown in Table 6.6, which serves as a base for the analysis of Chapter 7.

Tables 6.8 and 6.9 show the distribution of the informants by class, as compared to the distribution of the 312 native speakers in the MFY survey, moved and remaining. This comparison shows the relative proportions of speakers of various classes in the total, and also relative success or failure in gaining representation in that class. The chief discrepancies lie in two sections of the scale. Class 2 is higher in the ALS sample, and class 3 is lower than in the MFY sample. If both of these classes are treated together, the discrepancy will in part be resolved. On the other hand, if classes 3 and 4 are combined, the total of 24 percent will not be far from the 25 percent of the original sample. The under-representation of class 6 can similarly be compensated for if classes 6 and 7 are combined. Thus by the same combination used in the original sampling we have Table 6.7.

Since the total picture shows approximately equal thirds in all cases, it is apparent that the fluctuations do not add up to a cumulative bias, but rather cancel each other out. However, it was noted above that the rate of moving for the higher classes was regularly higher than for the lower classes. (The figures were 26, 38, and 42 percent for 0–2, 3–5, and 6–8.) For us now to arrive at comparable distribution in the population must mean that the completion rates are in an inverse progression. The actual rate of completion by class groups is 59, 72, and 65 percent. (The addition of the three supplementary informants to the upper group, and the subtraction of the three working class AA speakers, are the steps responsible for the final uniformity.)

Table 6.8   *Class distribution of ALS respondents*

| Class | ALS | | | MFY |
	New Yorkers	Non-New Yorkers	Total respondents	Total native speakers
0	7	5	12	30
1	7	3	10	30
2	9	7	16	32
3	13	1	14	43
4	10	5	15	37
5	5	5	10	25
6	8	2	10	40
7	9	2	11	21
8	2	4	6	18
9	11	3	14	36
Total:	81	37	118	312

Table 6.9   *Class distribution of ALS respondents*

	Percentage		
0	8.5	10.0	10.0
1	8.5	9.0	9.5
2	11.0	13.0	10.0
3	16.0	11.5	13.5
4	12.5	12.5	11.5
5	6.0	8.0	8.0
6	10.0	8.0	13.0
7	11.0	10.0	7.0
8	2.5	5.0	6.0
9	14.0	11.5	11.5
Total:	100.0	100.0	100.0

Ethnic distribution of the ALS respondents

The distribution by ethnic groups for the ALS respondents is compared with the total MFY native speakers in Table 6.10.

Here the situation is not so favorable. Whereas the sample is over-represented for the orthodox Jewish population, it is under-represented for the Catholic group. The basis for this is a low rate of completion for the Catholic respondents in the ALS sample population. The percentage of ALS respondents as against the ALS target sample is shown in Table 6.11.

Table 6.10   *Distribution of ALS respondents by ethnic group*

| | Percentage | | | |
	Total ALS respondents	Total MFY native speakers	Total ALS respondents	Total MFY native speakers
African–American	32	67	26	24
Jewish, Orthodox	23	49	19	16
Jewish, Cons. & Ref.	24	58	19	19
Catholic	35	104	29	33
Protestant	8	25	7	8
	122	303	100	100

Table 6.11   *Percent completed interviews by ethnic group*

	% completed
AA	71
Jewish, Orthodox	71
Jewish, Conservative or Reform	63
Catholic	58
Protestant	89

This difficulty in interviewing Catholic, especially Italian, subjects, was first encountered by the MFY survey. It was overcome by special efforts; in our case, the information in the television interviews will help to reduce this gap. Fourteen of the thirty-three television interviews are of Catholic informants. The relations of Catholic and Jewish informants must, however, be examined carefully for each of the variables as discussed in the next chapters. Since the class distribution of these groups is radically different, such relationships must be examined within each class; this can be done in the distributional analysis of Chapter 8.

The most serious bias in the sample population is that of men vs. women. The considerable gap which existed in the ALS target sample between men and women has become a major problem in the sample of 122 informants. For all adult linguistic interviews, including the three supplementary upper middle class interviews, we find the numbers of men and women shown in Table 6.12.

The overall record shows that we reached 92 percent of the female population, but only 71 percent of the males. The overbalance of women in the ALS interviews themselves is two to one. Again, the only approach to solving this problem will lie in the detailed analysis of distribution within each class. Wherever indications of a difference by sexes is suspected, it will be necessary to study each group separately.

Table 6.12   *Distribution of ALS and television interviews by gender*

	Men	Women
ALS linguistic interviews	42	83
Television interviews	14	19
Remaining	25	15
	81	117

Table 6.13   *Distribution of NYC speakers by class and gender*

Class	0	1	2	3	4	5	6	7–8	9
Men	2	2	2	4	3	1	2	4	4
Women	4	7	8	9	7	4	6	7	4

Table 6.14   *Ethnic distribution by gender*

	Catholic	Jewish	African–American	Protestant
Men	7	18	1	1
Women	14	22	7	2

Chapter 7 will be concerned with the class stratification of the variables. If men and women are unevenly concentrated in the various classes, then what appears to be class stratification may in reality be due to a difference in the sexes. It is therefore imperative that the imbalance of men and women be checked for each class. For the sample of New York speakers, the numbers of men and women by class are shown in Table 6.13.

Considering the size of the numbers, we could not ask for a more even distribution than this. The only anomaly is the even percentage in class 9. If, however, we check the total number of men and women in the original group of native speakers (column 3 of Table 6.4) we find that this is one category where men are in the majority: eighteen men against seventeen women. However, the addition of the three supplementary informants to this class, all males, biases the situation more towards the preponderance of males, and all class 9 values need to be checked carefully for distortion on this point.

The ethnic distribution of the sexes is as shown in Table 6.14.

Here we see a higher percentage of men in the Jewish group, and a lower percentage for AAs. The two male AA speakers rejected from the sample must therefore be used to check the results against bias on this point.

Interviewing other members of the household

The MFY adult survey population was selected for those in the household over twenty years old. A second MFY survey was conducted among the adolescent children of the 911 informants. Of 706 potential informants, 555 were interviewed, or 79 percent.

In the present survey, it was considered impractical to aim for a systematic coverage of youth as well as adults. Any children of the principal informant who could be interviewed were included in the study. If an appointment was made beforehand, the informant was asked to have his children, especially the oldest, be present if possible. In a few cases, children were interviewed separately. Table 6.15 gives a view of other persons present and participating in the interview. As a result of this procedure, we obtained information on the linguistic behavior of sixty-eight children of the informants, ranging from eight to thirty-five years old.[23] The data from interviews with children will be brought forward in dealing with differentiation through age groups, in Chapter 9 and thereafter, to extend the time depth of the study.

Summary of possible sources of error

In the course of this detailed examination of the sampling procedure, we have found a number of points where the possibility of bias in the results must be considered. All of these problems stem from the difficulties of surveying a large population with limited resources.

The loss of a large part of the population of native speakers through removal has been considered. No serious bias to the ethnic composition of the population was found, but there was a depletion of the higher ranking social classes and a corresponding increase in the proportion of the lower classes remaining.

This bias was compensated for by an inverse relation in the rate of completion of interviews, with worst results for the lower class. The net view of the population matches the original group of 312 native speakers in class

---

[23] Information was also obtained from thirty-five associated persons such as parents, wives, husbands, and friends of the informant. Finally ten replacement interviews with families randomly selected to replace informants who had moved were also completed. In the present study, the information gathered from associated persons and replacement interviews will not be utilized, as it did not bulk large enough to be studied as a separate category.

Table 6.15   *Other members of household participating in ALS interviews*

	Number of interviews
Informant alone	50
Spouse only present	15
Children present	51
1 child	42
2 children	5
3 children	2
4 children	1
5 children	1
Parent of informant present	5
Friend of informant or of children present	10
Brother or sister of informant present	6
Informant not present	7
One child of informant present	3
Two children of informant present	3
Five children of informant present	1

distribution. The ALS informants are grouped in thirds as lower, working, and middle class.

A lower rate of completion for Catholic residents was not matched by any compensating process, and this remains a possible source of bias. A more serious bias of the population lies in the proportions of men and women.

Despite these problems, we can say that the group of 122 informants has reasonably good representation from all classes, and all ethnic groups in the original population. The under-representation of some groups is not enough to prevent us from detecting the speech patterns of these groups as a whole.

We are not using quantitative methods in order to make an overall estimate of the amount of (r-1) used in the Lower East Side, or in New York City as a whole. For that purpose, the differential rates of completion would raise serious obstacles. The use of quantitative methods in this work is for a different purpose: to show the structure of stylistic and social variation within the language of New York City. For that purpose, we need representation from all those who use the language in different ways. The great value of the secondary study, based on the firm foundation of the MFY survey, is that we are in no danger of omitting entire social groups from the discussion. If there was a linguistic or social type which had eluded us entirely, to be found only among the refusals or other non-respondents, this goal would be defeated. However, the various approaches to the non-respondents discussed in Chapter 8 will cut sharply into the likelihood of such a loss.

We are now ready to analyze the results of the survey. In Chapter 7, the class differentiation of the five variables will be shown in detail. This will be the most exacting test of the hypothesis first stated for (r) in Chapter 3, which can be generalized for all of the variables as a result of the material to be presented.

Part II

Social differentiation

7   Class differentiation of the variables

The original problem which we faced in the opening pages of this study was to discover in the apparently irregular fluctuations in the speech of New Yorkers, a coherent linguistic structure. So far we have found evidence of a regular pattern of social variation and a regular pattern of stylistic variation. These were first viewed in isolation, in the speech of small sections of the community (Chapter 4). In this chapter, we will use the results of the survey of the Lower East Side to describe the double pattern of variation in a representative section of the community. Instead of studying one axis of variation at a time, both will be seen together as part of a two-dimensional structure. Instead of a rough indication with a few examples, we will have quantitative statements where the sources of error can be estimated and minimized.

The meaning of *stylistic variation* has been defined and illustrated in Chapter 3, and the independent variable of contextual style has been given an operational definition within this study. Now it will be necessary to examine the concept of *social variation* and give the independent variable along this dimension a correspondingly precise operational definition.

Social class as a measure of social stratification

The social stratification of New York City is considered here as a structure in two dimensions. On the one hand, there is social differentiation, which is the focus of this chapter and the following three. On the other hand, there is the *social evaluation* of such differences, which will be considered in Chapter 11. A consistent pattern of differentiation, which has social significance for the native residents of the community, will therefore be termed social stratification.[1]

---

[1] The terminology in which *differentiation* is opposed to *evaluation* is utilized at many points throughout this study. The present chapter, for example, is concerned solely with differentiation of the variables, and not evaluation. The existence of *social stratification*, as here defined, cannot be established without considering both differentiation and evaluation. However, throughout Part II, the term *stratification* will be used in a slightly different sense,

129

[This is the main focus of the New York City study: generating the patterns of social and stylistic stratification that started the quantitative study of linguistic change and variation. The diagrams produced in this section have been reproduced in great numbers: they speak eloquently of the main theme: that the speech community is a highly structured object. Furthermore, we cannot easily speak any way we choose; sociolinguistic variables and their complex conditioning are social facts, which we are not free to ignore, as the case of Nathan B. will testify. There is not a whole lot of mathematical sophistication in this chapter, but there is a great deal of careful work.]

The evaluation of this pattern takes the form of some kind of hierarchy, with ranking of better and worse on some evaluative scale. The scale of evaluation need not be linear: there can be, for instance, many lines of descent from one highest ranking group, or many lines of ascent from a lowest ranking group. These different lines may not be ranked in relation to each other by the community as a whole. Nevertheless, the concept of a single community implies that linear scales are possible, and most of the approaches which we will attempt will involve the matching of linguistic variables against a linear social ranking.

The social variable need not be conceived as socio-economic class, though this is the usual association of the term "social stratification." It will be useful to begin with this concept as an independent variable, for some form of socio-economic differentiation is strongly suggested by the exploratory interviews and by the department store survey. In Chapter 8, we will test other social variables, to see if the abstract construct of *social class* is required to account for the facts of linguistic variation, or if some simpler parameter can be found.

Two approaches to social variation in language

We can take two different routes to the description of social variation in language, no matter what means of describing social groups is chosen. On the one hand, we can consider various sections of the population, and determine the values of the linguistic variables for each group. In this way,

Footnote 1 (*cont.*)
　　to designate differential structures which show a "horizontal" layering. For example, the diagrams for the differential distribution of the variables shown in this chapter are called *class stratification* and *style stratification* diagrams, because they have the horizontal structure which these terms suggest. It is then useful to speak of *sharp stratification*, meaning a wide separation of a few discrete levels on the vertical scale, as opposed to *fine stratification* which indicates a matching of one continuum with another, with an almost unlimited number of horizontal layers separated by almost vanishingly small distances on the vertical scale. These are the extreme types: normally we will be dealing with relatively sharp or fine stratification.

we can determine what kind of speech a person would be apt to hear if he associated with college-trained professionals, what kind of speech he would hear if he worked all his life among longshoremen. The alternate approach is to chart the overall distribution of the variables themselves, and then ask, for certain values of each variable: what are the social characteristics of the people who talk this way? This is equivalent to looking for the social significance of a speech pattern as we first hear it; when we meet a New Yorker for the first time, what can we infer about him from the way he talks?

Thus the first approach will describe for us the type of speech we can expect from a given group of New Yorkers, and the second will tell us what group membership we can expect from a person who talks in a certain manner.

Both approaches will be helpful in determining the particular social factor or combination of factors which is correlated most closely with linguistic behavior. However, the first approach, through social groups, seems more fundamental and more closely tied to the genesis of linguistic differentiation.

[It was helpful to lay out these two complementary approaches at the beginning. Many sociolinguists have chosen to follow one path or the other, without considering the advantages of both. Do we put together all the people who speak in the same way, and see who they are? Sometimes an atheoretical approach of factor analysis pays off, and many of the studies that I've done recently have made good use of factor analysis (principle components) (Labov 1994: Ch. 18; *Atlas of North American English*, Ch. 11). But if our main interest is in language, we will want to see how linguistic forms are distributed across the social landscape. If our main interest is in explaining society, it would be helpful to work the other way around, and discover what social groups are identified by a common linguistic pattern. The great majority of sociolinguistic studies have taken the first route: language as the dependent variable, and social categories as the independent variables.]

The evidence of this survey as a whole reinforces the idea that the social group of peers in which a speaker spends his pre-adolescent years is the main force in establishing his linguistic pattern.

While parents may be the primary source for the basic language pattern which is common to all English speakers, they have little influence as a rule on the child's native speech or social dialect variations. In the latter respect, a child's native speech pattern is determined by his immediate friends and associates.[2] Contrast with outside groups, which comes later, is important in

---

[2] I have tested this hypothesis again and again in dealing with the contrasting usage of several generations within one family, and it is rarely that the influence of the parents appears as primary. For example, I recently interviewed a family in which the parents were raised in Waco, Texas; the son, now thirteen years old, grew up in Omaha, Nebraska; they are now living in Berkeley, California. Before the son appeared, I predicted to the parents that he would show no trace of their distinction between *which* and *witch*, or *four* and *for*, and that

consolidating this native pattern or in imposing modifications from without. However, the most coherent system remains that which was established in the early years by the sanctions of the immediate group. Therefore, in asking about the language characteristics of a social group, we are dealing with an abstraction which has clearly observable correlates in the history of the individual and the structure of the neighborhood. When we have finished this type of analysis, we may turn to the second approach, and use the concept of *linguistic class* as a first step towards establishing the overall structure of New York City English. In following this procedure, we will be able to avoid any error which would arise in assuming that a group of people who speak alike is a fundamental unit of social behavior.

The socio-economic class index

[A great deal of ink has been spilt over the issue of how to define social class. It is not unusual for American sociolinguists to reject the work of sociologists on this question as if it were irrelevant to their concerns. They share the general tendency of most Americans to think of *social class* as an unpleasant word, or to think that if we describe class stratification, we are accepting or approving all of its consequences. The particular index of social characteristics used here is useful for a study of a big city, but it is not used in a fixed manner. In fact, the next two chapters take it apart and put it back together in many ways. It will turn out that occupation is more closely correlated with some variables and education with others. In the 1970s study of Philadelphia, occupation was by far the most powerful determinant of linguistic behavior, but an index that combined occupation with education and house value was more stable and regular (Labov 2001: Ch. 5). One of the most interesting parts of the New York City study is the examination of status incongruence: how people speak whose education, occupation, and income aren't correlated in the usual way.

Sociolinguists who operate in other societies sometimes begin with the notion that the New York City study assumed or projected that this

Footnote 1 (*cont.*)

> he would show a merger of *caught* and *cot*, *hawk* and *hock* which was foreign to them. Their disbelief was belied by the evidence of the son's speech. In New York City, the case of the certified public accountant and his family, mentioned in Chapter 2, is a typical instance of the parents' bewilderment at their son's use of many stigmatized speech forms which they themselves never use, despite his success in high school and his strong orientation towards college. My own children show many dialect characteristics which are quite different from those used by either my wife or myself, despite the fact that we were both raised in the same county of New Jersey in which we are now living. The first vowels of *mirror* and *nearer*, for example, have coalesced, together with all similar sets: such an innovation cannot be accounted for by any theory which places parental influence on language in a primary position.

particular socio-economic index should fit every society in the world, but there is no basis for such a hasty conclusion. Even the generalization that all societies are stratified must be set aside. There is no substitute for working close to the ground in determining what social categories are most relevant. A classic example is Rickford's (1979) study of CaneWalk in Guyana, which established two major social divisions: the Estate Class of cane-cutters, and the Non-Estate Class including everybody else.

Other recent approaches to social categorization have classified people according to the type of social networks in which they are engaged (Milroy 1980, Bortoni-Ricardo 1985). There can be no doubt that this is a sensitive index of linguistic behavior, and necessary to understand the mechanism of linguistic transmission and diffusion. One of the limitations of this New York City sample is that it is basically a study of isolated individuals. The Philadelphia study combined the analysis of social stratification with the study of social networks, and found that the one did not replace the other in terms of explanatory value: in fact, they were additive (Labov 2001, Ch. 5).

Finally, we should not forget that one important approach to social class (Warner 1960) is subjective: a matter of how people see and talk about each other. In a more detailed, long-term study of a speech community, we will want to gather up all the threads of gossip, rumors, and social histories that we can find. Our gifted Philadelphia field worker, Anne Bower, once drove through North Philadelphia with her central sponsor and close friend from South Philadelphia, who said, "You'll recognize an Irish neighborhood – a bar on every corner."]

The operational definition of socio-economic class which will be used in this chapter is the ten point scale set up by MFY on the basis of their adult survey. This scale has already been introduced as the basis for the stratified sampling procedure described in Chapter 6. The theory behind this index, the procedures which were followed, and evaluation of the results are set forth in detail by John Michael (see footnote 14 to Chapter 6). Since this material is unpublished, I shall quote extensively from it, and reproduce some of the tables which will help to explain the concept of class behind the index.

Michael's initial approach to stratification is through the concept of social rank.

An individual's standing in terms of a hierarchy of positions can be called his social rank.

An individual may be ranked on a number of different scales; his combined social rankings represent his overall or general social standing.

Since this is a community study, the individuals must be ranked by their standing in the local community. Yet to preserve the utility of comparisons with national patterns, the scale must be related to the larger social systems of city, state, and nation.

. . . We shall keep both local and national hierarchies in mind as population referents since both play some (unascertained) role in determining a person's social position.

Faced with a choice of two orders of stratifying dimensions – those concerning production, and those concerning consumption – Michael chooses the former.

The productive aspect of social rank (i.e., social class) involves the degree to which an individual possesses wealth, knowledge, power, and authority, relative to other members of his society. In indices of class these hierarchies are most commonly represented by income, education, and occupation. Simply stated, social class is an individual's life chances stated in terms of his relation to the production and acquisition of goods and services. The consumptive aspect of social rank (i.e., status) involves an individual's expression of his life chances in a particular style of life. The emphasis here is on *how* the person spends his money, *where* he was educated, *how* he exerts his will over others. . . .

   To avoid contamination of status with our measure of social class, then, we construct the index of social class from variables reflecting *only* its productive aspect.[3]

A single indicator, such as occupation or education, might have been used for the social class index. Most of the indicators are closely related; Michael refers to a study of Horwitz and Smith which showed that two separate indicators of class predicted attitudes with roughly equal force in the same direction.[4] However, the decision to use a weighting of three indicators is based on considerations of accuracy and reliability.

. . . while indicators of class are interchangeable, we can combine indicators to achieve greater accuracy by eliminating fluctuations in social ranks from one hierarchy to another. Using more than one indicator of class also minimizes the errors accrued from measurement.

The three indicators chosen are occupation, education, and income. Each of these are determined on a scale of 8–10 levels in the survey, and then

---

[3] Language may be thought of as an expression of style of life as well. It is quite distinct from the pattern of values, affiliations, and interactions which are used to define social class from the consumptive aspect, but it seems to be on the same level. Therefore correlations with the productive indicators seem to explain more than correlations with other indicators of style of life. The productive indicators will also be more useful as we try to gain some historical depth in our view of linguistic processes; styles of life are hard to compare from generation to generation, but positions in the productive hierarchies are more comparable. The linguistic survey will therefore benefit from the firm separation of indicators established by the MFY index.

[4] Hortense Horwitz and Ellas Smith, "The Interchangeability of Socio-economic Indices," (1955), pages 73–77.

Table 7.1

Occupational rank	
IV	Professionals, managers, and officials (salaried and self-employed)
III	Clerks and salesmen
II	Craftsmen and foremen; self-employed white and blue collar workers
I	Operatives, service workers, laborers and permanently unemployed persons

grouped into four broad categories. The categories for occupational rank are listed in Table 7.1. (A more detailed description is given in Chapter 8, under the discussion of occupation as a single parameter.)

The occupation of the chief breadwinner was used for the entire family.[5]

The categories for occupation given above are derived from the ones used by the Bureau of the Census. One important change from the Census usage is the separation of the small shopkeeper from the owner of a large business. Instead of appearing in the highest rank, the candy store owner here appears in rank II. The decision to rank clerks and salesmen ahead of this group was based on the observation that "head work" is still accorded more social prestige than "hand work," or at least, most people still behave as *if* this is the case.

The categories for educational rank are shown in Table 7.2.

Here too, the policy was followed of assigning the education of the chief breadwinner to the entire family, with a set of rules similar to that used for occupation. This policy was not followed for the linguistic survey. Instead, the education of the individual being interviewed was used in ascertaining his or her position on the social class index. This seemed to be more in line with the purposes of the linguistic survey, where the focus was on the adult individual rather than the family as a conditioning factor in the behavior of youth. However, when the final analysis of the linguistic variables was made, the many small adjustments in social class position produced by this change in the rules had no appreciable effect. The number of changes which increased the correlation of linguistic behavior with social class

---

[5] The following rules were followed in this policy: 1) Husband's occupation was used for all married women except in cases where the wife is working and the husband is retired; 2) widows who do not work were classified by their dead husband's occupation; 3) college students were assigned the highest occupational rank to represent their probable occupational destinations.

Table 7.2   *Educational rank*

IV	Completed some college or more
III	Finished high school
II	Completed some high school
I	Finished grade school or less

standing were equal in number to the changes which decreased that correlation.[6]

The indicator for income was calculated by a complex procedure which is given in detail in Michael's report. Essentially, the following steps summarize the construction of this indicator:

1) The total income for the family, and the number of adults and children who are supported by that income were determined.
2) The number of "equivalent adults" in the household was determined from a chart which gave less weight to children than adults, following figures on the relative costs of supporting children and adults.
3) The income per equivalent adult was determined by dividing total family income by the number assigned under 2) above.
4) This figure was adjusted downward by $5.00 weekly, representing the common household expense for all sizes of families. The remaining figure is the adjusted income per equivalent number of adults.

The results of this procedure give us the rankings in Table 7.3.

The three indicators are now given equal weight in the derivation of a ten-point linear scale, in the matrix shown as Table 7.4. The distribution of the original MFY informants on this array shows a considerable amount of scattering among the various possibilities. Thus in classes 4 and 5 we find twelve possible configurations of occupation, education, and income, running the gamut from the highest to the lowest category in each variable. On the other hand, classes 0 and 9 are the most uniform: only informants with the lowest and highest category for all three variables are included.

---

[6] There were 37 shifts in the assignment of social class through the use of the informant's own educational rank, as opposed to the use of the chief breadwinner's education. Nineteen of these shifts were in the direction of a higher social rank, and 18 towards a lower social rank. Twenty-eight shifts were only one rank on the scale; 8 showed a change of two ranks, and 1 of three. Twenty-four of these changes of social class were in such a direction as to favor or disfavor the class stratification of the variables. The net result for New Yorkers was as follows: favoring stratification of (r), 6 yes, 7 no; of (th), 6 yes, 7 no; of (dh), 7 yes, 6 no. For out-of-town speakers, favoring stratification of (th), 7 yes, 4 no; of (dh), 7 yes, 4 no.

Table 7.3   *Income rank*

		Adj. weekly income per equiv. adult
IV	More than nation's median	$37.32 and above
III	More than the LES median, but less than nation's median	$25.01 to 37.31
II	More than minimum wage, but less than the LES median	$18.01 to 25.00
I	Less than minimum wage	$18.00 and less

Table 7.4   *Weights of occupational, educational, and income rankings combined*

	Income rank															
	(High) IV Occupational rank				III Occupational rank				II Occupational rank				I (Low) Occupational rank			
Educational	(High)		(Low)		(High)		(Low)		(High)		(Low)		(High)		(Low)	
rank	IV	III	II	I	IV	III	II	I	IV	III	II	I	IV	III	II	I
(High) IV	9	8	7	6	8	7	6	5	7	6	5	4	6	5	4	3
III	8	7	6	5	7	6	5	4	6	5	4	3	5	4	3	2
II	7	6	5	4	6	5	4	3	5	4	3	2	4	3	2	1
(Low) I	6	5	4	3	5	4	3	2	4	3	2	1	3	2	1	0

Michael gives considerable attention to the problem of dividing the continuum of social class; this will be a major question for the linguistic survey as well, when we do turn to the question of cutting the final ten-point scale into sections.

. . . classes are ideal types of constructs so the society is viewed as sequentially ordered clusters of variables. But empirically, indicators of the productive aspect of social class are distributed on a positively skewed curve without sharp breaks between different strata.

In order to set up cutting points for the ten-point scale as a whole, Michael utilizes the discussion of class characteristics given by Joseph Kahl;[7] Michael's summary is shown as Table 7.5. Both productive and

[7] Joseph A. Kahl, *The American Class Structure* (1957).

Table 7.5   *The distribution of the population and their educational, occupational, and income characteristics, according to Kahl's social class divisions*

	Class title	Educational characteristics	Occupational characteristics	Income characteristics	Percentage of the national population
V:	Upper class	College graduate of the *right* school	First rate professional manager, official or proprietor of a large business	Don't bother to count it	1
IV:	Upper middle class	College graduate	Careermen in professions, managerial, official or large business positions	Equally high but they count it	9
III:	Lower middle class	High school graduate, frequently with specialized training thereafter	Semi-professionals, petty businessmen, white collar, foreman and craftsmen	Enough to save for children's college education	40
II:	Working class	Some high school	Operatives: blue collar workers at the mercy of the labor market	Enough for cars, TV, etc.	40
I:	Lower class	Grade school or less	Laborers: last to be hired and first to be fired. Frequent job shifts	Struggle for bare existence	10

consumptive characteristics are combined on Table 7.5 to give a common sense view of class levels. In Table 7.6, Kahl's estimate of the size of these classes on a national scale is compared with the distribution of the ALS informants.

Table 7.6 indicates, as predicted in Chapter 6, that the major differences between the Lower East Side and the nation as a whole are reduced by studying only the native speakers of the area. Though the distribution of ALS informants is still shifted towards the lower end of the scale, the only serious discrepancy is in the shortage of lower middle class speakers.

Table 7.6   *Comparison of ALS informants with Kahl's classes*

Social class index	All ALS informants	New York ALS informants	MFY informants	Kahl's description	
MFY	%	%	%	%	Name
0	10	8.5	12.9	10	Lower class
1	9	8.5	17.3		Mixed lower class and working class
2–5	46.5	45.5	49.6	40	Working class
6–8	22.5	23.5	15.3	40	Lower middle class
9	12	14	4.9	9	Upper middle class
–	–	–	–	1	Upper class
	100	100	100	100	
[N:	118	81	988]		

Fortunately, this group displays relatively consistent behavior, and the 23 percent we do have will yield clear insight into the linguistic pattern characteristic of the group. As far as the upper class is concerned, we would not expect to find representatives of this group living on the Lower East Side, and any study of their speech must come from a different approach.

[This is certainly so. Upper class speakers are not interviewed by writing letters, knocking on doors, or hanging out on street corners. Such a study requires a carefully orchestrated series of introductions, beginning with upper middle class friends who are close to the investigator. See Kroch 1996 for the study of the Philadelphia upper class.]

The labels used above will be applied informally to designate the four main sections of the social class scale, no matter how the cuts are made. The lowest portion, which may be shown as 0–1 or 0–2, will be called *lower class*; the group centering around 3 and 4 will be called *working class*, whether or not classes 2 and 5 are attached to it; classes 6–9 will be called *middle class;* when 6–8 are considered separately they will be called *lower middle class*, and when class 9 is treated separately, it will be called *upper middle class*.

The main part of the discussion to follow will concern the eighty-one New York respondents to the ALS interview. Aside from the difference in regional background between them and the out-of-town respondents, there is a great difference in racial composition, as shown in Table 7.7.

When the out-of-town respondents are considered, black-white differences must be taken into account. Any discussion which refers to the

Table 7.7

	New York	Out-of-town
White	72	16
African–American (AA)	9	21

Table 7.8   *Class stratification of the variables*

Class group 0–2

	Style					N:				
	A	B	C	D	D′					
(r)	02.5	10.5	14.5	23.5	49.5	18	22	14	17	17
(æh)	23.0	27.0	29.0	32.0		13	21	13	17	
(oh)	23.0	24.0	24.0	21.0		16	22	13	15	
(th)	78.0	65.0	43.5			18	22	13		
(dh)	78.5	56.0	49.0			17	22	13		

Class group 3–5

						N:				
(r)	04.0	12.5	21.0	35.0	55.0	26	28	26	27	26
(æh)	25.0	28.0	30.5	32.0		21	27	26	27	
(oh)	19.5	22.0	23.0	24.0		23	28	26	27	
(th)	68.0	53.5	27.0			15	28	26		
(dh)	63.5	44.5	34.0			22	28	26		

Class group 6–9

						N:				
(r)	12.5	25.0	29.0	55.5	70.0	21	30	29	29	29
(æh)	27.0	30.0	34.0	35.0		23	30	29	29	
(oh)	20.0	23.5	26.5	29.5		27	30	29	27	
(th)	25.5	16.5	10.0			23	30	29		
(dh)	29.5	16.5	13.0			27	30	29		

out-of-town informants, or includes them, will state this fact specifically: otherwise, only the New York City informants are considered in the discussion to follow.

Class 8 is extremely small in the New York sample, with only two informants. It will be treated here in every case along with class 7, as 7–8, since without exception, these two speakers show the same pattern of linguistic behavior as the nine speakers of class 7, rather than the 14 members of class 9.

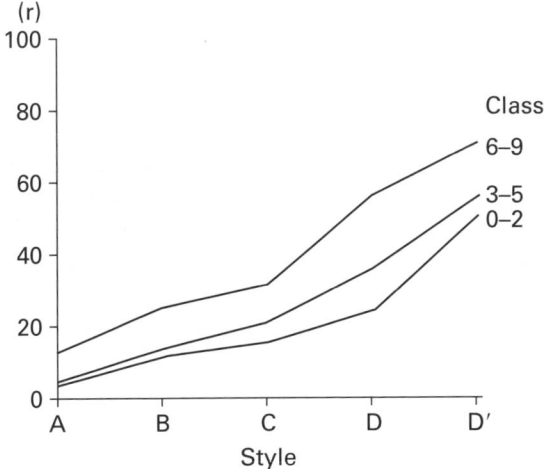

Figure 7.1   Class stratification of (r)

Class stratification of the five variables

As a first step in the study of class distribution of the variables, we will simply follow the original division into three roughly equal parts of the scale: 0–2, 3–5, and 6–9. These total 23, 28, and 30 informants respectively. If the original view of the social variation of these variables is correct, we should find clear-cut separation of these three groups. Later, we may refine our view by dividing the continuum in other ways, but this first step will give us a base.

Table 7.8 gives the values for the array of the five variables for three class groups, following the arrangement used in Chapter 4. Figures 7.1 through 7.5 show the type of graphic display which we will use for studying class stratification. In these diagrams, the vertical axis is the phonological index, and the horizontal axis shows the stylistic levels which are utilized for that variable. The values for each class group are plotted on the diagram and connected along horizontal lines. This type of figure will be called a *class stratification diagram*.

These diagrams show both stylistic stratification and class stratification. The uniform direction of the lines, with steadily changing values as we progress from left to right, show a stratification of styles on the axis of informal to formal. The separation of the class strata is shown by the separation of the 0–2, 3–5, and 6–9 lines.

In Figure 7.1, we see a steady rise in the use of (r) with increasingly formal styles. This relation holds for all fifteen points on the diagram.

Similarly, at each style the three class strata are differentiated. It may be seen that values for the use of (r) start at a very low point for casual speech. This reflects the basically *r*-less pattern of the language of the streets which we have noted in the exploratory interviews. Only the middle class 6–9 shows any degree of (r-1) pronunciation at this level. The rise of (r) indexes is quite steady through Style C; these first three styles are the only ones which represent connected speech. The sharp upturn of the 6–9 group for Style D, and a similar upturn for the others at D′, shows habits in the pronunciation of individual words which are not characteristic of connected speech.

Figure 7.2 shows a relatively fine separation of the three strata, with the lower class and working class reaching the same point for Style D. The gap between the middle class and the rest is widened in this reading of word lists, just as in Figure 7.1 for (r). The regular progression of values indicates a shift from the high, close vowel of (æh-2) towards the lower, open vowel of (æh-4).[8]

Figure 7.3 is altogether different from these two. Whereas the 3–5 line and the 6–9 line show separation along the same lines as in the (æh) diagram, the lower class line starts on the lower side, and crosses the diagram with no apparent direction, ending at a relatively high point. This situation is best viewed in a different type of diagram, such as the one shown in Figure 7.6 for the same (oh) data. Here the vertical axis shows the (oh) index, as before, but the horizontal axis is occupied by the three class groups. On the diagram, the values for each stylistic level are plotted and connected along straight lines. This type of figure will be termed hereafter a *style stratification diagram*.

Figure 7.6 shows us that the (oh) pattern is essentially curvilinear for the three class groups. The highest vowels are those of the working class, and the two extreme groups both use lower vowels. Furthermore, we see a regular pattern of stylistic stratification for the working class and middle class, but no such pattern for the lower class. Thus the pattern for (oh) differs from (æh) in three respects:

a)   The highest vowels are shown by the working class, not the lower class.
b)   The lower class shows no pattern of stylistic variation.
c)   The differentiation of middle class from working class increases rapidly in Styles B through D.

---

[8] In all diagrams for (æh) and (oh), the scale of the phonological index runs from *40* at the bottom to *10* at the top. Thus low values of the variables appear at the top of the diagrams, and high values at the bottom. This arrangement reflects the fact that (æh-10) and (oh-10) are vowels with *high* tongue position, and (æh-40) and (oh-40) vowels with *low* tongue position. Low (æh) and (oh) values correspond to high vowels, and high (æh) and (oh) values correspond to low vowels.

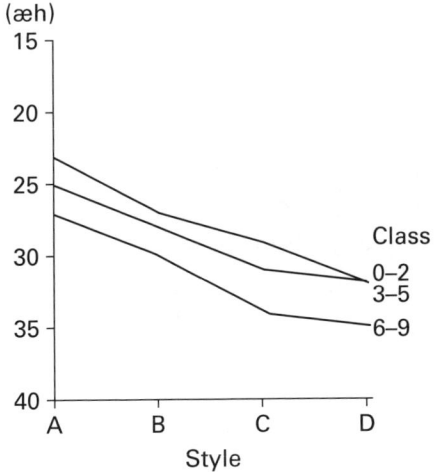

Figure 7.2   Class stratification of (æh)

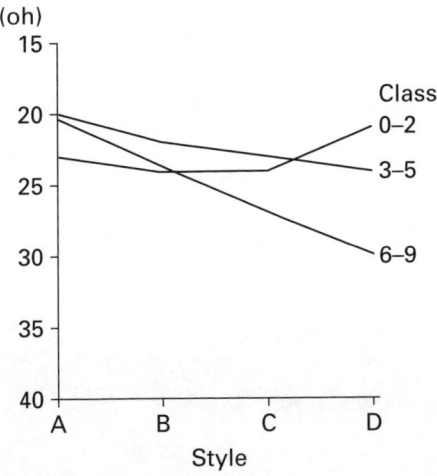

Figure 7.3   Class stratification of (oh)

Figures 7.4 and 7.5 are the class stratification diagrams for (th) and (dh). Here we see a regular separation of the three class groups and the three stylistic levels. Furthermore, the spacing of the three class groups remains relatively constant, through the three styles, as compared to the situation shown in Figures 7.1 to 7.3. It would be too soon to connect this fact to the

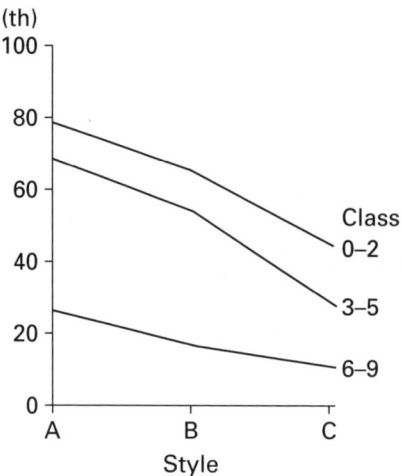

Figure 7.4   Class stratification of (th)

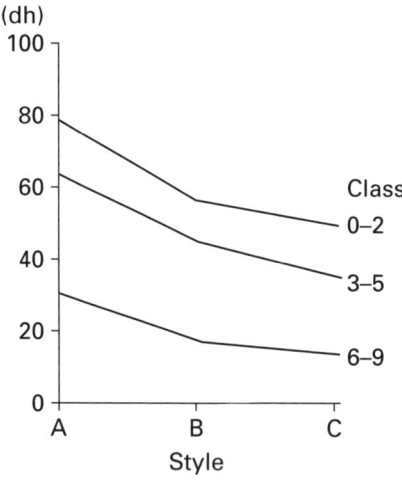

Figure 7.5   Class stratification of (dh)

stability of the (th)-(dh) pattern in respect to linguistic change, but this possibility may be investigated by a number of other routes to confirm the suggestion seen here.

In these six diagrams, the basic outlines of social differentiation are established. The first hints of the exploratory interviews, the marked regularities

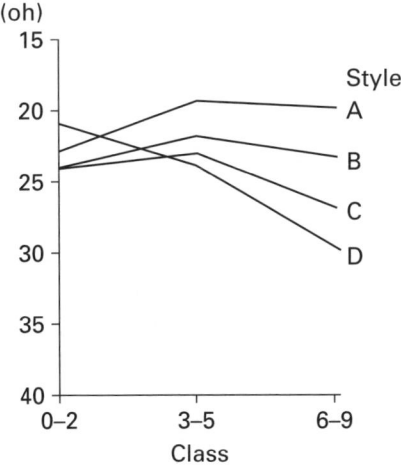

Figure 7.6   Style stratification of (oh)

of the stylistic investigation, here culminate in a clear demonstration of a stylistic-social structure. Given ten to twenty utterances of a speaker in several stylistic levels, we find a regular progression of the variables; when this speaker is placed with ten or twenty others of the same social class, the combined values of the variables fall into a relatively fixed position in this structure. This restriction on the possible values of an averaged variable may be illustrated by examining the working class value for (dh), Style B, in Figure 7.5. It must lie somewhere between (dh)-64 and (dh)-34 if the structure of stylistic variation is to be preserved, and between (dh)-56 and (dh)-17 if the structure of class variation is to be preserved. The actual value is (dh)-45.

There are a number of open questions which remain. First, the divergence of the 0–2 group in Figure 7.3 must be accounted for, especially as compared with the convergence of 0–2 and 3–5 in Figure 7.2. Second, we must ask whether the divisions into 0–2, 3–5, and 6–9 represent natural cutting points of the scale of class as far as language is concerned. Will some other division show clearer stratification, or is this the most effective in that respect? Third, we would like to follow up the suggestion stemming from the differences in the behavior of the middle class 6–9 in Figures 7.1–7.3 as against Figures 7.4–7.5.

These questions are all connected, and may be studied here, by closer examination of the data. First, we may wish to consider whether the cross-overs shown in Figure 7.3 would be resolved by any different arrangement of the classes. For example, there are a number of divisions of the class continuum which will show good stratification for (r), (æh), but not (dh). If we cut 0–1, 2–5, 6–9, we will see a cross-over in the (dh) diagram: the 0–1 line will come down below the 2–5 line at Style B, and then cross back up again, as in Figure 7.7. In this case, we might have concluded that the (dh) variable divided the community into only two distinct strata, instead of three. Such a conclusion would be unjustified, however, because it was produced by a division of classes that was quite arbitrary, and a different division shows a higher degree of structural organization in the complex of social and stylistic variation. We may call such a deviation as that shown in Figure 7.7, an *apparent deviation*. In the course of working with the data, a good many apparent deviations from class and stylistic variation may occur. Some are due to mechanical errors; some to the presence of marginal informants who do not fit the pattern; some to the division of the class continuum. All of these can be resolved into the regular pattern of stratification shown in Figures 7.1, 7.2, 7.4, and 7.5.

However, no re-division of the data, no re-shuffling of informants will resolve the deviation shown in Figure 7.3. For example, Figure 7.8 shows the class stratification of the (oh) variable with the class groups 0–1, 2–5, 6–9. The situation remains the same, because this behavior is characteristic of the core classes, 0–1, 3–4, and 6–8. We may call such a deviation from regular structure a *real deviation*.

Real deviations from regular structure can often be the source of new theoretical gains. We may note that Figure 7.3 is a case of a double deviation. Not only does the 0–2 group deviate from class stratification, but it also deviates from stylistic stratification. It is oriented neither towards the class structure nor the stylistic structure. We may therefore infer that for lower class speakers, (oh) is not a phonological variable as (æh) is. These informants are seemingly immune to the various pressures towards stratification of (oh). We will be able to examine this suggestion more closely below, but first we may follow up the idea inherent in the fact that the only real deviation in this series is a double deviation. The combined evidence in the study thus far leads to the following general hypothesis:

For the phonological variables, real deviations from class stratification are consistently and reciprocally associated with real deviations from stylistic stratification.

The implication of this hypothesis is that the factors which produce both types of stratification are the same. This is not an obvious fact. There is no reason, on the face of it, for the lower class not to use high, close (oh) vowels, higher than the working class, and yet show no stylistic stratification. Nor is

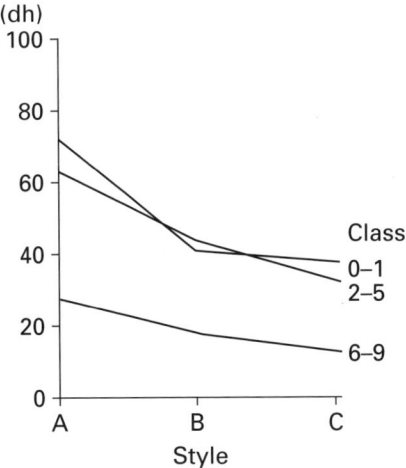

Figure 7.7   Apparent deviation from class stratification of (dh) with alternate grouping of classes

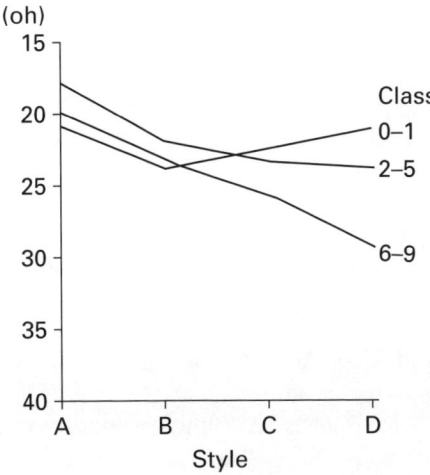

Figure 7.8   Real deviation from class stratification of (oh) with alternate grouping of classes

there any reason, on the face of it, why the lower class could not use intermediate values of (oh), and yet preserve stylistic variation.

We have seen that (oh) does not behave like a socially significant variable for the lower class, that it neither marks them nor stigmatizes them.

In Chapter 9 we will study the evidence for linguistic change in the distribution and social significance of (oh); the present position of the lower class in regard to (oh) will be seen as characteristic of an early stage of change from below.

[There is a fair amount of discussion here of "regular structure" and "real deviations." It hasn't aged well, and five following pages of the first edition are deleted. Yet the ideas are used to find out some very interesting properties of (æh) and (oh). But the very clear delineation of sharp vs. fine stratification has survived well, and the following discussion has been echoed in many succeeding publications.]

The possible relations of class to language

At this point, we might ask whether we have any theoretical reason to suppose that all of the cutting points for all of the variables would fall along the same lines. This depends upon our view of the possible relations between class and language. If we think of class as a rigid series of categories, in which the marginal cases are rare or insignificant, then a proof of class correlation with language would require equally discrete categories of linguistic behavior (in our terminology, *sharp stratification*). Language traits characteristic of AA and white groups in the United States, for example, would necessarily show a pattern with only two or three discrete categories. If, on the other hand, we think of class as a continuous network of social and economic factors, in which every case is marginal to the next one, we would expect that language would also show a continuous range of values, and the number of intermediate points of correlation would be limited only by the consistency and reliability of the data (in our terminology *fine stratification*). A correlation of smoking habits with death rates, for example, shows this matching of one continuum against the other.

It is clear that class and language relationships will be somewhere between these two extremes. The usual meaning of *class*, as opposed to *caste*, presupposes a degree of vagueness in boundary lines, and an amount of mobility which produces many marginal and mixed cases.[9] But though Michael refers to his objective class index as a continuum, he is aware of the fact that the social phenomenon he is trying to classify is not a continuum, but shows a certain degree of discrete structure. Hence his concern with a theoretical justification for cutting points. However, these considerations are admittedly weak ones, and the types of correlation used to justify

[9] See W. Lloyd Warner, *Social Class in America* (1960), page 20; John Dollard, *Caste and Class in a Southern Town* (1957), pages 61–63.

such cutting points are much weaker than the linguistic evidence we will introduce. In this chapter, the independent variable is treated as a continuum, which we will divide in several ways to show the clearest pattern of stratification for each variable. This may involve several reorganizations of the class groups shown above. From this procedure, we will gain on two theoretical grounds:

1) The linguistic variables which are most clearly stratified by the same divisions of the continuum may be understood as associated in the overall linguistic structure.
2) The cutting points where the linguistic evidence shows the greatest internal agreement will be indicated as the most natural divisions of the class continuum – to the extent that language is a measure of class behavior.

In such decisions, the evidence of Style B will be considered first, as the most stable measure with the maximum number of responses, and considerations from the other styles will be used as auxiliary information.[10]

The social structure of (r)

Though the information given by Figures 7.1–7.6 seems to be very substantial, there are a great many half-truths concealed in these simplified statements. One such half-truth is that (r) stratifies the population into three distinct class groups. In Figures 7.9 through 7.11 we present detailed evidence to show that (r) shows fine stratification: it differentiates the New York community into a great many strata. In fact, the resolution of the population into intermediate classes is so fine that we seem to be approaching the model of the continuum suggested above as a limiting case.

Figure 7.9 is a style stratification diagram which shows the data for all nine classes for each of the five styles (Classes 7 and 8 are always grouped together). The fine breakdown will be used in each for a preliminary view of the distribution of the linguistic facts: it is assumed that the individual classes are too small to show regular stratification in every case, and our aim will be to divide the class scale: 1) into more groups than the three shown in Figures 7.1–7.5; and 2) at the most natural divisions in the linguistic pattern. Since we have between three and five stylistic levels, it is assumed that the same amount of data will be able to discriminate three to five class strata.

---

[10] See Table 7.8 and the frequencies for the various styles. These frequencies represent the number of speakers represented in the average. Style B is regularly the highest, and Style A is the least reliable in this respect, especially for the 0–2 group.

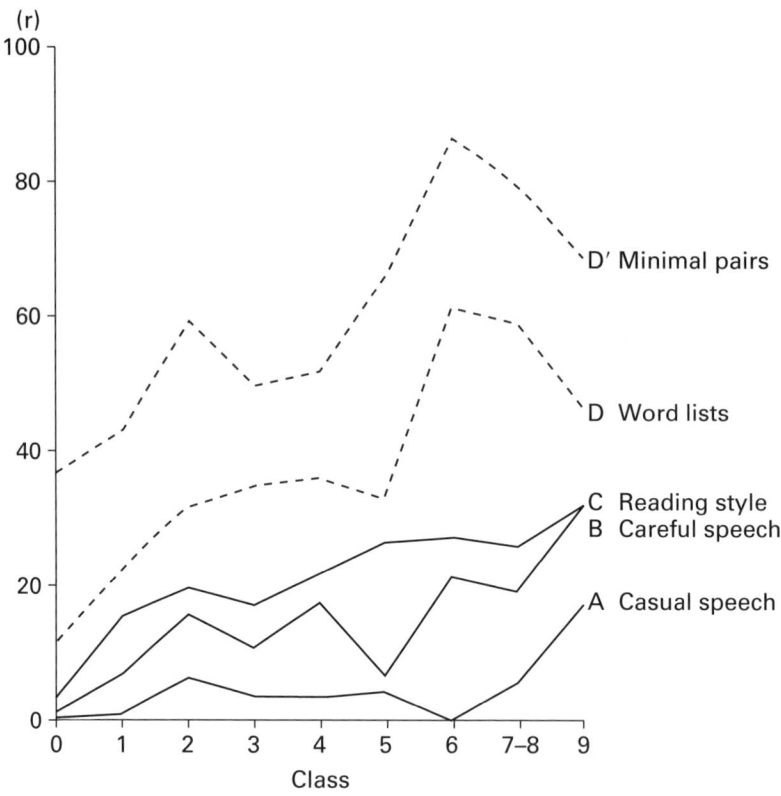

Figure 7.9   Detailed style stratification of (r): nine classes

The fluctuations in Figure 7.9 are small: except for a slight high point for the marginal class 2, and a dip for the marginal, low-frequency 5, we see smooth progressions upward from zero almost to 90. We do note that there is a sharp decline from this high point to class 9, but as we shall see, this decline is itself a recurrent deviation.[11]

This smooth progression indicates that we can cut at many points along the class continuum, and obtain good stratification. Figure 7.10 shows a second style stratification diagram for (r) in which the class continuum has been simplified only slightly, to six points instead of nine. Now the progression departs from regular structure only in the downturn for Styles D and D′, which we will see below is recurrent. The grouping of the social classes

---

[11] This deviation from regular structure will appear as a cross-over pattern in style stratification diagrams, and will recur for variables (æh), and (oh) below.

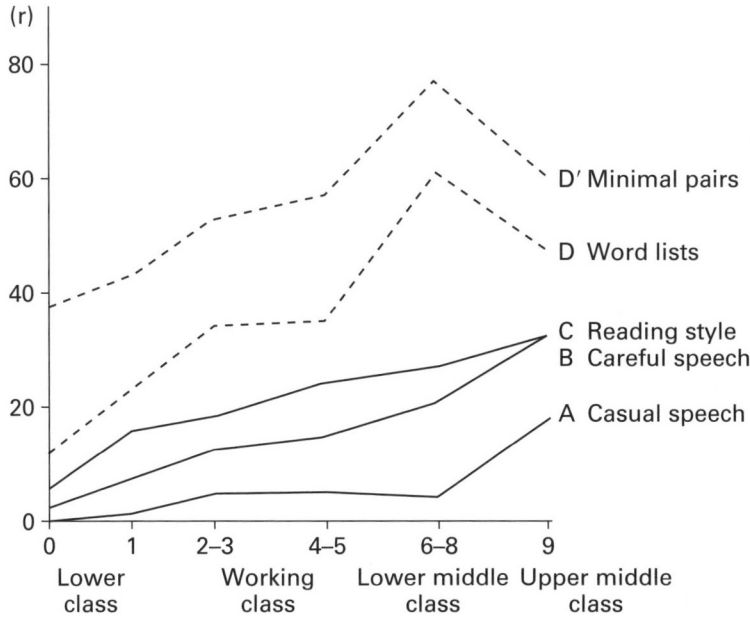

Figure 7.10   Simplified style stratification of (r): six class groups

actually conforms closely to the division made by Michael, following Kahl.[12]

In Figure 7.10, we see that the lowest line, that for Style A, runs very close to zero until class 9 is reached. On the other hand, as the formality of the styles increases, we find that the discrepancy between 9 and the other classes decreases. Finally, for Style D', the lower middle class is much higher in (r) index than the upper middle class.

We can now see the social stratification of (r) more clearly if we look at the class stratification diagram of Figure 7.11. Here the six strata run parallel to each other in a very fine structure of stylistic and social stratification. There is one cross-over in the pattern: the sudden upward jump of the 6–8 class, which goes beyond the class 9 line for Styles D and D'.

[The cross-over pattern, recognized here for the first time in New York City, has appeared quite often as a general characteristic of a second-highest status group. Over and over again, we see that in the most

---

[12] Whenever a grouping of the classes places one of the classes for which 100 percent of the sample was studied together with a class for which 67 percent was studied, the averages are weighted accordingly. This is the case in the present example for the group 2–3.

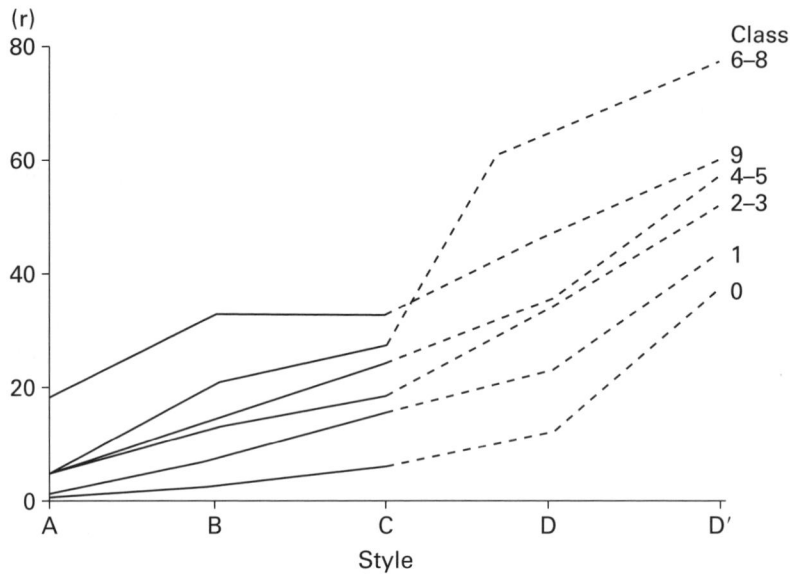

Figure 7.11   Re-defined class stratification of (r): six class groups

formal styles, this group over-shoots the mark of the highest status group. In fact, this quantitative type of "hypercorrection" may be related to one of the fundamental driving forces in linguistic change (see Labov 1966b).]

In all of these diagrams, the lines leading to Style D and D' are shown dotted, to indicate that these values do not represent connected speech. Instead, they may be thought of as a kind of *phonic intention*, illustrating the norms of the speaker, in part, rather than a reliable indication of performance.

At the extreme left of Figure 7.11, we see that most of the strata are grouped very near to the zero index for (r). The lowest group, class 0, never uses any (r-1) in casual speech, the others practically none. Group 9, on the other hand, shows an (r) index of 18, averaging one out of every five vowels with (r-1). This is a very noticeable amount, enough to distinguish class 9 speech in everyday life. This figure covers groups with very opposite tendencies: in the discussion of differentiation through age groups we will find that (r-1) has become even more of a marker of upper middle class speech for younger speakers than for older ones.

This left hand edge of Figure 7.11 confirms the impressions of everyday life in New York City. Since the upper middle class speakers are few in number, and do not talk loudly in public places, we might conclude that New York is completely (r)-less in casual speech. But close attention to casual speech in such surroundings will reveal the pattern seen here.

Appendix B presents some brief examples of casual speech collected anonymously on the Lower East Side. The material on (r) in the lunch counter episode may be studied for comparison with Figure 7.11.

In Figure 7.11, we see that the behavior of lower middle class and upper middle class is almost totally opposed. The lower middle class uses no more (r-1) in casual speech than the great majority of New Yorkers. In careful speech and reading style, it follows the same gradual increment in (r) index as classes 0–5, but at a higher level. The sudden upward jump for isolated words carries the lower middle class from a low of (r)-04 to a high of (r)-78. We may contrast this type of hypercorrection with the relatively steady pattern followed by the upper middle class. Starting at a moderate value of (r) index in casual speech, there is a slight increase to reading style and careful speech, and then a less extreme rise for isolated words.

We may note that the working class groups are not immune from the sudden increase in Style D′: the direction of class 5 echoes the more extreme example of class 6.

The disparity between intention and performance is one of the significant themes which will appear in many parts of this study. Without studying the evidence from schools or mass media, or even comparing the usage of various classes, we may interpret the sudden jump upward between Style C and D as an indication of the social prestige of (r-1). In other words, both axes of variation reflect the establishment of a prestige feature. Along the axis of stylistic variation, we see the use of (r-1) penetrating the habits of an individual; along the axis of social variation, we see it penetrating the population as a whole.

In summary, the following features of the social distribution of (r) appear in Figure 7.11 which were not seen in Figure 7.1:

1) (r) shows fine stratification: the use of (r-1) differentiates the class continuum into at least six groups, and there is no sign of a sharp break in behavior between classes 0–8.

2) The middle class group 6–9 is not a coherent unit with respect to (r); it is differentiated into a lower middle class which uses little (r-1) in casual speech, but a maximum amount in the most formal styles, and an upper middle class group which is the only class to use a significant amount of (r-1) in casual speech.

3) The lower middle class shows a crossing of class lines between Styles C and D. This appears to be a real deviation from regular structure as long as class 6 is differentiated from class 9.

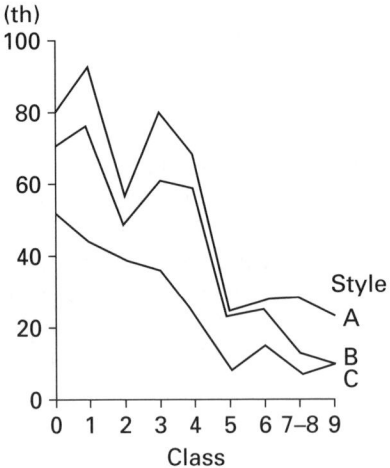

Figure 7.12   Detailed style stratification of (th): nine classes

The social structure of (th) *and* (dh)

We will now turn to a completely opposite type of linguistic variable. Whereas (r-1) is a feature of a new prestige pronunciation, (th-3) and (dh-3) are long-established signals of a stigmatized speech pattern. (Chapter 11 will establish this point in detail.)

In Figures 7.12 and 7.13, we see style stratification diagrams for (th) and (dh), where the data for all nine classes is shown at three stylistic levels. The two diagrams have much in common, but differ in some important respects.

The (th) variable shows a very steep decline from the high point set by class 1 in Style A: (th)-96. The marginal class 2 shows a much lower value than the general shape of the curve suggested, at least in Styles A and B. Style C shows a much smoother progression.

The fluctuation which we see here in the lower class section is typical of many which will be found throughout the present chapter. There are many complex causes for this uneven behavior which will be examined further when we come to social evaluation. For (dh), the pattern of the lower class is almost reversed, with the marginal group 2 showing a peak rather than a valley, and class 0 and 1 falling behind the working classes 3–4.

Both variables share a sudden drop for the small group 5, and we see an extreme difference between classes 4 and 5 which could hardly be greater. Since class 5 is small, we cannot treat this point too closely; for the moment, we can say that this group of speakers behaves very differently in regard to

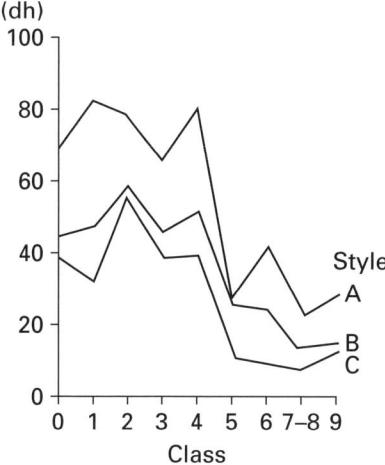

Figure 7.13   Detailed style stratification of (dh): nine classes

these variables as compared to (r). It is difficult to avoid placing them with the lower middle class.

The overall view which we derive from Figures 7.12 and 7.13 is summed in the class stratification diagrams of Figures 7.14 and 7.15. Here we see the class continuum divided into four groups for (th) and three for (dh), both examples of regular structure.

We are under no obligation to treat each variable in the same way; there is no reason to assume that each is affected by the class structure to the same extent, or that stigmatized values of each variable are rejected by the various classes to the same degree. However, it is reasonable to proceed on the assumption that the cutting points for each variable will be the same, until the fact of distribution clearly contradicts this assumption. In the case of (th) and (dh), which are paired in their articulation as well as in their history, we need especially good reason to use different cutting points for the social continuum.

The discrepancy between (th) and (dh) cutting points is justified as we examine the fluctuations of Figure 7.13; there is no point between class 0 and 4 where it would be reasonable to divide working class from lower class. Whereas it is possible to make a sharp distinction between 0–1 and 2–4 for (th), yielding even better stratification than for the original Figure 7.4, this is not possible in the case of (dh). We now see that the solution of Figure 7.5, cutting 0–2, 3–5, 6–9 was really quite artificial. By placing the 5 class with 3–4, the average values of these classes brought them below the 0–2 level. But from Figure 7.14, it is quite evident that class 5 falls with the lower

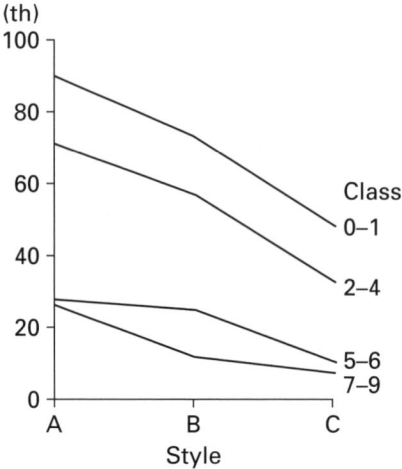

Figure 7.14   Re-defined class stratification of (th): four class groups

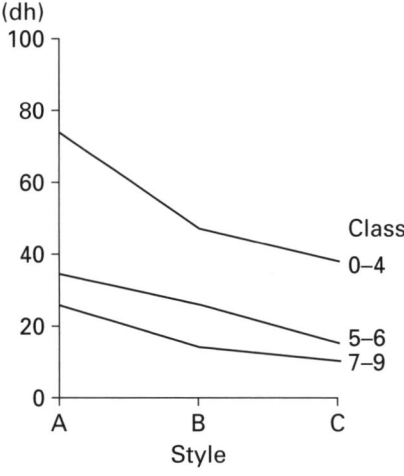

Figure 7.15   Re-defined class stratification of (dh): three class groups

middle class. The great gap between working class and lower middle class in the use of (dh) is obscured by the original Figure 7.5; in the present Figure 7.15, this gap is quite plainly shown.

The comparison of (th) and (dh) illustrates the fact that a stop consonant used as the initial sound of *think* and *thing* is characteristic of lower class speakers much more than working class speakers. These words often occur in stressed position. However, the use of stops and affricates in words such as *then* and *the*, which use (dh) in unstressed position, is a characteristic of both working class and lower class. That is not to say that the whole body of speakers from class 0 to class 4 is uniform: there are other ways of differentiating these 46 speakers. But class stratification of (dh) does not discriminate among them. (In Chapter 8, we will discuss a method of analyzing this large group through a combination of occupational and educational rank.)

We see that unlike (r), these two variables do not space the strata evenly. The (th) variable, which shows four strata, groups them two and two. On the other hand, there are no sharp deviations from the overall pattern of class stratification, such as we saw in the (r) diagram. Most of the strata continue along fairly straight lines. Thus we have *regular, sharp stratification.*

This may be a reflection of the comparative stability of the (th) and (dh) distribution, as mentioned before. However, it is somewhat surprising to find that there are not more strata in this picture. We have only found one more division for (th), and no more for (dh). It is particularly surprising to find no difference between the lower middle class 7–8, and the upper middle class 9, which was so clearly differentiated in the case of (r). The reason for this anomaly lies in a single deviant case: from a close examination of this case, we may learn a great deal more about social stratification of language.

The deviant case of Nathan B.

[Many aspects of the NYC study influenced linguists' later work, but one aspect did not. There are no people in most of the sociolinguistic studies that followed – just means, charts, and trends. Although I have campaigned to bring people back into the field of sociolinguistics there has been only a limited response on this front. This book has already included quite a few people in Chapter 4, like Steve K., Josephine P. and Martha S. The person cited most often from this volume is Nathan B., whose inability to control (th) and (dh) is the topic that follows. The case of Nathan B. illustrates the fundamental Durkheimian notion of a social fact: we are free to talk in any way we want, but there will be social consequences if we depart too strongly from the norms. Beyond that, Labov 1966 demonstrated that the case of Nathan B. was effectively masking the fineness of social stratification, and once he was set aside, the pattern appears far more regular.

Table 7.9   *Values of the NYC variables for Nathan B.*

	Styles					No. of tokens				
	A	B	C	D	D'					
(r)	03	09	12	23	42	35	55	48	26	12
(æh)	35	37	40	38		4	19	25	13	
(oh)	29	27	28	25		14	19	17	11	
(th)	88	93	88			18	38	24		
(dh)	107	89	114			67	103	42		

In general, trying to explain exceptional cases is a dangerous procedure, unless we put the same effort into studying unexceptional cases. Nevertheless, this use of an individual case paid off. The Philadelphia study (Labov 2001) devotes a whole chapter to the characterization of individual leaders of linguistic change. There it is not the exceptional but the prototypical individuals who are in focus. For other memorable characters in the sociolinguistic literature, see Reefer in Rickford 1979, and the leaders in the palatalization of /t/ and /d/ in Cairo (Haeri 1996).]

The class 9 informant we will now consider is a life-long native of the Lower East Side. There is nothing marginal about his demographic characteristics: his parents were Russian and Polish Jews who came to New York City well before he was born. He grew up on the Lower East Side, played with boys from the neighborhood, and went to school there. He completed college by attending evening school, and went on to obtain a Ph.D. in political science. He is married, and lives in the high rent cooperative apartments where many of the other upper middle class informants are to be found. At forty years old, he has published several books on Jewish political history, and though he works in local government to some extent, his principal occupation is writing and research.

From the first few words that Nathan B. spoke, it was obvious that he used an extraordinarily high percentage of stops for (th) and (dh). He commented on this himself at the very beginning: "I have a speech problem with *th*'s."

The indexes for his speech are shown in Table 7.9.

The indexes for the first three variables are not uncharacteristic of other New Yorkers of his age and class background. However, the very high values of (th) and (dh) are matched only by some lower class or working class speakers. The frequencies are more than enough to substantiate the (th) and (dh) values in all three styles. What is most remarkable is that the values do not fall: they are essentially constant despite the strenuous efforts of the speaker to pronounce fricatives.

In this case, we see a real deviation on the part of an individual, which answers the requirements of the hypothesis: class deviation is associated with stylistic deviation.

Nathan B.'s difficulty is not confined to speech production alone, but concerns phonemic perception as well. At one point in the interview, I asked him to pronounce the numbers from one to ten, and then asked where was the top of his tongue as he started to say *ten*. When he answered, I continued:

INTERVIEWER: And *den?*
NATHAN B.: Den. Den. I have trouble with *th*'s.

At another point in the interview, I asked a question about the feeling many people have that "whatever is going to happen is going to happen."[13]

INTERVIEWER: The word *fate* doesn't ring a bell with you?
NATHAN B.: It rings a very strong bell . . . I'm very proud of my Judaic heritage, and when you mentioned the word [feɪt], to me this means Judaism.
INTERVIEWER: I didn't . . . I don't . . . that would not have occurred to me originally . . .
NATHAN B.: [feːt] or [feːtʰ]?
INTERVIEWER: Not (feː θ).
NATHAN B.: F-A-I-T-H.
INTERVIEWER: F-A-T-E.
NATHAN B.: Oh, well, that's quite different. *Fate* in itself – I don't give it much thought (th-3).

A further element in this deviant pattern is that when Nathan B. tries very hard to say (th), aiming at the fricative, he often uses an /f/. (This is ranked as a (th-2) in the index.) This characteristic, while common post-vocalically among AA speakers, is otherwise rare among adult New York speakers. It appears to be a common trait of young children of four or five, who are still learning to pronounce (th).

We have now documented the deviant nature of Nathan B.'s behavior. The question is, how can such a speech pattern, whether it is physiologically or culturally conditioned, fit in with the situation of an upper middle class person? We can readily conceive of a lower class person getting along (in his later years) with a prestige style of speech, though he will be considered an eccentric by those who know him. Can the upper middle class accept such a linguistic eccentric as Nathan B.?

---

[13] This question on *fate* was appended to the Danger of Death question in some of the later interviews.

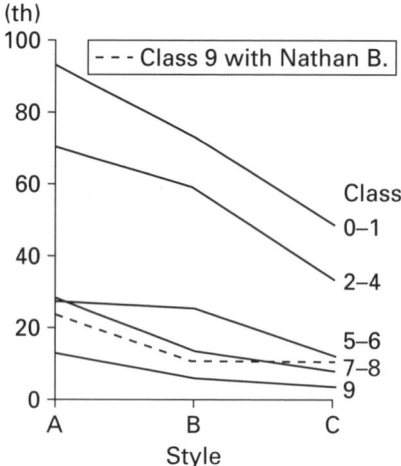

Figure 7.16   Class Stratification of (th) without Nathan B.: five class groups

The answer is that Nathan B. was not accepted. He has been rejected from the upper middle class role which would normally have been assigned to him. When he was attending college, it is said that he broke all academic records for evening students. He captained a debating team, but his written speech had to be delivered by another student. Several times in his college career he stubbornly refused to take speech courses, as he considered them unimportant to his main purpose. As he approached the award of the Ph.D. degree, he was considered a most eligible candidate for a teaching appointment at the university. A professor in the political science department had an informal conversation with him, in which he told Nathan B. that he had a promising future at the university, and that he would be glad to see him continue on the staff. However, he would have to take corrective courses to improve his speech. Nathan B. abruptly refused to do anything of the kind, and the academic world was closed to him. He continues, not unhappily, working in political science, but primarily as a writer and not as a speaker.

Whatever the reasons may be for Nathan B.'s eccentric behavior, it is evident that some sections of upper middle class society cannot tolerate a speaker who uses such a high percentage of socially stigmatized forms.[14]

---

[14] This is not a small section as far as we are concerned, for eight of the fourteen upper middle class informants in the ALS interviews are in academic work. From their subjective evaluation tests, reported in Chapter 11, it is evident that they too would have rejected Nathan B. as a member of that community.

Table 7.10   *Effect of Nathan B. values on class 9*

		A	B	C		A	B	C
Class 9 with Nathan B.	(th)	23	10	10	(dh)	29	15	14
Class 9 without Nathan B.		12	5	2		21	6	4

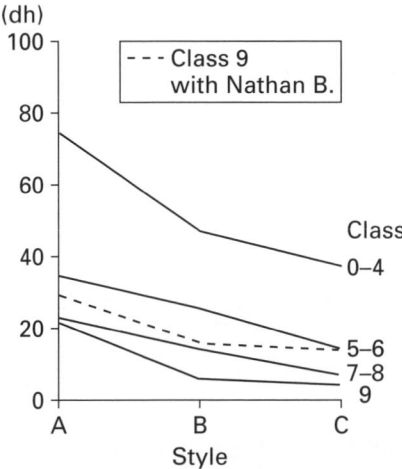

Figure 7.17   Class Stratification of (dh) without Nathan B.: four class groups

If we now re-examine the (th) and (dh) diagrams in this light, it becomes apparent that stratification is more precise than Figures 7.14 and 7.15 showed. Figures 7.16 and 7.17 separate class 9 from 7–8. The dotted line shows class 9 as it is measured with Nathan B.'s results included; the solid line shows class 9 at the much lower level which represents the usage of the other ten speakers in this group. The contrast may be emphasized by the figures in Table 7.10.

This discussion is not meant to indicate that the case of Nathan B. is unique; it is only logical to assume that if one of twelve upper middle class speakers in the sample was deviant in this way, then there must be dozens of such individuals in the population of 20,000. However, such deviant cases cannot perform all of the normal functions of upper middle class persons, and there are sanctions imposed upon those who deviate greatly from the norm represented by the solid line in Figures 7.16 and 7.17. This is the upper middle class stratum which society recognizes.

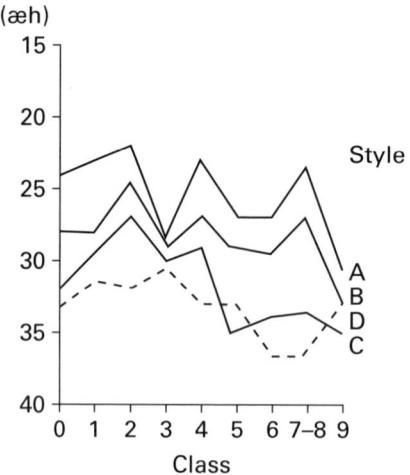

Figure 7.18   Detailed style stratification of (æh): nine classes

The social structure of (æh)

The initial view of the (æh) variable, in Figure 7.2, was quite clear. This simple view was an illusion, however, for Figure 7.18 shows a great deal of irregular fluctuation in this variable. The general overall trend is recognizable as the gradual downward movement which we saw in Figure 7.2, but the regularity in the style stratification diagram of (r) is missing. There are alternate rises and falls, with the successive peaks and valleys following the direction of the variable as we saw it originally.

The structure of stylistic stratification seems fairly well preserved, for lower class as well as middle class. There are two crossing points: for class 5 as well as class 9, Style D has crossed Style C. In the case of class 5, we have become accustomed to such fluctuations; we do not expect regularity from this small unit. In the case of class 9, however, we must accept this crossover as part of the pattern for the moment. Whether or not it is a real deviation remains to be seen.

When we examine Figure 7.18 for any opportunity for finer stratification, as compared to Figure 7.2, the only possibility lies in the separation of lower middle class, 6–8, from upper middle, 9. Figure 7.19 is the class stratification diagram which shows the results of this division. The lower middle class starts at a high point, above the working class, and cuts sharply downward to the extreme low point of (æh)-36.5. It cuts across the upper class between Style C and D, just as we observed in the case of (r).

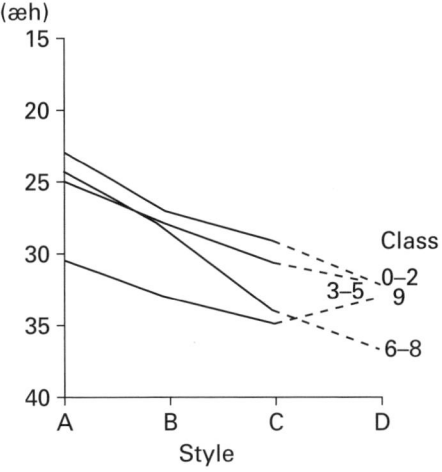

Figure 7.19   Re-defined class stratification of (æh): four class groups

Thus there are a number of questions about (æh) which must be answered:
1) Why is there such irregular fluctuation along the axis of class variation?
2) Why does the lower middle class group cut across two other class lines?
3) Why does the upper middle class value reverse direction for Style D?

The first question can only be answered by the distributional analysis of Chapter 8. Before approaching the other two questions, it will be useful to look at (oh).

The social structure of (oh)

The style stratification diagram of Figure 7.20 is quite different from anything which we have seen before. Despite some apparent confusion, it seems to fall naturally into four sections. For classes 0–2, there is no clear structure of stylistic stratification, and no structure of class stratification. The chaotic situation seen there confirms the earlier impression that this variable does not have social significance for the lower classes. With the working class, 3–5, we see the beginning of a structure. Style A rises to a maximum for class 4; Styles B, C and D fall below this, but are not clearly distinct. The marginal class 5 is the first to show the four styles in their normal order, leading to the very different pattern for the lower middle class. The (oh) values for Style A are just as high as for the working class; but the other styles show a sudden increase in the range of stylistic variation.

Once again, we see that the upper middle class is more moderate in stylistic range than the lower middle class. Styles A, B, and C are considerably

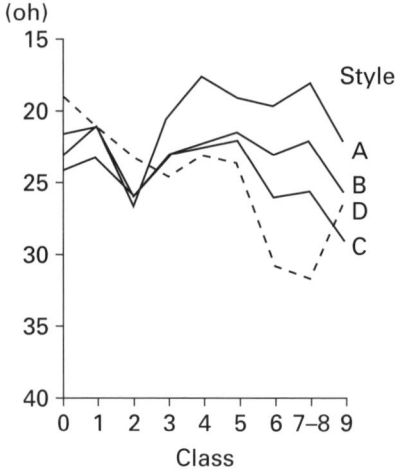

Figure 7.20   Detailed style stratification of (oh): nine class groups

lower than for the 6–8 group, and here too we find a stylistic cross-over, with Style D between B and C.

The parallel between the (æh) and the (oh) variables is carried further by the class stratification diagram of Figure 7.21. Because the lower class does not enter into this structure, it is not shown here. Once again, we find the lower middle class starting above the working class, and ending well below all other class groups. The only difference between the structure of Figure 7.21 and that of Figure 7.19, is that the lower class is missing in the latter diagram.

The pattern shown by (oh) is a clear example of a curvilinear distribution, with the two center classes leading. Whether the high values of (oh) in casual speech were first developed in the working class, or the lower middle class, or both, we see them at a position well beyond the (oh)-20 mark. Unlike the variable (æh), the (oh) variable is not recognized as socially significant by all sections of society. Comparing Figures 7.18 and 7.20, it is clear that the lower class and working class speakers are perfectly capable of following a regular pattern of stylistic variation for (æh) – but have apparently not instituted such a regular pattern for (oh).

We have now observed three cases where the lower middle class has shown a cross-over pattern. For (r), only the upper middle class line was crossed. For (æh), both working class and upper middle class lines were crossed. Finally, for (oh), the lower middle class lines ran the full gamut, from the very highest point on the graph to the very lowest.

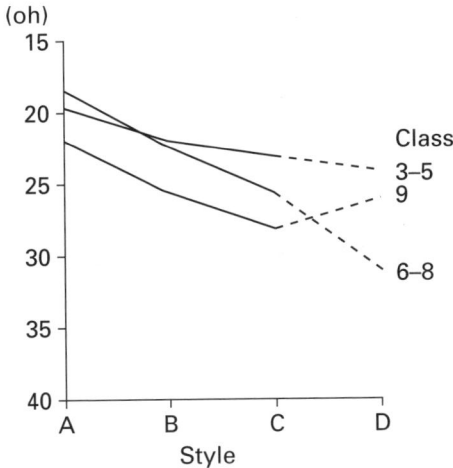

Figure 7.21   Re-defined class stratification of (oh) without lower class

Two aspects of the (oh) distribution suggest a process of linguistic change in progress: the exclusion of the lower class from the pattern of social and stylistic variation, and the hypercorrect behavior of the lower middle class. This aspect of (oh) distribution will be examined carefully in Chapter 9. The cross-over is also a sign of linguistic insecurity, as indicated in the index of linguistic insecurity discussed at the conclusion of Chapter 11. Neither of these factors would be apt to show up strongly in a long-established pattern of social stratification which was not subject to change. It is not surprising, then, that we have found the cross-over only for (r), (æh), and (oh), but not for the (th) and (dh) variables. The latter variables were originally introduced into our study primarily because they were considered likely to show a stable pattern, one not involved in the linguistic changes of the other variables.

This reasoning has a flaw, however. The cross-over we are primarily interested in is to be found between Styles C and D. Yet (th) and (dh) have only Styles A, B, and C. No word list was presented for these variables. It is possible that the lower middle class would show a sudden downturn for (th) and (dh) if we had data for Style D. The interpretation of the cross-over as a synchronic sign of linguistic change rests upon further proof in Style D.

Fortunately, there is enough data on (th) to resolve the question. In the (æh) word list, we find *bath*; in the days of the week, there is *Thursday*; in the numbers from one to ten, there is *three*. With these three items, we can build an index for (th) in Style D; the number of items is only a little less than that used for (r) in D′.

Table 7.11   *Distribution of* (th-2) *and* (th-3) *in style D by class*

	SEC								
Class	0	1	2	3	4	5	6	7–8	9
No. of informants	7	7	9	13	10	5	8	11	11
No. using stops or affricates	3	3	2	5	1	0	1	1	0

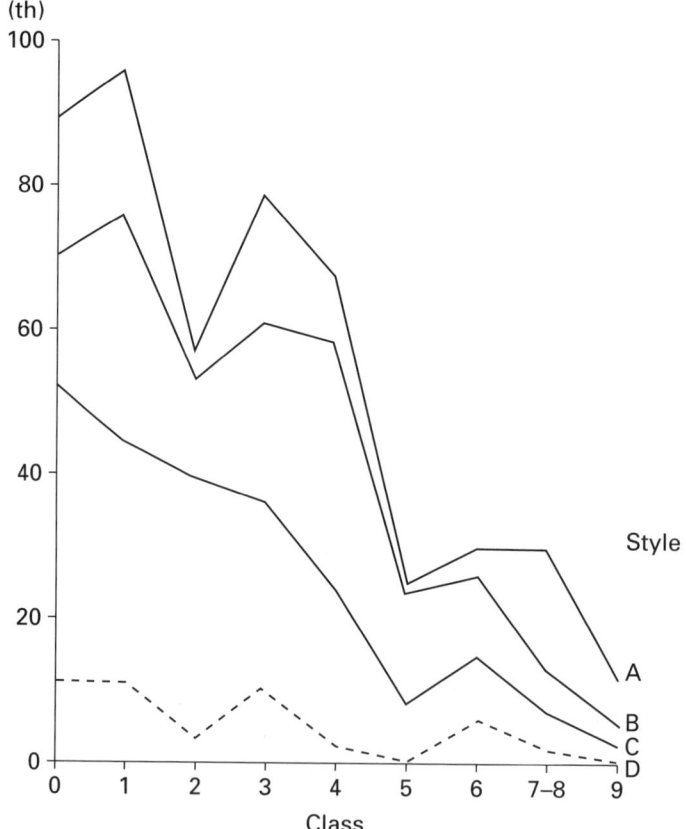

Figure 7.22   Addition of Style D to style stratification of (th)

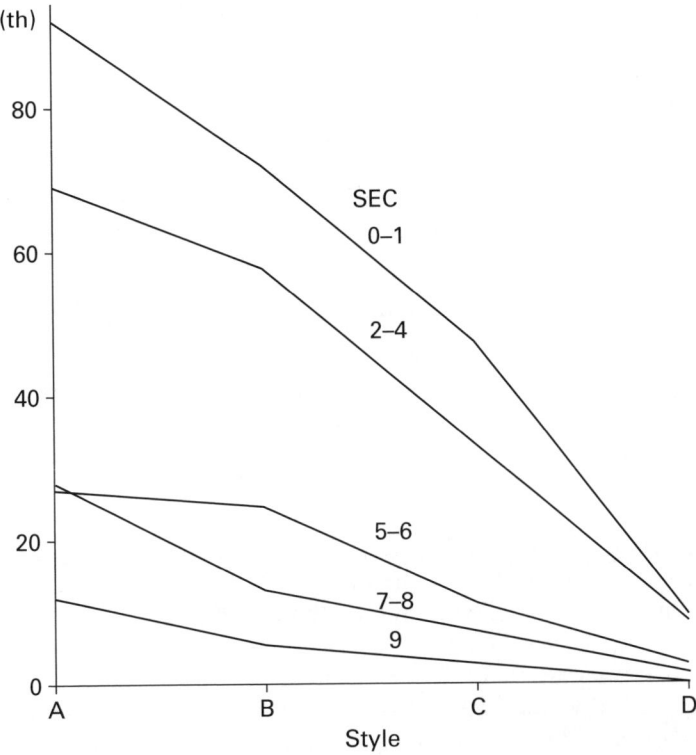

Figure 7.23   Addition of Style D to class stratification of (th)

The numbers of individuals who used either stops or affricates in the three words listed are shown in Table 7.11.

In Figure 7.22, the information for all nine classes is entered on a style stratification diagram, along with the other three stylistic levels. It is satisfying to note that the fluctuations in the Style D line match the irregularities of the other styles quite closely. The economical index for (th)-D has apparently measured the behavior of the informants with some accuracy.

Figure 7.23 shows the Style D information added to the class stratification diagram. We find that the values for Style D are extended along straight lines for most of the cases. We can therefore say that the middle classes 5–6 and 7–8 show no hypercorrect behavior, nor any tendency to simulate the cross-over pattern of (æh), (oh), and (r).

We can therefore say with some confidence that the cross-over pattern of the lower middle class is a synchronic sign of a linguistic change in progress.

[It's not hard to see why two diagrams have been extracted from this book over and over: Figure 7.11 for (r) and Figure 7.23 for (th). They show an astonishing degree of regularity – especially when we recognize that the cross-over pattern of (r) is part of a repeating and predictable pattern. The distinction between stable variables and variables involved in change in progress – just by the pattern itself – is a basic and recurrent theme. The discussion also touched on the distinction between change from above and change from below, which will become an even more important issue.]

The hypothesis of real deviation

We now have the data required to re-assess the hypothesis raised earlier in this chapter: that real deviations from a regular structure of class stratification are consistently and reciprocally associated with real deviations from a regular structure of stylistic stratification. Does the evidence support this hypothesis?

In Figure 7.20, the double deviation of the lower class from the regular structure for (oh) was shown even more clearly than in Figures 7.3 and 7.6. We also saw an illustration of a double deviation on the part of an individual, Nathan B., for (th) and (dh).

On the other hand, we now have three examples of a lower middle class cross-over, in Figures 7.11, 7.19, and 7.21, and two examples of a reversal of stylistic progression for class 9, Figures 7.19 and 7.21. We might defend the hypothesis by claiming that Figures 7.19 and 7.21 show double deviation of the upper middle class 9, but this is a desperate expedient. It is the lower middle class which deviates from the others on these diagrams, cutting several class lines.

The repetition of the deviation is seen in Figures 7.11, 7.19, and 7.21; what then is the set which includes these three structures? It is the homogeneous set formed by the operation of selecting all variables which show linguistic change in progress.

There is a circularity in the argument here, for we used the repetition of the pattern to assert the change in progress. Therefore the hypothesis is not confirmed in this chapter: we must wait for independent evidence of the existence of change for (r), (æh), and (oh) as opposed to (th) and (dh), in order to support the hypothesis. This evidence will be provided in the discussion of differentiation through apparent time, in Chapter 9.

We have still not yet accounted for the reversal in style progressions for class 9. The similarity in Figures 7.19 and 7.21 for both the lower middle and upper middle classes suggests that these two structures form a set as opposed to Figure 7.11 for (r). What single selection defines such a set? The most relevant consideration which will appear is that these represent the results of linguistic change originating from below, as opposed to Figure 7. 11 for (r), which shows the results of linguistic change from above. The definitions of these terms, and the evidence for these statements, will be provided in Chapter 9.

Evidence of the out-of-town informants

The evidence we have used for this study of class differentiation of the variables is based entirely on the speech of eighty-one New York respondents. The speech of those informants who were raised outside of New York City can serve as a valuable check on the validity of our conclusions. For those variables which are associated with the native speech pattern of New Yorkers, acquired in pre-adolescent years, the out-of-town informants should show entirely different patterns. This is the case for (æh) and (oh). In Appendix E, the out-of-town respondents are analyzed by the same techniques which we have used in this chapter, and it is clear that there is no relation between their use of (æh) and (oh) and that of the New Yorkers.

For those variables which have the same social significance throughout most of the United States, there should be little difference between New Yorkers and out-of-towners. In Appendix E, we find that this is the case for (th) and (dh). Finally, for those variables which are part of an acquired speech pattern common in New York City, the out-of-town respondents should show some tendency towards the new prestige pattern, though not as much as New Yorkers. The study of (r) in Appendix E shows that the expected relationship holds for out-of-town and New York respondents, both for those who were raised in an r-pronouncing dialect area and those raised in an r-less area.

The study of the out-of-town respondents therefore provides an additional step towards establishing the reliability and validity of the evidence as well.

Summary

In this chapter, we have shown a series of close correlations between the distribution of the five phonological variables, and the socio-economic index established by MFY. We have explored the concepts of stratification, and regular structure, and given partial confirmation to a hypothesis which associates social and stylistic variation as part of a single overall process. We have shown that (r) exhibits a fine stratification on the basis of socio-economic class, while (th) and (dh) show sharp stratification. The variable (æh) shows an overall pattern of class stratification with considerable internal irregularity; the variable (oh) shows a curvilinear distribution in which the working class and lower middle class seem to form the leading edge of a linguistic change in progress.

In this chapter, the abstract construct of social class has been used as a unitary independent variable. In Chapter 8, we will re-analyze the concept of social class into its component parts, and determine which factors are most closely correlated with linguistic behavior. In addition, we will examine the distribution of the variables within each social class for evidence of the influence of sex or ethnic group upon the linguistic pattern.

8   Further analysis of the variables

In Chapter 7, the five phonological variables were correlated with the socio-economic index developed by Mobilization for Youth (MFY) to analyze the social structure of the Lower East Side. All five of the variables entered into regular structures, or near-regular structures. Not all of the variables participated in identical structures, and we found that the most clear-cut stratification was obtained in each case by using slightly different cutting points. The variable (r) showed the finest stratification; (th) and (dh) showed the sharpest differentiation of the class scale into two distinct halves; (æh) showed only slight class differentiation with considerable internal fluctuation; (oh) followed a curvilinear distribution, with the two center classes at the peak.

We also found that patterns of stylistic and class differentiation divided the variables into two types: (th) and (dh), in which the relations of the classes in all styles were relatively constant; and (r), (æh), and (oh), in which the lower middle class showed an abrupt crossing of the upper middle class line in the more formal styles. The behavior of (æh) and (oh) was very similar, except for the fact that the lower class does not share in the (oh) structure of stylistic and social variation. This view of linguistic differentiation seems satisfactory, not only because a difference has been found in the linguistic behavior of various classes, but because the evidence is consistent with our knowledge of the linguistic history of the city, based on the writings of Babbitt, Thomas, Frank, and Hubbell. The suggestions of linguistic change afforded by the evidence of Chapter 7 will be spelled out in detail in Chapter 9.

It is now necessary to re-examine the use of the socio-economic index as an independent variable. At this point, we have no proof that such an index, constructed from three indicators of productive status, is the social measure most closely correlated with the phonological variables. It was first adopted by MFY as a more reliable measure of social ranking than any single indicator. However, it is possible that one of the three indicators which compose this index is more closely correlated with linguistic behavior than the others, for one or more of the variables. When this question has been examined, we will also examine the other two independent variables which were discussed in the analysis of the sample: sex and ethnic group.

The logical ordering of the independent variables in time

In the introduction to Chapter 9, it was argued that the most important influence upon a person's native speech pattern is the group of friends and associates of his own age, during his pre-adolescent years. This statement will be assumed as probably true for the discussion to follow.

We would then expect that the social characteristics which date from those years would have the most influence on all of the variables. However, not all of the variables are a part of the "native" speech pattern: the language structure we are studying consists of acquired patterns as well as the native one. We might therefore order the phonological variables in three groups, according to the relative ages in which their patterns are set. The characterization of the variables is drawn from various sources in the Lower East Side survey, and may be also considered as assumed for this discussion.

(th) and (dh): The initial level is established early in life, according to social differentials which are quite general; ability to modify this pattern must accordingly be acquired quite early.

(æh) and (oh): The initial levels are set as a part of the pre-adolescent pattern, but according to social differentials now in flux, and not general across the community; it is not possible to estimate how late in life the native speech pattern can be modified with consistent results.

(r): The initial level is zero for most New Yorkers; (r) pronunciation is acquired after the pre-adolescent years and is therefore never consistent. Modifications of the amount of (r) can probably take place quite late in life.

We can make a corresponding analysis of the logical order in which the independent variables can establish or modify the speech pattern of the individual. At the outset, we can say that a person's childhood associates are largely determined by his sex, ethnic group, and parent's social status. If his own status continues that of his parents, then all of these factors will also continue to give us a good measure of social influences on his speech. If the initial pattern is modified, the first influence in this direction would most likely be education. His occupation, on leaving school, and later in life, would follow next as a measure of possible modifying influence. Finally, the one factor which reflects most accurately his present status is his income. Matching these two sets of assumptions, we might say that these influences may be correlated with the language features in the following way:

1) An individual's use of (dh) and (th), as part of the pattern determined by his sex, ethnic group, and parental background, will be modified

more by education than by occupation, and more by occupation than by income.

2) An individual's use of (r) will be relatively independent of sex, ethnic group, and parent's background, and more closely correlated with his occupation, education, and income as indicators of his current social position.

3) The position of (æh) and (oh) in this respect would fall somewhere in between, but we do not as yet know enough about the age at which these patterns are set.

   (The expression "modified by education" may be taken as shorthand for, "modified by influences of associates during the period of his education, and therefore measured by the highest educational level attained.")

   These assumptions will be useful in interpreting the results of this chapter.

   [The further history of sociolinguistic studies shows two problematic relations to socio-economic indices. One is to use them automatically, without reflection or examination of their component parts. The other is to reject them as a whole, in favor of a measure that is intuitively closer to communication – like the linguistic market place. Chapter 7 suggested that the combined index gives us a more regular view of social stratification than individual indicators; this chapter argues that different indicators are more valuable for particular variables. Here we approach a question that has drawn a great deal of attention in recent decades: changes in linguistic behavior across the lifespan.]

Education of respondent as an independent variable

The educational scale which is used to classify the informants is the one used by MFY. It is a nine-point scale in terms of the number of years *completed.*

0	None
1	Some elementary school
2	Elementary school (8th grade)
3	9th grade
4	10th grade
5	11th grade
6	12th grade; high school graduate
7	Some college
8	Graduated college or more

In order to assess the usefulness of this indicator alone, we can choose one of the variables which was not handled altogether adequately by the socio-economic index. In the case of (dh), we noted that the index could not

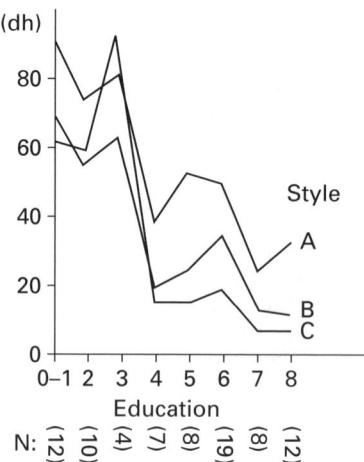

Figure 8.1   Style stratification of (dh) by respondent's education

distinguish the (dh) usage of a very large body of speakers: those from class 0 to 4. We will therefore test education of the respondent alone as a correlate of (dh).

Figure 8.1 shows the style stratification diagram for (dh) with education as the independent variable. The number of respondents for Style B (the maximum) is indicated below each educational rank. (In order to test each independent variable for discrimination of the highest and next to highest group, it will be useful to exclude the figures for Nathan B. in any arithmetic averages for (dh) and (th). The effect of his high (dh) and (th) readings obscures any smaller differences brought about by change of indicators. His position will be shown on any distribution diagrams, however.)

Figure 8.1 shows that there is one major break in the values of the variable – between educational level 3 and 4. This means that the first year of high school has some significance, for in New York City, the 9th grade is included in junior high schools. It may be relevant that elementary schools are restricted to smaller neighborhoods than high schools, and one may surmise that in high school, the individual has an opportunity to measure himself or herself against speakers from a wider range of environments than in grammar school or junior high school.

To the left of this break, we find no significant differences in the (dh) usage of levels 1, 2, and 3. (There is only one level 0 speaker, and 0 is always combined with 1 here.) Moreover, the style stratification of these levels is quite mixed. For levels 2 and 3, Style C actually shows more stops and affricates than A or B; thus we can infer that most of these speakers do not

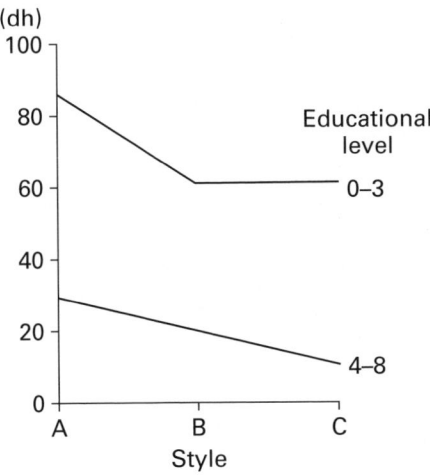

Figure 8.2   Educational stratification of (dh)

adjust their usage to suit the formality of the context. To the right of the break, we see the possibility of a division between levels 4, 5, 6 on the one hand, and 7, 8 on the other – but it is a small difference compared to the 3–4 break.

Figure 8.2 is therefore the fairest representation of the stratification of (dh) with respect to education: two widely separated strata. Thus we find that education is a sharp differentiator of (dh) behavior, but it cannot provide as many levels of stratification as the original index.

Occupation of respondent as an independent variable

The scale of occupation used here is essentially the four-rank scale used to construct the index of Chapter 7, now expanded to seven units:

1)   Professional, semi-professional
2)   Proprietors, managers, and officials
3)   Clerical, sales, and kindred workers
4)   Craftsmen, foremen, and kindred workers
5)   Operatives and kindred workers
6)   Service workers
7)   Laborers

(This scale is adopted from the MFY Codebook, which is in turn an adaptation of the Bureau of the Census practice – there is only one small proprietor in the sample, so that 2 is always shown with 1.)

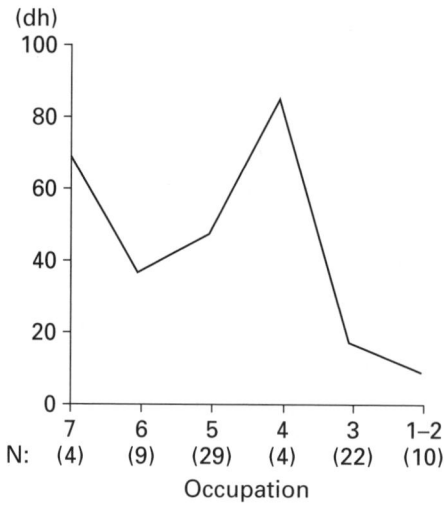

Figure 8.3   Distribution of (dh) in Style B by respondent's occupation

Figure 8.3 shows the distribution of (dh) with respect to occupation for Style B only. The peaks shown for occupations 4 and 7 are associated with very small numbers; on the whole, we would have to be content with the distinction between occupations 1–2, professionals and proprietors; 3, clerical and sales; 4–7, manual workers. Thus occupation alone does not give us as many subdivisions as the combined socio-economic index.

Occupation and education combined

We have seen that both occupation and education showed sharp breaks at a particular point. These breaks do not divide the population into the same groups, so by a combination of the two indicators, we may improve our results. Table 8.1 shows the distribution of informants by occupation and education.

As Table 8.1 shows, there is a close correlation between occupation and education for the two upper ranks; but the manual workers are about equally divided between those who have had at least one year of high school, and those who have not.

We will develop four classes from Table 8.1 by the following procedure: first, considering that the presence or absence of some high school experience is the most determining factor, we will divide the population into two parts: those with and those without one year of high school (SC1). Second,

Table 8.1   *Distribution of ALS informants by education and occupation*

		Occupational level		
		1–2	3	4–7
Educational level	8:	9	1	–
	4–7:	2	18	24
	0–3:	–	2	23

Table 8.2   *Social class (SC) distribution*

		Occupational level		
		1–2	3	4–7
Educational level	8:	SC 4	SC 3	SC 2
	4–7:	SC 4	SC 3	SC 2
	0–3:	SC 1	SC 1	SC 1

we will divide the remaining group by occupation, into a professional class (SC4), a white collar class (SC3), and a blue collar class (SC2). This gives us Table 8.2.

We will provisionally refer to these four classes as *social class* (abbreviated SC) as opposed to the MFY *socio-economic class* (abbreviated SEC). Figures 8.4 and 8.5 are bar graphs which illustrate the difference between the two indexes, in regard to (dh). While SEC does not differentiate the two lower classes, the index of social class gives us an evenly spaced distribution.

[This "Social Class" alternative to the SEC index will be used in Chapter 9 to register the development of (æh) and (oh) in apparent time. The first edition devoted a good ten pages of further discussion to show how it provided more regular stratification than SEC, but these are small differences. I have abbreviated this on the reasoning that I laid out in the introduction: the value of each part of the book can be judged by what others have done with it. In the very many studies of the speech community that followed – see Chapter 15 – there are no further uses of this alternate measure of class stratification. The concept of a "working population" used in Figures 8.4 and 8.5 does reveal gender and class stratification even more clearly than the methods of Chapter 7. This concept may not have taken root in sociolinguistics since the numbers of women who were not included in that group has shrunk in the decades that

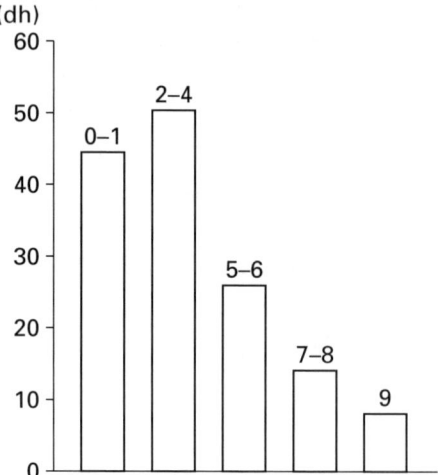

Figure 8.4   Distribution of (dh) in Style B by socio-economic class index

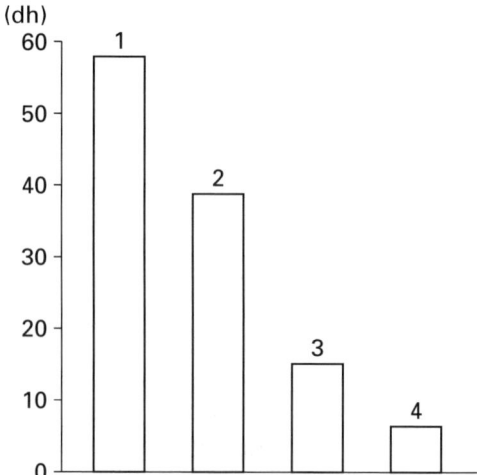

Figure 8.5   Distribution of (dh) in Style B by social class index

followed. Next, the discussion plunges into the productive and stimulating study of ethnic and gender differences.]

When we consider the occupations of those who are working actively, we obtain a very striking correlation with the informants' occupations. The concept we will set up here is the *working population*: this will include all

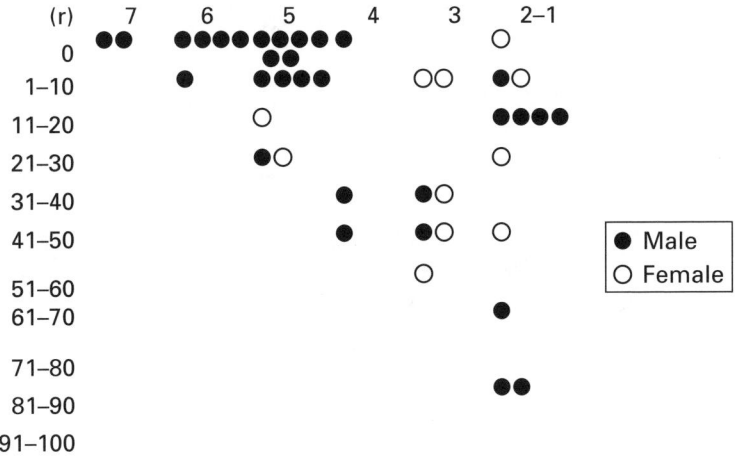

Figure 8.6   Detailed distribution of (r) in Style B by occupation of the working population

those who are now working actively, and also those men recently retired who worked actively all their lives. By *working actively*, we mean holding a job outside of the family environment which occupies a full working day. Figure 8.6 shows the distribution of (r) for the working population of forty New York subjects. Though the numbers are small, the main sequence is well established. Most striking is the absence of any deviant cases in the lower left half. The group in the upper right corner shows the division of the upper middle class into an older group, with little (r), and a younger group with a high percentage of (r). We will consider this in more detail in Chapter 9.

If we consider the distribution of (th) for the working population, we find a sharp division into two distinct types, as in Figure 8.7. Here we find a group of fifteen men with (th)-40 or higher, and clearly separated from them, a group of twenty-five men and women with (th) of 30 or lower. There are six subjects with manual occupations in the upper left group: two of the women are Catholics, both are beauticians. The men are Jewish: one is Abraham G., the taxi driver whose careful speech is described in Chapter 4. The other is Steve K., the philosophy student who became a copyreader's assistant in a print shop.

We next turn to the examination of (æh) and (oh). We found originally that the class stratification of (æh) was not as sharp as with the other variables, and that there were more fluctuations from class to class. We shall

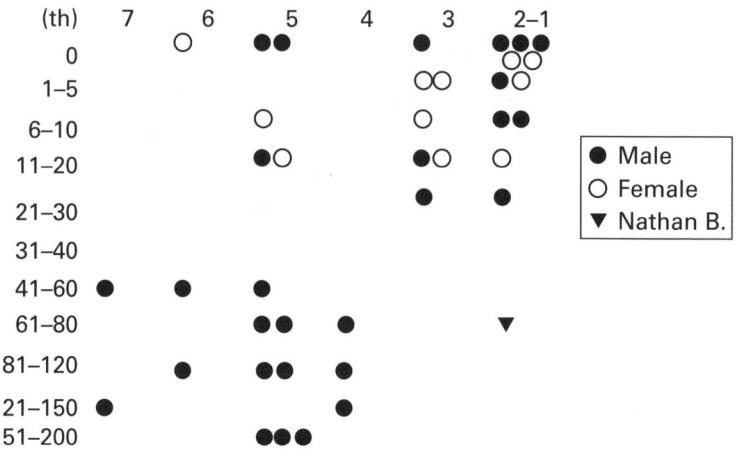

Figure 8.7   Detailed distribution of (th) in Style B by occupation of the working population

therefore turn to a different independent variable which is more relevant to (æh) and (oh): ethnic membership.

Ethnic group as an independent variable[1]

There are three ethnic groups large enough to be studied in the sample of eighty-one New York City speakers:

Jews	45
Italians	19
African–Americans	9

The balance of the population consists of eight informants of various backgrounds: two Ukrainians, and one each of Irish, German, Greek, Spanish, and Norwegian backgrounds. One subject came from an African–American (AA) background but is now a part of the white group

---

[1] The ethnic group as it exists in New York City is not to be identified with the ethnic groups of European society. "The ethnic group in American society became not a survival from the age of mass immigration but a new social form . . . Ethnic groups then, even after distinctive language, customs and culture are lost . . . are continually recreated by new experiences in America. The mere existence of a name itself is perhaps sufficient to form group character in new situations, for the name associates an individual, who can actually be anything, with a certain past, country, race. But as a matter of fact, someone who is Irish or Jewish or Italian generally has other traits than the mere existence of the name that associates him with other people attached to the group. A man is connected to his group by ties of family and friendship. But he is also connected by ties of *interest*. The ethnic groups in New York are also *interest groups*." Glazer and Moynihan (1963) pages 16–17.

Table 8.3   *Class distribution of ethnic groups*

				SEC					
	0	1	2	3	4	5	6	7–8	9
Jews	4	4	3	6	4	4	5	6	9
Italians	2	1	3	4	3	–	2	3	1
African–Americans	–	1	2	4	2	1	–	–	1

	0–2	3–5	6–9
Jews	11	14	20
Italians	6	7	6
African–Americans	3	7	1

for all practical purposes. In order to supplement the AA population, we will re-introduce the two New York speakers who were removed from the original sample in order to reduce the AA working class group to 67 percent, along with the Jewish and Catholic groups.

The class distribution of the three main ethnic groups is shown in Table 8.3 above.

The relative percentages of Jews and Italians reflect fairly accurately the proportions in the original population, despite the generally lower rate of completion for the Italian group. There are two weak points in this distribution: class 5 and 9. The first deficiency may account for the shifting behavior of class 5, in its orientation towards 6–9 for (th) and (dh), and towards 0–4 for (r), (æh), and (oh). The deficiency in class 9 is not a product of any sampling bias, but reflects accurately the real situation. Of the total Italian population in the original MFY sample, only one was class 9. Therefore any Jewish-Italian differences which are emphasized by the behavior of class 9 represent an indissoluble link between ethnic membership and class behavior.

The distribution of the AA group has been discussed in Chapter 6. The weakness in the upper middle class, while probably a good reflection of the overall distribution of AA subjects, represents the loss of speakers during the two-year lag between MFY and ALS surveys. Most of the lower class AA speakers are not native New Yorkers, and appear in the out-of-town studies in Chapter 7.

It will not be sufficient to study Style B alone in dealing with (æh) and (oh), because much of the relevant structure is displayed in the shift of styles. Style A will give us the nearest approach to the native speech pattern; Style B is again the most reliable in number of cases; Style C or D will show the end-point of formal shifting.

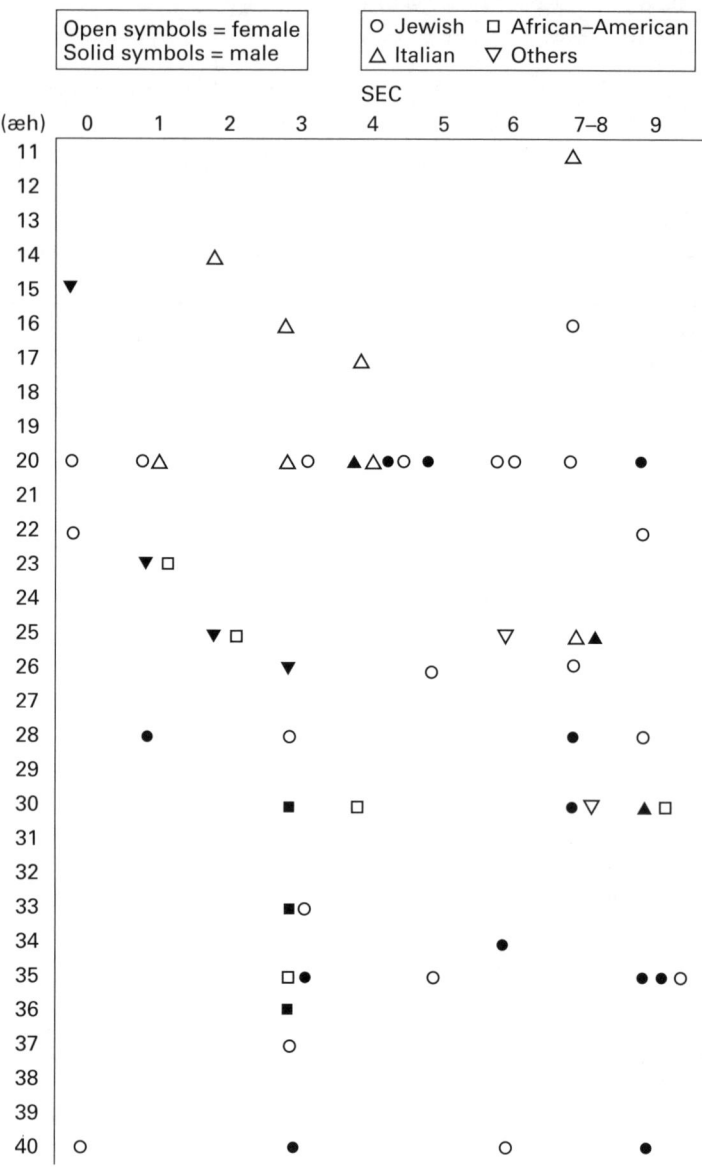

Figure 8.8   Detailed distribution of (æh) in Style A by SEC, ethnic group, and sex

Table 8.4   *Distribution of* (æh) *by ethnic group*

	Jews			Italians			African–Americans		
Age	A	B	D	A	B	D	A	B	D
10–17	1	1	–	4	1	–	–	–	–
19–21	10	3	–	4	7	1	–	1	1
22–26	4	10	4	2	3	3	2	2	1
27–32	6	10	8	1	6	2	3	5	5
33–39	8	12	13	–	–	6	3	3	1
40–42	4	8	12	–	–	5	–	–	–
	33	44	37	9	17	17	8	11	8

Figure 8.8 gives the complete data for the distribution of (æh) in casual speech by ethnic group, socio-economic class, and sex. Although we can detect a general diagonal structure, from upper left to lower right, the chief structure in this diagram seems to be a horizontal layering. There is first of all a group of speakers who use very high, close vowels from (æh)-10 to (æh)-17. Then there is a heavy concentration of fourteen speakers at exactly (æh)-20. Another group of twelve is to be found between (æh)-22 and (æh)-26; we can more or less arbitrarily divide this group from the ten speakers who are centered around (æh)-30. Then there is an even lower group of eleven speakers between (æh)-33 and (æh)-39, and finally a set of invariant speakers at (æh)-40.

It is immediately apparent that there is a great difference between Italians and Jews. Four of the six speakers in the high (æh) range of 10–17 are Italians; while Jewish speakers are heavily concentrated at (æh)-20, and are then scattered downward. There are no Italian speakers below (æh)-33, but there are twelve Jewish speakers.

Figure 8.9 shows the pattern, or lack of pattern, characteristic of (æh) in Style B. It may be seen that all groups – except the AAs who are relatively stable around (æh)-30 – are shifted downward, but the Italians are still relatively higher than the Jews. There is a definite trend towards the lower right section, although the presence of the row of lower class speakers on (æh)-40 disguises this.

Table 8.4 shows a comparison of Jews, Italians, and AAs for Styles A, B, and D. In Styles A and B, the Italians are concentrated higher than the Jews, but by the time we reach Style D, there is little difference. According to this table, the AAs do not treat (æh) as a variable, since they are centered around (æh)-30 in all three styles.

Figure 8.10 shows graphically the relative positions of Jews and Italians on the scale of height of (æh) for Styles A, B, and D. The hatched portion

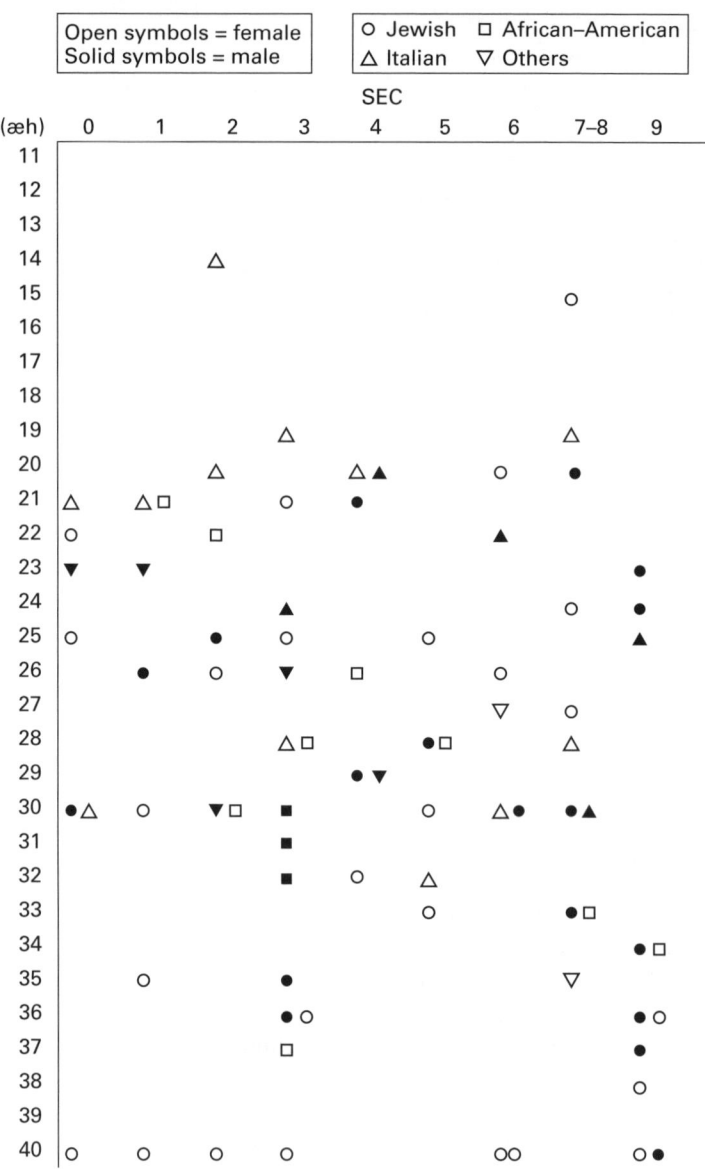

Figure 8.9   Detailed distribution of (æh) in Style B by SEC, ethnic group, and sex

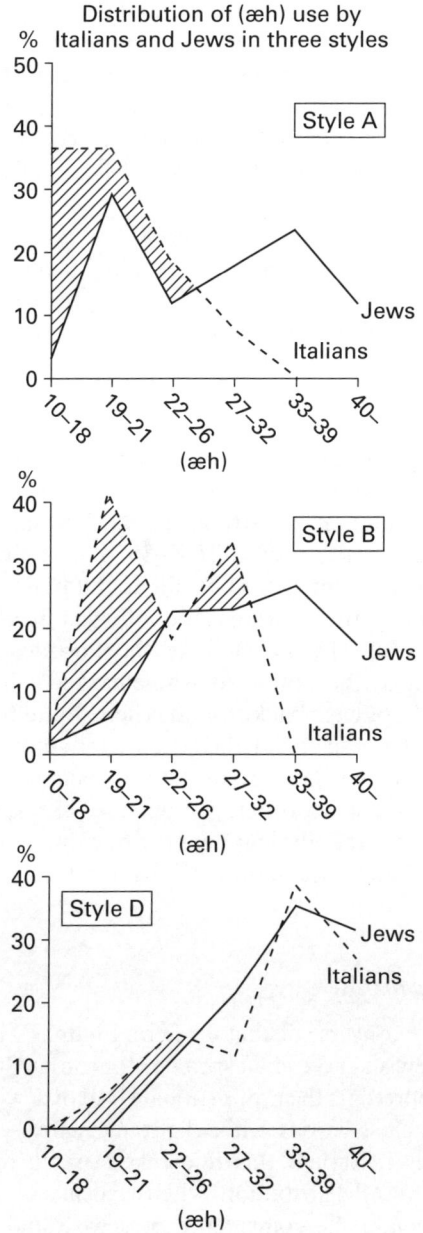

Figure 8.10   Distribution of (æh) use by Italians and Jews in three styles

indicates that proportion by which Italian speakers lead the Jewish speakers in height of (æh). In Style A, there is a great difference at the left hand side, (æh)-10–17. Conversely, there are many Jewish speakers in the right hand area, (æh)-33–39, where no Italians are registered. In Style B, the concentration of Jewish speakers around (æh)-20 has disappeared, while the Italian group is concentrated at this point. The Jewish speakers still are represented alone in the (æh)-33–40 area.

A marked change is found in Style D. Both groups follow essentially the same distribution in this style, with the Italians only slightly higher in (æh) values than the Jews.

Here we see confirmed the earlier suggestion that New York forms a single speech community, quite diverse in everyday speech, but united by a common norm – in this case, expressed by the standardization of the most formal pronunciation.

[Before systematic sociolinguistic studies began, it was assumed that the dominant influences on the speech of New Yorkers would be the parents' language, the result of massive immigration from Ireland, Germany, Italy, Poland, Greece, Russia, etc., in the period 1850–1924. But linguistic influence turned out to be the least important of all, as children turned a deaf ear to the foreign accents of their parents, and followed the *doctrine of first effective settlement* (Zelinsky 1992). Like the Portuguese and Indians on Martha's Vineyard, they plunged wholeheartedly into the local sociolinguistic system. Language background is here found to be far less important than age, gender, and social class. In a later study, Labov (1976) compared closely matched second and third generation New Yorkers, and found that it made no difference whether the speaker's parent spoke another language. Yet ethnic influences remain, as Figures 8.8 and 8.9 show, in a subtle re-orientation of the symmetry of the system.]

Relation of ethnic membership to (oh)

The distribution of (oh) is the converse of that for (æh). Figure 8.11 shows the progressive relations of Jewish and Italian speakers for (oh) in Styles A, B, and C. The hatched area represents the proportionate lead of Jewish over Italian speakers for the high, close vowels, while the Italians are seen to be using lower, more open vowels. In Style B, this difference is greatly reduced. Both groups show the same overall distribution, with two peaks of concentration. In Style C, we see again the coincidence of Jewish and Italian speakers in the accepted norms, centering on (oh)-22–26. The coincidence in the proportions of speakers using the higher vowels, (oh)-13–21, is very marked.

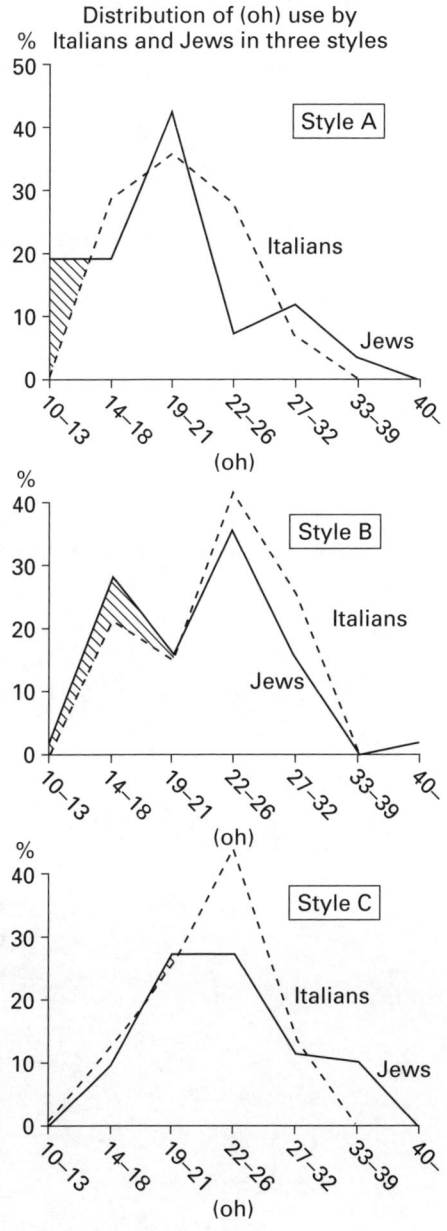

Figure 8.11   Distribution of (oh) use by Italians and Jews in three styles

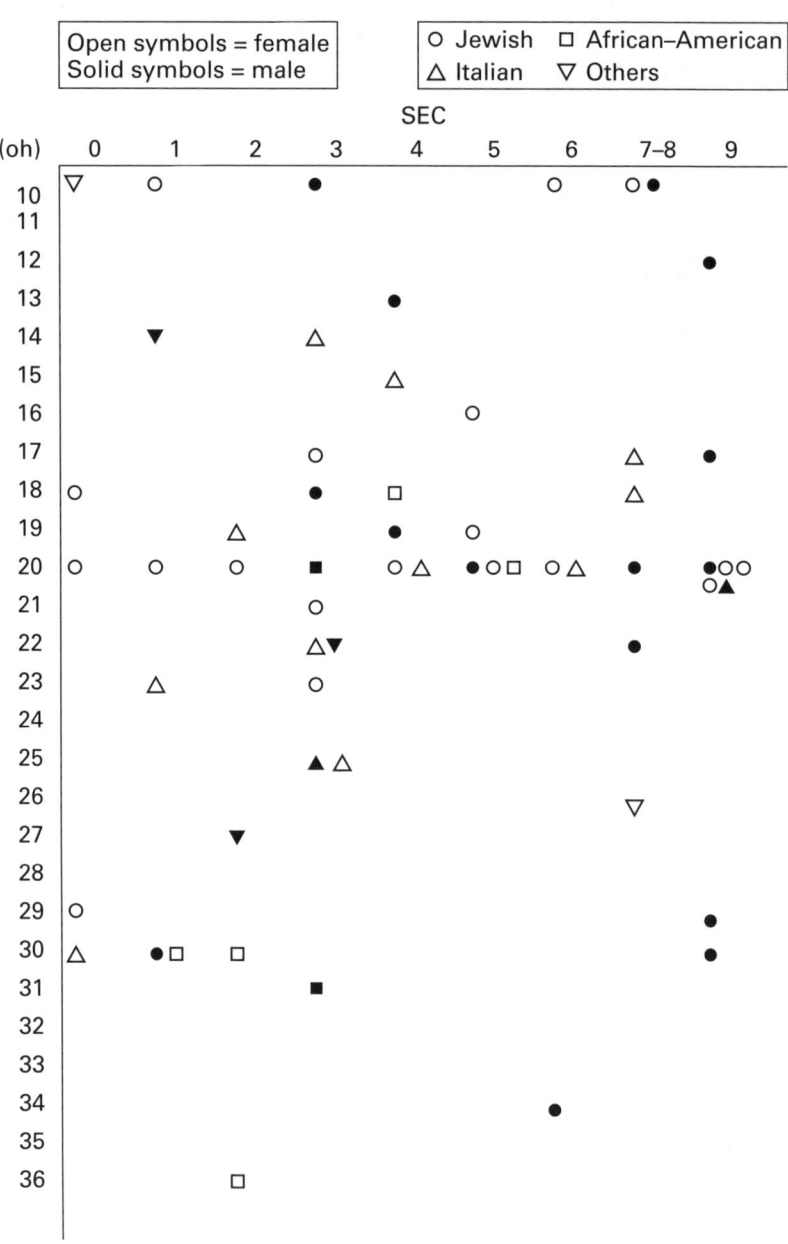

Figure 8.12   Detailed distribution of (oh) in Style A by SEC, ethnic group, and sex

Table 8.5   *Average values of ethnic groups for* (æh) *and* (oh)

	(æh)				(oh)			
	A	B	C	D	A	B	C	D
Jews	28	33	36	37	20	21	23	24
Italians	22	23	27	33	21	24	23	25
African–Americans	30	28	31	31	26	29	31	29

Table 8.6   *Comparison of Jewish and Italian Speakers for* (oh) *without the lower class*

Age	A		B		C		D	
	Jews	Ital.	Jews	Ital.	Jews	Ital.	Jews	Ital.
10–13	5	–	1	–	–	–	1	–
14–18	4	3	7	2	2	1	3	–
19–21	12	4	7	–	4	2	8	3
22–26	1	–	8	6	7	5	3	4
27–32	3	–	5	2	9	1	8	1
33–39	1	–	–	–	3	–	4	1
40–	–	–	1	–	1	–	1	–
	26	7	27	10	26	9	28	9

Figure 8.12 is an overall view of the distribution of (oh) in Style A. Here the curvilinear pattern, first seen in the arithmetic averages of Chapter 7, is revealed more clearly. The lower classes show a general scattering of (oh); the upper portions of the working class, and the lower middle class show uniformly high vowels; the beginning of a fall is seen in class 7–8, and class 9 has generally more open vowels, comparable to those of the lower class.

The position of the AA speakers in regard to (oh) again shows no participation in the stylistic stratification of this variable. Table 8.5 summarizes the relations of the three ethnic groups.

Because the lower class group does not react to (oh), the figures on the right do not reveal the full extent of variation.

In Table 8.6, the actual distribution of Jewish and Italian speakers for (oh) is compared, without the lower class group 0–2. This table may be compared with Table 8.4 for the regular progression of stylistic variation of (æh).

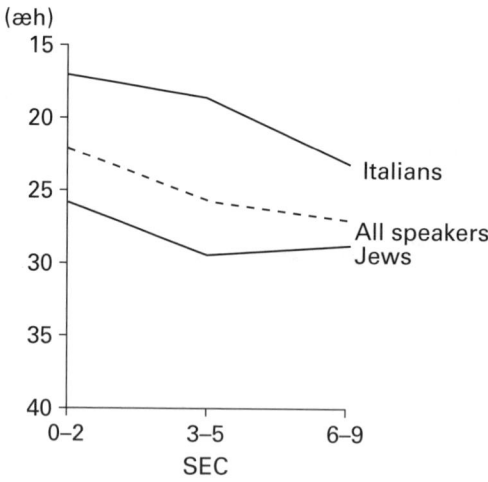

Figure 8.13   Ethnic stratification of (æh) in Style A by SEC groups

The parallel behavior of Jews and Italians preserves the pattern of stylistic variation despite the fact that the groups start from different average values of the indexes.

[Table 8.6 is an elegant demonstration of the power of cross-tabulation. Today we tend to use multivariate analysis to get at the intersecting influences of age, ethnicity, and style. But it would be hard to think of an assembly of factors and weights that would show so neatly the difference in the behavior of Italians and Jews.]

Relations of ethnic groups to socio-economic class

We have noted that the class stratification of (æh) was more gradual and less marked than with the other variables. Since we find that Jewish-Italian differences are very important in the structure of this variable, we may find that a clearer pattern emerges by combining ethnic group and class. Figure 8.13 shows a style diagram for casual speech which compares Jewish and Italian usage for the three class groups 0–2, 3–5, 6–9. The combined values for all speakers are shown by the dotted line. The lack of direction of the Jewish group as a whole is compared to the uniform tendency of the Italian group. In Figure 8.14, the view of Style B is amplified by using all nine class groups. The Italian group shows a fairly smooth curve, with a peak for lower class speakers, and gradually lower values for the others. The Jewish group, on the other hand, shows fluctuations, with

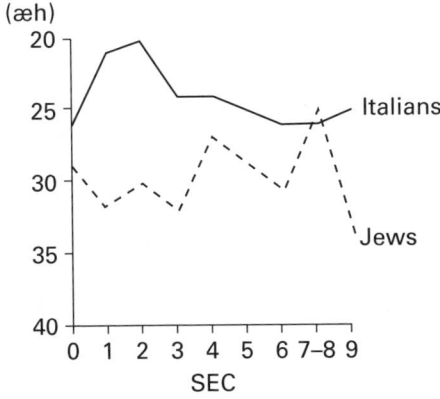

Figure 8.14   Ethnic stratification of (æh) in Style B by nine SEC units

a gradual rise to the lower middle class, and a fall for the upper middle class.

Figure 8.14 suggests that most of the fluctuations in the original diagram of Figure 7.18 are due to the Jewish group. The presence of the older Jewish speakers, who seem to use very open (æh) vowels in their natural speech, may be responsible for this pattern in part.

Figure 8.15 combines style stratification for Style A and Style B, for both Italians and Jews. The regularity of the Italian pattern, in terms of even spacing of the classes, and a regular progression from left to right, is quite marked in comparison to the Jewish group.

We have thus made some progress in explaining the irregularities of the (æh) distribution, isolating a regular Italian factor from the less regular Jewish one. Ethnic differentiation is seen to be a more powerful factor than class differentiation, though both exist in addition to marked stylistic variation.

As far as the (oh) variable is concerned, Italians and Jews follow the same pattern; the Jewish speakers show the most extreme curvilinear distribution. Figure 8.16 gives us a comparison of Jewish and Italian usage of (oh) which is the correlate of Figure 8.15 for (æh).

In comparing (æh) with (oh), we find that the group which leads in the use of high, close vowels, is also the group which shows the most regular stylistic and social variation. The Italian group is most regular for (æh), and the Jewish group for (oh), as shown in Figures 8.12 through 8.16, and Table 8.5. Unfortunately, we have no real Italian group 9 to pursue the comparison in greater detail: the study of the lower middle class cross-over presumes a steady base in the upper middle class figures.

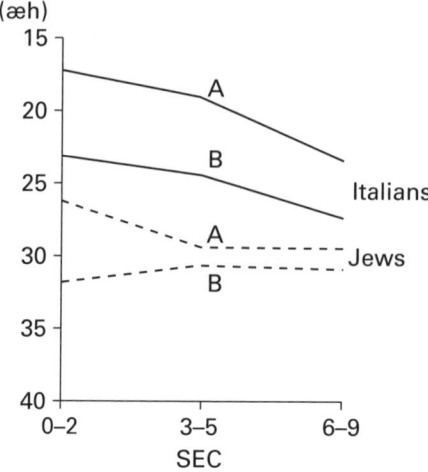

Figure 8.15   Ethnic stratification of (æh) in Styles A and B by SEC groups

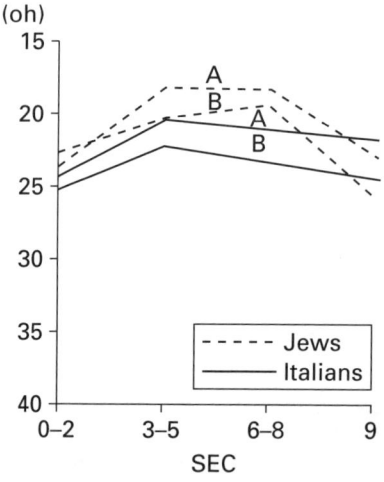

Figure 8.16   Ethnic stratification of (oh) in Styles A and B by SEC groups

So far we have not raised the question of why the Italians should have shown a tendency to use higher (æh) vowels and Jews to use higher (oh) vowels. An important consideration must be the possibility of influences from the structures of the Italian and Yiddish vowel systems. That pressures can be exerted on a language by a *substratum language*, which was spoken by previous generations, is a point of view often employed in historical linguistics. In New York City we have the existence of continued contact with native Italian and Yiddish speakers, which argues even more strongly for a cross-linguistic influence.[2] The possible role of underlying Italian and Yiddish influence is one of the problems which will require further study, beyond the present work.[3] On the other hand, it will be shown (in Chapter 9) that the pattern of (oh) and (æh) variation was present in the speech pattern of the most traditional "old stock" families. Undoubtedly the influence of the substratum language is to be seen in the acceleration of trends already present in the English of New York City rather than the introduction of new variants or new structural relations.

[As interesting as these substratum differences may be, it must be admitted that very few of them have succumbed to the linguist's desire for explanation. Chapter 7 of Labov 2001 collects a sizeable number of such unexplained substratum effects, as for example, the fact that Italians in Philadelphia show a persistent tendency to interchange *make* and *let*, with no clear explanation apparent in the structure of Italian. Here however there seems to be some light on the horizon. Footnote 3 develops a strong argument on why Jews raise /oh/. It is not unrelated to the hypercorrect pattern of the lower middle class that plays such a prominent role in Chapter 7.

---

[2] The great majority of the ALS informants were familiar with a second language, since their parents or grandparents had been born and raised in Europe. In many cases, the informants had learned their parents' native language first, and continued to use this language in speaking to their parents, or to other elderly persons. English was used with brothers and sisters as a rule, and with friends of the same age level. It was rare for an informant to report that he had used any language besides English with peers, or in thinking to himself, or in dreaming.

[3] No simple difference in phonemic inventories of Yiddish and Italian will account for the differentials in the use of English that have been noted. Neither Yiddish nor Italian have a low front vowel /æ/, and both have a short low back rounded vowel, an allophone of /o/ used in checked syllables with the value [ɔ]. One possible mechanism for the Jewish raising of [oh] was suggested to the author by Marvin Herzog, of the staff of the *Language and Culture Atlas of Ashkenazic Jewry*. Many native speakers of Yiddish do not distinguish in English the low back rounded vowel /oh/ from the unrounded vowel /ʌ/. Thus *a cup of coffee* may be [a kɔp kɔfi]. The children of speakers with this pattern may react by over-differentiating /ʌ/ and /oh/, leading to an [oh-1] pronunciation with a high, over-rounded long vowel as opposed to the lower, unrounded short /ʌ/. This type of hypercorrection, in which the speaker over-compensates for the influence of a stigmatized foreign pronunciation, may be responsible for the Jewish lead in the raising of [oh]. If this suggestion could be extended to the case of the front vowels, it would appear even more probable – that is, if the raising of /æh/ could be seen as a comparable overcompensation for the foreigner's use of /æ/. Yiddish accents in English seem to favor the use of /e/ for /æ/, with a homonymy of *bad* and *bed*, and we have seen a number of older, second-generation Jewish speakers who use a low [eh-4], even in casual speech. Native Italian speakers, using English as a second language, seem to favor a forward variant of their /a/ phoneme for words of the *bag, ask, dance* class. If this explanation is correct, the second and third generation with Italian-born relatives would tend towards higher /æh/ as a form of hypercorrection.

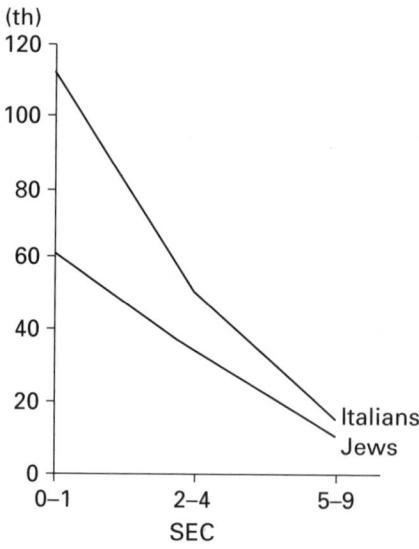

Figure 8.17   Ethnic stratification of (th) in Style B by SEC groups

The tendency for Jewish speakers of English to raise /oh/ reappears in Laferriere's study of Jewish and Italian ethnicity in Boston (1979) – though here the raised /oh/ is the prestige marker, and lowered /oh/ is stigmatized. It also appears in Knack's study of Grand Rapids (1991), where the social situation is again quite different.]

The evidence of this chapter, and Chapter 9, point to unconscious pressures for continued ethnic group identification as the primary mechanism in these linguistic developments. The selection of a particular linguistic variant is of minor significance compared to the social values which are afterwards assigned to it.[4]

Jewish and Italian differences for other variables

The initial assumptions of this chapter would lead us to believe that there are no serious ethnic differences in the usage of (r). This is the case. In all of the distributional diagrams for (r), Italians and Jews are seen to follow the same patterns at the same levels. This is in marked contrast to the situation with (th) and (dh), where Catholics, and particularly Italians, are seen to

---

[4] Thus the mechanism of hypercorrection, suggested above, might account for the origin of a trend, which would continue as high /æh/ became a symbol of group identification for New Yorkers with Italian backgrounds, and high /oh/ for those with Jewish backgrounds.

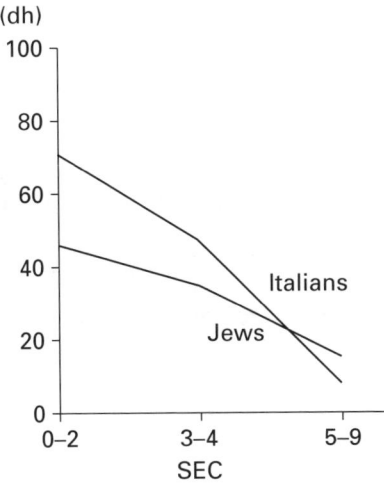

Figure 8.18   Ethnic stratification of (dh) in Style B by SEC groups

use a much greater percentage of stops and affricates. Figure 8.17 compares Italians and Jews in their use of (th) in Style B, and Figure 8.18 for (dh) in Style B. The differences for (th) are quite extreme, and show that for each class group, Italians use more stops and affricates. The middle class usage of (dh) reflects a slight reversal in the relations of the two groups; since there are only six Italians in this group, we cannot lean too heavily upon this fact for further interpretation.

We can now estimate the type of error involved in the main distributional weakness of the ALS sample of completed interviews: the lower proportion of Italians, and particularly, Italian men. These speakers generally use higher (æh), and more stops and affricates in (th) and (dh) than the population as a whole, if we can judge from the nineteen subjects in our sample. It is important to note, however, that they follow the same patterns of social and stylistic variation as the rest of the population. The difference is one of relative level. We can therefore infer that any attempt to gauge the absolute level of the usage of (th) and (dh), (æh) and (oh), or (r) in the population as a whole might show some error due to the difficulty of estimating the values for the non-respondents. However, there is no reason to believe that the structure of social and stylistic variation would be at all changed by the complete record of the population that moved and could not be reached.

We can now consider the second serious weakness in distribution of the sample and see if there are important differences between men and women – in their use of the five variables.

Comparison of men and women

The comparison of the sexes for the five phonological variables must be made for two distinct parts of the population: the upper middle class on the one hand, and the rest of the informants on the other. This is necessary, not only because the proportions of men and women have been reversed for the upper middle class, but also because the relations of the sexes in these two parts are different for some of the variables. For example, the difference between all men and women in the sample for (dh), Style B are:

	average (dh) index
men (30)	54
women (52)	31

If we exclude class 9, we have:

men (22)	68
women (48)	34

Thus men are now seen to be twice as high as women in their use of stops and affricates for all but class 9.

In Figure 8.7, we see the relations of men and women in the working population for their use of (th) in Style B. Here the women are uniformly concentrated in the upper half of the diagram, with no sign of a sharp differentiation by occupation. However, the three women in manual occupations cannot give us a firm base for comparison. A much larger group of factory workers would be necessary here.

Men and women follow the same patterns in the use of (r). Figure 8.6 shows the relations of men and women in the working population. The women fit fairly well into the predominantly male pattern. In a more complete view of the sample, we find no significant differences between the sexes in their use of (r).

In Figures 8.8, 8.9, and 8.12, we can study the relations of the sexes for (æh) and (oh). There is no immediate pattern of sex differences by class. However, a close examination will show that women show more concentration in the extreme values, especially for (oh). This tendency is illustrated by Table 8.7, which compares men and women for both variables in Styles A, B, and D. The progressions of the numbers of informants in each category show that men and women follow the same stylistic variation, but that the total shift of the women speakers is much greater. Class 9 is not included. The tendency of women to follow an extreme pattern of stylistic variation, which we may call hypercorrection, is an important aspect of the structure of New York City English. One of the most difficult problems to explain is

Table 8.7   *Comparison of* (æh) *and* (oh) *distribution for men and women*

		Style					
		A		B		D	
		Men	Women	Men	Women	Men	Women
(æh)	10–13	–	1	–	–	–	–
	14–18	1	4	–	2	1	–
	19–21	3	10	3	9	1	2
	22–26	4	6	7	9	–	5
	27–32	3	4	11	12	8	9
	33–39	4	4	3	5	4	14
	40–42	1	2	–	6	4	16
		16	33	24	43	18	46
(oh)	10–13	3	4	–	1	–	3
	14–18	3	10	4	10	2	5
	19–21	4	14	7	7	5	13
	22–26	3	5	8	16	5	4
	27–32	3	4	5	10	5	8
	33–40	1	1	–	2	1	10
		17	38	24	46	18	43

the mechanism of the steady rise of (æh) and (oh) through successive generations, which will be detailed in the next chapter. It is possible that the hypercorrect behavior of women plays a vital role in this procedure.

[The differentiation of men and women was not foregrounded in the New York City study, though the consistent and complex patterns that appeared in later work are all laid out here. Labov 1966 might well have devoted a separate chapter to gender. We observe the tendency of women to favor prestige forms (Figure 8.14); their extreme shift in formal styles (Table 8.7); and most importantly, their leading position in change from below (Table 8.7).]

Temporal relations of the variables

The findings of this chapter confirm the initial assumption of the logical order of social influences on the variables. We can summarize the relative positions of the independent variables in this way:

Sex and *ethnic group membership* seem to operate on the variables in much the same way. They play an important part in the overall level of (th) and (dh). Ethnic group seems to be the principal determinant of the initial level of (æh) and (oh), as shown in Style A, while sex partly determines the overall range of correction under stylistic shift. Both sex and ethnic group seem to have relatively little influence on (r).

The respondent's *occupation* and *education* are the most important determinants of (th) and (dh) usage in all three styles. They have less relevance for (æh) and (oh) except in determining the type of correction found under shift to more formal styles. Both factors play a part in determining the usage of (r), as they reflect the current status of the individual.

Income appears as a necessary element in the fine stratification of the population with respect to (r), reflecting the current status of the speaker.

In these statements, the expression "determines" must of course be read as an abbreviation for "is closely correlated with and appears to measure social influences which are logically and temporally prior to linguistic behavior."

This chapter has presented some of the detailed influences which underlie the larger view of class stratification of the variables as presented in Chapter 7. The findings of the present chapter supplement rather than correct this view of class differentiation of language. They bring us closer to the description of a uniform linguistic structure for the New York community, and the processes of linguistic change which have created that structure.

Distribution of the variables in apparent time

[The first eight chapters of this book concern synchronic patterns of variation in the speech community, with the linguistic variable as the working tool of analysis. There have been hints about linguistic change in progress but it is not until this chapter that sociolinguistics takes on the study of change and variation as its central problem. The concept of apparent time, and its relations in real time, had been explored in the Martha's Vineyard study, but here it is analyzed and explored in much greater detail.

We now have much more information than we had at that time on the extent to which adults change their language as they grow older. It is important to note that from the outset, there was no assumption that they did not: the task is "to distinguish the effects of linguistic change from the invariant effects of aging and from the modifying effects of the present situation upon older speakers."]

The study of small differences in language behavior is concentrated upon the variable elements in linguistic structure; this procedure brings us inevitably to indications of linguistic change. Variability itself is change: but some types of variation are themselves invariant from generation to generation. We are particularly interested in gradual alterations of the linguistic habits of a population through the course of time, which will be referred to here as *linguistic change*.

The explanation of linguistic change on a large scale is one of the primary goals of linguistics, and in the present work we hope to contribute to that end by the close examination of linguistic change in progress. Throughout the last several chapters, it has been suggested that some attributes of the variables are correlated with linguistic change: the social differential in the use of (r), the cross-over pattern of the lower middle class for (æh), (oh), and (r), and the fine stratification of (r) as against the sharp dichotomies imposed by (th) and (dh). In this chapter, evidence from the objective distribution of the variables through age levels will be brought forward to explore this question in detail.

Methods for the synchronic study of change

The ideal method for the study of change is diachronic: the description of a series of cross-sections in real time, either by an independent set of random samples of the same population (a trend survey), or by re-interviewing the same individuals over a period of years (a panel survey). These are expensive methods, in terms of time and energy as well as money, and it is not often that they are carried out with full rigor. We have referred to earlier studies of New York City speech, and this chapter will refer to the Linguistic Atlas and Hubbell's records, as well as Babbitt's earlier report.

However, the method of selecting informants, the type of informants, and the context of the interviews were so different from the present study that caution must be used in drawing comparisons.[1] Differences between these earlier records and our own could be due to many other factors besides linguistic change. Therefore, until such time as the entire procedure, or a procedure similar to the present survey, is repeated after an interval of years, our best evidence for linguistic change will be internal evidence, drawn from the survey itself.

By studying the differences between the linguistic behavior of successive age levels in our sample, we can make inferences about linguistic change. This type of approach may be referred to as a *pseudo-trend study*, it is a series of cross-sections in apparent time as opposed to real time. The dimension of apparent time lies along the axis of the age levels of present-day informants, taken as representatives of the native speech pattern of the years in which they grew to maturity. It is obvious that such a method will give an accurate report of change only if apparent time is isomorphic with real time. This condition is fulfilled only: 1) if there are no differences between older and younger speakers which are repeated in each generation;

---

[1] Some important differences in method between the LA, Hubbell's survey, and the present study may be summarized as follows: 1) *Population*: Both the Atlas and Hubbell studied only white speakers descended from several generations of NYC residents. There are no representatives of the three principal ethnic groups of the city – Jews, Italians, or African-Americans – in either study. 2) *Sampling*: Neither the Atlas nor Hubbell followed any systematic procedure. The language of the 25 Atlas informants was used in classifying them by age levels and cultural types, so the information on distribution by age level and class is partly redundant. Among the few lower middle class informants, Lowman included a brother and sister from the same family. Hubbell's 30 informants were apparently selected by convenience: 14 of them are male Columbia College students, and 5 are teachers in the city schools. Besides these, there are 4 upper middle class informants, 2 lower middle class, no working class, and 5 lower class representatives. Except for the students, and one 31-year-old elevator operator, all of the informants are over 55. Thus the main body of working class and lower middle class residents of New York City are unrepresented in either study. 3) *Contexts*: The Atlas records are entirely Context B, and primarily the stressed words from that context needed for lexical studies. Hubbell relies primarily on reading, Context C, but uses some records of Context B as well.

and 2) if the older speakers remain isolated from the effects of the language used by younger speakers. Since these conditions are rarely fulfilled, the study of apparent time must be refined to distinguish the effects of linguistic change from the invariant effects of aging and from the modifying effects of the present situation upon older speakers.

The effects of aging may be either physical or cultural. Studies of the physiological process of vocal aging have shown that pitch and tempo alter regularly with advancing years;[2] but the possible effects of aging upon vowel and consonant production remain unknown, except for the obvious results of the loss of teeth. To control for possible effects of extreme old age, we will examine differences in speech production at three or four age levels, rather than rely too heavily upon the evidence of the very old informants. We can also rely to a certain extent upon comparison of our oldest informants with the oldest Atlas informants, who would presumably show similar effects of aging.

[In 1996 I followed through on this question by a series of re-interviews of Philadelphians who had been recorded seventeen years earlier. The same interviewer asked the same question to elicit the same story. There was no measurable difference in the realization of the variables of the Philadelphia vowel system (Labov and Auger 1998). It should be noted however that this was a study of normal aging based on the older members of the sample: speakers who were in their fifties and sixties when they were first recorded. Studies of young adults show varying degrees of shift (Sankoff 2002).]

Studies in apparent time may be most successful in communities where single-style speakers prevail, and where it is not normal for a person to adjust his speech radically to fit the social situation around him. In the previous study of linguistic change on Martha's Vineyard, cited above, this condition prevailed, and inferences from apparent time were comparatively straightforward. But as we have already seen, quite opposite conditions govern New York City. The extraordinary malleability of speech under shifts of social context may indicate a corresponding tendency of speakers to adjust their styles to fit a changing linguistic climate.

To minimize the effects of such adjustment, I will rely principally upon Style A, casual speech, which is most closely related to the native speech pattern of the pre-adolescent speaker. There is no doubt that for some persons, this pattern can shift in the course of twenty years. However, there is evidence that the shift is relatively small. The record of the out-of-town speakers as a whole, as reviewed in Chapter 7, shows no evidence that this group has made a radical adjustment to the native New York City pattern. On the contrary, the (æh) and (oh) vowels of the out-of-town respondents

---

[2] See Edward D. Mysak and T. D. Hanley, "Vocal Aging" (1959).

showed no relation to the New York vowel structure. Many individual cases can be cited to show vowel systems of out-of-towners preserved intact after thirty or forty years in the city, despite the sharp contrast between these systems and the New York structure.[3] As we have seen, it was even necessary to reject most of the marginal cases who had come to New York City in the latter part of their pre-adolescent years, because their characteristics departed so markedly from the main sequence of New York City speakers.

Despite the relative stability of casual speech, we must be prepared to find some degree of shift which is proportional to the length of time of exposure to an alien environment. Before we can utilize the data on distribution of the variables by age levels, a certain amount of preliminary analysis is necessary. We will use the evidence presented so far on the characteristics of various classes in order to construct models of the possible relations of real time to apparent time.

The relative stability of class patterns

There are a number of social forces which may produce a shift in the overall speech pattern of New Yorkers as they grow older. Contact with a wider range of class types, better acquaintance with the language of the upper middle class, exposure to the standard of broadcast media – all these may have some effect in moving the everyday speech of the average citizen away from his neighborhood pattern, and towards the prestige norm. We would expect that those who show the most linguistic mobility in their stylistic shifts would be most likely to show such an overall shift as they advance in years. The lower middle class speakers would be preeminent in this respect, and working class speakers next.[4] In contrast, the older speakers from the lower class and the upper middle class should serve as our best sources

---

[3] For example, a woman in one of the exploratory interviews was born in 1914 in the state of Washington of Ukrainian parents. She moved to North Carolina in 1926, and then to New York City in 1927. The vowels of *cot* and *caught, hock* and *hawk, Maud* and *Dodd* were still identical; this phonemic merger had been preserved intact from her pre-adolescent pattern, despite thirty-six years on the Lower East Side. Her 13-year-old daughter showed no trace of her mother's speech pattern. A similar case is that of an old lady of Polish background, born near Scranton, Pennsylvania in 1903. She left Scranton when she was 16, and lived in Utica until 1945, when she came to New York City. Though she has not been in contact with her original dialect area for forty-four years, she preserves a system with only one low-back phoneme. Her pronunciation of *caught* would be mistaken by New Yorkers for *cot* and vice-versa.

[4] Throughout this chapter, the terms *upper middle class, lower middle class, working class*, and *lower class* will be used informally to designate four divisions of the social spectrum ranked in that order. For the discussion of some variables, these will be operationally defined as SEC 9, 6–8, 2–5, and 0–1; for others, they will be defined as SC 4, 3, 2, and 1. The relations between these two scales are set forth in Chapter 8. In order to study distribution in

of historical information, since they show the least degree of stylistic variation.

The lower class speakers may show less shift for several reasons. They are less in contact with the prestige norm, as a result of their limited education. They are relatively isolated from the clerical and business world, and their attitude towards upward social movement may be negative or anomic.

The upper middle class speakers have greater linguistic security by all of the measures used in this study.[5] They have less tendency to shift their speech in later life, partly because they have incorporated into their everyday speech a large measure of the prestige norm. This assimilation may not have been accomplished in their pre-adolescent years, especially if they come from families of lower social status, but a considerable amount of the prestige pattern is acquired in the late teens in the college environment. At eighteen or nineteen, one cannot expect the acquired speech traits to be perfectly consistent, but upon graduation from college, the upper middle class speakers have probably obtained maximum exposure to the prestige norm. Their acquisition of these traits, the approval of their associates, and their general linguistic security would all tend to diminish any future shift of their everyday speech.

The possible relations of apparent time and real time

[At this point, the argument plunges into an analysis of the possible relations of apparent and real time outlining the linguistic patterns across age and class that follow from the presence or absence of change. It introduces two other concepts that have played a major role in the study of change and variation: *change from above* and *change from below*. Perhaps it would have been better to call them "change from without" and "change from within," since "below" tends to be confused with the notion of lower social class, but the terms are well established now.]

Before we examine the actual usage of the variables over several age levels, it will be useful to ask what kind of distribution we can expect in various cases if linguistic change has or has not been taking place. The simplest of all cases would be for a variable which has no social significance, is not involved in stylistic variation, and has not been stigmatized or awarded

Footnote 4 (*cont.*)
　　apparent time, it seems best to treat each variable by the social parameters which show the sharpest stratification for it, in terms of the criteria used in Chapter 8.
[5] We have already seen that the degree of shift from casual speech to more formal styles is less for the upper middle class than for other classes. This will be further demonstrated in this chapter. In Chapter 12 it will be seen that the upper middle class has high linguistic security by the lexical test of eighteen disputed words. In the discussion of linguistic attitudes a similar result will appear.

prestige of any sort. In such a case, we would expect either no difference between age levels, meaning that no change was in progress, or a uniform change from level to level, without any differences in social class or ethnic group, indicating a gradual linguistic change. This would be the model of a change through random drift, as discussed in the opening chapter. While it is a theoretical possibility, no such case has come to our attention in the study of New York City English.

A case which frequently does occur is that of a language feature which has been socially stigmatized as a mark of uneducated or uncultivated speech, or has been associated with a minority of low status. We may call this *Case I*. If no linguistic change in the social significance of this item has taken place, we would expect a distribution such as the following: the groups of higher social status would show no trace of the feature, or very little; the uneducated members of lower status groups, who were closely tied to their own neighborhood, would use this feature extensively, and show little change in their usage as they grew older, so that both older and younger speakers would show a relatively high degree of this trait, however, the middle ranking members of lower status groups, such as the upper sections of the working class, or the lower middle class, will come into broader contact with the prestige forms, and we would expect some weakening of their use of the stigmatized form as they grew older. Thus even a static situation can produce variations from one age group to another.

If linguistic change is in progress, the effect of increasing stigmatization may reverse the situation described above. The older speakers will show greater use of the newly stigmatized feature, and the younger groups less, especially among the middle ranking of the lower status groups. We can thus show two contrasting schemes for Case I in Table 9.1.

A second case which frequently occurs is that of a prestige feature which is not used in everyday language by the majority of the population. We may refer to this as *Case II, change from above* (see Table 9.2). If no change is taking place, we would expect that the highest status group would show a uniformly high level of this feature through all age groups. The lowest status group would probably show none. The middle ranking groups would show none for younger speakers, but tend to acquire some smaller amounts of this characteristic in later years, as they came into contact with the prestige norms. This effect might be observable in everyday speech, but would be considerably magnified in more formal styles.

If the prestige feature is not invariant, but has been recently introduced, we should see a different distribution. The highest ranking group will show us the plainest signs of linguistic change: the older speakers will adhere to the older prestige norm, and be relatively unmoved by the newer norm.

Table 9.1   *Case I: A stigmatized language feature*

I-A. No change in progress

	Lower class	Working class	Lower middle class	Upper middle class
Younger	high	higher	higher	low
Older	high	lower	lower	low

I-B. Change in progress

	Lower class	Working class	Lower middle class	Upper middle class
Younger	(lower)	lower	lower	low
Older	(higher)	higher	higher	low

Table 9.2   *Case II: Change from above: a prestige feature*

II-A. No change in progress

	Lower class	Working class	Lower middle class	Upper middle class
Younger	low	lower	lower	high
Older	low	higher	higher	high

II-B. Change in progress

	Lower class	Working class	Lower middle class	Upper middle class
Younger	low	lower	lower	high
Older	higher	higher	higher	low

Younger speakers will show much greater use of the new prestige form, and contrast sharply with older speakers of high status.

Traces of this newer norm will be found in the middle ranking group, but not among young speakers who have acquired only the traditional pattern. It is the older speakers from the middle ranking group who show the greatest malleability, and the least linguistic security: it is they who will adopt some of this new prestige marker. It is not likely that the oldest speakers of this class will show the same adjustability as the middle-aged ones: the evidence from the present study indicates that the greatest degree of stylistic fluctuation, and linguistic insecurity, occurs in middle-aged speakers from the middle ranking groups.[6]

---

[6] As shown in Figure 9.5, it is the 40–49 age level which is the principal focus of such hypercorrection. This age level probably extends from 40 to 55, since indications are that women in this class report their age as lower than their chronological age.

Thus the contrast for a prestige feature, between the effects of no change and of change, depends primarily upon the behavior of the highest ranking group.

If we compare these diagrams with those for the stigmatized feature, we see that we cannot look for evidence of linguistic change in the same groups in both cases. The key to change of the stigmatized feature is in the behavior of the lower ranking groups, especially the working class and lower middle class. Their behavior is quite opposite for the cases of change or no change. But for the prestige feature, the behavior of these lower ranking groups gives little information. Quantitative differences may prove helpful in analyzing the situation, but qualitatively, the relations are the same. We must look to the highest ranking group for primary information on linguistic change in this case.

Once we have determined the situation for casual speech, we can further amplify our understanding by investigating more formal styles. The information gained here will be particularly useful in showing the details of change for the prestige feature, for formal styles of speech respond most directly to this type of language trait.

The two cases discussed above are relatively simple examples of the pressure of society upon language. These forces are applied from above – they are the product of overt social pressures consonant with the social hierarchy. The process is out in the open for us to observe, in public performances, in the attitudes of teachers in the schools, and in the conscious reactions of some middle class persons. Ordinarily, such forces are exerted upon individual elements of a language system, rather than upon the system as a whole. The item in question may be the use of a single word, such as *ain't*, or the pronunciation of a word, such as *vase*, or *aunt*, or it may be an entire allophone, such as the upgliding central diphthong in *bird*, or the (æh-2) of *bad*, *ask*, and *dance*. The *results* of public pressure from above are sometimes highly systematic, as the shift of one feature may have systematic consequences if the feature is important enough. We see this case in the introduction of (r) into the phonological system of the language, with the systematic developments to be explored in Chapter 14.

There is another type of linguistic change, correlated with social factors of a different nature. We may describe this as *change from below*, because it is expressed as a gradual shift in the behavior of successive generations, well below the level of conscious awareness of any speakers. In most cases, the shift begins with a particular group in the social structure and is gradually generalized in the speech of other groups. Usually the initiating group has low status in the social hierarchy – otherwise the change would be transformed into overt pressure from above. Social reaction may afterwards fasten on the results of such a change, and force a reversal in whole or in part by pressure from above. However, the change itself is accomplished without public attention, and is usually subject to overt pressure from above at a late stage.[7] The upward transit of slang terms in the language is the aspect of change from below which is most familiar to us in everyday life. The reasons for such a progression are obscure, and many speculative explanations have been advanced without the support of empirical tests. It is safe to say that the explanation for this upward movement, which I have called change from below, is one of the most important open questions in the study of linguistic change. The relations between social classes are not the only types of differentiation associated with change from below. We have already seen that the distribution of (æh) and (oh) is closely associated with systematic ethnic differences. Since the relations of Jews, Italians, and Irish (and now African–Americans and Puerto Ricans) have formed one of the principal themes of social dynamics in New York City, we can believe that such linguistic correlates can lead to generalized changes in the speech of the city as a whole.

What kind of distribution through apparent time can we expect from changes from below? If the situation is not complicated by a corresponding correction from above, we would expect to see a steady progression along at least one social dimension as well as the dimension of apparent time. For example, Table 9.3 for Case III-A shows a pattern rising in the working class, and spreading to other classes.

This pattern in its simplest form is seldom to be found in actuality. The differential behavior of ethnic groups, of the sexes, and other factors will complicate the pattern. Furthermore, the new forms may be stigmatized from above at a certain stage. We would therefore have to superimpose the pattern of Case I-B on the result (see Table 9.4). A possible later stage of III is therefore given in Table 9.4.

The ensuing complications may become so great that we would be forced to give up the attempt to analyze apparent time, and rely instead upon whatever evidence we have from earlier studies in real time.

For change from below, there is no important distinction between stigmatized and prestige forms: the speech form assumed by each group may be

---

[7] There are many such examples in the history of the English language. The loss of (r) apparently began as a change from below, and the dropping of /h/ in the initial combination /hw/ in *which* and *when* seems to have proceeded upwards. The "broad a" in *father*, *ask*, *France*, *dance*, etc., seems to have originated as a vulgar pronunciation, according to John Walker in his *Principles of English Pronunciation*, first published in 1791. Many such examples may be found in H. C. Wyld, *A History of Modern Colloquial English* (1936).

Table 9.3   *Case III-A. Change from below: early stage*

	Lower class	Working class	Lower middle class	Upper middle class
Youngest	high	high	high	medium
Young adults	medium	high	medium	low
Middle-aged	low	medium	low	low
Oldest	low	low	low	low

Table 9.4   *III-B. Change from below: late stages with correction from above*

	Lower class	Working class	Lower middle class	Upper middle class
Youngest	high	high	high	low
Young adults	high	high	high	medium
Middle-aged	medium	high	low	high
Oldest	low	medium	low	medium

taken as an unconscious mark of self-identification. We therefore have the possible types of linguistic change corresponding to distributional patterns in apparent time (with examples) shown in Table 9.5.

We may now proceed to examine the distribution of the variables in apparent time, and interpret the results in accordance with the considerations given above. We will therefore examine the social characteristics of the sample population by age level.

[This exposition of the relations of "higher" and "lower" across age and social class is well confirmed by the data sets to follow. It seemed too complicated to work with, and I later used a simpler model, where the absence of change was shown by flat distribution in age and a monotonic distribution in social class, while the presence of change would show a monotonic distribution in age and a curvilinear class pattern (Labov 1980). But as predicted here, a stigmatized variable will be used more freely by younger speakers than older speakers – at least for the upper working class and lower middle class. The study of Philadelphia in the 1970s included a good complement of teenage working class youth who regularly produced an adolescent spike for (th) and (dh), while the adult age distribution was flat (Labov 2001: Ch. 3).]

Table 9.5   *Types of linguistic change*

		Incidental	Systematic
Change from above	Stigmatized forms	/ʌy/ in *bird*	–
	Prestige forms	/ah/ in *vase*	(r)
Change from below	Self-identification	*keen, cool* as slang	(æh), (oh)

The distribution of the population by age

Figure 9.1 shows the distribution of the eighty-three New York informants by age level, social class, sex, and ethnic group.[8]

In Figure 9.1, we can immediately note certain weak points in the distribution. The entire diagram is plainly skewed, with the oldest speakers represented in classes 0–3 only, and the youngest primarily in classes 4–9. The heaviest representation is in the 40–49 age level. More men are found in the younger age levels, and more women in the middle-aged rank, while the oldest subjects are men.

This distribution is characteristic of the entire sample population of native speakers, and not the result of a failure to locate a particular group. Table 9.6 shows the distribution of the various sample populations by age level.

The first column is the ALS target sample: the native English speakers who had not moved, including New Yorkers and out-of-towners, minus the four marginal cases discussed in Chapter 6. If we compare the sample of New York subjects actually interviewed in the ALS survey, we see that the distribution is not very different. The sample of eighty-three is slightly higher for the youngest speakers, and weaker for the 35–39 group and 50–59 group.

The shortage of younger informants is not a product of the survey procedure; it is partly due to the fact that all of the MFY informants are two years older than they were when the adult sample was first constructed. Secondly, a shortage of speakers between 30 and 39 has developed because this group has shown the highest rate of moving. In any case, we will need more younger speakers to study change through apparent time.

We can find the younger informants we need in the 13 adult children of informants studied in the ALS interview. Twelve of these were New Yorkers. Furthermore, 25 of the 33 subjects studied in the television interviews were New Yorkers. We thus have 120 informants, as shown in the third column of Table 9.6.

---

[8] These include the supplementary informants for class 9, and two African–American speakers who must be eliminated for comparisons of working classes across ethnic lines. The four marginal speakers eliminated in Chapter 6 will not appear in this chapter.

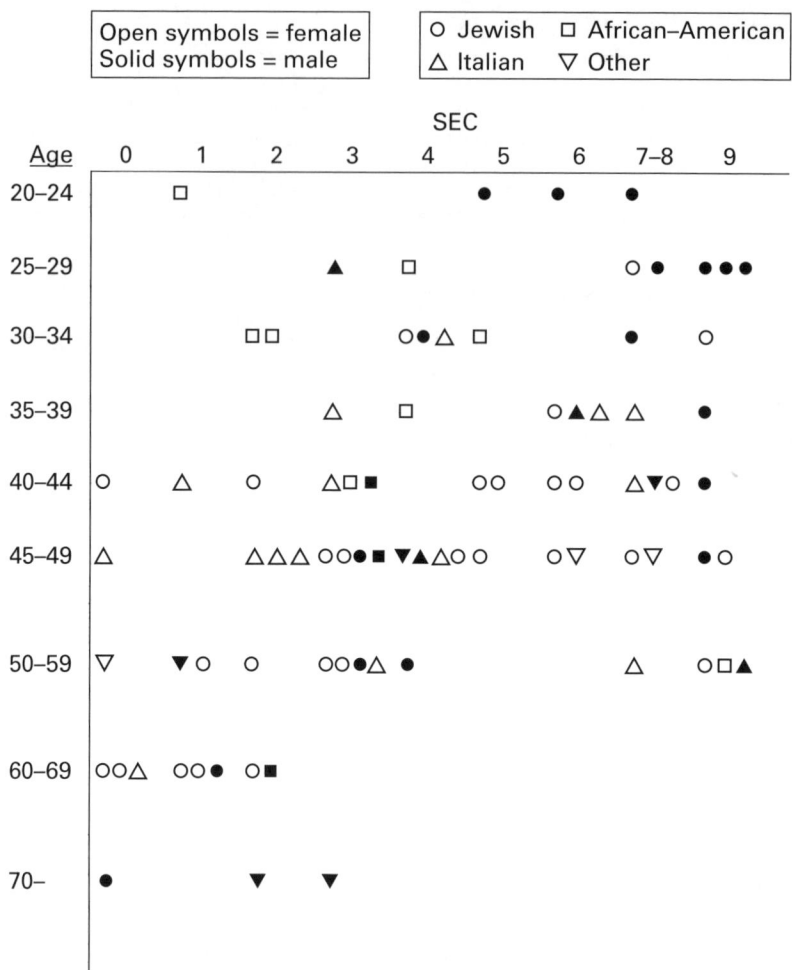

Figure 9.1   Distribution of 83 adult New York ALS informants by age, SEC, sex, and ethnic group

This addition leaves us with a shortage of older speakers in the 50–59 age range, and of the very oldest subjects. We have a fairly good sample of the middle-aged group, but there is little we can do to supplement the oldest group. Losses through death and disability, combined with low numbers to begin with, have reduced this group to the point that we must combine it with the group aged 60 to 69.

The resulting distribution is shown in Figure 9.2. The adult children of ALS informants are seen here as supplementing the distribution of

Table 9.6   *Percentage distribution of populations by age level*

Age	ALS target sample	Native NY ALS subjects	All NYC subjects	Completion rate for ALS + TV	Died or moved population
20–24	02	05	10	100	05
25–29	07	08	08	93	11
30–34	07	09	09	93	13
35–39	13	08	10	83	18
40–44	16	17	16	97	12
45–49	20	23	21	84	15
50–59	20	16	15	63	15
60–69	08	10	08	75	08
70–	07	04	03	69	03
	100	100	100		100
	[N: 191	83	120		117]

Figure 9.1 at the points where the original pattern was weakest. The children of informants are shown at the top of the diagram. The distribution of those eight to nineteen years old seems fairly even, with more male than female subjects, and representation from all ethnic groups. But we cannot consider this sample as reliable as our adult sample. As noted in Chapter 6, the youth interviews were not pursued systematically, and convenience played a considerable part in the final results. I did not sample the young people who are never found at home, nor even the ones who did not happen to be available when I wanted them. Therefore the youth sample may be used to suggest trends which are positively present in the data, but not to exclude any possibilities which we do not find.

However, we will want to utilize the information from the twelve adult children of informants throughout this chapter. These subjects have a well-established social position of their own, and it is possible to assign them socio-economic rankings as reliably as the regular ALS informants. Since their evidence is needed for the study of the younger sections of the adult population, it is necessary to see if they follow the same linguistic patterns as the main body of adult speakers, or if their addition to the sample will result in a completely different overall distribution.

We can check the effect of adding this group to the population by re-tabulating style and class stratification arrays for (r). As we have seen, the variable (r) is the most sensitive and regular indicator of socio-economic status. The structure of stylistic and social variation which we have seen in Figures 7.9, 7.10, and 7.11 is preserved for this combined population with only slight changes. One deviation from regular structure is

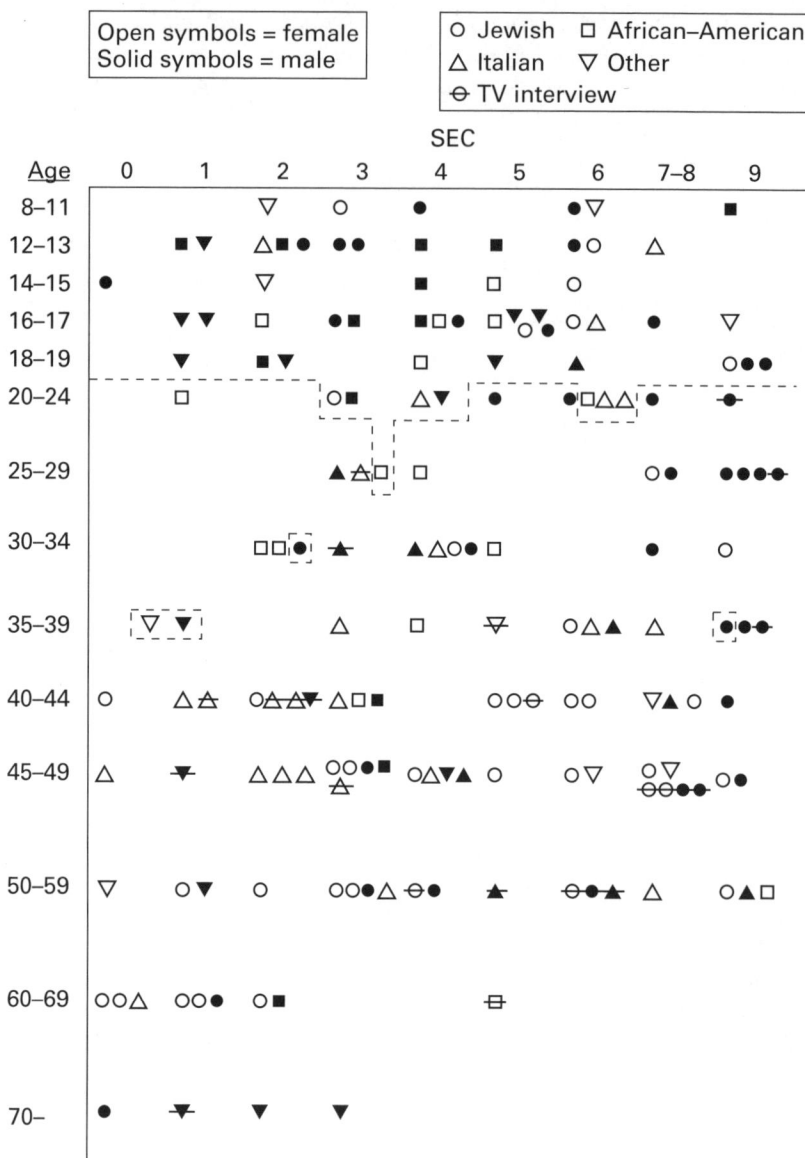

Figure 9.2   Distribution of 169 New York informants including children and television interviews. Dotted lines indicate children of ALS informants.

eliminated: the equality of Styles B and C for class 9. A deviation in the relations of class 0 and 1 in Style D' appears. Otherwise, the overall stratification of the population is sharpened, for the (r) values are slightly lower for the lower ranking classes and for the less formal styles, and slightly higher for the higher ranking classes and more formal styles.

We can conclude that this addition to the sample will allow us to investigate distribution in apparent time for an expanded sample population: the younger informants fit the overall pattern of behavior for (r) quite well, and even sharpen the view of stylistic and social stratification.

A case of stigmatization: the upgliding vowel of third

In order to check the general views of the relations of apparent time and real time set forth above, we may take first a simple and clear-cut example of Case I, a stigmatized phonological feature. The most well-known example of a stigmatized New York City trait is the upgliding central diphthong in words like *third*, *bird*, and *shirt*, *curl* and *worm*, *verse* and *worse*, which has come to symbolize New York City speech in folk mythology under the name of *Brooklynese*. The upgliding central diphthong may be written phonetically as [əɪ], and as /ʌy/ in the phonemic notation of Chapter 2.[9]

This sound is still frequently heard in New York City for the words just listed. A few lower class and working class respondents used this diphthong for *oil* and *voice*, as well as *Earl* and *verse*. But this merger of word classes is rare today; middle class speakers have apparently never used /ʌy/ for the *voice* group of words, even when they used it regularly for *verse*. We will therefore be studying the occurrence of /ʌy/ in words such as *third*, *bird*, *curl*, and *verse*.

The use of /ʌy/ in any context is now heavily stigmatized, although at one time it was a pronunciation used regularly by New Yorkers of all classes. For reasons that are not entirely clear, it has met with an extreme form of social pressure from above, and has receded rapidly under this social correction.[10]

---

[9] The upgliding diphthong may be pronounced by beginning with the final vowel of *sofa*, and adding to it the final vowel of *city*.

[10] Babbitt's records, summarized in Chapter 14, show /ʌy/ as the regular form in 1896. No earlier data on /ʌy/ in New York City is quoted by George Philip Krapp, in his review of the situation, in *The English Language in America* (1952), II, pages 185–186. Krapp adds: "Historical evidence for the origin of this diphthong is lacking, and though statistics showing the extent of its use are not available, it is a matter of common observation in New York that the pronunciation is widespread and is making its way from the lower popular level to the general popular level." There is no other evidence for this statement of Krapp, and we have no reason to believe that /ʌy/ is a late stage of change from below. In Map 25 of Kurath and McDavid, *The Pronunciation of English in the Atlantic States*, we see that /ʌy/ is perfectly regular in South Carolina and other parts of the Lower South studied: cultivated as well as uncultivated informants used this vowel. A scattering of occurrences is found elsewhere in the south, but the only other solid concentration is in New York City. See also Allan E. Hubbell, " 'Curl' and 'Coil' in New York City" (1940), for the situation just before World War II.

Table 9.7   *Percentage using any /ʌy/ by age and SECs: overall distribution*

Age	0–1	2–5	6–8	9		N:		
20–39	75	35	09	00	4	16	11	7
40–	85	57	35	00	13	35	17	7

Table 9.7 gives the percentages of speakers who used any instances of this stigmatized form in any style during the interview, by class and age level. The population studied includes the ALS informants, adult children of informants, and those studied in the television interview.[11]

Table 9.7 conforms in detail to the pattern of Case I-B: a stigmatized language feature showing change in progress.

This overall view can be confirmed by a closer examination of the data. Table 9.8 shows the distribution for five age levels and five class levels, in which the numerator of the fraction represents the number who used some upgliding centralized diphthongs, and the denominator the total number of cases. Informants under twenty are added on the top line, so the total number of cases here is 162.

The marginals of Table 9.8 show a steady progression along both axes, indicating that the use of /ʌy/ is systematically correlated with both age and class. In order to judge the relative influence of these two independent variables, we can examine Figure 9.3, an age stratification diagram, and Figure 9.4, a class stratification diagram. A comparison shows us immediately that age is stratified more clearly than class. There are four deviations from regular structure in the relations of class groups, but only two deviations for age levels in the same array. Figure 9.3 indicates that the age level 60–75 shows no contrast (upper middle class speakers being missing); the 40–59 groups show only a coarse pattern of stratification, not at all regular for the lower class and working class; the age level 20–39 shows regular class stratification, and the younger speakers use no /ʌy/ at all except for the lower class. Thus the impact of social stigmatization has produced such a swift change that only one generation shows the regular class stratification that we have observed for the other phonological variables. For the oldest

[11] Hereafter, the term *ALS New York City informants* will be used to indicate the 83 regular ALS informants and their children. Only the 12 adult children are included, unless the age level 8–19 is specifically mentioned. The term *all New York City informants* includes these respondents, plus the 25 respondents raised in New York City who were studied by means of the television interview. The two African–American speakers excluded from the study of class distribution are automatically included whenever ethnic groups are studied separately.

Table 9.8   *Speakers using any /ʌy/ by age and SEC: detailed distribution*

Age	0–1	2–3	4–5	6–8	9	0–9	%
8–19	2/7	0/11	0/12	0/16	0/5	2/51	04
20–39	3/4	3/7	3/10	1/11	0/7	10/39	24
40–49	1/3	5/14	4/8	4/13	0/4	14/42	33
50–59	3/3	2/4	3/3	2/4	0/3	10/17	59
60–	7/7	5/5	1/1			13/13	100
8–60	16/24	15/41	11/34	7/44	0/19	49/162	
%	67	38	32	16	00		

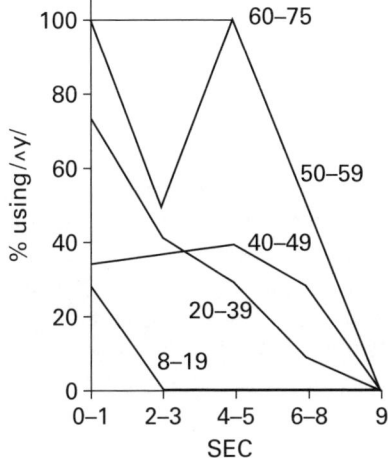

Figure 9.3   Age stratification of /ʌy/ by class

speakers, /ʌy/ is used regularly by all but the highest ranking class. For our youngest speakers, the stigmatized feature has disappeared for all but the lowest ranking class.

This rapid change covers the whole range of social contrast in four generations: for the speakers raised before World War I, the use of a constricted [ɚ] in *bird*, *work*, and *worm* is a prestige mark of upper class speech: for those who are growing up today, the once common standard /ʌy/ is a highly stigmatized mark of lower class speech.

Our interpretation of the distribution in apparent time is confirmed by earlier records. The Linguistic Atlas records of 1941 show /ʌy/ in the speech

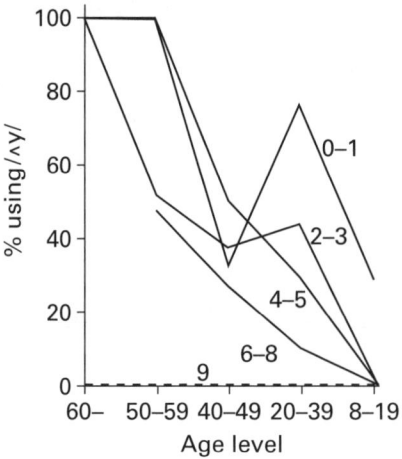

Figure 9.4   Class stratification of /ʌy/ by age

of nineteen of the twenty-five informants. Those who did not use this phoneme used the constricted [ɚ] which is common today: five of these six speakers were classified as cultured informants, and one as intermediate[12]. Hubbell's studies were made only a few years later, but they include speakers thirty years younger than the youngest Atlas informants. Table 9.9 summarizes his findings for the thirty informants; the social class categories are assigned by me in accordance with the information given by Hubbell. The numerator of the fraction is the number using /ʌy/, the denominator the total number.

Thus we see that the process of stigmatization has made further progress since Hubbell's studies of the 1940s. The limited data of earlier studies are consistent with our analysis of the relations of apparent time and real time for Case I-B, and with the more complete data provided in Table 9.8.

[This record of the rapid extinction of the major NYC stereotype is certainly accurate as far as it goes: r-less /əy/ has disappeared. Yet close listening to New Yorkers over the years has convinced me that it lingers on in a modified form. Many New Yorkers today can be heard to use a palatalized form of a well contracted, mid-central [r] in *first* and *work*.]

---

[12] For the meaning of the Atlas categories *cultured*, etc., see below in the section concerning (r).

Table 9.9   *Use of /ʌy/ by Hubbell's informants according to SC index & age*

	SC 1	SC 3	SC 4
15–29		5/6	2/7
30–49	1/1		
50–59	1/1	1/1	1/3
60–69			3/3
70–	3/3	0/1	3/3

The distribution of (r) in apparent time

We can now turn to an example of Case II, a language feature with social prestige. The case of (r), one of the most important of the five variables, illustrates this type as precisely as the previous example illustrated Case I. The overall distribution of (r) in apparent time is shown in Table 9.10 for ALS New York informants.

If we now refer to the diagram for probable distribution of features in the Case II-B, we see that Table 9.10 corresponds in every detail to that abstraction. The growing stratification of (r) is shown by considering the percentages of those who used some (r-1) in casual speech (see Table 9.11).

In casual speech, the great majority of New Yorkers remain completely *r*-less. Of the twenty-five speakers between 20 and 39 years old who are not class 9, only one used (r-1) in casual speech – and he only used (r-1) once. For older speakers, we see that small amounts of (r-1) pronunciation have crept into their speech. Although 31 percent used some (r-1) the average value of the index remains at only (r)-05.

The upper middle class values are based on small numbers: only thirteen speakers are actually represented in Style A. However, their use is extremely consistent. Of the speakers in the 20–39 group, one of the six used no (r-1), but the rest all used high values. For the older speakers, most of the average (r) value is in the speech of one subject who was exactly 40 years old – a borderline case. His index was (r)-40: of the other speakers, four had indexes of 00, one 03, and one 16.

If we examine the younger speakers, 8–19, we find a comparable situation. There are only two upper middle class speakers who gave values for Style A: one at (r)-87, the other (r)-67. Two other speakers who did not actually give samples of casual speech were used with extrapolated minimum values to give the figure shown above. For the twenty-eight speakers from other classes in the youth group, only two showed slight traces of (r-1).

Thus the overall development of (r-1) in New York City in casual speech has not been a general increase in the use of this feature but rather an

Table 9.10   *Average indexes for* (r) *in style A by age and class: overall distribution*

	SEC					N:		
Age	0–1	2–5	6–8	9				
8–19	00	01	00	48	6	16	6	4
20–39	00	00	00	34	3	13	9	4
40–	00	06	09	09	10	25	8	7

Table 9.11   *Sharp stratification of* (r) *by age and two SEC groups*

Age	SEC 0–8	SEC 9
20–39	06%	87%
40–	31	43

increase in sharpness of stratification. For the older speakers, (r) was apparently not a feature of prestige pronunciation, and did not serve to differentiate class groups. For younger speakers, there is a great gap between upper middle class and the rest, with (r) serving as a marker of this particular class alone.

We may now benefit from a closer examination of the distribution of (r) in apparent time. Figure 9.5 shows the distribution of average (r) indexes for four age levels and four class groups in Style A for ALS New York City informants. The broken horizontal line shows the level of (r) for the upper middle class, and the height of the bars shows the average (r) indexes for the three other class groups.

Figure 9.5 illustrates graphically the lack of contrast between the upper middle class and other classes for the older age levels, and the extreme contrast for the lower age levels. It is introduced here primarily for comparison with Figure 9.6, which shows the same diagram for Styles B, C, D, and D'.

From top to bottom of Figure 9.6, we see stylistic variation, with more (r-1) used regularly by all sub-groups. From left to right, there is a larger pattern of age variation imposed on a pattern of social variation. The age variation is itself divided along two contrasting lines: the upper middle class moves up from left to right, and the other classes move down from left to right, starting with the second age level. For the three classes shown as 0–1, 2–5, and 6–8, the amount of (r-1) used increases steadily in that order for nine of the fifteen cases.

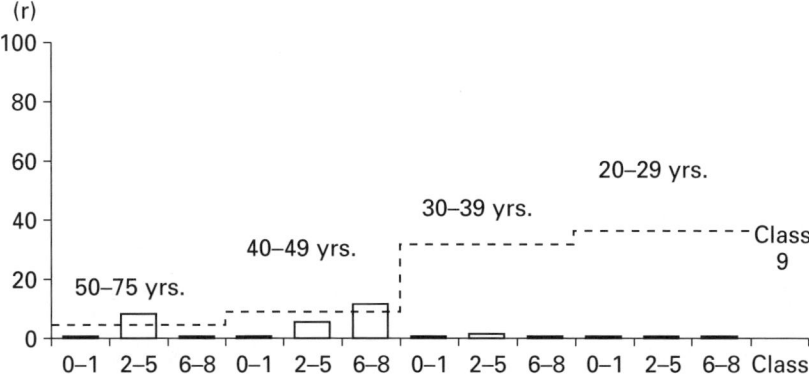

Figure 9.5   (r) indexes for classes 0–8 in relation to (r) for class 9 by age in Style A

This pattern confirms in detail the mechanism suggested in the discussion of Case II. In Style A, it was difficult to see the shift of the middle-aged members of the lower middle class with the same clarity that is seen in the whole stylistic range. As far as the oldest speakers are concerned, all of the values are at a very low level for Styles A, B, and C, so that the question of which is higher is not particularly meaningful. However, when we examine Style D′, we see that there is a tendency for even the oldest speakers of class 0–8 to go beyond the (r) level of the upper middle class speakers.

The hatched portions of the bars indicate the proportion by which speakers from class 0–8 go beyond the (r) index of the upper middle class. The hypercorrection of the lower middle class carries it beyond the highest level of any upper middle class speakers in Styles D and D′. However, it is worth noting that even the lower class moves in this direction among the speakers 40–49 years old in Style D′.

As we examine the record for Style D′, it is plain that the source of (r-1) pronunciation for the 40–49 group is not the upper middle class of their own age level. On the contrary, this group of lower middle class speakers seems to be oriented towards a prestige norm maintained by younger speakers, such as those in the 20–39 age level. In this age level, the upper middle class does seem to represent the maximum use of (r-1) at which all other groups are aiming in formal styles. This indicates a more stable relationship between the four classes than the situation in the older age levels.

One of the problems of this analysis is that in dividing a sample of ninety-four speakers into fifteen groups, we have a great many unreliable cells. These are represented by bars with broken lines in Figure 9.6 – groups with less than five speakers. We can correct this situation for Style B by

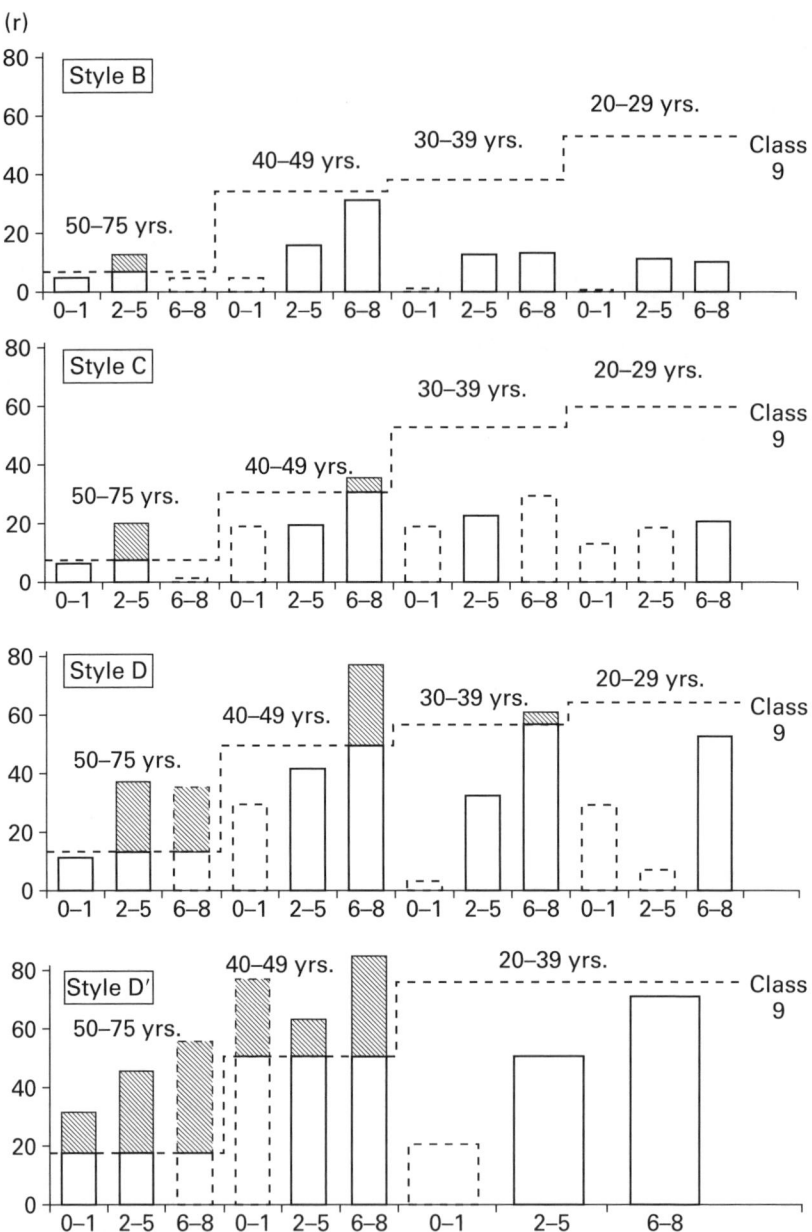

Figure 9.6   (r) indexes for classes 0–8 in relation to (r) for class 9 by age and style

Table 9.12   *Distribution of* (r) *indexes in style B by age and class for television interviews*

Age	0–1	2–5	6–8	9		N:		
20–29	–	00	–	63	0	1	0	2
30–39	00	02	–	–	1	2	0	0
40–49	03	02	15	28	3	5	4	2
50–	00	–	16	–	1	0	4	0

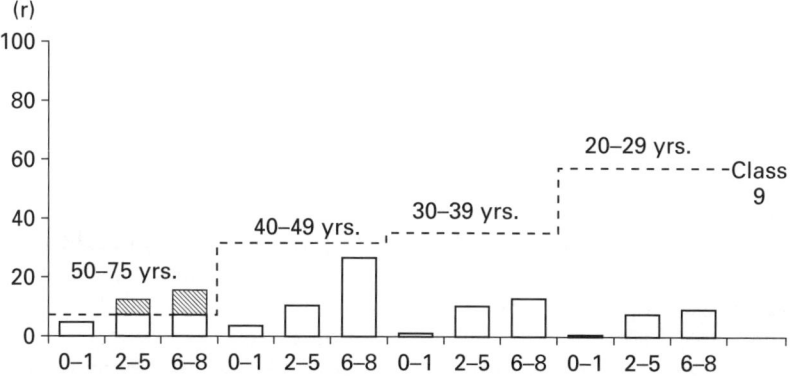

Figure 9.7   (r) indexes for classes 0–8 in relation to (r) for class 9 by age in Style B: all New York City informants

augmenting the sample with the twenty-five subjects interviewed in the television survey. Altogether, these twenty-five informants display the rough outlines of the pattern of age and class stratification in Style B. Table 9.12 shows the average values for the television interviews alone.

It should be noted that the context of the television interviews lies somewhere in between Context B and Context A of the ALS interviews, though somewhat closer to B. Appendix C correlates the ALS interviews and television interviews for ten speakers randomly selected who were interviewed by both methods. In the light of Table 9.12, we can feel justified in adding these twenty-five speakers to the ALS New York informants in Style B. The result is Figure 9.7. The bars with broken outlines can now be replaced by solid bars, and all four age levels are seen to be arranged in the order of 0–1 lowest, 2–5 next, and 6–8 highest. Each increment to the sample has thus produced greater rather than less regularity in the social stratification of (r), lending additional confirmation to the initial statement of Chapter 7.

Comparison with the department store survey

In Chapter 3 the results of a survey of department store employees were presented to show the stratification of (r) within a single occupational group. This procedure was quite apart from the methods, materials, and population of the Lower East Side Survey. It involved errors of approximation due to several factors: the small amount of data per informant, the method of notation, the method of sampling, the estimation of age of the informant, and the lack of background data on the informants. To compensate for these sources of error, we had the uniformity of the interview procedure, the location of the informants in their primary role as active employees, the relatively large number of cases within a single cell, the simplicity of the data, and above all the absence of the biasing effect of the formal linguistic interview. The ALS survey is strong in precisely those areas where the department store survey is weak, and the sources of error are exactly the opposite. These two approaches to the social distribution of (r) are therefore complementary: if the results converge, we will have reduced the likelihood of bias or error to a very low point.

One of the problems in the department store survey was that the interviewer was simultaneously the transcriber and the maker of the initial hypothesis. However, the initial hypothesis did not go beyond the facts of simple social stratification. The distribution of (r) in apparent time was not analyzed at that time. Therefore the results shown in Figure 3.5 were unexpected and difficult to understand. Instead of a uniform increase of (r) with decreasing age for each department store, we obtained such a result only for the highest ranking store. The middle ranking store showed the reverse progression, with the older speakers showing most (r-1) and the younger speakers the least. Finally, the lowest ranking store showed no direction of change at all. The explanation given at that time, as quoted in Chapter 3, was considered only tentative, without sufficient evidence. The hypercorrect pattern of the lower middle class, and its role in linguistic change, had not been demonstrated by the quantitative methods of Chapters 7 and 8. The cross-over pattern of the lower middle class provides the synchronic evidence for the analysis of Case II-B in the present chapter, which places the role of this class in the larger context of the relations of aging and adjustment to the native speech pattern.

We can now make a direct comparison of the department store survey with the results of the ALS survey. Figure 9.8 is an adaptation of Figure 9.7 for that purpose. When this is compared to Figure 3.5, the results are identical.

Despite the fact that the populations studied were different, that the methods were totally opposed, and that the sources of error were comple-

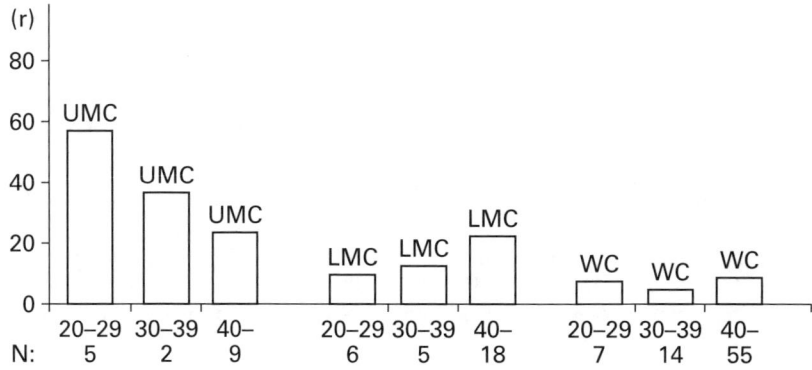

Figure 9.8   (r) indexes by age and class in Style B: all New York City informants

mentary, both diagrams show the abstract structure of Case II-B. Point by point, the structure of these two figures match. The adoption of a prestige factor by the highest ranking group, the corresponding shift among the older members of the middle ranking group, and the relative indifference of the lowest ranking group are the main features of linguistic structure which display the effects of linguistic change.

[The convergence of the department store study and the Lower East Side study is an impressive demonstration that we can bypass the surface phenomena to arrive at a more abstract structure that is independent of the particular surface details. Not only does the complex pattern of Figure 9.8 agree with Figure 3.5, but the same pattern was obtained in Fowler's replication of the department store study (Labov 1994: Ch. 4). The model of two approaches with complementary sources of error was also used in Harlem in the 1960s (Labov, Cohen, Robins and Lewis 1968), and in Philadelphia in the 1970s (Labov 1980, 2001).]

We may now turn to the evidence of the Linguistic Atlas on the use of (r) in New York City before World War II. The twenty-five Atlas informants for New York City were selected as individuals whose parents and grandparents were born in New York City, and as representatives of the following social levels:[13]

I)   Persons of little formal education, little reading and restricted social contacts.

II) Persons of better formal education (usually high school) and/or wider reading and contacts.

[13] From Hans Kurath, *Handbook of the Linguistic Geography of New England* (1939).

III)   Persons of superior education (usually college), cultured background, wide reading and/or extensive social contacts.

These mixed criteria evidently offer wide latitude for the subjective judgment of the field worker, who was not so much sampling a population as searching for predetermined types.

The informants for the Atlas may also be classified according to their age:

A)   Aged, and/or regarded by the field worker as old-fashioned.
B)   Middle-aged or younger, and/or regarded by the field worker as more modern.
C)   The youngest Atlas informants, 45 to 48 years old (a distinction added by Frank).

Again, we see that the definitions are extremely informal, and give the field worker ample room to set aside chronological age in favor of his subjective impressions.

Although the limited numbers of the Atlas survey, and the informal nature of the categories, set obvious limitations on the use of the data for a study of social stratification, we may obtain some broadly qualitative indications of the direction of linguistic change from these records.

The evidence on final and pre-consonantal (r) is summed up by Frank (1948) in the following manner (p. 84):

The post-vocalic /r/ is almost regularly actualized as the non-syllabic sonorant [ə]. In words of the type of *har* and *burr* it is usually actualized as vowel prolongation. However, two informants use [ə], a weakly constricted postvocalic /r/, less frequently strongly constricted [ɚ] in two-fifths to two-thirds of the test words. One of these is the Queens County informant who was educated in areas where /r/ is usually of the constricted type. The other is the younger informant on Staten Island, an area partially under New Jersey influence.

This statement brushes aside a good deal of the data which is presented in the chart which Frank herself supplies. Not two, but nine of the twenty-four speakers listed on this chart show some constricted forms. Four of these are old (three I-A, one II-A), four are middle-aged (three II-B, one III-B), and one is from the youngest group (I-C). Instead of accepting the fact of variation as an inherent tendency of the population, Frank attempts to explain away the major deviations and ignores the minor ones, in the interest of regularity. Yet for the ten test words listed, and the twenty-four informants listed, we have 11 percent constricted forms: 27 out of 240. And this sample is intended as the most homogeneous group of native New Yorkers which could be assembled.

We can conclude from the Atlas records that the raw material for the social stratification of (r) was present in New York City before World War

II, and we need not think of the sudden rise of the prestige of (r) as the creation of a new structure ex nihilo. But in the 1890s, Babbitt gives no indication of any variation from the *r*-less pattern of the city.

Hubbell's records show slight traces of (r-1) in the speech of five out of his nine informants over 60 years old; all five are in his upper middle class group. Three of his four middle-aged speakers showed some (r-1). We can divide the fourteen college students into an upper middle class group of eight and a lower middle class group of six, depending on the family background. Six of the former group showed some (r-1), and three of the latter.[14] In these reports, we see a little more resemblance to the structure which governs the use of (r) among our respondents. However, the limitations of the data and the informal method of reporting make it difficult to interpret this material, and we must be careful not to impose too much structure upon it.

The most reliable record for the beginning of the present structure of (r) is in the usage of the upper middle class ALS informants in casual speech. Their record points to a sudden change for the New Yorkers under 40 years old. The dividing line seems to be closely associated with the period of World War II. The age group which is now 40 to 49 years old was born in the years 1914–1923, and was educated in the New York City schools in the years immediately preceding World War II. A person who was 41 years old in 1963 would have graduated from high school just before the outbreak of the war. On the other hand, a person who was 35 years old in 1963 was only 16 when the war broke out. Most of the group between 20 and 39 years old were educated in schools during the war and directly after. The youngest adult in our sample, 20 years old, was born in 1933, and entered high school just at the end of the war. Thus the period of World War II coincides with the sharp break in (r) usage. We may explore this question further in Chapter 11, when we examine the development of subjective reactions towards (r).

[There seems to be no doubt that World War II was a punctuating event for the development of the English language. The large-scale movement of population involved – primarily among men – was certainly one factor. Another is the radical shift in the relative power and status of Britain and the U.S. Whatever the reasons, this change in the use of constricted /r/ was not restricted to New York City: we find the same trend in Boston,

---

[14] Hubbell does an unusually thorough job of describing the principal forms used by his thirty informants for a long list of variables. However, the amounts of the variable used are reported so informally that it is unwise to attempt any comparisons with quantitative methods. Hubbell never gives any explanation of how he arrives at the few numerical estimates he makes, and our experience shows that unless every instance is accounted for, the report is likely to have no resemblance to actual usage.

Providence, Richmond, Charleston, and Savannah, as the *Atlas of North American English* shows. In the southern cities, however, the change is a radical one, affecting the vernacular of all youth across social classes. In the northeast, the change has so far affected only the upper middle class vernacular; for others, it is a phenomenon of careful speech.]

The distribution of (æh) and (oh) in apparent time

We now proceed to the analysis of the difficult cases of (æh) and (oh), which should correspond to Case III according to previous indications. In the discussion to follow, Style A will be used for all tables, with the exception that for those under 16, the highest value recorded will be used.[15] Instead of using socio-economic class for (æh) and (oh), as we did in Chapter 8, we will use the social class index. There is little difference for these variables, but the social class groups seem to correspond to groupings which are closer in time to the pre-adolescent period, and therefore more appropriate for a study of linguistic change.

The overall distribution of (æh) by social class and age for ALS New York City informants is shown in Table 9.13. The relations of the classes here conform not to Case III, but to Case II-B: a prestige marker with linguistic change in progress.

The upper middle class has shifted towards more open (æh) vowels, and the other classes towards higher, closer variants. The resulting diagram is not that of a shift in the native pattern of (æh), but rather the progress of a prestige marker. The prestige marker is the correction of (æh-2) to (æh-4), which is an extremely common tendency among all classes in more formal styles. The upper middle class shows (æh-2) and (æh-3) in the speech of its older members; younger members have begun to incorporate the open vowel of (æh-4) into casual speech. We might say that the other classes show the reverse pattern, with the older speakers acquiring some of the prestige element (æh-4) in their own speech.

However, such an explanation would not predict such a progression for the lower class, which is normally less sensitive to prestige markers. Yet we have a regular rise in the height of (æh), as shown in Table 9.14 .

We are therefore probably dealing with a case of III-B, change from below with the addition of a later reaction from above. The pattern of the lower class would represent the later stages of the increase of height of (æh) which has reached the lower class later than the other classes. At the same

---

[15] The pattern of stylistic variation is not consistently set for many children under fifteen, and it may fluctuate in an irregular fashion. For many in this age range, it is not possible to draw a distinction between casual and careful speech – yet the data recorded under Style B may show all the marks of uninhibited and spontaneous speech.

Table 9.13   *Average (æh) indexes by social class and age: overall distribution*

Age	SC				N:			
	1	2	3	4				
20–39	24	24	22	35	2	11	5	4
40–	27	26	25	31	17	8	10	6

Table 9.14   (æh) *values for the lower class SC-1 by age*

	SC 1
8–19	20
20–39	24
40–49	26
50–59	28
60–	28

time, the lower class would remain less affected by the more recent addition of the corrective factor imposed from above.

Earlier analyses of (æh) showed that ethnic factors were more important than socio-economic factors in the overall social stratification. We may therefore benefit from a reconsideration of the age distribution of (æh) in terms of ethnic groups rather than social class, for all but the upper middle class.

Table 9.15 does not have enough cases to show detailed distribution for older speakers, except in the case of the Jews. Sufficient information is available, however, to show that the pattern of linguistic change is quite regular for Jews and African–Americans, but not for the Italians. Since the Italians have by far the highest vowels (corresponding to the lowest (æh) indexes) we may consider that the upward shift has more or less been completed for them.

It is evident that the lower class speakers over 60 have not participated in this process.[16] We may therefore conclude that the upward movement of (æh) began sometime before World War I, affecting the Italians first, then the Jews, and the African–Americans. Babbitt's evidence on (æh), to be

[16] All eight speakers in the sample who are in this age category are also in SC 1. Their (æh) values in Style A (or in Style B where no separate Style A was recorded) are as follows: 20, 25, 25, 26, 28, 30, 30, 40. No other age level shows this tight grouping around (æh)-25–30.

Table 9.15   *Average (æh) indexes by age and ethnic group: detailed distribution*

Age	SC 1–3			SC-4
	Jews	Italians	African–Americans	(All ethnic groups)
8–19	22	20	24	33
20–39	23	19	28	35
40–49	27			
50–59	29	18	33	31

examined in detail in Chapter 14, indicates an even earlier raising in the nineteenth century, in which *bad, bag, hand*, etc. were consolidated with *ask, bath, dance*, etc., at a mid-front position. The upper middle class has begun to move in the opposite direction, in response to the stigmatization of the high vowels, and the new forms of low (æh) vowels have been accepted as prestige markers. We have already seen that hypercorrection of the lower middle class is a powerful factor in more formal styles for (æh). The result of such hypercorrection is a structure similar to Figure 9.6, for (r).

Thus the pattern formed by social class in the dimension of apparent time illustrates the progress of the prestige marker (æh)-4. The pattern formed by ethnic groups in apparent time illustrates the upward movement of the vowels in accordance with the general model of change from below.[17]

We may now consider the overall distribution of (oh). Table 9.16 shows the average indexes for the ALS New York informants.

Table 9.16 does not indicate any pronounced contrast between older and younger speakers. However, if we now construct a table (9.17) in which ethnic group is the principal factor for the three lower status groups, a definite pattern emerges.

[17] The Atlas records must be questioned as far as (æh) is concerned. Lowman did not record any speakers as using (æh) vowels as high as the vowel of *where, scarce*, etc. But Hubbell's re-assessment of the phonograph records of nine Atlas informants showed that six of them did use vowels of this height (æh-2), and for at least two it was the principal variant. On the other hand, it is sometimes difficult to determine in Hubbell's records if the phoneme /æə/ is meant to be the same height as the vowel of *bat*, or higher. The following regularities appear, however. The eastern New England prestige form (æh-5) is used mainly by older upper class informants. Upper middle class informants use a range of variants from (æh-2) to (æh-4); for the older speakers, the main variant seems to be (æh-2); for the younger, the emphasis is shifting to (æh-3). Among the younger lower middle class informants, (æh-4) is becoming the principal variant (in Style B). The lower class shows the most tendency towards uncorrected (æh-2). This evidence supports the interpretation we have given above, with the exception that (æh-2) seems to have a more solid position among older lower class speakers from a traditional New York background.

Table 9.16   *Average* (oh) *indexes by age and social class: overall distribution*

	SC							
Age	1	2	3	4	N:			
20–39	21	22	18	22	3	12	6	5
40–	23	22	19	22	17	9	12	6

Table 9.17   *Average* (oh) *indexes by age and ethnic group: detailed distribution*

	Social classes 1–3			SC 4
Age	Jews	Italians	Others	
8–19	17	18	22	23
20–35	18	18	(16)	22
36–49	17	20	18	22
50–59	15	20	15	22
60–	25	30	25	–

Table 9.17 corresponds to the abstract pattern of Case III-A. It shows change from below at an earlier stage than the case of (æh). Although there has been a reaction from above against the high vowels of (oh), it is not yet pronounced enough to show in these average values for casual speech. It seems that the rise in (oh) started with the Jews, and that the Italians show a corresponding rise later in apparent time. The African–Americans do not show a regular pattern for this variable, either in stylistic or in social variation, and data for them is not shown here.

It should be pointed out that the values for the oldest groups reflect the usage of lower class speakers only. If we had speakers of that age from SC 2 and 3, we might find that the rise has been less sudden than Table 9.17 would indicate.

Figure 9.9 shows the distribution for Italian speakers, with the general pattern of increasing height of (oh). There appears to be a break in the age dimension at about 35. The barred symbols in Figure 9.9 represent Italian speakers interviewed in the television survey. The context of the television interview is somewhat more formal than Context A, but the overall pattern formed by these speakers is the same as the pattern formed by the regular ALS subjects.

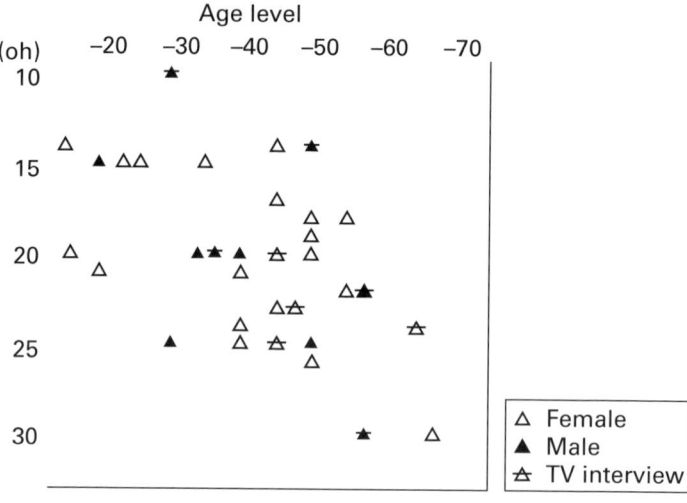

Figure 9.9   Distribution of (oh) values for Italians by age and sex

The records for previous studies of (oh) are difficult to interpret, since the description of the variants in articulatory terms differ from one investigator to another, and there are no phonemic levels to which the reports may be tied.[18] Babbitt's evidence points to a general level of (oh) lower than (oh-3). The Atlas records show a raised form of (oh), and a lowered form, in addition to the principal variant written as [ɔ:] or [ɔ:ᵊ]. The lowered variant appears to be the Eastern New England type, (oh-5), and there is some indication of its use by older, "cultured" informants. The raised variant, (oh-2) or (oh-3), is used most by younger "uneducated" informants and the older "intermediate" informants. Such a distribution does not present a clear view of change, though Frank has the impression that raised (oh) is gaining ground. Hubbell's records show a much less ambiguous picture. The oldest informants use the most open vowels, and the youngest informants the highest, or in Hubbell's description, "most retracted." The extreme forms seem to have been used by three college students: two that we might rank as SC 3, and one as SC 4. The indications of change are much plainer than in the case of (æh), if we interpret the remarks of Hubbell correctly.

[18] The Atlas records show only variations in the height of (oh) and the presence or absence of an off-glide. Hubbell refers to the variant used by younger speakers as "retracted." We have described the extreme forms as raised, fronted, and over-rounded, with a distinct off-glide. More moderate forms, such as (oh-2), are raised and only slightly fronted, but never retracted, as British variants are. I would suspect that all three descriptions refer to similar sounds, since over-rounding can convey the impression of retraction to some listeners.

We have seen two examples of change from below. In both cases, we must ascribe to the linguistic features a measure of social significance. As indicated above, the social significance of most changes from below is a form of self-identification, of group membership, which establishes the speaker as an authentic representative of a sub-group within the community. Since identification as a Jew or an Italian has long been an important social theme for New Yorkers, it is understandable that (æh) and (oh) should be involved in this opposition. We see now that the contrast between Jew and Italian in the use of (æh) and (oh) is diminishing, and at the same time the social class identification afforded by these variables is gaining in importance. It is not possible to document the social history which parallels these linguistic developments within the pages of this study. However, it appears that the traditional orientation of New Yorkers into a three-cornered structure of Jews, Irish, and Italians is giving way to new social patterns. The white population is now contrasted as a whole with AA and Puerto-Rican groups.[19] This contrast is reinforced by social and economic patterns of increasing stratification, in which the privileged groups are sharply opposed to the underprivileged. We may find linguistic parallels for these developments in the examination of the distribution of (æh) and (oh) for those under 20 years old.

Figure 9.10 shows the distribution of these two variables by age, ethnic-group and socio-economic class.[20] We see that the concentration of (æh) at (æh)-20 is greater than that of the corresponding group at (oh)-20. Both diagrams show some tendency for young children to use higher vowels than older children. The most significant fact, however, is the social distribution below (oh)-22. The speakers who use (oh) forms of this range consist exclusively of three types:

1)   Upper middle class.
2)   All of the AA informants.
3)   Lower class white informants.[21]

The clustering of lower class white values with those of AA speakers is part of a general tendency in New York City English which was observed in exploratory interviews. The gradual evolution of New York City speech

---

[19] Perhaps the most objective view of this development may be seen in *Income, Education, and Unemployment in Neighborhoods*, published by the Bureau of Labor Statistics, U.S. Department of Labor in January, 1963. The contrast between the income, educational status, and unemployment record of white, AA, and Puerto Rican is developed here on the basis of the 1960 Census.

[20] SEC is used here insead of SC, because it is the parents' present situation which determines the social position of the children, and the SEC is more closely related to the current status of the family.

[21] Five of the SEC-1 youth on this diagram are members of a single Irish-Italian family, and the evidence is therefore not as strong as if they were representatives of different families.

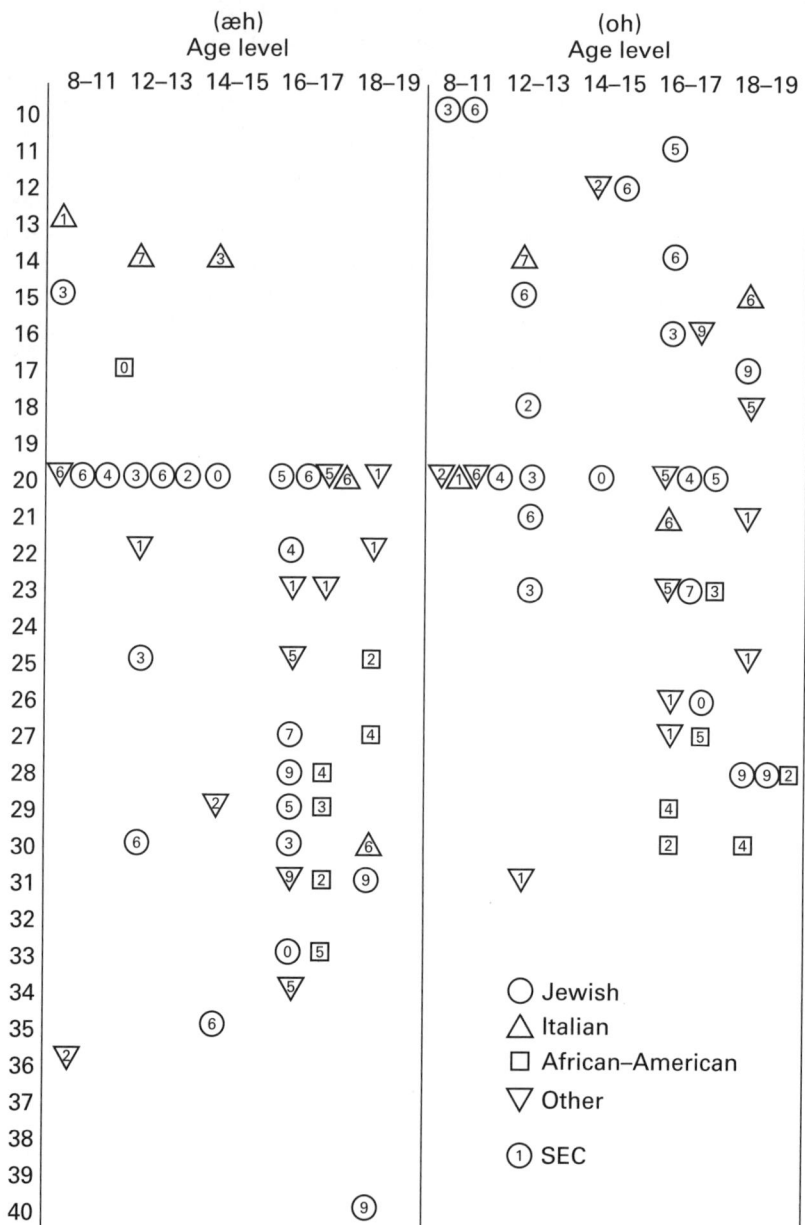

Figure 9.10   Distribution of (oh) and (æh) for age levels from 8 to 19 by sex, SEC, and ethnic group

towards higher (oh) forms has not been followed by AA speakers, and there is a group of lower class whites whose speech resembles that of African–Americans in several ways.[22] The situation for (æh) is not as clear, and there are other speakers from the working class and middle class who are found in the same area. It is (oh) which follows the curvilinear pattern to perfection, with lower class, AA, and upper middle class in close juxtaposition. (There are three other upper middle class speakers at exactly the same level in the 25–29 age level.)

The discussion of other variables in Chapter 10 will show further instances of the grouping of AA and lower class white speakers.

The distribution of (th) and (dh) in apparent time

The great majority of New Yorkers use some stops and affricates in their everyday speech for the variables (th) and (dh). However, there are few native speakers who rely primarily upon stops and who rarely use fricatives. There can hardly be any question that the stop form of (th) or (dh) is an example of a stigmatized feature: what we have to determine is whether any change can be inferred from the distribution in apparent time. The overall distribution of (th) and (dh) for ALS New York informants in Style A is seen in Table 9.18.

The consistent pattern of differences that we see here is in accord with the discussion of Case I-A (stigmatized feature – without linguistic change) as concerns relations of older and younger speakers of classes 1–3. However, the fact that the upper middle class speakers show a reverse trend was not predicted for this case. We might then interpret Table 9.18 as Case II-B: the introduction of a prestige feature. A style of speech without any stops or affricates for (th) and (dh) would be the new prestige feature. But such an interpretation runs against the grain of our native intuition; the experience of this study shows that it is not the pronunciation of fricatives which has social significance, but rather the use of stops or affricates. (See Chapter 11 for evidence on this point.) Furthermore, there are some concrete facts of distribution which argue against this interpretation.

1) The patterns of (th) and (dh) for age distribution are much less marked than that of (r). If we sum the three lower classes, we reverse the relations of the age levels for (th) and (dh), but not for (r).

---

[22] One of the most striking incidents which illustrate this tendency occurred when one of the members of the lower class Irish-Italian family was giving an account of a fight with AAs in reply to the Danger of Death question. In his spontaneous speech, he began to use intonation, vocabulary, and syntax which sounded more like AA speech than white. One of his brothers mentioned that he sounded like an AA himself, and he was quite surprised, since he was not deliberately imitating AA speech.

Table 9.18   *Average* (th) *and* (dh) *indexes by age and social class: overall distribution*

	Age	Social class				N:			
		1	2	3	4				
(th)	20–39	111	46	34	06	3	12	6	5
						19	5	7	3
	40–	92	30	23	18				
(dh)	20–39	109	59	41	10	3	12	6	6
						20	8	10	5
	40–	87	45	18	32				

Table 9.19   (th) *and* (dh) *indexes for SC1–3 compared to* (r)

	(th) SC 1–3	(dh) SC 1–3	(r) SC 1–3
20–39	57	59	00
40–	69	61	05

In Table 9.19 we see that the older groups use more stops and affricates than the younger groups. This shift is a product of the skewed distribution of the informants, but it illustrates that there is a qualitative difference between the relations of the age levels for (r) on the one hand, and for (th) and (dh) on the other.

2) The age distribution of (th) and (dh) does not have the regularity of the (r) pattern. Figure 9.11 shows the type of age differences that prevail for (dh) in Style A which allows us to compare sixteen different groups, paired as younger and older halves with the same social class and sex. In order to build up the number of cases, the data for television interviews have been included, and the out-of-town speakers as well (since we have seen that stratification for out-of-town speakers is essentially the same as for New Yorkers). The values for the television interviews are undoubtedly low for Style A, as discussed in Appendix C, but they may be taken here as minimum values.

It is difficult to make comparisons for SC 1, because we do not have enough younger speakers. However, for SC 2 and 3, for both men and women, the tendency for younger speakers to have higher values is evident.

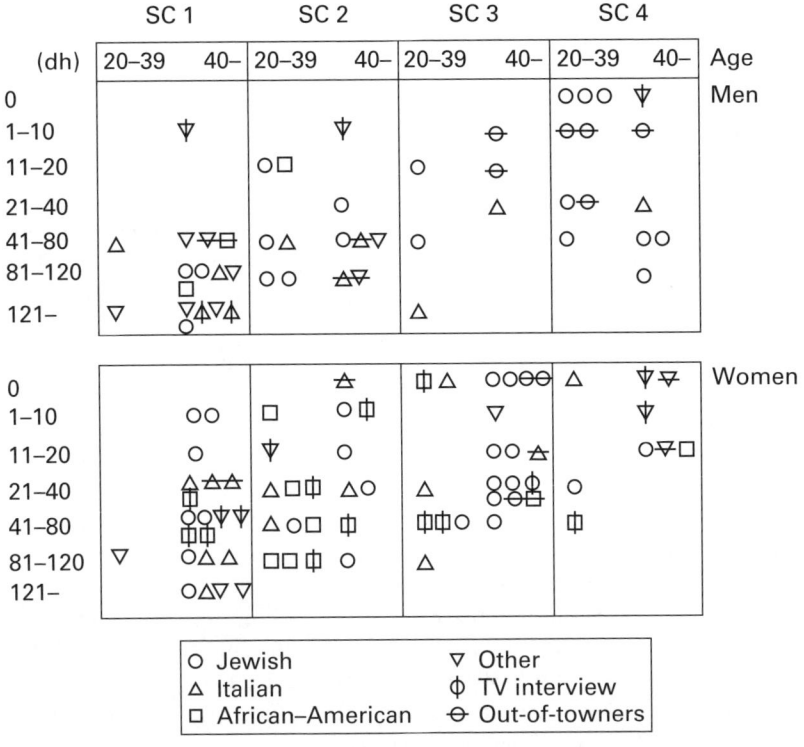

Figure 9.11   Distribution of (dh) in Style A by age, sex, ethnic group, and social class: all informants

This is in accord with the analysis for Case I-A. If change in the social significance of (th) and (dh) had been in progress, we would expect to find the reverse relationship for age levels in SC 1–3.

The situation for SC 4 does not show the uniformly low values which we would expect for a long-standing reaction to a stigmatized feature. The upper middle class men show a tendency to reverse the relations of the other classes, and indicate an increasing sensitivity to (dh) in apparent time. The addition of the television interviews does not eliminate this tendency. According to the evidence presented here, there has been some change in the social significance of (dh) for the upper middle class. As far as women are concerned, there is no such trend to be inferred from the data, but we have insufficient numbers in SC 4 to permit any close comparison.

The Linguistic Atlas was not greatly concerned with these consonants. Only one page of Frank's monograph is devoted to (th) and (dh), reflecting the general lack of interest in consonants for the Atlas as a whole.

Frank notes that the affricate (th-2) occurs in the speech of young uneducated New York City informants in all positions – word initial, medial and final. She adds that the dental [t̪] – that is, (th-3) – occurs in free variation with (th-2) in the speech of these informants in initial or final position (page 80). This agrees well with the data of the present survey, if we consider that only the stressed replies to questions about lexical items enter into the Atlas results. A great many of the (th) forms occur in phrases such as *something like that* or *I think*, and (th) is relatively rare when these are eliminated from the data.

The information on (dh) is no doubt defective. Frank (1948) writes that "two instances of the voiced stop /d/ for /ð/ occur in the speech of two young uneducated informants as in *without* and *the both of us*. This feature has probably been borrowed recently from non-English speech" (page 81).

In the speech of native New Yorkers, the variant (dh-3) is seldom to be confused with the phoneme /d/, as it has neither the slight aspiration nor the degree of voicing associated with /d/. It may also be noted that since the Atlas records rarely contain unstressed forms, (dh-3) in words such as *the, then, this, that*, would not appear at all. We do find that the same distribution of (th) existed in the 1930s as today: younger uneducated informants use more than older uneducated informants. This evidence does suggest once again the stability of the (th) and (dh) pattern.

In Hubbell's records, we find a class distribution not too dissimilar from that in the ALS survey. He found traces of (th) stops in the speech of only two of his sixteen upper middle class informants, and none for (dh). The lower middle class informants showed more stops: only four of the nine showed none, and two speakers showed moderate to heavy use of stops for both (th) and (dh). All of the lower class informants used some stops, and two of them showed very heavy use. The limited data given by Hubbell do not indicate any clear evidence for difference in age levels, though the younger speakers show higher percentages of stops for the two lower ranking groups.

Interpretation of the relation of (th) and (dh) to linguistic change becomes more problematic after considering the evidence of Hubbell and the Linguistic Atlas. While both show a pattern which our analysis has associated with stability – the younger informants showing more of the stigmatized forms than the older ones – the general frequency of stops and affricates seems to be much lower than in the ALS survey. It is very difficult to accept the notion that a high level of stops and affricates in New York City speech is a new development. Writers have noted this characteristic of working class speakers for many decades. For example, O. Henry describes the speech of a New York City boy at the turn of the century in this way:[23]

There was a smart kind of a kid in the gang – I guess he was a newsboy. "I got in twenty-fi' mister," he says, looking hopeful at Buck's silk hat and clothes. "Dey paid me two-fifty a mont' on it. Say, a man tells me dey can't do dat and be on the square? Is dat straight? Do you guess I can get out my twent-fi'?"

Babbitt's report on (th) and (dh) could have been written today. He describes these consonants as social variables, which native speakers sometimes pronounce as fricatives, and sometimes as stops.

The most striking and important peculiarity in consonants is the substitution of *t* and *d* for *θ* and *ð*. This does not take place in all words, nor in the speech of all persons, even of the lower classes; but the tendency exists beyond doubt. . . . I observed very few cases of natives who could not, and did not in some words, pronounce the interdentals correctly; and the substitution of *d* and *t* for them . . . is not heard in the speech of the better classes.

Babbitt then notes that there is no phonetic rule for the occurrence of the stop form; he believes that it is tied to frequency.

The definite article, the pronouns *this* and *that*, the ordinal numerals in *th*, and such everyday words, are almost uniformly pronounced with the *d* or *t*, while anything in the nature of a "book-word" keeps the orthodox interdental.

In the ALS interviews, stops and affricates were used most often in the most frequent words, although this is undoubtedly connected with the fact that the rarer elements of the vocabulary occur primarily in careful speech. For instance, *method* and *parenthesis*, Babbitt's examples of words used with fricatives, do not occur in casual speech as a rule. The fact that the Linguistic Atlas reported such a low frequency of stops and affricates is probably due to two factors: 1) a bias of availability, leading to a selection of informants whose speech habits were not representative; and 2) a concentration upon stressed lexical items, rather than the entire speech production of the informant.

Not only is the usage of (th) and (dh) reported by Babbitt the same as observed today, but the social significance of these variables appears to be the same. Babbitt notes that newspapers ridicule working class speech by writing *De Ate* for *The Eighth* (Assembly district), just as they ridicule the use of /ʌy/ as "*goil*" and "*woild*." The social distribution of (th) and (dh) variants has not, however, undergone the rapid evolution of /ʌy/, but remains almost as it was at the turn of the century.

[23] From "The Tempered Wind," *The Complete Works of O. Henry*, New York: Doubleday, Page, 1926, page 259.

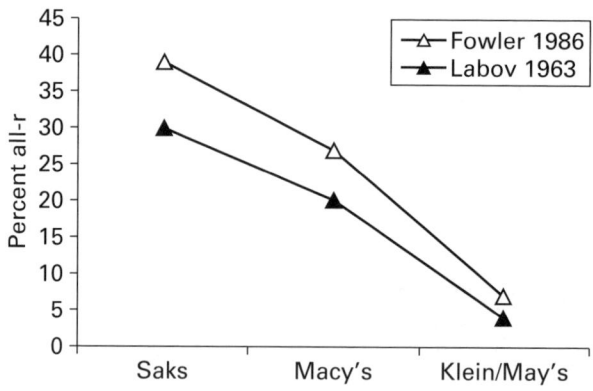

Figure 9.12   Percent all-r in the department store study of 1963 and Fowler's 1986 replication

Thus the evidence of Babbitt confirms the analysis of distribution in apparent time, that (th) and (dh) are variables which show little indication of linguistic change in progress.

[At the time that this chapter was written, real-time evidence had to be drawn from whatever records could be found in the past, since there were no real-time quantitative replications. This was necessarily qualitative evidence. For example, I concluded that the centralization of /aw/ on Martha's Vineyard was new because all the variants in Linguistic Atlas records were between [ao] and [æo]. The NYC situation was richer in records of the past, but considerable effort had to be put in to the evaluation of what was said or written. Fundamentally, the task was no different from the interpretive work required of any historical linguist.

The first deliberate return to the same community was the work of Hermann, who re-studied in 1929 the village of Charmey that Gauchat had investigated in 1899–1905. Four of the variables that Gauchat had described had advanced further; two were found to show the same age distribution and were plainly cases of age-grading.

In the 1980s, students of the speech community began quantitative re-studies in real time. In 1984, Henrietta Cedergren reported a re-study of her 1973 work on Panama City, and in 1988, Peter Trudgill added a real-time component to his 1974 study of Norwich. (For some of the results, see Chapter 4 on Real Time Studies in Labov 1994.) In 1986, Fowler replicated the NYC department store study in exact detail, with the overall results of Figure 9.12. All the other relations reported in Chapter 3 were reproduced, at a level 10–20% higher in (r-1). In 1987, a Montreal team headed by Thibault and Vincent (1990) managed to re-interview a remarkable 50 percent of the random sample of 120 subjects interviewed in 1971, plus 12 younger speakers; a smaller re-study was done by Vincent in 1995. Since then, important re-studies have been done in Martha's Vineyard, Glasgow, Eskilstuna, Helsinki, Tours, Rio de Janeiro, and Springville, Texas. The details are given in Table 2 of Sankoff's review article on "Age: Apparent Time and Real Time" (2002).

From these dozen or so studies, some important general conclusions have emerged. A few reports in real time show no further change – like two of the variables studied by Gauchat, and Macaulay's re-study of Glasgow – but in most cases, the interpretation of apparent time as an indication of change in progress was confirmed. But in every one of these cases, there was some advance in the adult population. The general finding is that some adults do alter their speech in the direction of the ongoing change, but the changes are smaller and less regular than in the pre-adolescent and adolescent population. It follows further that apparent time will normally underestimate the rate of change.]

Summary

This chapter has been devoted to the interpretation of age differences in the values of the five phonological variables. In order to utilize this information, we analyzed the possible relations between the dimensions of apparent time and real time. We then used the results of such analysis to interpret the facts of distribution. Because variation through the age levels of the population is imposed upon stylistic variation, class variation, and differences in ethnic groups and the sexes, this distribution is necessarily complex. The presuppositions about the behavior of the various classes which we used were admittedly speculative, and the evidence of previous chapters could only be adduced for probable indications of the directions in which the classes would move. However, the convergence of the department store survey and the survey of the Lower East Side decreased the likelihood of error in the interpretation of (r) to the point where we may regard this as firmly established as any of the findings in Chapters 7 and 8.

In Chapter 7, it was pointed out that there were two deviations from regular structure which were recurrent: the lower middle class cross-over, and the style reversal of the upper middle class, both in Style D. The first was found in the structure of (r), (æh), and (oh); the second in (æh) and (oh). If the cross-over was to be considered as re-defining regular structure, then (r), (æh), and (oh) must be considered a homogeneous set as opposed to (th) and (dh). We posited that the first three variables were involved in linguistic change, and the second two were not. The evidence of this chapter has given the needed confirmation to this proposal. It was also posited that (æh) and (oh) represented change from below, and that the upper middle class reversal in Style D was associated with this set. This conclusion must still be regarded as tentative, since the interpretation of the (æh) and (oh) patterns in apparent time was complex and required larger sampling of Italian respondents for a definitive solution.[24]

Chapter 10 will briefly examine the distribution of some interpersonal variables which show no systematic variation on the stylistic axis, but which are a part of the structure of social variation. The analysis of the relations of apparent time and real time as developed in this chapter will be applied to these variables as well.

---

[24] Some further remarks on the concepts of *linguistic change from below*, and *linguistic change from above*, may be helpful. These concepts are based upon linguistic processes, rather than social distinctions. The dimension of *above vs. below* run parallel to the dimension of stylistic variation, rather than social variation. A change from above is exerted by overt pressure upon formal styles of speech, with results that are sporadic or unsystematic from a linguistic point of view. A change from below occurs below the level of conscious attention, affecting all members of a word class, and parallel elements in the phonological system. Because the upper middle class is usually the first to react to social pressure from above, and some members of this class are instrumental in promoting such social pressure, such linguistic change is sometimes thought of as proceeding from the top of the social scale, downwards. This is not necessarily the case: sometimes the lower middle class leads in such correction, as on the use of spelling pronunciations. Although change from below gradually affects all classes, it appears to originate with some particular group; this group is most often a lower ranking social group, though not necessarily. [Further studies indicate that the originating group is most often a centrally located group in the socio-economic range – lower middle class or upper working class (Labov 1980, 2001).]

10   Other linguistic variables

In the survey of the Lower East Side, a great many other linguistic variables were studied in addition to the five main phonological variables. The stylistic and social differentiation of morphological variants, of syntactic forms, and many consonantal variants, were analyzed in the speech of the ALS informants.[1] The distribution of many of these variables confirmed the linear array of the set of stylistic contexts, and the ten-point scale of socioeconomic classes. The distribution patterns of non-standard grammatical forms, such as double negatives, and person–number disagreements, showed a regular structure of stratification by socio-economic class which could not be duplicated by any single social parameter.[2] The morphological variants of the suffix -ing showed a regular and fine structure of stylistic and social stratification. In addition, the distribution of the -ing variable in apparent time provided a case of stigmatization without linguistic change which confirmed in detail the analysis of Case I-A in Chapter 9.

The mid-central vowel in her

Chapter 9 has presented data on one variable which is closely associated with (r): the vowel of *bird* and *work*. This variable occurs in all contexts

[1] Some of the other phonological variants studied are the loss of contrast of /i/ and /e/ before nasals as in *pin* vs. *pen*; contrast between /iw/ and /uw/ as in *dew* and *do*; contrast between [ŋ] and [ŋg] as in *singer* and *finger*; contrast of /i/ and /e/ before intervocalic /r/ as in *mirror* and *nearer*; contrast of /eh/ and /e/ before intervocalic /r/ as in *fairy* and *ferry*; contrast of /hw/ and /w/ initially, as in *which* and *witch*; contrast of final [dθ] and [θ] as in *width* and *with*. The case of *beer* vs. *bear* and *sure* vs. *shore* will be taken up in Chapter 14. The loss of final /l/ as in *school* was studied; the substitution of glottal stop for /t/ as in *total* and *bottle*; the release of final /t/ and the explosion of initial /t/; the simplification of consonant clusters; the occurrence of word-final, intervocalic /r/; the occurrence of [ðə] and [ə] instead of [ðiy] and [ən] before words beginning with vowels. A great many morphological forms serve as socially significant differentiators: among the most important are the forms of *ask*, *isn't*, and *didn't*.
[2] The SC scale was not quite as sensitive as the SEC scale to differences in the peak of concentration of non-standard grammatical forms of different types, although it showed regular stratification for all.

where historical (r) followed a mid-central vowel and was followed by a consonant. We will now consider the parallel case of historical *final* (r) preceded by a mid-central vowel: that is, words of the type *her, were, occur, stir*. The most important of these words is *her* since it occurs more frequently than any of the others except *were*, and the latter is usually unstressed.

The most common pronunciation of this class of words among the ALS informants is the same as that used by most American speakers. In stressed position, the mid-central constricted form [hɜ˞] is used, and in unstressed position, [hə˞]. These are the same vowels as the forms most commonly used in *bird* and *work*, and similar to the forms used in *r*-pronouncing dialects. However, there are many speakers who use an *r*-less form in some or all instances of *her, were,* etc.

The *r*-less form is a mid-central vowel, which varies in position from [ɨ], slightly higher than the final vowel of *sofa*, to [ʌ], the vowel of *tub*.[3] It may be short, or half-long; the longer forms of [ʌ] are sometimes monophthongs, and sometimes show a centering glide, [ʌ ᵊ]. The forms which differ from the common standard [hɜ˞] most strikingly are those with the nucleus [ʌ], and in the following discussion, we will therefore concentrate upon the incidence of [ʌ] in this word class. Since the great majority of these forms were actually found in the word *her*, I will refer to the incidence of [hʌ], and the inclusion of a few [wʌ] and [əhʌ] forms will be understood, as well as such slight variants as [hʌ⁺⁺] and [hʌᵊ].

In casual speech, we do not find stressed forms of the *her* class variable as often as the variable of *bird* and *work*. Only 23 of the 80 white ALS New York City informants used the word *her* in casual speech. Eleven of these used one or more instances of [ʌ], a total of 26 occurrences in all. The situation in careful speech is much the same. However, the standard reading texts contain a number of occurrences of stressed *her*, and we therefore have in this style information on 68 out of the 80 white adult ALS New York City informants, and 38 young people: a total of 106 in all. Table 10.1 shows the number of those who used one or more instances of [hʌ] (as the numerator of the fraction), and the total number of cases who used the word class of *her* (as the denominator). Three age levels are shown and five SEC levels, the same divisions of the scale that were used for the stratification of (r).

Table 10.1 can be presented in somewhat simpler form as Table 10.2, showing three social groups, which appear in the following percentages of [hʌ].

This presentation shows some tendency for a reduction in the use of [hʌ] with decreasing age and increasing social rank, but the trend is not regular.

---

[3] The vowel of *tub* is also occasionally heard before /r/, as [hʌr].

Table 10.1   *White ALS informants using* [hʌ] *in style C by age and SEC*

	SEC					
Age	0–1	2–3	4–5	6–8	9	Total
8–19	2/5	5/11	1/9	3/8	0/5	11/38
20–39	1/4	1/3	0/4	3/10	1/4	6/25
40–	3/7	7/10	1/11	4/10	1/7	16/45
	6/16	13/24	2/24	10/28	2/16	33/106

Table 10.2

Age	SEC 0–3	SEC 4–8	SEC 9
8–19	43	24	00
20–39	30	22	25
40–	59	24	14

Table 10.3   *Instances of* [hʌ] *per informant for white ALS speakers by age and SEC in style C*

	SEC		
Age	0–3	4–8	9
8–19	.69	.24	.00
20–39	.43	.57	.20
40–	1.59	.29	.43

The social significance of [hʌ] is indicated a little more clearly in Table 10.3 which shows the ratio of total number of occurrences of [hʌ] to the total number of informants who used some members of the word class of *her*.

The extreme figures for Table 10.3 are located at opposite corners. The older, lower class informants use by far the most [hʌ] in this presentation, and the younger class 9 informants use none at all. However, the usage of the other sub-groups seems to fluctuate, and it is clear that if social pressure is being exerted against [hʌ], it is only just beginning. The younger group of upper middle class speakers seem to indicate such a trend.

In the records of previous surveys, [hʌ] seems to predominate. Babbitt's early observations of 1896 seem to indicate that an upgliding form was used in the *her* class, but there are no relics of such a pronunciation, and both Hubbell and Frank show [hʌ] as the principal form.

Among African–American speakers, the vowel of [hʌ] is used only by two upper middle class subjects. Most African–Americans favor the mid-central vowel [ə] without constriction in stressed forms, and this is common among those with northern as well as southern background.

[The New York City pronunciation of *her* as [hʌ] has a special fascination: it is a unique violation of the English constraint against ending a word with a stressed short vowel. In every other case, the vowel nucleus is followed by a glide, or a consonant, or is lengthened. So there are no words of the form [hɪ, hɛ, hæ, ho, hu]. But there is a [hʌ], at least among New Yorkers, along with [fʌ, wʌ, stʌ]. The structural constraint is fundamental to English phonology, which retains this distributional restriction on short vowels, no matter what phonetic forms are realized by sound change. Where and how the New York City exceptional forms were generated remains a mystery.]

The social distribution of (ay) and (aw)

There are two speech variables which will have considerable importance for the analysis of the overall structure of New York City English, and the changes that are takinayg place in that structure. These two variables are the positions of the first elements of the diphthong /ay/ as in *my*, *nine*, *ride*, etc., and the diphthong /aw/ as in *mouth*, *loud*, etc. The variations do not follow a detailed pattern of stylistic variation as the five main phonological variables do. The values for any given individual hover close to a central norm, and the fluctuations that do occur are not systematic by styles. However, these variables do follow a very regular pattern of social variation, and as such may be referred to as interpersonal as opposed to intrapersonal.

The axis of phonological variation is the degree of differentiation of the first and second elements of the diphthongs, which we may call *nucleus-glide differentiation*. For the front-gliding diphthong /ay/, this occurs as positions of the first element which are progressively further back in the vowel quadrangle; for the back-gliding diphthong /aw/, this occurs as positions of the first element which are progressively further front. Figure 10.1 locates these vowels in the vowel quadrangle. The point marked zero on this diagram corresponds to the position [a˞], the most common position of the first elements of both /ay/ and /aw/ in the surrounding regions of New Jersey, New York State, and Connecticut.[4] The successive numbers to the left indicate the index for (aw), and the numbers to the right, the index for

---

[4] See Kurath and McDavid (1951) Maps 26 and 28.

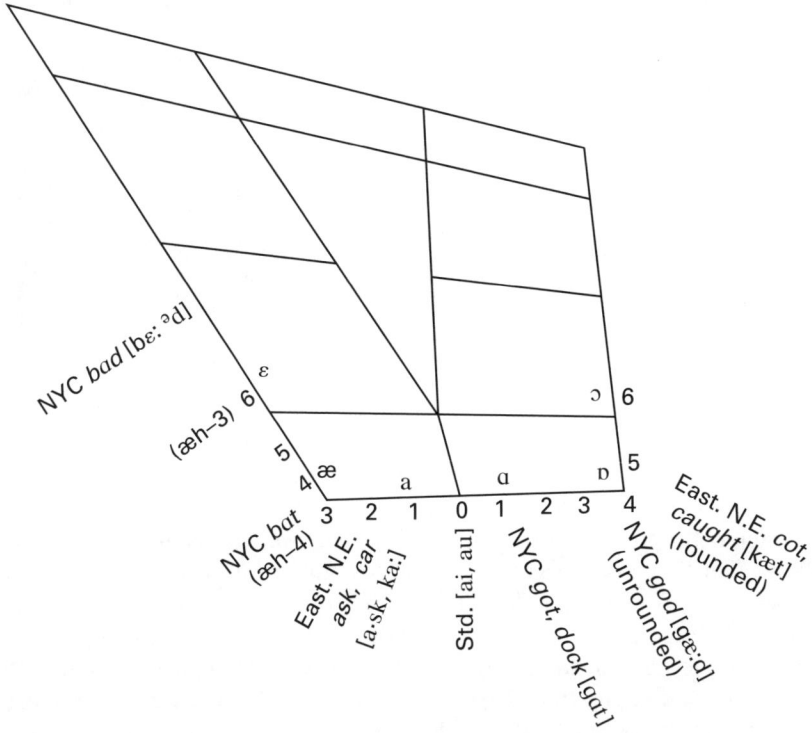

Figure 10.1   Phonetic scale for nucleus-glide differentiation of (ay) and (aw)

(ay). The positions of various simple vowels that have been discussed previously are indicated on the diagram with identifying words opposite the index numbers. To identify (ay-1) in *guy*, for example, one would pronounce the word *got* with the vowel used most commonly in New York City (and most parts of the northeastern United States) symbolized [ɑ], with the addition of a front upglide.

For the extreme values of both variables, the diphthong tends to show a slower upglide with a more distinct second element, and the glide usually ends at a higher point. The difference might be symbolized as [gaˑɪ], fast, as against [gɒːi], slow.[5]

---

[5] When the extreme forms are heard in isolation, many American speakers think of them as "Cockney." The phonological shift which we are observing here follows the same route as the Cockney vowels for *eye* and *ow*, *my* and *now*, and in some cases, are no less extreme.

Table 10.4   *Average* (ay) *and* (aw) *indexes by SEC for all adult white NYC informants*

SEC	(ay)	(aw)	N
0	06	03	7
1	05	01	10
2	06	03	9
3	16	07	14
4	17	06	13
5	17	10	7
6	17	08	12
7–8	11	13	12
9	18	03	16
			100

[Acoustic analysis of these long upgliding vowels showed that they were even more complex than this. Labov, Yaeger and Steiner 1972 examined the characteristic productions of stressed *my, by, why,* of New Yorkers and found that they often began with a steady state of about 60 msec, in the upper low back position indicated here, then descended to a point of inflection in low central position, and without pausing, proceeded to the end point of the glide in lower high front position. Similar articulations are found in London and Philadelphia. This is a challenging case for the effort to represent the central tendency of a vowel by a single point, since it is still not clear whether the steady state or the point of inflection has a greater perceptual weight.]

The same tendencies towards nucleus-glide differentiation can be noted before all types of consonants, but the effect is more extreme and more easy to observe in final position and before voiced consonants and voiceless fricatives. Thus the values of the variables which were assigned to each informant were the most common variants used in words such as *my, why, surprise, ride, side,* and *mouth, loud,* etc. Conversely, the pronunciation of *light, right, about,* etc., was not used for this variable. A series of values was assigned to successive utterances until it became plain what the central tendency for that speaker was.

[The value assigned to each speaker was more precisely the modal value of the first five occurrences of the variable. The study of /ay/ and /aw/ was not given as much attention as the five major variables. Yet they seem to be clear cases of change in progress, and would certainly deserve further study. Chapter 3 of Labov 1994 did re-examine the (ay) and (aw) data from the 1966 book, with results to be summarized below.]

Table 10.5   *Average* (ay) *and* (aw) *values for all adult NYC Jews and Italians*

	(ay)	(aw)	N
Jews	13	05	66
Italians	14	06	26

Table 10.6   *Average* (ay) *and* (aw) *values for all adult white NYC informants by sex*

	(ay)	(aw)	N
Men	08	02	43
Women	18	08	57

The index for a group of speakers is the mean value of the individual indices multiplied by ten. Thus five speakers with (ay) values of 0, 0, 1, 1, 2 would yield an index of (ay) -08.

The sample population which will be used for the study of (ay) and (aw) includes all New York informants except African–Americans. This group follows an entirely different pattern with fronted variants of (ay) and reduction of the upglide.[6] Since there are no stylistic considerations in the assignment of (ay) and (aw) values, the data from television interviews can be considered on a par with the data from all other interviews.

Table 10.4 gives the values of (ay) and (aw) for 100 white adult New York informants by socio-economic class. It shows that there are only two major groups in the scale of (ay) values: 0–2 and 3–9. Class 9 is slightly higher in (aw) values that the rest. As far as (aw) is concerned, we have three, or perhaps four divisions. Classes 0–2 show a low (aw) index; classes 3–6 are higher; 7–8 shows the maximum value; and class 9 is low, at a level with the lower class group.

In the use of (ay) and (aw), Jews and Italians are not very different from each other, as shown in Table 10.5. This situation contrasts sharply with the case of (æh) and (oh), where the ethnic factors were larger than the class differentials.

There is a great difference between men and women in the use of (ay) and (aw), as shown in Table 10.6.

---

[6] This is of course a continuation of southern patterns of speech, and is strongest among those AA speakers who have the closest connection with the south.

Table 10.7 *Average (ay) and (aw) values for all white NYC informants by SEC and age*

Age	(ay)				(aw)				N			
	SEC				SEC							
	0-2	3-5	6-8	9	0-2	3-5	6-8	9				
8-15	9	25	28	—	13	20	22	—	8	4	6	—
16-19	5	20	15	12	0	20	10	8	6	3	4	4
20-39	5	17	23	14	0	5	8	4	2	17	10	7
40-44	10	22	25	15	3	11	11	0	4	5	4	2
45-49	7	16	10	13	7	6	8	0	6	9	4	3
50-59	7	10	10	15	3	7	5	5	3	6	4	2
60-69	4	—	—	—	1	—	—	—	7	—	—	—
70-	0	—	—	—	0	—	—	—	4	—	—	—

It has been noted that the upper middle class shows a different distribution for men and women than the other classes. It is also true that the usage for (ay) and (aw) is quite different for the upper middle class. If we consider only classes 0–8, we find that the men have an (ay) index of only 05, as low as the lowest value recorded for an individual social class in Table 10.4. In the case of (æh) and (oh), women showed more extreme values of those variables; in the case of (ay) and (aw), the differences are even greater.

From the foregoing discussion, we would assume that (ay) and (aw) will follow the model for Case III: change from below. No evidence has been seen for overt social pressure from above; in the discussions of linguistic attitudes which concluded our interviews, it appeared that only at the college level are extreme values of (ay) and (aw) noted and stigmatized. Since Jewish–Italian differences are not pronounced, it is most likely that a class differential in apparent time will appear, which gives the impetus of social identification to these developments. For the investigation of these variables in apparent time, we will use the SEC index. The values for the youth group will be particularly crucial in this development, and we have already noted that it is simpler to assign the young people positions by their parents' SEC level than their own occupation and education. (If the children's education has already surpassed that of their parents, their SEC status is adjusted upward by that degree of change.)

Table 10.7 shows the distribution of (ay) and (aw) values for eight age levels and four class groups.

The pattern here seems to be that of Case III-A – the early stages of a linguistic change from below. There is a definite progression towards higher values of both indices. The oldest speakers show the lowest values: this is particularly notable for the four oldest lower class speakers. On the whole, the lower class shows the smallest rise in (ay) and (aw) values until the level of the youngest children is reached. On the other hand, both the working class and lower middle class show a rise for ages 50 through 40, then a slight fall for the 39–20 group, and the highest values of all for the younger children. The two variables generally follow the same outline, though (aw) is at a lower level than (ay). This relation is not merely an artifact of the scale, for the zero readings of (aw) would indicate no change from the original position on any scale.

The alternation of the pattern seems to indicate a relation of alternate half-generations, such as the following:

Generation IIB [5–19]

Generation IIA [20–34]

Generation IB [35–49]

Generation IA [50–64]

Table 10.8   *Average* (ay) *and* (aw) *values for all white NYC informants by half-generations*

	(ay)				(aw)			
Generation	0–2	3–5	6–8	9	0–2	3–5	6–8	9
II-B	7	23	22	12	8	20	17	8
II-A	5	18	24	10	–	7	10	4
I-B	8	17	18	20	4	7	8	1
I-A	5	10	10	15	2	7	5	5
0	0				0			

The children of Generation IA are the adult children of our sample, and the children of Generation IB are the youth of our sample. The suggestion of the feedback system, brought forward at the end of Chapter 9, is still present in this possibility. If we rearrange the age levels of Table 10.7 according to this pattern, we obtain the arrays of Table 10.8.

The regularity shown here is close to the paradigm for Case III-A. A suggestion of a reverse pattern for (ay) is seen in the trend of the upper middle class, particularly when we compare alternate half-generations. The relations of the three lower ranking groups in alternate half-generations show a fairly general rise of (ay) and (aw). We can interpret Table 10.8 as evidence for a change from below which began in the two center classes, and spread outwards. It should be emphasized that this type of systematic change does not lend itself to the clear and decisive confirmation which we saw for Cases I and II, and all inferences may be considered quite tentative except the existence of change from below itself. We will resume the discussion of (ay) and (aw) in Chapter 14, the discussion of the structure of the New York City vowel system.

The records of previous studies are consistent with the view of gradual change as presented above. Hubbell's thirty informants are sharply divided into two groups, as we have seen: college students, and informants over 50. Of the older informants, only two showed traces of (ay) differentiation; both from working class backgrounds, with only elementary school education. Of the fourteen younger informants, only four showed no backing of (ay), and these were from upper middle class families; three of the four who showed the most extreme forms of backed (ay) were students from lower middle class families, and the fourth was a lower class man of 31. As far as (aw) is concerned, the situation is even more regular. Two older informants showed traces of fronting, but most showed *backed* forms of (aw), that is [ɑʊ] alternating with [aʊ]. All of the college students showed some fronting of (aw).

The records of the Linguistic Atlas show that the backed variant of (ay) was used among uneducated and intermediate informants in New York City in the 1930s. The phonetic representation of this variant in the Atlas notation is [ɑɨ] or [ɑ⁺ɨ], which would correspond to our (ay-6, 7). There are 15 out of 116 occurrences of this variant among uneducated speakers of all ages, and 8 out of 45 for the intermediate informants (Type II). The cultivated informants did not use any of these (ay) forms.[7]

The Atlas evidence points to the beginning of a change from below which has now, in 1963, made substantial progress. It was noted above that the (aw) shift seems to have begun later than the movement of (ay). The Atlas does not show any slightly fronted forms for (aw), although a number of extreme types [æʊ] were recorded. We do not find such forms in our own records except for the very youngest ALS informants, and it is likely that the forms we have observed are the product of a separate evolution that is totally unrelated to the LA [æu]. The latter was the typical recessive form used by aged, rural, and old-fashioned informants throughout the northern United States, and was not probably transmitted to succeeding generations from these speakers.[8]

Babbitt's early observations of 1896 indicate some variation of (ay) in which the low central position of the first element is used, a centralized form, and also backed forms. For (aw), a position which is the opposite of the present tendency is indicated:

au has much variation in the first component, but in no case shows "fronting" of the vowel [to *æ* or a mixed vowel near *æ*] as in the South. What is heard is generally a regular *a* or something approaching *ɒ*.

[Chapter 3 of Labov 1994 re-examines the principles governing the study of apparent time, and takes the case of (ay) and (aw) in New York City as an example. It may be useful to show how the data can be further explored with tools that were not available in 1966. The original data from 158 Lower East Side speakers is reviewed, and summarized in the form of the scattergram of Figure 10.2. The horizontal axis is age; the vertical axis is a combined scale of frontness or backness of the nuclei. Each point represents the modal value for the first five occurrences of the variable. The two regression lines show a differentiation of (ay) and (aw) across apparent time. The r^2

---

[7] The cultivated informants did use a certain amount of another variant: a slightly centralized diphthong for /ai/. This feature was found in the other social levels as well – among the same speakers who used the backed variant.

[8] "In New England [æu], [ɛu] are rare except in some rural northern areas; in parts of New York State and the northern counties of Pennsylvania they are somewhat more common. There, as in New England, this type of pronunciation is regarded as rustic and old-fashioned and is being repaced by [au]." Kurath and McDavid (1951), page 110.

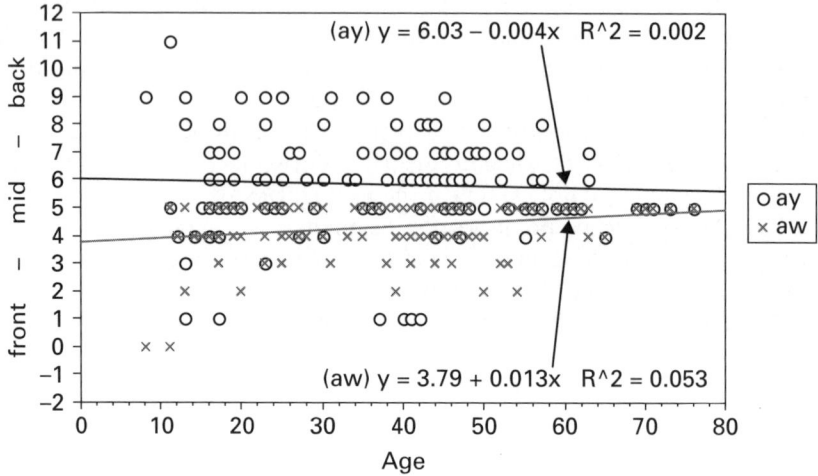

Figure 10.2   Distribution of NYC (ay) and (aw) in apparent time for all speakers (N=158)

figures show that the (aw) line accounts for 5 percent of the variance, and the (ay) line almost none. The (aw) regression does mark a significant trend (p < .001) for a population of this size, but it is nonetheless a small one. Furthermore, there seem to be two opposite trends among younger speakers, eight circles appear in the lower half of the diagram, indicating a fronting of (ay).

However, when the 31 African–American speakers are examined separately, the regression lines move in the opposite direction (see Figure 10.3). There are no significant trends on the whole, but it turns out that all 8 of the fronted (ay) values were AA speakers..

As in so many other studies of North American speech communities, there is a sharp division between black and white: African–Americans do not participate in the sound changes that are active in the majority population. Once African–Americans are removed from the sample, both (ay) and (aw) show a significant change in apparent time, both accounting for 11 percent of the variance, p < .0001. There is a notable contrast between the oldest speakers, with identical central nuclei for (ay) and (aw), and the youngest, with widely separated means (see Figure 10.4).

Since Table 10.6 showed that the lower class and the upper middle class did not participate in these sound changes in progress, the next step is to remove them and examine the sound change in the central social class groups that do so. Figure 10.5 from Labov 1994 shows the increase in the

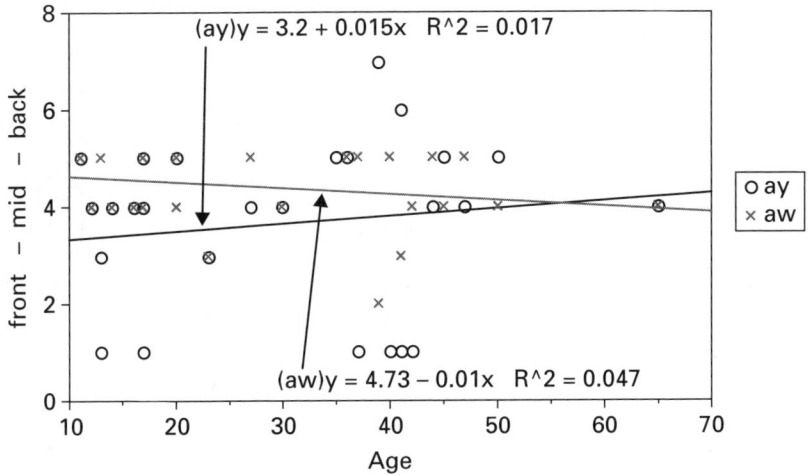

Figure 10.3 Distribution of (ay) and (aw) in apparent time for African–American NYC speakers (N=31)

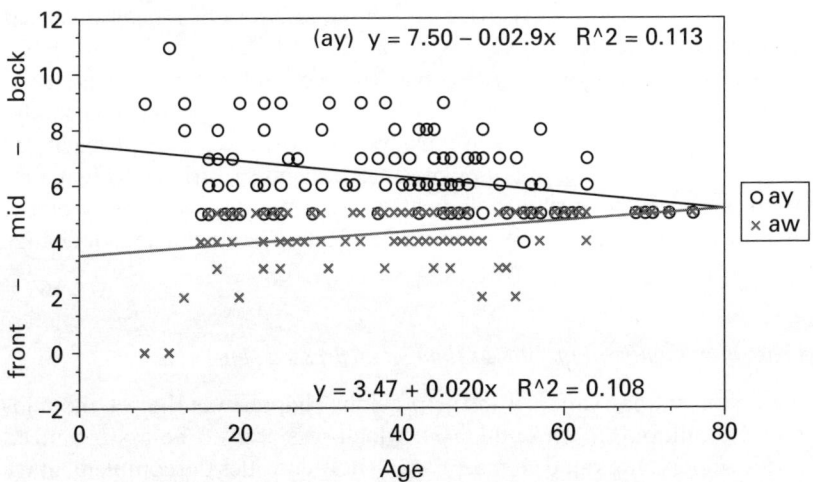

Figure 10.4 Distribution of (ay) and (aw) in apparent time for all white NYC subjects (N=127)

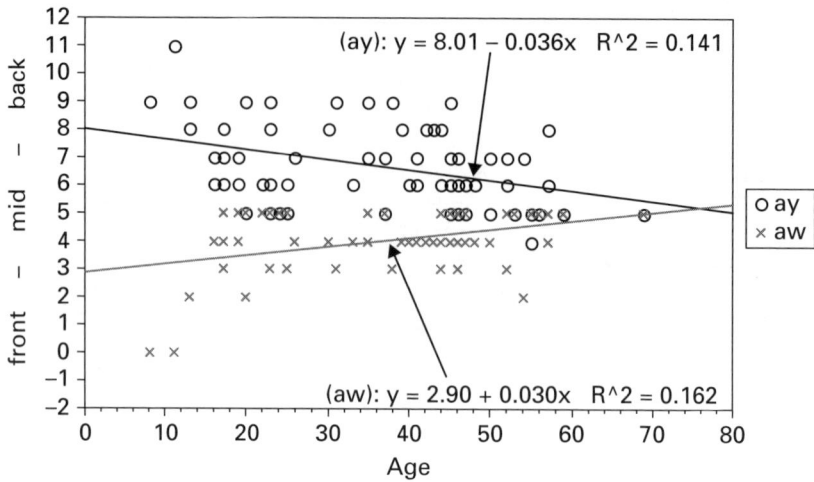

Figure 10.5   Distribution of (ay) and (aw) in apparent time for UWC and LMC only (N=70)

steepness of the lines and the increase in the amount of variance accounted for. The r-correlation of (ay) with age (the square root of r^2) has advanced to .38 and to .40 for (aw).

These scattergrams and regression analyses provide a more concise treatment of the general strategy of the NYC study. Applying a statistical analysis to the entire population is not always the most revealing approach. By systematically reducing the population for any given variable to that subgroup in which the variation is greatest, we obtain a clearer view of the processes at work, whether it is social stratification, style shifting, or change in progress.]

A case of stigmatization without change: unstressed (ing)

The first example examined in the previous chapter was that of the mid-central diphthong in *bird* and *shirt*, which was seen to be a stigmatized feature undergoing rapid change. We will now consider the complementary case of a stigmatized feature which does not show change of social significance or social distribution, but appears to have remained essentially stable in the past sixty years; this variable will help to clarify doubtful points which remain in regard to (th) and (dh).

We will be dealing primarily with the form of the suffix -*ing*, used to form participles and verbal nouns, as in *going* and *hunting*. There are two distinct traditional pronunciations of this form. One such pronunciation may be symbolized /in/. The other uses the velar nasal stop and is usually written phonemically as /iŋ/. Because this consonant usually corresponds to the spelling -*ng* in English, most native English speakers think of it as a combination of /n/ and /g/, and refer to the variant /in/ as "dropping the g." Since the great majority of New York speakers do not distinguish between *finger* and *singer*, there is no phonemic distinction for this regional dialect between [ɪŋ] and [ɪŋg], and the two variants do appear phonemically as /in/ versus /ing/.

Both of the variants correspond to old traditions. Wyld finds spelling evidence for /in/ in letters written as early as the fourteenth century.[9] There is every reason to think that this was the most common pronunciation for all social classes for the early modern period of English. The reaction which stigmatized this form, and favored the /ing/ variant as closer to the spelling, seems to have gathered momentum at the end of the eighteenth century. Walker's rulings on the matter (1806) are quite hesitant: he recommends /in/ for the present participles of words which contain -*ing* in the root, such as *singing*, *ringing*, but /ing/ for all other words.[10] The early decades of the nineteenth century seem to have witnessed a decisive preference for the /ing/ form as far as grammarians and school teachers were concerned.

[The stability of the (ing) variable has become an issue of some importance. The absence of any phonological conditioning and the discovery of strong grammatical conditioning indicated that the variation takes place at the morphological rather than the phonological level. Labov 1989 proposed that it is the result of an allomorphic alternation that is at least 1,000 years old: the Old English verbal noun -*inge* vs. the participle -*inde*. Houston (1985, 1991) explored the issue in detail and confirmed the likelihood of historical continuity, although the present social and stylistic stratification, documented here, dates from the eighteenth century. Chapter 3 of Labov 2001 adds further data to support the stability of this variable.

There remain some unresolved issues on the stability of linguistic variation. Weinreich, Labov, and Herzog (1968) argued that change always involves variation, but that variation need not imply change, despite the efforts to infer the direction of change without evidence from apparent time (Bailey 1972). More recently, emphasis on the blocking principle (Williams 1997) has led to the view that all variation is intrinsically unstable, and will be resolved in favor of invariant relations. We still need to determine under what conditions inherent variation can remain stable over long periods of time.]

---

[9] H. C. Wyld, *A History of Modern Colloquial English* (1936), pages 289–290.
[10] John Walker, *Rhetorical Grammar*, cited in Wyld (1936).

The same general development is found in America, as shown by the evidence gathered by Krapp.[11] He finds spellings in New England records as early as 1654 which point to /in/ as the prevailing form. Dearborn's *Columbian Dictionary*, published in Boston in 1795, lists /in/ as "an impropriety."[12] The situation as it now exists in New York City seems to be approximately the same as it was in Krapp's time, and the form /in/ seems to have been decisively marked as typical of uneducated speakers. Yet unlike the upgliding diphthong of *bird* and *work*, it maintains a steady position. The social significance of the /in/ variant seems to have remained unchanged for at least a hundred years, and changes in its distribution seem to have been minor. Frank (1948: p. 92) finds that in the speech of the Atlas informants in the 1930s, "this feature is limited almost entirely to the speech of the uneducated." The chart given by Frank shows that intermediate and cultivated informants (Types II and III) rarely use it. The chart may be summarized by the following ratios of /in/ pronunciation to the total instances of the suffix:

Type I	Uneducated	30/108
Type II	Intermediate	1/50
Type III	Cultured	1/50

There is of course nothing about the (ing) variable which is peculiar to New York City. The pronunciation /in/ has the same distribution in many parts of the United States. Fischer studied the use of the /in/ and /ing/ forms among a group of New England school children[13] and found that boys favored /in/ more than girls; that "model" boys used much more /in/ than "typical" boys; and that /in/ was used for informal situations much more than /ing/. The distribution of the two forms was found to follow the same lines in the English of Martha's Vineyard, in the study already cited.

We therefore have good documentation for the established status of the /in/ variant: it is a feature stigmatized by many educated American speakers as "incorrect" or "uneducated," and yet it has a well-defined place in the overall scheme of English usage.

In the survey of the Lower East Side, (ing) follows a regular pattern of stylistic variation, just as the five main phonological variables do. The index for (ing) will be the percentage of /in/ forms used of the total number of -*ing* suffixes. In addition, occurrences of the morpheme -*thing* will be added to the data when it occurs in combination as *something, anything, nothing,*

[11] George Philip Krapp, *The English Language in America* (1925), II, pages 214–215.
[12] Benjamin Dearborn, *Columbian Grammar* (1795), page 136. Cited in Krapp (1925).
[13] John L. Fischer, "Social Influences on the Choice of a Linguistic Variant" (1958).

Table 10.9   *Percent /in/ in two stylistic contexts*

	Style B	Style C
All adult white NYC	31	13
All adult white out-of-town	37	08
All AA NYC	62	18
All AA out-of-town	77	42

etc., but not when it occurs as the free form *thing*. The average indexes for all white adult New York City informants for Styles A, B, and C are:

Style A: 50   Style B: 31   Style C: 13

Fischer defined three stages of formality of the context in his study of schoolchildren: his corresponding indexes would be:

Least formal: 63   Intermediate: 52   Most formal: 03

African–American subjects were omitted from the averages given above because they show a much higher use of /in/ than white speakers. New York AA speakers have exactly twice as high a use of /in/ for careful speech as white speakers, and out-of-town AA informants use /in/ even more. On the other hand, out-of-town white speakers show almost the same averages as New Yorkers. All of these groups follow the same pattern of stylistic variation of (ing): it is only the absolute level of /in/ usage which varies (see Table 10.9).

There is no serious difference between young and adult speakers in respect to (ing). When we add to the ninety-four adult white NYC speakers who give us figures for (ing) in Style B, the twenty-five white informants under 20, the index shifts upward by only one percentage point.

In New York City, we do not find that /in/ pronunciation is preeminently a male usage, as appeared in Fischer's study and on Martha's Vineyard. The average index for all male New York City speakers (N:56) is 36 in Style B, as compared to 31 for the males and females combined (N:119). Most of the difference is in the lower class. However, no large differences appear for other classes, and in the middle class, men appear to use slightly less /in/ than women.

If the stigmatized (ing) variable is historically stable, it should show the same kind of style and class stratification diagrams as (th) and (dh). Figures 10.6 and 10.7 show style and class stratification diagrams for (ing) for all white New York City informants. The pattern is remarkably similar to Figures 7.22 and 7.23.

The distribution of (ing) in apparent time should also match that of (th) and (dh). Table 10.10 does in fact show the same pattern as Table 9.18.

Table 10.10   *Average (ing) indexes by age and social class for adult white NYC informants*

	Style A					Style B			
	SC					SC			
Age	1	2	3	4	Age	1	2	3	4
20–39	90	60	43	00	20–39	75	45	50	02
40–	85	48	21	23	40–	50	27	12	02
[N:	2	10	6	4	[N:	4	14	5	9
	24	8	10	5]		22	12	21	10]

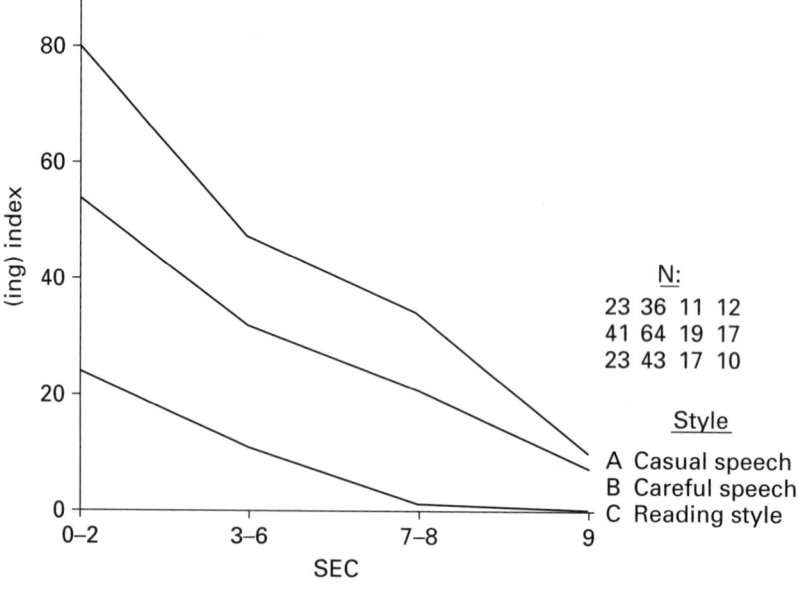

N:
23 36 11 12
41 64 19 17
23 43 17 10

Style
A Casual speech
B Careful speech
C Reading style

Figure 10.6   Style stratification of (ing)

The older members of the three lower ranking classes show less /in/ than the younger members. The only difference between Table 10.10 and the abstract construction for Case I-A (a stigmatized feature not involved in change) is that in Style A the older members of the highest ranking group do not show a minimal use of the stigmatized feature. In Style B there is no such

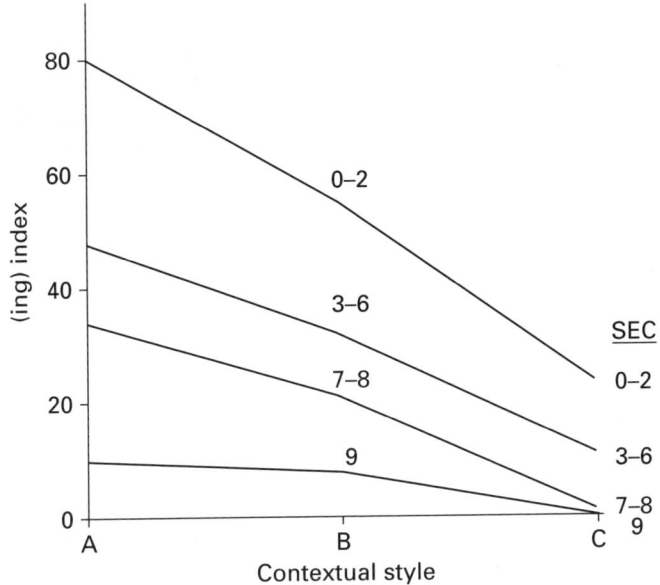

Figure 10.7   Class stratification of (ing)

difference, and the table matches Case I-A. On the whole, the evidence of (ing) strongly reinforces the interpretation already given to the data for (th) and (dh).

[Of all the variables studied in this book, (ing) has been found to have the greatest generality over the English-speaking world, and has been the subject of the most fruitful study. It was explored first by Fischer (1958) in the small study of a New England town that laid out the fundamental axes of variation. After the NYC study, Trudgill 1974 repeated the NYC study in Norwich, in a detailed and elegant way, with results quite similar and yet different from the American pattern. Figure 10.8 shows that the Norwich data preserves the regular structure of social and stylistic stratification but with much greater separation between the working class and middle class levels. The behavior of the upper working class is particularly interesting: in formal styles, this group switches to the very low level of apical /in/ characteristic of the middle classes, so that the sharp division between the two groups takes a different form. It is clear that this difference in sociolinguistic behavior corresponds to a difference in the sharpness of social stratification in England and America, and reinforces the view of sociolinguistic variation as a sensitive indicator of social structure.

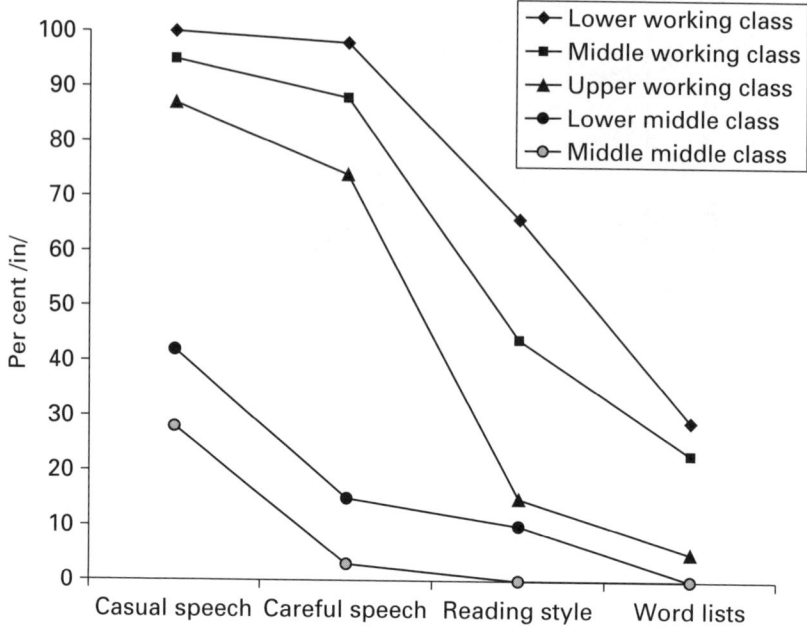

Figure 10.8   Social stratification of (ing) in Norwich (Trudgill 1974)

The variable (ing) was explored in Philadelphia (Cofer 1972, Labov 2001), in Australia (Peterson 1985), and Northern Ireland (Douglas-Cowie 1978). Houston (1985) found a similar structure of the variable in interviews by Labov in twenty British cities as well as American sites. Only in the American South was there found a markedly different system, where high levels of the /in/ variable are maintained in formal speech. Labov 1989 and Roberts 1993 traced the acquisition of (ing) among young children; it was found that the stylistic variation of the adult community was acquired by children as young as three years old, while other structural conditions were not learned until later.]

With this view of a wider range of linguistic variables, we have completed the survey of the differentiation of the linguistic variables in speech. The second part of the inquiry will be undertaken in Chapter 11, as we investigate the subjective evaluation of the variables by our informants. In the studies of differentiation, we have been led inescapably to conclusions about social significance. However, it is one thing to draw inferences about social significance from circumstantial evidence, and another to determine this directly from the native speakers themselves. Chapter 11 will describe a subjective reaction test which was designed to solve the many technical and theoretical problems of determining evaluative reactions by a reliable and quantitative measure. The results of this test will confirm many of the indications of linguistic change which we have already found, and display patterns which are even more regular than those of objective performance.

Part III

Social evaluation

11   Subjective evaluation of the variables

[Part III of the book, dealing with "Social evaluation" incorporates results from a series of field experiments that formed an essential part of the methodology. The experimental approach did not take hold in sociolinguistics in any way comparable to the studies of speech production that formed the basis of Part II. Though each of these experimental methods has had a history of replication and development, the studies that incorporate experiments are few by comparison with those that do not.

The simplest experimental approach involves the reading of texts and word lists, and this of course is not uncommon. Minimal pairs are one step more complicated, since they involve a comparison of production and perception – complicated by the need to label those perceptions. The self-report test (Chapter 12) is not difficult to prepare – a simple recording of the range of phonetic variants that have already been coded for the study of speech production. Linguistic insecurity tests (Chapter 12) need somewhat more preparation. The matched-guise experiments that are the subject of this chapter demand the most time and effort for the production of the stimuli. The resources and information needed to prepare matched guise recordings will usually require a good year of exploratory work. I hope that the results of this chapter will justify that effort, and reinforce the view that a successful study of the speech community must give considerable attention to normative behavior.]

We have completed our survey of social differentiation of five phonological variables in New York City, and we will now turn to the more obscure and difficult question of the subjective evaluation of the variables by our informants. We have seen a pattern of social variation and a pattern of stylistic variation which fit together closely: in general, a variant that is used by most New Yorkers in formal styles is also the variant that is used most often in all styles by speakers who are ranked higher on an objective socio-economic scale. The connection between these two axes of variation was further illustrated by the close correlation between real deviations from stylistic variation and real deviations from social variation. The combination of both types of variation into a single structure suggests to us that most New Yorkers think or feel that particular variants are better, or more correct, or are endowed with superior status. Our task in this chapter is to investigate such subjective reactions among the native English speakers of the Lower East Side.

Most reactions to phonological variables are inarticulate responses, below the level of conscious awareness. They occur as a part of an overall reaction to many variables. There is no vocabulary of socially meaningful terms with which our informants can evaluate speech for us. We therefore need to proceed not by direct questions, but by eliciting some kind of evaluative behavior that is sensitive enough to reflect the influence of many variables, and is subject to quantitative measurement.

Direct questions are almost useless. Some informants will be ready and willing to answer questions about a certain variable; a few will even volunteer their opinions on this subject. But the great majority of respondents show no conscious awareness of the variables we have been studying. In the discussions of linguistic attitudes which took place at the end of our interviews, many respondents showed strong opinions about New York City speech in general, but only a few were able to mention specific words, sounds, or phrases which characterized the language of the city or of groups within it. Direct questions will tap the reactions of only a handful of exceptionally articulate middle class speakers.

The type of evaluative behavior which we wish to measure is more systematic, more completely internalized than any reply we might elicit by the overt discussion of speech. We are searching for the evaluative norms which reflect the complex and regular structures seen in Part II of this study. In order to measure the internal evaluative processes of our respondents, we must construct a chain of inference which leads to a quantitative measure of overt behavior. Should the results of this construction coincide with the structures described by the methods of Part II, the confirmation will be even more striking than the convergence of the department store survey and the Lower East Side survey. In that case, we approached objective performance by two different survey methods; here we approach the structure of the speech community on two different levels of behavior.

The chief problems which we must solve are three: 1) to isolate the subjective reactions to particular values of a single variable; 2) to reduce these reactions to a quantitative measure; 3) to find the overall structure reflected in the pattern of the resulting measurements.

Our first aim in designing the subjective reaction test is to expose each informant to utterances with contrasting values of the variable in which all other variables would be held constant. This might be done with synthetic speech, or with practiced utterances of the interviewer. But we would then have to prove that the phonetic detail of the variant was equivalent to that of the natural variants, and also, that the artificiality of the utterance did not itself introduce a new variable that disturbed subjective reactions.[1]

It seems preferable therefore to approach the problem by using natural utterances of native speakers to elicit reactions. In casting the net a little wider, we will inevitably draw in some extraneous variables; but we will be certain of the main object – those values of the variables which are in fact used by Lower East Side speakers.

The initial material for the subjective reaction test (hereafter abbreviated SR test) was forty versions of the standard reading, "When I was nine or ten . . ." This reading is given in its entirety in Appendix A, with the relevant occurrences of the variables underlined.

The five variables are concentrated in successive paragraphs. As noted in our earlier description of this passage, the first paragraph contains none of the variables; the second contains (oh); the third, (æh); the fourth (r); and the fifth, (th) and (dh) .

It would be possible to obtain reactions from a respondent by playing the reading a paragraph at a time, and testing his reactions to the speaker after each paragraph. We could then see how the listener's evaluation of the speaker rose or fell as the listener reacted to the speaker's treatment of separate variables. However, there would then be no way to estimate how much of the listener's reaction to the values of (oh) was carried over to his evaluation of the (æh) paragraph, and so on through the list. If, on the other hand, each variable was treated by a different speaker, we would not know how much of the listener's reaction was due to the speaker's voice quality and treatment of other variables.

To solve these problems, it was decided to select one sentence from each paragraph for five different speakers, and play the sentences from each paragraph with the speakers in mixed order. As the listener reacted to a particular sentence, he would not be able to know exactly how he had rated the same speaker in a previous utterance. In analyzing the results, however, the comparison between utterances of the same speaker's use of different variables would be retained.

The five informants selected as speakers for the SR test were all women whose voices were recorded in the exploratory interviews. If both men and

---

[1]   In some exploratory interviews, I used my own imitation of the sound (oh-1) in some test sentences to elicit reactions. A number of informants told me that my pronunciation sounded effeminate. From this one might conclude that high, fronted (oh) vowels were considered inappropriate for male speech. However, it soon appeared that I had been using an over-rounded variant of (oh-1) that is made with pursed lips. The equivalent male form, with equal height and fronting, is articulated without any noticeable pursing of the lips. No one can say how many slight differences may remain unnoticed in the attempts of the interviewer to imitate the pronunciation of a given class or region. Therefore, even if the reactions of the informants are immediate and strong, they may be reactions to unsuspected features of the utterance.

women had been used, it would not have been difficult for the listener to identify a particular voice as it recurred.

The speakers were selected not for their social characteristics, but for their treatment of the variables.[2] It was necessary to obtain sentences with consistently high values of each variable, and others with consistently low values of each. In addition, some sentences with inconsistent use of a variable were contrasted with sentences in which the same speaker used the variable consistently.

Twenty-two sentences from the five speakers were copied onto a test tape for the SR test in its final version. On the tape, the number of the sentence is first given in my own voice, and then two copies of the test sentence are heard twice in succession, separated by a short pause. The first five sentences, from the zero paragraph, allowed the listener to hear each of the five speakers once. The order and structure of the succeeding test sentences will be discussed under the individual variables.

The tape was played to the subjects after they themselves had completed all of the reading under Context C, including a reading of "When I was nine or ten . . ."[3] The respondents were told that this test was the most

[2] The social characteristics and voice qualities of the five speakers may be described briefly as follows.

Speaker 1 is a middle-aged, Jewish woman with a high, quavery, and uncertain voice. She lives in a middle-income cooperative; her husband is a certified public accountant. She had some college education.

Speaker 2 is a middle-aged Jewish woman. She lives in a low-income project; her husband is a carpet-layer. She attended two years of normal school, and is a part-time substitute teacher. Voice quality is nasal and penetrating; consonants are formed with considerable pressure and exploded with sibilance.

Speaker 3 is a young woman of Italian-born parents. She lives in a tenement apartment; both her husband and herself are semi-skilled workers. She has only a grammar school education and reads with considerable hesitation. Voice quality is husky and low; consonants are dark and velarized.

Speaker 4 is a middle-aged Jewish woman, living in a middle-income cooperative apartment. Of the five speakers, she is the one who would be described as "cultured" in Atlas terms. Her voice quality is fairly low and well-modulated; speaking and reading styles are not very different; consonants are usually formed carefully, but without the heavily aspirated and sibilant release of Speaker 2.

Speaker 5 is a middle-aged woman of Italian-born parents. She lives alone in a tenement apartment, and works at a factory job as an unskilled operator. She completed only the sixth grade in grammar school. Her voice quality shows a slight rasp, but is felt by many people to be "warm." She shows vivacity in her reading style, with a tendency to break into laughter, in contrast to the level and colorless tones used by Speaker 3 in reading. (æh) vowels are very high; (oh) is moderate; (r) is consistently (r-0) in Style C. (th) and (dh) show moderately heavy use of stops and affricates.

[3] It was found to be important for the success of the test that the respondents read the text themselves beforehand, or hear someone else read it. Otherwise, many listeners will find it difficult to realize that the speaker on the tape is only reading words which were written for her, rather than speaking for herself, and they will downgrade her for phrases such as "He was a funny kid, all right." They may remark in this connection, "I would never say anything like that."

important part of the interview: since we had already learned how they themselves used the English language, we then wanted to know how they felt about the way other New Yorkers used it.

Respondents were asked to imagine themselves in the position of a personnel manager, interviewing people for a large corporation. They were given the form shown as Figure 11.1, on which to rate the speakers – for their speech only. On the left of Figure 11.1 is an index scale of occupational suitability of speech: for each sentence, the respondent was asked to indicate his reactions by drawing a horizontal line across the vertical scale, marking the first scale for the first sentence, the second for the second, and so on. The marks might be made on a line, or in between lines if they felt there was an in-between case. A mark across the scale at a certain job meant that the person speaking could hold that job, as far as her speech was concerned, and all those jobs listed below, but none of the jobs above. For example, the first mark shown on Figure 11.1 indicates that the speakers of the first sentence could not hold any job higher than that of a factory worker because of her speech. A mark at "None of these" meant that the speech was so poor that the person could not even hold a factory job.[4] The marks shown on Figure 11.1 represent the median ratings for middle class respondents (SEC 6–9) from 20 to 39 years old.

Most of the respondents agreed with the hierarchy expressed by the scale: that each job listed required better speech than the ones below, and did not require as good speech as the ones above. However, in case respondents had some reservations on particular items, it was explained to everyone that the index was to be thought of as a continuous scale running from perfect speech at the top to terrible speech at the bottom, with all degrees in between. It was also explained that the listener was not trying to judge what job the speaker actually held: that some factory workers, for example, spoke well enough to hold any of the jobs shown. The respondent was to judge what was the highest job on the scale which the speaker *could* hold, speaking as she did. The complete instructions to the respondents are given in the questionnaire form in Appendix A.[5]

---

[4] It is plain that such a rating cannot be taken literally. Many respondents needed this rating as an outlet for their strong negative feelings about certain sentences. I originally inserted this rating as a bottom rank which no one would choose, in line with the principle that some people hesitate to mark anything as the very worst. However, many informants went even beyond this mark, to the bottom of the line, which must then be considered as rank *0*.

[5] After Sentence 5 was played, the listener was asked to mention aloud any particular words which came to his attention and influenced him in making his final judgment. After Sentence 11, the test was interrupted briefly to allow the respondents to rest; during this time, the respondent was asked a few general questions about his reactions, and the type of cues for which he was listening. The sentences from 12 to 22 were then played without interruption.

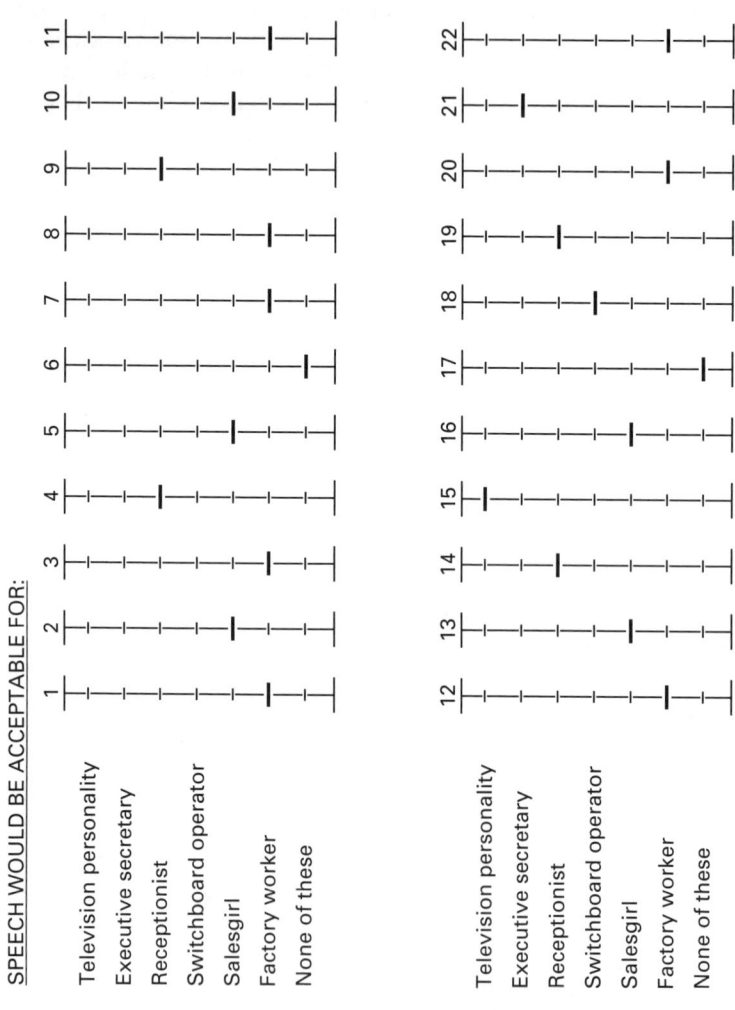

Figure 11.1 Subjective evaluation form with median ratings for SEC 6–9, age 20–39

It should be evident that this subjective reaction test does not measure all subjective reactions. The scale of occupational suitability is plainly designed in accordance with the requirements of the socio-economic hierarchy, and reflects values which are best exemplified by speakers with middle class orientation. It will be shown that almost all members of society share these values, to a greater or lesser extent: one of the recurrent themes of this study is that the speech community as a whole is unified by a common set of norms of this type. However, there are other values which are conferred on speech forms, that are not represented here. The particular reactions which are measured here are those which respond to pressure from above – reactions to prestige norms and stigmatized language features. Those subjective reactions which accompany the more subtle and obscure changes from below are not measured here. It may be possible, in the future, to devise tests for these reactions as well – tests for emotional response on the basis of group identification – but these are beyond the goals that are set in the present study.

[The matched guise experimental approach was developed by Wallace Lambert and his associates at McGill (Lambert 1967). Their elegant and ingenious experiments demonstrated and replicated the finding that members of a speech community share a set of unconscious norms of great strength and generality, shared by both the dominant and the dominated sections of society. Subjects are asked to make personality judgments of the same speaker in several linguistic guises. Both English and French speakers shared the perception that those who speak English are taller, more intelligent, more dependable, and more honest than those who speak French. An essential feature of this methodology is that the subjects not be aware that the same speaker is presented in different guises. An alternation of three or four intervening subjects is sufficient to ensure that this be so. Every once in a while someone carries out a matched guise experiment with a single speaker, not realizing the force of this condition, and the results are very pale by comparison.

Matched guise experiments proved equally successful in evaluating dialects of the same language. From a linguistic point of view, such matched guise experiments carried out by cognitive psychologists have one

Footnote 5 (*cont.*)
    It seemed at first that the SR test would be a difficult and fatiguing one, and that it would not be easy to get most respondents to complete it. Experience showed that this was not the case. With the presentation described above, most respondents seemed to grasp the purpose of the test readily, and give their full cooperation. Many lower class speakers who had little education, and whose speech would be ranked at the bottom of the scale by most judges, took great pleasure in the SR test; and completed it with zest. Only two subjects failed to complete the test once they had begun it. In many cases, the SR test was administered to several people at once – in one case, to eight members of the family and friends. Altogether, two hundred SR tests were completed, including ALS informants, their children, and supplementary informants.

glaring weakness: we do not know what variables produced the effect on the judges. The methods first developed in the New York City study were designed to solve this problem by concentrating the linguistic variables in short texts, and comparing reactions to these with "zero" passages that contain none of the variables. No such test is ever perfectly controlled, and the final sections of this chapter will look closely at the possibility that other factors were responsible for the results.]

The results which we will present here are based on SR tests completed by 122 native New York informants: 85 adults and 49 children of informants under 20 years old. The distribution of these informants by age and socio-economic class, sex and ethnic group, follows that of the sample population displayed in Figures 9.1 and 9.2. The television interview sample is of course not included. Of the original 83 New York ALS informants, only 7 did not take the SR test; 7 out-of-town informants did not take the test, and 2 adult children of ALS informants who were included in the sample of Chapter 9.

In addition to these losses, which were much smaller than originally expected, there were three cases of persons who can best be described as "dialect deaf." With the best will in the world, these respondents could not hear any significant difference between the speakers on the test tape: as far as they were concerned, the test sentences were all perfect, and were marked at the top of the scale, since they did not contain any words which were obviously mispronounced, or any grammatical mistakes. For these three subjects, the variables which we have been studying in this work did not exist. One of these respondents was an old Jewish lady, SEC 0; another was an African–American boy 16 years old, SEC 2; a third was the husband of an informant, an Italian man of 60, born in Brooklyn, SEC 3. A few other informants showed tendencies in this direction, but the great majority heard clear-cut differences between the test sentences, and showed a pattern of ratings which followed well-defined norms.

The zero pattern

We will consider first the patterns formed by the ratings given to the first five sentences, taken from the zero paragraph of the standard reading. The ratings in this section will be used as reference points for any later changes in the ratings given to the same speaker as she reads a sentence containing many instances of a particular variable. In this way, the effect of reading style, voice quality, recording quality, preciseness of articulation, and intonation patterns, will be effectively cancelled out, as these do not vary significantly from one sentence of the standard reading to another.

Table 11.1   *Average ratings for the zero section of the SR test by socio-economic class*

	Speaker				
SEC	1	2	3	4	5
6–9	2.6	3.3	2.7	4.8	3.2
3–5	3.0	3.8	3.5	4.9	3.9
0–2	4.0	4.6	4.3	5.0	3.8

In the discussion to follow, we will not be concerned with the absolute values of the ratings. We will be interested in patterns of relationships between ratings rather than absolute values, just as in most of the previous analyses in this study.

There is general agreement on the relative rankings of the five speakers as they are first heard. We may call this set of relations the *zero pattern*. The five speakers, identified by the position of the sentence in which they are heard, fall into three levels according to the average rankings given them by all respondents:

Level 1			Speaker 4	
Level 2		Speaker 2		Speaker 5
Level 3	Speaker 1		Speaker 3	

Although the zero pattern is quite constant, there is a regular progression in the absolute differences of rankings assigned by socio-economic class groups. Table 11.1 shows the average ratings for the three class groups for the zero section.

The rating of the speakers does not match their socio-economic ranking very closely. However the recurrent zero pattern is related to the class status of the judges. Only one deviation from a regular relation appears – the lower class rating of Speaker 5. In this structure the zero pattern becomes gradually shallower. The absolute ratings of Speaker 4 are almost the same, but the differences between her and the others are less for the working class than the middle class, and less still for the lower class. We may say that the middle class stigmatizes the speech of all but the most cultured speaker, and the other classes do not penalize these speakers to the same extent. Despite such differences, the zero pattern seems to describe the norms of all classes.

Subjective reactions to (oh)

The structure of the (oh) section of the SR test is shown in Figure 11.2. Test sentences 6 through 9 were taken from the (oh) paragraph of the standard

Table 11.2

Sentence	Speaker	*always*	*chocolate*	*coffee*	*afternoon*
6	1	(oh-1)	(oh-1)	(oh-2)	(æh-4)
7	2	(oh-2)	(oh-1)	(oh-1)	(æh-4)
8	5	(oh-2)	(oh-2)	(oh-1)	(æh-2)
9	4	(oh-2)	(oh-3)	(oh-5)	(æh-4)

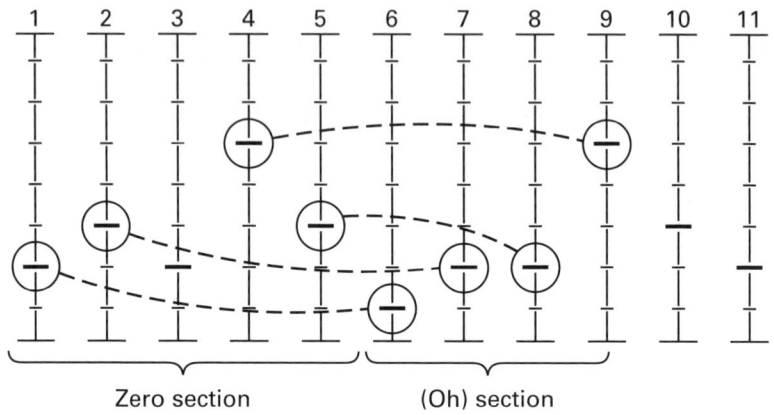

Figure 11.2   Structure of subjective evaluation form for (oh)

reading; they were read by the same voices as sentences 1, 2, 5, and 4, respectively. The sentence was the same for all four speakers: "We always had chocolate milk and coffee cake around four o'clock in the afternoon."

The relevant values of the variables are listed in Table 11.2.[6] The speakers will be identified hereafter as 1, 2, 3, 4, 5, according to their position in the zero section.

The occurrence of (æh-4) in *afternoon* is not heavily stressed for any speaker; the corrected (æh-4) of Speakers 1 and 2 is not prominent, and did not attract any overt notice. The (æh-2) in *afternoon* of Speaker 5 in Sentence 8 was remarked by some listeners, although it receives only

---

[6] The word *four* is not listed, since (oh) before intervocalic (r) is regularly close to (oh-3) for most speakers, and never rises to (oh-1). The syllable -er- in *afternoon* is regularly (r-0) for all four speakers, but a very sharp listening is required to detect the value of the variable here, and it may be counted as a small but constant factor in all four sentences. Speakers 1 and 2 use a tense, over-rounded form of (oh-1) which is particularly prominent in "chocolate milk and coffee cake." As pronounced by Speaker 2, *chocolate* and *coffee* occur with a rhythmic extra stress that many listeners commented on: a "sing-song" effect.

Table 11.3 *Number of ratings higher, equal or lower than the zero section for sentences 6–9*

Sentence	Relation to zero section equivalent		
	Higher	Equal	Lower
6	18	34	30
7	15	19	50
8	18	16	50
9	22	28	34

secondary stress. We will therefore find in Sentence 8 some effect of (æh-2) as well as (oh); the comparison of Sentence 8 with Sentence 11 in the next section will resolve any ambiguity.

Finally, it may be noted that Speaker 4 does not show a consistent (oh) value, proceeding from (oh-2) to (oh-3) and (oh-5). This inconsistency is normal, since we did not find any speakers in the exploratory interviews or the survey itself who used a lowered version of (oh) consistently.

The results for each sentence may be analyzed first by listing the total number of ratings which were higher than the corresponding sentence in the zero section, those that were the same, and those that were lower. Only adults are considered in Table 11.3.

The overall results show that the pronunciations of (oh-1) are associated with a pronounced fall in the ratings. At first glance it seems as if Sentence 7 received the brunt of this effect. However, Speaker 1, who now appears in Sentence 6, was rated quite low to begin with. We might consider that there was more room for a listener to raise his rating of Sentence 6, and less room to lower it. Yet the number who showed higher ratings for Sentence 6 was almost as small as Sentence 7. Those who rated Sentence 6 at the same low level as Sentence 1 were not reacting in a manner inconsistent with the stigmatization of (oh-1).

Following this line of reasoning, we can say that a consistent negative reaction to high (oh) vowels such as (oh-1) will produce a consistent response to Sentences 6, 7, and 8 in which these ratings will be equal or lower than Sentences 1, 2, and 5 respectively. A response to all of the sentences examined which is equal or lower than the response to the corresponding sentence in the zero section will be termed *(oh)-negative*. The test described for an (oh)-negative response will be termed a *three-choice test*. Table 11.4 shows the percentage of (oh)-negative responses for all nine SECs by the three-choice test.

Table 11.4 shows a close parallel to Figure 7.20, a style stratification figure for (oh). It shows that classes 0–2 display no separation of styles for (oh),

Table 11.4   *Percentages of (oh)-negative response by class*[7]

				SEC				
0	1	2	3	4	5	6	7–8	9
37	20	13	59	56	80	100	73	58

Table 11.5   *Percentage of (oh)-negative response by social class and age*

	Social class								
Age	1	2	3	4			N		
20–39	(50)	67	100	71		1	15	7	7
40–59	43	45	67	67		16	9	15	6
60–	29					7			

Table 11.6   *Percentage of (oh)-negative response by SEC and five age levels*

	SEC								
Age	0–2	3–4	5–8	9			N		
8–15	25	37	67	(100)		8	8	6	1
16–19	43	67	78	75		7	6	9	4
20–39	25	80	100	60		4	10	11	5
40–59	18	60	62	57		11	15	13	7
60–	33	(00)				6	1		

indicating by both stylistic and social deviation from the overall structure that (oh) is not a variable for this class group. Similarly, Table 11.4 shows that the percentages of (oh)-negative response for classes 0–2 are much lower than for other classes. In Figure 7.20, classes 3–4 show the beginning of high (oh) values in casual speech, and a separation of Style A from more careful styles. Styles B, C, and D, however, do not show stratification. Similarly, in Table 11.4, classes 3 and 4 show intermediate values of (oh)-negative response.

[7] The numbers of cases for this table are the same as those shown in Table 11.3. This will hold for all subjective reaction tabulations by individual SEC. In all of the tables of this chapter, only adults from 20 to 75 are included unless otherwise specified in a table showing age levels.

In Figure 7.20, classes 5 through 8 show high values of (oh) in casual speech, and rapidly increasing values of (oh) in more formal styles, with regular stratification of styles. In Table 11.4, these classes show the maximum (oh)-negative response. Finally, class 9 in Figure 7.20 shows only moderate (oh) values and in Style D does not show the very open, hypercorrect vowels used by classes 6–8. In Table 11.4, class 9 also shows moderate (oh)-negative response, lower than the response of classes 6–8.

These detailed parallels between subjective reactions and objective performance indicate that the (oh) section of the SR test has indeed isolated subjective reactions to that particular variable.

We may now consider the distribution of subjective reactions to (oh) in apparent time. Table 11.5 shows the distribution of (oh) response for four class groups and three age levels.[8]

Table 9.16 shows that the lowest values of the variable, corresponding to the maximum height of (oh) vowels, are by the younger group of SC 3 speakers. Correspondingly, we find that maximum sensitivity to (oh) – the greatest percentage of (oh)-negative response – is shown by this group. In the relations of the other class and age levels, Table 9.16 matches Table 11.5. The upper middle class showed no change in Table 9.16; it can be seen here that older and younger speakers of class 9 have approximately the same (oh)-negative response.

We can expand the view of the relations of the age levels by showing a table for the youth as well as adults. Table 11.6 shows five age levels, using the SEC scale for class divisions, as we regularly do whenever youths below 20 are included in the comparison; the same SEC groups as in Table 11.4 are used.

For all age levels, the lower middle class shows the highest level of (oh)-negative response. For the two center class groups, the young adults 20 to 39 years old show the highest degree of (oh)-negative response among age levels. From this point, the values for the younger children decline. We will show other evidence of this type to indicate that young people below the age of 19 or 20 have not yet acquired full sensitivity to the socially significant dialect features of their community. Nevertheless, the rule seems to hold that those who show the highest values for (oh) in casual speech will also show the greatest (oh) sensitivity in the SR test. There is a connection between: 1) high vowels in casual speech; 2) correction over a wide range in formal styles; 3) a regular pattern of stylistic stratification; and 4) strong (oh)-negative response.

---

[8] In order to match the presentation of Chapter 9, Table 11.5 of this chapter shows the percentages by social class rather than socio-economic class. The pattern of SC groups is the same as that for SEC groups, but comparison with Table 9.16 will be made more precise by using the SC scale.

Table 11.7   *Percentages of (oh)-negative response by ethnic group and age*

Age	Jews	Italians	N	
20–39	88	100	8	8
40–	52	40	25	10

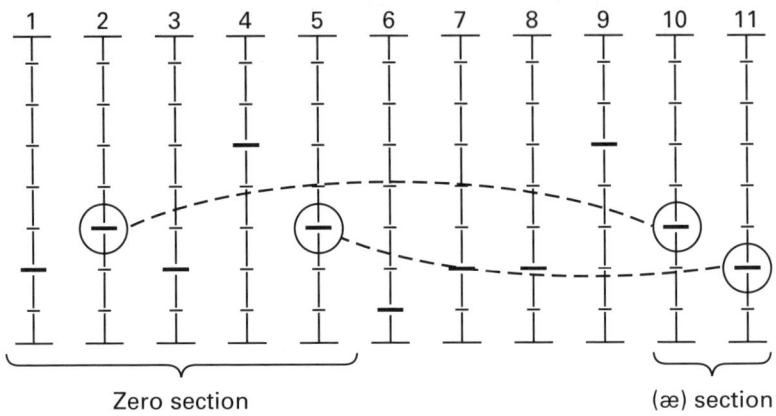

Figure 11.3 Structure of subjective evaluation form for (æh)

This surmise may be explored further by considering the relations of Jews and Italians in the SR test for (oh). Chapter 9 showed that the Jewish–Italian contrast was more evident in the development of (oh) in apparent time than class contrast. Judging by our limited evidence, the high (oh) vowels seemed to have occurred earlier among the Jews than the Italians. If this is so, we would expect that older Jews would show a higher (oh)-negative response than older Italians, but that the younger groups of both Italians and Jews would show strong (oh)-negative response. Table 11.7 shows that this is indeed the case. As in the corresponding Table 9.17, only three lower classes are shown: the upper middle class is excluded. It appears that the Italians have actually surpassed the Jews in (oh)-negative response among the younger people, although the numbers here are too small to put much emphasis on the fact.

Table 8.7 showed that women used higher (oh) vowels than men in casual speech, but in formal styles showed an even greater shift to the more open vowels, thus reversing the relationship. From these facts, we

Table 11.8   *Sentences testing responses to* (æh)

Sentence	Speaker	
10	2	We used to play Kick-the-Can. You run past
		<div style="text-align:center">(æh-4) (æh-4)</div>
		the man as fast as you can and kick a tin
		(æh-4) (æh-3) (æh-4)
		can so he can't tag you.
		(æh-4) (æh-4) (æh-4)
11	5	"Bad boy!" but he was too fast. Only my aunt
		(æh-2) (oh-2) (æh-2) (æh-2)
		could catch him. She even taught him to ask
		(oh-2) (æh-2)
		for a glass of milk and jump into a paper bag.
		(æh-2) (æh-2)

should expect that women would show a greater (oh)-negative response. There is a difference between men and women in the SR response, although the value of the difference is small. Fifty-four percent of the men show (oh)-negative response in the three-choice test, and 60 percent of the women.

[Reviewing this treatment of subjective evaluations of (oh) it appears that the data from social class, ethnicity and gender coincide to establish the underlying principle that those who use the highest level of a stigmatized variable in their vernacular show the greatest tendency to stigmatize it. This might be encapsulated as the *Reflexive Stigma Principle*. It is a principle of some generality that should be taken into consideration in constructing a model of how the sociolinguistic monitor operates and what it does.]

Subjective reactions to (æh)

Sentences 10 and 11 will be used for an examination of subjective response to values of the (æh) variable. The structure of the (æh) section is illustrated in Figure 11.3, and the relevant values of the variables are shown in Table 11.8.

In Sentence 10, Speaker 2 is heard using the corrected (æh-4) vowel. This is a long, low, fronted version of the vowel of *bat*, which conveys to many listeners the impression of tenseness. Her only inconsistency is the word *fast*, in which the vowel is (æh-3).

Sentence 11 is spoken by Speaker 5, the working class woman who was rated fairly high in the zero section, but who was rated lower in Sentence 8 by most respondents. In the (oh) section, Speaker 5 used moderately high (oh) vowels with one semi-stressed high (æh). Here she uses a number of

Table 11.9   *Responses to Sentence 11 in relation to Sentence 5 by SEC*

	SEC									
Relation to S.5	0	1	2	3	4	5	6	7–8	9	Total
Higher	3	1	1	3	1	1	1	1	3	15
Equal	2	0	0	4	0	1	3	2	1	13
Lower	2	4	7	8	8	3	6	8	8	54

Table 11.10   *Comparison of responses to Sentences 11, 5 and 8*

	Higher	Equal	Lower
Sentence 8 compared to 5	18	16	50
Sentence 11 compared to 5	15	13	54

Table 11.11   *Comparison of responses to Sentences 8 and 11*

8 lower than 11	8 equal to 11	8 higher than 11
12	26	35

stressed (æh) vowels, quite long, at the level of (æh-2), the vowel of *where*, and two examples of (oh-2) under secondary stress.[9]

In reacting to Sentence 11, the listener is responding to the most common value of (æh) to be heard in casual speech in New York City. Figure 8.8 (the distribution chart for (æh) in Style A) shows a high concentration exactly at (æh)-20. In Figure 7.18, all classes show regular style stratification for (æh). In contrast to (oh), we should therefore expect to see a uniform reaction to (æh) in the SR test.

For the simplest case of an (æh) negative response, we need only compare Sentence 11 to Sentence 5. Table 11.9 shows the numbers of responses for each socio-economic class which were higher, equal, or lower than Sentence 5.

If this response is compared to the overall response of the informants to Sentence 8 (again as compared to Sentence 5), it appears that the reaction

[9] Speaker 5 inserted the word *dog* in place of *boy*, in "Bad boy!" Despite this unwelcome intrusion, her reading was used because the versions of (æh-2) were highly characteristic of the forms to be heard in casual speech from many New Yorkers. Few informants would read a standard text with this variant consistently reproduced.

Table 11.12   *Percentage of responses to Sentence 11 equal to or lower than Sentences 5 and 8 by SEC*

				SEC				
0	1	2	3	4	5	6	7–8	9
50	50	88	86	67	60	80	73	75

Table 11.13   *Percentage of (æh) negative response by SEC and age*

	SEC groups					N		
Age	0–2	3–5	6–8	9				
8–15	100	75	100	(100)	7	8	6	1
16–19	86	100	100	75	7	12	4	4
20–39	75	90	100	80	4	10	11	5
40–	75	80	70	71	16	15	10	7

against (æh-2) is even stronger than that against (oh-1) and (oh-2) (see Table 11.10).

The reaction against (æh-2) can be shown to be stronger in another sense. We may ask if Sentence 11 is not only equal or lower than Sentence 5, but also if it is equal or lower than Sentence 8. For responses to Sentence 11 lower than Sentence 5 see Table 11.11.

If we now consider the class distribution of this complex characteristic, we have Table 11.12.

Table 11.12 shows that the working class exhibits the maximum (æh)-negative response. This table highlights the fact that (æh) is the uppermost consideration for the working class speakers who wish to be correct in their speech, while (oh) plays a smaller part in their unconscious reactions.

The distribution of (æh)-negative responses (lower than sentence 5) to Sentence 11 in apparent time is shown in Table 11.13. The comparatively high values show that we are dealing with a late stage of change from below, where social reaction from above has been imposed on almost all groups.

Table 11.13 confirms the expectation that (æh)-negative reaction would be more general over class and age levels than (oh) reaction. Among the younger adults, the lower middle class and the working class show the highest level of (æh)-negative response. This fits the general view of the development of (æh) put forward in Chapter 9.

Table 11.14   *Percentage of (æh)-negative response for Jews and Italians by age*

Age level	Jews	Italians	N	
20–39	86	100		
40–	81	88	14	6
All ages	82	91	28	15

Table 11.15   *Responses to Sentence 10 as compared to Sentence 2 by SEC*

	SEC			
Relation to S. 2	0–2	3–5	6–8	9
Higher	9	7	5	5
Lower	6	15	13	4

In Table 8.2, Jews showed somewhat lower (æh) vowels than Italians in casual speech; Figure 8.10 gave us a graphic view of this relationship. The situation is just the reverse of the relations of Jews and Italians with regard to (oh). The subjective reactions of the two groups also show a reversal. Whereas the Jews were slightly higher in (oh)-negative response, the Italians show a greater (æh)-negative response (see Table 11.14).

The reactions to Sentence 10 are of an entirely different order from the reactions to Sentence 11. In Sentence 10, Speaker 2 uses a fairly consistent (æh-4), but it does not seem to satisfy a great many listeners. Reactions to Sentence 10 were quite mixed: they may be summed up in terms of higher and lower ratings as compared to Sentence 2 (see Table 11.15).

It appears that the working class and middle class definitely reject Speaker 2's version of (æh). However, the lower class and the upper middle class respondents do not share this reaction, and perhaps lean in the other direction. Overt comments on Sentence 10 were that the pronunciation seemed unnatural, or that Speaker 2 was trying too hard. When we compare Sentence 10 to Sentence 7 – that is, Speaker 2 pronouncing (æh)-4 as compared to (oh-1), we find that Sentence 10 is rated only slightly higher. In 32 cases. Sentence 10 was rated higher than Sentence 7, and in 25 cases, Sentence 7 higher than Sentence 10. It can be concluded that most New Yorkers – and in particular members of the two center class groups –

are not satisfied with the pronunciation which they themselves use in formal contexts. There is nothing unusual about Speaker 2's (æh-4). This half-long, low front tense vowel may be heard in Styles C and D from most of the respondents who downgraded this usage when they heard it. It is possible, however, that the mixed reaction to (æh-4) as spoken by Speaker 2 is not entirely due to the fact that the vowel is over-tense and fronted. The one inconsistency shown by Speaker 2 on the word *fast* may have been insufficient to produce a negative reaction. Similarly, we may recall that Speaker 4's inconsistent use of (oh) did not meet with general approval. Here there is no question of over-rounding, or length, but simply an oscillation of variants. On the one hand, Sentence 9 which contained these versions of (oh), was ranked higher than Sentences 6, 7, and 8 which contained (oh-1, 2). On the other hand, there were more respondents who rated Sentence 9 lower than its correlate in the zero section than respondents who rated it higher.

The fact that New Yorkers are sensitive to inconsistency of this type will be shown conclusively in the following section.

Subjective reactions to (r)

The structure of the SR test in respect to (r) is shown in Figure 11.4. We will examine Sentences 14, 15, 18, and 19 for subjective reactions to this variable. Sentences 14 and 15 represent consistent (r-1) pronunciation by Speakers 2 and 4. Sentences 18 and 19 show inconsistent (r-1) pronunciation by the same speakers.[10]

We may consider that there are two possible sets of responses to these sentences which are consistent with the recognition of (r-1) as a prestige marker: rating Sentences 18 and 19 lower than 14 and 15 respectively, or in view of the fact that they represent the same speakers, rating Sentence 18 the same as 14, and 19 the same as 15. Either of these reactions, or a combination, we will treat as (r)-positive. If in either case, the subject follows a contrary direction, rating 18 higher than 14, or 19 higher than 15, we will call his reaction (r)-negative. This test for subjective reaction to (r) will be called the *two-choice test*.

[10] There is also included in the SR test a pair of sentences showing consistent (r-0) pronunciation – spoken by 5 and 3. No significant social differences appeared in the reactions to these sentences. The most common response was for those who had rated the speakers very low to give them a slightly higher rating for their use of (r), and vice-versa. The neutral reaction to these sentences confirmed a view which can be drawn from Chapter 7: that r-less pronunciation by working class speakers is relatively colorless in New York City, and has little social significance. It is the prestige marker (r-1) which is the marked feature, and which has social impact when it is used.

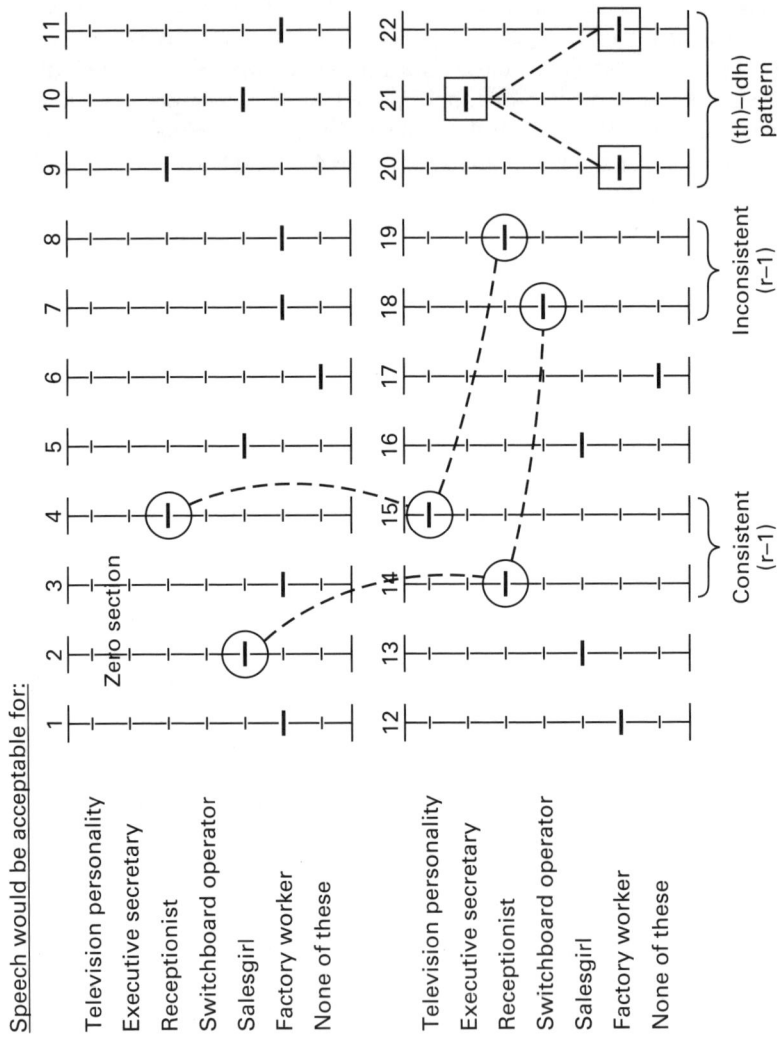

Figure 11.4   Structure of subjective evaluation form for (r)

Table 11.16   *Sentences testing responses to* (r)

Sentence	Speaker	

14	2	He darted out about four feet before a car,
		          (r-1) (r-1) (r-1)
		 and he got hit hard.
		          (r-1)

15	4	(Same as above)

18	2	He darted out about four feet before a car,
		          (r-1) (r-1) (r-1)
		 and he got hit hard.
		          (r-0)

19	4	We didn't have the heart to play ball, or (r-1) (oh-3) cards, all morning. (r-0) (oh-3) (r-1)

Table 11.17   *Percentages of* (r)-*positive response to the two-choice test by SEC and age*

	SEC							N			
Age	0–1	2–3	4–5	6–8	9	Total					
8–17	16	57	67	89	(50)	61	6	14	12	9	2
18–19	100	–	100	100	100	100	2	–	2	1	3
20–39	100	100	100	100	100	100	3	6	7	11	5
40–	63	67	50	70	57	62	8	18	8	10	7

Table 11.17 shows the percentages of (r)-positive response to the two-choice test for four age levels, and five divisions of the socio-economic scale (the same divisions used for the original class stratification of (r) in Chapter 7). In this table, our attention is immediately taken by a regularity more absolute than any that has been encountered so far. One hundred percent of the speakers from age 20 to 39 showed (r) positive reactions to the two-choice test, but only 62 percent of those over 40. Furthermore, this regularity is extended to the respondents who were 18 and 19 years old. A simple four-cell table (11.18) shows a remarkable distribution of respondents who show (r)-positive and (r)-negative response for two age levels.

The zero cell of Table 11.18 demonstrates the uniformity of the New York City speech community on the plane of normative evaluation.

In Table 11.17, class differences have largely disappeared, and only differences in age level stand out. This is a particularly striking fact, since in

Table 11.18   (r)-*positive and negative responses of two age groups*

Age	r-positive	r-negative
18–39	42	0
40–	32	10

Table 11.19   *Percentages of* (r)-*positive response to the four-choice test by SEC and age*

			SEC						N		
Age	0–1	2–3	4–5	6–8	9	Total					
8–17	00	36	33	67	(50)	37	6	14	12	9	2
18–19	50	–	100	100	100	88	2	–	2	1	3
20–39	75	84	86	100	100	87	3	6	7	11	5
40–	38	44	25	70	57	48	8	18	8	10	7

Chapters 7 and 8, (r) showed the finest and most regular class stratification of all of the variables. We now find that this uniform stratification of (r) in performance is accompanied by a uniform evaluation of the prestige norm by younger speakers of all classes. In Chapter 9, the objective evidence of speech pointed to a sharp break in the use of (r) between those 30 to 39 years old, and those 40 to 49. The data presented here confirm this discontinuity.

A more difficult test may now be constructed to include the two zero Sentences 2 and 4. Consistent recognition of (r-1) as a prestige marker should lead to the rating of Sentences 14 and 15 equal or higher than the zero level of Speakers 2 and 4. Instead of a two-choice test, a *four-choice test* will be used to establish an (r)-positive response. For an (r)-positive rating the subject must rate the consistent use of (r-1) equal to or higher than the zero level, and the inconsistent use equal to or lower than the consistent use. A reversal in any one of these four choices will give the subject an (r)-negative rating. Table 11.19 shows the data for the four-choice test which corresponds to Table 11.17 for the two-choice test.

The more difficult four-choice test reduces the overall percentages slightly, but preserves the relationships intact. The results of the four-choice test are more impressive in several ways. If we take the total number of choices which respondents had to make, for Sentences 14, 15, 18, and 19, the contrast between age groups in Table 11.20 appears.

Table 11.20   *Recognition of (r) as a prestige marker for two age groups*

Age	Choices consistent with recognition of prestige marker	No difference from zero level	Choices inconsistent with recognition of prestige marker
18–39	128	35	5
40–	108	48	48

The consistency of the younger group is the more remarkable when one considers that Sentences 14 and 15 are widely separated from Sentences 2 and 4 in the course of the SR test. Only five deviations from the pattern of (r)-positive response appear for younger speakers. Furthermore, these deviations were all in class 4 and below, so that it is evident that minor differences in sensitivity to (r) still exist among the several class groups.[11]

From the results of Tables 11.17 and 11.19, there can be no doubt that the age differences in (r)-positive response are well established. There is little room for differences of sex or ethnic group, or even socio-economic class, in the face of such a general change in apparent time. Socio-economic differentiation, obscured in the two-choice test, reappears to some extent in the four-choice test in Table 11.19. The differences in age groups are repeated in every class, however, and they are larger in magnitude than any difference between classes.

The break is actually sharper than it appears in Tables 11.17 and 11.19. Figure 11.5 shows the percentages of (r)-positive response for nine age groups; the two-choice test responses are indicated by the solid line, and the four-choice responses by a broken line. The break seems to come exactly with those who were born in 1923 as far as our sample is concerned. No

---

[11] Differences exist in the fineness of reaction to Sentences 18 and 19. For all of the variables, the average values of the absolute differences in ratings of the same speakers are correlated with class. In the present case, the higher ranking classes seem to hear the difference between Sentences 14 and 18, 15 and 19, as slight differences; the ratings of the speakers drop one or two ranks only. Lower ranking respondents react as a rule in an exaggerated fashion, and penalize the inconsistent utterances by rating them much lower than Sentences 14 and 15. If we sum the absolute differences between 14 and 18, 15 and 19, for all respondents between 18 and 39, we obtain the progression shown in the table below:

Working class and Lower class 0–5	Lower middle class 6–8	Upper middle class 9
3.9	3.5	3.1
[N: 20	12	8]

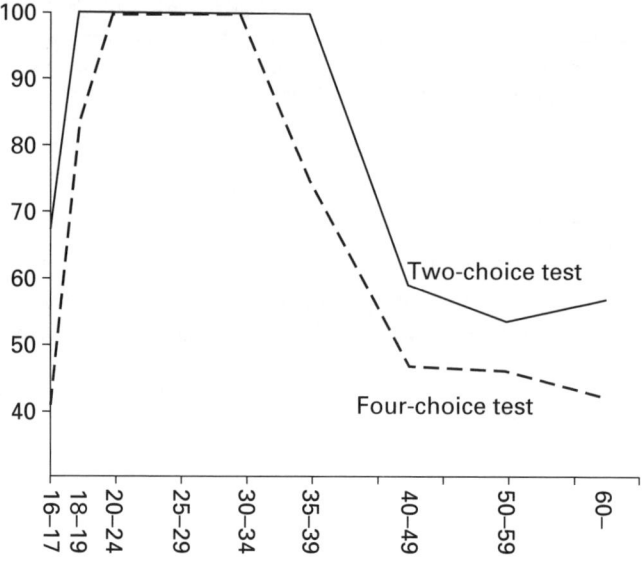

Figure 11.5   Subjective evaluation of (r) by age

particular direction for those over 40 is shown in this figure, while at the
other end of the scale, it seems to be just about at the age of 18 that young
people learn to recognize the social significance of this feature.

The data presented so far lead to the tentative conclusion that New
Yorkers under 40 react in a uniform manner to a single inconsistency in
the use of (r-1), while those over 40 show a mixed reaction. This conclusion has considerable importance for a general explanation of the mechanism of the linguistic change which is taking place. We must therefore
study any possibility that the pattern of Tables 11.22 and 11.25 is due to
other causes. There are two classes of extraneous factors which may
account for the patterns observed besides subjective evaluation of (r-1) as
a prestige marker.
1) Other differences between the age levels besides differences in chrono-
    logical age.
2) Other differences between Sentences 14 and 18, 15 and 19, besides
    inconsistency in the use of (r).

A number of these points may be checked by correlating (r) response
with response to another variable: subjective reactions to (th) and (dh). We
will therefore interrupt the discussion of (r) to present the results for (th)
and (dh), and then return to the analysis of (r)-positive response.

Table 11.21   *Sentences testing responses to* (th) *and* (dh)

Sentence	Speaker	
20	3	There's something strange about that – how I (dh-1) (r-0) (th-1) (dh-1) can remember everything he did: this thing, (r-0) (th-1) (dh-1)(th-2) that thing, and the other thing. (dh-1) (th-1) (dh-3) (dh-3) (th-1)
21	4	There's nothing strange about that – how I can (dh-1) (r-1) (th-1) (dh-1) remember everything he did: this thing, that (th-1) (dh-1)(th-1) (dh-1) thing, and the other thing. (th-1) (dh-1) (dh-1) (th-1)
22	3	I suppose it's the same thing with most of us. (dh-1) (th-3) (th-3)

Subjective reactions to (th) *and* (dh)

Instead of comparing the zero section to the sentences at the end of the test, we will study the relations of the ratings given to these three sentences alone.

In Table 11.21, the numbers of the variants do not convey the full contrast between Sentences 20, 21, and 22. In Sentence 20, Speaker 3 seemed to sense the approaching problem of (th) and (dh), and she used considerable effort in pronouncing the first instances of these variables. She paused a moment before *this thing*, pronounced *that thing* clearly, and then apparently succumbed to fatigue. She finished with a rush on *the other thing*, using (dh-3) twice. The (dh-3) on *other* is the most prominent, and it brought comments from many listeners.

In Sentence 21, Speaker 4 reads with clarity: the quality of all her (th) and (dh) variables is unambiguously fricative. Despite the fact that she misreads *nothing* for *something* (she was reading without her glasses), the articulation of this sentence, its phrasing and cultivated intonation pattern, led many listeners to rate it highest of all the 22 test sentences.

In Sentence 22, Speaker 3 is heard again, reading the next sentence from the standard reading. Her low, husky voice quality contrasts with the clear tones of Speaker 4, and the articulation of consonants is noticeably less forceful. The (th-3) of *thing* and *with* is quite prominent.

For the (th) and (dh) variables, a minimal SR test is established. If speakers are sensitive to the stigmatized forms of (th-3) and (dh-3), they should rate Sentence 21 higher than 20 or 22. There may be other factors besides these variables which would influence a person to rate Sentence 21 higher than the

290 III Social evaluation

Table 11.22 *Percentages of* (th)-*insensitive response by age and social class*

Age	Social class				N			
	1	2	3	4				
20–39	(50)	13	29	00	2	15	7	5
40–	43	33	20	14	23	9	15	7

other two, since the voice qualities and the articulations of the two speakers are different. But if subjects do *not* rate Sentence 21 higher than the other two, we can conclude that either they do not hear the difference between fricatives and stops for (th) and (dh), or else they are not sensitive to the social significance of this difference. We are not interested in those who react to the distinction so much as those who do not react.[12]

The patterns shown by Sentences 20, 21, and 22 may be classified into a number of sub-types. However, the most clear-cut distinction between the various patterns in terms of social distribution is that between those that respond to Sentence 21 higher than both 20 and 22, and those that do not. Any response in which Sentence 21 is rated higher than both 20 and 22 will be called (th)-sensitive. All other responses will be called (th)-insensitive.

For the study of (th) and (dh), the index of social classes will be used, since it was found in Chapter 8 that this scale gave a clearer view of the class stratification of these variables. Table 11.22 shows the percentages of (th)-insensitive speakers for two age levels of the four social classes.

In Table 11.22 the lowest social class shows by far the greatest number of (th)-insensitive respondents. For the younger subjects, it is surprising to find that the white collar workers show less sensitivity than the blue collar workers (with some high school), despite the fact that the latter use far more stops and affricates.[13]

[12] There is a special problem of considerable social interest in the speech of those who have been exposed to a standard dialect for many years, and yet find themselves unable, or unwilling, to utilize it in formal situations. The parallel between this deviation from social norms, and the deviation of those who have not accepted the norms of educational aspiration, may be quite close.

[13] The results seen by using the SEC index are quite similar:

SEC					SC			
0–2	3–5	6–8	9		1	2	3	4
42	24	19	08	All ages	44	21	23	08

Table 11.23

	Average (dh) index in style A	% of (th)-insensitive respondents
Men	54	9
Women	22	30

In the relations of the age levels in Table 11.22, no regular trend appears. For SC 2, the younger speakers show more sensitivity to (th) and (dh), but SC 3 does not repeat this relationship. Both age levels of SC 4 are high in sensitivity to this variable, although the younger group shows a slight edge. This situation contrasts sharply with that of the three variables already discussed: (oh), (æh), and (r). In all three, there was a steady increase of sensitivity to the marked feature across all class groups. There is a contrast between the variables involved in processes of linguistic change, and those which are essentially stable. The developments were somewhat obscured in Chapter 9, since the older respondents tend to acquire the newer prestige pronunciation to some extent. Careful analysis of the possibilities enabled us to reveal the pattern of change which lay behind the distribution of the variables in apparent time. However, no such problems obscure the development on the plane of subjective reactions. Here the imposition of new norms from above may be traced without interference, and the patterns of change are clearer than in the case of behavior itself. This was most striking in the case of (r), but a review of the entire SR test justifies such a view for each case.

There is therefore a recurrent pattern in the behavior of New Yorkers who use a high degree of a stigmatized form in their casual speech, yet recognize the social significance of this form by a shift in formal styles, and even more clearly, in their subjective reactions to the speech of others. We may see reflected in this opposition two contrasting social influences on language behavior: 1) the pressure towards identification with a particular ethnic, neighborhood, or occupational group; and 2) the need to conform to the overall hierarchy of values imposed by the community. Our studies of casual speech show the influence of both pressures; the SR test measures only the force of the latter. Thus the contradiction we have noted is a product of our approach more than of the informants' behavior. Their behavior may be described as response to the tensions created by opposing pressures rather than a series of internal contradictions.

We may continue the study of these opposing forces by considering the differences between men and women for (th) sensitivity (see Table 11.23). In

Table 11.24   (th) *and* (dh) *production and sensitivity for Jews and Italians*

	(th) index in style A	(dh) index in style A	% of (th)-insensitive respondents
Jews	61	47	27
Italians	115	72	14

Chapter 8 it was found that men used far more stops and affricates than women. The relations are reversed in the SR test.

Here again it appears that those who show the greatest use of a stigmatized form also show the greatest sensitivity to it. Though it may be socially appropriate for men to use more stops and affricates, among their friends, or on the job, they are seen here to have a clearer perception about the social significance of the forms which they use.[14]

In Chapter 8 it was also shown that Italians used more stops and affricates than Jews (Figures 8.17 and 8.18). We should now be able to predict that Italians will show a lower percentage of (th)-insensitive speakers than Jews.

Table 11.24 shows as predicted that even though Italians use more stops and affricates, they show only half the proportion of (th)-insensitive respondents. The relationship between high use of a stigmatized form and high sensitivity to it seems to hold in every case for the relations of men and women, Jews and Italians.

[The Reflexive Stigma Principle receives considerable support from the figures on gender and ethnicity. These are not common sense expectations. The principle doesn't apply quite so simply in the social class figures of Table 11.22, and it might well be modified by excluding members of the lower class who show limited recognition of societal norms. One might precede the principle by the caveat, "In so far as speakers are aware of sociolinguistic norms . . ."]

Further analysis of (r) *response*

We may now return to the resolution of the questions raised on the analysis of (r)-positive reactions. We would like to ascertain that there is no other explanation for the sudden increase in apparent time of (r)-positive response besides a change in the linguistic structure of the speech community.

1) *Other differences between the age levels* In Figure 9.1, it was seen that the age levels of respondents are skewed in relation to class; however, Tables

---

[14] We are dealing with a situation in which men are evaluating women speakers. It is possible that the situation would be different if men were evaluating men, or women evaluating men, but we have no data to compare such responses with the SR test as completed.

Table 11.25   *Percentage of four-choice* (r)-*positive response by age and* (th)-*sensitivity*

Age	All respondents	(th)-sensitive respondents	(th)-insensitive respondents	N		
20–39	87	92	80	34	29	5
40–	48	46	50	51	35	16

11.17 and 11.19 showed that the relationship of age levels is repeated for each class; it may be concluded that the change in (r)-positive response is independent of class.

It is also possible that the older speakers simply do not hear as well as the younger speakers. They may also show a tendency to tire more quickly as the SR test progresses, or they may have less interest in the test. All of these possibilities can be checked by considering the pattern of (th)-sensitivity. The three sentences for (th) occur at the end of the test, when fatigue is at a maximum. The (th) and (dh) sounds are more difficult to hear than the other variables, because they have the lowest acoustic energy.[15] We can say that those respondents who are hard of hearing, or who are fatigued by the test, or who show little interest in the test, are more likely to give (th)-insensitive ratings than the other respondents.

If we now study the reactions of the respondents to (r) in relation to (th)-sensitivity, these questions can be resolved. For the sub-group of respondents who showed (th)-sensitive response, the factors of fatigue, loss of hearing, or lack of interest, should be considerably less than for the (th)-insensitive group. If there is a connection between these factors and (r)-response, the difference between age levels in (r)-response will appear significantly reduced for respondents who were uniformly (th)-sensitive.

It appears that (r)-positive response is independent of (th)-sensitivity. The pattern of (r)-positive response by age levels could hardly have been repeated more closely for the (th)-insensitive group than Table 11.25 shows. Only five younger respondents showed (th)-insensitive ratings: four of them were (r)-positive on the four-choice test. Sixteen older respondents were (th)-insensitive: eight of these were (r)-positive, and eight (r)-negative.

---

[15] In the television interviews conducted over the telephone, for example, we obtained lower (th) and (dh) indexes in many cases than when the same informants were interviewed in person. The low energy of these variables was responsible for a number of distinctions being obscured by losses and noise in telephone transmission.

We may conclude that the (r)-positive response which was measured is a function of date of birth, and that the factors of hearing loss, fatigue, or lack of interest in the test are not likely to have played a part in this result.

2) We may now consider the possibility that other variables associated with Sentences 14 and 15, 18 and 19 were responsible in whole or in part for the differential reaction of the age levels to the pairs of sentences.

When a speaker shows an inconsistency in (r), she is likely to show other pronunciation features which are less typical of careful speech. For example, in Sentence 19, Speaker 4 hesitated after the word *ball* (trouble with her eyesight); her consonants were not formed or released as forcefully in 19 as in 15: she did not, for example, pronounce the final /t/ in *didn't* in Sentence 19, and one or two respondents noticed this.

Sentence 18 was taken from a first reading of the text by Speaker 2, and in this reading she was a little further away from the microphone than in the second reading, from which Sentence 14 is taken. Such differences as these may account for a part of the reaction which placed Sentences 14 and 15 higher than Sentences 2 and 4, 18 and 19. However, if this is true, there is no reason to suspect that out-of-town speakers would react any differently than native New Yorkers to the test. They should be able to hear such differences as preciseness of articulation, speed of reading, or distance from the microphone, just as well as New Yorkers. We may therefore turn to the out-of-town respondents to check this point. Table 11.26 shows the following percentages of (r)-positive response to the four-choice test.

The older out-of-town speakers show about the same response as New Yorkers did, but the younger speakers, instead of showing *more* (r)-positive response, actually show *less*. This relationship is exactly what we would expect if the test does measure the special New York response to (r-1) as a new prestige marker. The older out-of-town respondents have had about as much exposure to the new prestige form in New York City as the native New York respondents. But the younger out-of-town subjects were raised outside of New York, away from this influence, and have only had a brief exposure to it. The distribution of (r)-positive response among out-of-town speakers therefore confirms the fact that it is the variable (r) which is the focus of subjective reactions.[16]

We can use the out-of-town speakers to check this question in another way. If (r) is indeed the variable which is being measured in the SR test, then

---

[16] A majority of the out-of-town respondents were African–Americans. This group is therefore not comparable to the New York respondents, and it is possible that the special (r) response of AA subjects was responsible for the difference. However, when we compare only AA out-of-town subjects with only AA New York subjects, the difference in (r) response holds. The younger New York AA respondents showed even more consistent (r)-positive response than the younger New York white respondents.

Table 11.26   *Percentages of* (r)-*positive response to the four-choice test for New York and out-of-town respondents*

Age	New Yorkers	Out-of-town	N	
20–39	87	40	34	10
40–	48	50	51	22

Table 11.27   (r) *sensitivity of out-of-towners by r-lessness of region*

	Out-of-town respondents	
	from *r*-pronouncing region	from *r*-less region
(r)-positive	10	5
(r)-negative	7	10

speakers who come from an (r)-pronouncing region should have more tendency to show (r)-positive response than those who come from an (r)-less region, where an (r)-less dialect has prestige. This is indeed the case, as shown in Table 11.27. For the four-choice test, out-of-town respondents show very different results depending on whether they come from an *r*-less or an *r*-pronouncing region.[17]

The evidence that we have presented shows that the reactions to Sentences 14 and 15, 18 and 19, are indeed reactions to the use of (r). The evidence for a sudden change in the norms of *r*-pronunciation cannot be explained by the presence of associated variables. The original presentation of subjective reactions to (r) in this chapter showed a sudden increase in (r)-positive response in apparent time, and this increase points to a corresponding change in the structure of the New York City speech community in real time. As noted before, the change seems to be closely associated with the period of World War II: all those in the sample who were raised during and after the war show a uniform (r)-positive response in the test.

[This sudden break in normative behavior at the time of World War II gives further weight to the argument that social evaluation has to be studied

---

[17] In this case, we do not expect to find that the low use of (r-1) among younger speakers is associated with high sensitivity to this prestige feature. The younger out-of-town subjects who were raised in an area where the prestige norm was an *r*-less dialect, would have no reason to stigmatize sentences 18 and 19, or award high ratings to 14 and 15 on the basis of consistent (r-1) pronunciation – except in so far as they have absorbed the New York City standard. It seems natural that they could apply this standard less accurately than those who had been born and raised in the city.

along with social stratification of speech production. Informal studies in Boston indicate a parallel shift, with /r/ incoming as a marker of formal speech, but with little effect on everyday speech. A much more thorough-going revolution in the treatment of (r) has occurred in the south. Feagin (1987) reported that the city of Anniston, Alabama, had shifted from *r*-less to *r*-full in three generations. The *Atlas of North American English* (Labov, Ash & Boberg 2006 Ch. 7) finds that the shift to consistent *r*-pronunciation has swept over every southern city. The wholesale shift of *r*-constriction in the south contrasts with the limited character of the change in the north. The replications of the department store study indicate an increase in formal speech of no more than 1 or 2 percent a year.

My own understanding of the shift of norms in New York City is that it reflected the abandonment of the earlier prestige form of Anglophile English. When Great Britain lost its status as a world power, it could no longer be claimed that Received Pronunciation was "International English." But note that Bonfiglio (2002) argues that the shift away from *r*-lessness was triggered by its association with AAVE. It is certainly true that in every city, the (r) index for AAs is much lower than for whites (see, for example, Myhill's study of (r) in Philadelphia (1988)).]

The convergence of social differentiation and social evaluation

At the beginning of this chapter, it was pointed out that a coincidence of patterns from the study of subjective evaluation and the patterns of social differentiation of speech would provide good confirmation of the analysis that has been presented so far. A great many close correlations between these two areas of behavior have been found. This summary will review these correlations as they apply successively to the previous findings on the differentiation of the variables.

1) In Chapter 7, it was found that all five variables followed consistent patterns of stylistic and social variation. It was seen that the variable (oh) did not exist as a socially significant feature for the lower class: in the SR test, the lower class shows the minimum (oh)-negative response. The relations of working class, lower middle class, and upper middle class to the structure of (oh) differentiation were reflected closely in their degrees of (oh)-negative response. The hypercorrect pattern of the lower middle class, shown by the cross-over in style stratification diagrams, is paralleled here by maximum (oh) sensitivity.

    The variable (æh) was shown to differ from (oh) in Chapter 7 in that all classes participate in the use of this feature as a socially significant variable. The SR test showed a uniform high degree of (æh)-negative response (with the exception of class 0). The cross-over pattern of the lower middle class also appeared in the SR test since the lower middle class showed higher (oh)-negative response than the upper middle class.

The variable (r) showed a fine-grained stratification of all levels of society, according to their differential use of (r-1). In the SR test, we find a consistently high level of (r)-positive response for all classes. Thus the penetration of society by the (r) variable is almost complete, and its status as a prestige marker is established.

The (th) and (dh) variables showed a regular pattern of social differentiation in Chapter 7, without any tendency for a crossing of class lines. In the SR test, there are three clear-cut levels of (th)-sensitivity. The pattern differs from that of Chapters 7 and 8 only in that the upper section of the working class (SC 2) is at the level of the lower middle class, rather than at the level of the lower class. The lower middle class does *not* exceed the upper middle class in (th)-sensitivity; this is the most significant parallel, since it indicates in the SR test the relative stability of the social significance of these variables, just as shown in their class differentiation.

2) Chapter 8 showed an alternation between Jews and Italians in their relations to (æh) and (oh). In casual speech, Jews used higher (oh) vowels, and Italians higher (æh) vowels. In more formal styles, there was a tendency towards convergence at the more open variants. In the SR test, Jews showed higher sensitivity to (oh), and Italians to (æh). The degree of correction which occurs in speech is thus paralleled by the consistency of negative response to stigmatized forms. A similar parallel was shown for (th) and (dh), where the Italians use more stigmatized forms in casual speech, and a higher degree of (th)-sensitivity in the SR test.

In the relations of men and women, a similar set of parallels was found between the differentiation of (æh), (oh), and (th)-(dh), and sensitivity in the SR test.

3) In Chapter 9, we found that the distribution of (r) usage in apparent time pointed to a sudden increase in the use of (r) in casual speech about the time of World War II. This pattern is revealed in even greater clarity in the SR test. The variable (oh) was found to show a distribution in apparent time characteristic of relatively early stages of a change from below: only the highest ranking class showed signs of correction in casual speech, while only in more formal styles did the lower middle class show hypercorrection. In the SR test, younger respondents showed a higher degree of (oh)-negative response than older ones, for all classes, although the lower class response was on a level so low as to be almost negligible.

The distribution of variable (æh) in apparent time was found in Chapter 9 to resemble the result of a change from below at a more advanced stage, where correction even in casual speech was evident. In the SR test, all classes showed a high level of negative response, and the continuing trend was evident in that the younger speakers showed even more (æh)-negative response in each class.

Finally, the variables (th) and (dh) showed some small indications of a trend towards increase of social significance in Chapter 9, although they were essentially stable as compared to the other variables. We may draw similar conclusions from the evidence of the SR test, though again, any evidence of a change is uncertain.

The most general principle which appears from this review is that subjective reactions to phonological variables form a deeply embedded structure which is recognized by the entire speech community. The variable (oh) is the latest arrival in this structure, and is not fully integrated for all classes. In several respects, we have seen that some lower class New Yorkers do not participate fully in the structure of stylistic and social variation of all the variables. With these exceptions, we can say that New Yorkers recognize a common structure of social stratification of the variables. When New Yorkers use a high degree of a stigmatized form, it is not because they do not recognize the same norms as the other members of society: we have found that they are usually even more aware of the social significance of this variable than others. The forces which preserve the structure of social differentiation of New York City are probably related to the need for self-identification with particular sub-groups in the social complex. This structure of social differentiation is not supported by the isolation of social groups, nor by their relative ignorance of each other's norms. We observe the process of increased differentiation of language behavior despite close contact of the social groups concerned, and their participation in a relatively uniform set of social norms.

[The interpretation of the results of this chapter must take into account that the subjective reaction test was an experiment which necessarily focuses on language and normative behavior. It found significant differences and shifts in the responses of subjects, but the consensus displayed here is a consensus on proper and formal behavior. It gave no evidence for the existence of "covert norms" that were suggested throughout the New York City study to account for the maintenance of non-standard forms over long periods of time.

The subjective reaction test developed in the Lower East Side study was followed by one dealing with the variables of AAVE in the study of South Harlem (Labov et al. 1968, Labov 1972b). That study also made use of the variation found in spontaneous speech. All speakers were male, and all judges African– American. The Harlem subjective reaction test added two new dimensions. In addition to a question on "What is the highest occupation this speaker could hold, speaking as he does?" the subjects responded to "If this person was in a street fight, how likely would he be to come out on top?" and "If you got to know this person over a period of time, how likely would he be to become a friend of yours?"

The results showed, as we expected, that the fight dimension was the complement of the job dimension. The zero paragraph showed that the higher a speaker was rated on the job dimension, the lower he was rated on the fight scale. But this effect was heavily differentiated by class. It was strongest for middle class adult subjects, and not significant for working class subjects born in the south. In other words, the stereotype that speakers of AAVE are all good street fighters is held most strongly by those who are most remote from the street.

Another interesting feature of the Harlem results was the nature of the Friend responses. For middle class and upper working class subjects, the level of response was close to the job responses; for working class subjects, it was the other way around. This variation adds another aspect to the search for covert norms that may support non-standard dialects.

A subjective reaction test was constructed for the study of Linguistic Variation and Change in Philadelphia (Labov 2001, Ch. 6). Four female speakers were selected from exploratory interviews, reading a text in which five Philadelphia variables were successively concentrated. Four of these were changes in progress in the vowel system: the raising and fronting of (æh), the raising and fronting of (aw), the fronting of (ow), and the raising of (ay) before voiceless consonants. Only one of these – (æh) – was ever the subject of overt comment; there was far less overt consciousness of the variables than in New York City. Nevertheless, Philadelphian subjects showed a consistent negative reaction to advanced forms of these changes in progress, differentiating them significantly from the zero passage.

In Philadelphia, the Friend question did not produce a different pattern of responses from the Job question. No further evidence for covert norms appeared. At least within the formal framework of the SRT, Philadelphians showed a negative response to the progress of sound change for new and vigorous variables on both the Job and Friend scales. However, this consensus was not uniform across the speech community. Subjects younger than 19 years were quite different from adults, and showed far less recognition of these prestige norms than adults did. This fits in with some of the results from New York City, where the full set of sociolinguistic norms were not acquired for most social groups until adult status was reached.]

12   Self-evaluation and linguistic security

Chapter 11 demonstrated that New Yorkers showed surprisingly consistent response to the subjective reaction test. In their reactions to the speech of other New Yorkers, they detected stigmatized features with great regularity, and demonstrated uniform recognition of prestige markers. We were able to measure these reactions, despite the fact that few of the respondents consciously perceived the values of the variables which caused their reactions.

In the conscious report of their own usage, however, New York respondents are very inaccurate. There is little correlation between their self-evaluation and their use of the five variables, in any style. Nevertheless, we can learn a great deal about attitudes towards the variables from these reports. For this reason, the test to be described is not referred to as a "Self-recognition test," but rather a "Self-evaluation test." We shall see that when average New Yorkers report their own usage, they are basically giving us their norms of correctness. There is no conscious deceit in this process. It appears that most New Yorkers have acquired a set of governing norms which they use in the audio-monitoring of their own speech. We have reason to believe that the process of stylistic variation described in Part II of this work is governed by the degree of audio-monitoring which is superimposed upon the motor-controlled patterns of native speech.[1] The audio-monitoring norm is the form which is perceived by speakers themselves as they speak. They do not hear the actual sound which they produce, but the norm which they impose. We will return to this hypothesis after the evidence on self-evaluation and linguistic security has been presented.

The self-evaluation test

[The most common term for the test described in this section is a "Self-report test." The very fact that there is a self-report test has considerable

---

[1] The experimental evidence which bears upon this hypothesis is summarized in footnote 15 to Chapter 4.

implications for the sociolinguistic enterprise. If self-report were accurate, the self-report test would be uninformative, or redundant with the evidence of speech. In fact, there would be no need to elicit spontaneous speech or conduct sociolinguistic interviews. One could simply do as most linguists do in the field: ask the informants how they say things.

In 1951, Carl Voegelin and Zellig Harris outlined the competition between two basic approaches to linguistic field method. One approach, that of Boas and Sapir, is to ask the informant – that is, to tap the intuitions of the native speaker by direct elicitation. The other would be to record what the informant says, a long and painful procedure which had not been favored until then. They pointed out that the newly invented tape recorder would bring about a change in the balance between these two options. The record shows that this shift did not take place until ten years later, and was then limited to the new and small area of sociolinguistics. A shift to the study of recorded corpora of speech is now beginning to gain momentum, some forty years later. The balance between the two approaches still needs to be informed by more research on the problem of when and where self-report is a reliable index of the linguistic system.]

Immediately after the subjective reaction test was concluded, the interviewer introduced the self-evaluation test in the following way:

I'd like to give you an idea of what we were trying to do in this test, but first I have to get some idea of how you hear yourself.

The respondents were given the form shown as VI.C. in the questionnaire of Appendix A, with seven words listed as follows:

cards	1	2	3	4
chocolate	1	2	3	4
pass	1	2	3	4
thing	1	2	3	
then	1	2	3	
her	1	2	3	
hurt	1	2	3	

The respondents listened to four variant pronunciations of the first three words, and three variants of the last four. These variants were values of (r), (oh), (æh), (th), (dh), (her), and (hurt) for the seven words in that order. They were pronounced by myself – in person, in the interviews which I conducted, and on a tape recording for the interviews conducted by Michael Kac. The informants were asked to circle the number of the pronunciation which came closest to the way they usually said the word themselves. If they heard no difference between variants, they circled all numbers; if they used several of the variants, they circled each.

There had been no discussion of these words or these variables prior to this test, though the reading and the SR test had inevitably focused some attention on them. Nothing said by the interviewer would lead the respondent to think that one or the other variant was considered better or worse.

The base for most of the discussion of this test is the population of eighty-one adult ALS New York City informants, together with the twelve adult children of these informants: a total of ninety-three. Of these ninety-three informants, fourteen did not take the Self-evaluation test (hereafter referred to as the SV test). There is no serious bias in the sex or ethnic composition of the sample as a result of the loss of fourteen non-respondents. But as far as class is concerned, there is a bias: nine of the non-respondents were from the lower class, and five from the working class, but none from the middle class. One must therefore examine the result in the breakdown by SEC to see if the overall result has been distorted.

The analysis will also refer to out-of-town respondents: thirty-seven ALS adult out-of-town informants and one adult child of an ALS informant. Eight of these did not take the SV test: six African–Americans from Southern, *r*-less regions, and two white informants from *r*-pronouncing regions. We will consider these categories separately in the discussion.

The sample population for the SV test is therefore seventy-nine adult New Yorkers and thirty out-of-town respondents. Unless the out-of-town respondents are specifically mentioned, the discussion will refer to the New Yorkers. Whenever a discussion of ethnic group is given, two New York African–American speakers will be added to the nine in the sample.

Self-evaluation for (r)

The four variants which were presented for (r) were as follows:

1	2	3	4
[kɑɽdz]	[kɑɚdz]	[kɡ̪ədz]	[kɒːdz]

The first variant used the retroflex [r] of midwestern English (r-1). The tongue tip is curled back, close to the roof of the mouth; the vowel is colored by this retroflexion as well as the constriction of the [r].[2] The second variant uses the humped [r] more common in the east, where the tongue is widened and contracted, and the blade approaches the roof of the mouth while the tongue tip is lowered. This is the (r-1) which is used by New Yorkers.

---

[2] A common pronunciation in the Midwest, and in other areas where retroflex tongue position prevails, is a retroflex vowel where there is only one phone to represent the phonemes /a/ and /r/, rather than a vowel followed by a consonant. In the SV test, however, the pronunciation was clearly a vowel followed by a retroflex central constriction.

Table 12.1   (r) *variants reported*

	Variant		
1	2	3	4
17	31	16	10

Table 12.2   (r) *reported vs.* (r) *used in careful speech for adult New Yorkers*

	Variant reported			
(r)-B index	1	2	3	4
0–10	8	16	10	6
11–30	5	8	5	2
31–60	2	4	1	2
61–100	2	3	–	–
	17	31	16	10

The third variant is one of the common (r-0) forms heard in New York City, where the vowel is only slightly retracted and is followed by a distinct centering glide. The fourth type is a long, monophthongal back vowel, the (r-0) form which is used most frequently by traditional speakers from most classes.

The following discussion will be chiefly concerned only with the seventy-four who circled one variant, and the relation between reported (r) and the actual use of (r). The total number of forms reported by the seventy-four New Yorkers are shown in Table 12.1.

Three respondents circled several forms, indicating that they used both (r-1) and (r-0). Two circled all forms, indicating that they could hear no difference.

Sixty-one percent of all New Yorkers identified their own usual pronunciation as (r-1), and 32 percent as (r-0). There is no similarity between these results and the data for Style A; we have already seen in Part II that all but a few of the subjects use only (r-0) in casual speech. Therefore we will compare this result to the indexes for careful speech, Style B. Table 12.2 shows the distribution of the seventy-four informants by the amount of (r) used in Style B, and their self-evaluation for (r).

From Table 12.2, it is evident that the distribution for variants 1 and 2 are very similar, and the distributions for 3 and 4 are also very much alike. We

Table 12.3   *Model of accurate self-evaluation of* (r)

		(r) used	
		(r-1)	(r-0)
(r) reported	(r-1)	100	0
	(r-0)	0	100
		100	100

Table 12.4   *Percentage of* (r) *reported by New York informants vs.* (r) *used in style B*

		(r) used	
		(r-1)	(r-0)
(r) reported	(r-1)	79	62
	(r-0)	21	38
		100	100
	N	14	60

will therefore sum variants 1 and 2 as *(r-1) reported*, and variants 3 and 4 as *(r-0) reported*.

If the subjects circled the form actually used more than half the time, we can consider this performance an accurate report of their usage. But very few New Yorkers attained over 50 percent (r-1) in Style B; it would be more realistic to allow a report as "accurate" if the subject used over 30 percent (r-1) in Style B. Therefore, in the following tables, (r-1) will be shown as the (r) "used" if the subject was rated at (r)-30 or above in Style B. Despite the leniency of this criterion, we will find many more New Yorkers who report (r-1) than use it.

We may therefore set up a four-cell table (12.3), showing the relation of the form reported to the form used if reporting were completely accurate.

The actual percentages obtained from the New York informants are quite different, as shown in Table 12.4. It appears that there is little relation between the amount of (r) which New Yorkers actually use, and their impressions of their own speech.

Table 12.5   *Reports of own* (r) *usage vs.* (r) *actually used according to SEC groups*

	SEC groups							
	0–2 (r) used		3–5 (r) used		6–8 (r) used		9 (r) used	
(r) reported	(r-1)	(r-0)	(r-1)	(r-0)	(r-1)	(r-0)	(r-1)	(r-0)
(r-1)	0	7	3	17	2	9	6	4
(r-0)	0	3	1	12	2	6	0	2
	0	10	4	29	4	15	6	6
% Inaccurate reports	70		55		58		33	

Self-evaluation for (r) *by class.*   In Chapter 7, we saw that there was a close relation between objective position on the SEC scale and objective use of (r). Chapter 11 showed that class was almost irrelevant to the subjective evaluation of (r). If it is true that the norm of subjective evaluation governs the SV response, we can expect that class will show very little relation to the pattern of (r) reported to (r) used. Table 12.5 shows that this is the case. Here actual numbers of respondents must be used rather than percentages, for many of the cells are almost empty.

In Table 12.5, the same overall pattern is followed by the three lower ranking classes. In each case, the majority of the respondents reported (r- 1), and most of these were reporting inaccurately. The only difference between these groups and the upper middle class is that half of the class 9 speakers actually did use (r-1). Thus the pattern of inaccurate (r-1) reporting runs through all classes. This pattern undoubtedly reflects the same subjective attitude towards (r) which appears in the high percentage of (r)-positive response to the SR test.

If we now consider only those who use (r-0), and set aside those respondents who actually do use (r-1), we will have a fairly homogeneous set of sixty speakers whose tendency to report (r-1) inaccurately is independent of class. This group can be used to investigate the other independent variables.

Self-evaluation for (r) by sex.   There are no striking differences in the SV test for (r) as reported by men and women. For the group of (r-0) speakers, 13 out of 19 men reported (r) inaccurately, and 24 out of 41 women: 69 percent of the men and 59 percent of the women.

Self-evaluation for (r) *by ethnic group.* We find pronounced differences as far as ethnic group is concerned. Eight out of 8 African–Americans reported (r-1) inaccurately, 16 out of 27 Jews, and only 9 out of 18 Italians.

We have already seen in the discussion of subjective evaluation that the African–Americans of New York City show a uniform (r)-positive response. Their special position is part of a repeated pattern which will appear again in the examples to come for other variables, and in the discussion of linguistic attitudes in Chapter 13.

Self-evaluation for (r) *by age levels.* Chapter 11 showed a sharp difference between older and younger respondents in their subjective reactions to (r). Similarly, we find that the contribution of the younger speakers towards inaccurate (r-1) reporting is much greater than that of the older speakers. Only a bare majority of the (r-0) users among the older respondents reported (r-1). But among the younger informants, 18 out of 22 followed this pattern: only 53 percent of the 40 respondents over forty years old were inaccurate (r-1) reporters, while 82 percent of those under forty fell into this category. This pattern resembles the results for the four-choice test for (r) in the SR section. There the younger speakers showed twice as high a rate of consistent recognition of the prestige of (r-1); here, the younger speakers show a similar margin for those who inaccurately claim (r-1) as their own usage. This finding supports the hypothesis that the SV test reveals the evaluative norm of the respondents rather than their actual usage.

Self-evaluation for (r) *by out-of-town informants.* For the out-of-town respondents, we find that the relationships between (r) used and (r) reported are somewhat different. Table 12.6 presents data for these thirty subjects in two groups: those who were raised in an *r*-pronouncing region, and those raised in an *r*-less region. For the former, we find that those who both use (r-1) and report (r-1) predominate. For the latter, we observe a tendency to report (r-1) inaccurately, but the tendency is weaker than with New Yorkers, as one would expect.

The greatest tendency in this group to report (r-1) inaccurately was among southern African–Americans. The two speakers on the left of Table 12.6 who reported (r-1) inaccurately were from northern states. The seven speakers on the right who did so were all from the south; This continues the pattern observed for New York City African–American respondents.

The two respondents who reported (r-0) inaccurately were older informants; at least one had considerable trouble in hearing.

Table 12.6   *Reports of own* (r) *usage vs.* (r) *actually used by out-of-town respondents*

(r) reported	From r-pronouncing region (r) used		From r-less region (r) used	
	(r-1)	(r-0)	(r-1)	(r-0)
(r-1)	8	2	1	7
(r-0)	2	1	0	9
	10	3	1	16

Table 12.7   *Characteristics of deliberate* (r-0) *users by age*

Age	No.	% (r)-positive 2-ch.	4-ch.	% using no (r-1) in any style	% reporting (r-1) inaccurately
20–39	9	100	84	55	55
40–59	7 (6)	50	33	29	43
60–	5 (4)	25	00	80	00

Analysis of the deliberate (r-0) *users.* We have been very much concerned with those speakers who lean towards (r-1) as the norm of correct usage, since these represent the majority of our informants. It may be instructive to search for the remnants of the older pattern of (r-0) pronunciation, in which this variant had prestige. To do this, we may analyze the behavior of the twenty-one informants who used no (r-1) whatsoever in Style D′. Whether or not they used small amounts of (r-1) in other styles, these subjects deliberately returned to the (r-0) pronunciation when faced with the comparison of *dock* and *dark*, *god* and *guard*, etc. Table 12.7 shows the characteristics of this group (numbers who took SR test in parentheses).

Table 12.7 shows two opposite types of deliberate (r-0) users, and one intermediate type. Like all of the respondents under forty, the nine subjects on the top row show 100% (r)-positive response for the two-choice test. They show the same high percentage of (r)-positive response for the four-choice test as other younger speakers – 84% compared to 87% for the rest. They also show strong (r)-positive tendencies in the SV test, where more than half inaccurately reported (r-1).

The very oldest respondents display a set of characteristics which is quite the opposite in every respect. They show minimal (r)-positive response, to the SR test; 80% use no (r) in any style, and not one claimed (r-1) as their one usage.[3]

The middle-aged set shows intermediate characteristics on all counts but one: the use of (r-1) in other styles. This result fits with the view of the behavior of middle-aged informants developed in Chapter 9 – they are the ones who show the most tendency to acquire (r-1) in their careful speech.

Only the very oldest respondents show immunity from the influence of the new prestige form. This result demonstrates the importance of the subjective dimension for the study of linguistic change. If the analysis had ended with Chapter 9, we would have been unable to discriminate between two very different sets of (r-0) pronouncers. The younger set is deliberate only in appearance: their use of (r-0) stems from a lack of motor control over the prestige form which they recognize, or possibly from other, more obscure forces not yet analyzed. But in any case, the SR test and the SV test demonstrate that their linguistic behavior is quite opposed to that of the older group, which is truly deliberate in its use of (r-0). It would have been difficult to support the claim for linguistic change for this particular sub-group of New York speakers without the data provided in Part III.

The class distribution of the r-less speakers shows the sharpest differentiation yet observed. Table 12.8 shows the percentage of those who use no (r-1) in Style D' in four age levels and four SEC groups.

The lower middle class slot is empty: there are *no* speakers who fail to use some of the new prestige marker in their most formal style. The lower middle class is differentiated most sharply from the other classes by the pattern displayed here.

Two distinct groups show a high percentage of (r)-00 speakers in Style D': the youngest and oldest members of the lower class and the working class. As we have seen, the first is r-less *despite* the speakers' recognition of the new prestige marker. The older speakers are r-less *in conformity with* their subjective attitudes.

We have thus penetrated, step by step, to an understanding of the underlying processes which accompany the objective distribution of (r) in New York City. We now understand a great deal about the mechanism of linguistic change and the structure of New York City as a speech community, which we could not have learned from the initial presentation of the social stratification of (r) in Chapter 7. Other variables will now be

---

[3] One of these informants was deaf to this dialect feature, but the others were not. If the inability to hear the distinctions were responsible for the r-less performance of these older speakers, we would not expect to see a uniform choice of a single variant in the SV test for the entire group. In actual fact, the four who took the SV test all reported variant 4 as their own usage.

Table 12.8   *Percentage of* (r)-*00 speakers in style D' by age and SEC*

	SEC			
Age	0–1	2–5	6–8	9
20–39	67	75	00	20
40–49	20	18	00	25
50–59	33	14	00	33
60–	71	50	–	–
[N:	3	17	11	5
	5	17	9	4
	3	7	1	3
	8	4	–	–]

Table 12.9   (æh) *forms in the SV Test*

	1	2	3	4
pass:	(æh-1)	(æh-3)	(æh-4)	(æh-5)

explored in the same manner. In the discussions to follow, the seventy-nine New York City adult respondents will be the principal population analyzed and the social class (SC) scale will be used to study class differentiation.

Self-evaluation for (æh) and (oh)

The four forms which were presented to the respondents for (æh) are as shown in Table 12.9.

In the exploratory interviews, it appeared that most informants would choose (æh-4). Therefore a choice on each side of this form was offered, and as a first variant, the extreme (æh-1) to contrast with the rest.

Seven informants reported (accurately) that they varied between several forms. On the other hand, not one respondent reported that they could not hear the differences between the variants. The variable (æh) is the only one for which no such reports were made. This result correlates with many other findings about (æh): that all classes are involved in the structure of stylistic variation; that subjective reactions to (æh) show the highest agreement in (æh)-negative response; and that the distribution of (æh) in apparent time reflects an advanced stage of a change from below, with widespread recognition of the corrective pressure from above.

Table 12.10   *Social class distribution of* (æh-3) *and* (æh-4) *responses*

Reported	SC 1	SC 2	SC 3	SC 4
(æh-3)	9	8	4	5
(æh-4)	8	14	10	6

Table 12.11   *Reported* (æh) *usage for ethnic groups*

Reported	Italians	Jews	African–Americans
(æh-3)	11	7	10
(æh-4)	7	24	0
(æh-5)	0	5	0

Only two informants reported (æh-1) as their own usage.

Five informants chose (æh-5) as representing their own usage: that is, the vowel lower than the sound of *bat*, close to the eastern New England forms of *ask*, *past*, *dance*, etc. None of these informants actually used such forms: most used some (æh-2) alternating with larger numbers of (æh-4) in Style B. Two of these informants were among the very few who failed to show (æh)-negative response in the SR test, and it is possible that their choice of (æh-5) was conditioned by a certain degree of dialect deafness in this area.

The majority of the respondents selected (æh-3) or (æh-4): thirty-eight reported (æh-4), and twenty-six reported the slightly higher form, (æh-3). The majority followed a pattern which we would predict after our study of (r): they inaccurately reported their subjective norm (æh-4) as their actual usage.

Most of those who reported (æh-3) did so accurately, in so far as they indicated that their usage was a closer vowel than (æh-4). The class distribution of this group was concentrated at the two extremes. Again this fits in with previous data which shows that the center groups are more apt to correct their usage to the open vowel of (æh-4) (see Table 12.10).

The preponderance of (æh-4) choices among the two center classes is of course in direct contradiction to their actual use in everyday speech, and careful conversation as well.

The ethnic composition of the sub-group that reported (æh-3) as its own usage is quite different from that of the sub-group that chose (æh-4) (see Table 12.11).

Previous data on (æh) has shown ethnic differences to be sharper than class differences. There have also been indications that the SV test shows

Table 12.12   (oh) *forms in the SV test*

1	2	3	4
(oh-1)	(oh-2)	(oh-3)	(oh-5)

Table 12.13   (oh) *forms selected in the SV test*

(oh-1)	(oh-2)	(oh-3)	(oh-5)
5	10	27	25

differences in subjective norms more clearly than any other test, even the SR test. Table 12.11 confirms these indications by showing that the three ethnic groups are sharply differentiated by the test for (æh). African–Americans accurately report their own usage centered around (æh-3); Figure 8.9 shows this grouping of AA speakers in Style B. Italians report their use of (æh) as considerably lower than their actual use; but the Jews show an overwhelming tendency to report (æh-4), despite the fact that two-thirds of these reports are inaccurate, and five Jewish respondents go beyond this to the form (æh-5) which is quite remote from the native speech pattern.

The SV test for (oh) presented the respondents with the variants shown in Table 12.12.

The four forms chosen out of a possible five represent those which are heard most often in the city. When New Yorkers do shift to an open form of (oh), they usually go to (oh-5) rather than (oh-4), which is quite rare. The (oh-5) form is familiar from New England models.

The test word used here was *chocolate*. It was found in the course of the survey that AA respondents used a different phoneme in their natural speech pattern for this word: /a/ as in *hot* or *chock*. I then substituted the word *office* for AA respondents, but the results were thus not consistent, and the data for African–Americans will not be utilized here.

The reporting for (oh) does not show the same concentration on a single value observed for (æh). The distribution of choices is as shown in Table 12.13.

Two subjects reported that they could hear no difference between the four variants. Only two subjects reported their own variation accurately. Five respondents reported the extremely high vowel (oh-1) as their own; only one of these actually used (oh-1) consistently – a lower class Jewish speaker. Four of the five respondents who did report (oh-1) had failed to

Table 12.14   *Reported* (oh) *values by social class*

Reported	SC 1	SC 2	SC 3	SC 4
(oh-1), (oh-2)	5	3	3	2
(oh-3)	11	7	4	4
(oh-5)	3	6	11	4

Table 12.15   *Reported* (oh) *values by ethnic group*

Reported	Jews	Italians
(oh-1), (oh-2)	9	4
(oh-3)	11	12
(oh-5)	18	3

show (oh)-negative response in the SR test. This small group is thus characterized by a combination of lack of ability to discriminate (oh) variants with insensitivity to the social significance of the (oh-1) form.

We have seen that most respondents reported (r) and (æh) inaccurately. For (oh), only twenty-two of the seventy-four respondents being considered here can be said to have reported their own speech accurately.

There is a general bias towards the lower values. All but one of the twenty-five respondents who selected (oh-5) were reporting inaccurately, even for Style D. The tendency to select variants more in the direction of the prestige norm is here carried to an extreme, for almost none of these speakers would use (oh-5) in their natural speech.

The class distribution of respondents for this variable is shown in Table 12.14 above.

The social class scale shows a type of progression to which we are now accustomed. The lower class chooses (oh-3), a fairly accurate report; the high school group of blue collar workers, SC 2, shows more of a tendency towards the unrealistic (oh-5), while white collar workers show an overwhelming preference for this illusion. The professional class, SC 4, shows a strong shift from their actual (oh) usage, but as before, their tendency is not as extreme as that of the white collar workers.

Equally sharp differences appear between the two ethnic groups that we are considering, as shown in Table 12.15. The Jews concentrate their reports towards the prestige pattern of (oh-5), while the Italians remain closer to their actual usage.

Here the parallelism of Jews vs. Italians, maintained in so many tests, has broken down. We saw originally that Jews used higher (oh) vowels, and Italians higher (æh) vowels; that the younger Jews showed an increase in (æh), and the younger Italians an increase in (oh); that the Jews showed the greatest sensitivity to (oh) in the SR test, and Italians to (æh). However, in the SV test, the Jews show the greatest tendency to report the ultra-correct, very open vowels for *both* (æh) and (oh). We must therefore avoid the concept of an automatic ethnic alternation; what we find is a parallelism that is most complete in the casual speech of the older generation, and which is overridden in areas of language behavior where subjective attitudes play a larger part. It is not subjective attitudes towards the speech of others that differentiates the Jews from the Italians so much as the image which respondents have of themselves in relation to language. We will return to this problem in the discussion of the index of linguistic insecurity.

The case of Mrs. Mollie S.

In the course of a survey, we sometimes meet certain individuals who are in an unusually favorable position to expose the mechanism of the overall trends observed. Such a case was that of Mollie S., 36, a lower middle class housewife of Jewish background, and her daughter Debbie, 13. This one interview reveals clearly the way in which New Yorkers combine an extraordinarily keen perception of the speech of others with a completely unrealistic view of their own speech. The combination of outer perception with self-deception is fundamentally a product of the phonemic principle, as it applies to socially significant variation in language.

Mollie S. had undergone a series of eye operations for glaucoma and as a result she had not been able to read for three years. The operations had not been successful; she was all but blind, and the heavy expenses had reduced the family to straitened circumstances. Mollie S. and her daughter spent a great deal of time listening to television, and they had paid a great deal of attention to the voices of the announcers and actors. They played many word games together which centered about words which sounded the same or different. They had therefore developed an unusual sensitivity to speech which enabled them to identify the specific variables in the SR test more accurately than any other informants. Mollie S. identified the inconsistency in *r*-pronunciation in Sentence 18, which no other lower middle class informant had done. Her daughter showed an equally fine adjustment to the speech of others.

Both Mollie S. and her daughter were greatly amused by the stigmatized forms of speech used by the speakers on the SR test, and reminded each other of similar traits in the speech of their acquaintances or well-known personalities they often ridiculed. They were particularly entertained by (oh-1).

In direct discussion, Mollie S. laughed at the idea that she could ever use (oh-1), or (oh-2), even in the most spontaneous or casual speech. She thought that her daughter sometimes fluctuated in this direction. In actual fact, her daughter used (oh-2) and (oh-3), while Mollie S. alternated between (oh-1) and (oh-2), in careful as well as casual speech.

Debbie S. explained exactly why she thought it was impossible for her ever to say (æh-2).

When I read myself, and the words go into my mind, like – let's take *bag*. It doesn't go into my mind as [bɛːg] it goes into my mind as [bæːg] –
  (Interviewer: You might say it as [bɛːg]. . .)
  No! I'd say it the way it comes out of my mind as [bæːg]. Usually, if I'm reading a story, usually I say the words to myself, the way I picture it . . .

In the explanation of this unusually observant person, one finds an explicit statement of the process which can be inferred from the SV test. New Yorkers do not perceive the sound that they speak, but rather the norm that they have accepted as the result of pressure from above.

The case of Debbie S. and Mollie S. ends on an unhappy note. In the discussion of (r), both mother and daughter insisted that they always pronounced all of their *r*'s as (r-1). They had ridiculed the lower middle class speaker for dropping a single (r-1), and they could not believe that they would make such a mistake themselves. Unwisely, I played back the section of the tape in which Mollie S. recited, "Strawberry short cake, cream on top, tell me the name of my sweetheart." She could hear the consistent (r-0) pronunciation in her speech, but after a moment's thought she explained the situation as a psychological transference – she had imagined herself in her childhood setting, and had used a childish speech form. I then played a section of careful speech, the discussion of *common sense*, and also Debbie's reading of the standard text. When Mollie S. and her daughter at last accepted the fact that they regularly used (r-0) in their own speech, they were disheartened in a way that was painful to see. An interview which would otherwise have been an exhilarating experience for this lady and her daughter was thus terminated in a bitter disappointment for them both. Once the damage had been done, there was no way to restore their pride in their own speech. The actual (r) index for Mollie S. in casual speech was (r)-00, and in careful speech, (r)-23.

[The case of Mollie S. is to my way of thinking the most important of the various reports on individuals in this volume: Nathan B., Steve K., Dolly R., Emilio D. (to follow) and others. This incident demonstrates more forcibly than any other the way in which linguistic norms can intervene between production and perception. The study of near-mergers has recently provided strong experimental evidence on this point (Labov, Karan and Miller 1991),

Table 12.16   (th) *and* (dh) *forms in the SV test*

	1	2	3
(th)	the same thing (th-1)	the same thing (th-2)	the same thing (th-3)
(dh)	just then (dh-1)	just then (dh-2)	just then (dh-3)

but the special experience of Mollie S. and her daughter is a natural experiment of some importance.]

Self-evaluation for (th) *and* (dh)

Instead of a single word, a phrase was used for each of the variables to be discussed here. The respondents were presented with the sets in Table 12.16.

On the whole, the results of the (th) and (dh) tests showed that respondents report their expected norms instead of their actual usage, as with other variables. Only nine respondents reported that they used the stigmatized forms (th-3) and seven reported (dh-3). Most of these had shown (th)-insensitivity on the SR test. Four who reported (th-3) had actually used no affrication stops at all in Style B – in other words, their report was an error in hearing. However, all of those who selected (dh-3) showed high (dh) indexes in careful conversation, Style B.

Inability to hear (th) and (dh) variation plays a more important role in the situation than a similar inability for the other variables. The distinction between (th-1) and (th-2) seems to be obscure for some groups of the population; the Italian subjects in particular reported (th-2) much more frequently than other respondents did.

However, in the overall view, fifty-five out of eighty-three respondents did show the typical pattern of reporting the prestige variants as their own usage, despite the fact that they frequently used the stigmatized variants.

Self-evaluation for (her) *and* (hurt)

Before we conclude the report of the SV test, it may be useful to look briefly at the results for two other variables: (her), the vowel of stressed *her*, *stir, occur*, etc., as discussed in Chapter 10, and (hurt), the vowel of *bird, shirt, work*, etc., discussed in Chapter 9. These cases will give us additional confirmation of the fact that increasing sensitivity to the social significance of a stigmatized form will lead to increasing inaccuracy in self-reporting.

The forms presented to the respondent for (her) were as shown in Table 12.17.

Table 12.17   (her) *forms in the SV test*

1	2	3
I told her (her-1) [hɝ·]	I told her (her-2) [hɜ:]	I told her (her-3) [hʌ:]

Table 12.18   *Respondents using and reporting* [hʌ] *by class*

	SEC group		
	0–3	4–8	9
Number using [hʌ:]	19	12	2
Number reporting [hʌ:]	6	3	0
Number hearing no difference	2	0	0

The first variant uses a constricted (r), the second an unconstricted center-glide, and the third, the vowel of *but* and *tub* (without retroflexion).

Very few informants were willing to report the third form compared to the number who use it in actual speech. We may compare usage with self-reporting in Table 12.18, which shows only the numbers using or reporting [hʌ].

[The short vowel in this word is one of the most characteristic New York City forms, but it is not stigmatized in a way comparable to the palatalized vowel of *hurt*. Nevertheless, only a small fraction report themselves using it.]

There were *no* respondents who reported [hʌ] who did not actually use this form. On the other hand, there were twenty-four respondents who did use it, but who did not report it. We can see a gradual development of the social significance of this variable in the disparity between use and report. The disparity increases somewhat as we go from the lowest ranking section to the middle ranking and the highest ranking section of the class spectrum. However, the effect is much smaller than the comparable progression for the highly stigmatized form /ʌy/ of the variable (hurt) – phonetically [hʌɪt].

The forms presented to the respondent for (hurt) are shown in Table 12.19.

We are interested primarily in the third variant, which is the highly stigmatized form. In Table 12.20, we can observe the class distribution of the disparity between use and report.

Table 12.19   (hurt) *forms in the SV test*

1	2	3
it hurt	it hurt	it hurt
[hɚt]	[hɜɪt]	[hʌɪt]

Table 12.20   *Respondents using and reporting /ʌy/ by class*

	SEC group			
	0–1	2–5	6–8	9
Number using /ʌy/	9	18	5	0
Number reporting /ʌy/	4	5	1	0
% report/use	44	28	20	–
[N:	12	35	21	11]

Not only is there a close correlation between class and the use of the stig-matized form, but there is a parallel correlation between class and the will-ingness to report the use of such forms. This is a conclusive demonstration of the fact that the SV test does not measure the ability to perceive a given form. The working class speakers who use /ʌy/ can undoubtedly hear the stigmatized form as well as, or better than, the lower class speakers. The lower middle class speakers have a higher percentage of those who have adopted a new norm, and therefore they show a smaller tendency to report their actual use and a greater preference to report inaccurately the prestige norm as if it were their own.

[The use of SV tests was further developed by Trudgill in his study of Norwich (1974) with important results. See also the study of Australian vowels by Bradley and Bradley (1979). Another approach to self-report is found in the work of Di Paolo on the merger of vowels before /l/ in Salt Lake City (1988). The finding that merger is more advanced in perception than production is another aspect of the mismatch between these linguistic modes, even when no strong social motivation is present.]

The index of linguistic insecurity

We have presented a great deal of information to show that New Yorkers hear themselves not as they actually sound, but rather in accordance with the norms they acknowledge. We have also seen that the lower middle class shows the same hypercorrect tendency in the reports of its own speech as in actual usage, stylistic variation, and in the SR and SV tests.

The hypercorrect tendency of the lower middle class seems to be rooted in a profound linguistic insecurity. This insecurity is perhaps an inevitable accompaniment of social mobility and the development of upward social aspirations in terms of the socio-economic hierarchy. Hypercorrection is a term often used to refer to the familiar tendency of speakers to overshoot the mark in grammatical usage; in attempting to correct some non-standard forms, they apply the correction to other forms for which the rules they are using do not apply. Common examples of such hypercorrect forms are *Whom did you say was calling?* and *He is looking for you and I.* The tendency to spelling pronunciations such as [ɔftɪn] for *often*, or [pɑlm] for *palm* is another expression of the same process.

The development of linguistic insecurity has accompanied the development of the doctrine of correctness.[4] In the seventeenth and eighteenth century, many rising members of the English middle class found themselves in social situations where their native speech patterns were not appropriate. It was this aspect of social mobility which created a need for a doctrine of correctness, and led to the elevation of the schoolmaster and the dictionary as authorities for speech in both England and America.[5]

In general, we may say that those who adopt a standard of correctness which is imposed from without, and from beyond the group which helped form their native speech pattern, are bound to show signs of linguistic insecurity. For most New Yorkers, the reference group for linguistic behavior is not any group of which they are a member. Linguistic insecurity leads directly to hypercorrection, for insecure speakers have not internalized their newly acquired norms, and have no automatically applied rule to let them know where to stop in their corrections. Sometimes the structure of their own native pattern makes it very difficult for them to stop at the mark set by higher ranking social groups. In phonological matters, we see an example in the fact that lower middle class white speakers do not have the allophone (æh-3) in their system; therefore in attempting to correct their native (æh-2), they can only go to the next lower level which is established in their system, (æh-4); but as we have seen, this correction does not as a rule satisfy their own critical reactions.

In the course of this study, we have seen further indications of the linguistic insecurity of the lower middle class in their hypercorrect use of several variables in Style D; in their high degree of sensitivity to forms which are characteristic of the respondents themselves in natural speech;

---

[4] The history of the theory of correctness is given by Sterling A. Leonard, *The Doctrine of Correctness in English Usage, 1700–1800* (1929).
[5] See A. W. Read, "The Motivation of Lindley Murray's Grammatical Work" (1939).

and in the inaccurate reporting of the respondents' own speech pattern. In the light of this tendency to linguistic insecurity, one can predict that lower middle class speakers will acquire new prestige pronunciations in their middle years; this analysis was confirmed by the patterns of distribution in apparent time, both in the Lower East Side survey and the department store survey.

We may now consider a completely independent approach to the measurement of linguistic insecurity. At the end of the ALS interview, the respondents are presented with a test which measures their tendency to consider their own pronunciation wrong, and to accept a pronunciation which they do not use, as right. The form used for this purpose is shown in the questionnaire in Appendix A, Section VIII. Each of eighteen different words is pronounced by the interviewer in two different ways, in accordance with the phonetic forms shown in the questionnaire. The respondents are asked to circle the number of the pronunciation which they think is correct. Then they are asked to check the pronunciation which they actually use. The number of items in which the respondent circles one form and checks another is the index of linguistic insecurity (abbreviated ILI).

It is obvious that in many cases respondents will not admit to using a variant pronunciation which they consider sub-standard, even when they have already used this pronunciation in reading style. The tendency to claim the standard for one's own usage has been measured in the SV test, and we have seen that it is very strong. Now we are measuring a type of linguistic insecurity which is overt, where respondents are willing to admit to themselves and to the interviewer that their own usage is not the correct one. There is no direct necessity for these two measures to coincide: for example, people who consistently report the prestige form for their own speech will fall into the category of inaccurate reporters on the SV test; if they refuse to admit any difference between the standard and their own pronunciation of the eighteen words, they will be showing the same tendency as in the SV test, but will be ranked at zero on the scale of linguistic insecurity. We are therefore measuring *latent insecurity* in the SV test, and *manifest insecurity* in the ILI procedure. We would expect that Mollie S., for example, might rank high in latent insecurity in the SV test, but not necessarily in manifest insecurity in the ILI scale.[6]

Table 12.21 shows the distribution of index scores for four socio-economic groups.

In Table 12.21, the lower middle class group 6–8 stands out with the highest index scores. Approximately half of the lower class and working

---

[6] In actual fact, Mollie S. showed an ILI score of 5, close to the average score for the lower middle class group.

Table 12.21   *Percentage distribution of index of linguistic insecurity scores for adult New York respondents by SEC*

	SEC groups			
ILI	0–2	3–5	6–8	9
0	44	50	16	20
1–2	25	21	16	70
3–7	12	25	58	10
8–13	19	04	10	–
	100	100	100	100
[N:	16	28	19	10]

class groups had a zero score – they reported no difference between the "correct" form and the form they actually used. Very few of these respondents showed an ILI score of more than 1 or 2. (It is interesting to note that the working class group showed even lower scores than the lower class.) In sharp contrast, the majority of the lower middle class group showed high ILI scores. Again, we find the upper middle class in a more moderate position, with 70 percent showing only 1 or 2 "correct" items different from their own.

This performance of the lower middle class is consistent with other types of hypercorrect behavior found in other chapters; in all cases we see that this group defers to an exterior standard quite different from their own pattern – in this case, consciously so.

In Chapter 8 it was found that women show a more extreme range of stylistic variation than men – a much greater degree of correction in formal style. We would expect accordingly a higher score for women on the index of linguistic insecurity. This is indeed the case; as shown in Table 12.22, women are 50 percent higher than men in this category.

The distribution of the ILI scores among ethnic groups shows the pattern in Table 12.23.

This is a surprising result. One might have expected the Jews to show the highest degree of linguistic insecurity, judging by their record on the SV test. However, it appears that the latent insecurity of the SV test does not match the manifest insecurity of the ILI scale in this case.

Since there is no previous evidence from which to predict such a result, one cannot explain the special position of the Italians. However, a particular case which is the extreme expression of the tendency shown above may be helpful in understanding the significance of this result.

Table 12.22   *ILI scores by gender*

	Mean ILI score
Men	2.1
Women	3.6

Table 12.23   *ILI scores by ethnicity*

	Average ILI
Italians	3.8
Jews	2.4
African–Americans	1.3

The case of Emilio D.

The respondent in question is a plumber, of Italian background, thirty-seven years old. He lives in a cooperative middle class apartment; his income is high, and this fact combined with his high school education places him in class 6 on the socio-economic scale.

However, Emilio D. is exceptional in class 6, since he is a blue collar worker, and his speech pattern in many ways is more characteristic of class 3. He showed an exceptionally high (dh) and (th) index: 122 and 133 in careful speech, and almost as high in reading. He used the stigmatized form /ʌy/ in *bird* and *shirt* and, even in formal styles, used high uncorrected vowels for (æh) and (oh).

In the interview situation, Emilio D. was ill at ease. He spoke comparatively little, and his only really spontaneous comment was a brief denunciation of anti-segregation pickets. His (dh) score of 133 is completely isolated from others in SEC 6 – no one else in this class has an index higher than 75. This rating was quite independent of any considerations drawn from the index of linguistic insecurity.

From the results of the SR test for Emilio D., we can conclude that he is not insensitive to the language variables we are studying. He showed positive response to (r) in the four-choice test, (oh)-negative response, (æh)-negative response, and an extreme (th)-sensitive pattern.

In the index of linguistic insecurity, Emilio D. appeared as the least secure of any respondent. On 13 of the 18 items, he rated his own pronunciation incorrect, and some other pronunciation correct. No other respondent showed such a high score on this measure of manifest insecurity.

Emilio D. appears in the SEC matrix as an example of status incongruency, since his income rank is considerably higher than his occupational rank (and educational rank as well). The index of linguistic insecurity shows that he has not avoided the linguistic consequences of his exceptional position.

[In 1984, Owens and Baker replicated the linguistic insecurity test in Winnipeg. They first used the New York City form of the test exactly as it was used in this volume, and then adapted it to the variables most pertinent to Canadians. The major findings of the New York City study were strongly supported here. Most salient is the high ratings of women on the linguistic insecurity test, and especially those in the second highest status group. However, the label *linguistic insecurity* implies a mechanism and a motivation that may not describe the situation most accurately. At various points in the study of the speech community, it appears that social mobility is connected with the recognition of an exterior norm of correctness. In fact, the rise of the doctrine of correctness (Leonard 1929) was associated with the rise of the middle class in the seventeenth and eighteenth centuries. Another way of looking at the special concern of women for conformation to prestige norms is that women undertake more responsibility than men for the upward mobility of children. This may result in some of the superficial stigmata of insecurity – hesitation, nervousness, self-correction, extreme style-shifting – but this behavior takes on a more positive aspect when viewed as a concomitant of social mobility.

In 1966, I published a separate study which showed that an index of social mobility had as high a correlation with linguistic variables as the socio-economic indices (Labov 1966b). However, a similar index of mobility – comparing the subject's occupation with that of his parent(s) – did not prove equally useful in explaining linguistic variation in Philadelphia (Labov 2001). It proved significant only at one point in the analysis. Combined with house upkeep, upward social mobility was negatively correlated with the vocalization of (r), a characteristic of Italians in south Philadelphia which is still under investigation but still poorly understood (Labov 2001: Ch. 7.7). But in Philadelphia social mobility did not add to the understanding of the correlation of the stable sociolinguistic variables with socio-economic class, or with the sound changes in progress.]

Summary

This chapter developed one of the primary elements in the underlying structure of the New York City speech community: a profound linguistic insecurity. The lower middle class is the most seriously affected by this tendency, but all classes show the trait to a greater or lesser degree.

New Yorkers also showed a systematic tendency to report their own speech inaccurately. Most of the respondents seemed to perceive their own speech in terms of the norms at which they were aiming rather than the sound actually produced. The self-evaluation test and the index of linguistic insecurity helped to delineate further the normative structure which lies beneath the surface phenomena of New York City speech.

Chapter 13 will report the opinions, attitudes, and uneasy suspicions about the language of New York City which subjects offered in response to direct questioning. This discussion will provide overt evidence of the linguistic self-hatred which marks the average New Yorker and motivates many of the other types of behavior that have been studied here.

13 General attitudes towards the speech of New York City

[This chapter describes a form of sociolinguistic behavior where New York City is far from typical of the speech communities of the world. Chapter 9 pointed out that underlying attitudes towards language are evoked more accurately when the subject doesn't realize that language is in question. However, New York is at one extreme of a continuum of linguistic insecurity, and the effect is so strong that the negative assessment of the New York City vernacular emerges even under direct questioning.]

At many points in the course of this study, it has been emphasized that the behavior which we are studying lies below the level of conscious awareness. Very few of the informants perceive or report their own variant usage of the phonological variables, and fewer still perceive it accurately. This does not mean that New Yorkers do not give a great deal of conscious attention to their language. Most of the informants in our survey have strong opinions about language, and they do not hesitate to express them. But their attention focuses only on those items which have risen to the surface of social consciousness, and have entered the general folklore of language. Just as the reporting of usage in the self-evaluation test is essentially inaccurate, so most perception of language is not perception of sense experience, but of socially accepted statements about language.

It was common for our informants to condemn the language of a person, a group, or a whole city in very general terms: "sloppy," "careless," "hurried," "loud," or "harsh." When we asked for particular features in this style of speech which were offensive, most of the respondents could not think of any; the few examples which were given were morphological variants, such as *ain't* for *isn't*, *gonna* for *going to*, *whatcha* [wʌtšə] for *what are you*, or *aks* [æks] for *ask*. The only phonological form that was mentioned frequently and spontaneously was the stigmatized upgliding vowel in *bird, work, shirt*, etc.[1] Most voice qualities which the listener did not like were termed "nasal"; in

---

[1] Other phonological variables which were mentioned occasionally are: a strongly voiced [g] following [ŋ] in words such as *wrong, ringer, singer, Long Island*, called the "*ng click*" in college speech classes; "hard *t, d,* and *g*" in initial position (usually referring to velarized initial consonants); and the variables (æh) and (r) which we have been considering in this study.

Table 13.1   *NYC respondents participating in the linguistic attitudes section by class*

	SEC			
	0–2	3–5	6–8	9
Total ALS adult informants	27	32	22	12
Participating in linguistic attitudes section	15	24	18	11

New York City, this most frequently refers to a denasalized voice quality of lower class speech.

This chapter will be concerned with general attitudes toward New York City English, the kind of information which can be obtained from any informant directly: general approval or disapproval, comparisons with other regional dialects, feelings about correctness, and the need to change one's language. The data will concern emotional attitudes rather than cognitive statements; most of these attitudes may be seen as expressions of the linguistic insecurity of the New York City speech community.

Methods and the population studied

The questions on linguistic attitudes which were used in the survey of the Lower East Side are given in Section VII of the questionnaire in Appendix A. This section of the interview was not applied with formal rigor: for some informants, the discussions were long, and for others, very brief. In many cases, the interview had already lasted an hour or more before this section was reached, and the strenuous effort of the SR test had left the subjects in no state of mind for extended formal questioning. The linguistic attitudes section was therefore administered as if it were not a part of the formal interview, and the completion rate for various questions was somewhat irregular. If the informant had only a limited amount of time, other sections of the interview were given priority.

As a result of these limitations, only 68 of the 93 adult New York City informants gave responses to the section on linguistic attitudes, and there are usually only 40 to 50 responses for a given question. Twenty-eight of the 38 out-of-town respondents participated in this section of the survey, with comparable rates for particular questions.

There is a class bias in the losses, as Table 13.1 shows.

A breakdown by classes will therefore be required to assess the effect of the bias on the overall results. Since the data consists of single answers, and

Table 13.2 *Responses to questions on linguistic attitudes*

	Total	Adult New York respondents										Out-of-town respondents	
		SEC			Ethnic group			Sex		Age			
		0–2	3–5	6–9	I	J	AA	M	F	20–39	40–	W	AA
Recognition by outsiders as New Yorker													
Yes	24	8	9	7	10	9	–	8	16	7	17		
No	8	2	3	3	–	6	1	–	8	2	6		
As non-New Yorker	4	–	–	4	1	–	1	1	3	1	3		
Opinion on outsiders' view of NYC speech													
Not negative	15	4	6	5	6	6	2	7	8	6	9	6	4
Negative	30	5	10	15	5	15	2	11	19	11	19	4	–
Own attitude towards NYC speech													
Positive	14	2	4	8	3	5	4	7	7	7	7	5	5
Negative	23	6	6	11	6	13	1	5	18	4	19	6	2
Neutral	9	2	6	1	1	6	1	6	3	2	7	2	7
Own attitude towards southern speech													
Positive	8	2	3	3	2	4	–	2	6	1	7	–	–
Negative	12	2	3	7	3	3	4	5	7	4	8	3	7
Neutral	4	1	2	1	–	3	–	2	2	1	3	–	–
Efforts to change own speech													
Yes	32	4	9	19	5	19	3	10	22	14	18	4	5
No	14	3	6	5	3	6	–	8	6	4	10	3	–

lacks the quantitative reliability of the phonological indexes, only obvious and large-scale trends will be considered here.

The numerical data for the discussion is given in Table 13.2. In the following pages, the results will be discussed in general terms, with references to the figures in Table 13.2 only where necessary.

Recognition of New Yorkers by outsiders

The informants were asked if they had ever travelled outside of New York City, and if they had ever been recognized as New Yorkers by their speech. Some had never been outside of the city limits, even on a vacation; but for those who had left the city at times, it seems to have been a common experience to be recognized as New Yorkers by the evidence of their speech alone.

"It's the first thing you open your mouth," reported one of the oldest ALS informants, a 73-year-old Irishman. A middle class Jewish housewife admitted ruefully, "I know I sound like a New Yorker. I've been spotted instantly, innumerable times." A young Italian woman from a working class family had the same experience: "Oh definitely, wherever I go."

Three-quarters of the lower class and working class informants reported that they had been recognized as New Yorkers, but only half of the middle class informants did so. All but one of the Italian respondents had been identified by outsiders as New Yorkers, but only three-fifths of the Jewish group. But there were no Jewish respondents among the four middle class speakers who could say that someone outside of the city had thought that they were *not* New Yorkers. Those who made this report took considerable pride in doing so, for the overwhelming majority of respondents felt that recognition as a New Yorker was tantamount to stigmatization as a New Yorker.

Opinions on how outsiders view New York City speech

Immediately after the question on recognition, the subjects were asked if people who lived outside of the city liked New York City speech, and why these outsiders felt as they did. (I will refer to such outside residents as *outsiders*, in contrast to the ALS informants who were raised outside of the city and who are designated *out-of-towners* in this study.)

Two-thirds of the New York City respondents thought that outsiders did not like New York City speech. Only three thought that the speech of the city was looked on with the interest or approval of outsiders; the balance thought that the outsiders were neutral, or didn't care much one way or the other. Among the working class respondents, there was a higher proportion of respondents who felt that outsiders were neutral than for any other class. Yet even a majority of them voted for "dislike."

"They think we're all murderers," said the old Irish working man. "To be recognized as a New Yorker –" thought a middle class Jewish woman, "that would be a terrible slap in the face!" An older Jewish woman put it this way: "Somehow, the way they say, 'Are you a New Yorker?', they don't care so much for it."

Sometimes the New Yorker will pretend to be ignorant of the ridicule directed at his local speech pattern, but no one is deceived. An Italian girl in her early twenties, from a working class family, gave the following view of her identification as a New Yorker by her husband's friends.

Bill's college alumni group – we have a party once a month in Philadelphia. Well, now I know them about two years and every time we're there – at a wedding, at a party, a shower – they say, if someone new is in the group: "Listen to Jo Ann talk!" I sit there and I babble on, and they say, "Doesn't she have a ridiculous accent!" and "It's so New Yorkerish and all!" [laughter]

I don't have the accent. I'm in a room with fifty people that have accents, and . . . I don't mind it, but I *never* take it as a compliment. And I can tell by the way people say it, they don't mean it complimentary.

Although the general consensus is that outsiders do condemn New York City speech, there is an opposing point of view held by some New Yorkers. Most of these are men, and the experience they draw upon was usually obtained in the armed services.

A thirty-year-old Jewish truck driver denied that other servicemen disliked New York City speech.

Some got quite a kick out of it . . . I used to put on "thoity thoid 'n' thoid" [θɔɪti θɔɪdntθɔɪd] but I didn't really talk that way – I spoke that way because it was expected of me. Kidding, you know.

This minority point of view is stated even more strongly by Steve K., the ex-philosophy student whose special attitude is described in Chapter 4, page 79.

The people in the army – respected New York. They liked New York. They were fascinated by it, all from Ohio, Chicago – they enjoyed the fact that I was from New York. It was never said as a put-down . . . it was a matter of curiosity.

Views of the out-of-town ALS informants

What do the out-of-town informants in our survey actually think about New York City speech? Their view is almost exactly the contrary of the New York respondents. Only one in four reported that outsiders disliked New York City speech; most of the out-of-town informants believed that outsiders were neutral towards New York City speech, neither admiring it nor despising it. This was true for the white respondents as well as the

African–Americans, although African–Americans lean even more heavily in favor of New York City.

When the out-of-town respondents reported their own feelings about New York City, the result was still more favorable. Ten liked the speech of the city, nine were neutral, and less than a third said that they disliked it. Again, this tendency was strongest among African–Americans: 12 out of 14 AA out-of-town respondents said that they liked the speech of the city or were neutral towards it. (For all AA respondents, the figure is 17 out of 20.)

Sometimes the leaning towards New York was a part of a reaction against the respondents' own native region or town. "I don't like that midwestern drawl," said a post office clerk who was raised in Indiana. Some of the lower class subjects from eastern Pennsylvania found little to admire in the declining fortunes of the coal mining towns from which they came.

Pennsylvania? I wouldn't give five cents – too dead. I'm out of that graveyard. There's a lot of excitement in New York City.

But there is also the sincere desire to sound like a New Yorker. One woman who came to work in New York City as a young girl said: "When I came to New York City, I tried to talk like that, but I couldn't because my accent was too much Pennsylvania." When her aunt back home said that she spoke like a New Yorker, she took it as a compliment, which a true New Yorker would never have done.

There are some respondents who have spent most of their lives in New York City without showing any significant change in their native speech pattern. A teacher who had worked for thirty years in the New York City school system seemed to have preserved intact the phonological pattern of Beverly, Massachusetts, where she was raised. She said that when she was a little girl, a boy from New York City used to visit her:

He was always talking about his *aunt* [æh-3] Nelly – had to take a *bath* [æh-3] – we took the wrong *path* [æh-4] in the woods, and so forth. I just didn't like it, and when I came, I just made an effort not to change.

As a rule, upper middle class respondents from out-of-town showed the most resistance to the speech of the city, and lower class and working class subjects showed a more favorable response.

Attitudes of New York respondents towards New York speech

When most New Yorkers say that outsiders dislike New York City speech, they are describing an attitude which is actually their own. Whether or not their opinion about outsiders' views is a projection of their own feelings, New Yorkers show a general hostility towards New York City speech which emerges in countless ways. The term "linguistic self-hatred" is not too extreme to apply to the situation which emerges from the interviews. Only 14 New Yorkers expressed themselves favorably towards New York City; 9 were neutral, and 23 expressed dislike quite plainly. These overt reactions are the correlates of the phonological behavior and the unconscious subjective reactions which have been studied in the various chapters of the present work.

The terms which New Yorkers apply to the speech of the city give some indication of the violence of their reactions. "It's terrible." "Distorted." "Terribly careless." "Sloppy." "It's horrible." "Lou-zay!"

Again, we find that men express much less of this attitude than women. As Table 13.2 shows, a minority of the men expressed themselves negatively about New York City speech, but a large majority of the women respondents did so. Since our survey population is weighted somewhat in favor of women, it is possible that this aspect of the city's attitudes has been stressed too heavily. Yet it should be emphasized that men follow the same general pattern of stylistic variation and subjective reaction as women; their reactions are simply more moderate, and in this case, there is a third force which modifies their behavior even further in comparison to that of women. We will return to this discussion below.

The negative attitude towards New York City speech seems to have penetrated even to those who have never been outside of the city. An old Italian woman who had been only to the fifth grade, cannot read even today, and had never been outside the city limits, remarked in answer to the interviewer's question, "Out of town they speak more refined."

A more neutral attitude characteristic of working class men may be heard in a quotation from a working class Italian man, raised in Williamsburg: "I was brought up in New York, and if I would talk any other way it would seem strange."

One may wonder how the ALS interview question could be asked in terms of "New York City speech" in general. It would seem natural for the respondents to distinguish between many kinds of New York City speech, since they did distinguish sharply the usage of various informants in the subjective reaction test. However, very few respondents felt the need for such equivocation. There seemed to be a general understanding that there was such a thing as "New York City speech," and whatever the respondent perceived as that entity was the object of the statements quoted above.

Informants' dislike of their own speech; pressure from above

We find the negative attitude towards the city speech in general is directed by the respondents towards themselves as well. More than half of the respondents thought poorly of their own speech, and two-thirds had attempted to change their speech in some way or another.

The pressures towards conformity with middle class norms of speech are very strong. We have seen objective evidence of this tendency; in the course of the survey, respondents reported many incidents which showed the social contexts in which such pressures occur. An AA man reported the following situation among his immediate friends:

> I have some friends that speak very rough – when we are all together, with the careful group, we all try to be more careful.
> Some fellas never come down – they stay up all the time – and you find that the ones that don't speak well – are more or less quiet.

Another form of correction comes from the respondents' children. A number of the oldest informants, especially among the lower class subjects, had suffered for many years under the sharp corrections of their own children. A frequent comment is, "My son always laughs at me." One older Italian woman was particularly embarrassed at her own inability to distinguish *earl* and *oil*, which had apparently been a point of ridicule for many years in her own family. She cheered up considerably when she learned that this was once the prestige pronunciation of the highest levels of society.

As a rule, our informants show little tendency to respect the speech of their elders. "Lots of these words, they laugh at me," said one old Jewish woman. Another woman took a more hopeful view:

> I'll tell you, you see, my son is always correcting me. He speaks very well – the one that went to [two years of] college. And I'm glad that he corrects me – because it shows me that there are many times when I don't pronounce my words correctly.

Under such pressures, a tendency towards linguistic insecurity on the part of older New Yorkers is not difficult to understand.

Pressures from below

A great deal of the present study is devoted to delineating the effect of pressures from above upon language. It has been pointed out that equally powerful pressures must be exerted from below, since the pattern of class stratification of language is becoming sharper rather than tending to disappear. Many New Yorkers are conscious of the need for the style shifts that we have observed by means of the phonological indexes. One respondent who is the owner of a small advertising agency shows the effects of pressures from above and below, and is himself aware of both influences on his own language. He was very conscious of the need for correct speech for his office staff: he said that he would have refused to hire any of the speakers on the SR test tape except Speaker 4. "I think people have to have some respect for the way the language is written. Even if we all make mistakes,

I think we can't say *'cause* 'n' *dat* 'n' *di udda ting* [oh-1, dh-3, th-3]. It's no longer our language. I'm vehement about this." Yet he also said of himself:

As a performer – I change my style of speech. I will do a kind of gutsy talk, that's very different. It will not include four-letter words, but I change the pattern almost entirely, 'cause I'm very good at that, and I enjoy it.

In the examples that he offered ("I'm gonna talk plain . . ."), he used (r-0), (th-3), (dh-3), (oh-2). He found this style essential for dealing with customers:

I said, "Thank you" for something, and he was annoyed, 'cause I thanked him – 'cause he's a rough, tough kinda guy, y'know. So he says, "Aaah, ya fuckin' gentleman you!" 'Cause basically I am – he resents the fact that I'm courteous to him. So what I did was to put my head back in the door and say to him, "You know Jack, you're quite a character." He had a bunch of people – they're all close people, and he had made the remark in front of them. "What would you want me to do, take that thing from you, and call you a dirty name? Would that [dh-3] be a sign of respect to you?". . . So he smiled and says, "Go on, kiddo, I'll see ya."

A lawyer explained to the interviewer why he made no effort to change his own speech, and why his speech had actually "deteriorated" in recent years.

. . . most of the people I associate with in this area are men with very little schooling . . . mostly Italian-American . . . so that these are the men I've gone out drinking with, the ones I go out to dinner with, and when I talk to them, my speech even deteriorates a little more, because I speak the way they speak . . .

This speaker had preserved the traditional r-less pattern, with raised (æh), more consistently than any other class 9 speaker. He showed the mixture of feelings that are produced in any New Yorker who tries to go against the tide – yet the pressure from below was strong enough to allow him to resist the opposing pressure from his wife, his children, and their friends.

The people that I represent never criticize my speech – the only criticism I receive is primarily from my wife – I get it there – my children also . . . self criticism when I listen to myself. I find it important to be natural in my speech – I can express myself faster and clearer.

Pressure towards conformity with the native speech pattern is very strong among schoolchildren. Those who come to the city from out of town are quickly compelled to drop their own regional accents. One woman who had come from Atlanta as a ten-year-old, fifty years ago, could still remember how she had cried when the others made fun of her southern accent. The pressure is greatest against those who would attempt to use an acquired prestige pattern too early. A teacher who conducted a class of gifted children told me:

I had a boy of Greek parentage, and oh! he spoke beautifully in class, and I happened to hear him on the street one day. He sounded just like everybody else in

Chelsea, and when I mentioned it to him – the next day – he said that he knew which was correct, but he said: "I couldn't live here and talk like that."

One of the reasons for the resistance of children to the middle class norms is that their teachers advocate a language, and an attitude towards language, which is quite remote from everyday life. The teacher quoted above told me of her difficulties in explaining to children the importance of pronouncing the word *length* as [lɛŋθ] and not [lɛnθ].

Some children, you correct them – and they aren't anxious. They say, "What difference does it make?" And I try to tell them that it does make [a difference]. There might be two people applying for a position, and someone might talk about the length [lɛŋθ] of the room, and someone else about the [lɛnθ] of a dress, and I said the one who spoke correctly, probably, in many instances *would* get the position.

The phonological variables we have been studying are seldom discussed by teachers. Instead, many of them concentrate on individual words that have become major issues in their own thinking. One young man, of Polish background, who now worked in a furniture warehouse, remembered two rules of pronunciation on which the speech teacher had drilled his high school class.

I never paid attention to the rules of grammar until she started teaching to me, and I was so surprised at the way stuff is supposed to be pronounced . . . She wrote the word *butter* on the board, and she asked me how to pronounce it, and I said [bʌtɚ]. She told me that was wrong, and that's when I learned to pronounce *t*'s like a *t* – I used to pronounce them as *d*'s all the time.

The pronunciation he used with me was exactly the same pronunciation of *butter* which almost all Americans use – with a semi-voiced intervocalic consonant. When I asked him how the teacher had taught him to pronounce the word, he couldn't remember what it was supposed to sound like.

I haven't been in school for a while, and I'm reverting back to the *d*'s again.

The only other rule of pronunciation which the teacher had stressed was the use of [hw] as the initial consonant of *when* and *where*, instead of the normal [w] which is used by New Yorkers of all classes and age levels. This young man used a high percentage of stops and affricates in his careful conversation – (th)-95, (dh)-47 – but the teacher had never brought this feature to his attention.

[This incident is one of many examples of the great gulf between public discussion of linguistic variation and reality. Typical is the image of the high school teacher's campaign to reverse the flapping rule in American English. It was one aspect of the earlier preference for British or "International English" that was reversed after World War II, as outlined in the discussion of (r). Now the major focus of attention among English teachers has switched from the NYC vernacular to the contrast of minority and majority dialects, but most of the efforts to change pronunciation are equally divorced from reality.]

Almost everyone in the sample agreed that the speech of their high school English teachers was a remote and special dialect which had no utility for everyday life. A few looked rather wistfully back at the lost possibility of "improving" their own speech in those days, but hardly a word was raised in defense of the English teacher.

An African–American man gave me this view of the pressure exerted against working class children who adopt middle class standards of speech:

When I was small and going to school, if you talked that way, the kids would kid you, but we had a few kids that would do it, and we always kid them . . . There was a girl who was always very proper . . . so, she'd always walk up and say, "Pardon me." We'd all laugh, we knew it was correct, but we'd still laugh. Today, she end up successful.

One of the main factors which contribute support to the working class speech pattern of the city is its association with cultural norms of masculinity. A middle-aged Italian man who was raised in Massachusetts explained why he lost his outside speech pattern very quickly when he came to the city:

To me, I think [th-3] I got the [dh-3] New York speech. At one time, I had a good speech, and vocabulary too, when I first came from Massachusetts. But I lost it. When I first came here, to New York, they used to say, "You speak like a fairy – like they do in Massachusetts." When I kept going back to Massachusetts, they said, "Gee, you got the New York lingo."

The masculinity attributed to New York City working class speech is described directly in Steve K.'s account of a primitive painter who had abandoned his earlier career as an archaeologist, and with it, his middle class speech pattern.

If E. has consciously gone back to Brooklyn for his language – his reasons are not social, they're sexual. Because his vulgarity was sexual: he's aware of himself sexually, as a sexual person. His idea of success isn't the American idea of success – it's not the money . . . If he's gone back to Brooklyn, it's for the same reason, he wants to be there grappling.

Differences in linguistic attitudes of various sub-groups

Men vs. women As we compare the sexes' reports of linguistic attitudes, we find a series of significant differences. Only one man reported that he had not been recognized as a New Yorker when he left the city, but eleven out of sixteen women made this statement. Both men and women share the view that outsiders dislike New York speech, but women were more consistent in this respect. As we have seen, the sexes are opposed in their personal attitudes towards the speech of the city, with men favoring it slightly, and women heavily against. In the reports of efforts to change, women also show a more consistent tendency in this direction.[2] On every count, women show much greater linguistic insecurity than men. The masculine values associated with the working class speech pattern used by men do not seem to be counterbalanced by any similar positive values with which women endow their native speech pattern.

Class differences   We have noted that only a few New Yorkers reported that they had been identified as *not* being from New York, and all of these were middle class. The linguistic goal of most of the middle class speakers is to lose all resemblance to New Yorkers; almost all of them stated that they would be complimented if someone told them they did not sound like New Yorkers. There are also class differences in the perception of outsiders' views: three-quarters of the middle class respondents thought that out-of-towners disliked New York speech, but smaller percentages of working class respondents thought so, and even fewer from the lower class. In New Yorkers' attitudes towards their own speech, we find that the working class showed the smallest percentage of respondents who reacted negatively. This finding correlates with the results of the index of linguistic insecurity, where working class speakers showed the least linguistic insecurity. In the tendency to change one's language, again we find that the middle class led the others,[3] while the lower class showed the least effort in this direction.

We can summarize these findings by saying that the middle class shows the greatest linguistic insecurity, and the working class the least. But when we consider the recognition of norms imposed from above by the socioeconomic hierarchy, which we have called the social significance of the variables, the class groups are ranked in order: middle class highest, working class next, and lower class least. Despite their good knowledge of these unifying norms, the working class speakers show the least tendency to reject their native speech pattern in favor of the prestige pattern. The lower class

---

[2] There were three women who reported that their speech had "deteriorated" in their present surroundings, and who felt that they could do little about it. We may place these respondents among the ones who showed the most linguistic insecurity.

[3] The upper middle class respondents showed as great a tendency in this direction as the lower middle class. The reason is probably that most of the upper middle class had been required to take speech courses for the city school system and other academic work. The difference between these two groups is that the upper middle class respondents had usually made the changes earlier, and with more consistent results.

shows less ability to recognize middle class norms, and less confidence in the native speech pattern. Thus the lower class forms an outside group in two senses: 1) many lower class subjects fall outside the influence of the unifying norms which make New York City a single speech community; and 2) many seem to lack the cultural values which maintain the working class pattern of speech in opposition to massive pressure from above.

Ethnic differences We have already noted that Italians were almost unanimous in their report that they had been recognized as New Yorkers, while the Jews showed some exceptions to this rule. As far as our limited numbers of replies indicate, the Jews showed more tendency to think that outsiders disliked New York City speech, and to dislike it themselves. However, both groups showed equal dislike of their own speech, and equal effort to change their own speech.

The African–American informants, on the other hand, are separated from the rest of the sample population by more than a quantitative difference in trends. In almost all respects, the African–Americans reverse the pattern of attitudes shown by the others. The numbers of New York City AA respondents are too small to give us a very reliable report by themselves, but they seem to conform quite closely to the pattern shown by the out-of-town AA respondents, and the two sub-groups will be discussed together.

While most white New Yorkers thought that outsiders disliked New York City speech, almost all of the African–Americans who expressed an opinion thought that out-of-town residents did not dislike the speech of the city. While most white New Yorkers showed negative attitudes towards the New York speech pattern themselves, only three out of twenty AA respondents expressed this opinion, and nine reported that they liked it.

The sharpest opposition between AA and white occurred when the respondents were asked to compare their feelings about New York City speech with their feelings about southern speech. Eight white informants said they liked southern speech better, four were neutral, and only eight liked New York City speech better. As far as the African–Americans were concerned, none liked southern speech better than New York City speech.

A typical white attitude towards southern speech was expressed by a woman white collar worker:

[Southern speech?] I like the sound of it. A girl in the office comes from Kentucky, and people get me mixed up with her.

An old Jewish lady had grandchildren in Texas: "They sound adorable – I love to hear them talk."

An AA woman, fifty years old, born and raised in the Bronx, said this about southern speech:

When I was very young, and used to hear about some of the things that happened in the south, I had a physical reaction, as if my hair was standing on end . . . and if I would hear a white southerner talk, I was immediately alerted to danger, and so I never could see anything pleasant in it . . .

Although AA speakers share the white attitudes towards correctness, and are even more anxious to change their own speech, they reverse white attitudes towards the cultural values of New York City speech. For most AA speakers, any feature of speech associated with northern regional dialects (such as (r-1)), is considered good, cultivated, and educated usage, as opposed to southern dialect features, which are considered un-educated and "rough." But in the same way that many younger New Yorkers prefer the rough outlines of the working class dialect, many young AA speakers lean towards southern characteristics in their casual speech. Many older AA respondents told me that they were quite puzzled to find young AA people, raised in the north, of northern parents, talking "rough" just like southerners. For the older AA subjects, the sound of New York City English is a good sound, and the very qualities which make white New Yorkers shudder, seem perfectly acceptable northern speech to many African–Americans. Thus in the SR test, about half of the New York City AA respondents showed (oh)-positive response, and two-thirds of the out-of-town AA respondents did so. In the case of (æh), the majority showed negative response to (æh-2), but there was a much larger number of AA respondents who showed (æh)-positive response than white respondents.

Thus the African–Americans of New York City react primarily against features of southern English – the regional dialect speakers from the lower south form a negative reference group for them.[4] The white New Yorkers react against their own speech, and their image of it: to many of them, southern speech appears as attractively remote and not without glamor as compared to the everyday sound of New York City speech.

Age differences   In the limited data which we have available, there were no differences by age in the respondents' reports of being recognized as New Yorkers, nor in their views of outsiders' evaluations of New York City speech. The younger respondents did not seem to have absorbed as much negative feeling about New York City speech as the older subjects. Finally, the younger people reported more efforts to change their language; this may reflect the greater number who have been required to take speech courses at one time or another.

---

[4] This term is used in the technical sense developed by Robert K. Merton, *Social Theory and Social Structure* (1957), page 300.

The primary observation to be drawn from the data is that attitudes towards New York City speech have not changed radically in recent years, as attitudes towards (r) have. The strong feeling against the native speech pattern of the city seems to be shared by all age levels of the community.

The negative prestige of New York City speech

Preceding chapters have dealt with patterns of behavior which revealed negative evaluations of New York City speech. In this chapter, we have brought forward a relatively small body of evidence from conscious reactions which illustrate the same orientation. As far as language is concerned, New York City may be characterized as a sink of negative prestige. The reasons for this cultural bias fall outside of the province of the linguist. However, we can present some evidence to indicate that the pattern is not a new one, but originated well before the arrival of the immigrants from southern and eastern Europe whose descendents occupy the Lower East Side today.

In the earlier history of New York City, New England influence and New England immigration preceded the influx of Europeans. The prestige dialect which is reflected in the speech of cultivated Atlas informants shows heavy borrowings from eastern New England.[5] There has been a long-standing tendency for New Yorkers to borrow prestige dialects from other regions, rather than develop a prestige dialect of their own. In the current situation, we see that the New England influence has retreated, and in its place, a new prestige dialect has been borrowed from northern and midwestern speech patterns. We have seen that for most of our informants, the effort to escape identification as a New Yorker by one's own speech provides a motivating force for phonological shifts and changes.

The failure of the New York City speech pattern to expand into its own hinterland is another aspect of the process of negative evaluation which we have been studying. Most of the important dialect boundaries of the eastern United States fall along lines which are natural troughs in the network of communication.[6] The speech patterns of Boston, Philadelphia,

---

[5] Evidence for both migration patterns and dialect influence is provided in Frank (1948), Chapter I and *passim*.

[6] This statement is based upon the dialect boundaries shown in Kurath (1949), and Kurath and McDavid (1961), and calculations from traffic flow maps provided by the highway departments of all eastern states. An example of such a minimum line in the communication network is the line which divides northern speech from midland speech. It runs across Pennsylvania from east to west, separating the northern tier of counties from the rest. Even today, very few travelers go from Pittsburgh to Buffalo, or from Philadelphia to Schenectady, compared to the number that go from Albany to Buffalo, or from Philadelphia to Pittsburgh.

Richmond, and Charleston expanded throughout the eighteenth and nineteenth centuries, to a radius of 75 to 150 miles around each of these influential cities; today we find that the limits of dialect regions which surround them are located in the more or less remote mountainous areas that impede the flow of communication. But the New York City dialect area is an exception to this pattern, and a radical exception. The influence of New York City speech is confined to a narrow radius, hardly beyond the suburbs that form the "inner ring" of the city; and even today the speech pattern fails to expand as New Yorkers move in large numbers into the outer ring.[7] The dialect boundary which surrounds New York City is crossed every day by at least a million people: it has no relation to any minimal lines in the pattern of communication.

Thus we see that most other dialect boundaries of the eastern United States represent the limits of the expansion of prestige patterns, while the New York City boundary represents a circumscription of an area of negative prestige. This is not a recent pattern, but rather one which must date from at least the early part of the nineteenth century.

[In the study of the relation of lines of communication to dialect boundaries (Labov 1974), New York City proved to be an isolated exception to the general rule. For most of the eastern United States, dialect boundaries were found to be located in areas of minimum travel, as reflected in highway locations and average daily traffic flow. But it has remained fixed in a narrow belt around the city for over two centuries. Raven McDavid once pointed out that the location of this boundary coincides with the line of occupation of New York City by British troops in the war of 1812.

The limitation of New York City linguistic influence may be seen in the constriction of its special term for 'submarine sandwich.' While the specific Philadelphia term *hoagie* has spread to a number of areas (e.g., is well known in Florida), and New Orleans' *po' boy* has spread up the Mississippi and along the Gulf Coast, New York City *hero* is basically confined to the city itself.]

Summary

This chapter has concluded the study of the subjective evaluation of the speech of New York City. In this study, we have seen that subjective

---

[7] For the delineation of the terms *inner ring* and *outer ring*, see Edgar M. Hoover and Raymond Vernon, *Anatomy of a Metropolis* (1959). The process in which the New York pattern is rejected, and children follow the pattern of an *r*-pronouncing dialect despite the presence of a very large number of *r*-less New York City adults, may be seen in the area of Bergen County where I live. In the elementary schools of Closter, New Jersey, one can hardly find a single instance of an (r-0) form spoken by the children; among their parents, (r-0) forms predominate.

evaluation often precedes and out-runs changes in speech itself. Our view is that New York City is a single speech community, united by a common set of evaluative norms, though divergent in the application of these norms. The structures of fine stratification, sharp stratification, and ethnic diversity which have been found in the objective indexes of the variables, were correlated with a uniform pattern of subjective reactions. Changes in apparent time, however, appeared with greater clarity in subjective reactions to particular variables, than they did in the evidence of speech itself.

We have seen that the dominant theme in the subjective evaluation of speech by New Yorkers is a profound linguistic insecurity, which is connected with a long-standing pattern of negative prestige for New York City speech.

This chapter has also touched on some of the less obvious sources of pressure from below, which maintain the structure of stylistic and social variation, and even seem to be leading towards increased stratification of speech performance within the city. The preponderance of some stigmatized speech forms among male speakers, despite their clear recognition of the social significance assigned by pressure from above, reinforces the suggestion that masculinity is unconsciously attributed to the unmodified native speech pattern of the city, as it is used by men. Thus the pressure exerted in conformity with the socio-economic hierarchy is counterbalanced by a cultural tradition which we have described as pressure from below. The exact description of the covert values associated with the native speech pattern is one of the unfinished tasks which remain for future studies.

[In every discussion of the mechanism of linguistic change, there remains a certain tension between two types of explanation. One is purely mechanical, the effect of Bloomfield's principle of density. The other is social, following the demonstration of the social motivation of sound change in Martha's Vineyard in 1963.

It seems to be generally agreed that each act of face-to-face linguistic communication, particularly communication between peers, leads to some (mutual) adjustment. It follows that linguistic boundaries will fall along discontinuities in this network of communication, as indicated above. In general, people talk like those that they talk to most often. The logic of explanation requires that this mechanical effect take precedence over the effect of linguistic attitudes and social motivation, This principle is reinforced by the fact that those attitudes are widely divorced from the reality of linguistic production, as we have seen at many points in this volume. The resistance of the New York City vernacular to the incessant campaign against it, in the public domain and in private practice, must lead us to doubt the effect of social pressures from above. The question remains as to whether the vernacular system requires the explanatory force of "covert values" or the term used here, "pressure from below."

The answer seems to be "yes." New York City does not behave like other cities. On the positive side, we observe resistance of r-vocalization to the trend towards r-fulness elsewhere, which has successfully converted the coastal south, but not the everyday speech of New York. On the negative side, we observe that the largest city in the country, the acknowledged leader in fashion, finance, theater, and art, has had very little linguistic influence on the surrounding communities. With very few exceptions, New York phonology and lexicon are confined to the city limits and the New Jersey cities Weehawken, Hoboken, Jersey City and Newark. The linguistic attitudes associated with the speech of New York City have created both of these effects: stability and constriction, a stand-off that must be the result of two powerful and equally opposed forces. But because they are so powerful, we must not extrapolate too quickly to the situation of other cities. The study of social motivation must continually confront the fact that the mechanism of change lies well below the level of conscious perception, and each demonstration of the effect of such covert values will require the accumulation of empirical evidence.]

Part IV

Synthesis

14   The structure of the New York City vowel system

[In the years since SSENYC first appeared, many sociolinguistic studies have dealt with the social and stylistic stratification of linguistic variables, following the pattern of Chapters 7–10, with interesting and valuable results. The topic of this chapter, the relation of these variables to the linguistic system, has not been pursued with the same energy. One reason for the more limited influence of this chapter was the rather opaque method of presentation, involving a special vocabulary of "linear sets; first, second, third, and fourth order structures, variance analysis". The first part of this chapter has been rewritten in a more straightforward manner, but the rest of it needed less change. "Third order structures" emerge as two-dimensional arrays, and "fourth order structures" as three-dimensional arrays. The two different approaches to phonemic analysis – minimal pairs vs. distribution in spontaneous speech – have survived and are both well represented in the most recent approach to the problems raised here, in the *Atlas of North American English*.

Essentially, this chapter makes two contributions. It studies co-variation within the linguistic system in a manner that supports Martinet's approach to the functional economy of the linguistic system, with results parallel to the brilliant achievements of William Moulton in this area. Secondly, it puts together the various changes in real and apparent time to sketch out the mechanism of linguistic change, anticipating the paper with that title. It also introduces for the first time some statistical evaluation, which has been absent up to this point.

I was first tempted to eliminate the elaborate three-dimensional Figures 14.9, 14.11, and 14.12, designed to integrate social and stylistic sub-systems with the sub-sections of the New York City vowel system. But on reflection, I find that these intricate assemblies of triangles, pentagons, and rectangles, have considerable success in capturing the way in which patterns of style shifting and social stratification intersect with the phonemic system. They have been retained and might well have appeared on the front cover of this second edition. In any case, I hope that they will be reproduced as often as the simpler diagrams of Chapter 7.

The opening chapters of this study presented the problem of accounting for large-scale variation in the speech of New Yorkers. Inconsistencies and oscillations ranged over a large part of the phonology, to such an extent that it was difficult to construct a coherent system for the speech of most individuals. Thus we find Hubbell describing the use of /r/ by New Yorkers as "a pattern that might be described as the complete absence of any pattern . . . thoroughly haphazard . . . a matter of pure chance" (1950: p. 14).

In the previous studies, one can find many observations that reflect an awareness of the social significance of the variables that have been investigated here. Frank, Hubbell, and Bronstein are native New Yorkers, and they grew up with a native feeling for how these variables were used and who used them. However, they viewed such variation as deviations from the structure of speech which had to be eliminated or disregarded for a systematic presentation of linguistic patterns.

In the present work, this attitude is reversed. It conceives of the variation as an integral part of the structure of New York City speech.

In Chapters 7 through 10, the phonological variables were studied through average values of the indices. An individual's index for (æh) in a given style was averaged with those of other individuals for that style, giving a group index. The structures studied so far have been relations between average values rather than relations between the values used by single speakers. This procedure has given us reliable group indices for each style and social class that have in turn enabled us to analyze the differential behavior of many different variables.

This chapter will be concerned with the structural correlation among the variables and the distribution of those correlations in the population as a whole. This will incorporate the functional economy of the system with social variation, and show how many cognitive distinctions are maintained for each social class and style.

The New York City vowel system is displayed in Table 14.1, which indicates the maximum range of distinctions available to New Yorkers. The upper half shows the phonemes, with the variables studied here indicated in the parenthesis notation. The bottom half of the table illustrates the word classes involved.

The long and ingliding vowel system is composed of two sets of historical word classes. When /r/ is vocalized, it is a symmetrical set of six phonemes. When /r/ is fully constricted as a consonant, this sub-system shrinks to two main items: /æh/ in *bad, ban, pass, bath,* etc. and /oh/ in *law, bought, sawed, lawn*, etc.[1] Early in the history of New York City speech,

Table 14.1   *Vowel system of New York City*

			Short		Long			
			Upgliding				Ingliding	
			Front upgliding		Back upgliding			
	V		Vy		Vw		Vh	
nucleus	front	back	front	back	front	back	unrounded	rounded
high	i	u	iy		iw	uw	ih	uh
mid	e	ʌ	ey	oy	–	ow	(eh)	(oh)
low	æ	o	–	(ay)	–	(aw)	(æh)	ah

			Short		Long			
			Upgliding				Ingliding	
			Front upgliding		Back upgliding			
	V		Vy		Vw		Vh	
nucleus	front	back	front	back	front	back	unrounded	rounded
high	*bit*	*put*	*beat*		*dew*	*boot*	*beer*	*boor*
mid	*bet*	*but*	*bait*	*quoit*	–	*boat*	*bare*	*bore*/
								bought
low	*bæt*	*cot*	–	*bite*	–	*about*	*bad*	*bar*

/æh/ rose to mid position and merged with /eh/, so that *bad* and *bared,* were homonymous. In this chapter we will consider evidence that the new merged (æh) continued to rise and merged with /ih/ so that *bad, bared,* and *beard* were all homonyms, and that in parallel, (oh) rose to merge with /uh/ so that *more* and *moor* are homonyms.

In vernacular New York City speech, there is no distinction between /æh/ and /eh/: they are merged in the variable (æh). But in formal styles, the /æh/ class is often corrected to a low front position, longer and tenser than the

___
[1] Each of the other cells in the sub-system is represented by a marginal set that is too small to affect the functional economy of the system: /ih/ in *idea,* /eh/ in *yeah,* /uh/ in *skua.* The class of /ah/ in *father, palm, balm* is marginally opposed to /a/ in *bother, Pom(pom), bomb.*

lax class /æ/.[2] As the final section of this chapter will show, this creates a long and ingliding sub-system with six members.

Co-variation of (æh) and (oh)

In the preceding chapters, many parallels between the variables (æh) and (oh) were found.

1) Both follow a pattern of stylistic variation from high vowels in Style A to low vowels in Style D.
2) Both show a pattern of social variation in which the lower ranking classes use high, close vowels and the upper ranking classes use low, open vowels. The lower class participates in (æh) variation only.
3) Both show a cross-over pattern in Style D for the lower middle class, and a reversal of stylistic variation in Style D for the upper middle class.
4) Both variables are stratified more sharply by ethnic group than by social class indices. The Jews show higher (oh), the Italians higher (æh), and African–Americans show little participation in the social or stylistic variation of either.
5) Women show the most extreme values of both, using higher vowels than men in Style A, and lower vowels in Style D.
6) Both show distributions in apparent time which follow the model for linguistic change in progress, with (æh) showing a later stage. Ethnic groups show sharper differentiation in apparent time than class groups. The Jews show more increase of high (æh) by age level, and the Italians more increase of high (oh).
7) In the Subjective Reaction test, New Yorkers show negative subjective response to the high close variants of both (æh) and (oh); the greatest sensitivity is to (æh). The groups that use the highest vowels in casual speech show the most negative response to these forms in the SR test.
8) In the Self-evaluation test, New Yorkers report themselves as using lower vowels for both (æh) and (oh) than they actually do. Jews report lower vowels for both than Italians, while African–Americans report their usage accurately.
9) Out-of-towners do not show the patterns listed above for (æh) and (oh), neither in objective distribution or in subjective reactions.

Figure 14.1 shows the correlation of (æh) and (oh) in casual speech by sex and ethnic group for adult New York City informants. The rows and columns of Figure 14.1 were derived by beginning with the concentrations

---

[2] This hypercorrect tendency was found in Jewish students from New York City at Cornell University by C. K. Thomas, "Jewish Dialect and New York Dialect" (1932). Thomas reported many Jewish students using (æh-5) in *land, man, bad*.

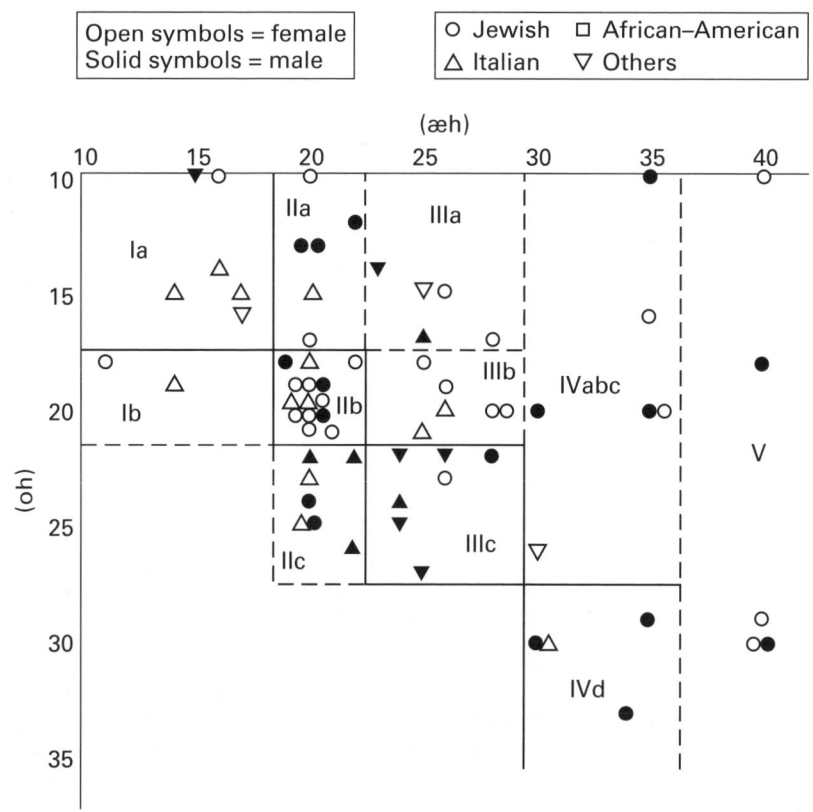

Figure 14.1   Co-variation of (æh) and (oh) in Style A for ALS New York City informants

that surround the (oh)-20, (æh)-20 point, and then drawing solid lines around those diagonally connected groups in which (æh) and (oh) have about the same values. The dotted lines extend these quadrangles to divide the field into five (æh) columns and four (oh) rows. The four cells in the lower left are empty, and the six in the upper right are so sparsely populated that they have been combined into larger cells. The central cells Ia, IIb, IIIc, IVd contain 45 percent of all the speakers; the parallel diagonals that are drawn to connect the corners of these central cells contain 83 percent of the speakers. There are no speakers below the diagonals, and only 12 above.

The correlation of (oh) and (æh) may be shown more precisely by tabulating (oh) values for each of the five (æh) columns in Figure 14.1.

Table 14.2   *Co-variation of* (æh) *and* (oh) *in Style A*

Column of Fig. 14.1	(oh) range	Mean (oh) index	N
I	10–17	16	8
II	18–21	19	27
III	23–28	20	18
IV	29–36	23	10
V	37–40	24	6

Table 14.2 shows a regular progression of increasing (oh) with increasing (æh). The r-correlation between (æh) and (oh) is not very large, .10, but it is significant at the p < .0001 level. We can learn more about the process by examining the progression from row to row.

For the first two rows, the values of the variables are in the same range; in the remaining three, the values of (æh) are increasingly greater than those of (oh). This reflects the influence of social correction on (æh). It has been shown that such correction goes far beyond the rate for (oh). The speakers whose values are located above the diagonals are almost all from the Jewish group. The tendency of some Jewish speakers to use low (æh) vowels in casual speech has been noted (footnote 2). It is possible that those in column V have this low vowel as part of their vernacular. But the speakers in column IV seem to have introduced (æh-4) into their speech pattern as a superposed variant, since they show sudden oscillations to (æh-2) in at least a quarter of the instances.

A number of Italian speakers are concentrated in cell Ia, those who use a preponderance of (oh-1) and (æh-1). Italian men are found mostly in the low central part of the main sequence, together with other Catholic men. Fourteen out of 18 in the three lowest cells – IIc, IIIc and IVd – are men. The tendency of men to use moderate values of both (æh) and (oh) is clearly displayed.

Co-variation of (ay) *and* (aw)

Chapter 10 found many parallels in the distribution of the interpersonal variables (ay) and (aw). Both follow a pattern of social variation with increasing nucleus-glide differentiation for the working class and the lower middle class. Both show comparable values for Jews and Italians, and lower values for men than women. Both show a pattern of distribution in apparent time that indicates early stages of a linguistic change in progress. Figures 14.2 and 14.3 display the co-variation of these two variables. The undifferentiated forms are located at lower right, and increasing

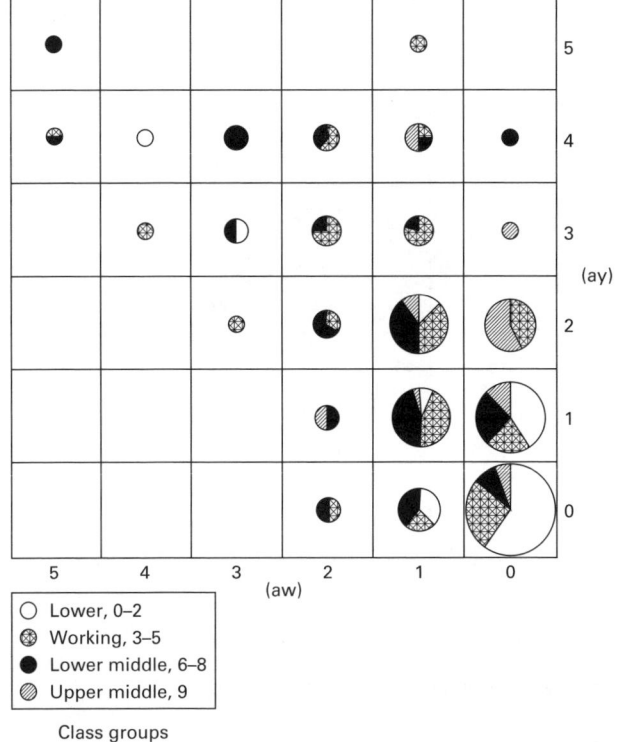

Figure 14.2   Co-variation of (ay) and (aw) by SEC for all New York City informants

nucleus-glide differentiation is shown in the sequence leading towards the upper left. All white New York City informants are included: regular ALS informants, children of ALS informants, and the television interviews.[3]

The area of the circles is proportional to the number of speakers in each cell. Thus the large circle at lower right represents 37 speakers with (ay)-00, (aw)-00, and the small circle at the upper left represents one person with (ay)-50, (aw)-50. In Figure14.2, the divisions within each circle indicate the percentage of each class group within each cell. It is evident from Figure 14.2 that lower class informants predominate among those with no differentiation of (ay) and (aw), while working class and lower middle class speakers show the greatest tendency towards extreme differentiation of

---

[3] African–Americans are not included in these figures, since the majority fall below the origin, as Chapter 10 indicated.

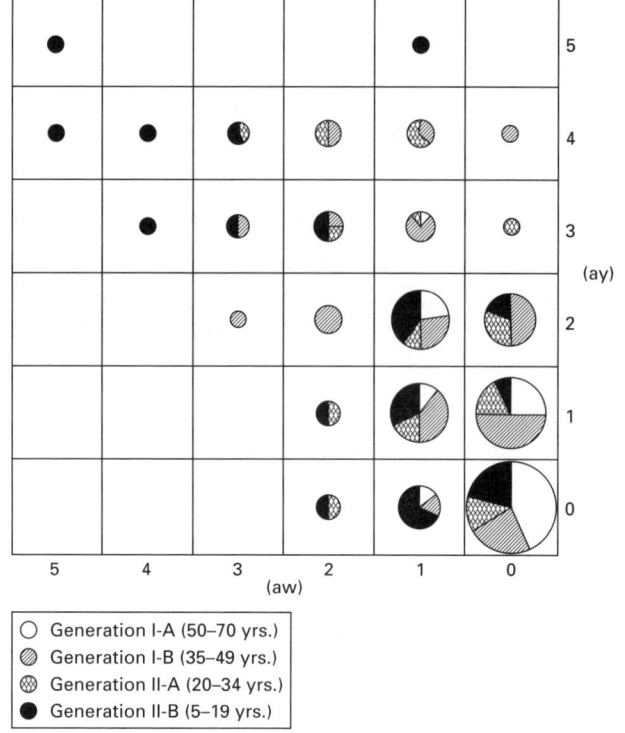

Figure 14.3   Co-variation of (ay) and (aw) by age for all New York City informants

these variables. The upper middle class does not treat the two variables symmetrically: the great majority of class 9 speakers are located in the three cells at the right which show some (ay) differentiation, but none for (aw).

In Figure 14.3, the same co-variation diagram is repeated showing the distribution of age groups within each cell. The half-generations tabulated in Table 9.15 are used here to give four age levels. The rapid development of nucleus-glide differentiation for the younger age levels is quite apparent in Figure 14.3: the oldest speakers are concentrated heavily at the lower right, and none appear in cells beyond (ay)-3 or (aw)-2. The four speakers at the upper left are all quite young; this portion of the diagram may therefore represent phonological habits not yet solidified, and these young people may retreat to less differentiated values of (ay) and (aw) as they grow older.

The co-variation of (ay) and (aw) may be shown in a numerical progression similar to that used for (æh) and (oh).

Table14.3   *Co-variation of* (ay) *and* (aw)

	(aw) levels					
	0	1	2	3	4	5
Average (ay)/10	0.7	1.8	2.3	3.2	3.5	5.0
N:	70	42	14	5	2	2

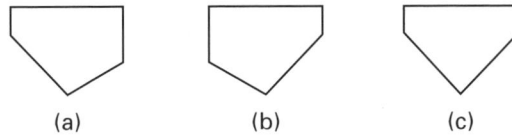

(a)   (b)   (c)

Figure 14.4

The *r*-correlation of these two variables is exceptionally high (.98); the (ay) values have been divided by 10 to show how they approximate the (aw) levels in each of the six categories shown. This correlation is not disturbed by correction of one member of the pair, as was seen for (æh) and (oh).]

Co-variation of (ah) *with* (oh)

There are some speakers in the community who use relatively high vowels for /oh/. Others use relatively high vowels for /æh/. A third group uses high vowels for both. Abstract representation of these quantitative relations within the pentagon may be shown in Figure 14.4.

If there is an internal economy of phonological space, which tends towards equal spacing of the phonemic units, then the loss of symmetry shown for the two left cases should produce a tendency towards a shift in the position of /ah/.

This possibility can be investigated from a structural point of view by data taken from the minimal pairs test and the reading of the standard text, where minimal pairs are inserted in close proximity. (". . . she told him to ask a subway guard. My god! I thought . . .). There is no evidence that the distribution of the phoneme /ah/ is sensitive to stylistic variation. On the contrary, if a person says [gɑ:d] for *god*, he will tend to say [gɑ:d] and [fɑ:ðə] and [hɑ:d] in any style. The only variation in the position of the vowel that we are likely to find will occur when (r-1) enters. In *r*-pronouncing systems, the low back vowel tends to be centered and slightly raised. In this case, the

Table 14.4

	without historical /r/	with historical /r/
ending in voiceless consonant	*dock, hot*, etc.	*dark, heart*, etc.
ending in voiced consonant	*god, hod*, etc.	*guard, hard*, etc.

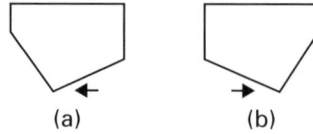

(a)   (b)

Figure 14.5

entire long and ingliding system itself tends to disintegrate, and therefore, only *r*-less patterns are relevant to this chapter.

Though the position of the vowel [ɑ] may be relatively constant, the distribution of the /ah/ phoneme is a variable (ah). There are a number of word classes which may be organized in different ways (see Table 14.4).

An analysis of the Linguistic Atlas records for New York City, carried out by Thomas Wetmore,[4] shows a distribution of the word groups given above which is similar in many ways to the distribution we find today. Words such as *barn* (or *guard*) occur with a speech sound which is both longer and further back than the one used in words such as *crop* or *pot*. The word class of *god* is intermediate in both respects, but overlaps the class of *crop* more than that of *barn*. (The class of *dark* is not shown in his records, but presumably follows that of *barn*.) In the present survey, *god* sometimes appears in this intermediate position, but more frequently it is found at either of the two extremes: in a center position, similar to *got* but longer, or in the low back position, identical to *guard*. The Atlas records did not record the full range of distributional variation which appears in the analysis to follow.

There are three principal (ah) options used in New York City, as shown in Table 14.5.

These options differ in the way in which the sub-classes of *hod, heart*, and *hard* contrast with the fixed point of the short vowel *hot*. In the back option I, all three classes contain back vowels. In the split option II, only *heart* and *hard* are back. And in the center option III, all three are center vowels.

If the pentagonal structure for the ingliding vowel system is correct, we would expect to find co-variation in phonological space of (oh) levels and

---

[4] Thomas H. Wetmore, *The Low-Central and Low-Back Vowels in the English of the Eastern United States* (1959).

Table 14.5

	Word class of:			
Option	*hot*	*hod*	*heart*	*hard*
I	center	back	back	back
II	center	center	back	back
III	center	center	center	center

the (ah) options. We can construct a 3 x 3 table by dividing the (oh) range
into three sections:

high	(oh)	< 20
mid	(oh)	20–25
low	(oh)	> 25

and correlate this with the three (ah) options. We would expect to find that
high (oh) is correlated with back (ah), mid (oh) with split (ah), and low (oh)
with center (ah).

As Chapter 8 showed, the (æh)-(oh) system of African–American speakers is completely diVerent from that of other New York City speakers, so
that evidence of these subjects is not relevant. There are also a few respondents who use a great deal of (r-1) and show no consistent (r-0) pattern in
Styles C and D. With these reservations, there remain seventy white New
York City ALS respondents who provide suYcient information to test the
hypothesis. The results are shown in Table 14.6 below.

It is immediately apparent from the modal values of Table 14.6 that the
hypothesis is sound: back (ah) is associated with high (oh); split (ah) with
mid (oh); and center (ah) with low (oh). Figure 14.6 illustrates this result
graphically by showing the percentage distribution of (oh) for each of the
three (ah) options.[5]

The pattern of Table 14.6 may represent a direct structural relation
between (oh) and (ah), such that the position of (ah) is a function of the
position of (oh). But there are two other possibilities: 1) that the correlation
is within the range of chance fluctuation; and 2) that both (ah) and (oh) are
determined by some third factor, logically or temporally anterior to both.

The possibility of chance fluctuation is tested by setting up a null hypothesis that the dimensions of height and backing of vowels are completely

---

[5] The demonstration given here is thus parallel to the presentation of the same principles in
dialect geography, given by W. Moulton, "Dialect Geography and the Concept of
Phonological Space"(1962). Moulton showed a close correlation between the phonetic
position of the low central phoneme and the phonetic positions of the mid phonemes in the
vowel systems of Swiss German dialects.

Table 14.6   *Co-variation of* (oh) *and* (ah) *for white NYC adults*

(oh) range	(ah) options			
	I [back]	II [split]	III [center]	Total
[high] < 20	13	13	4	30
[mid] 20–25	7	16	5	28
[low] > 25	1	4	7	12
	21	33	16	70

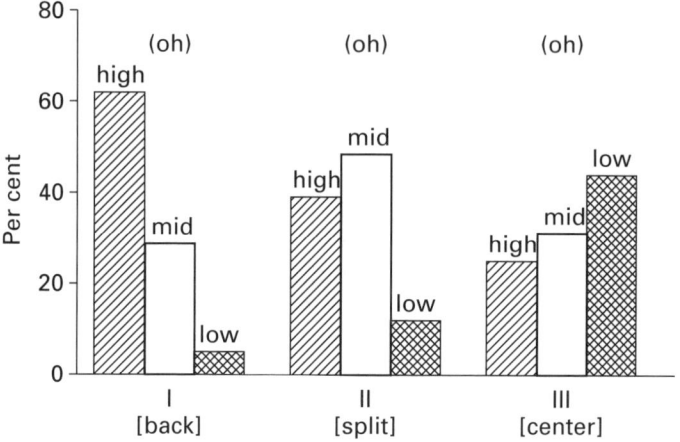

Figure 14.6   Percentage distribution of (oh) ranges for each (æh) option

independent. This hypothesis has a special interest because it is a general assumption behind most current feature theories of phonological structure. In this case, the probability of the null hypothesis is extremely low. This hypothesis would predict a distribution such as Table 14.7. The probability of Table 14.6 occurring as a chance fluctuation from a modal Table 14.7 is less than .001 ($\chi^2 = 20.1$).

The evidence for (oh) shows that this variable is a function of contextual style, of socio-economic class, age, sex, and ethnic membership of the speaker. To test the second possibility mentioned above, it is necessary to examine the correlation of (ah) with each of these factors. It was noted previously that (ah) shows no regular stylistic variation. Table 14.8 shows the distribution of the three (ah) options for various independent social variables: SEC, age, ethnic group, and sex.

Table 14.7   *Null hypothesis for independent variation of* (ah) *and* (oh)

(oh) range	(ah) options			
	I [back]	II [split]	III [center]	Total
[high] < 20	9	14	7	30
[mid] 20–25	8	13	7	28
[low] > 25	4	6	2	12
	21	33	16	70

Table 14.8   *Correlation of* (ah) *options with non-linguistic variables*

		Percentage distribution										
		SEC				Age		Ethnicity			Sex	
Option	Total	0–2	3–5	6–8	9	20–39	40–	J	I	Oth	M	W
I [back]	32	26	29	35	30	40	26	38	26	[17]	24	34
II [split]	45	21	58	53	60	45	48	47	53	[33]	48	46
III [center]	23	53	13	12	10	15	26	15	21	[50]	28	20
	100	100	100	100	100	100	100	100	100	100	100	100
[N:	70	19	24	17	10	20	50	45	19	6	29	41]

It appears that the center option is associated with the lowest SEC group and is more favored by the older age group (these two have been shown to be associated in our sample distribution: see Chapter 9). This fits in with the view to be developed later in this chapter that the backing of (ah) is a step in the evolution of the New York City vowel system. Further evidence along this line is provided by the asssociation of the back option with the younger group, and the split and center options with the older group over forty.

The tendency for men to use less Option I than women is not significant. There is also an ethnic difference in the use of the (ah) options. Jewish speakers are more apt to use Option I than Italian speakers, who show a strong tendency towards Option II.

The question to be answered is whether these correlations of (ah) with independent variables are secondary (products of the immediate dependence of (ah) on (oh)), or whether (ah) is directly associated with the social variables, just as (oh) is. This choice can be tested by isolating groups which are more homogeneous than the total sample of seventy, and examining the (ah)-(oh) correlation within these groups. For example, if the correlation of (ah) and (oh) is a product of the fact that Jews use high (oh) *and* back (ah),

Table 14.9   *Co-variation of* (ah) *and* (oh) *for Jewish NYC adults*

| | (ah) options | | | |
(oh) range	I [back]	II [split]	III [center]	Total
[high] < 20	9	9	2	20
[mid] 20–25	6	9	3	18
[low] > 25	0	3	4	7
	15	21	9	45

while Italians use low (oh) *and* center (ah), then the correlation would not appear among Jews themselves. (Or if we are dealing with a combined causal factor of several independent variables, the correlation would appear in a much weaker form when we examine the Jews alone.)

The correlation of (oh) and (ah) appears to be independent of these social variables, since it does reappear in each of the sub-groups. Table 14.9, for example, shows the distribution of (ah) and (oh) options for the forty-five Jewish respondents alone. Here we see a strong tendency towards the back option by those with high (oh); and on the other hand, the usual association of the center option with low (oh). Furthermore, the correlation of these two linguistic variables is not weakened by the selection of one ethnic group alone. The null hypothesis – that the observed correlation is due to chance – is almost as unlikely in this case; its probability is approximately .005. We can conclude that the relation of these two variables is virtually independent of both social and stylistic factors: the distribution of (ah) and (oh) positions is a purely internal product of the highly structured relationships within the phonological system.

Correlation of (æh), (oh) *and* (ah)

Empirical evidence has been presented to show that (æh) and (oh) are in fact parallel, as indicated in the pentagonal diagram, and we have just seen that the diagonal line from (ah) to (oh) represents an empirically confirmed functional relationship (equidistant spacing within the vowel system). If the pentagonal diagram is not an arbitrary fiction, the position of (ah) should be determined by *both* (æh) and (oh), and not just by one of the mid vowels.

We can investigate this possibility by relating (ah) options to the *relative* values of (æh) and (oh). If (æh) is higher than (oh), we would expect (ah) to remain in the center, while if (oh) is higher than (æh), we would expect that there is a stronger tendency for the backing of (ah). Figure 14.1 gives a

Table 14.10   *Co-variation of* (ah), (æh), *and* (oh)

(ah) options	Upper diagonal (oh) higher than (æh)	Lower diagonal (æh) higher or equal to (oh)	Total
I [back]	20	1	21
II [split]	17	16	33
III [center]	7	9	16
	44	26	70

graphic view of the relative positions of the mid vowels. The central diagonal represents that area where (æh) and (oh) are positively correlated, and the majority of respondents are located there. If we now divide the diagonal lengthwise with a line running from lower right to upper left, dividing the diagonal area exactly in half, these respondents will be divided into two categories. Those located in the upper diagonal have higher (oh) than (æh); those within the lower diagonal have (æh) higher than or equal to (oh) (since the diagonals are slightly skewed towards the high (oh) direction).

Table 14.10 examines the distribution of (ah) options for these two sets of informants. This is one of the most clear-cut correlations which have appeared in the course of this study in that the determination of Option I is almost complete. Of the twenty-one informants who use the back option, only one has (æh) higher than (oh). (This one subject is Emilio D., the case of status incongruence discussed at the end of Chapter 12.) χ^2 for this table is 15.0, and since we are dealing with only two degrees of freedom, the probability of the result being due to chance is well below the .001 level.

This result indicates that (æh) is indeed a controlling factor in the development of the low center vowel, and in particular on the occurrence of Option I. It is not difficult to understand why the combined effect of (æh) and (oh) has a greater effect in discriminating Option I than the other options: the backing of (ah) is the innovation in the system, and its development is encouraged by the bias towards high (oh). The center option is the original form, and is not a direct response to the raising of (æh) or of (oh). We are thus led to the inference that the differential raising of (oh) over (æh) was a cause of the backing of (ah).[6]

This result completes the empirical study of co-variation in the lower section of the pentagonal system of ingliding vowels. The data to be presented below will confirm the fact that continued raising of /æh/ and /oh/ has led to merger with the high vowels.

[6] Thus the behavior of /ah/ is completely consistent with the views of Martinet, cited above, in which the internal economy of the phonological system is the chief motivating agent in linguistic change. Moulton's study supports Martinet's position.

[It is worth re-emphasizing here the importance of William Moulton, whose brilliant work is the model for this study of co-variation. It is no accident that the determination of the phonetic position of (ah) was related here to the relative heights of (æh) and (oh), since Moulton's (1962) paper on "phonological space" anticipated this finding in the dialect geography of Swiss German vowels. In 1962, Moulton took leave of Princeton to teach a course on Dialect Geography at Columbia, and the notes I took were a constant reference throughout the writing of this chapter. No one has done more than Moulton to restore the intellectual prominence of dialect geography, and it is rewarding to find that the study of co-variation in an urban speech community can achieve the same results.]

Merger of /ih/ and /æh/, /uh/ and /oh/

The respondents who are shown in Figure 14.1 with (oh) values higher than (oh)-19, show an overlapping distribution of /oh/ and /uh/. For most of these speakers, particularly those at the very top of Figure 14.1, /oh/ and /uh/ are merged in casual speech. This is most certain for those ten respondents with (oh)-14 or lower.

In the speech of eight respondents to be found in (æh) Column I, the same considerations indicate a merger of /ih/ and /æh/. For example, a thirty-four year old Italian woman's speech shows the phonetic overlap of the two classes shown in Table 14.11.

When the phrase *girl's hair-cut* is isolated on the tape, and presented as *girl's hair*, it sounds like *girls here* to most people. The merger of /ih/ and /æh/ in this speaker is accompanied by a corresponding overlap of /uh/ and /oh/, with (oh-1) values that are clearly in the [ʊ] category. Correlated with these are Option I for /ah/, (ay-4) and (aw-3).[7]

The merger of the high and mid ingliding vowels is an unexpected finding of the ALS survey. Nowhere in the writings of Frank, Hubbell, or Bronstein is there any mention of such a merger. It may be that the development is so new that it did not exist at the time these reports were written. It is also possible that reliance on more formal styles did not allow the merger to appear. However, even in Style D the identity of high and mid ingliding vowels is reported by many informants.

There also are a number of speakers in (oh) level *b* who show a merger of /oh/ with lowered forms of /uh/. Only a few /uh/ forms occur in casual

---

[7] The informant described here is a fourth generation New Yorker, whose grandparents were brought to the United States from Italy when they were very young. She was raised in Brooklyn, and has worked as a bookkeeper in a bank, and as a checker in a supermarket. She graduated high school.

Table 14.11   *Overlap of /ih/ and /æh/ in the speech of Rose B., 34*

/ih/		(æh-1)	/æh/ (æh-2)	(æh-3)
years	[jɪ·z]		[jɛ··z]	
here		[he··ʳ]		
hair		[he··ʳ]		
there		[ðe··ʳ]	[ðɛᵊ]	
		[ðe·]		
yeah		[jeᵊ]		
man		[me˕ᵊn]		
fashion		[fe˕ᵊšən]		

speech, and for such a small number, it is difficult to say if we are merely witnessing a change of incidence (*poor, you're, sure* being used with /oh/) or the complete merger of phonemes distinct for other speakers. Similarly, there are speakers in (æh) Column II who use low forms of *here* and *beer* [usually as a centralized monophthong [bɨː][8] which coincides with the (æh-2) vowels.

The upgliding vowels

The list of upgliding vowels given by Hubbell may be shown as follows:

front-gliding			back-gliding	
/iy/ lead			/iw/ lewd	/uw/ food
/ey/ laid	/ʌy/ bird	/oy/ Lloyd		/ow/ load
	/ay/ lied		/aw/ loud	

Both /ay/ and /aw/ show nucleus-glide differentiation for many respondents. This cover term is more than a useful substitute for the expression "fronting and backing." The movement of the bottom elements of the structure shown above produces symmetrical structures.

A general upward compression of phonological space has led to this result. In the ingliding vowel system, the compression takes the form of a raising of /æh/ and /oh/ followed by a shift of /ah/ to a low back position. For the upgliding phonemes, the general upward contraction moves /aw/ up and front, while /ay/ and /oy/ move together to the same positions now held

---

[8] Many African–American respondents fall into this category, using fairly low mid vowels for both *cheer* and *chair*, *steer* and *stare*, *here* and *hair*. Kurath and McDavid (1961) show a merger of this type in many parts of the Lower South, especially in coastal South Carolina (Maps 34–41).

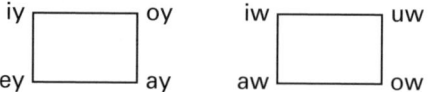

Figure 14.7   Upgliding subsystems

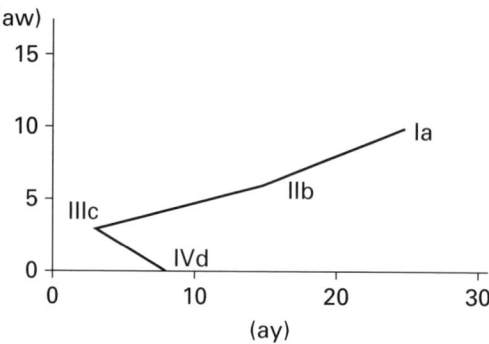

Figure 14.8   Co-variation of (ay) and (aw) for equivalent (æh)–(oh) groups

by /ah/ and /oh/. A general contraction of phonological space can cause radically different results in each sub-system, as the internal economy of the sub-system dictates. The holes in the patterns of the upgliding systems lead to the contrary and corresponding movements of the two low vowels /ay/ and /aw/. Figure 14.2 shows us that to the extent that /ay/ moves back, so /aw/ moves forward.

To prove that the movements of the three sub-systems are part of the same overall process, we must now establish a co-variation between (æh) and (oh), on the one hand, and (ay) and (aw) on the other. To do this, we first take the four quadrangles of Figure 14.1 in which (æh) and (oh) have approximately the same position: Ia, IIb, IIIc, and IVd. The thirty-one speakers in these quadrangles show a parallel movement of (æh) and (oh) vowels. If we now plot these quadrangles on a co-variation graph of average (ay) and (aw) values, we obtain Figure 14.8.

The lowest quadrangle, IVd, shows a deviation from the expected correlation for (ay), but with this exception, there is a regular progression of (ay) and (aw) values correlated with each other and with (æh) and (oh). The values of (ay) and (aw) for the entire field of (æh) and (oh) are shown in Table 14.12.

Table 14.12 shows fairly regular correlation between (ay) and the two variables (æh) and (oh). Column V does not fit the structure, but with this

Table 14.12   *Co-variation of* (ah) *and* (aw) *with* (æh) *and* (oh)

		(ay) values (æh)						(aw) values (æh)				
		I	II	III	IV	V		I	II	III	IV	V
[oh]	a	25	25	18			a	10	10	13		
	b	[30]	15	10	14	20	b	11	06	11	14	07
	c		10	3			c		05	03		
	d				8	13	d				00	00

exception, there is only one deviation from a regular progression of (ay) values with respect to (æh), and one in respect to (oh). However, the figures for (aw) values do not show a good correlation, except for the equal value cells Ia, IIb, IIIc, IVd. In this situation, we can see the effect of corrected (æh-2) in the large number of Jewish speakers in the shaded quadrangles IIa, IIIab, IVabc. Apparently the correction has become so deeply ingrained that these speakers use a great deal of (æh-4) even in casual speech.

While the parallel development of (æh) and (oh) is disturbed by this development, the parallel development of (ay) and (aw) is not. The latter variables have not yet become the subject of social correction. It is characteristic of changes imposed from above that they do not apply generally, to all of phonological space, but sporadically, and so disturb only parts of a phonological system. While New Yorkers are correcting one result of the general compression of phonological space, they are continuing to participate in other changes which may be subjected to correction at a later stage.

Vowel systems in formal styles

The systematic study of vowel systems in New York City must consider at least two distinct structures: one for casual speech, approximating the native speech pattern acquired in early years, and one for the most formal utterances, which approximate the subjective norms of the speaker in so far as he or she has attained some degree of motor control over them.[9]

The set of vowel phonemes which are derived from contrastive analysis of formal style do not form the same type of tightly integrated structure as that derived from study of casual speech. The direction and apparent goals of stylistic shifts may be uniform, but the degree of success in attaining

[9] The norms revealed in the SR test are more absolute than the ones shown here, but they are too far removed from the natural economy of the speech process. For example, African–Americans show the most uniformity in the evaluation of (r-1) as a prestige feature, but the least ability to use it in speech, even in Style D′.

these goals is irregular. The intermediate styles, careful speech and reading style, show intermediate stages of this style shift, with even less evidence of discrete clustering of speech sounds Figures 7.18, 7.19, 7.20, and 7.21 give this comparison in graphic form.

The formal structure of /r/-usage may be studied by examining three minimal pairs in Style D: *dock* vs. *dark*, *god* vs. *guard*, *source* vs. *sauce*.[10] Table 14.13 shows the percentages of New York informants who used (r-1) to distinguish all three pairs, one or two pairs, or none of the pairs, according to class, age, ethnic group, and sex.

Table 14.13 shows that the population falls into equal thirds as a whole by the use of /r/. As we have seen, no New Yorker is perfectly consistent in the use of /r/.[11] Table 14.13 repeats the end-point of stylistic and social variation which we have seen in Chapters 7 and 8. It shows us the futility of attempting to use contrastive analysis to isolate phonemic systems in such a complex environment as New York. Instead of the sharp, phonemic stratification of /r/ vs. no /r/ which we would like to see, there is the usual finegrained stratification of (r). For those variables which are subject to social pressure from above, the minimal pairs used in Style D will simply reflect the degree of the informant's recognition of these norms and his ability to meet them.

This limitation of minimal pairs applies to attempts to determine the status of /æh/ as well. The minimal pair (tin) *can* vs. (I) *can* was used in the questionnaire, but the results showed little relation to the native speech pattern of most respondents. Instead, we obtained a repetition of the informants' preference for (æh-4) in formal styles. It was even difficult to determine whether /æh/ was distinct from /æ/, since the effect of the identical spelling of the two forms tended to make informants equalize any small differences that might actually be used in formal speech. The best indication of the status of /æh/ could be found in the reading of the word list. The [æh-4] in this list was usually quite long for *bag*, quite short for *back*. The phonemic status of /æh/ thus depends upon the unpredictability of the long form in words ending in voiced fricatives [such as *jazz*, *razz*], and in polysyllables.

There are several areas in the phonemic system which can be illuminated by the analysis of contrast. One of these is the merger of *beer* and *bear* among working class and lower class respondents. Minimal pairs for these variables were inserted into the survey only at a late stage, but the results

---

[10] The pair *bared* vs. *bad* is excluded because it showed a radically different pattern. Many readers stumbled over this word, or interpreted it as *barred*, and the amount of (r-1) used is much higher than for the other pairs – a difference not consistently shown between this sub-class and the other sub-classes of (r) words in other styles.

[11] Only two New York respondents used all /r/ in Style C and Style D for *bared* vs. *bad* and the three sentences used in Table 14.3. In Styles A and B, these speakers were of course less consistent.

Table 14.13   *Use of /r/ to distinguish minimal pairs in Style D'*

| | Total | SEC | | | | Age | | Ethnic group | | | Sex | |
		0–1	2–5	6–8	9	20–39	40–	J	I	AA	M	W
% all /r/	33	00	25	52	43	32	32	34	30	10	29	33
% some /r/	33	67	25	37	33	32	37	39	24	30	22	40
% no /r/	34	33	50	11	25	36	32	27	47	60	50	27
	100	100	100	100	100	100	100	100	100	100	100	100
N:	74	6	36	19	12	28	41	38	17	10	29	45

Table 14.14   *Asymmetric contrast of /uw/ and /iw/*

	do	*dew*
/uw/	yes	no
/iw/	yes	yes

confirmed the view of phonemic merger presented above. Since low /ih/ and /uh/ have not become the objects of social correction, it is possible to use the analysis of contrast to determine merger for men who tend to use the lower form of the combined phoneme.[12]

A second area for effective contrastive analysis is the distinction between /iw/ and /uw/, as in *dew* and *do*, *yew* and *you*, *cartoon* and *soon*. Some New Yorkers make this distinction regularly; others use a semi-vowel for *dew* in Style D, as /dyu/ vs. /duw/; still others use /diw/ for both *do* and *dew* (in which the first element of the diphthong is an intermediate form, semi-rounded, semi-fronted). However, almost all New Yorkers agree that one can say "I do," as either /ay diw/ or /ay duw/, but that one cannot say /duw/ for "dew on the grass." The latter form makes most New Yorkers laugh, because the form /duw/ can only be *do*, which in this context means excrement. This asymmetric relation is seen in Table 14.14.

---

[12] In one interview with a young couple, both teachers in the New York City schools, I was able to document the merger of both sets of high and mid vowels. The husband had difficulty in passing the New York City oral English examination which is required for teachers; his wife, an English teacher in a junior high school, had coached him. The greatest difficulty she had was to teach him to distinguish *beer* and *bear*, etc. He has restored this distinction in formal style, but still merges /uh/ and /oh/ even in Style D. His wife told of an experience in teaching the meaning of the word *homonym* to her class, in which one girl volunteered the pair *sure* and *shore*; after twenty minutes of argument, the teacher had still failed to convince her of her error.

In other words, the word class which permits /iw/ is only a sub-set of the word class which permits /uw/. Despite this limitation in contrast, /iw/ must be considered a phoneme for most New Yorkers, on the basis of the irreducible contrast which does exist.

Despite the fact that some parts of the vowel system can be investigated successfully by the analysis of contrast, it is not possible to show a coherent structure for casual or formal speech styles through this method. For those phonemes which are *not* involved in socially significant variation, the study of contrast will show discrete structure: for those which are involved in a regular pattern of social and stylistic variation, the use of minimal pairs will only repeat one section of the variable structures shown in Chapters 7–9. It is necessary to find some measure of formal behavior in which large groups of New Yorkers will agree, and thus show discrete structures comparable to those of casual speech.

The structure of stylistic patterns

A more satisfactory approach to the formal structure of New York City English is to study the patterns of stylistic variation which the informants follow. Table 14.15 summarizes the information on stylistic variation by showing the percentages of individuals who follow patterns in a given direction. This table has no relation to absolute values of the variables, but only to the relations between contextual styles.

In the figures shown for Table 14.15, the African–American group is not included in any percentages except that for the AA ethnic group. The first line shows the percentage of those who follow the pattern of stylistic variation from less (r-1) to more (r-1) with increasingly formal styles. There is only one point where the population deviates from the general high level of agreement on this point: the lower middle class shows 100%[13] while the lower class shows only 50%. In the case of (æh), an even higher percentage of respondents favor a shift from high to low vowels for this variable. There are three points at which the 75–85% level of consistency varies: the younger speakers show complete consistency; the Italians, who show the highest values in casual speech, are also completely consistent in their stylistic shift; and the African–Americans show a very low level of participation in this stylistic pattern.

The fact that the AA group shows only 33% following the pattern of (æh) variation does not mean that a majority of these respondents follow the reverse pattern. Only one of the twelve AA informants could be said to reverse the (æh) pattern; the balance showed no variation, or an irregularly fluctuating pattern. This applies equally to other groups and other variants: only a very few respondents show a pattern which reverses the one shown in Table 14.15.

Table 14.15   *Percentage of respondents following patterns of stylistic variation for* (æh), (oh), *and* (r)

Variable pattern	Total	SEC				Age		Ethnic group			Sex	
		0–2	3–5	6–8	9	20–39	40–	J	I	AA	M	W
(r-0)→(r-1)	75	50	76	100	70	70	77	76	70	84	64	82
(æh-2)→(æh-4)	83	75	87	85	80	100	77	78	100	33	85	83
(oh-2)→(oh-4)	65	53	59	77	80	84	58	68	56	33	65	67

Finally, the (oh) variable shows a somewhat lower level of consistency in stylistic variation. As we would expect, the lower class shows the least consistency, and the middle class the most. The fact that younger speakers show much more tendency to follow this pattern is consistent with the hypothesis that social correction of (oh) has begun only recently. Finally, we see that the African–Americans show no participation in this pattern, the Italians a moderate amount, and the Jews the most. Once again, a pattern is followed in which the highest exponent of a stigmatized form shows the greatest correction.

Thus Table 14.15 sums up most of the trends that have been studied before, but indicates the very high regularity of behavior in formal styles in a way that the minimal pairs of contrastive analysis cannot show.

The three-dimensional structure of stylistic variation

The three-dimensional vowel structure of stylistic variation is shown as Figure 14.9. Only the ingliding phonemes are shown here, since the upgliding phonemes are not sensitive to stylistic variation.

---

[13] The converse of this absolute regularity appears in the group of respondents who used *no* (r-1) in Style D'. There are twenty-one such informants, and none of them are in the lower middle class. Table 14.16 shows that this type of speech behavior occurs primarily in the oldest and youngest respondents of the lower class and working class.

Table 14.16   *Percentage of* (r)-00 *speakers in Style D' by age and class*

Age	SEC				N:			
	0–1	2–5	6–8	9				
20–39	67	75	00	20	3	17	11	5
40–49	20	18	00	25	5	17	9	4
50–59	33	14	00	33	3	7	1	3
60–	71	50	–	–	8	4	–	–

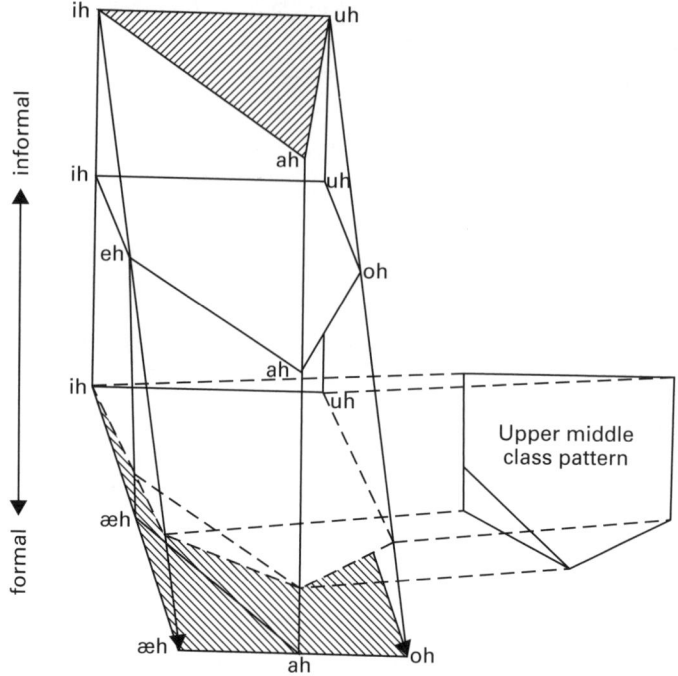

Figure 14.9   Structure of New York City vowel system: stylistic variation

The upper part of Figure 14.9 shows the two-dimensional structures used by New Yorkers in less formal situations. The triangle is the simplest pattern, with merged high and mid ingliding vowels. This is the system used by many younger informants, and by a great many middle-aged informants as well, in the most informal contexts. Thus the highest plane is related to the one underneath it by a development in apparent time, as well as a relation on the axis of stylistic variation. The lower part of the diagram indicates the *direction* of change in the more formal contexts, as indicated by the heavy arrows leading from /ih/ to /eh/ to /æh/, and from /uh/ to /oh/ to lower form of /oh/. The structure used in formal contexts is shown as a hypercorrect form of the prestige pattern, based primarily upon upper middle class usage. This prestige pattern is shown with an /æh/ phoneme at the position of (æh-3). It is true that there are some upper middle class informants in our sample who use a low /æh/ at (æh-4), and a similar form may be heard on radio and television. However, the most common form of upper middle class (and upper class) speech as shown in Hubbell's records, and our own, is (æh-3). Similarly, the upper middle class /oh/ is fairly stable at (oh-3).

The lowest plane of Figure 14.9 indicates that the direction of stylistic variation followed by New Yorkers frequently carries them beyond the level of the prestige pattern, to the form shown as the lowest plane. This represents the very low, tense, fronted form of /æh/, and the more or less irregular mixture of (oh-3) and (oh-5), which have been observed in Style D for (æh) and (oh) in Chapters 7 and 8. It should be noted that Figure 14.9 reflects the organization of the ingliding phonemes without considering the radical alteration in their status which is introduced through a frequent use of (r-1). Only for class 9 has the effect of *r*-pronunciation penetrated so deeply into the structure of the vowels that the system of phonemes shown here has been seriously weakened.

The totals of Table 14.15 show that 65 to 83 percent of the informants participate in this structure as they adjust their speech to more formal styles. Not everyone uses the entire range of variation: some never rise past the middle level, and others go little below that. A larger number follow the straight line that connects (æh-1) with (æh-4) than those that follow the line from (oh-1) to (oh-5). Women use a larger range of this structure than men.

The odd rectangular shape of the most formal plane indicates the relative lack of stability in this part of the structure. The stringent phonological economy which dominates the linguistic developments on the most informal plane does not operate on the most formal level, where the maximum degree of conscious attention is given to language. The weak position of /æh/ in the lower left has been noted. The odd mixture of long and short allophones which makes up the /oh/ phoneme in the lower right is another example of the instability of the formal plane. The most highly structured aspects of Figure 14.9 are: 1)the plane of casual speech; 2) the *direction* of shift of objective speech patterns as shown in Table 14.15 and the vertical axes of Figure 14.9.

The plane of casual speech is determined for each individual not by the highest plane shown here, but by the vertical position on the structure of Figure 14.9 which an individual assumes in his casual speech. Younger speakers from the central groups assume the highest position; the oldest speakers are found at a relatively low position, near the center, in the structure of their casual speech. Obviously a single diagram such as Figure 14.9 is too general to place most individuals on it with any degree of predictability.

Structural relations of ethnic groups   The relations of Jews and Italians can best be seen as an aspect of the development of the native speech pattern in real time.

The parallel asymmetries of the Jewish and Italian ingliding vowel systems has begun to disappear for the youngest speakers, as indicated by the merger into the triangular structure at the bottom of Figure 14.10.

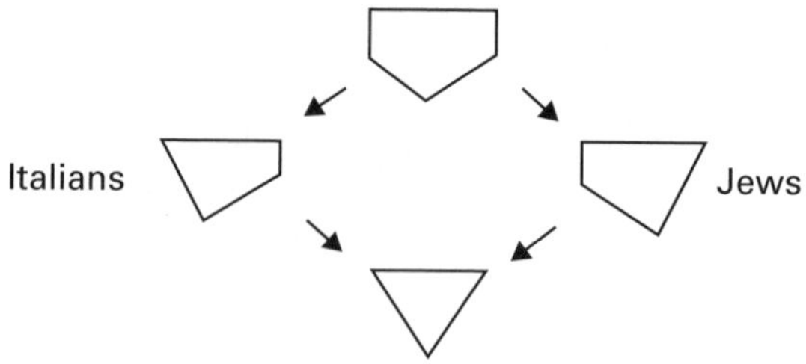

Figure 14.10

Class stratification of the New York City vowel system

The three-dimensional structure of stylistic variation shown in Figure 14.9 is of course not generally uniform for all classes. It is repeated for each class in progressively different forms. Since the class structure of New York City is now well established in our results, we need not hesitate to refer to this recurrent pattern.

Figure 14.11 displays the three-dimensional structure of the ingliding vowel systems, and the two-dimensional structures of the upgliding vowel systems. Just as in Figure 14.9, a certain amount of temporal development is built into this pattern, for the plane shown as the highest level of informality is actually the one used primarily by the younger informants; most informants over forty do not show the mergers of mid and high vowels indicated on this plane.

In Figure 14.11, the structure of New York City's vowel system is seen as forming three distinct sub-types, as determined by the plane of casual speech. The lower class shows a lowered system of ingliding vowels, with the high vowels merging with the mid vowels in mid position. The difference between this triangular structure, and that shown for the central groups, is not an isolated phonetic fact, since the mid position of /oh/ is reflected in the low position of /oy/ (and /ay/) in the upgliding system.

Both the working class and the lower middle class show a general tendency towards a raising of the mid vowels in casual speech. Although only a minority of the speakers may actually show a complete merger, this structural diagram indicates the general direction of stylistic and temporal variation in which the systems seem to be moving. The only structural difference shown here between the working class and the lower middle class is the low position of /oh/ for the lower middle class in the most formal style. The mixture of variants which occurs in this position undoubtedly

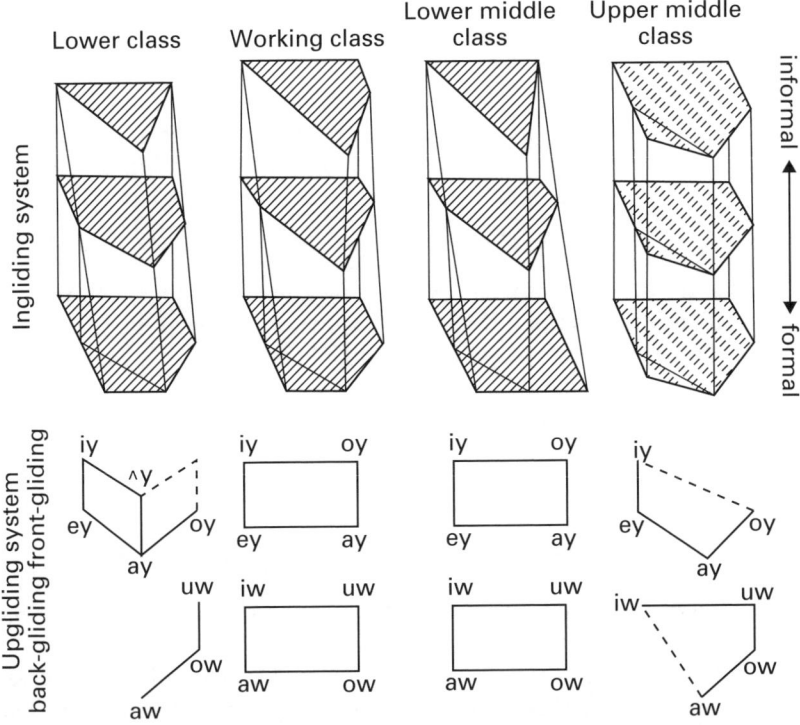

Figure 14.11   Three-dimensional structure of New York City vowel system: stylistic variation for four class groups

contains elements which most properly belong with the short vowels, and others which belong with the ingliding vowels.

In Figure 14.9, the relations of the upper middle class prestige pattern to the speech of most New Yorkers were indicated by projecting its outlines onto the formal plane of speech. In Figure 14.11, the upper middle class pattern is shown as only one of four patterns; the relationship to the speech of other classes is the same as that shown in Figure 14.9, as may be seen by comparing the three and four lowest planes in Figure 14.11.

The upper middle class is shown without any structural changes in stylistic variation. The entire system of ingliding vowels, however, is shown in dotted lines since for most of the younger speakers, it has been reduced to a series of allophones of short vowels before /r/.

Figure 14.11 reflects generally the detailed style stratification diagrams for (æh) and (oh), Figures 7.18 and 7.20. If one traces the locus of the /æh/ phonemes in the twelve positions shown here, one will reproduce the general outlines of Figure 7.18; similarly, the loci of /oh/ shown here reproduce the outline of Figure 7.20.

The patterns for the upgliding phonemes show even more clearly that the two center classes represent the continued evolution of the traditional New York City vowel system. The lower class represents the closest approximation to the older system, with the beginnings of evolution in a contrary direction; and the upper middle class shows the reversal of the evolution of the traditional system as a result of social correction from above and the introduction of /r/.

The lower class retains the center upgliding phoneme /ʌy/ in this diagram. The low positions of /ay/ and /oy/ match the low positions of /ah/ and /oh/ in the ingliding system. On the other hand, the central classes show the tendency to regularize the upgliding systems, following the general direction of the raising of the mid vowels.

The outlines of the style stratification diagrams for (oh) and (æh) can be traced on Figure 14.11. Similarly, the outlines of class stratification diagrams can be traced in a three-dimensional structure in which the usage of the various social classes are seen as horizontal levels in a two-dimensional structure which is repeated for various styles. Figure 14.12 shows such a representation for Style A and for Style D. Here the axis of stylistic variation is shown as the relationship between the two structures, while the axis of social variation is represented by the contrast of the successive planes. The outlines of the class stratification diagrams for (æh) and (oh) may be traced in the left and right forward edges of the structure. The curvilinear pattern appears here as an inward bend in casual speech, and an outward bulge in formal style.

Developments of the three-dimensional structure in real time

The three-dimensional structure shown in Figures 14.11 and 14.12 is of course the result of a long development in time, which in turn constitutes a four-dimensional structure. However, we do not have the data to show the details of the entire development, and it would be quite speculative to attempt such a complex description. We can make some fairly well-founded statements about the order of the most important developments in the phonological system which have led to the present structure. The basis for most of this discussion is the interpretation of stratification in apparent time, as presented in Chapters 9 and 10. The records of the Linguistic Atlas and Hubbell's study are utilized as well, within the limitations set by the sampling methods used. The basis for the earliest stage of the casual speech pattern is provided by Babbitt, whose observations were made just prior to the time when the oldest ALS informants were growing up in the city. It was pointed out in Chapter 2 that Babbitt's general approach to the language of

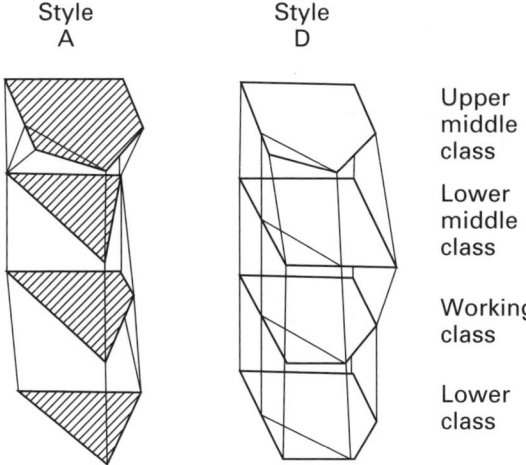

Figure 14.12   Three-dimensional structure of the New York City vowel system: social variation for two stylistic levels

the city seemed to be more realistic than the other studies reviewed: he alone of the previous investigators listened to the speech of the general population, rather than a small minority.

I   *Evolution of the pattern of casual speech*   Figure 14.13 is a schematic representation of the development of the casual speech pattern which has led to the structure portrayed in Figures 14.11 and 14.12.

Stage 1   The four diagrams at the top of Figure 14.13 show the earliest system of vowels for which we have evidence. It is based primarily upon Babbitt's evidence, which on one important point, carries us back even further than 1896. In regard to /æh/, Babbitt writes:

Among the older New Yorkers this very high vowel is used in all the set of words pronounced in New England with the broad vowel [*ask, half, pass,* etc.], and is really higher in these words than in *man, cab,* etc. But this distinction is now lost and the general vowel has quite overtaken the special one [*hend,* hand, *keb,* cab, *dens,* dance, *helf past,* half past].

For the earliest stage of New York City speech, Figure 14.13 therefore shows a vowel /æh/ in casual speech distinct from /eh/, and the first change noted is the raising of /æh/ to merge with /eh/. Babbitt had a sure instinct for the phonemic principle, which was often lacking in later investigators; he continually looks for evidence of contrast between words, rather than attempting to fix an absolute phonetic value.

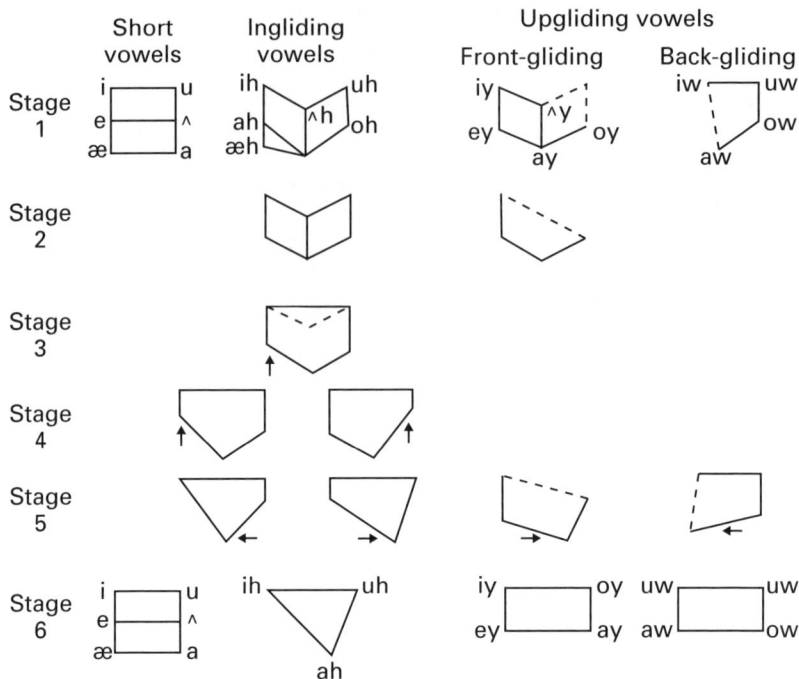

Figure 14.13   Stages in the evolution of the New York City vowel system in casual speech: working class and lower middle class

On such firm evidence, we can be sure that the system shown in Stage 1 is *r*-less. Babbitt reports that *father* is homonymous with *farther*, *lodge* with *large*, *God* with *guard*, that *four* and *war* rhyme with law. Babbitt's evidence supports the analysis of the Linguistic Atlas, in that a glide /ə/ is reported only after [i, e, æ, u] but not after [ɑ, ɔ, ə]. In the case of [ɔ] Babbitt implies that a glide is sometimes heard, but not always, in which case *war* and *four* rhyme with *law*.

The evidence of Babbitt points to a comparatively low position for /oh/, lower than (oh-3): "The quality of the vowel [in ɔr] tends . . . to be higher in many individuals than the ɔ when not followed by *r*."

Babbitt leaves the question of /ʌh/ somewhat in doubt. He does not mention the word class of *her, were* directly. He does take up the question of /ʌy/ in great detail, as quoted in Chapter 9, and, in the course of his discussion, mentions that he used to illustrate the sound of French *feuille* by having a New York boy pronounce *fir*. Since every example given for /ʌy/ is a word in which historical /r/ is followed by a consonant (*curtain, first, word, girl, world, incontrovertible, Stern*) it is possible that Babbitt meant *fir* as the first part of *first.* In that case, all other indications point to /ʌh/ as the vowel in *her, were,* etc.

The evidence that Babbitt gives for /ʌy/ as the uniform New York City pronunciation in *first,* etc. is completely convincing. The entire front-gliding system seems to have been lower and more central than the present one, since Babbitt reports that /iy/ is not very high, that /ey/ begins low (and centralized), that the beginning of /ay/ varies from [ə] to [a] to [ɒ] and that /oy/ is very close to /ay/. In the back-gliding system, Babbitt reports a very firm position for /iw/: "*iu* . . . is the usual American *iu* [not *ju*], with stress on the first component."

Stage 2   The earliest change recorded is that noted by Babbitt: a continued raising of /eh/ so that *man, cab* are mid vowels, as well as *ask, half, bath.*

The stigmatization of /ʌy/ began quite early; Babbitt records the fact that the comic newspapers had ridiculed it as "the Bowery dialect," using the spelling "goil," "woild." The developments in apparent time as shown in our survey confirm the early date of the stigmatization of /ʌy/. The weakening of this element may have had repercussions in the ingliding system; if a corresponding diphthong /ʌh/ existed, its position was less secure as a result of the disappearance of /ʌy/.

Stage 3   The weakening of /ʌh/, indicated here by the use of dotted lines, is a process that is now continuing, and cannot be placed in any firm sequence with the other changes. However, it is not improbable that the disappearance of these phonemes in the speech of many people was a precondition for further raisings and mergers in the ingliding system.

Stage 4   The alternate use of high /æh/ and high /oh/ by Italians and Jews has been documented in this study in several places.

Stage 5   The result of continued raising of /æh/ and /oh/ is seen in a merger of /ih/ and /æh/ on the one hand, and /uh/ and /oh/ on the other. The internal economy of phonological space is then reflected in forces exerted upon the other members of the system; the lower member of the /æh/-/oh/ pair begins to move up, and the position of /ah/ shows a corresponding adjustment.

Similar forces operate upon the upgliding vowels, producing a nucleus-glide differentiation of /ay/ and /aw/ which contributes to the symmetry of the respective sub-systems.

Stage 6   This stage shows the vowel structure found in the speech of many younger members of the working class and lower middle class. Merger of both sets of high and mid vowels eliminates much of the contrast between Jews and Italians. In the extreme form shown here, complete symmetry is attained, but at the cost of considerable differentiation from the prestige pattern.

II   *Reversal of the evolution of the system under social pressure from above*   As a consequence of the developments described in the previous section, a whole set of retrograde movements in formal styles may be documented, responding to social correction from above.

a) The stigmatization of /ʌy/ was listed above as an important step in the evolution of the system; at the same time, it also represents one of the most powerful examples of the influence of social correction.

b) A social reaction against (æh-2) is shown in the speech of all but the oldest informants. Retrograde movement of (æh) coincides with the direction of imitation of the earlier prestige forms, aiming at (æh-5) of New England. Evidence has been cited from Thomas to indicate that (æh-5) in the careful speech of Jewish college students was common in 1932.

c) The introduction of /r/ into the New York City system as a dominant element in the prestige dialect may certainly be traced in the 1930s, but apparently made a great step forward in the years coinciding with World War II.[14] The chief consequences of this step are:

1) Reduction of the ingliding vowel system to the status of variants of the short vowels plus /r/.

2) Reversal of the backing of /ay/, fronting of /aw/, backing of /ah/, raising of /æh/, raising of /oh/, and movement of all of these to more central positions.

---

[14] The highly specific nature of this historical development invites us to explore the social changes which may be correlated with the introduction of /r/ as a prestige feature. Changes have certainly taken place within the institutional structures: a generation of speech teachers who followed the British standard seems to have passed away, and schoolteachers with midwestern patterns have appeared in the city with increasing frequency. This is an area of study which deserves a careful, independent investigation. It should also be considered that the general broadening of the social horizon which accompanied the induction of millions of New York City men into the armed forces must have affected the evaluation of speech patterns.

   We might argue plausibly that such extensive exposure to other *r*-pronouncing dialects was an important factor in the shift of prestige dialects in New York City. However, the significance of such "external" events appears less certain when we consider that women, not men, show the greatest tendency to adopt /r/; that many men report that their New York City speech was not ridiculed in the armed services, while vacationers and tourists do report such reactions; and that the overall change appears as an increase in stratification rather than an increase in the use of /r/. It is possible that the shift in the schools, and in the broadcast media, may best be considered as symptomatic of a larger process of urban stratification, accelerated by the long-standing negative prestige of New York City speech.

   [For a view attributing the importation of [r] to racism and anti-semitism, see Bonfiglio (2002).]

3) Elimination of /ʌy/ entirely, and a rapid reduction in the frequency of /ʌh/. Thus the introduction of /r/ is apparently correlated with a reversal of every one of the changes shown under I above.

III   *Deviation of the lower class*   The view of New York City speech in Figures 14.11 and 14.12 indicated that lower class speech is not following the same tendencies seen in the main body of the working class and lower middle class. The most important developments that have been noted are the relatively low positions of /æh/ and /oh/; when a merger with /ih/ and /uh/ takes place, it is at a low mid position, rather than a high position such as [ɪːə] or [ʊːə]. This tendency coincides with the usage of many young African–American people who have not followed the northern, New York pattern, but rather show relatively strong southern influence in their speech. The implication of AA influence is even stronger when we observe a tendency towards the fronting of /ay/ in white and Puerto Rican speakers, rather than a backing. This is a characteristic of AA speech which is strongest where southern influence is the strongest.

The questions which are raised by this tendency cannot be explored fully within the compass of the present study. However, they do represent one of the main lines of further inquiry that are suggested by the findings of this study, and which may be followed with the techniques developed here.

The mechanism of linguistic change

The evolution of the New York City vowel system, as outlined in the previous section, displays a wide variety of phonological shifts, and mergers. Many of the developments displayed here illustrate a strong tendency towards symmetry and the equalization of distances in phonological space. They give strong empirical confirmation to the analysis of linguistic change set forth by Martinet, in *Economie des changements phonétiques*. However, there is much more to the mechanism of linguistic change than pressures between phonemes as functional units of cognitive communication. In stage 3 of Figure 14.13, the system was quite symmetrical. No arguments for further symmetry, holes in the pattern, or front vs. back asymmetry, explain the continued raising of /æh/ in stage 4.

In the present study, we have documented the role of ethnic groups and social class groups in the type of development shown in stage 4 and beyond. In the absence of any reasonable substratum effect, the unconscious tendency of speakers to increase the measure of their identification with their immediate group may be stated as the probable mechanism of these changes. In the study of /ay/ and /aw/ on Martha's Vineyard, it was found that continued hypercorrection of such linguistic tokens of group identification was the mechanism for a change that lasted over several generations. So far in the present study, I have used the term hypercorrection to describe the lower middle class tendency to outdo the upper middle class in the use of prestige features in formal styles. Hypercorrection can operate in a more general sense as the mechanism of change in response to pressures from below.

We have seen a great deal of evidence for the fact that linguistic behavior is highly normative, or goal directed. The need for a target, a set of norms, is evident in the casual speech of our informants as well as in their formal styles. In cognitive communication, such norms are provided by a stable set of functional units. But the units by means of which expressive and other non-cognitive functions of language are carried out, are not so discrete. In aiming at such targets, it is only natural that the speaker will go beyond them. Driven by the fear of not conforming, and the need to establish oneself as an authentic member of one's immediate group, the members of the speech community can gradually push these labile norms further and further in the direction that they first began to move. Pressures of this sort can be exerted on individual words; or upon entire phonemes; or most likely, series or orders of phonemes. Pressure can also be exerted upon the whole structure of phonological space, compressing it, expanding it, or altering its dimensions in a systematic way that affects the status of all phonemes.

Such pressures upon phonological space take place in the form of an articulatory gesture, or in less dynamic terms, a phonological posture. The developments on Martha's Vineyard revealed a general constriction of phonological space from all sides, producing a centralization of vowels in all sectors of the system. In New York City, the pressures upon phonological space cannot be expressed simply in terms of raising, backing, or fronting. There is also an element of rounding, lengthening, and lip-spreading, as seen in the cases of /oh/, /ah/, and /æh/. The overall tendency may best be described as centrifugal, in which all of the dimensions of phonological space are expanded to their limits. Thus the merger of /ih/ and /eh/ does not represent a contraction of phonological space, but rather a tendency of the front ingliding vowels to reach the extreme position of the triangular pattern. Rounded vowels become more rounded, front vowels become more fronted, low back vowels come closer and closer to the extreme point of cardinal /ɒ/. Such pressures upon phonological space are exerted primarily by women rather than men, and some of the evidence given here indicates that women lead in the evolution of the New York City speech pattern for the two central classes.

If we continue the line of thinking suggested by this hypothesis, the deviation of the lower class from the main line of evolution may be seen as a reversal of this centrifugal movement, leading to a general lowering of the mid vowels and a centering of the low vowels. The quite different reversal represented by the introduction of /r/, on the part of upper middle class speakers, is clearly accompanied by a centripetal movement which is especially strong in vowels preceding strongly constricted (r). The parallel positions of the upper middle class and the lower class are then seen as two forms of a reversal of the centrifugal direction of the main line of evolution of the vowel system.

These speculations on the mechanism of linguistic change carry us as far as the nature of the data will permit, and perhaps a little farther. The principal task has been to demonstrate a consistent and coherent structure for the New York City speech community. In this chapter, that task has been carried to its conclusion.

15   1966–2006

Judging from the literature and general opinion, SSENYC had consider-able impact on the field of sociolinguistics. It initiated a field of quantita-tive, linguistically-oriented sociolinguistics, or as it is commonly referred to today, the study of linguistic change and variation. The annual meeting of NWAVE (New Ways of Analyzing Variation) has reached its thirty-fourth year, and the organizers of the most recent session at NYU (for the first time in New York City, as it happens) announced that over 300 abstracts were received. The journal devoted to quantitative analysis, *Language Change and Variation*, is in its eighteenth year. The common theme that unites the authors of these papers is that considerable insight can be gained into the structure of language by the study of linguistic variables, usually in spontaneous speech, rather than by accepting the limitation to invariant behavior that is characteristic of introspection.

These papers draw upon data from groups of various sizes, but the main body of data that they draw from is normally a research project of a scope comparable to SSENYC, designed to record and analyze a sample of speakers that is representative of a speech community. The common under-standing that unites the field – what I have called the central dogma of sociolinguistics – is that language is located in the speech community, not the individual. Drawing upon the larger perspective set forth by Weinreich, Labov, and Herzog (1968), we can say that the linguistic behavior of individuals cannot be understood without knowledge of the communities that they belong to. These community studies are to be found in a long suc-cession of research reports, dissertations, and book-length publications dating from 1966 to the present. This chapter will present a brief review of that stream of work. It will focus on how the researchers set about sampling the community, the samples they created, the linguistic variables analyzed, the range of contextual styles considered, what changes in progress they may have found, and a few of the results that bear on general linguistic principles. It will then consider the issues more generally.

The list is inevitably partial. SSENYC is concerned with the stratification of a large city, and so I will not be examining the many studies of small towns and rural areas, which require a certain degree of participant observation and judgment samples. Nor will I be considering here studies of communal groups within the city, African American and Latino minorities, unless they are designed to study the social stratification of language within those groups. We will be looking at answers to the question: how can we represent a city's speech? This leaves out many important bodies of sociolinguistic work, like the studies of rural North Carolina by Wolfram and his colleagues, Eckert's study of high schools in the Detroit area, and Rickford's and Baugh's research in African–American communities of the West Coast.

The list will be organized by date rather than geography, to give some sense of the progress of the field and the development of the methods used. The dates are usually the year of the major publication that followed the completion of the work (often several years after); this can be found in the bibliography under the name of the researcher and that date. There are a few cases where the dates are in parentheses, if there was no single main publication or it followed long after. In such cases, particular references are listed in the entry. There is no effort to achieve completeness here; these are the items that I have found most relevant to my own work.

1967 Detroit: Roger Shuy, Walt Wolfram, and William K. Riley

This large-scale research project began with a sampling of schools within census tracts selected for socio-economic characteristics. Within each school, students were selected randomly and their families contacted by letter (public schools) or by the field worker going directly to the home address (private schools). If the person was not suitable as a subject or not available, the field worker went to the next person on the list. 702 speakers representing 250 families were recorded with an instrument that included many of the techniques of SSENYC. Of these, 36 speakers were analyzed for negative concord, pronominal apposition, relative clause complementizer, and nasalization of pre-nasal vowels, and studied for social stratification by four social classes, age, gender, and race. Wolfram (1969) is a more detailed study of 36 African–American subjects, often cited to show social stratification of negative concord, and the sharper slope of correction among lower middle class women.

1968 Harlem: William Labov, Paul Cohen, Clarence Robins, John Lewis

The individual interviews of SSENYC show considerable differences between white and black speakers, but it was evident at the time that the effect of the outside observer was much greater for black than white subjects, and occasional observations of speech within the black community showed that we were far from recording African–American Vernacular English (AAVE). The study of Harlem reported in Labov, Cohen, Robins, and Lewis (1968) and in Labov (1972b) was designed to obtain a representative sample of the AAVE community and record the vernacular with a minimal observer effect. A local club-house was rented as a research site, and all of the named adolescent and pre-adolescent groups in a two-block area were contacted and recorded individually by John Lewis, an African–American in his mid-twenties with a background similar to the youth. The equivalent of casual speech in an interview was obtained by recording party-like group sessions, following methods used by Gumperz (1964) in Norway, but with each subject recorded on a separate tape recorder. Isolated and peripheral youth were also studied, along with a complete census of one high-rise apartment building.

Harlem adults were studied by sampling four neighborhoods with a total population of 5,365. Two of these were the neighborhoods of the adolescent groups. From the residences of every third block, a random sample was constructed. If the resident was not available, did not fit the design, or refused, the interviewer went successively to the left and right apartments until a suitable person was found. Refusal rates were moderate, about 18 percent. The interviewer was an African–American male in his thirties (Clarence Robins), and the interview design adopted the techniques of SSENYC to the African–American community. The subjective reaction Job scale was expanded to include the likelihood of the speaker to win in a street fight, or become a close friend on further contact. The pattern of complementary reactions to the Job and Fight scales was found to be characteristic of middle class subjects but not lower working class (Labov 1972a:250).

The Harlem study was the first to consider internal constraints on linguistic variables, and introduced the concept of variable rule, in which probabilities were associated with these constraints as well as the social characteristics of the speakers (Labov 1972b: Chs. 1–4).

1972 Philadelphia: Thomas Cofer

The interviewing techniques of SSENYC were replicated in West Philadelphia in Cofer's dissertation. He recorded 46 men and selected 20 for analysis: 5 groups each of white middle class speakers, white working class, black middle class, and black working class. He examined (dh), variable use of the *that* complementizer, and the variant realizations of the relative pronoun.

(1972) Montreal: Gillian Sankoff, David Sankoff and Henrietta Cedergren

By far the most rigorous and systematic community sampling was that used by the Montreal group in 1972 (Sankoff and Sankoff 1973). Unlike SSENYC, which sampled the Lower East Side to represent the city, the Montreal group undertook to represent the entire population of 988,000 francophones in a stratified sample with equal representation from all socio-economic levels. They divided the 188 census tracts with over 65 percent francophones into 6 groups by income level, and randomly selected from a street directory 20 subjects from each sixth. The 20 subjects were distributed with 5 in each of 4 age groups, with gender split alternately as 2 to 3 or 3 to 2.

Field workers went to the address selected; if the person was not of the age or gender needed to fill the cells, they went to the next left or right house systematically. The Montreal group also introduced the social dimension of the linguistic marketplace (Bourdieu 1977), used in many of their analyses. They found that it correlated .96 with objective socio-economic indices.

The Montreal sample was also the first computerized sociolinguistic corpus, and was the first body of material to be extensively analyzed with logistic regression. The group has studied phonological variables like diphthongization of vowels (Cedergren, Clermont, and Cote 1981), elision of (l), syncope of devoiced vowels (Cedergren and Simoneau 1985), and grammatical variables like the negative particle *ne* (Sankoff and Vincent 1977), and the alternation of *qu'est-ce que* with *qu'osque* and *ce-que* (Kemp 1979).

In 1984, 60 of the 120 original subjects were re-interviewed with 12 additional younger speakers, and in 1995, 14 were re-interviewed again. A description of the entire corpus, including a lengthy list of studies published, is provided in Thibault and Vincent (1990). In recent years, the Montreal corpus has been the site of several studies comparing real time with apparent time views of change.

1973 Panama City: Henrietta Cedergren

Cedergren represented the population of Panama City by sampling 13 barrios proportionately to their population. Of the 100 households targeted from addresses chosen at random, she interviewed 91. The interviews differentiated conversation from a reading passage. Cedergren dealt with a range of Spanish variables: lenition of intervocalic (D), lenition of (R), aspiration and deletion of (S), and the lenition of (CH). This was the first study to use the logistic regression program developed by David Sankoff (Varbrul: 1988), which permits the analyst to assess the simultaneous influence of many internal and external influences on the dependent binary variable. Cross-tabulation diagrams like those displayed in SSENYC then gave way to single numbers for each factor in a group, and the interactions of class, gender, and age largely disappear from the scene.

In the Cedergren study, the lenition of (CH) in *mucho, muchacha,* etc., was found to be a change in progress, displaying the curvilinear social class pattern characteristic of NYC (ay) and (aw). In 1983, Cedergren returned to Panama City and repeated her sampling methods to create a trend study. It was found that the lenition of (CH) had advanced further, but that adults had also shifted their use in that direction to some degree.

1973 Glasgow: Ronald K. S. Macaulay and Gavin Trevelyan

The approach to sampling the community followed the same technique as Shuy, Wolfram, and Riley in Detroit. Names and addresses were obtained from neighborhood schools. A total of 130 speakers were recorded, stratified by four social classes, and Protestant and Catholic adherence. Five phonological variables were analyzed for 48 speakers: (i), (u), (a), (au), (glottal stop). Results are presented for ages 10, 14, university students, parents of schoolchildren and those over 50. Religion was not a significant factor, but regular stratification was found throughout.

1974 Norwich: Peter Trudgill

One of the most important research projects that built upon and developed the model of SSENYC was Trudgill's study of the medium-sized city of Norwich in East Anglia. A random sample of 25 persons from each of 5 districts was drawn from the register of electors, and ultimately 50 of those who were native to East Anglia and had lived in Norwich at least 10 years were interviewed, along with 10 schoolchildren between 10 and 20 years old. These 60 subjects were classified into 5 social classes and 7 age groups. Four contextual styles were used, comparable to SSENYC.

Trudgill's results for the (ING) variable were quite comparable to SSENYC, except for the greater gap between middle class and working class groups in speech styles, reflecting the sharper stratification of English society. He studied a wide range of Norwich phonological variables, as well as the variable absence of third singular (s), and found regular stratification in most of them. One phonological variable – the backing and lowering of /e/ before /l/ – was found to be a change in progress, with the upper working class in the lead. Trudgill (1972) developed the self-report test of Chapter 12, and found a consistent pattern of under-reporting for men and over-reporting for women that reinforced the notion of covert prestige of vernacular forms.

*(1977) Philadelphia: William Labov, Matthew Lennig, Donald Hindle,
Arvilla Payne, Anne Bower, Elizabeth Dayton, Gregory Guy*

The project on Linguistic Change and Variation (LCV) in Philadelphia was
designed to determine the social location of the leaders of the many linguistic changes in the city's vowel system, testing the curvilinear hypothesis that
this location would be in the interior groups of the socio-economic hierarchy. Instead of the sample of individuals characteristic of SSENYC, the
focus was on neighborhood networks, and the effort to explain individual
behavior by social interaction. After a year of exploratory interviewing, ten
neighborhoods were selected for extended study, stratified by income and
house values, with repeated interviewing of individuals and groups over
two to three years. Individual interviews included subjective reaction tests
isolating the effects of five variables. 180 speakers were interviewed in the
Neighborhood Study, and analyzed for stable sociolinguistic variables. The
vowel systems of 120 speakers were analyzed acoustically, and correlated
through multiple regression analyses with a wide range of social variables.
Interviews with twenty members of the upper class conducted by Anthony
Kroch (1996) were included. The leaders of linguistic change were found to
be upwardly mobile women of high local status groups, with a high density
of interaction within the neighborhood and a high proportion of contacts
outside the neighborhood (Labov 1980, 1990, 2001).

To verify whether the ten neighborhoods represented the city as a whole,
a random sample of 60 telephone users was interviewed, covering all
geographic areas. The relatively short telephone interviews produced the
same curvilinear social pattern as the neighborhood studies (Hindle 1980).

The relatively new suburb of King-of-Prussia was selected as the upper
middle class neighborhood. Payne (1976, 1980) studied the acquisition of
children in this neighborhood from out-of-state families and found that those
who arrived before the age of nine acquired most of the Philadelphia sound
changes but only those whose parents were born in Philadelphia acquired the
grammatically and lexically conditioned pattern for the tensing of short-*a*.

Results of the LCV study of Philadelphia were published in a number of
articles beginning in 1976. Particularly relevant to this chapter is the
description of field methods (Labov 1984). The most complete report is to
be found in Labov (2001).

1978 Buenos Aires: Beatriz Lavandera

Lavandera was concerned with the alternations in the tense/mood system that
occurs in the *si-* clauses of Buenos Aires Spanish: the standard imperfect subjunctive and the colloquial use of the conditional and the present indicative.

After six years of exploratory work as a native speaker of the local dialect, she interviewed 87 speakers, stratified by gender, age, and three educational classes (primary, secondary, college). There were 4 or 5 subjects in each cell.

In her exploratory interviews, Lavandera found very few *si*-clauses (an average of 2.5 per fifty-minute interview. She then developed a variety of techniques tested in real-life situations without a tape recorder, such as the uses of silence and repeated questions in getting people to express themselves hypothetically without her using the target construction herself. She then obtained a total of 1418 *si*-clauses, an average of 16 per subject. The conditional was a minor use throughout. The results showed a strong shift away from the imperfect subjunctive towards the use of the present indicative by men and by younger subjects. A combined education/occupation index showed a u-shaped distribution, with maximimum use of the present indicative by the lowest and highest social classes.

In a later publication (1978), Lavandera raised important questions about whether these variants have the same meaning, and how we can deal with the co-variation of form and meaning. For further discussion of this issue, see D. Sankoff and Thibault (1981).

1978 Teheran: Yahya Modaressi

Modaressi undertook a study of Teheran along with Ghazvin, a smaller provincial capital 150 km from the capital. Half of the sample of 53 subjects were selected from schools, one-quarter randomly, and the last quarter through personal contacts. Twenty-one subjects were interviewed in Ghazvin. Subjects were distributed across four educational levels, and the interviews included four contextual styles. The Farsi variables that Modaressi investigated included the raising of /a/ to /u/ before nasals, simplification of consonant clusters, and the use of the third singular possessive /æsh/. They showed regular social stratification, with a very sharp drop off of the colloquial forms in passing from speech to reading. The variation from /an/ to /un/ was found to be a change in apparent time, with Ghazvin trailing behind Teheran. However, the social stratification in the smaller city was reversed. In Teheran, the higher the social class, the lower the frequency of /un/. In Ghazvin, the use of /un/ is highest with the highest educational group, and falls off regularly to the lowest.

1978 Paris: Matthew Lennig

Lennig gathered data on the Parisian French dialect in two periods, 1975 and 1977. In his first visit, he followed a series of social networks, but failed to get the social stratification he was looking for. He returned with a design for 75 subjects in three neighborhoods but re-oriented his work to take advantage of the possibility of interviewing workers in the Honeywell-Bull factory (CHB). He obtained permission from the director of personnel to interview workers at various skill levels on the job, and conducted 27 one-hour interviews, six per day. With the addition of 10 office employees at the administrative office, he interviewed a total of 90 subjects.

Lennig's focus was on the Parisian vowel system. He carried out an acoustic analysis of 52 speakers, normalized by the log mean algorithm on the basis of those vowels for which he obtained three tokens from each speaker. He found that the "Parigot" rotation of back vowels upward and forward was generally reversed. The initiating change was the merger of front and back /a/ phonemes, with the upper middle class leading.

1979 Anniston, Alabama: Crawford Feagin

Over several decades, Feagin has produced many studies of language stratification and language change in Anniston, the home city of her grandparents. Her 1979 book analyzed 82 speakers out of the 205 recorded, representing two social class groups: the upper class from personal networks, the working class from church, labor union leaders, and schools contacts. The sample was stratified by age, sex, and two social classes (upper class and working class), and urban vs. rural location. Feagin's original focus was the comparison of the speech of white southerners with previous studies of African–American English, analyzing progressive *a*-prefixing, perfective *done*, double modals, *liketa*, person-number agreement, and negative concord. For other papers on social stratification and language change in Anniston see Feagin (1986, 1987a, 1987b).

1979 Ottawa: Howard Woods

Woods began the study of Ottawa with a classification of census tracts into those with high, mid, and low economic characteristics. He then went to the geographic midpoint of a selected tract on the north side and requested an interview. If the person was not suitable or refused, he called on the next highest street number. This procedure netted 89 interviews and only 9 refusals, and with 11 additional subjects from the Urban Valley gave a total of 100. The interviews included word lists and minimal pairs. Woods gathered information on a wide range of phonological variables, including flapping, (ING), consonant cluster simplification, and Canadian raising. Grammatical variables included *between you and I*, Canadian (eh), *have* vs. *got*, and the pronunciation of many individual words like *again, aunt*, and *either*.

1979 Buenos Aires: Clara Wolf and Elena Jiménez

This study of the porteño dialect of Spanish was based upon three groups of very different kinds: 36 speakers of tertiary educational level; a much smaller group of 12 lower class adults; and 240 students from nine to eighteen years old. The corpus was derived from a larger study of cultivated Buenos Aires speech. The focus was on a single variable: the devoicing of /ž/ to /š/ in *calle*, *llama*, etc. It was a change in progress, practically complete for the students, but hardly begun among the oldest speakers. The lower class speakers were more advanced than the educated group, but by far the largest differences had to do with gender. Women were very much in the lead in this change, and men were generally one generation behind women.

1980 Rio de Janeiro: Anthony Naro et al.

Anthony Naro trained an important group of sociolinguists at several universities in Rio de Janeiro and environs in the late 1970s (Lemle & Naro 1977). Members of this group interviewed a sample of 48 speakers in Rio between 1980 and 1983. The sample was stratified by sex, age, education, and economic level of the neighborhood (de Oliveira e Silva & Scherre 1998). A panel sample was constituted of 16 of these speakers, who were re-interviewed in 1999, and 32 new speakers were interviewed in 2000 to form a new trend comparison (de Paiva & Duarte 2003).

1980 Belfast: Lesley and James Milroy

The Milroys carried out their study of Belfast at the height of the troubles that disrupted social communication in that city. They contacted speakers in three neighborhoods through social networks, beginning with friends and friends of friends. an essential technique at a time when knocking on strange doors was a dangerous procedure. They recorded 46 speakers drawn from one Protestant and two Catholic neighborhoods: Ballymacarrett, the Hammer, and the Clonard. Eight phonological variables were analyzed in the initial study, primarily in the vowel system. Their focus on social networks led to an appreciation of the influence of multiplexity and density of networks on language stratification and resistance to change, and the importance of weak ties across networks in the spreading of change.

1981 Amman: Hassan Abdel-Jawad

Abdel-Jawad prepared a stratified random sample of Amman neighborhoods, selected for their social class concentrations, including "first class" areas, popular areas, and refugee camps. Subjects were also selected to represent urban, fellahHiin, and Bedouin origin. The variables studied included the palatalization of /k/ and the variants of Qaf (typically classical /q/, urban /ʔ/, peasant /k/, Bedouin /g/). Abdel-Jawad found that women used less of the classical uvular variants than men, and more of the modern urban glottal stop, at all educational levels (see also Abdel-Jawad 1987).

1982 Ottawa-Hull: Shana Poplack

Poplack and her research group at the University of Ottawa undertook a systematic sample of the francophone community of Ottawa, the capital of Ontario, and the nearby city of Hull in Quebec, assessing both the effects of social stratification and of long-term stable bilingualism. Three neighborhoods in Ottawa and two in Hull were selected, and a random sample constructed following the method used by the Montreal group ten years earlier. Interviewers approached each address and looked for a subject to fill a stratified design of two men and two women to represent each of six age groups, raised in the target city from ages six to thirteen years. As the sample neared completion, the field worker asked for help in finding someone of the desired demographic description, but no friends or relatives of subjects already interviewed were accepted. Once the desired person was located refusal rates were low, and the probability of obtaining a complete interview was .95. A total of 120 subjects were interviewed. The main emphasis was in obtaining a large volume of highly informal speech. A total of 270 hours was recorded and transcribed to form a computerized corpus of 3.5 million words, the subject of many analytical papers that followed.

A great many papers have been produced at the Ottawa Sociolinguistics Laboratory by Poplack and her associates, proceeding from this and studies of other speech communities. They may be accessed at www. sociolinguistics.uottawa.ca.

1982 Rio de Janeiro: Solange de Azambuja Lira

Lira studied a sample of 60 speakers in Rio de Janeiro, stratified by age, sex, and three socio-economic levels. The study also included group interviews with teenagers. The stylistic levels opposed narratives to the main body of the interview. The linguistic variables were pro-drop and subject postposing. Lira found that the most important constraints were same vs. switch reference, aspect, and animacy.

1983 São Paolo: Fernando Tarallo

Tarallo interviewed 40 speakers in São Paolo, half over thirty-five and half under thirty-five, in three social classes. The study concerned three strategies for oblique relative clauses: the standard pattern with pied piping, resumptive pronouns, and a chopped variant that eliminated the preposition with a consequent loss of information in some double object verbs. The interview included elicitation tests and subjective reaction tests. Tarallo also included information on the use of this variable in the mass media: sports broadcasts and novellas.

1983 Belo Horizonte, Brazil: Marco de Oliveira

De Oliveira studied the Portuguese of this medium-sized Brazilian city during a period of political tension, where recording fresh contacts was difficult. Working through personal contacts, he recorded 50 of 76 informants, drawn from four social classes (excluding the upper class). His focus was on extensive variation in the liquids /r/, /rr/ and /lj/; change in apparent time was located in the fricativization and vocalization of /rr/. His finding that the changes were most advanced in the lowest social class led him to suggest a modification of the hypothesis that associates a curvilinear pattern with change from below. He argued that change is initiated by the leading social class in terms of numerical domination: the lower class in Brazil, the upper working class and lower middle class in the U.S. and western Europe.

1983 San Pedro Sula, Honduras: Alma Leticia Lopez Scott

Lopez studied the commercial center of the second-largest city in Honduras, with a population of 342,000 in 1980. She was able to interview 43 of 47 speakers targeted, representing four socio-economic and three age groups. The focus of this study was on the phonetic conditioning and social stratification of the aspiration and deletion of Spanish /s/. The Lopez study is one of the few which showed change in apparent time for this variable, spreading from syllable final to syllable initial position.

1985 Sydney: Barbara Horvath

The Sydney Social Dialect Survey was designed to obtain a sample stratified for three socio-economic groups, age (adults and teenagers), gender, and ethnicity (Anglo-Celtics, Italians, and Greeks). The goal was to fill each cell with 5 speakers. One hundred and seventeen speakers were interviewed in 1977 and a further 60 in 1980. The main focus was on the vowel system of Australian English, especially the vowels (iy, ey, ow, ay, aw), classified phonetically into the Cultivated, General, and Broad categories first established by Mitchell and Delbridge (1965). An unusual feature of the Sydney study was the inclusion of recently arriving groups including L2 speakers who came to the city after the age of twenty. In addition to "accented" or non-native vowel forms, Horvath identified an "Ethnic Broad" category, which for some vowels (particularly /aw/) was more advanced in the direction of change in progress.

A second unusual feature of the Sydney study was the use of principal components analysis, which established groups on the basis of their linguistic similarity, followed by an effort to determine the social membership of these groups. One of the most remarkable results of this analysis was the recognition of two widely separated groups of speakers as a "core" and "periphery."

The high rising intonation in declarative clauses, widely reported across English speech communities, was first described and studied in detail by Guy, Horvath, Vonwiller, Daisley, and Rogers (1986) in the Sydney community. It was found to be a vigorous change in progress. The curvilinear pattern in the socio-economic scale was found for males, but not for females; and for the Anglo-Celtic speakers, but not for Greeks or Italians.

1988 Tokyo: Junko Hibiya

Hibiya studied Tokyo by sampling a single neighborhood, Nezu, which was located between the upper middle class area Yamanote and the lower-middle, working class area Shitamachi. She began with 9 personal contacts, and then constructed a random sample by taking every fifteenth person from the municipal office residence lists. A total of 88 subjects were interviewed out of 294 eligible; only 30 refused the interview.

Hibiya focused on two changes in progress, both representing a shift towards the general standard. One was the replacement of the traditional Tokyo velar nasal [ŋ] in non-initial position by standard [g]. The other is the replacement of the Shitamachi realization of underlying /h/ before /i/ as laminal [ʃ] instead of palatal [ç]. To track these variables across stylistic contexts, Hibiya adapted the conversational modules developed in Philadelphia to the Japanese context. Though it has been said that Japanese are reluctant to tell narratives of personal experience except in the most intimate situation, Hibiya had considerable success in eliciting narratives from most speakers, and was able to correlate narrative style with higher values of the vernacular forms. She also showed a correlation of the frequency of honorifics with the use of the standard variants.

There was no notable difference between men and women in their use of the velar nasal, but a strong interaction between gender and class in the use of [ʃi]: working class men were the main users of this vernacular variant and working class women used standard [ç] like middle class women. Among the Nezu residents, Hibiya was able to show strong differences in the frequency of [ʃi] according to whether they were born in Shitamachi, Nezu, or Yamanote, except for her highest group, the middle class.

In her study of the replacement of the velar nasal by [g], Hibiya found a sizeable difference in the historically embedded classes of native Japanese words (19%) and Sino-Japanese vocabulary (59%), a distinction dating from the sixteenth century.

1991 Cairo: Nilofaar Haeri (published 1996)

Haeri undertook the study of the colloquial Arabic of Cairo with a sample of 100 speakers located from a series of networks through friends and extended contacts. The sample was stratified by gender and four social classes; the upper class was the group most strongly oriented towards western culture. One part of Haeri's study was aimed at the stable sociolinguistic variable Qaf (as previously studied by Abdel-Jawad and others), where men consistently used more of the traditional uvular stop. Haeri showed that this use was essentially a series of lexical borrowings from classical Arabic rather than inherent variation in Egyptian Arabic. She also studied a new change in progress, palatalization of apical stops by following high vowels, and found that the leaders of linguistic change were intrepid women who resisted the pressures to conform to traditional social constraints.

1991 Cairo: R. Kirk Belknap

A second study of Cairo was carried out by Belknap, who had three native speakers interview 26 persons, divided into three age groups, about half male and half female, of three educational levels. With this limited sample there were only one or two speakers in each category. His investigation centered on the variation between plural and feminine singular agreement with both human and non-human plural heads. The variation was found to be con-strained by a number of internal factors, but no social stratification emerged.

1991 Seoul: Yunsook Hong

The first representative study of an Asian city was carried out by Hong in Seoul (in 1991). She interviewed 52 subjects in four social classes, contacted through the university, welfare homes, relatives in their homes, and in one particular site that is particular to Korean cities: real estate agencies, a favorite place for people to sit and gossip. Hong studied the social class distribution of the mid-front vowel merger (/æ/ and /e/), the variation of word-initial liquids, and the reduction of consonant clusters.

1991 Lille: Anne Lefebvre

Lefebvre carried out a sociolinguistic study in the phonological framework of Martinet. She sampled the speech of the industrial city of Lille with 103 speakers, categorized in nine occupational classes. The variables were a quantitative treatment of the traditional phonological oppositions of French in four speech styles: conversation, reading, questionnaire, and minimal pairs.

1991 Copenhagen: Frans Gregerson and Inge Lise Pederson

The team headed by Gregerson selected the central Nyboder neighborhood to represent Copenhagen. A total of 40 interviews were analyzed at three levels of style: non-casual, casual, and sentence reading. In addition, 18 subjects were recorded in 11 group sessions, to get a closer approximation to the vernacular. Phonological variables included the realization of (A) and vowels before /r/, with particular attention to narrative and discourse analysis in the second volume of the report.

1994 Milton Keynes: Paul Kerswill and Ann Williams

Kerswill and Williams studied the "new town" of Milton Keynes, which was created in 1969 with an initial population drawn from many areas of England, as a laboratory for the creation of new dialects. A sample of children in the local schools was drawn, with 8 males and 8 females at ages four, eight, and twelve. A caregiver for each child was also interviewed, for a total of 96 speakers. A process of dialect leveling was observed to take place, largely between the ages of eight and twelve. At the age of four, children tended to resemble their caregivers. A radical shift towards the newly formed local norms was found beginning at age eight and more or less complete at age twelve. Among the many findings concerning the formation of new dialects, they observe that a child's rate of adoption of second-dialect features depends on the strength of his or her peer group orientation. For other reports on this project, see Kerswill (1996, 2002) and Williams and Kerswill (1999).

1995 Seoul: Seo-Yong Chae

The second study of Seoul was done by Chae on the basis of two selected neighborhoods, Kahoy and Wense-tong. Since a Korean privacy law bars lists of residents, Chae made contacts through convenience stores, bakeries, old peoples' club houses, and houses with open gates. Many recordings were made on the street, where Seoul residents feel free to conduct extended conversations. A total of 48 subjects was interviewed, with a strong emphasis on obtaining personal narratives. Chae identified five styles: narrative, careful speech, response to the interviewer, reading passage, and reading sentences. The main variable studied was the raising of (o) to [u] in bound morphemes. As in the Teheran study, reading styles showed a very sharp decline in the use of the raised form. A matched guise test was devised: two female speakers using [o] were judged to be more avant-garde, more intelligent, and taller.

1995 Tokyo: Kenjiro Matsuda

A second study of Tokyo by Matsuda overlapped with that of Hibiya, using some of her data together with Matsuda's own field work and data from Sachiko Ide's Housewife Corpus. The sample design included males and females in two age groups, over and under forty, from uptown Yamanote and downtown Shitamachi. Matsuda focused on a single linguistic variable: the occurrence of the object marker *o*, which is more often than not absent in everyday speech. The class and gender differences were small, but all groups shifted significantly towards greater deletion in casual speech. Casual and careful speech were distinguished on the basis of the eight-membered decision tree (Labov 2001). All sub-classes of careful speech (Response, Language, Soap Box, Interview style) showed lower rates of deletion than all sub-classes of casual speech (Tangent, Kids, Group, Narrative).

1998 Memphis: Valerie Fridland

Fridland's study of Memphis was based upon a sample of 100 volunteers, recruited from local churches and businesses. They were interviewed briefly and asked to read word lists and minimal pairs. An acoustic analysis of the major vowel classes was carried out on the material from word lists and minimal pairs, showing that the major features of the southern shift were well represented in Memphis, particularly the lowering and centralization of /ey/. Stage 3, involving the corresponding change of /iy/, is not found in Memphis (Fridland 1999). In later studies with re-synthesized speech tokens, Fridland showed that Memphis residents identify the lowering of /ey/ as a southern feature (Fridland, Bartlett, and Kreuz 2004).

2004 Montreal: Charles Boberg

With the help of a cohort of student interviewers, Boberg designed a pilot study of the English of Montreal. Given the minority status of English in that city, and the coherence of ethnic enclaves, the sample of 35 speakers was carefully stratified by three ethnic groups (9 Irish, 15 Italian, 11 Jewish), and equally divided by gender. The interviews covered a wide range of topics in spontaneous speech as well as word lists and minimal pairs. The report on ethnic differences focused on word lists, arguing that any differences found there are likely to be magnified in spontaneous speech. Acoustic analysis of formant positions did show a number of significant differences, especially for Italians, who showed much less fronting of /uw/ than other groups. Boberg found a mean F2 of /uw/ for Italians that was 253 Hz lower than the Jews and Irish. The Philadelphia analysis of F2 of /uw/ assigned a regression coefficient for Italian ethnicity of -226 Hz (Labov 2001).

2005 L'Aquila: Christopher Cieri

Cieri studied the Italian spoken in the small city of L'Aquila in the Abruzzo region of Italy. He gathered the sample of 60 interviews in three periods of field work through a series of social networks that are traced in great detail. The interviews included minimal pairs and word lists as well as question modules. Changes in the vowel system of 35 speakers were analyzed acoustically, using the automated system for the analysis of large corpora developed at the Linguistics Data Consortium. Cieri found evidence for change in progress with lower values of /e/ for younger speakers in the lowest socio-economic class, but working class females shifted to high values in a hypercorrect manner. In general, females were in the lead, and even more so for the parallel lowering of open /o/.

Cieri paid close attention to interviewer effects. Half of the interviews were conducted by a local speaker of L'Aquila Italian. In this case, the outside interviewer (Cieri) appeared to elicit speech closer to the vernacular, as the style of the local interviewer produced less speech and variants more characteristic of formal style.

2006 Charleston, South Carolina: Maciej Baranowski

The city of Charleston, South Carolina, was represented in the *Atlas of North American English* (Labov, Ash & Boberg 2006) by three speakers; it appeared to be outside of the mainstream of southern speech but showed extreme fronting of /ow/ as in the midland. Baranowski undertook a complete sociolinguistic study of the city, beginning with a judgment sample of four areas selected for their socio-economic and social stratification. He recorded interviews with 100 speakers, stratified into four age groups and five social classes, including 20 speakers from the Charleston upper class. In addition, he carried out rapid and anonymous studies of (r) and (ay) in downtown Charleston. Acoustic analysis, using the methods of the *Atlas*, was carried out for 43 Charlestonians, and for all 100, the rates of monophthongization of /ay/ and syllable final /r/ were measured.

Baranowski found that the traditional dialect of Charleston, most characteristic of the upper class, was in rapid decline – as shown by the replacement of monophthongal and ingliding forms of *say, go*, etc. with upgliding diphthongs. The decline followed with a high degree of precision the logistic form of an s-shaped curve for this and many other features of the Charleston dialect, including the reversal of the merger of *beer* and *bare*, etc., along with the importation of coda /r/. Most of these changes took place at the same time, with the generation maturing after World War II showing the most dramatic change. The replacing dialect is distinct from that of the south, but similar to that found in the south-eastern super-region, uniting the Midland and the periphery of the South. It is characterized by the nasal short-*a* system and extreme fronting of /ow/. Remarkably enough, the upper class is leading in this process. As the three speakers of the *Atlas* first showed, Charleston has more extreme fronting than any other dialect region.

2006 North America: William Labov, Sharon Ash, Charles Boberg

All of the studies described above deal with a single city. The most recently completed project is the *Atlas of North American English* [ANAE], a study of all the cities (above 50,000 population) in the continent of North America. North America is of course a single speech community in one sense, but the *Atlas* was designed to determine what areas of diversity exist within it, as defined by ongoing sound changes. This was done by a telephone survey. The cities to be studied were originally identified as centers of Zones of Influence, as determined by the geographic extent of the area where the city's newspaper was the most widely read. Names were selected from telephone directories, selecting by preference clusters of family names representing the majority ethnic groups of the area. The first two persons who answered the telephone and said that they had grown up in that city from the age of four or earlier, were accepted as representing that city (four or six persons for the largest cities). A total of 762 subjects were interviewed with an instrument that obtained the pronunciation of particular words and minimal pairs. Considerable amounts of spontaneous speech were recorded, focused largely on developments in the city and the downtown area. Acoustic analysis of 439 subjects mapped the major chain shifts taking place across the continent.

ANAE contrasts with the output of SSENYC and the many studies that followed in displaying large areas of uniform structure, sharply divided from its neighbors, as for example, the area dominated by the Northern Cities Shift which stretches from Rochester to Milwaukee. The division between North and Midland, or North and Canada, appears to be a profound barrier to linguistic influence. ANAE is not a study of sociolinguistic variation, like SSENYC, but rather of the constituent patterns in which the variation is played out. In this volume the variable raising of (oh) is a major theme. Chapter 8 shows how lower middle class women have the highest vowels in spontaneous speech, but the lowest in formal styles. The chapter also demonstrates how Jews have relatively higher (oh) vowels than Italians (and vice-versa for (æh)). But ANAE's maps show New York City as part of a continuous belt of high (oh) users, ranging from Fall River to Baltimore. This is the only part of the continent where (oh) is an upper mid vowel with $F1 <$ 700 Hz in the normalized system. While New York City has a higher mean (oh) than any other city, its resistance to the low back merger is equivalent to that of Philadelphia, Wilmington, and Baltimore in raising (oh) far from /o/.

Where are we heading?

Social stratification   This review of thirty-seven studies that followed SSENYC has emphasized the methods and findings that are special to each study rather than the parallel findings that have emerged. But the parallelism is there: significant social stratification of language variables is found in all but one study. This result gives rise to the question, what next? What does a sociolinguistic investigation of a new variable in a new city add to our understanding of language? To pursue this question, we must note that the common thread is not the existence of social stratification, but rather the pattern of combined and independent stylistic and social stratification. (SSENYC might have been more accurately called *The Stylistic and Social Stratification of English in New York City*.) The pattern was unexpected; until 1966 the general understanding was that "functional varieties" that differentiate styles were different variables from the features that defined "cultural levels" (Kenyon 1948). The combined pattern and the variations within it have consequences for our understanding of the speech community, and for education and social policy as well.

Consensus   The pattern of social and stylistic stratification for (ing), Figure 10.7, shows that all social classes are different in their use of this variable, and this differentiation repeats at each stylistic level. But it shows equally well that all social classes are the same, in following the same pattern of style shifting. There is a consensus that the /in/ variant is most appropriate for casual speech, and least appropriate for formal styles. Weinberg (1974) and Cedergren (1973) find that this holds equally true for the deletion of /s/ in Argentina and Panama. Consider for a moment what other patterns might emerge. If there were no stylistic stratification, we would have a strict social stratification that divides social groups precisely by their language use. Social mobility would then require abandoning one's home vernacular and adopting a new form of speech. No such case has been found here, but there are situations where style shifts are much stronger than social differences. In Modaressi's study of (an) in Teheran or Chae's study of (o) in Seoul, the major shifts are between speech and reading. Almost everyone can control the standard form in reading, and the frequencies that differentiate social groups in speech are minor barriers to social movement. Since most of the studies of social stratification reviewed here have incorporated a wide range of stylistic contexts within the interview, it is possible to make such rigid stratification from the New York City pattern.

All such studies of social stratification are relevant to the goal of reducing social inequality. In general, linguists favor the adoption of standard language forms in so far as they serve as avenues to social mobility, but oppose them when they operate as barriers to mobility. Unrealistic linguistic shibboleths, which do not reflect actual speech patterns, are likely to operate as social barriers. If the standard is defined as the usage of educated speakers, a democratic society demands that anyone should be able to acquire the standard by listening to that form of speech, in the mass media or in personal contact. The rule that insists on number agreement to the predication of presentational sentences, condemning *There's a lamp and a book on the table*, cannot be learned from listening to educated speech, but only by attending schools where such rules are taught (Meechan and Foley 1994).[1]

On the other hand, the (dh) variable does reflect a real world consensus on the preference for interdental fricatives in formal or educated speech, though all social groups depart to some extent from that norm. Chapter 7 showed that Nathan B.'s inability or disinclination to follow that norm prevented him from realizing his professional potential. The various studies of social and stylistic stratification show that all sociolinguistic variables do

---

[1] Among the 37 studies, we note that Belknap's study of Arabic agreement is the only one that found no evidence of social differentiation, as opposed to the many findings of social stratification of subject/verb agreement in Spanish and Portuguese.

not operate in this way. Matsuda's study of the deletion of the object marker in Japanese indicates that it varies only slightly across social classes, with a gradual and moderate shift to more deletion in casual speech.

Change in progress   The majority of the studies cited have noted some type of change in progress in the speech community. Some register change from above, the loss of vernacular forms, or (as in the case of SSENYC (r)) the importation of new prestige forms. The most challenging are the changes from within the linguistic system, like SSENYC raising of (aeh) and (oh), fronting of (aw), and backing of (ay). Such changes from below have been found by Trudgill, Cedergren, Wolf & Jiménez, Modaressi, Horvath, Haeri, and Baranowski, as well as the Philadelphia LCV project and the *Atlas of North American English*. These are the processes that can most clearly illuminate the basic mechanism that underlies the diversity of dialects, languages, and language families, and remain as mysterious in their motivation as in their origins. Such changes occur well below the level of social awareness, and are far more systematic than stereotyped linguistic variables or changes from above. Because they operate at such an unconscious level, it takes several years of exploratory study to locate them and to detect their effects upon the rest of the system. Each time a new change in progress is located, we make further progress towards a general understanding of linguistic change. The most recent study, Baranowski's investigation of Charleston, had two unexpected findings: (1) a merger has been effectively reversed, and (2) that this reversal was led by the upper class, both challenges to the general principles that have been put forward so far.

How to sample the city   These 37 studies show a fairly sharp division between two approaches to this question: random sampling of individuals or selection through social networks. In Poplack's Ottawa study, social networks were explicitly banned: a subject's recommendations of friends and neighbors were not followed through, but only referrals from those who were not eligible to be subjects. (SSENYC targeted individuals, but included interviews with other members of the family.) This is not the result of prejudice against social networks, but rather from the recognition that members of the same social network are likely to be more similar to each other than to non-members. In that sense, a study that interviewed three social networks is a study of three extended individuals, and is not as likely to represent the community as a study of 100 individuals. On the other hand, interviews with single speakers give us no view of the social context that has molded their speech patterns, and explanations of how the resultant patterns were produced is largely speculative.

It is clear that we need to carry out explorations of social networks to understand the diffusion of linguistic influence from the leaders of language change. Such studies are most informative when they deal with groups that share a common linguistic history. Members of close-knit groups that interact daily may be radically different in their linguistic behavior if they were raised in different areas (Labov and Harris 1986). Thus the study of social networks must be controlled by the same considerations that lead us to accept or reject an individual as representative of the community we are studying.

It must be acknowledged that many studies of social networks took place in a context where no other method was possible – in Belfast or Belo Horizonte at a time of great political tension. Given unlimited resources and opportunity, everyone would prefer a combination of both methods: a random sample of social groups. Unfortunately, there is no known method of enumerating all the groups in an area – unless one considers only named groups, as in the Harlem research of the 1960s. The other possibility is to carry out two separate samples, as in the Philadelphia design which supplemented ten neighborhood studies with a random sample of sixty telephone interviews.

The beginning of this chapter focused on the speech community as the central object of sociolinguistic research, as opposed to the study of individuals. The study of social networks is a welcome step away from a focus on the individual. But unless the social networks we study are firmly located in the larger speech community that generates their use of language, we will be saying more and more about less and less.

The neighborhood and the city   Inspection of these thirty-seven studies shows that most of them, like SSENYC, selected one or several neighborhoods to represent the city as a whole. Only a few (like the Montreal or Ottawa projects) examined all the neighborhoods. In the case of SSENYC, the choice of the Lower East Side was justified by the department store study, since the customers of Saks, Macy's, and Klein's were drawn from the entire population, not just one neighborhood, and the results patterned closely with the intensive survey of the one neighborhood. All of these results put together support the remarkable finding that great cities of a million or more are geographic unities. Any given neighborhood may differ linguistically from another but such differences are correlated with socioeconomic class differences in the population. Though to say so loses all credence in the public forum, it must be asserted that "Brooklynese" is nothing but a convenient geographic label for working-class New York City speech.

Size of the sample   How big a sample do we need? All of the studies put together show that from 60 to 100 speakers are needed to register social stratification by age, gender, and social class of a given city. On the one hand, we do not need the 705 speakers who were first interviewed in Detroit. On the other hand, samples of less than 50 have not proved adequate to the task, and what trends appear often fail to show statistical significance. SSENYC had 81 speakers in the basic sample, and behind this, a much larger number including other family members, exploratory interviews, out-of-towners, and refusals. None of the other studies have followed SSENYC in sampling those who refused the interview, but in general, refusal rates have been low.

The 120 speakers of the Montreal sample can be considered the ideal, bearing in mind the care with which the sample was constructed. It is almost a miracle of effort and ingenuity that 60 of the same subjects were located in real-time re-interviews thirteen years later; if the sample had been much smaller, the real-time studies that followed would have been inadequate. Size is almost secondary to design. To complete a carefully stratified random sample, major efforts are needed to fill the cells as the study nears completion, as the experience of Montreal, Ottawa, and ANAE shows.

Impressionistic vs. acoustic measurement   SSENYC introduced a technique of categorizing impressionistic notations into a small number of levels and carrying out numerical calculations on the means of these records. As acoustic measurements became faster and more accurate, the direct assessment of vowel timbre came into wider use, as in the Fridland and Baranowski studies. The democratization of acoustic measurement through the free program Praat (Boersma et al. 2006) has given even further impetus to the use of acoustic tools. We can expect that this trend will grow and develop in the years to come.

Multivariate analysis vs cross-tabulations   SSENYC began with the concept of the linguistic variable, but no statistical support for the analysis of results. Only the extreme regularity and independence of the social and stylistic factors made it possible to present a convincing view of the results. The Harlem study introduced the analysis of internal constraints and the search for evidence on underlying forms, along with the construct of the variable rule. Probabilistic weights were attached to both the output and the constraints themselves in the analysis of (t,d) deletion and the contraction and deletion of the copula. All of these patterns were displayed by cross-tabulations and their graphic transformations. Multivariate analysis, which could take into account the simultaneous effects of many dimensions of influence, was not then generally available for the binary data that are the results of linguistic choice. Cedergren's (1973) study of Panama was the first to introduce multiple logistic regression in the form of the Varbrul program.

This was a great step forward for the analysis of internal constraints, but not always as helpful when it incorporated social factors. Since the assumption of independence is inherent in the Varbrul program, it provides no general mechanism for detecting the interactions that are typical of gender, social class, and age. The assignment of a single numerical weight to "Male" or "Female" is equivalent to asserting that the difference between male and female is constant for all styles, social classes, and age groups, an assertion that is contradicted by almost all the studies cited.

There are three solutions to this problem. One is to have samples large enough to permit finer cross-tabulations, examining male/female differences for different social classes and ages. The other is to run separate multivariate analyses for the social groups most likely to show such interaction. The third is to search systematically for all possible interactions – a procedure easier in some statistical packages than others. In any case, it is not possible to return to univariate analysis, summing up separately the differences in the population by gender, social class, education, or style. A judicious choice of cross-tabulations in graphic form will display the pair-wise independence of such factors as style and social class, bearing in mind that it is the regularity of the diagrams in Chapter 7 of this book that first conveyed the systematicity of sociolinguistic data and led to the research tradition summed up in this chapter.

Accounting for the social stratification of language   A first question raised by SSENYC is how social stratification of language is maintained. Despite the negative prestige reported for the New York City vernacular in Chapter 13, ANAE and other recent studies show a great stability of this system in the everyday speech of 2006. If there is a consensus on what are proper ways of talking, then one would expect the gradual disappearance of non-standard forms over time, just as in the dialect leveling reported for most parts of western Europe. As one woman put it to me, "Why do I say [ɒi] when I don't *want* to?" The obvious answer, brought to the fore in SSENYC and Trudgill (1972), is the construct of *covert prestige*, associated with non-standard forms just as overt prestige is attributed to standard forms. The stable graduated stratification we find would then be the result of a balance of opposing forces. Though I have no doubt that such covert prestige exists, there is less evidence for it than one might think. In SSENYC it emerges primarily from Steve K. in Chapter 13. The subjective reaction test of the Harlem study in 1968 showed indications of covert prestige: as ratings on the Job scale fell, ratings on the Fight scale rose. However this effect was strongest among middle class subjects and disappeared for those at the lower end of the social scale. Thus the covert prestige of nonstandard forms may be felt more by those who don't use these forms than by those who do.

What competing explanation may there be for the maintenance of linguistic stratification? One must always consider the simple mechanical effect of the principle of density in the form enunciated by Bloomfield: that people who talk to each other the most tend to resemble each other in their forms of speech (1933). As reported in Chapter 4, I attempted at several times to get people to pronounce constricted [r] consistently in a reading passage, and success was marginal at best. To control a new form of speech a great deal of practice is needed, no matter how clear its social value.

A parallel problem arises in regard to the role of social strata in change from below or resistance to change from above. Sturtevant 1947 suggested that the spread of a linguistic change through a society from the originating group is the result of neighboring groups adopting the forms associated with membership in that group and symbolic of the group's values. The Philadelphia LCV project found that the new and vigorous changes like the raising and fronting of checked /ey/ were led by upper working class speakers. It is not inconceivable that the closely associated lower middle class followed behind, as the parallel partial regression lines suggest. However, we find the same parallel upward slope for the upper middle class, and behind them, an exactly parallel slope for the upper class. It would be difficult to support the notion that upper class speakers change their language as a symbolic adoption of working class values.

The problem is even more formidable for the linguistic changes that sweep across vast territories as displayed in ANAE. The Northern Cities Shift may indeed be symbolic of local practices for high school youth in a Detroit suburb (Eckert 1999), but that does not help us understand how and why it proceeds in the same way for 34,000,000 people across the entire Inland North. To understand such phenomena, we may have to turn to structural factors that are independent of social stratification, or social factors of a wider scope than we have considered before.

Glossary of linguistic symbols and terminology

I   Brackets, parentheses, and virgules

[ ] phonetic notation, symbolizing speech sounds
/ / phonemic notation, symbolizing phonemes
( ) variable notation, symbolizing phonological variables
    (æh)   a variable in general
    (æh-4)   a particular value of a variable
    (æh)-22 index score or average index score for a variable

II   Phonetic symbols

The phonetic notation used in the present work is that of the International Phonetic Association. The symbol [ʊ] is used in place of IPA [ɷ]. The position of the low vowels is indicated in Figure 10.1. The symbol [ɒ] is regularly used for a low back *unrounded* vowel; where the low back rounded vowel is indicated, the symbol is specifically marked as rounded. The low back-central vowel is indicated by [ɑ], and the low front-central vowel as [a].

Present Study	Linguistic Atlas
[a]	[a]
[ɑ]	[ɑ]
[ɒ]	[ɑ]
[ɒ.]	[ɒ]

III   Values of the variables

(r)

(r-1)	[r, ɚ, ɹ]	constricted consonant or glide
(r-0)	[ə, ᵊ, ɐ, ʌ, -]	unconstricted glide, lengthened vowel, or no corresponding phonetic element

404

	(æh)		
(æh-1)	[ɨˀ]		NYC *beer, beard*
(æh-2)	[ɛˀ]		NYC *bear, bared*
(æh-3)	[æ⌄]		
(æh-4)	[æ:]		NYC *bat, batch*
(æh-5)	[a:]		Eastern New England *pass, aunt*
(æh-6)	[ɑ:]		NYC *dock, doll*

	(oh)		
(oh-1)	[ʊˀ] [oˀ]		NYC *sure*
(oh-2)	[ɔˀ]		
(oh-3)	[ɔ⌄ˀ]		General American *for, nor*
(oh-4)	[ɔ:]		IPA cardinal /ɔ/
(oh-5)	[ɒ,] (rounded)		Eastern New England *hot, dog*
(oh-6)	[ɑ]		NYC *dock, doll*

	(th)	*(dh)*	
1	[θ]	[ð]	an interdental fricative
2	[tθ]	[dð]	an affricate
3	[t]	[d]	a lenis stop

IV   Standard linguistic terms and terms defined in this study

To help make these sociolinguistic findings accessible to social scientists outside of linguistics, the following definitions of linguistic terms are provided.

affricate: a consonant with a sudden, stop-like onset which continues with a scraping, fricative-like sound; the initial consonants of *chip, judge, tse-tse* are affricates, as well as the sound which corresponds to -*t y*- in *paint your wagon*, in rapid colloquial style.

allophone: one of several distinct speech sounds which do not contrast with one another in distinguishing words, and are members of the same *phoneme*. A rapidly pronounced diphthong [aʳ] with a slight glide, and a slow diphthong [ɒ:i] with a distinct glide are both allophones of /ay/ in *I'll*.

checked syllable: a syllable which ends in a consonant or a consonant cluster, such as *hit, burst, butler*; opposed to *free* syllable.

constriction: narrowing of the space available for the passage of air in the articulation of speech sounds, without shutting off the flow of air entirely; *constricted (r)*, is articulated with the tongue close to the roof of the mouth, and only a very narrow central passage for air remaining; *weakly constricted (r)*, sometimes written [ɚ], is a less narrow constriction, but not so open as a central vowel glide [ə].

contrastive analysis: (as defined in Chapter 14) an approach to *phonemic* analysis which relies upon minimal pairs and near minimal pairs to establish contrast between functional units.

fine stratification: see *stratification*.

free syllable: a syllable ending in a vowel, as *be*, *law*, *law*ful; the opposite of a *checked syllable*.

fricative: a narrowly constricted consonant characterized by a continuous hissing or scraping noise, produced by turbulent motion induced in the air stream; the initial consonants of *fin*, *vim*, *thin*, *then*, *sin*, *shin*, *Zen*, and medial consonant of *pleasure*.

fronting: a shift of articulation in which the highest part of the tongue is placed closer to the mouth, and further from the throat.

glide: a rapidly articulated, resonant speech sound, pronounced more quickly than the syllable *nucleus* to which it is adjacent; the first sound of *you're* or the last sound of *Roy*.

ingliding: terminating in a mid-central glide, as ingliding vowels [eᵊ] and [uᵊ].

morpheme: the smallest meaningful unit of language, such as a root, a suffix; *dragging* contains two morphemes, *dragon* only one.

nasal: a speech sound articulated with the passage between the throat and nasal chamber partly open, thus adding nasal resonance to the usual oral resonance. In English, the consonants /m/ and /n/ are nasal consonants; the vowel of *can't* is a nasal vowel, though it is not a separate *phoneme*.

nucleus: the most sonorous part of a syllable; the vowel which is longest and receives most stress, as opposed to the *glide* of a diphthong which is shorter and less stressed.

nucleus-glide differentiation: (as defined in Chapter 10) a shift of articulation (from a more common standard) in which the place of articulation of the nucleus is increasingly different from that of the glide, as in the fronting of the first element of /aw/ and a backing of the first element of /ay/.

phoneme: a functional unit of the sound system of a language: the minimum unit which distinguishes *morphemes*, words, or word sequences. Thus the final sounds of *wreath* and *wreathe* are two different phonemes, /th/ and /dh/, since only the contrast of these two sounds distinguishes the two words.

A phoneme may be represented by a number of speech sounds which are equivalent in their function of distinguishing words: these are *allophones* of the phoneme in question. The differences between allophones may be: 1) conditioned by the phonetic environment, as when the final glide of *buy* is longer than the pre-consonantal glide of *bite*; 2) part of a structure of stylistic or social variation, as in the difference between (oh-2) and (oh-3); 3) conditioned by physiological differences, as in /s/ pronounced by those without teeth; 4) a slight variation in sound which shows no systematic pattern, and for which no social, stylistic, or cognitive significance is immediately apparent.

phonemic: concerning phonemes, as in *phonemic notation*.

phonetic: concerning speech sounds, as in *phonetic notation*, which registers speech sounds without regard to functional importance in distinguishing words.

phonological space: the range of variation in the articulation of speech sounds which is utilized by a language in the discrimination of functional units, along such dimensions as fronting, backing, raising, or lowering of the tongue; rounding or unrounding of the lips; stopping, obstructing, or releasing the passage of air, etc.

phonological system: the set of phonemes, their relations to each other and to phonological space, and the structure of non-distinctive units within and across phonemes.

sharp stratification: see *stratification*.

speech sound: a relatively homogeneous section of articulated sound.

stop: a type of consonant characterized by a total interruption of the flow of air from the lungs, and a sudden release; the initial consonants of *pin*, *bin*, *tin*, *din*, *kin*, *gun*, etc.

stratification: (as defined in Chapter 7) the separation of sets of characteristics into distinct levels. *Sharp stratification* is a wide separation of a few discrete layers (necessarily by comparison with at least one pair of narrowly separated layers); *fine stratification* is a correlation of two continuous or near-continuous variables into an (indefinitely large) number of narrowly separated layers.

upgliding: terminating in a high glide (front or back), as upgliding vowels [eʳ] and [oᵘ].

Appendix A   Questionnaire for the ALS Survey

I.   "Some information on your language background"

A.   1. What was the first language that you learned to speak? [if not *English*, go to page 2, question 2a.]
      2. What country were you born in?
         [ALL such questions to be specified as follows: if U.S.A., what city? if NYC, What neighborhood?]
      3. What country was your father born in?
      4. What was his native language?
      5. Did he learn any other language when he was growing up?
 6–8. [Same questions for mother.]
      9. What country was your father's father born in?
     10. What was his native language?
11–16. [Same questions for father's mother, mother's father and mother. NOTE: Questions 3–16 to be pursued until first generation born outside U.S.A.]
     17. When were you born? [Year]
     18. Are you married?
19–20. [If yes] what country was your wife born in? What was her native language?
     21. Have you any children? [If so], what are their ages?
     22. Can you give me an idea of the places you have lived, starting from the time you were first learning to speak?
     23. Where did you go to elementary school? to high school? to any further schooling?
     24. Did you speak any other language besides English when you were growing up? [If yes, go to page 2, question 15a.]

I. B.   For those whose first language learned is not English
    2a.   What country were you born in?
3a-4a.   What country was your father born in? your mother?
5a-6a.   Did they come to the U.S.? When?
    7a.   What year were you born?
    8a.   When did you come to the U.S. [if not born here]?
    9a.   Where have you lived since you came to the U.S.?
    10a.   Which language is most natural to you now?
    11a.   [If there has been a change] when did this change take place?
    12a.   Are you married?
    13a.   [If so], what is your wife's native language?
    14a.   Do you have any children? what ages?
    15a.   Can you give me an idea of how much you use your other lan-
           guage in the following situations [not at all, a little, less than half
           the time, half the time, more than half the time, almost always,
           all the time]
           talking to your parents [now or in the past]
           parents talking to you   "   " " "   "
           at school or at work
           with friends around home
           reading newspapers
           in church
           dreaming

II.   Lexicon: traditional

"Now I'd like to ask you a few questions about some of the words you use today for everyday objects, and some others you used when you were growing up."

A.   1. What do you call the round cake, shaped like a tire, covered with powdered sugar, that some people dunk into coffee? [If *doughnut:*] Is there a difference between a doughnut and a cruller? In traditional NYC speech, a doughnut was called a *cruller* (<Dutch *kroeller*). Younger speakers use *cruller* for a twisted pastry.
         2. What is the name of the soft, white, very lumpy cheese that some people eat with sour cream, or else with green salads? [If *cottage cheese*,] what is *pot cheese?* In traditional NYC speech, cottage cheese is called *pot cheese* (<Dutch *pot kees*). Younger speakers use *pot cheese* for large curd cottage cheese.
         3. When you go to the movies, and you find a great many people waiting to get in, you may have to wait with them. You would say that you were waiting or standing . . . [*in* or *on* line]?
         4. If you accidentally knock into someone on the street, and you find that you know that person, and stop and talk a while, you might say on coming home that you had . . . [*bunked* into him?] [Did you ever hear someone say *bunked*?]
         5. When a little boy puts his head down on the ground, and falls head over heels, he is doing a . . . [If *somersault*,] is that the same as a *tumblesault?* [If so,] how do you say that?
         6. Did you ever go riding on a small sled in the winter? [If *yes*,] if you took the sled in both hands, ran down the hill, and threw yourself face down on the sled, what would you call that kind of a ride? [If no name,] what would you call a dive into a swimming pool in which you land flat on your stomach? The traditional NYC term is *bellywop(per)*.

II.   Lexicon: children's.

B.   1. If you should come out of your house with a piece of cake or candy in your hand, a friend sees you, what one word could he say to claim half or a part of it? That is, if he says this, you have to give it to him, but if you say something first, you don't have to?

[Check list: *thumbs up*, *heggies*, *akios*, *whacks*, *havesies*, *divvies*, *some*, *goodies*] The oldest NYC claiming term was *akios*, followed by *heggies* and then *thumbs up*.

2. Suppose two boys are fighting, and one wants to call time out, what does he say? [*Fingers?*] What if he has had enough, and wants to quit? [*I give*, *uncle?*]

3. In a game like hide-and-seek, or kick-the-can, What would you holler out to bring everybody in? [*False alarm?*]

4. Did you play marbles very much?
    a.   What did you call a big marble?
    b.   A glass marble?
    c.   A steel marble?
    d.   Your favorite shooter?
    e.   What was the main game you played? How did you play it?

5. There is a game played on the city streets with 13 numbers in a big square; you flip bottle caps or checkers from one number to another. Did you play that game? What is the name of it? Can you tell me how it is played? The NYC term for this game is *skellies*.

6. In this game, or in marbles, suppose your marble or bottle cap was stuck behind something so you couldn't shoot. What would you say to
    a.   Be allowed to move around it?
    b.   Be allowed to remove whatever was in the way?

III.   Folklore

"Now I'd like to ask you about some of the customs or rules you followed when you were a youngster. Children don't learn these from radio, or television – or from books or teachers – but from each other. Languages used to be learned that way, and that's one of the reasons that we are very much interested in these things."

A.   [For males]

1. Did you ever get into fights when you were a kid?
    Did you have any rules about what was considered fair?
    [Kicking or stomping, biting, hitting below the waist, etc.]

2. Do you remember any particular fight that was very crucial?
    Did you ever fight with someone much bigger than you were?
    Did you ever go into a fight fairly certain that you would lose?
    [continue here until informant talks spontaneously]

3. What were some of the names that were used for people of different nationalities? Italians, Negroes, Puerto Ricans, Jews . . . Which of these were "fighting words," and which could be used in kidding around?

4. What was the term for a very pretty girl? A very ugly one? The usual slang term for a girl among boys? Could you use that in front of a girl?

5. [If the informant's temperament seems to permit]
    what was the most direct word for a girl's sex organs? The most common word? Any slang words? [If you take the words *pussy*, *snatch*, *cunt*, *hole*, *nooky*] which of these do you think might possibly be the oldest, a word that could have been used by your great-grandfather if he spoke English? It is a general finding that people do not know that *cunt* is by far the oldest of these (<Middle English *cunte*).

6. Do you know a game where one boy stands in the middle and tries to catch one of the gang that runs past?
    [Check for various games: Three Steps to the King, King in the Middle, Father and Son, Red Devil, Johnny Jump Up . . .]
    [Try to get informant to tell you how some of these are played.]

III.   Folklore

B.   [For girls]

1. Suppose you were telling somebody something that you didn't want to count, what could you do with your hands or some part of your body? [Could you cross any other part of your body beside your fingers?] [Could you say anything so that this couldn't be done?]

2. How would you convince someone that you were telling the truth, by some sign or saying that something would happen if you were lying?

3. What would you do if you and a friend said the same thing together at the same time?

4. How would you decide who was *it*? What rhymes would you say:

[See check lists for these and questions below]

5. Did you jump rope? What rhymes did you use?

6. Did you know any clapping games? What songs went with them?

7. Did you use any rhymes to make fun of people?

IV.   Semantics and Syntax

"Now I'd like to turn to some more serious questions, about some words that we use every day, but don't always think too much about what they mean."

A.   Common sense.
  1. What is common sense?
  2. Do most people have it?
  3. Have you met anyone who you thought had a great deal? What kind of thing would he do, what kind of a person is he?
  4. What about some who had none, or very little?
  5. If I say that 2 and 2 are 4, is that common sense, or is it something else?
  6. If a little girl fell into the river, would it be common sense to jump in and pull her out?
  7. Do people get more common sense as they get older, or is it just something you're born with?
  8. Could you say of someone, "he is very intelligent but he has no common sense?"
  9. . . . "He's very smart, but has no common sense?"
  10. . . . "He's very wise, he has wisdom, but no common sense?"
  11. . . . "He has good judgment, but no common sense?"

B.   Danger of Death.
  1. Have you ever been in a situation where you thought there was a serious danger of your being killed? That you thought to yourself, "This is it?"
  2. What happened?
  3. How did you feel afterwards?

C.   The shoelace.
"Now I'd like you to do something for me, in the way of a puzzle, or rather to do something difficult with language. You tie a shoelace every day. Can you tell me how to tie a shoelace, without using your hands, as if I were blind, or on the other end of a telephone?"

D.   Successful man.
  1. Finally, I'd like to ask you to define something. A successful man. What is a successful man?

V.   *Pronunciation.* [text of readings on the following pages]

1.   [Give informant 5 cards for "when I was 9 or 10 . . ."] We'd like you to read this as naturally as possible. In other words, we don't want you to read this as if you were in a school room, but to give us an idea of how you might actually say this if you were telling the story yourself.

2.   "Now would you please read this list of words, as rapidly as you can." [Hand informant "bat, bad . . ." list]

[+ indicates words that are normally tense in Style A]

bat	pad	have
+bad	+pass	has
back	pal	razz
+bag	+cash	jazz
batch	can	hammer
+badge	+half	hamster
+bath	+past	fashion
bang	+ask	national
pat	+dance	family

3.   "And this short list . . ." [Hand informant "Paul, all . . ." list]

paul	coffee	talk
all	office	taught
ball	chalk	dog
awful	chocolate	forty-four
	chock	

4.   "Thank you. Would you please count from one to ten."
"Where is the tip of your tongue when you first <u>begin</u> to say 'ten'?"
"When you start to say '<u>den</u>'?"

5.   "Now would you please say for me the days of the week and the months of the year . . ."

6.   "Here's one more thing I'd like you to read for me if you will. It's another story, perhaps a little better than the other one." [Hand informant cards (a–e) for "Last Saturday night . . ."]

7.   "You've just used the pairs of words you see printed on this card." [Hand "same or different sound" card to informant.]
"Would you please read these words again, and after each pair, say whether they <u>sound</u> the same or different?" [When informant reads last two items, add, "Do they rhyme?]

dock	dark	Mary	merry	sure	shore
pin	pen	guard	god	since	sense
which	witch	"I <u>can</u>!"	"tin <u>can</u>"	do	dew

beer	bear	voice	verse	source	sauce
ten	tin	poor	pour	mirror	nearer
		finger	singer		

Text for concentrating five phonological variables.
[Underlining added to indicate concentration of the variables.]

Zero

When I was nine or ten, I had a lot of friends who used to come over to my house to play. I remember a kid named Henry who had very big feet, and I remember a boy named Billy who had no neck, or at least none to look at. He was a funny kid, all right.

(oh)

We always had chocolate milk and coffee cake around four o'clock. My dog used to give us an awful lot of trouble: he jumped all over us when he saw the coffee cake. We called him Hungry Sam.

(eh)

We used to play Kick-the-can. One man is "IT": you run past the man as fast as you can, and you kick a tin can so he can't tag you. Sammy used to grab the can and dash down the street – we'd chase him with a baseball bat, and yell, "Bad boy! Bad! Bad!" But he was too fast. Only my aunt could catch him. She had him do tricks, too: she even taught him to ask for a glass of milk, and jump into a paper bag.

(r)

I remember where he was run over, not far from our corner. He darted out about four feet before a car, and he got hit hard. We didn't have the heart to play ball or cards all morning. We didn't know we cared so much for him until he was hurt.

(th)
(dh)

There's something strange about that–how I can remember everything he did: this thing, that thing, and the other thing. He used to carry three newspapers in his mouth at the same time. I suppose it's the same thing with most of us: your first dog is like your first girl. She's more trouble than she's worth, but you can't seem to forget her.

Text for phonemic contrasts.

[Underlining added to indicate members of minimal pairs.]

Last Saturday night I took Mary Parker to the Paramount Theatre. I wanted to go and see The Jazz <u>Singer</u>, but Mary got her <u>finger</u> in the pie. She hates jazz, because she can't <u>carry</u> a tune, and besides, she never misses a new film with <u>Cary</u> Grant. Well, we were waiting on line about half an hour, when some farmer from Kansas or somewhere asked us how to get to Palisades Amusement Park.

Naturally, I told him to take a bus at the Port Authority Garage on 8th Avenue, but <u>Mary</u> right away said no, he should take the I.R.T. to 125th St., and go down the escalator. She actually thought the ferry was still running.

"You're certainly in the <u>dark</u>," I told her. "They tore down that <u>dock</u> <u>ten</u> years ago, when you were in diapers."

"And what's the <u>source</u> of your information, Joseph?" She used her sweet-and-sour tone of <u>voice</u>, like ketchup mixed with tomato <u>sauce</u>. "Are they running submarines to the Jersey <u>shore</u>?"

When <u>Mary</u> starts to sound humorous, that's <u>bad</u>: <u>merry</u> hell is <u>sure</u> to break loose. I remembered the <u>verse</u> from the Bible about a good woman being worth more than rubies, and I <u>bared</u> my teeth in some kind of a smile. "Don't tell this man any <u>fairy</u> tales about a <u>ferry</u>. He can't go that way."

"Oh yes he <u>can</u>!" she said. Just then a little old lady, as <u>thin</u> as my grandmother, came up shaking a <u>tin</u> <u>can</u>, and this farmer asked <u>her</u> the same question. She told him to ask a subway <u>guard</u>. My <u>god</u>! I thought, that's one sure way to get lost in New York City.

Well, I managed to sleep through the worst part of the picture, and the stage show wasn't too hard to <u>bear</u>. Then I wanted to go and have a bottle of <u>beer</u>, but she had to have a <u>chocolate</u> milk at <u>Chock</u> Full O'Nuts. <u>Chalk</u> this up as a total loss, I told myself. I bet that farmer is still wandering around looking for the 125th St. Ferry.

VI.   Subjective evaluation

A.   Subjective reaction test.
"Now I'd like to get your reactions to some samples of speech from New York City. On this tape, I have some sentences read by New Yorkers, from the same story which you have just read. Let us suppose that you were a personnel manager, and one of your points on which you rated everyone is their speech. Of course, you wouldn't hire them on their speech alone, but you would take it into consideration. This form shows the kind of rating scale you might use. [Explain.] You might think of it as a scale going from perfect speech on the top, to absolutely terrible on the bottom.

Each sentence will be spoken once, and then repeated. Listen to the first time, make up your mind, then hear it again, and if you have decided then, make a mark across the line at any point, on a dash or in between."

[Play test tape from "When I was 9 or 10 . . ." readings.]

[Pause at No. 11 for a rest; ask the informant what he is listening for, if he notices any words . . . or if he is just reacting to the overall impression. Compliment him on the ease with which he makes up his mind.]

B.   How many different speakers do you think were on this tape? [Write this in the lower right corner.]

C.   Self-evaluation test.
[Play sample pronunciations, and write down informant's opinion, with any new versions of his own, on the reverse.]
[On second series of each word, count "1, 2, 3, 4" after each pronunciation.]

"cards"	1	2	3	4
	[kɑrdz]	[kaɚdz]	[kaˡʔdz]	[kɒːdz]
"chocolate"	1	2	3	4
[1st vowel:]	[oːˀ˕]	[ɔˑˡ]	[ɔˑ]	[ɒˑ]
"pass"	1	2	3	4
	[pɪˑ ˀs]	[pæˡs]	[pæˑs]	[paˡs]
"thing"	1	2	3	
	[seɪmθɪŋ]	[seɪmtθɪŋ]	[seɪmtɪŋ]	
"then"	1	2	3	
	[džʌsðɛn]	[džʌsdðɛn]	[džʌdɛn]	
"her"	1	2	3	
	[aɪtoldhɝˑ]	[aɪtoldhɜ]	[aɪtoldhʌ]	
"hurt"	1	2	3	
	[ɪt hɝˑt]	[ɪt hɜː t]	[ɪt hɔɪt]	

VII.   Linguistic attitudes

1. What do you think of your own speech?
2. Have you ever tried to change your speech? What particular things about it?
3. Have you ever taken any courses in speech? What did the teacher mention in connection with pronunciation?
4. a.   What do you think of New York City speech?
   b.   Have you traveled outside of New York City? [If so] did people pick you up as a New Yorker by your speech?
   c.   Do you think that out-of-towners like New York City speech? Why?
   d.   What do you think of Southern speech as compared to New York City speech? [If Negro, distinguish Negro vs. white speech]
   e.   Have you heard Mayor Wagner talk? As far as his speech is concerned, not his politics, but his way of talking, how do you like it? [Same question for Rockefeller]. Which do you like better? [Probe if time permits for opinions on other speakers the informant thinks are good or bad.]
5. Going back to the time when you were growing up, I'd like to get some idea of the kind of speech that your friends used. Were most of your friends [same race or religion as informant]? Did you have any friends who were [other races and religions].
6. [If time permits, probe for any incidents where speech was a factor in disagreements of the group.]

VIII. Variant pronunciations.

"If someone should come to you, say a high school student, and ask you which of these pronunciations is correct, which would you say?" [After first item, add: "Is this the way you would usually say it? Let me know if there's a difference between the correct way, and the way you might usually say it, for any of these words."]

1. [džoʊsɪf]   or   [dˇzoʊzɪf]
2. [kætš]   or   [kɛtš]
3. [təmeɪto]   or   [təmɑto]
4. [daɪpɚz]   or   [daɪəpɚz]
5. [ɑnt]   or   [ænt]
6. [ɔftən]   or   [ɔfn]
7. [gərɑdž]   or   [gərɑ:ž]
8. [hjumərəs]   or   [jumərəs]
9. [veɪz]   or   [vɑ:z]
10. [lɛnθ]   or   [lɛŋθ]
11. [fɛbruɛri]   or   [fɛbjuɛri]
12. [kætšəp]   or   [kɛtšəp]
13. [ɛskəleɪtɚ]   or   [ɛskjuleɪtɚ]
14. [nɬu]   or   [njɬu]
15. [tjɬun]   or   [tɬun]
16. [ævənɬu]   or   [ævənju]
17. [bikɔs]   or   [bikɔz]
18. [hæf]   or   [haf]

IX.   Form for self-evaluation test and index of linguistic insecurity

You are about to hear several different pronunciations of the words listed below. All of these are used by some speakers of American English. Circle the number of the pronunciation which is closest to the one you usually use.

"cards"   1   2   3   4
"chocolate"   1   2   3   4
"pass"   1   2   3   4
"thing"   1   2   3
"then"   1   2   3
"her"   1   2   3
"hurt"   1   2   3

You are about to hear two possible pronunciations of the words listed below. Circle the one you believe is *correct*. Then check the one you usually use.

Joseph	1	2	length	1	2
catch	1	2	February	1	2
tomato	1	2	ketchup	1	2
diapers	1	2	escalator	1	2
aunt	1	2	new	1	2
often	1	2	tune	1	2
garage	1	2	avenue	1	2
humorous	1	2	because	1	2
vase	1	2	half	1	2

Appendix B   Anonymous observations of casual speech

One of the fundamental problems which is treated in this study is that of eliciting casual and spontaneous speech in the context of the formal linguistic interview, which normally evokes careful speech only. In Chapter 4, methods for obtaining records of casual speech within this framework were described. In order to verify the results, it is necessary to compare them to records of casual speech gathered outside of the context of the linguistic interview. The department store survey described in Chapter 3 is one such method. Another source for such casual speech is the large bulk of anonymous observations on the streets of the Lower East Side, made in the course of the exploratory interviews. The first excerpt given below shows a section of spontaneous speech of working class and lower class young adults which may truly be called the language of the streets. The second is a set of observations made in a middle class area, showing the type of (r) usage which may be heard in everyday conversation.

I.   The punch-ball game

At the corner of Stanton and Ridge Streets on the Lower East Side of Manhattan, there is a punch-ball game organized every Saturday in reasonably good weather. Fifteen to twenty young men, from about seventeen to twenty-five years old, take part. The area is a tenement district, and most of the residents are members of the lower class or working class. All ethnic groups of the Lower East Side are represented here; in a nearby playground, I interviewed several groups of youngsters who included Polish, Czech, Jewish, Puerto Rican, English, Irish, and African–American (AA) boys. No AAs actually took part in the punch-ball game: most of the white ethnic groups, however, seem to be represented among the players.

This session of the punch-ball game was recorded on August 11th, 1962. I was one of many bystanders by the curb, and the microphone and recorder were concealed in a small satchel.

The punch-ball game is played in the middle of Stanton Street, across the intersection of Ridge Street. A man from the team that is batting is stationed at Ridge Street to hold up the game when a car approaches, or hold up the car if necessary. Punch-ball is played without a pitcher: the batter bounces the ball once (at which point runners can move) and hits it with his fist.

The speech that is recorded here is the language of the streets in its most literal sense. The content falls into two major categories: 1) a running stream of chatter ("Let's go!"), disparagement ("Hey Sol, you stink!"), encouragement ("Atta baby!"), irony ("A miracle, a miracle!"), instructions to the outfielders ("C'mon in, Louie!"), and warnings of cars approaching ("Hol' it, Walter!"); 2) arguments and instructions related to specific points in the game: instructions to base runners ("Hey Walter, try'n' get to third!"), arguments about who was up ("Waddayoulookin'at me for? I tol'ya I was up!"), about whether a ball was thrown from the outfield to the plate, or whether it was cut off by an infielder, thus allowing the man at third to advance to home, and finally, the calculations of the winners ("Double money, double money!"). The material in the second category is generally clearer in the recording, and gives the best phonological information.

The phonology of this excerpt may be summed up in the following average values, combining the usage of all speakers:

(r)-00
(æh)-22
(oh)-25
(th)-61
(dh)-101

This data fit the information yielded by Chapters 7 and 8 on the casual speech of younger men from the lower class and working class. The total absence of (r-l) is accompanied by a preponderance of long monophthongs: [dɛː], *there*; [fɔː], *for*; [skɔː], *score*, with only occasional off-glides. The (æh)-(oh) usage of the speakers places this group in the IIc quadrangle of Figure 14.1, along with other younger Catholic male speakers from the two lower classes. The use of (th) and (dh) is typical of the younger speakers of these two classes, as shown in Table 9.18.

The /ʌy/ phoneme occurs freely in this record, especially in *third*, but the constricted vowel [ɜ] is also heard. From the information given in Table 9.8, we can infer that those who use the former vowel are probably lower class speakers, while the latter is more apt to be used by working class New Yorkers of this age group.

For some of these speakers, (ay) and (aw) show no nucleus-glide differentiation, parallel with the group indicated in Figure 14.2. Others show a slight tendency towards the backing of (ay), but more show fronting of (aw). This tendency is in accord with the correlated (æh) and (oh) values shown above. This group of speakers uses only moderately high (oh), and obeys the general correlation of the four variables shown in Figure 14.8. If, on the other hand, one records the casual speech heard in the Grand Street area, the (oh) usage tends to (oh-1) quite frequently and (æh) shows lower vowels.

The high ingliding vowels /ih/ and /uh/ heard in this section are frequently long, lowered, and centralized monophthongs, indicating the low merger with the mid vowels discussed in Chapter 14. The vowel /ih/ of *here* is heard several times as a central vowel, not far from [ɜ] and rounded, as in [lɛsgɛsmovəhɜ:] *let's get someone over here.* Only one example of /uh/ is heard, in *just to make sure*, as (oh-1).

The text is given on the right in phonetic transcription, and on the left in regular orthography. Since a great many diacritics would be needed for the various values of (oh), these values are indicated here as superscripts for [o], using the code numbers for the values of the variables as used in this study. No intonation or stress patterns are indicated, except for occasional extra-heavy stress. The word breaks are to give an approximate idea of timing.

Text of the punch-ball game

Hey Walter, try 'n' get to third!	[hei wɔ³ łtə trainɨgɛt: ə θɜ˥ˈd
Hey I'll coach myself!	hei aɪł koutš maisɛłf
Hol' it, Walter, hol' it!	houlɪt wɔ³lə houlɪt
Tag up, Walter, tag up!	tɛ: ˥gʌp wɔ³lə tɛ:˥gʌp
Run, run! Score now!	rʌn rʌn skɔ:² nau
Hol' it, hol' it, hol' it!	hőʊ ɪt hőʊ ɪt hőʊ ɪt
Atta baby!	ǽţə beɪ •bi
One out, one out. . .	wʌn a˧ ʊt wʌna˧ʊt
A miracle, a miracle!	əmɨ rə kəł əmɪrə kə ł
Hey, you stink Sol!	hei: just ĭŋk sɑ••ł
Whatayouthink I'm running-	wʌtə juţɪŋkamrʌnɨŋ-
along to get to third	lɔŋt tgɛt³θɜ ˈd
base for?	beɪsfɔ²
He just threw it. I was	hidžsʌsθruɪt aiwəz
standing around. . What	sţɛ•ndɪn araʊnd wʌţ
a thing to do. . .	ətɪŋtəduʊ
C'mon in, Louie!	kᵊmanɪn lu:i
Awright, hol' it! There's	ɔraɪt hőʊ lɪt ðəz
one out.	wʌnæ˧ʊt
Two out. Awright, Al,	tu aʊt ɔraɪt æ:ł
you're up. . .	jɚˑʌp

You're up, Allen, you're up!   jɚʌp ælən jɚʌp

Allen, you're up!   ælən jɚʌp

Gotta get this out. . .   gɑṭə gɛt ðɪs aˈʊt

Hey – good thing I did go. . .   hej gʊd ðɪŋ aɪ dɪd gʊu

You ain't kiddin'. . .   jʊu eɪnt kɪdɪn

otherwise he'd a been out. . .   ʌðəwaiz hidəbɪn aʊṭ-

Somebody picks the ball up. . . Go!   sʌmbʌdi pɪks ðə bɔ³l ʌp gʊu

Out, out!   aˈʊt åʊt

. . .didnget up! Hey, you didn't get up?   dɪŋgɛṭʌp heiju dɪᵈŋgɛḍʌpᵢ

Why'nyousayyouwzup? I said I was up here. . .   wainjusei juwzʌp ai sɛdaiwəzʌphiə

Whaddayoulookinatmefor? I tol'ya I was up!   wʌdəjulʊkɪŋəmifɔ³ai tʊʊl jəiwᵊzʌp

I ain't up yet!   ắi eɪnt ʌpjɛːt

A man over here!   ə mɛ̃ːn oʊvᵊ hɨːᴸ

Le's have a man overtohere!   l ɛshæᵀvəmæ̃ːᴸn oʊvətəhɜːᴸ

Le's get someone over here!   l ɛsgɛsmoᵁ vʌhɜːᴸᵀ

Hey, I'm up this series!   hei aᵕmʌp ðɪsː iriz

Atta baby! Atta baby!
[applause]   æṭəbeibi

Attawaygo, Bref. . .   æṭ əwe jgoʊ brɛf

Hol'it Al!   hoʊ́l ɪt æːᵀɫ

Run!   rʌn

Run it, run it!   rʌnɪt rʌnɪt

Stay there!   sṭei dɛ•

C'mon, c'mon, c'mon!   kmɑn kmɑn kmɑn

run it, run it, run it!   rʌnɪt rʌnɪt rʌnɪt

Safe, safe!   seɪf seɪf

C'mon to third! Stay there!   kmɑnt əθɜ³ᴵ sṭej dɛ•

Third!   θɜᵛd

Who's up?   huᵈzʌp

We're all mixed up here!   wi ɔːᵌlmɪkstʌphɨːᵎ

They got the whole side over here!   ðeigɑtðə hoʊl saɪd oʊvəhiᵊ

Wait, wait, wait!   wei wei wei

. . .in the infield, Carmine! You was throwin' to the plate!   ɪn ði ɪnfɨld kɒᵕmaɪn juwztrowɪntd pleɪt

Get outa here! You threw the ball home!   gɛːḍa ˈʊṭəhɨ jutru ḍəbɔlhoʊm

. . .t'the plate!
Nobody made a cut-off that
  ball!
There were three guys over
  there!
Nobody was hol'in the plate
  at all.
Hey, Carmine, you threw
  that ball right in the
  infield!
. . .nobody cut off th' ball!
  Charles ain't at fault.
Hey Winky, you playin' a
  kid game?
  You throw the ball home?
There was nobody at home!
You threw the ball to the
  infield!
You were standin' on second!
You threw the ball home.
They know it! Nobody cut
  off that ball!
  Nobody cut off that
  ball!
Call it!

All right, go back to second!
  Go ahead!
What an umpire!
All right, two outs.
Le's go!

Hol' it up, hol' it up!
Two outs, two out. . .
Hey Joe, hold that guy at
  third! Hold that kid!
All right, I'll watch him!
Watch the line, Rich! Go
  back a step, just to
  make sure!
All right, y' ready?

These guys come jumpin'
  out. . .

Hol' it up, Walter!
Hold it up, Walter!
I got it, I got it!
One out!

Hey, Joe!

tdə plɛɪt
nobʌdi meɪdəkʌtɔfðə
  bɔː²
ðɛw θrigaizoʊvə
  dɛ̞ə
nobʌdi wez hoʊɬn ðə plɛɪt
  ətɔɬ
heɪ kamaɪn jutθru
  d̞æt bɔ²l raɪtɪnði
  ɪnfil
nobʌdi kʌt̞ɔfdbɔɬ
  tšaz eɪnt ə fɔɬt
hejwɪŋki jʊuple jɨnə
  kɪd geɪm
jəθroʊ də bɔ²l hoʊm
ðɛwəznoʊbʌdiː hoʊm
jutruwdəbɔ• tədəɪn
  fɪ²ɬ
juwstæn̞nansɛkɨnd
jutrudəbɔlhoʊm
dəɪ noʊɪt nobʌdi kʌt̞
  ɔ³f dᵒæ bɔː²
  nobʌdi kʌt̞ ɔf d̞æt
  bɔᵊ
kɔlɪt

əʔaɪt goʊbæktə sɛkɨŋ
  go˧ᵊhɛʔ
wʌt̞ə ʌmpaɪᵊ
araɪt tu aʊts
les goʊ

hoʊlɪt̞ʌphoʊlːʌp
tu a˧ʊts tu a˧ʊt
heɪ džoʊ hoʊl d̞æt gai ət
  tθ3id hoʊl d̞æt kɪd
ɔraɪʔ alwætšɨm
wʌtšðəlaɪn rɪtš goʊ
  bæk a stɛp džʌstə
  mek šɔ¹
əraɪʔ jᵊrɛdi

dᵒiz gaiz kʌm džʌmpɨn
  aʊt

hɔlɪt̞ʌp wɔ³lə
hoʊld ɪt̞ʌp wɔ²ltʌ
aɪgat̞ɪtaɪgat̞ ɪt
wʌn aʊt

heɪ džoʊ

All right, le's go! One out. . .	ɔrailɛs gou wʌn aʊʔ
Hey, Joe!	hei džou
All right, ready?	ɔrai rɛdi
Watch the line!	watšðəlɑin
Straight away!	streɪt̹əwɛi
All right, go ahead, Joe. . .	ərait gʌ•ᵊd džou
All right, kid's up, Red's up!	ɔ:rai kɪdzʌp redʐ ʌp
. . .see what I mean?	siwʌt̹aimin
All right, when he hits the ball, go!	ɔraiʔ wɛnihɫtsðᵊbɔ²l go
Bounces it, when he bounces it!	ba⊣ʊnsɫz ɪt wɛniba⊣ʊnsɫz ɪt
Bounces the ball, when he bounces it!	ba⊣ʊnsɫz də bɔl wɛni ba⊣ʊnsɫz ɪt
Hol' it up, Red! Hol' it up, hold it up!	houlɪt̹ʌp rɛəʔ houlɪ ʌp houldɪt̹ʌp
Go, go, go!	gou gou gou
Run it, run it!	rʌnɪt rʌnɪt
Atta baby!	æt̹əbebi
That's all, that's all!	ðætsɔ³ɫ ðætsɔ³ɫ
How many innings that game?	haʊmɛniɪnŋz ðæt geɪm
Twelve innings, double money, double money!	twɛlvɪnɪŋs dʌbɫ mʌni dʌbɫ mʌni
Double up the money! Double money. . .	dʌbɫ ʌpðə mʌni dʌbɫ mʌni
Good hit, Red!	gʊd hɪt red
C'mon, double up!	kəmɑn dʌbəɫ ʌp

II.   The lunch counter

The following record of (r) pronunciation in casual speech was made at a lunch counter on the corner of Grand and Madison Streets, on September 5th, 1963, between 8:30 and 9:00 p.m. This location is in the center of the middle class cooperative apartment area, but also borders on a lower class project area, the Vladeck project.

The transcriber, myself, was seated at the lunch counter. Most of the speakers who were recorded were buying something at the candy counter, or buying soda to take out from the counterman at the lunch counter.

Table B.1

Sex	Race	Age	(r) values	Notes
F	W	40–50	0000000000	leather jacket, gold sandals
F	W	40–50	0	
M	AA	20–50	00	
M	W	20–25	00	
M	AA	20–25	0	
M	W	14–15	01	Orthodox Jewish: wears yarmulke
M	W	8–12	00	
M	AA	8–12	0	
M	AA	20–30	1111	tending counter
F	W	15–18	00	
F	W	40–50	0	
F	W	40–50	0000000	
M	W	15–16	00	
M	W	20–25	0	
M	W	30–35	1	tie, hat, white short sleeve shirt
M	W	50–60	1	

The sparsity of notes which might identify the class position of the speaker illustrates the difficulty of using such data as primary evidence of speech patterns. On the other hand, in the light of Chapter 7, we can see some regularity here. The young counterman who used all (r-1)'s was evidently a college student; his manner was cultivated, and he approached each customer with, "Good evening, may I be of service to you?" The other clear identification of middle class status – the hat, tie and white shirt – was also associated with (r-1).

Appendix C   Analysis of losses through moving of the MFY sample population

This discussion is an analysis of the type of losses sustained by the original Mobilization for Youth (MFY) sample population through moving in the two-year period between the MFY survey and the American Language Survey (ALS). The sample population of native English speakers which was selected for study consisted of 312 individuals. Eight of these died, or became incapacitated, and 109 moved, leaving the ALS target sample of 195 subjects. By analyzing the social characteristics of the group who moved, we will be able to determine in what way the ALS target sample does or does not represent the original population of native speakers present on the Lower East Side in 1961.

The distribution of speakers who had moved or died, according to racial and ethnic group, may be seen in Table C.1.

The only serious discrepancy here is with the Protestant group, which shows twice as high a rate of moving as the others. This is what we would expect from the rootless character of this group as described above. The losses from the Protestant group in the sample need not be a serious source of concern. It appears that not more than one or two of the sixteen who had moved were natives of New York City, and therefore would in any case not have appeared in the most important of the studies to follow Chapter 6.

The other groups are approximately the same as far as rate of moving is concerned, with the Catholics showing a somewhat higher figure. It now appears that 15 percent a year is closer to the rate of moving which is characteristic of a large part of the sample, and we need not anticipate any serious distortion in the ethnic composition of the sample through the loss of the 109 who had moved.

The actual numbers of those who had moved and those who had died are given in column 4 of Table 6.4. Inspection of this table shows that there is a more serious problem in the socio-economic composition of those who had moved. The distribution is illustrated in Table C.2.

Table C.1 *Losses from moving within each ethnic group*

	% for 2-year period
AA	31
Jewish	30
Orthodox 30	
Conservative 30	
Catholic	38
Protestant	64

Table C.2 *Losses from moving in each class group*

	% for 2-year period
Lower Class, 0–2	26
Working Class, 3–5	38
Middle Class, 6–9	42

Table C.3 *Losses through moving for ethnic and class groups*

Class	AA	Jewish, Orth.	Jewish, Cons. & Ref.	Catholic	Protestant
0–2	21	33	33	32	00
3–5	23	23	28	40	100
6–9	75	36	37	40	75

This progression shows a regular pattern, and the loss of the moved population therefore prevents us from obtaining as good a representation from the higher social classes as compared with the lower.

A closer examination of the data in Table 6.2 shows that the progression noted above is not due to factors which affect all ethnic groups equally, but rather to the differential behavior of the two marginal groups: the African–American (AA) and the white Protestants.

Table C.3 shows a breakdown of the moved population by both ethnic and class divisions. The three central groups have lost approximately the same percentages in the three class division. However, the AA group has moved out almost entirely as far as the 6–9 class group is concerned, and the Protestant group shows a total loss of the small 3–5 group representation.

As far as the AA population is concerned, this loss is a serious drawback in an attempt to depict the original composition of the MFY survey. The loss is heaviest in the upper middle class group (9 on the MFY socio-economic

Table C.4   *Percentage of males in sample populations*

	%	N
Total MFY sample	45	1225
MFY respondents	46	988
Native speakers studied for ALS	38	312
Remaining ALS population	41	195

index), where five out of seven had moved and could not be located. However, it should be noted that this group was heavily over-represented in the original MFY survey as compared to the AA population of the city as a whole. The mean income of the AA MFY respondents was approximately $1,000 higher than the mean income of AA families in New York City. Therefore the view of AA speech obtained in this survey will not be as seriously impaired as if the original sample had been more representative of New York City.

The complete loss of the working class Protestant group of six speakers is also unfortunate, but again, it may be noted that these informants were mostly not native to the city.

One of the most serious problems in the composition of the population is the proportion of men and women. In the original sampling of the Lower East Side, it was found that women outnumbered men by five to four. The percentage of male respondents in the population through the various selections is shown in Table C.4.

We see that a slightly higher percentage of males responded to the MFY survey, closing the gap between male and female. However, the proportion of males among the native speakers is considerably less, only a little more than a third of the total population of native speakers. The loss of subjects through death and moving readjusted the balance slightly in favor of men. Thus in the ALS target population there are 79 men and 116 women.

So far, it appears that the peculiar problem of a secondary survey – the loss through death and mobility – has not shown any serious biases in the remaining population, as far as the three central ethnic groups are concerned. There is another consideration which must be studied – the relationship of the subjects to the city and the neighborhood. Here we find more serious differences in the moved and remaining population.

Local status of the moved population

One of the most important characteristics of a population, as far as linguistic behavior is concerned, is its relation to the older traditions of the community. Individuals who move in and out of an area in the course of a

Table C.5   *Relation of moved and remaining population to the Lower East Side*

	Native to LES	Lived on LES over 10 yrs.	Lived on LES less than 10 yrs.
Moved	30%	26%	44%
Remaining	47%	28%	25%

Table C.6   *Relation of Jewish and Catholic population to Lower East Side by moved and remaining groups*

	Native to LES	Lived on LES over 10 yrs.	Lived on LES less than 10 yrs.
Moved	37%	40%	23%
Remaining	64%	23%	13%

few years do not participate in the local culture which is usually associated with characteristics of local speech, while groups that remain in one neighborhood for generations may have many special features of culture and language. For the entire MFY population of 1961, who responded to the MFY survey, we have data on how many years they have lived in the Lower East Side, and on the country of birth. We would most like to know their relation to New York City – whether they were born in New York or some other part of the country. However, this question was not asked in the MFY survey, and we only know the answer for the subjects we have interviewed in the linguistic survey. We can compare the moved and remaining population for its relation to the Lower East Side, and note any significant differences (Table C.5).

Relationship of the subjects to the Lower East Side was determined by the same criterion used for relationship to New York City: if the subject had been born on the Lower East Side, or had come to the Lower East Side before the age of eight, he was considered a native of the area (Table C.6).

This redistribution of the sample population in its relation to the local community, through loss of the less stable elements, is much more marked than Table C.5 shows. The two marginal groups, originally 75 AAs and 25 Protestants, each included only one speaker who was native to the Lower East Side. The comparison of moved and remaining groups is therefore meaningless for the AA and Protestant groups, and we can reorganize the table as Table C.6 to include only the central groups – the Jews and Catholics.

Table C.7   *Percentage of speakers native to the Lower East Side for Jewish and Catholic Groups*

	Jewish, Orth.	Jewish, Cons. & Ref.	Catholic
Total speakers before moving	77	54	52
Remaining speakers after moving	88	60	55

Table C.8   *Percentage of speakers native to the Lower East Side for Socio-economic groups*

	0–2	3–5	6–9
Total speakers before moving	65	56	55
Remaining speakers after moving	67	64	64

Table C.9   *African–Americans moved and remaining by number of years spent on the Lower East Side*

	Native to LES	Over 20 yrs. on the LES	10–20 yrs. on the LES	Under 10 yrs. on the LES
Moved	1	0	3	25
Remaining	0	6	14	26

Table C.6 shows a reversal in the relationship of native and non-native as far as the Lower East Side is concerned: one-third of those who moved were born on the Lower East Side, while two-thirds of those who stayed were native East Siders.

The effect of this loss on the native status of the three central groups may be seen in Table C.7. This represents the resulting increase in the percentage of subjects who are local East Siders as a result of the moving of part of the population.

The effect upon the various socio-economic groups of this shift is concentrated in the two upper sections, as shown in Table C.8, and the total effect is to make these three divisions more comparable in their proportions of local speakers.

The AA group has very little connection with the Lower East Side from this point of view. If we examine the number of years spent on the Lower East Side by the AA speakers who have stayed and those who remained, we might be able to see some trend towards the development of a stable population. If AA speakers who have remained are concentrated among those who have spent more years on the Lower East Side, this would be evidence of such a trend.

Table C.9 shows the actual number of AA subjects who moved from the East Side, or remained on it, according to their local status. This chart shows some evidence of the development of neighborhood ties among the AA residents, or at least that the group which has moved out is more mobile than the group which remained – from the point of view of past record as well as present. The effect is more striking when we realize just how mobile is the group of twenty-five AA residents who had lived less than ten years on the Lower East Side and have since moved.

Came to LES less than 1 year before MFY survey	11
Came to LES 1–2 years before MFY survey	4
Came to LES 3–10 years before MFY survey	10

Assessment of the effects of losses through moving

The effect of the two-year lag between the first selection of the sample and the execution of the linguistic survey cannot be overlooked. Most of the losses have been in that section of the community which has the least connection with the traditional speech pattern – if relation to the Lower East Side is an indication of relation to New York City as a whole. In one sense this may make the task of constructing a coherent view of the language system somewhat easier, since it stands to reason that the most highly structured cultural patterns are apt to be those which belong to the most stable sections of the community.

However, the removal of disproportionately large numbers of middle class subjects is a part of a continuing pattern that is altering the social structure of the city. The existence of this pattern gives rise to other considerations on the effects of the loss through moving.

A certain percentage of those who had moved in the two-year interval will have left New York City for the surrounding suburbs, or moved even farther afield. We have seen that the middle class shows the largest percentage of movers, and this is the group which is most likely to have left the city entirely. In that case, they are no longer a part of the New York City speech community which we are attempting to describe through the survey of the Lower East Side and other means. In this light, we can say that a part of the apparent loss through moving represents those who have removed themselves from the universe under study, and the actual loss through the two-year lag is less than the total described above.

We may also consider that the middle class speakers who had moved out of the city, or moved to areas in Queens or Jamaica which are predominantly middle class, have followed a pattern which is more typical of those with upward social mobility than the group which has remained behind. Those who have fled to the suburbs have differentiated themselves from the large working class population in the Lower East Side even more sharply than those who remain in the Lower East Side. It is also probable that the language behavior of the middle class group that had moved shows even greater differentiation from the working class language pattern.

It would be possible to study the composition of those who had moved by several ways. They might be pursued by mail or telephone to distant parts of the city. However, such methods will result in a heavy bias towards those speakers who are easily located, have telephones listed, or who care to reply to mail forwarded. Another approach would be to interview families which have moved into the vacated apartments, since these replacements are also presumably more mobile than the average. However, in the Lower East Side, a large number of these replacing families are Puerto Rican, and not native speakers of English. We will therefore rely on internal comparison of the speakers who remain in order to assess further the effect of this loss of mobile subjects on the total results.

The death of six of the informants in the course of the two-year lag was an additional loss to the survey, particularly since all six of the speakers were native to the Lower East Side. The effect of the loss, however, was in a direction contrary to the loss of informants through moving, and therefore offset this larger defect in the population studied. There is therefore reason to believe that the social stratification of language which we will observe in the remaining population is a minimal stratification: that if the population had been surveyed in 1961, we would probably have found stratification that was equally sharp or sharper.

Appendix D   Analysis of the non-respondents: the television interview

In Chapter 6, the derivation of the sample for the Lower East Side survey was discussed, and the characteristics of the ALS target sample given. The regular ALS linguistic interview was completed for 63 percent of that sample. The non-respondents will be analyzed in this appendix – first for their social characteristics, and then, by means of the television interview, for their linguistic behavior. The television interview was described generally in Chapter 6: the questionnaire itself is given at the end of this appendix.

Characteristics of the non-respondents

Table 6.4 showed an ALS target population of 195 individuals. A total of 122 were interviewed through the regular ALS survey procedure, and 33 of the remaining 73 by the television interview. Six of the 195 individuals in the target sample are eliminated when one-third of the AA working class group is set aside to match the other working class groups. The total ALS response for this comparable sample is then 119 out of 189, or 63 percent. Of the 70 non-respondents, 33 were studied through the television interview, and 37 were not sampled. The non-respondents were basically of two types: refusals, and those who could not be reached.

Reasons for non-response   About half of those who refused mentioned the previous survey as a reason for their refusal (although no connection with the MFY survey was stated by the ALS interviewer). Several of the MFY informants had been inconvenienced by the primary interview, or found it long and tiresome. (Among those who did respond to both surveys, many reported favorably on the MFY interview.) Some informants could not be reached because they were seldom home, worked long hours, or were never located. Another group of those who could not be reached might have been interviewed by the ALS procedure if the time allotted for field work had been extended. Most of the latter are represented in the seventeen informants who are labelled *can't reach*, but who were sampled by the television interview.

Table D.1

	Refused	Can't reach	Total
Sampled through the television interview	16	17	33
Not sampled	11	26	37
Total	27	43	70

Table D.2 *Social characteristics of the non-respondents*

	Television interviews		Not sampled		Total non-respondents	
	Refused	CR	Refused	CR	Refused	CR
Total	16	17	11	26	27	43
SEC Groups						
0–2	7	3	4	11	11	14
3–5	5	7	4	5	9	11
6–8	3	4	2	9	5	13
9	1	3	1	1	2	4
Ethnic Groups						
Jews	4	11	2	12	6	23
Italians	4	3	3	5	7	8
AAs	5	1	1	5	6	6
Sex						
Men	5	10	5	18	10	28
Women	11	7	6	8	17	15
Age						
20–39	6	4	3	5	9	9
40–59	8	12	7	14	15	26
60–	2	1	1	7	3	8

About a dozen of the informants who were not interviewed made one or more appointments with the interviewer, but did not keep them.

Social characteristics of the non-respondents.   The social characteristics of the non-respondents by class, ethnic group, age and sex, are shown in Table D.2.

Table D.2 shows that the losses through refusals and through inability to reach the respondents were greatest among the lower class subjects. A large portion of the losses through refusal were recouped by means of the television interview, so that the major loss remaining is the group of 14 lower class speakers who could not be reached. Many of these subjects were Italians and AAs; the overall completion rate (as shown in Table 9.6) was higher for Jews than AAs or Italians. Table D.2 shows that Jews showed a much lower tendency to refuse the ALS interview: only one-quarter of the Jewish losses were through refusal, but about half of the Italian and AA losses. A number of the Jews who could not be located worked in stores until ten o'clock at night. The fact that there was greater difficulty in interviewing Italians and AAs than Jews repeats the experience of the MFY interview.

The losses in the male population, considered in Chapter 6, are seen primarily due to unavailability in Table D.2. Men showed far less tendency than women to refuse the ALS interview: only one-quarter of the male losses were due to refusal, while over half of the women non-respondents refused. The tendency to refuse was also higher among younger informants, while most of the losses in the older age levels were due to inability to locate the informants.

The tendencies to refuse, or the difficulties of locating informants, vary somewhat from group to group. However, the television interview cut across all group lines, and the proportion of those interviewed to those not sampled is roughly equal for most of the categories shown in Table D.2. We may therefore conclude that the television interview provided an efficient device for sampling the speech of those who did not complete the longer ALS interviews. If the results of the television interviews show the same patterns of social variation which were shown for the ALS informants, then it may be concluded that the ALS survey as a whole reported the speech of the target sample accurately.

Analysis of the television interview

First, it is necessary to consider the reasons why all of the non-respondents were not sampled through the television interview. There was only one abrupt refusal to the television interview which prevented us from obtaining sufficient data on the speech of the subject, and this person was afterwards studied by other means.

A certain number of subjects simply refused to come to the door, or to the telephone. In some cases, their wives or husbands had apparently taken on the task of protecting them from any contact with strangers, and it was not possible to overcome this barrier. Others could not be located: they apparently worked odd hours, and were not home at any time that the interviewers could reach them. Another group of non-respondents were junior members of the household, and spent most of their time elsewhere. A majority of these subjects could have been reached if additional time was assigned to the problem. However, the results of the department store survey, the ALS survey, and the television interview indicate that further field work would not be likely to yield data significantly different from that already on hand.

In conducting a linguistic survey there is always the suspicion that those who refuse do so because they are less interested in language, less sensitive to linguistic differences, or perhaps hostile to universities and the pursuit of knowledge in general. Such a description fits only a small minority of the non-respondents to the ALS survey. Many of those who refused did so because they were busy, suspicious, or annoyed by the primary survey. In the cases where such suspicions were overcome, the informant often showed an abrupt change of attitude, and great interest in the survey. Most of the group who could not be reached did not appear to differ in social or personal characteristics from the population as a whole except in their working hours.

By means of the television interview, it was possible to check the speech behavior of the rudest and roughest of the refusals, since most of them were sampled by this device. It might be said, as a result of studying Table D.2, that lower class AA and Italian women were prone to refuse the ALS interview because they are self-conscious about their lack of education, or else because they are less interested in language than most people. Nine of these subjects are included in the television interview. It might be said that the ALS interviews as a whole show a shortage of men, especially Italian working class men. There are fifteen men in the television interviews. In general, the television interviews represent that portion of the non-respondents who showed the lowest rates of completion for the ALS interviews. Therefore the following discussion will report the speech of those subjects who were the most different in their social characteristics from the 122 ALS informants.

Calibration of the television interviews   In order to compare the results of the television interviews to those of the ALS interviews, it was necessary to calibrate the former against the latter. This was done by selecting by a random process ten ALS informants who had already been studied through the regular linguistic interview, and re-interviewing them through the television interview. In no case did any of these informants show any suspicion that there was a connection between the two interviews, and the results of the television interview are therefore independent of the ALS interview. (These interviews were all conducted over the telephone, and in the cases where the interviewer was the same as in previous contacts, appropriate adjustments in voice quality and intonation were made.)

The average index values for the ten respondents' use of the five main phonological variables are shown in Table D.3, as compared to the results of the ALS interview in Contexts A and B.

The results for (r) show that the context of the television interview seems to fall between Context A and Context B. The average value for (æh) tends to confirm this, although all three index values for (æh) are very close. The

Table D.3   *Comparison of ALS and television interviews for ten ALS respondents*

Variable	ALS Style A	TV interview	ALS Style B
(r)	17	27	40
(æh)	27	27.5	28
(oh)	21	24	24
(th)	18	13	23
(dh)	38	14	17

value for (oh) is that of Style B. Finally, the values for (th) and (dh) are lower than either Style A or Style B.

The reliability of these five measures can be assessed by listing the number of individual cases in which the value for the speaker was within 5 percent of Style A or Style B or in between – but *not* higher or lower than both Style A or Style B. Only those cases where the variable actually appeared as a variable are considered: where (r) is always 00, or (th) and (dh) always 00, there is little confirmation of the reliability of the television interview.

Table D.4 shows that (r) is the most reliable measure, and (th) the least reliable. Since the number of instances of (æh) and (oh) were relatively low, it is understandable that the results for any given individual might not be consistent. The number of instances of (æh) and (oh) were less than five in most cases. However, the greatest number of instances of the variable were provided for (dh), and (th) is often represented by more than five occurrences. The reason for the anomaly in (th) and (dh) results is that there is a considerable loss in the audible signals for these consonants over the telephone; all of the sample interviews described above were conducted over the telephone, and most of the television interviews as a whole. In all but one of the consistent cases of (th) and (dh), the value was the lower alternative, that of Style B, contrary to the evidence of (r). Consistent with this hypothesis is the fact that (th) shows the greatest loss: the unvoiced stops and affricates are the most difficult to hear. There is therefore a tendency to hear the affricates as the more common fricatives. If we adjust the values of (th) and (dh) upward by 50 percent – the margin required to match the results of (r) and (æh) – we then find that all of the (dh) discrepancies are eliminated, and all but one of the (th) discrepancies.

In the following discussion, the absolute values of the variables are of less interest than the social patterns formed by the distribution of the variables. The adjustment of (th) and (dh) made above merely illustrates that these variables continue to be relatively consistent indicators of speech behavior, despite the losses through telephone transmission.

Table D.4   *Consistency of results for five variables*

	Number of variable cases	Number of consistent results	
			%
(r)	9	7	78
(æh)	9	6	67
(oh)	10	6	60
(th)	6	3	50
(dh)	8	5	63

Table D.5   (r) *values by SEC*

	SEC			
	0–1	2–5	6–8	9
(r)	02	09	23	53
[N:	3	14	7	3]

Six of the thirty-three informants studied, sampled in the television interviews were not raised in New York City. The following discussion therefore concerns twenty-seven New York City television informants.

Social distribution of (r)   The class distribution of (r) for the twenty-seven informants follows the same pattern as that for the ALS informants in Figure 7.11.

The distribution of (r) pronunciation in other respects is also similar to that of the ALS informants. Excepting class 9 (which is primarily a male category), the average performances of men and women are the same: (r)-12 and (r)-10 respectively. Ethnic comparisons are difficult to make because all but one of the Italian speakers are working class or lower class, and most of the Jews are middle class. As far as age is concerned, the television interviews again show the same pattern as the ALS informants.

Table D.6 shows the same general outlines as Table 9.10. The relations of the younger and the middle-aged informants generally match the paradigm of case II-B of Chapter 9, showing the introduction of a prestige feature.

Social distribution of (æh) *and* (oh)   The class distribution of these variables is not as regular as that of (r). The general outlines of Figures 7.17–7.20 may be seen in Tables 7–9, but with some irregularities. This is understandable

Table D.6   (r) *by age and SEC*

Age level	SEC 0–8	SEC 9		N:
20–39	12	66	6	2
40–59	13	35	16	1
60–	02	–	2	0

Table D.7   (æh) *and* (oh) *by SEC*

	SEC			
	0–2	3–5	6–8	9
(æh)	24	24	30	27
(oh)	24	22	25	23
[N:	6	11	7	3]

Table D.8   (æh) *and* (oh) *by ethnicity*

	Jews	Italians	AAs
(æh)	26	22	29
(oh)	24	20.5	28
[N:	12	8	3]

since even the larger sample showed a great deal of internal fluctuation.

The relations of ethnic groups for these variables are seen to be more important than class; yet the present data are again subject to the limitation that the Italians are primarily lower class and working class, while the Jews are middle class. Since the style here is more formal than Style A, the middle class Jewish tendency towards correcting both (æh) and (oh) is strongly marked.

In Table D.8, the Jews show lower vowels for both variables than the Italians; the AA speakers considerably lower than either, as we would expect from the results of Chapter 8.

The relations of the age groups in Table D.9 fit the patterns shown in Chapter 9 quite closely.

The middle-aged group shows the tendency towards correction of (æh) which was noted in Chapter 9. However, (oh) shows no such reversal of the characteristic steady upward movement which illustrates the early stages of change from below. In Table D.9, the television interviews may be consid-

Table D.9   (æh) *and* (oh) *by age*

	Age		
	20–39	40–59	60–
(æh)	24	27	21
(oh)	20.5	24	26
[N:	8	17	2

Table D.10   (th) *and* (dh) *by SEC*

SEC		0–2	3–5	6–8	9
(th)		55	30	06	03
(dh)		55	28	14	12
	[N:	6	11	7	3]

Table D.11   (th) *and* (dh) *by finer division of SEC*

	SEC				
	0–1	2–4	5–6	7–8	9
(th)	[100]	40	21	00	03
(dh)	91	25	35	07	12
[N:	3	11	5	5	3]

ered to have shown a close parallel to the ALS interviews.

Social distribution of (th) and (dh)   The initial view of class stratification of (th) and (dh) in Chapter 7 used the class grouping shown in Table
D.10.

Table D.10 shows the regular pattern of sharp class stratification which is
typical of (th) and (dh). A re-grouping according to Figures 7.14 and 7.17
produces even sharper stratification, but is somewhat less regular, as shown
in Table D.11.

Although the numbers here are a little too small to allow such a fine division, it may again be seen that the very high values of (th) and (dh) are
typical of the lower class.

The analysis of Chapter 8 indicated that the social class scale, using occu-

Table D.12　(th) *and* (dh) *by social class*

	SC			
	1	2	3	4
(th)	58	47	00	03
(dh)	48	40	10	11
[N:	6	10	9	4]

Table D.13　(dh) *values for ALS and television interviews*

	ALS Style A	Television interviews	ALS Style B	Television interviews plus 50%
SC 1	93	48	70	72
SC 2	44	40	37	60
SC 3	25	10	14	15
SC 4	20	11	07	16

pation and education only, gave more regular stratification for (th) and (dh), and resolved the irregularities seen among the lower class groups. A similar distribution appears for the television interviews.

Table D.12 shows the sharp division between the white collar workers [SC 3] and the blue collar workers (SC 2) of the same educational background, and also the differentiation of blue collar workers with different educational backgrounds (SC 1 and 2).

In the light of the evidence on the calibration of (th) and (dh), the comparison of (dh) against the results of the ALS interviews shown in Table D.13 is instructive.

It is apparent that there is a loss of (dh) perception in the television interviews. However, the important question is that of the overall pattern of social distribution; it is impressive confirmation that even with the small number of twenty-seven informants, the same general pattern emerges in both groups of interviews.

In Chapter 8, it appeared that men used more stops and affricates than women. The results of the television interview show the same distribution, as shown in Table D.14.

Table D.14   (th) *and* (dh) *by gender*

	Men	Women
(th)	31	25
(dh)	39	22

Table D.15   (ʌy) *by SEC*

		SEC			
		0–2	3–5	6–8	9
% using /ʌy/		75	45	29	00
	[N:	4	11	7	2]

Table D.16   (ay) *and* (aw) *by SEC*

	SEC			
	0–2	3–5	6–8	9
(ay)	06	18	04	20
(aw)	00	06	03	00

Social distribution of /ʌy/   The use of /ʌy/ by the television informants is parallel to that of the ALS informants. A regular class stratification may be seen in Table D.15, showing the percentage of informants using /ʌy/ in the television interviews.

Social distribution of (ay) *and* (aw)   The class distribution of (ay) and (aw) is not as regular as that found in the larger ALS sample. The working class shows more nucleus-glide differentiation than the lower middle class, as shown in Table D.16.

There is agreement here with the ALS survey in the fact that the upper middle class shows a high level of (ay) differentiation, but no (aw) differentiation. This pattern may be seen in Figure 14.2. The development of nucleus-glide differentiation in apparent time is perfectly regular, as shown in Table D.17.

In Chapter 10, it was shown that men used somewhat less differentiation of (ay), and considerably less for (aw), than women. Similarly, the television

Table D.17   (ay) *and* (aw) *by age*

	Age level		
	20–39	40–59	60-
(ay)	19	08	00
(aw)	04	02	00

survey shows (ay)-12 for women, (ay)-11 for men; (aw)-05 for women, (aw)-01 for men.

Summary

The television interview was designed to study the speech of the non-respondents, in order to confirm the representative nature of the sample of 122 ALS informants actually interviewed. The results of the discussion above show that the agreement is quite close for most patterns of class distribution. The closest agreement is shown by (r); the absolute levels of (th) and (dh) are lower than the ALS sample, but the patterns of social distribution are the same; (æh) and (oh) are not as regular in class distribution, which was marginal for the ALS sample; because of the disparate social membership of the Jewish and Italian groups in the television sample, close comparison of ethnic distribution is not possible.

For those variables which are involved in linguistic change, the television survey shows a distribution in apparent time which matches that of the ALS survey. The patterns shown by (r), (æh), (oh), (ay), (aw), are almost sufficient in themselves to draw inferences about developments in real time.

It may therefore be concluded that the 27 New York City television informants show the same linguistic behavior as the 81 New York City ALS informants. If the previous studies of New York City had followed a systematic method of selecting informants, the 25 or 30 cases described would have been sufficient to show the outlines of a systematic structure of stylistic and social variation. We may conclude that the structure of social and stylistic variation of language can be studied through samples considerably smaller than those required for the study of other forms of social behavior.

Questionnaire
for the Television Interview

A.   *Introduction*

"We are checking radio and television reception in your part of New York City: that is, we'd like to find out what kind of a picture the television companies are getting onto your screen."

B.   *Elicitation of particular forms*

1. What channels give you the best reception? the worst? which channels do you watch most often? least often?

four:	(r):	(oh):
thirteen:	(th):	(ʌy):
nine, five:	(ay):	

2. Would you say that the trouble you are having with Channel _____ is *very* bad, or *not so* bad? [use (æh-3)]

bad	(æh):

3. At two o'clock in the afternoon, would you say your television set is usually *on* or off? [use (oh-3)] at four o'clock? at ten in the morning? ten at night?

off	(oh):

4. What kind of an antenna do you have?

antenna	(en):

5. What floor of the building do you live on?

floor:	(r):	(oh):

6. When you look out of the window of the room in which your television set is, what direction do you face? what do you see?

north	(oh):	Empire:	(r):	(ay):
south	(aw):	*River*:	(r):	

7. When the picture on your set isn't quite right, what do you do to make it a little better?

turn	/ʌy/:

C.   *General conversation*

"That gives us the information we need on reception. If you have another minute, we've been asked to pick up a little information on the programs."

1. Is there any particular show that's been taken off the air recently that you'd like to see back on?
2. Is there any series of programs that you used to watch all the time that you don't watch any more, that you've lost interest in?
3. Is there any particular *kind* of program that you'd like to see more of?
4. Is there any particular *kind* of program that you think takes up too much time on the air?
5. There's been some criticism of commercials: some people say that there are too many of them, or that they're too long. How do you feel about that?
6. There's another point that some people criticize: they say that some of the shows on daytime programs are not right for young children. What's been your experience on that? (If *bad* has been omitted above, ask: Do you think that horror shows are good or bad for young children?)
7. Did your children watch a lot of television when they were growing up? Did you let them watch anything, or did you more or less tell them what they could watch?

D.   *To determine regional background of informant*

1. Some people say that television reception in other cities is better than in New York.
2. Did they have television when you were growing up? Did you listen to the radio a lot? Where was that, in New York City?

E.   *To determine occupation of informant [to follow B. 7]*

1. You know, it seems to be hard to design television sets to suit everybody. It seems to be that people with different occupations use the dials in different ways. Can I ask what is your occupation? (your husband's?)

Appendix E   The out-of-town speakers

This discussion will analyze the linguistic behavior of the thirty-seven respondents in the ALS survey who completed full linguistic interviews and who were not raised in New York City. Despite the fact that many of them have spent more than twenty years in New York City, they cannot be considered native speakers; during their formative years, they were not exposed to the traditional dialect of the city. Therefore this group can be used as a valuable check upon the validity of the discussion of New York respondents in Chapters 7 and 11.

Any phonological variable which is known to be widespread throughout the United States should show the same patterns for the eighty-one New Yorkers and the thirty-seven out-of-towners.

Any phonological variable which is being superimposed upon a partially acquired New York City pattern, will also affect the out-of-towners. It may not affect their speech to the same degree, but the general direction of stratification should be similar.

Any phonological variable which is a part of the native New York City pattern, as acquired in pre-adolescent years, should not show stylistic or class stratification in the speech of the out-of-towners.

Thus in accordance with the three requirements set forth above, we must expect to find the same pattern for (th) and (dh), a similar pattern for (r) in some respects, and no similarity for (æh) and (oh).

As indicated at the beginning of Chapter 7, a majority of the out-of-town speakers are African–Americans. The out-of-town evidence must therefore be analyzed for AA-white differences, whenever these differences are relevant to the questions raised above.

The areas in which the out-of-town speakers were raised are shown in Table E.1 below. (The identification of the areas as *r*-less or *r*-pronouncing is based upon Map 156 in Kurath and McDavid 1961).

The three informants from Eastern Pennsylvania are from the coal mining areas around Wilkes-Barre. They are lower class informants with Italian or Slavic background, who have been in New York City over twenty years.

Table E.1   *Regional origins of out-of-town speakers*

AAs		Whites	
r-less regions			
Upper south	2	Eastern New England	3
North Carolina	7		
Lower south	8		
r-pronouncing regions			
New Jersey	2	North outside of eastern New England	5
Philadelphia	1	Kansas, Oklahoma	2
Pittsburgh	1	Eastern Pennsylvania	3
	$\overline{21}$	Midwest and west	3
			$\overline{16}$

Table E.2   *Class distribution of white and AA out-of-town speakers*

		White	AA
Lower class	0–2	5	10
Working class	3–5	2	9
Middle class	6–9	9	2
		$\overline{16}$	$\overline{21}$

The white speakers from out-of-town fall into two radically different types: those from the lowest social classes and those from the middle class. On the other hand, the AA speakers are well represented in both lower class and working class, with few middle class speakers.

We can turn first to the (th) and (dh) variables. As far as we know, these are not limited to New York City in their distribution, and we should be able to see the same type of stratification in out-of-town speakers as in New Yorkers.

Figure E.1 shows the stratification for white speakers for (th) and Figure E.2 for (dh). The two working class speakers are included with the lower class; with the small numbers of informants on hand, it would be difficult to show any finer stratification. Since the working class is missing, we can expect to find a very great gap between the upper and lower levels of the diagram. This produces the highly differentiated results of Figures E.1 and E.2, with a group of speakers who use a great many stops and affricates, a lower middle class group with very low use, and two upper middle class speakers who used none at all. This pattern is not dissimilar to that seen in

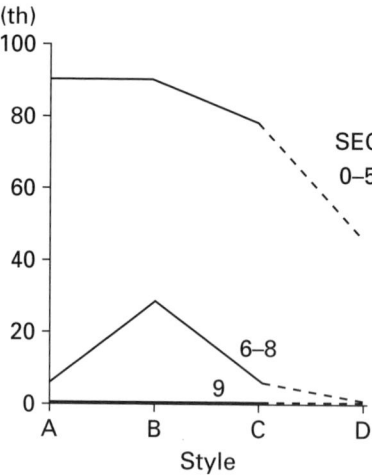

Figure E.1   Class stratification of (th) for white out-of-town speakers

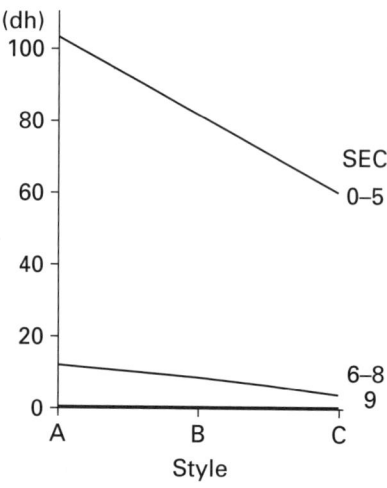

Figure E.2   Class stratification of (dh) for white out-of-town speakers

Figures 7.4 and 7.5, for New York City, but with even greater extremes for these variables.

The situation for the AA speakers is quite different. Figure E.3 shows that (th) is not a social variable at all for AA speakers. Indeed, most of the items which are responsible for the level of the index above zero are the

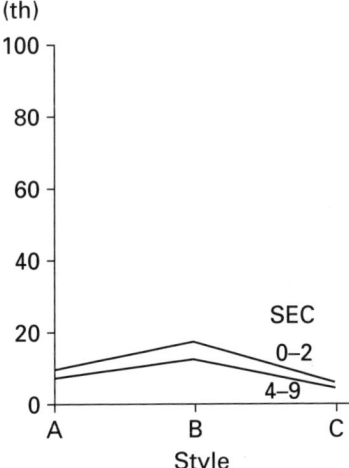

Figure E.3   Class stratification of (th) for AA out-of-town speakers

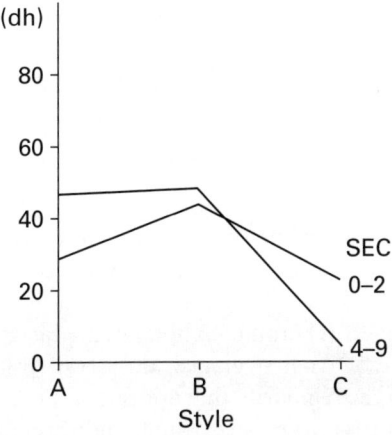

Figure E.4   Class Stratification of (dh) for AA out-of-town speakers

substitution of (f) for (th). Stops and affricates are seldom heard. In the case of (dh), Figure E.4, there is widespread use of stops, though not as much as with white speakers. Affricates are rare.

There is no tendency for the level of the index to fall from Style A to Style B, but there is a sharp decline for Style C. The reason for this pattern (which is repeated for lower frequencies of (th)) may be that AA speakers do not

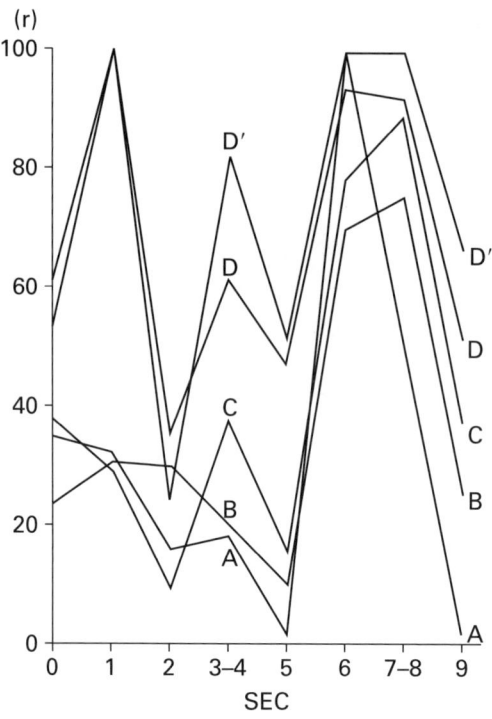

Figure E.5   Style stratification of (r) for all out-of-town speakers

have the control over this usage that white speakers do. However, it is also likely that they do not use a truly casual style in the presence of a white interviewer.

When we turn to the question of (r) pronunciation, we are faced with the unpromising data of Figure E.5. At first glance, this style stratification diagram seems to have none of the regularity that appears in Figure 7.9, for New Yorkers. The number of cross-overs is very high, indicating a lack of stylistic regularity, and the fluctuations on the social dimension are very great. However, the five stylistic levels are ordered in the normal sequence for classes 3–4, 5, 7–8, and 9.

As we examine Figure E.5 from left to right, we seem to find: first, a very mixed pattern of lower class speakers from 0–2; second, a group of working class speakers with a large range of stylistic variation; third, a group of lower middle class informants who pronounce almost all of their (r)'s; and finally, some upper middle class speakers with a very wide stylistic range for (r).

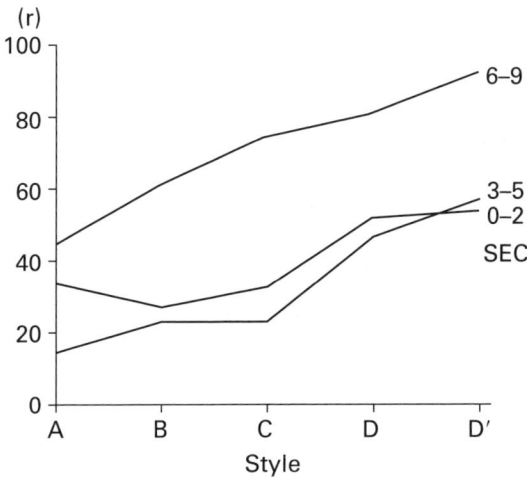

Figure E.6   Class stratification of (r) for all out-of-town speakers

A marked simplification appears in the class stratification diagram of Figure E.6. Here there are three class groups, all showing a fairly regular increase of (r) index with increasing formality. The working class section is on the bottom – since this group is almost entirely composed of southern AA speakers, this is to be expected. What is remarkable is that the two lower lines come very close to the pattern set by the New York speakers in the beginning of Chapter 7. Such a similarity is not at all apparent in the style stratification diagram of Figure E.5.

The opposition of AA versus white is not as pertinent to the study of the (r) variable as the question of the area where the informants were raised. In Figure E.7, we have resolved the class stratification diagram into four elements: an upper and lower class group for those who were raised in an r-pronouncing area, and another set for those raised in an r-less area. Here all deviation from stylistic regularity has disappeared, and similarly, the reversal of lower class and working class stratification has vanished. We see that the influence of the normative (r) is felt most strongly by the upper half of the speakers from r-less regions, but that all sections of the population respond to this influence.

There are two possible explanations for this regularity. First, it may be that the adoption of an r-pronouncing prestige pattern has taken effect in many other r-less areas besides New York City. The second possibility is that the influence of the New York City pattern has been brought home to these informants during the time that they lived in the city. Since

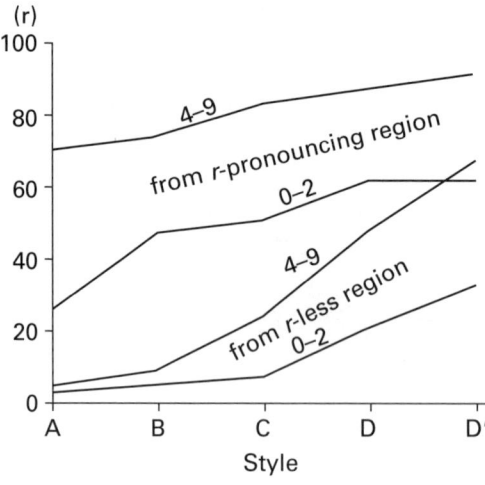

Figure E.7   Class stratification of (r) for out-of-town speakers by region of origin

r-pronunciation is an acquired form for New Yorkers as well, there is no reason to suspect that the out-of-towners should not share equally in this norm. The speakers from *r*-pronouncing areas will begin with a much higher level of (r-1) to start with; lower class subjects in particular may have begun to follow New York City practice of dropping *r* in casual speech, but the re-introduction of (r-1) in formal speech will be quite natural. The eastern Pennsylvania informants mentioned above fit this description quite well.

So far, the results of the out-of-town study fit in with our expectations. As we come to the (æh) and (oh) variables, we should expect to find no similarity between out-of-towners and New Yorkers. For a New Yorker, the whole structure revolves around the high (æh) and (oh) vowels which he acquires natively in his pre-adolescent years. Since the non-New Yorkers do not have this basic pattern to adjust, it is not likely that we will find either stylistic or class stratification.

Figure E.8 shows the raw data for the (oh) variable in a style stratification diagram. This is truly a mixed pattern. It has no observable relation to any previous treatment of (oh); here every possible order of the stylistic levels can be observed, with sixteen cross-overs on this diagram. Comparison with Figure 7.20, satisfies us that none of the structure characteristic of the New York treatment of (oh) is to be found here.

This diagram shows vowels at an altogether different absolute level from the New York City situation. Figure E.9 shows the overall values for New

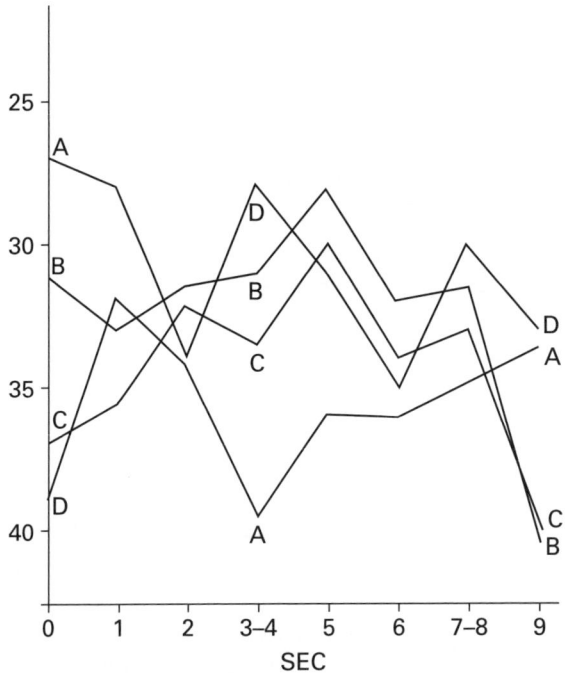

Figure E.8   Style stratification of (oh) for all out-of-town speakers

Yorkers and out-of-towners for all classes combined, in each of the four stylistic levels. There is about ten points' difference on the index between these two averages. Figure E.10 is the converse, showing the sum of all stylistic levels combined for each of the four class groups. The only trace of the New York City pattern which we see here is in the sharp drop at the right for the upper middle class. This represents the presence of two eastern New England speakers who use a very open vowel natively. The working class maximum for (oh) is entirely missing.

Finally, we may compare the New Yorkers and the out-of-town speakers for their use of (æh). The figures in Table E.3, showing the four stylistic levels for all New Yorkers and all out-of-towners, illustrate the point very well.

Thus the three requirements for the validity of the procedure have been answered in full. We can say with some assurance that the data for native New Yorkers does indeed describe some processes taking place in the city alone. We have taken an additional step towards establishing the reliability and validity of the evidence as well.

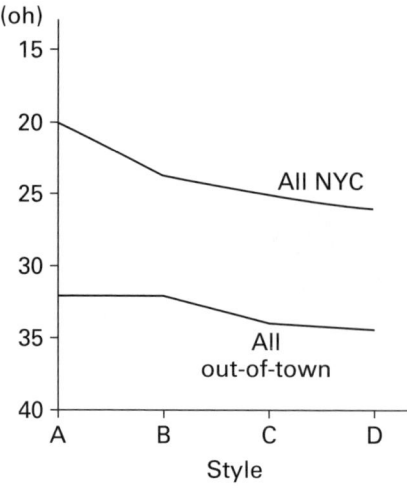

Figure E.9   Average (oh) for all classes by style: NYC vs. out-of-town speakers

Table E.3   (æh) *values by style for N YC and out-of-towners*

	38 out-of-town informants	81 New York City informants
Style A:	30	24.5
B:	30	29.0
C:	30	31.5
D:	30	33.5

Subjective reactions of out-of-town respondents

In Chapter 11, the subjective response of the out-of-town informants to (r) was compared with that of the New York informants. In this section, the reactions of out-of-town respondents to other variables will be considered.

As far as the zero pattern is concerned, the response of out-of-town informants was quite similar to that of the New Yorkers, as one would expect. The out-of-town treatment of (oh), however, was partly different from that of New Yorkers, as shown in Table E.4.

We see that the out-of-town speakers reacted in the same way as New Yorkers to Sentence 7, but showed no clear-cut reaction against the high (oh) vowels in Sentences 6 and 8. The percentage of (oh)-positive response by the three-choice test is forty-one for the out-of-town speakers, and

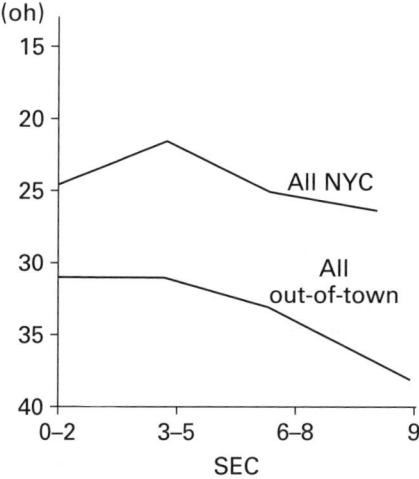

Figure E.10   Average (oh) for all styles by class: NYC vs. out-of-town speakers

Table E.4   *Response of out-of-town and New York subjects to* (oh) *sentences*

	Relation to zero pattern	
	Higher	Lower
Sentence 6		
Out-of-towners	10	11
New Yorkers	18	30
Sentence 7		
Out-of-towners	6	21
New Yorkers	15	50
Sentence 8		
Out-of-towners	8	13
New Yorkers	18	50

fifty-eight for New Yorkers. However, this difference is primarily due to the AA respondents: they showed only 24 percent (oh)-positive response to the three-choice test, while the white speakers showed 60 percent, about the same as New Yorkers.

The out-of-town speakers showed subjective reactions to (æh) that were similar to New Yorkers. The lower class out-of-town speakers did not

Table E.5   *Percentage of* (æh)-*negative and* (oh)-*negative response for
New York and out-of-town respondents by age level*

Age	(æh)		(oh)	
	New Yorkers	Out-of-towners	New Yorkers	Out-of-towners
20–39	90	70	76	40
40–	75	84	49	41

stigmatize (æh-1) as sharply as the working class and middle class did, and
tended to accept Speaker 2's version of (æh-4) more readily than the other two
classes. No important differences between AA and white speakers appeared.

It was shown in Chapter 7 that out-of-town speakers showed little resemblance to New Yorkers in their treatment of (æh) and (oh) in speech. They
followed different patterns of stylistic variation, and their average values
were at a lower level for casual speech. However, we pointed out that this
was due to the fact that out-of-towners did not have high values of (æh) and
(oh) in their native speech pattern to begin with. The negative reactions to
high values of (oh) and (æh) which we are studying here are not acquired
early in life, but are learned later, absorbed under the influence of pressure
from above. It is therefore possible for out-of-towners to acquire these
social reactions during their exposure to the New York City norms.
However, we would *not* expect the out-of-town speakers to duplicate the
relations of the age levels which we saw for New Yorkers: for (oh) and (æh),
the younger age levels regularly showed more negative response than the
older. In the case of (r), it appeared that the relations of the age levels were
slightly reversed for out-of-town respondents. Exactly the same condition
holds for (æh) and (oh), as shown in Table E.5.

We find that the critical factor in comparing (oh) and (æh) response for
New Yorkers and out-of-towners is not the absolute level, but rather the
relations of the age groups. The comparison of out-of-town respondents
with New Yorkers shows that this relationship of age levels is characteristic
of the native New York developments.

Out-of-town subjects show a surprising high level of (th)-insensitive
response. Twenty-one of thirty-two out-of-town respondents showed (th)-
insensitive patterns in the rating of Sentences 20, 21, and 22. This would not
have been predicted on the basis of our previous information. It was shown
that most out-of-towners follow the same pattern of (th) and (dh) stratification that New Yorkers do. Both white and AA out-of-town respondents
show the same high level of (th)-insensitivity: eleven out of fifteen white
respondents; ten out of seventeen AA respondents.

It is possible that the versions of (th) and (dh) which were used in the SR test follow a phonetic pattern that is slightly different from that used by out-of-town speakers, but there is no evidence to support such a view. It seems therefore that there is a trend in New York City towards greater sensitivity to (th) and (dh). We have seen evidence for such a trend at several points in the present study: first, in the slightly higher use of affricates and stops on the part of older upper middle class informants; second, in the SR test for (dh) among New Yorkers, where it was found that younger respondents from SC 3 and SC 1 showed smaller percentages of (th)-insensitive patterns than their older counterparts; and third, in the fact that New Yorkers as a whole show greater (th) sensitivity than out-of-town respondents. In no case has the evidence been clear-cut and consistent across all social groups, and we must conclude that if a trend exists, it is not a strong one.

Bibliography

Abdel-Jawad, Hassan (1981) *Lexical and Phonological Variation in Spoken Arabic in Amman.* University of Philadelphia dissertation.
—— (1987). Cross-dialectal variation in Arabic: competing prestigious forms. *Language in Society* 16:359–367.
Anisfeld, Moshe, Norman Bogo and Wallace E. Lambert (1962) Evaluational reactions to accented English speech. *Journal of Abnormal and Social Psychology* 65: 223–231.
Atwood, E. Bagby (1953) *A Survey of Verb Forms in the Eastern United States.* Ann Arbor: University of Michigan Press.
Avis, Walter S. (1961) The 'New England short *o*': a recessive phoneme. *Language* 37: 544–558.
Babbitt, E. H. (1896) The English of the lower classes in New York City and vicinity. *Dialect Notes*, 1: 457–464.
Bailey, Charles-James (1972) The integration of linguistic theory. In R. Stockwell and R. Macaulay, *Linguistic Change and Generative Grammar.* Bloomington: Indiana University Press. pp. 22–31.
Baranowski, Maciej (2006) *Phonological Variation and Change in the Dialect of Charleston, S.C.* University of Pennsylvania dissertation.
Barber, Bernard (1957) *Social Stratification.* New York: Harcourt, Brace and Co.
Bell, Allan (1977) *The Language of Radio News in Auckland: a Sociolinguistic Study of Style, Audience and Sub-editing Variation.* PhD thesis, University of Auckland.
—— (1984) Language style as audience design. *Language in Society* 13:145–204.
Belnap, R. Kirk (1991) *Grammatical Agreement Variation in Cairene Arabic.* University of Pennsylvania dissertation.
Bernstein, Basil (1959) A public language: some sociological implications of a linguistic form. *British Journal of Sociology* 10: 311–326.
—— (1960) Language and social class. *British Journal of Sociology* 11: 271–276.
Bloch, Bernard and George L. Trager (1942) *Outline of Linguistic Analysis.* Baltimore: Linguistic Society of America.
Bloomfield, Leonard (1933) *Language.* New York: Henry Holt.
Boberg, Charles (2004) Real and apparent time in language change: late adoption of changes in Montreal English. *American Speech* 79:250–269.
Boersma, Paul and David Weenink (2006) Praat: doing phonetics by computer. http://www.fon.hum.uva.nl/praat/
Bonfiglio, Thomas (2002) *Race and the Rise of Standard American.* Berlin: Mouton/de Gruyter.

462

Bortoni-Ricardo, Stella M. (1985) *The Urbanization of Rural Dialect Speakers: a Sociolinguistic Study in Brazil.* Cambridge: Cambridge University Press.

Bottliglioni, Gino (1954) Linguistic geography: achievements, methods and orientations. *Word* 10: 375–387.

Bourdieu, Pierre (1977) L'économie des échanges linguistiques. *Langue française* 34:17–34.

Bradley, David and Maya Bradley (1979) Melbourne vowels. *Working Papers in Linguistics* 5. University of Melbourne, Linguistics Section.

Bright, William and A. K. Ramanujan (1962) "Socio-linguistic Variation and Language Change," Proceedings of the Ninth International Congress of Linguists, 1962.

Bronstein, Arthur J. (1962) Let's take another look at New York City speech. *American Speech* 37: 13–26.

Brown, R. and Gilman, A. (1960) The pronouns of power and solidarity. In T. A. Sebeok (ed.) *Style in Language.* Cambridge, Mass: The Technology Press, pp. 253–276.

Cedergren, Henrietta (1973) *The Interplay of Social and Linguistic Factors in Panama.* Unpublished Cornell University dissertation.

—— (1984) Panama revisited: sound change in real time. Paper given at NWAVE, Philadelphia.

Cedergren, Henrietta, Jean Clermont and Francine Cote (1981) Le facteur temps et deux diphthongues du français montréalais. In D. Sankoff and H. Cedergren (eds.) *Variation Omnibus.* Alberta: Linguistic Research, pp. 169–176.

Cedergen, Henrietta J. and Louise Simoneau (1985) La chute des voyelles hautes en français de Montréal "As-tu entendu la belle syncope?". In H. Cedergren and M. Lemieux (eds) *Les Tendances Dynamiques du Français à Montréal.* Montreal: Office de la Langue Française, pp. 55–144.

Chae, Seo-Yong (1995) *External Constraints on Sound Change: The Raising of /o/ in Seoul Korean.* University of Pennsylvania dissertation.

Chomsky, Noam (1957) *Syntactic Structures.* The Hague: Mouton and Co.

Cieri, Christopher (2005) *Modeling Phonological Variation in Multidialectal Italy.* University of Pennsylvania dissertation.

Clopton, Sarah (2005) *Social Stratification of Castilian Spanish in Barcelona, Spain: A Study of the Social Meaning of /s/, a Variant Pronunciation of /θ/.* University of Pennsylvania Honors Thesis.

Cloward, Richard A. and Lloyd E. Ohlin (1960). *Delinquency and Opportunity: A Theory of Delinquent Gangs.* Glencoe, Illinois: The Free Press.

Cofer, Thomas (1972) *Linguistic Variability in a Philadelphia Speech Community.* University of Pennsylvania dissertation.

Conn, Jeff (2005) Of "moice" and men: The Evolution of a Male-led Sound Change. University of Pennsylvania dissertation.

Cooper, Franklin S. et al. (1952) Some experiments in the perception of synthetic speech sounds. *Journal of the Acoustical Society of America* 24: 597–606.

Dollard, John (1957) *Caste and Class in a Southern Town.* New York: Doubleday Anchor Books.

Douglas-Cowie, Ellen (1978) Linguistic code-switching in a Northern Irish village: social interaction and social ambition. In P. Trudgill (ed.) *Sociolinguistic Patterns in British English.* London: Edward Arnold, pp. 37–51.

Eckert, Penelope (1999) *Linguistic Variation as Social Practice*. Oxford: Blackwell.
Eckert, Penelope and John Rickford (eds) (2001) *Style and Sociolinguistic Variation*. Cambridge: Cambridge University Press.
Feagin, Crawford (1979) *Variation and Change in Alabama English*. Washington D.C.: Georgetown University Press.
—— (1986) More evidence for major vowel change in the South. In David Sankoff (ed.) *Diversity and Diachrony*. Amsterdam/Philadelphia: John Benjamins, pp. 83–96.
—— (1987a) A closer look at the southern drawl: variation taken to extremes. In Keith M. Denning et al. (eds.), *Variation in Language: NWAV-XV at Stanford*. Stanford, CA: Department of Linguistics, Stanford University, pp. 137–150.
—— (1987b) The dynamics of a sound change in southern states English: from R-less to R-ful in three generations. In J. Edmondson et al. (eds.) *Development and Diversity: Linguistic Variation across Time and Space*. Arlington: SIL/University of Texas, pp. 129–146.
Ferguson, Charles A. and John J. Gumperz (eds.) (1960) *Linguistic Diversity in South Asia: Studies in Regional, Social and Functional Variation*. Publication of the Research Center in Anthropology, Folklore, and Linguistics, No. 13. Bloomington, Indiana: Indiana University Press.
Fillmore, Charles J., Daniel Kempler and William S-Y. Wang (eds) (1979) *Individual Differences in Language Ability and Language Behavior*. New York: Academic Press.
Finegan, Edward and Douglas Biber (2001) Register variation and social dialect variation. In Eckert, P. and J. Rickford (eds) *Style and Sociolinguistic Variation*. Cambridge: Cambridge University Press, pp. 235–267.
Fischer, John L. (1958) Social influences on the choice of a linguistic variant. *Word* 14: 47–56.
Fowler, Joy (1986) The social stratification of (r) in New York City department stores, 24 years after Labov. NYU term paper.
Frank, Yakira A. (1948) The speech of New York City. University of Michigan, Ann Arbor, dissertation.
—— (1998) *The Southern Vowel Shift: Linguistic and Social Factors*. Michigan State University dissertation.
Fridland, Valerie (1999) The southern shift in Memphis, Tennessee. *Language Variation and Change* 11:267–285.
Fridland, Valerie, Kathryn Bartlett and Roger Kreuz (2004) Do you hear what I hear? Experimental measurement of the perceptual salience of acoustically manipulated vowel variants by southern speakers in Memphis, TN. *Language Variation and Change* 16:1–15.
Gardner-Chloros, Penelope (1991) *Language Selection and Switching in Strasbourg*. Oxford: Oxford University Press.
Gauchat, Louis (1905) *L'unité phonétique dans le patois d'une commune*. Halle.
Glazer, Nathan and Daniel P. Moynihan (1963) *Beyond the Melting Pot: The Negroes, Puerto Ricans, Jews, Italians, and Irish of New York City*. Cambridge: The M.I.T. and Harvard University Press.
Goidanich, P. G. (1926) Saggio critico sullo studio de L. Gauchat. *Archivio Glottologico Italiano* XX: 60–71.

Gregersen, Frans and Inge Lise Pedersen (eds) (1991) *The Copenhagen Study in Urban Sociolinguistics. Parts I and II.* Copenhagen: C. A. Reitzels Forlag.

Grootaers, William A. (1959) Origin and nature of the subjective boundaries of dialects," *Orbis*, 8: 355–84.

Gumperz, John J. (1958) Dialect differences and social stratification in a north Indian village. *American Anthropologist*, 60:668–682.

—— (1964) Linguistic and social interaction in two communities. In J. Gumperz and D. Hymes (eds) *The Ethnography of Communication,* (American Anthropologist Vol. 66, No. 6, Part 2.) pp. 137–153.

Guy, Gregory (1980) Variation in the group and the individual: the case of final stop deletion. In W. Labov (ed.) *Locating Language in Time and Space.* New York: Academic Press. pp. 1–36.

Guy, Gregory, B. Horvath, J. Vonwiller, E. Daisley and I. Rogers (1986) An intonational change in progress in Australian English. *Language in Society* 15:23–52.

Haeri, Niloofar (1996) *The Sociolinguistic Market of Cairo: Gender, Class and Education.* London: Kegan Paul International.

Halle, Morris (1962) Phonology in a generative grammar. *Word* 18:54–72.

Harris, Zellig S. (1951) *Methods in Structural Linguistics.* Chicago: University of Chicago Press.

Hermann, M. E. (1929) Lautveränderungen in der Individualsprache einer Mundart. *Nachrichten der Gesellschaft der Wissen-schaften zu Gottingen, Philosophisch-historische Klasse*, XI:195–214.

Herzog, Marvin (1964) The Yiddish language in northern Poland: its geography and history, Columbia University, New York, dissertation.

Hibiya, Junko (1988) *Social Stratification of Tokyo Japanese.* University of Pennsylvania dissertation.

Hindle, Donald (1980) *The Social and Structural Conditioning of Phonetic Variation.* University of Pennsylvania dissertation.

Hockett, Charles F. (1958) *A Course in Modern Linguistics.* New York: MacMillan Co.

Hong, Yunsook (1991) *A Sociolinguistic Study of Seoul Korean.* Seoul: Research Center for Peace and Unification of Korea.

Hoover, Edgar M. and Raymond Vernon (1959) *Anatomy of a Metropolis.* Cambridge, Mass.: Harvard University Press.

Horvath, Barbara (1985) *Variation in Australian English: The Sociolects of Sydney.* Cambridge: Cambridge University Press.

Horwitz, Hortense and Ellas Smith (1955) The interchangeability of socio-economic indices. In Paul F. Lazarsfeld and Morris Rosenberg (eds.) *Language of Social Research.* Glencoe, Ill.: The Free Press.

Houston, Ann (1985) *Continuity and Change in English Morphology: the Variable (ING).* PhD dissertation, University of Pennsylvania.

—— (1991) A grammatical continuum for (ING). In P. Trudgill and J. K. Chambers (eds) *Dialects of English: Studies in Grammatical Variation.* Longman, London and New York. pp. 241–257.

Hubbell, Allan F. (1940) 'Curl' and 'coil' in New York City. *American Speech*, 15:372–376.

—— (1950) *The Pronunciation of English in New York City. Consonants and Vowels.* New York: King's Crown Press, Columbia University.

Hymes, Dell (1962) The ethnography of speaking. In T. Glodwin and W. C. Sturteuant (eds.) *Anthropology and Human Behavior.* Washington, D. C.: The Anthropological Society of Washington pp. 13–53.

Janson, Tore and Richard Schulman (1983) Non-distinctive features and their use. *Journal of Linguistics* 19:321–336.

Kahl, Joseph A. (1957) *The American Class Structure.* New York: Holt, Rinehart and Co., Inc.

Kemp, William (1979) L'histoire récente de ce que, qu'est-ce que, et qu'osque à Montréal, trois variantes en interaction. In P. Thibault, ed., *Le français parlé: Etudes sociolinguistiques.* Edmonton: Linguistic Research, Inc., pp. 53–74.

Kenyon, John (1948) Cultural levels and functional varieties of English. *College English* 10:31–36. Reprinted in Allen, Harold B. (ed.) *Readings in Applied English Linguistics.* 2nd Ed. New York: Appleton-Century-Crofts, pp. 294–302.

Kerswill, Paul (1996) Children, adolescents, and language change. *Language Variation and Change* 8:177–202.

—— (2002) Koineization and accommodation. In J. K. Chambers, Peter Trudgill, and Natalie Schilling-Estes (eds.) *The Handbook of Linguistic Variation and Change.* Malden, MA: Blackwell, pp. 669–702.

Kerswill, Paul and Ann Williams (1994) A new dialect in a new city: children's and adults' speech in Milton Keynes. Final report to Economic and Social Research Council.

Knack, Rebecca (1991) Ethnic boundaries in linguistic variation. In P. Eckert (ed.) *New Ways of Analyzing Sound Change.* New York: Academic Press.

Kontra, Miklos (1993) The messy phonology of Hungarians in South Bend: A contribution to the study of near-mergers. *Language Variation and Change* 5:225–231.

Krapp, George P. (1952) *The English Language in America.* 2 vols. New York: The Century Co.

Kroch, Anthony (1996) Dialect and style in the speech of upper class Philadelphia. In G. Guy, C. Feagin, D. Schiffrin and J. Baugh (eds.) *Towards a Social Science of Language.* Vol. 1. Philadelphia: John Benjamins. pp. 23–46.

Kufner, Herbert L. (1957) History of the Middle Bavarian vocalism. *Language* 33:519–529.

—— (1960) History of the Central Bavarian obstruents. *Word* 16:11–27.

Kurath, Hans (1939) *Handbook of the Linguistic Geography of New England.* Providence: American Council of Learned Societies.

—— (1949) *A Word Geography of the Eastern United States.* Ann Arbor: University of Michigan Press.

Kurath, Hans and Raven I. McDavid (1961) *The Pronunciation of English in the Atlantic States.* Ann Arbor: University of Michigan Press.

Kurath, Hans et al. (1941) *Linguistic Atlas of New England.* Providence: American Council of Learned Societies.

Labov, William (1963) The social motivation of a sound change. *Word,* 19:273–309.

—— (1966a) The effect of social mobility on linguistic behavior. In S. Lieberson (ed.) *Explorations in Sociolinguistics.* Bloomington: Indiana University Press, pp. 186–203.

—— (1966b) Hypercorrection by the lower middle class as a factor in linguistic change. In W. Bright (ed.) *Sociolinguistics.* The Hague: Mouton, pp 84–113. Also in *Sociolinguistic Patterns* (Ch. 5).

—— (1972a) *Sociolinguistic Patterns.* Philadelphia: University of Pennsylvania Press.

—— (1972b) *Language in the Inner City.* Philadelphia: University of Pennsylvania Press.

—— (1974) Language change as a form of communication. In Albert Silverstein (ed.) *Human Communication.* Hillsdale, NJ: Erlbaum. pp. 221–256.

—— (1976) The relative influence of family and peers on the learning of language. In R. Simone et al. (eds) *Aspetti Sociolinguistici Dell' Italia Contemporanea.* Rome: Bulzoni.

—— (1980) The social origins of sound change. In W. Labov (ed.) *Locating Language in Time and Space.* New York: Academic Press. pp. 251–266.

—— (1981) Resolving the Neogrammarian controversy. *Language* 57:267–309.

—— (1984) Field methods of the Project on Linguistic Change and Variation. In J. Baugh & J. Sherzer (eds.) *Language in Use.* Englewood Cliffs: Prentice Hall, pp. 28–53.

—— (1989) The child as linguistic historian. *Language Variation and Change* 1:85–97.

—— (1990) The intersection of sex and social class in the course of linguistic change. *Language Variation and Change* 2:205–254.

—— (1994) *Principles of Linguistic Change.* Volume 1: *Internal Factors.* Oxford: Blackwell.

—— (2001) *Principles of Linguistic Change. Volume 2: Social factors.* Oxford: Blackwell.

Labov, William, S. Ash, M. Baranowski, N. Nagy, M. Rabindranath and T. Weldon (2006) Listeners' sensitivity to frequency. *Penn Working Papers* 8.

Labov, William, Sharon Ash and Charles Boberg (2006) *Atlas of North American English: Phonology and Sound Change.* Berlin: Mouton/de Gruyter.

Labov, Ash & Boberg (2005) [to follow]

Labov, William and Julie Auger (1998) The effect of normal aging on discourse: a sociolinguistic approach. In Brownell, Hiram H. and Yves Joanette (eds.) *Narrative Discourse in Neurologically Impaired and Normal Aging Adults.* San Diego, CA: Singular Publishing Group. pp. 115–134.

Labov, William, P. Cohen, C. Robins and J. Lewis (1968) *A Study of the Non-standard English of Negro and Puerto Rican Speakers in New York City.* Cooperative Research Report 3288. Vols I and II. Philadelphia: U.S. Regional Survey (Linguistics Laboratory, University of Pennsylvania.).

Labov, William, Mark Karan and Corey Miller (1991) Near-mergers and the suspension of phonemic contrast. *Language Variation and Change* 3:33–74.

Labov, William and Wendell A. Harris (1986) De facto segregation of black and white vernaculars. In D. Sankoff (ed.) *Diversity and Diachrony.* Philadelphia: John Benjamins, pp. 1–24.

Labov, William, Malcah Yaeger and Richard Steiner (1972) A Quantitative Study of Sound Change in Progress. Philadelphia: US Regional Survey.

Laferriere, Martha (1979) Ethnicity in phonological variation and change. *Language* 55:603–617.

Lambert, Wallace (1967) A social psychology of bilingualism. In J. Macnamara (ed.) *Problems of Bilingualism. Journal of Social Issues* 23:91–109.

Lambert, Wallace E. et al. (1960) Evaluational reactions to spoken languages. *Journal of Abnormal and Social Psychology*, 60:44–51.

—— (1963) Evaluational reactions of Jewish and Arabic adolescents to dialect and language variations (mimeographed).

Lavandera, Beatriz (1978) Where does the sociolinguistic variable stop? *Language in Society* 7:2:1971–1982.

Lefebvre, Anne (1991) *Le Français de la Région Lilloise*. Paris: Publications de la Sorbonne.

Lemle, Miriam and Anthony Naro (1977) *Competencias básicas do portugues*. Rio de Janeiro: MOBRAL.

Lennig, Matthew (1978) *Acoustic Measurement of Linguistic Change: the Modern Paris Vowel System*. University of Pennsylvania dissertation.

Leonard, Sterling A. (1929) *The Doctrine of Correctness in English Usoge, 1700–1800*. Madison: University of Wisconsin.

Lerman, Paul (1962) *Issues in Subcultural Delinquency*. New York School of Social Work, Columbia University dissertation.

Lightfoot, David (1997) Catastrophic change and learning theory. *Lingua* 100:171–192.

—— (1999) *The Development of Language: Acquisition, Change, and Evolution*. Oxford & Malden, Mass.: Blackwell Publishers.

Lira, Solange de Azambuja (1982) *Nominal, Pronominal and Zero Subject in Brazilian Portuguese*. University of Philadelphia dissertation.

Lopez Scott, Alma Leticia (1983) *A Sociolinguistic Analysis of /s/ Variation in Honduras Spanish*. University of Minnesota dissertation.

Macaulay, Ronald K. S. and Gain D. Trevelyan (1973) *Language, Education and Employment in Glasgow*. A Report to the Social Science Research Council.

MacDonald, Jeff (1984) The social stratification of (r) in New York City department stores revisited. *Paper written for Anthropology* 150, Anthropological Linguistics, for Nancy Bonvillain.

Mahl, George (1972) People talking when they can't hear their voices. In A. Siegman and B. Pope (eds) *Studies in Dyadic Communication*. New York: Pergamon Press, pp. 211–264.

Martinet, André (1952) Function, structure and sound change. *Word* 8:1–32.

—— (1955) *Economie des changements phonétiques*. Berne: A. Francke.

—— (1962) Structural variation in language. Proceedings of the Ninth International Congress of Linguists.

Matsuda, Kenjiro (1995) *Variable Zero-marking of (o) in Tokyo Japanese*. University of Pennsylvania dissertation.

McDavid, Raven I. (1948) Postvocalic /r/ in South Carolina: a social analysis. *American Speech* 23:194–203.

Meechan, Marjory and Michele Foley (1994) On resolving disagreement: linguistic theory and variation – there's bridges. *Language Variation and Change* 6:63–85.

Meillet, Antoine (1921) *Linguistique historique et Linguistique générale*. Paris: La Société Linguistique de Paris.

Merton, Robert K. (1957) *Social Theory and Social Structure*. Second Edition. Glencoe, Illinois: The Free Press.

MFY (1962) *A Proposal for the Prevention and Control of Delinquency by Expanding Opportunities*. 2nd ed. New York: Mobilization for Youth, Inc.

Mills, C. Wright (1956) *White Collar*. New York: Oxford University Press (Galaxy Book).

Milroy, Leslie (1980) *Language and Social Networks*. Oxford: Basil Blackwell.

Milroy, James and John Harris (1980) When is a merger not a merger? The MEAT/ MATE problem in a present-day English vernacular. *English World-Wide* 1:199–210.

Milroy, James and Lesley Milroy (1978) Belfast: change and variation in an urban vernacular. In P. Trudgill (ed.) *Sociolinguistic Patterns in British English*. London: Edward Arnold, pp. 19–36.

Mitchell, A. G. and A. Delbridge (1965) *The Pronunciation of English in Australia*. Sydney: Angus & Robertson.

Modaressi, Yahya (1978) *A Sociolinguistic Investigation of Modern Persian*. University of Kansas dissertation.

Moulton, William G. (1960) The short vowel systems of northern Switzerland: a study in structural dialectology. *Word* 16:155–183.

—— (1961) Lautwandel durch innere Kausalität: die Ostschweizerische Vokalspaltung. *Zeitschrift für Mundartforschung*, 28:227–251.

—— (1962) Dialect geography and the concept of phonological space. *Word* 18:23–33.

Myhill, John (1988) Postvocalic /r/ as an index of integration into the BEV speech community. *American Speech* 63:203–213.

Mysak, Edward D. and T. D. Hanley (1959) Vocal aging. *Geriatrics* 14:652–656.

Nagel, Ernest (1961) *The Structure of Science*. New York: Harcourt, Brace and Co.

Oliveira, Marco de (1983) *Phonological Variation in Brazilian Portuguese*. University of Pennsylvania dissertation.

Oliveira e Silva, Giselle de and Maria Marta Scherre (1998) *Padroes Sociolingüísticos*. Rio de Janeiro: Departamento de Lingüístico e Filologia-UFRI.

Owens, Thompson W. and Paul M. Baker (1984) Linguistic insecurity in Winnipeg: validation of a Canadian index of insecurity. *Language in Society*, 13:337–350.

Paiva, Maria de and Maria Eugenia Duarte (2003) *Mudança Lingüística em Tempo Real*. Rio de Janeiro: Capa.

Paolo, Marianna di (1988) Pronunciation and categorization in sound change. In K. Ferrara et al. (eds) *Linguistic Change and Contact: NWAV XVI*. Austin, TE: Dept of Linguistics, University of Texas. pp. 84–92.

Paolo, Marianna di and Alice Faber (1990) Phonation differences and the phonetic content of the tense-lax contrast in Utah English. *Language Variation and Change* 2:155–204.

Payne, Arvilla (1976) *The Acquisition of the Phonological System of a Second Dialect*. University of Pennsylvania dissertation.

—— (1980) Factors controlling the acquisition of the Philadelphia dialect by out-of-state children. In W. Labov (ed.) *Locating Language in Time and Space*. New York: Academic Press. pp. 143–178.

Peterson, Peter G. (1985) -ing & -in: The persistence of history? Paper given at ALS Annual Conference, Brisbane.

Peterson, Gorden E. and H. L. Barney (1952) Control methods used in a study of the vowels. *Journal of the Acoustical Society of America* 22:175–184.

Pfalz, Anton (1918) Reihenschritte im Vokalismus. *Akademie der Wissenschaften in Wien, Philosophisch-historische Klasse, Sitzunqsberichte, 2. Abhandlung,* 190:22–42.

Pilch, Herbert (1955) The rise of the American English vowel pattern. *Word* 11:57–93.

Poplack, Shana (1978) Dialect acquisition among Puerto Rican bilinguals. *Language in Society* 7: 89–104.

—— (1979) Function and process in a variable phonology. University of Pennsylvania dissertation.

Preston, Dennis (2001) Style and psycholinguistics. In Eckert, P. and J. Rickford (eds), *Style and Sociolinguistic Variation.* Cambridge: Cambridge University Press, pp. 279—304.

Putnam, George N. and Edna M. O'Hern (1955) The status significance of an isolated urban dialect. *Language* 31–4, Part 2.

Read, Allen Walker (1936) American projects for an academy to regulate speech. *Proceedings of the Modern Language Association,* LI:1141–1179.

—— (1938) The assimilation of the speech of British immigrants in colonial America. *Journal of English and German Philology,* XXXVII:70–79.

—— (1939) The Motivation of Lindley Murray's Grammatical Work, *Journal of English and Germanic Philology* XXXVIII:525–539.

—— (1963) The first stage in the history of *O.K. American Speech* 38:5–29.

—— (1977) The grammar of double talk. *American Speech* 52:122–127.

Reed, David W. and John L. Spicer (1952) Correlation methods of comparing idiolects in a transition area. *Language* 28:348–360.

Reichstein, Ruth (1960) Study of social and geographic variation of linguistic behavior. *Word* 16:55.

Roberts, Julia L. (1993) *Acquisition of Variable Rules: (t,d) Deletion and (ing) Production in Preschool Children.* University of Pennsylvania dissertation.

Roberts, Julie (1997) Hitting a moving target: Acquisition of sound change in progress by Philadelphia children. *Language Variation and Change* 9:249–266.

Roberts, Julie and Labov, William (1995) Learning to talk Philadelphian: acquisition of short *a* by preschool children. *Language Variation and Change* 7:101–112.

Roedder, Edwin C. (1926) Linguistic geography. *Germanic Review* I, 4:281–308.

Sankoff, David (1988) Variable rules. In U. Ammon, N. Dittmar and K. Mattheier (eds) *Sociolinguistics: An International Handbook of the Science of Language and Society,* Vol. 2. Berlin: de Gruyter, pp. 984–997.

Sankoff, David and Gillian Sankoff (1973) Sample survey methods and computer-assisted analysis in the study of grammatical variation. In R. Darnell (ed.) *Canadian Languages in their Social Context.* Edmonton, Alberta: Linguistic Research. pp. 7–64.

Sankoff, Gillian (2002) Linguistic outcomes of language contact. In J. Chambers et al. (eds) *The Handbook of Language Variation and Change.* Malden, MA: Blackwell, pp 638–668.

Sankoff, D. and P. Thibault (1981) Weak complementarity: tense and aspect in Montreal French. In B. B. Johns and D. R. Strong (eds.) *Syntactic Change. Natural Language Studies* 25:205–216.

Sankoff, Gillian and Diane Vincent (1977) L'emploi productif du ne dans le français parlé à Montréal. *Le français moderne* 45:243–256. (English version published as Ch.14 in *The Social Life of Language.*)

Santa Ana, Otto and Claudia Parodi (1998) A speech community model: configurations and variable types in the Mexican Spanish setting. *Language in Society* 27:1–48.

Saussure, Ferdinand de (1916) *Cours de linguistique générale.* Fourth edition (1949). Paris: Payot.

Schatzman, Leonard and Anselm Strauss (1955) Social class and modes of communication. *American Journal of Sociology.* LX:329.

Shuy, Roger, Walt Wolfram and William K. Riley (1967) *A Study of Social Dialects in Detroit.* Final Report, Project 6-1347. Washington, D.C.: Office of Education.

Sommerfelt, Alf (1930) Sur la propagation de changements phonétiques. *Norsk Tidsskrift for Sproqvidenskap*, IV:76–128.

Sturtevant, Edgar (1947) *An Introduction to Linguistic Science.* New Haven: Yale University Press, Ch. VIII, esp. pp. 81–84.

Tarallo, Fernando (1983) *Relativization strategies in Brazilian Portuguese.* PhD dissertation, University of Pennsylvania.

Thibault, Pierrette and Diane Vincent (1990) *Un Corpus de Français Parlé.* Montreal: Recherches Sociolinguistiques.

Thomas, Charles K. (1932) Jewish dialect and New York dialect. *American Speech* 7:321–326.

—— (1942) Pronunciation in downstate New York. *American Speech* 17:30–41, 149–157.

—— (1951) New York City pronunciation. *American Speech* 26:122–3.

Trager, George L. (1942) One phonemic entity becomes two: the case of 'Short A'. *American Speech* XVII:30–41.

Trager, George L. and Henry L. Smith (1957) *An Outline of English Structure.* Washington, D. C.: American Council of Learned Societies.

Trudgill, Peter (1972) Sex, covert prestige and linguistic change in urban British English. *Language in Society* 1:179–195.

—— (1974) *The Social Differentiation of English in Norwich.* Cambridge: Cambridge University Press.

—— (1988) Norwich revisited: recent linguistic changes in an English urban dialect. *English World-Wide* 9:33–49.

United States Bureau of Labor Statistics (1963) *Income, Education, and Unemployment in Neighborhoods.* Washington: Department of Labor, January, 1963.

Voegelin, C. F. and Harris, Zellig S. (1951) Methods for determining intelligibility among dialects of natural languages. *Proceedings of the American Philosophical Society* 95:322–329.

Warner, W. Lloyd (1960) *Social Class in America.* New York: Harper Torchbook.

Weinberg, Maria Beatriz Fontanella de (1974) *Un Aspecto Sociolinguistico del Espanol Bonaerense: la -S en Bahia Blanca.* Bahia Blanca: Cuadernos de Linguisticca.

Weinberg, Maria Beatriz Fontanella de and Myriam Najt (1968) *Los pronombres de tratamiento en el espanol de bahia blanca.* Separata de las Actas de La Quinta Asamblea Interuniversitaria de Filología y Literaturas Hispánicas.

Weinreich, Uriel (1951) *Research Problems in Bilingualism, with Special Reference to Switzerland*, Columbia University, New York dissertation.

—— (1953) *Languages in Contact.* New York: Linguistic Circle of New York.

—— (1954) Is a structural dialectology possible? *Word* 10:388–400.
—— (1959) Review of Charles F. Hockett *A Course in Modern Linguistics. Romance Philology*, XIII:329–332.
Weinreich, Uriel, William Labov and Marvin Herzog (1968) Empirical foundations for a theory of language change. In W. Lehmann and Y. Malkiel (eds.) *Directions for Historical Linguistics.* Austin: University of Texas Press, pp. 97–195.
Wells, Rulon S. (1947) De Saussure's system of linguistics. *Word*, 3:1–31.
Wetmore, Thomas H. (1959) *The Low-Central and Low-Back Vowels in the Eastern United States.* American Dialect Society Publication No. 32. University, Alabama: University of Alabama Press.
Williams, Ann and Paul Kerswill (1999) Dialect levelling: continuity vs. change in Milton Keynes, Reading and Hull. In P. Foulkes and G. Docherty (eds.) *Urban Voices.* London: Arnold.
Williams, Edwin (1997) Blocking and anaphora. *Linguistic Inquiry* 28:577–628.
Wolf, Clara and Elena Jiménez (1979) El ensordecimienteo del yeismo porteño, un cambio fonológico en marcha. In A. M. Barenchea et al. (eds) *Estudios Linguisticos y Dialectologicos.* Buenos Aires: Hachette, 1979.
Wolfram, Walt (1969) *A Sociolinguistic Description of Detroit Negro Speech.* Arlington, VA: Center for Applied Linguistics.
Woods, Howard (1979) *A Socio-dialectology Survey of the English Spoken in Ottawa: a Study of Sociological and Stylistic Variation in Canadian English.* University of British Columbia dissertation.
Wyld, Henry C. (1936) *A History of Modern Colloquial English*, Third edition. Oxford: Basil Blackwell.
Zelinsky, Wilbur (1992) *The Cultural Geography of the United States.* A Revised Edition. Englewood Cliffs, NJ: Prentice Hall.
Zwicky, Arnold (2002) Seeds of variation and change. Paper presented at NWAVE 31, Stanford.

Index

Note: References to figures, tables and notes are indicated as 51*f*, 34*t*, and 31 n8. References to the glossary are in *italic.*